GOLD, GREED AND GLORY

The Territorial History of Prescott and the Verde Valley 1864-1912

by
KATE RULAND-THORNE

with foreword by Elisabeth Ruffner

PublishAmerica
Baltimore

First printing

At the specific preference of the author, PublishAmerica allowed this work to remain exactly as the author intended, verbatim, without editorial input.

ISBN: 1-4137-9322-3
PUBLISHED BY PUBLISHAMERICA, LLLP
www.publishamerica.com
Baltimore

Printed in the United States of America

DEDICATION

To Nick, Alicia and Katie
My earth angels

BOOKS BY KATE RULAND-THORNE

LION of REDSTONE

EXPERIENCE SEDONA LEGENDS AND LEGACIES

UPON THIS ROCK: Margaret Brunswig Staude and her Sedona Chapel

ADVENTURES IN ARIZONA

THE LEGACY OF SEDONA SCHNEBLY

THE YAVAPAI: People of the Red Rocks, People of the Sun

GOLD, GREED AND GLORY

TABLE OF CONTENTS

FOREWORD

For a definitive narrative and some first person accounts, all well researched and colorfully written, of the history, characters and conditions of North Central Arizona, one needs look no further than this latest and finest work by Kate Ruland-Thorne.

Sensitive and as historically accurate as closely as verbal legend can be, Thorne's stories of the first known inhabitants bring to life a nearly lost civilization. The elders who are willing to share the stories of their people provide a factual, but entertaining saga confirmed as far as possible by the contemporary work of ethnologists, archaeologists and anthropologists.

Trail blazers, explorers, trappers and gold-seekers were the first Europeans to arrive in the region which was historically mapped as part of the Territory of New Mexico. American military records have been carefully noted by the author providing accuracy in the recounting of the early period of domination of the indigenous people.

A civilian government party accompanied by a military detail founded the territorial capital of Arizona where a town had not been present. Their backgrounds and customs as Middle Westerners and Easterners determined the grid pattern of the layout of the town of Prescott as well as the predominant architectural styles.

The pioneering years are particularly well described in this book and the individual settlers and adventurers lives are carefully detailed, bad times and all.

Of particular interest to this writer is Chapter Four, as I have read in this fine book accounts of actual lives of people I have known, either personally or through family connections.

A study of history often leads one to identify in time with the players and events. In this regard, I can write without concern for challenge that the last half of the Twentieth Century in the state and especially the Central Highlands is mine, as I have lived these times in this place.

I commend Kate Ruland-Thorne for writing an adventure all may enjoy through her vivid characterizations drawn from original sources and for her sense of place in describing the life and times of a colorful era.

Elisabeth Ruffner

In 1940, Elisabeth Friedrich arrived in Arizona from Cincinnati to meet her fiancé's family, the Ruffners, a pioneer family whose Prescott heritage began in 1869. After marrying Lester Ward 'Budge' Ruffner, Elisabeth proceeded to make her own mark on Arizona's history for the next 66 years.

A dedicated steward of Prescott's heritage and historic preservation, Elisabeth has been recognized statewide and nationally for her efforts, and garnered numerous prestigious awards in the process. Among them are the Arizona Culture Keepers Award in 2003; The Cultural Achievement Award from the United States Department of the Interior in 1980; She was appointed by President Gerald Ford in 1977 to be a member of the White House Conference on Library and Information Services, and in 1976 was awarded Trustee of the Year from the American Library Association. In 1969 the Prescott Business and Professional Woman's Club declared her Woman of the Year; and in 1969 she was presented with the Rosenzweig Award from the Arizona State Library Association for outstanding citizen participation in the development of community libraries. After helping found the Heritage Foundation of Arizona in the late 1960s, Elisabeth was instrumental in rescuing more than 689 of Prescott's historic buildings and securing their listing in the National Register of Historic Places.

Currently she hosts a weekly radio program, a public access television interview program and writes a monthly history page for *Yavapai Magazine.*

PREFACE

Prior to 1864, the vast lands located north of the Gila River in Arizona County, New Mexico Territory were known as Tierra Incognita, unknown lands. It was a dangerous place inhabited only by the Yavapai and fierce Tonto Apache people, none of whom took kindly to trespassers. The few brave souls who survived their ventures there returned to utter warnings and whisper of seeing gold.

Gold remained a rumor until the spring of 1863 when two famous mountain men, each leading separate expeditions, discovered rich bonanzas of gold within 30 miles of one another. By 1864, Tierra Incognita was replaced on old maps with new words: Prescott and Yavapai County. President Abraham Lincoln declared Arizona a Territory and separated it from New Mexico. He needed the gold to help finance the Civil War.

The stampede for gold was well underway when the soldiers and government officials arrived in North Central Arizona 1864 to organize the new Territory of Arizona. With rare exceptions, most of those men were as greedy for gold as any of the prospectors.

Of course the inevitable conflict with the Native population seriously interfered with all of their endeavors. For several years, the Indians had the upper hand until the arrival of General George Crook in 1872.

Soon to follow the prospectors, soldiers and government officials were the pioneers, entrepreneurs, outlaws, lawmen and Ladies of the night. GOLD, GREED AND GOLRY exams many of their lives, gives them flesh and blood and invites the reader along on their many glorious adventures.

ACKNOWLEGMENTS

During the three years that it has taken me to research and write this book, a number of people have earned my deepest appreciation for their insights, suggestions, researching, and editing skills. Elisabeth Ruffner's invaluable knowledge, guidance, and scrutiny helped keep me on track regarding the historical content, and punctuation. Kudos, also, to another pioneer descendant, Babs Monroe, who made sure I told the true story of her family, the Wingfields of Camp Verde.

Two illustrious newspaper editors, Barclay Jameson (Pueblo Chieftan—retired), and Greg Ruland, my son, and the managing editor of Arizona's Larson Newspapers, kept me on my toes regarding sentence structure and punctuation. Commas still drive me crazy.

Since I moved from Arizona to Colorado while in the middle of this project, I relied heavily upon my two able research assistants, Karen Schuhmann and Frieda Weber, to make numerous trips to Sharlot Hall Museum to check on, and look up, a variety of subject matter. What a great job, ladies. Thank you.

Thanks, too, to my two good friends, Aliza Caillou and Gretchen Burkey, both of whom are professional editors, for checking, reviewing and correcting the final draft of this book. They are amazingly astute and detail oriented editors. Thanks also to my writing support group, Inside/Out of Grand Junction, who, although fiction writers, suggested ways to make the information far more palatable and interesting for my future readers.

Last but certainly not least, many thanks to a fine artist and my dear friend Ron Henry who not only created the cover art but also is responsible for all maps and illustrations.

"When White Painted Woman got out of the shell, Giver of Life told her to kneel down in the sand. She kneeled (sic) down three times, but nothing happened. She was discouraged, but Giver of Life told her kneel a fourth time. She became pregnant and immediately gave birth to Son of Sun. She thought that is all there would be and the two of them would be alone. But Giver of Life told her to kneel four times again, and after the fourth time, let water drip into her. She did, and gave birth to Child of Water."

—Western Apache creation story

CHAPTER ONE - AHAGASKIAYWA
Before White Contact: The Yavapai and Tonto Apache People of Yavapai County

Ahagaskiaywa (aha-gas-ke-wea) is where "the people came out first."

This is the beginning of the emergence story of the Yavapai and Western (Tonto) Apache people. Although their versions of the story may vary, on one thing they do agree: *Ahagaskiaywa* is the most sacred place in all of Arizona.

Pioneer white settlers gave this sacred place another name— Montezuma Well. They mistakenly believed that the great Aztec leader once lived there with his people.

Montezuma Well located near the town of Camp Verde
—photo by Kate Ruland-Thorne (KRT)

The emergence story of the Yavapai and Tonto Apaches explains how they divide time into four cycles:

Cycle One was when the people emerged from the underground of Montezuma Well. It terminated when a great flood welled up and covered the land.

Cycle Two was during the time of the goddess, *Komwidapokwia* (K-weden-buk-wea), or "White Shell Woman," who survived the flood. It is also the story of her grandson, *Sakarakaamche* (Skara-ga-umja), the heroic monster slayer who made the world safe for all the people. The Apache version calls First Woman, "Changing Woman," and First Man, "Killer of Enemies."

Cycle Three ended when coyote stole the sun and started a great world fire.

Cycle Four is the present time.

"Our legends are teaching tools," explained Mabel Dogka, the oldest member of the Yavapai-Apache tribe. "They teach right from wrong, to be proud, to be strong…things that apply to life. When we think about these legends, we look at ourselves and decide whether we are good, bad, or a damn fool."

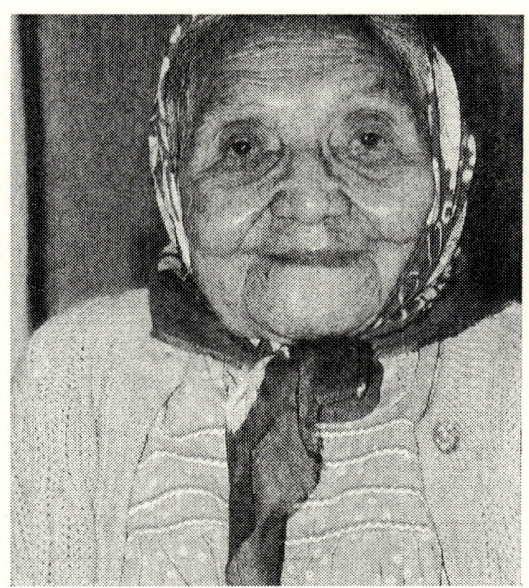 

***Mabel Dogka in 1990 by KRT and* 1952**
—photo courtesy of Mabel Dogka

Although the Yavapai and Tonto Apache people originate from two different language groups, they share more than an emergence legend. Their close proximity through the centuries allowed them to borrow from one another's life-ways. After white contact, pioneers lumped them together as all one people and referred to them as "Yavapai-Apache." These two distinctly different groups of people have been trying to correct that mistake ever since.

Since ancient times, the Yavapai called themselves *"abaya"*—the people. The region where they roamed on their hunting and plant gathering forays remains one of the most lush and magnificent in Arizona. Before white contact, they were a wealthy people in terms of their environment, and in their well-defined cultural ways.

In the 1500s, three hundred years before their contact with Americans, the Yavapai and Tonto Apache people encountered the Spanish, who ventured into north central Arizona in search of gold and a route to the sea. The Spanish referred to the Yavapai as *"Niojoras"* or *"old"*—a people who have been here a long time, and they described the Yavapai as "friendly" and their land as "full of abounding game, fertile valleys and tall pines."

The Spanish viewed the Western Apaches in a different light. They named them "Tonto," which means 'crazy'. These people, the Spanish decided, were a people to be feared because they gave no quarter and were ferocious and courageous fighters.

The Tonto Apaches call themselves "*Inde*," the people. Their two northern Arizona clans were known as the Red Rock Clan and the White Land Clan.

There are three groups of Yavapai: The *Wi-puk-abaya* of northeastern Arizona, also known as 'the people of the red rock country'. The *Tol-ke-abaya* (south below people), and the 'elsewhere people', (*Kwev-ik-abaya*). All three Yavapai groups collectively call themselves the "People of the Sun."

For centuries the Tonto Apache and Yavapai people lived peacefully with one another, and on occasion intermarried. The children born into such a union were identified as Apache or Yavapai depending upon which group of people their mother came from.

In terms of language, stature, customs, and origins, the two groups differ considerably. The Yavapai are a Yuman-speaking group whose ancestral cousins are the Mojave, Yuma, Cocopa, Walapai, Havasupai, and Maricopa. It is believed they migrated into Arizona approximately 12,500 years ago during the first migration of people from Asia across the Bering Strait. Their ancestors have been identified as the ancient Patayan, a hunting and gathering group who are related to the Iroquois. It is also believed they are related to the prehistoric Sinagua, a belief supported by the Yavapai's own oral history traditions. The Yavapai say their ancestors were here during the time of the huge mammoths and mastodons, giant beaver, grizzly bears, camels, horses, and large bison, all of which died off during the last ice age in 6,000 B.C. All Sinagua sites are sacred to both Apache and Yavapai, including Montezuma Castle, Tuzigoot, and the ruins in Sedona's Boynton Canyon.

For the early Yavapai, 'dream power' played an important role in all of their decisions, from going to war, to going on a hunt. Shamans interpreted these dreams.

War was a serious business among the Yavapai, and usually was entered into only to protect their territory or avenge a wrongdoing. Four days of purification was required after a battle if any deaths occurred.

Some anthropologists believe the Apache arrived in the area around 800 A.D. They are an Athabascan-speaking people whose cousins and historical enemies are the Navajos. Their nearest linguistic relatives are located in Canada and Alaska.

Other anthropologists believe the Apaches reached the Southwest in the thirteenth century and may have been at least partially responsible for raiding the ancient Indians and forcing them to abandon their northern cliff dwellings and pueblos.

There are seven distinct groups of Athabascan-speaking people in the Southwestern United States: Navajo, Western Apache (including Tonto), Chiricahua, Mescalero, Jicarilla, Lipan, and Kiowa Apache. Economically, these groups depended upon hunting, gathering and raiding. Raiding was a recognized and necessary part of their economy, particularly after they acquired horses from the Spanish in the 1600s. The Apaches wanted loot, not glory. They stole whatever they could lay their hands on; food, clothing, horses, cattle, mules and women and children. Without plunder, they would have starved.

Horses were only necessary to the Apaches in order to get from one place to another. They typically ran their ponies to death, then cooked and ate them.

For the Yavapai, the usual purpose behind raiding and warfare was to avenge the death of a kinsman. Initially the Yavapai did not take booty, as the Apache customarily did, because they believed they might be haunted by the dead person's personal effects. After contact with the Americans, the Yavapai lost all prior compunctions about taking booty, and revenge became their primary reason to raid and kill.

It was rare for either the Yavapai or Apache to kill a blood relative or clan member. Such an act was looked upon with horror. They believed it would be like taking vengeance upon oneself. Only if a family or clan member committed incest, the most heinous of all crimes, was such a killing justified.

The topic of incest was avoided entirely in the belief that it, and all irregular sex practices, was linked to witchcraft. Anyone caught in such acts was marked for life and either ostracized or killed.

It became everyone's duty to look after one another's children. It was considered an inexplicable abnormality to abuse a child.

Yavapai warrior prior to white contact
— **drawing by Yavapai artist David Sine, original owned by author**

All Apache and Yavapai groups looked upon the Pima, Maricopa, Havasupai and Walapai Indians as hated enemies, and often made vicious raids upon these people. These traditional enemies did not hesitate to retaliate. Their enmities had been going on for centuries. In the 1870s, General George Crook took advantage of these hostile relationships during the Indian wars, which led to the eventual downfall of most of them.

The Yavapai enjoyed cordial relations with the Navajo and Hopi people, with whom they carried on a lucrative and beneficial trading activity. The Navajo and Hopi particularly valued the finely tanned hides the Yavapai offered. Three Hopi or Navajo blankets fetched one Yavapai hide.

The Yavapai skinned their deer from chin to anus, then down the inside of each leg. Once removed, the hide was waved toward the east as good luck. No part of the animal was wasted. Its brains were preserved by cooking them in ashes, then spread over grass and dried into a cake-like substance. These brains were essential for tanning the hide.

Every portion of the animal's body had a particular purpose and use. Men made all the buckskin clothing. Most garments worn by the Yavapai and Apache people were made with these supple hides. Many rolls of tanned hides indicated that a man was a good hunter and that his family was wealthy.

In summer, the men wore only a breechclout and knee or hip high moccasins with a flap that came up over the toe and protected their feet on long runs. Women were required to be more modest. They wore two pieces of buckskin. The one in front was worn like a butcher's apron. The back piece hung from the waist and was tied with a buckskin belt. These sleeveless dresses were fringed along the sides and worn throughout the year. A blanket shawl kept them warm in the winter. Until they turned ten, children wore nothing at all in the summer months.

Tattooing was commonly practiced among the Yavapai groups in order to distinguish family and clan relationships, and to avoid marriage among members who might be too closely related. After her first menses, a close relative tattooed a young Yavapai woman on her arm, chin and forehead with cactus needles and charcoal pigment. Traditionally her mother was not allowed to perform this delicate operation. Meat eating was forbidden until the tattoos healed. When young men came of age they were tattooed as well.

Mabel Dogka's face and arms were tattooed in this manner when she was a young girl. "This is a clan design," she explained. "All *abyas* used tattoo marks to identify themselves."

To this day, the most important ceremony among the Apaches is the annual "Coming Out Ceremony" for pubescent girls, in which they become Changing Woman, the Apache's greatest cultural hero. Changing Woman is also called White Painted Woman or White Shell Woman. During the course of this four-day ceremony young girls acquire magical powers while being transformed into women of marriageable age.

After they turn ten, boys begin their training to become strong men. In the early days, both Yavapai and Apache boys were required to run in winter with snowballs under their armpits. The purpose of this not only was to teach endurance, but prevent the growth of auxiliary hair. They were not allowed to drink water except in the morning and evening, thereby training them to endure long periods without water while hunting or going on the warpath. They were not fed much for the same reason.

Another endurance test was running to the top of a mountain or high hill without stopping. Elders or grandfathers trained these young boys, preparing them for the harshness of life. A boy was not considered a man until he was 25 or 30 years old.

The Yavapai called their brush homes '*gwa-bun-ya-v*', the Apaches say '*ko-wa*', or 'tipi house'. Their homes were not carried from place to place as the people traveled, but freshly built at each camp. It took a full day to build one. The openings always faced east. When someone died the hut and all of its belongings were burned. This kept the dead person's spirit from hanging around, and allowed it to move on to the spirit world. The dead person's name was never mentioned again.

Mescal, taken from the root of the agave plant, was a staple of the Indian's diet and was cooked for three days in a fire pit. Mabel Dogka remembered eating mescal as a child and enjoying it. "When it is first removed from the fire pit," she recalled, "it is sweet like candy. After you peel it, you have to chew it, because it has lots of fiber. It's like eating sugar cane. After it hardens and dries, it can make your tongue raw if you chew it too long. My people don't even know what mescal is any more," she added.

Mabel also recalled getting rabbits and wood rats out of their holes when she was a child.

"We all stood around the hole with sticks. When the rat or rabbit tried to run from us, we were supposed to hit it. I remember just hollering. I couldn't hit it. My parents got after me for that. We also stole pinion nuts from the wood rat's holes. Sometimes we ran into rattlesnakes doing that."

The Yavapai and Apache people cultivated beans, corn and squash. They also gathered wild tobacco but men were not allowed to smoke it until after the age of 40. Tobacco, they believed, was once a beautiful woman who was jilted by a young man. In order to spite him she turned into tobacco, so all men would desire her forever.

The sacred beings of both the Yavapai and Apache people are the *Gaans* (Ga-hans), a class of supernatural beings who possess the power of the Great Spirit Himself. They are spirit messengers equivalent to the Hopi "*Katcinas*" and the Navajo *Yei.* It is believed the *Gaan* were builders of certain prehistoric sites, and that they still inhabit specific mountains and caves.

The *Gaan* visit earth and are called upon in time of war, sickness, death, and for special ceremonies. They were once a people who left because of disrespect, and went to live where eternal life could be lived without evil things.

The *Gaan* has no known face. When the Crown Dancers imitate them, they wear masks with eyes only. The Apaches consider the *Gaan* to be deities.

The Yavapai say that their people learned about the *Gaan* from the *Kakaka,* or 'little Indians'. The Apaches say they learned of the *Gaan* from the Almighty.

The *Kakaka* are known to have dwelled in all sacred ruin sites. The Yavapai point to the doors of the ruins as being designed for very little people. The *Kakakas* taught the Yavapai all their dances and songs, and had the power to foretell the future and heal the sick. They left important messages on stones.

Mabel Dogka said these little people are like the wind. "They cannot be seen, but their presence can be felt in the movement of the clouds, bushes, grass, and trees. They only communicate with shamans."

The most significant legend shared by all the Yavapai and Western Apaches is their belief that the first people emerged from *Ahagaskiaywa*—Montezuma well. All the land surrounding this ancient limestone sink, which extends from Prescott, throughout the Verde Valley and Sedona to Boynton Canyon, is still considered very sacred ground.

Unfortunately, beginning in 1863, these and other sacred sites would be desecrated with bloodshed during the Indian wars, and the life-ways of the Native people would be altered forever.

That was because a powerful new tribe had entered the area. This new tribe called themselves "The Americans."

"I encourage the troops to capture and root out the Apaches by every means, and to hunt them as they would wild animals." General Ord, September, 1869

"It is useless to negotiate with these Apache Indians. They observe no treaties, agreements or truces. With them there is no alternative but active and vigorous war 'til they are completely destroyed or forced to surrender as prisoners of war." General Halleck, 1869

"THE ONLY GOOD INDIAN IS A DEAD ONE." General Phillip h. Sheridan 1869

CHAPTER TWO
White Eyes, Long Knives and Renegade Indians—The Indian Wars

"With malice towards none and charity for all."

At the close of the Civil War in 1865, President Abraham Lincoln's eloquent words, spoken at his second inaugural address, were not intended for the Native people of the American West. He often used the word "savage" whenever he referenced the Indians in most of his speeches both before and after his presidency. "Savage" was a popular allusion to Indians used by most people in those days.

While campaigning for the presidency in Springfield, Illinois, on February 22, 1860, Lincoln inferred the superiority of whites based on their discovery of gold in territories on which Indians and Mexicans had lived for generations; he rhetorically asked "why did Yankees almost instantly discover gold in California, which had been trodden upon and overlooked by savages and Mexican greasers for centuries?" Included in that same speech, Lincoln explained that phonetic writing was what separated whites from 'savages', "and from that talent we have derived the fruits of our civilization."

Throughout his presidency, Lincoln's attitude towards Indians sometimes implied sympathy for their plight, yet his true philosophy was firmly rooted in the concept of "Manifest Destiny" a popular belief that claimed that 'God intended North America to be under the control of Americans'.

In the 19th Century, Indians were not considered "Americans." (American Indians did not acquire the right to vote until the 1940s).

Manifest Destiny conceptualized a passionate and long-held belief among the majority of Americans that white American men were superior to all other people. The phrase also promoted genocide, a government policy that had existed since the time of President Thomas Jefferson. The spirit of Manifest Destiny and the genocide it encouraged originated on this continent with the arrival of Christopher Columbus who subdued, enslaved or murdered all the Indians he encountered.

The term Manifest Destiny was coined by journalist John L.O. Sullivan who wrote in the July 1845 issue of the Democratic Review: "The United States has a Manifest Destiny to overspread the continent with its multiplying millions." His purpose was to justify our pending war with Mexico in 1846.

When our war with Mexico ended, we added Texas, California, Arizona and New Mexico to the Republic, and our multiplying millions did indeed start overspreading the continent. From 1848 to 1880, over 250,000 immigrants made the overland journey into the West.

Long before the Mexican War started, and for decades afterwards, the blood of Native people and their American adversaries drenched the deserts, mountains and plains of the American West.

Hostilities between Native people, and the increasing waves of fortune seekers and settlers who encroached upon their lands, began in earnest with the discovery of gold in California in 1849. Twelve

U.S. Presidents would come and go before our wars with the western tribes ended in 1890 at *Chankpe Opi Wakpala*, the creek known as Wounded Knee.

* * * *

"LONG KNIVES" — THE FRONTIER SOLDIERS

Once the Civil War ended in 1865, Washington turned attention to the desperate pleas for help from the western immigrants. Prompted by the need to complete the transcontinental railroad; the continual discoveries of valuable mineral resources in the west; and the desire to open more and more land for settlement there, the government initiated a major recruiting campaign in order to send soldiers to protect these interests.

Many Civil War veterans re-enlisted, along with raw recruits. For some the motivation was adventure and the opportunity to begin life anew in the untamed lands west of the Mississippi where new areas of settlement had opened up. Unfortunately the majority was fleeing misfortune of one kind or another. *The New York Sun* observed in 1865, "the Regular Army is composed of bummers, loafers, and foreign paupers."

The Army provided little incentive to attract men of higher caliber.

Their average age was twenty-three for first enlistments and thirty-two for re-enlistments. Often from the bottom rung of the economic ladder and illiterate, unskilled laborers formed the largest occupational group. Unable to find even menial jobs paying more than $2.00 a week in the East, the Army's monthly allotment of $13.00 seemed attractive.

Fewer than half the recruits were native born. The majority were recent emigrants from foreign countries, particularly from Ireland. Many had seen service in Europe and the U.S. Civil War.

Their officers were a mixture of West Point graduates and veterans of the Civil War Volunteer Service. Officers commonly were elevated from the ranks, having earned their commissions during the war. Approximately thirteen percent of the new officers were Irish or

German born. These officers, in particular, were a rough, hard drinking bunch whose influence did not always enhance the reputation of the western Army.

An exception was the Buffalo Soldiers of the 9th and 10th Cavalry, and 24th and 25th Infantry. So named by the Indians, and led by white officers, these recently freed slaves brought certain strengths and weaknesses to their units.

They excelled in discipline, morale and patience. Their ability to maintain good humor even under the harshest conditions inspired tremendous admiration from their white leaders. They also were sober, and performed well in combat where their service in the field proved outstanding.

Due to their slave heritage, they were illiterate, lacked initiative and were completely dependent on their white officers for leadership. Nevertheless, artist Frederick Remington, who traveled with them, reported that an officer once confessed to him that when on long, monotonous field service, and troubled with depression of spirits, he had only to go about the campfires of the Negro soldiers to be amused and cheered by the clever absurdities of the men.

As the years passed, black regiments included a large proportion of re-enlisted veterans. They took extreme racial pride in their own black units, and had no desire to be incorporated into the regular Army. As Secretary of War Redfield Procter observed in 1889, "the Army often offered a mere refuge for most men. For the black man, it offered a career."

Yet even the roughest and most seasoned veteran, black or white, was ill prepared for the intense guerilla warfare effectively being staged by the hostile tribesmen from Canada to Mexico and from Nebraska to beyond the Rocky Mountains, who tried to defend their lands. In the case of the Apaches of the American Southwest, their nation of approximately 5,000 not only disrupted western expansion for three decades, they successfully managed to thwart half the troops of the United States Army before there was an end to their tenacious warfare.

* * * *

JOSEPH WALKER, GENERAL CARLETON, AND THE BETRAYAL OF MANGAS COLORADAS

On February 24, 1863, Congress separated Arizona from New Mexico Territory, creating Arizona Territory. Gold discoveries prompted their decision, and the desire to use the gold to replenish Washington's dwindling treasury. The war of rebellion had two more years to go.

It was in that same year that Captain Joseph R. Walker of California and his party of miners discovered the gold that initiated Arizona as a territory. Walker was a formidable leader who stood over six feet and weighed 200 pounds. He helped establish the Santa Fe Trail in the 1820s, led the first successful wagon train from St. Louis to California in 1843, and was a guide for John C. Fremont during his western explorations. It was often said of him: "Walker didn't follow trails, he made them." He was 64 years old and suffering failing eyesight when he led his miners into the territory.

Mountain man Joseph Rutherford Walker
—courtesy of Arizona State Library Archives (ASLA)

Earlier that year, Walker had made an unsuccessful prospecting venture into Colorado Territory. He and his men left Colorado and entered New Mexico where he was required, due to the wartime conditions, to get permission from General James Henry Carleton, Commander of the Department of New Mexico, before he could proceed into what was to become Arizona Territory. Suspecting they might be spies for the Confederacy, Carleton required the entire Walker Party to take an oath of allegiance to the Union.

Two years before the Walker Party arrived in New Mexico Territory, General James Carleton and his troop of California Volunteers had marched into the Valley of the Rio Grande. Their purpose in that spring of 1861 was to protect the region from any new Confederate incursions. But the "Greycoats" had already fled back into Texas by the time he arrived, so he and his soldiers found themselves with little to do. Surveying the Rio Grande country, Carleton proclaimed it a "princely realm—a magnificent pastoral and mineral country."

An avowed believer in Manifest Destiny, Carleton started looking for Indians to fight. The Mescalero Apaches, one of several major groups of Apaches, were his first target.

In September of 1862, Carleton sent out an order:

"There will be no council held with the Indians, nor any talks. The men are to be slain whenever and wherever they are found, the women and children taken as prisoners."

When the Military Division in Washington was informed of Carleton's policy of extermination, it made no attempt to stop it.

Following several ruthless campaigns of relentless slaughter, what remained of the small beleaguered bands of Mescalero Apaches were marched off to Bosque Redondo, a desolate reservation Carleton had prepared for them on the Pecos River in east central New Mexico.

Next, he turned his attention to the Navajos whom he referred to as "wolves who run through the mountains and must be subdued." However, there were ten times the number of Navajos than there were of Mescaleros. This task would be more daunting.

Messengers supposedly were sent to inform the Navajos they were to voluntarily surrender to Carleton at Bosque Redondo on the exact date of June 23, 1863. Carleton knew it was unlikely that the thousands of Navajos scattered throughout the territory would get the message, and certainly none of them carried calendars. Nevertheless, when they ignored his demand to surrender, he ordered Col. Kit Carson to prepare his troops for war against the Navajos.

Carson refused. He promptly sent his resignation to Carleton complaining he'd volunteered to join the Army to fight Confederate soldiers, not Indians.

A rough and illiterate former mountain man, Carson liked Indians. He had lived among them during his famous mountain man days, and even had fathered a child with an Arapaho woman. Among most western tribes, Kit Carson was an admired man of legendary proportions. Unfortunately, he was no match for General Carleton.

Domineering and contentious, Carleton was notorious for tormenting his superiors and terrorizing his subordinates. Civil officials often succumbed to his bullying and citizens who stood up to him were harassed into submission. General Carleton refused to accept Kit Carson's resignation.

By then, Kit Carson had become a prominent citizen of Taos and was properly married to Josefa, daughter of Don Francisco Jaramillo. As one of New Mexico's leading citizens, Don Francisco's influence and support helped Carson to become prosperous and respectable.

Because the citizenry of Taos applauded General Carleton's policy to rid the area of Indians, Carson realized that by defying the powerful General Carleton's orders, he would lose the respect of not only his family, but other leading citizens of Taos. Reluctantly, he withdrew his resignation and took to the field against his old friends the Navajos.

He knew the only way to conquer them was to destroy their crops and livestock…and scorch their earth. By autumn he'd succeeded in laying waste most of their herds and crops between Canyon de Chelly and Ft. Canby.

In late March of the following year, more than eight thousand starving and defeated Navajos were forced upon their "Long Walk" to Bosque Redondo.

They never took up arms against the whites again. Nor did they forgive Kit Carson for his betrayal. Most unforgivable of all, was his destruction of their beloved peach orchards.

* * * *

THE BETRAYAL OF MANGAS COLORADAS

When the Walker Party asked permission to proceed into Arizona in 1863, Carleton immediately became suspicious that the Walker Party might be Confederate sympathizers. After making them swear an oath of allegiance to the Union, he sent a group of men along to keep an eye on them, headed by A.C. Benedict. Now thirty-six men rode west from Albuquerque.

Carleton was not the only one keeping an eye on the Walker prospecting party.

Mangas Coloradas, the mighty leader of the Chiricahua Apaches, had his band of warriors keep the prospecting party under constant surveillance from the time they left Albuquerque. Once the Walker Party became aware of this, their agitation grew to hair-trigger proportions. A plan was implemented to seize an Apache leader and hold him hostage while they pushed further west.

Fifty years later while in captivity, Geronimo, a member of the Mangas band of Chiricahuas, told the story of what happened. He said the prospectors sent a message that they would give Mangas' people blankets and food. Mangas consulted with the other leaders of his band, including Geronimo and Cochise. They all pleaded with him not to accept the offer. None of his band trusted the "white eyes."

Geronimo had no explanation as to why Mangas ignored the warnings of his people. Perhaps by then the 60 year-old Mangas was simply weary of war and knew, since it was winter, his people desperately needed the offered goods. They would never learn his true reasons for meeting with the Walker Party, because Mangas did not return to tell them. Only one reliable account of what happened during that meeting exists, written by a member of the Walker Party.

With three or four of his warriors in tow, Mangas met with the Walker Party on the morning of January 18, 1863 at their camp near Silver City, New Mexico. The prospectors hoisted a white flag, a sign of peace, as Mangas and his warriors approached. Negotiations took place in broken Spanish. Their exchange was long and tedious.

Mangas eventually dropped his guard and moved closer to the prospectors. Immediately the prospectors raised their rifles and told Mangas he was their prisoner, and if his warriors left them alone for ten moons, he would be released and could return in safety to his people. They told the warriors who accompanied Mangas to go and carry their message back to his people. How sincere this promise was, will never be known.

A detachment of General Carleton's soldiers were camped near the Walker Party, and when their commander, Brigadier General Joseph West learned of Mangas' capture, he rode into Walker's camp and demanded to take charge of this valuable captive. As recalled by one of Walker's party:

"The General walked out to where Mangas was in custody to see him, and he looked like a pigmy beside the old chief who towered above everybody in stature (Mangas was over six feet tall). He looked careworn and refused to talk and evidently realized he had made a great mistake in trusting the pale face on this occasion."

As General West took charge of Mangas, he reminded his soldiers of the Indian policy espoused by General Carleton five months earlier. The soldiers had no doubt as to what was expected of them. That night, two soldiers were put in charge of guarding the shackled Mangas.

The night was a bitterly cold. Mangas lay on the ground beside a campfire, wrapped in a flimsy blanket. A sentry on duty witnessed what happened next.

The two guards heated the tips of their bayonets in the fire and began poking the chief's legs and feet with them. Mangas rose up and yelled in Spanish that he was not a child to be played with. The guards promptly fired six shots into the old chief's body. The great chief of the Chiricahua Apaches fell dead by the fire.

The next morning, a soldier scalped Mangas with a butcher knife and pocketed it as a souvenir. Mangas' body was thrown into a gully where it lay for three days.

Then several soldiers decided to cut Mangas' head off and boil it in a pot. His skull was subsequently sent to a phrenologist in New York who later wrote that Mangas' cranial capacity was greater than that of Daniel Webster's. In the meantime, General West sent word to Carleton that Mangas had been shot trying to escape.

The Chiricahuas waited in vain for word of their chief. It never came. Apparently the messengers did not make it back to camp either.

Eventually news of Mangas' death filtered back to his band. When they learned that his head had been boiled in an iron pot, they were horrified. They pictured their beloved chief wandering headless in the afterlife. Geronimo later recalled that it was the greatest wrong ever done to the Indians.

Cochise, who took over Mangas' leadership, vowed to kill one hundred whites for every Apache killed. Thereafter, he and his warriors set out on a relentless and murderous rampage that lasted for another decade.

* * * *

THE ARIZONA GOLD RUSH AND
THE ESTABLISHMENT OF A TERRITORY

In the meantime, the Walker Party eventually made it unharmed to the San Francisco Mountains near present day Flagstaff. There they turned south and soon established a base near the area that eventually would be named "Prescott."

By May of 1863, they discovered a rich bonanza of gold in Lynx Creek. Over time, the Walker Mining and Prospecting Company enjoyed a yield of $2,000,000 in gold from their Lynx Creek digs, and many members of the Walker Party remained in the area and made a name for themselves in the development of Prescott.

When General Carleton received the report of the discovery, he sent a special party to verify the claims. Captain Nathaniel Pishon,

First Regiment, Cavalry, and California Volunteers accompanied New Mexico Surveyor General John A. Clark to the site. When Pishon verified the rich mineral field to Carleton, he included the following glowing statement: "The new government of Arizona, if it will ever come, will be at these new gold fields, not the insignificant village of Tucson."

Immediately two companies of California Volunteers 1st infantry, numbering 180 officers and men, were ordered to establish Camp Whipple in Little Chino Valley 20 miles north of what would later become Prescott. Carleton assigned Major Edward B. Willis to accomplish the task of establishing the camp, along with commanding officers Captains Joseph P. Hargrove and Henry M. Benson. These "long knives" as the Indians called the sword-wielding soldiers, were sent to open the area for settlement and protect the newcomers from Indian raids. Protecting the Indians from the settlers was not on the Army's agenda.

The camp was named for Major General Amiel W. Whipple who had surveyed the territory in the mid-1850s and later was mortally wounded at Chancellorville during the Civil War. The trails established by Whipple in the 1850s made the soldiers march into the area much easier.

Carleton, always the opportunist, quickly laid claim to several mines of his own in the area. Once he was able to focus his attention on Arizona, he arrogantly determined to rid it of the Yavapai and Apache people just as quickly as he had rid New Mexico of the Mescaleros and Navajos.

Instead, he stirred up Arizona's native people like a nest of enraged hornets.

One year after the gold discoveries were confirmed in Arizona Territory, John N. Goodwin was dispatched to administer the affairs of this new territory.

John Noble Goodwin, who was to become Arizona's first territorial governor, was born at South Berwick County, Maine, on October 18, 1824. He graduated from Dartmouth College in 1844, and returned home to Maine to read law in the office of John Hubbard. He was admitted to the bar four years later. In 1854, he served in the Maine State Senate where he was appointed special commissioner to revise the laws of Maine.

He married Susan Howard Robinson at Augusta, Maine, on October 27, 1857, and by 1861 was elected as a Republican from Maine to the 37th Congress under President Abraham Lincoln. In March of 1863, Lincoln appointed him Chief Justice of the United States Court for the Territory of Arizona. Following the sudden death of the original appointee, Representative Gurley of Ohio (who had helped push for legislation to make Arizona a separate territory), the U.S. Senate confirmed Goodwin's appointment by President Lincoln as Governor of Arizona Territory.

However, Goodwin had already set out for Arizona Territory prior to his confirmation. Accompanied by a group of Territorial officials and a military escort, he began his journey at Fort Leavenworth, Kansas, on September 25, 1863. They arrived in Chino Valley, the original site for the capital, on January 22, 1864.

Prior to their arrival, Major Willis negotiated a peace treaty with a band of three hundred Tonto Apaches who lived near Camp Whipple in Chino Valley. He then went to Santa Fe to meet the Goodwin party and escort them into Arizona. Unfortunately, when some soldiers from Whipple encountered a band of Tontos, they opened fire and killed twenty of the bewildered Indians, thus setting the Tontos on a relentless campaign against all white eyes.

Escorted by Major Willis, the Goodwin party toured most of the Territory with little resistance from the Indians. After visiting Tucson, the only established town in the territory, they confirmed Congress' enjoinder not to make it the capital, even though it was a logical choice. At the time of his visit, Tucson was a Confederate stronghold and Goodwin and his entourage, Republicans to a man, could not stomach the large number of Democrats and Confederate sympathizers who made up the majority of Tucson's population. It was notoriously lawless to boot. So gold was not the only reason Goodwin established Prescott as the first territorial capital on May 30, 1864. William Hickling Prescott, for whom the Capital was named, was a prominent historian of the time, who wrote the *History Of The Conquest Of Mexico* in 1843.

Prescott's original location in Chino Valley was moved 22 miles to the west in order to be closer to the mining activity. Game abounded in the new location and the land was rich with lumber and water. Numerous white settlers already had descended on the new location to stake their mining claims.

In a speech delivered to the first joint session of the First Territorial Legislative Assembly on September 30, 1864, Governor Goodwin spoke of Prescott's future and implied his advocacy of the doctrine of Manifest Destiny:

"We are clothed with the power to make laws which forever shape the destiny of the Territory, to lay the foundations of a new state and to build a new commonwealth. We are entrusted not only with the present interests of a small constituency and amendable to them alone, but we are trustees of posterity and responsible to the millions who in time shall come after us.

"Where the foot of the Anglo Saxon is once firmly planted, he stands secure, and before the clang of his labor the Indian and antelope disappear together. The tide of our civilization has no refulgent wave but rolls steadily on over ocean and continent.

"To the Apaches has been transmitted for a century an inheritance of hate and hostility to the white man. He is a murderer by hereditary descent and a thief by prescription. He and his ancestors have subsisted on the stock they have plundered. They have exhausted the ingenuity of fiends to invent more excruciating tortures for the unfortunate prisoners they may take, so that the traveler acquainted with their warfare, surprised and unable to escape, reserves the last shot in his revolver for his own head.

"When troops were removed from this territory at the commencement of the rebellion, it was nearly depopulated by their murders. They have made southern Arizona and northern Mexico a wilderness of desolation. But for them mines would be worked, innumerable sheep and cattle would cover the plains, and some of the bravest and most energetic men that were ever pioneers of a new country, and who now fill bloody and unmarked graves, would be living to see their brightest anticipations realized.

"It is useless to speculate on the origin of this feeling, or inquire which party is right or wrong. It is enough to know that it is relentless and unchangeable. They respect no flag of truce, ask and give no quarter, and make a treaty only that under the guise of friendship they may rob and steal more extensively and with greater impunity. As to them one policy only can be adopted. A war must be prosecuted until they are compelled to submit and go to a reservation."

These strong words carried the unmistakable message of genocide.

John N. Goodwin continued to live in Arizona Territory for three more years, serving as an elected delegate to the 39th Congress from 1865 to 1867. Afterward he moved to New York City and established a law firm. Among his clients was the Northern Pacific Railroad. He died on April 29, 1887, at the age of 62, in Paraiso Springs, Monterey County, California, where he had retired to seek relief from the gout.

* * * *

SOLDIERS, "SAVAGES" AND CITIZENS— THE ATROCITIES BEGIN

Governor Goodwin's passionate diatribe against the Apaches during the First Legislative Assembly was nothing new in the Territory…or the country. Newspapers from coast to coast called for the abolition of Arizona's Indian agencies, referring to them as: "Feeding stations and depots of supplies where the hostile Apaches can rest and gather strength while planning their next wave of atrocities."

The popular outcry common to every Arizonan was "Death to the Apaches!" The view towards them was exaggerated and unreasonable. As far as the Indians were concerned, the feelings were mutual.

Both sides were crazy for blood and revenge. Each became a ruthless and bitter foe to the other. Any hope for reform or reconciliation was still years away.

If that wasn't enough, friction grew between settlers and the Army and only escalated as the Army continued to show little progress against the Indians. Troops were blamed and their officers declared unfit as more and more settlers suffered extreme losses of life and property.

The Army was equally at odds against the citizenry, accusing them of constant treachery against the Indians and of lumping all Indians together, refusing to recognize the difference between hostile and non-hostile tribes.

Initially the Walapai and Yavapai people tried to avoid war, and on several occasions sat down to talk peace with the citizens. Instead, their peaceful assemblies faced instant treachery and all out murder. Provoked into unwanted hostilities, these Native tribes became as equally fierce adversaries as their Apache allies.

Another complaint the Army had against the citizenry was their economic dependence upon the troops. General O.C. Ord bluntly described the situation:

"Almost the only paying business the white inhabitants have in that territory is supplying troops. If the paymasters and quartermasters of the Army were to stop payment in Arizona, a great majority of white settlers would be compelled to quit it. Hostilities are therefore kept up with a view to protecting the inhabitants, most of whom are supported by the hostilities."

Thus the citizens damned the Army for not doing its job, and the Army damned the citizens for keeping the Indians stirred up, and then benefiting from their hostilities.

The truth of the matter was that the Army relied on the citizens more than they wanted to admit. Supplies shipped by the Army arrived erratically or not at all.

The starting point was San Francisco where supplies were shipped south along the Pacific coast and around the Baja Peninsula to Fort Yuma located on the Colorado River. There they were hauled overland for great distances under heavy escort to forts that were separated by miles and miles of impossible Terrain. This provoked General Sherman to declare to Congress in 1869: "The cost of the military establishment in Arizona is all out of proportion to its value as part of the public domain." Sherman was not the first high-ranking officer to question the military's presence in Arizona.

From 1865 to 1885, posts were established in Arizona, then abandoned, moved or renamed with dizzying speed. Location depended on where the Indians were more threatening, supplies were more accessible, water was more abundant, or because disease threatened to wipe out the troops. For example, Fort Lincoln on the Verde River was moved in 1868 to a more healthful location near the present site of Camp Verde and renamed Fort Verde. Malaria plagued the troops at the old site, which was situated near marshes along the sluggish Verde River where mosquitoes bred in abundance.

By 1866, all unified command in Arizona had disappeared completely after General McDowell, who replaced General Carleton, separated Arizona into four different districts.

This fragmentation of command only benefited the Apache and Yavapai. McDowell was severely criticized by an Inspector General who charged that there were too many small posts in the territory and "the scouting is uncoordinated and proving futile."

McDowell defended his structuring by blaming the character of Arizona. "Its deserts are too vast," he claimed, "its mountains too precipitous, there are too many canyons and uncertain sources of water, not to mention the cactus, snakes, poisonous insects and temperatures which often hover above 120 degrees." He, along with Generals Mason and Carleton contended that only troops who were skilled in guerilla warfare, and were as perfectly attuned to their environment, as were the Indians, could possibly prevail in Arizona.

Where were such men, they asked, or the officers to lead them? Even General Ord commented: "We have developed a greatly improved rifle, but I rather think we have a much less intelligent soldier to handle it."

There were citizens of the Territory, however, who believed they were up to the challenge. One such man was John Townsend whose method of operation was to go alone into the mountains and hide out until he could locate his "game." He indulged in killing Indians as a sport and was absolutely obsessed with it. He wanted to kill Indians more than he wanted to do anything else. Judge Edmund Wells wrote about him in Argonaut Tales, 1870:

"The more Indians Townsend killed, the more popular he became with his fellow settlers. They wanted the Indians killed as badly as he wanted to do away with them. His law was the law of reprisal, an eye for an eye, and a tooth for a tooth. With the violent loss of every white man, woman or child that came to his knowledge, a living Apache man, woman or child paid the penalty in kind, and the list registered on his rifle stock was a long one."

In an open meeting in 1866, the appreciative citizens of Prescott presented Townsend with a handsome Winchester rifle and a thousand rounds of ammunition, for which Townsend was profoundly touched. A few days later, the *Arizona Miner* printed tidings from him that "the gun was doing good work, and was a dandy."

With all his cunning, however, Townsend fell victim of the Indians after putting his foot in the same kind of trap he had laid for them so many times. Upon hearing of his death the *Arizona Miner* called for vengeance, the headlines urged killing..."the devilish foe until sufficient of them are offered as sacrifices to the spirit of the great departed."

The *Arizona Miner* was quick to report any and all Indian depredations as well:

"ONE HUNDRED INDIANS ATTACK ELEVEN WHITE MEN, WOUNDED SIX OF THEM, CAPTURED 24 HEAD OF CATTLE AND 4 TONS OF HAY:

The hell-hounds of the reservation are on the war path, and our citizens will do well to look for them. About 3 o'clock on the afternoon of the 6th fully 100 painted savages attacked at the foot of Grief Hill within plain sight of Camp Verde on the Verde River, in this country, a party of 11 whites—9 soldiers and 2 citizens, who were escorting and driving two ox teams and wagons containing corn. The men had passed what they considered the most dangerous place, when, of a sudden, a volley of bullets was poured on them from the vicinity of a juniper tree near the road. At the first fire from the Indians, six men were wounded and two head of cattle killed. Two of the men were said to have received dangerous wounds, and in one or two cases at least, amputation will have to be resorted to. The soldiers fought the savages until their ammunition ran out, when they were forced to abandon everything to the Indians and retreat to Camp Verde." (May 8, 1867)

On July 27, 1867, the *Arizona Miner's* flamboyant publisher John H. Marion admitted the Indians were swarming like bees around Prescott:

"Just now, our red brethren are awful thick hereabouts. They are seen in the woods...Close to town, on Granite Creek, in fact everywhere. So keep your powder dry and whenever you see an Indian that says 'Americano mucho bueno...' kill him; he don't mean it."

The inventive torture tactics of the Apaches, which always led to inflaming the angry passions of the citizens, was typified by the death of a 21-year-old Scotsman named George Taylor, who was captured by a group of Tonto Apaches near Wickenburg in the 1870's. According to John Bourke:

"The Apaches slaughtered three whites, one by torture, not far from Wickenburg. The Tonto Apaches who did it were actually waiting to plunder the Arizona-California Stage, but it was several hours late and to amuse themselves, they captured George Taylor, a 21 year-old Scot.

They led him to a secluded place, stripped and bound him, and began shooting arrows into his naked body, taking care not to hit a vital spot. In his agony, the young man rolled over and over, breaking off the arrows until more than 150 had been shot into him. When he could move no more, they finished him in a manner so beastly and excruciating that I could not, if I would…hint of the method of his final demise."

* * * *

THE CITIZENS TAKE CHARGE

The Indian Wars had reached such intensity in the Prescott area by 1864 that Major Edward B. Willis, writing from Fort Whipple to his superior officer, reported an estimated 150 animals had been stolen in Central Arizona, including numerous government mules. Citizens reported more than 400 of their horses and 40 of their mules had been stolen. Two prominent ranchers in the area, Abraham H. Peeples and King S. Woolsey together lost 33 head of cattle and 28 mules in a matter of weeks.

In an editorial that same year by *Arizona Miner* publisher John H. Marion, he addressed the citizen's dissatisfaction with the military's efforts to protect them:

"Arizonians! All of you are aware that it is the duty of the government to protect lives and property and you also know that it has failed to do so…perhaps after hundreds more lose their lives in unequal combat and thousands of dollars worth of property are stolen and destroyed, the government may send a few more companies of soldiers to help the few already here to carry on this miserable, abortive war."

The citizens considered their situation intolerable. Because of this, Peeples and Woolsey volunteered to lead a group of men to recover the livestock from their "new owners." Their motive was simply stated:

"We are determined, if possible, to punish the guilty Indians. Otherwise, unless the government takes a hand, we will have to leave this country and let the Indians have it."

They believed their very survival depended upon stopping the Indians no matter what the cost.

With Fort Whipple in short supply of soldiers, several brave companies of citizens organized as "Rangers" under Woolsey's leadership, and with guidance from the remaining military, set out on several expeditions to rout the area of "savages." They had two more motives in mind while on these numerous expeditions against the Indians: take note of future areas for settlement, and locate any potential gold deposits.

Brigadier General Carleton reported on their first such expedition in March of 1864. In summary he stated: "A party of 30 Americans and 14 Maricopa and Pima Indians (traditional enemies of the Apaches) under Col. King S. Woolsey, attacked a band of Gila Apaches…killed 19 and wounded others."

In the second campaign, later that same March of 1864, more than one hundred ranchers and miners joined forces to, as the *Arizona Miner* described it, "create a formidable movement against savages, and eager to chastise the wily foe." Two months after that in May of 1864, the Arizona Miner carried a request from King Woolsey for a third expedition. He tempted volunteers by stating: "There's lively work ahead."

Men like Woolsey typify the hardships, determination and courage needed to open the way for settlement in Central Arizona. Yet by today's standards, he might be considered a terrorist and a candidate for crimes against humanity.

Much like John Townsend, Woolsey's war against the Yavapai and Apache people became a personal vendetta, conducted without remorse and laced with such atrocities that he later shocked even some of his own contemporaries.

Although primarily remembered for his fights with the Apaches, this was just a small part of his activities. Woolsey also was a miner, rancher, farmer, road builder, real estate dealer and politician. He accomplished his numerous vigorous activities despite a serious heart condition.

Woolsey spent the last part of his life trying to justify his participation in the Battle at Bloody Tanks, the Pinole Massacre, and his abandonment of his Spanish wife and four children. Historians still question his depredations. For years after his death, his aging widow Mary continued to defend him. Nevertheless, he remains one of Arizona's most colorful, accomplished, and honored pioneers.

King S. Woolsey - Fort Verde State Park
—FVSP

* * * *

THE LIFE AND TIMES OF KING S. WOOLSEY

King S. Woolsey was born in Alabama around 1832. He arrived at Fort Yuma sometime in 1860 with two companions: Calvin Jackson (1827-1880) and A.C. Benedict (1830-1880). This is the same Benedict who, a few years later, was sent to spy on the Walker Party for General Carleton who suspected they were Confederate sympathizers. Woolsey, an avowed secessionist, later became a member of that same Walker Party.

When Woolsey arrived in Yuma, he quickly found work as a mule driver for Henry Grinnell who owned the Stanwix station on the Butterfield stage route. Eventually Woolsey bought Grinnell's interest in the Stanwix Station, and continued to own it for the rest of his life.

After the Civil War broke out in 1861, instead of rushing to join the ranks of his southern brothers, Woolsey stayed in Yuma and made a small fortune selling goods and supplies to the Union Army. By 1862, he had profited enough to move into other areas of endeavor.

With his new partner George Martin, he paid $1800 in gold for what was to become the Agua Caliente Ranch. The ranch took its name from a hot springs which bubbled up from the ground. Located near the Gila River in what is now western Maricopa County, the Agua Caliente Ranch became a popular and famous gathering place for travelers, dignitaries and Indian fighters. It also evolved into a small settlement with a number of people living and working there.

Soon after Woolsey acquired the Aqua Caliente Ranch in 1863, the Walker Party passed nearby. It's evident that his old friend A.C. Benedict, traveling as a spy with the Walker Party, knew about Woolsey's ranch and contacted him, After learning they were prospecting for gold, Woolsey eagerly joined this famous group. The Walker Party was among the first in 1863 to mine along the Hassyampa River and its tributary, Lynx Creek, where the famous gold discovery was made.

Woolsey eventually acquired a large number of claims in the area, but few brought him success. They did provide substantial wealth for others in later years.

In the meantime, after three years, Woolsey's partner, George Martin, sold his interest in the Agua Caliente Ranch to Woolsey and moved to Yuma. There he soon married Delfina Redondo, a member of a prominent Old Spanish family who bore him eight children. George established a drug business in Yuma and became prominent in local affairs. He served as county supervisor, county treasurer, city treasurer and was a member of the city council of Yuma before his death in 1907. One son, Andrew, served in the Upper House of Arizona's Second State Legislature.

In 1863, Woolsey formed another partnership with John H. Dickson, also a member of the Walker Party. They laid claim to a large section of land along the Agua Fria, approximately fourteen miles due east of Prescott. Dickson remained a partner with Woolsey for less than a year before moving on to other endeavors.

On the Agua Fria land, Woolsey built the first ranch house in northern Arizona. His Agua Fria ranch was in many ways a version of a southern plantation, yet well fortified with high walls built with stones gathered from Indian ruins. It provided ample refuge to many a person needing protection from the warring Indians. It also was the place from which the Rangers gathered to set out on their expeditions against the Indians. An early description of the ranch was found in a letter from Charles Poston:

"On the northeast we could see a stream called the Agua Frio (sic), shining in the sunlight like a thread of silver; and a single green spot marked the rancho of Colonel Woolsey, the frontiersman and Indian fighter who lives on the very edge of civilization, and defies the barbarous Apaches in their homes."

Woolsey and his Rangers' first major foray against the Indians occurred in January of 1864 when the infamous Battle of Bloody Tanks took place. The name would be derived from the fact that there were pools of water on the ground that became clouded with blood during the fight. The exact location of this battle is not known, but is believed to be halfway between Globe and the Silver King Mine.

On that day, according to Woolsey's version of the story, the Rangers found themselves facing almost 500 Apaches (participants later claimed the number to be less than half that many). Regardless, the Indians were in the clear majority and "painted for war," according to Woolsey. He decided to try and parley with the Indians.

Tonto Jack, a Yuma Indian who worked for Woolsey, was called upon to interpret. Six Apache leaders agreed to parley. Woolsey met them with four of his Rangers. He'd instructed the remaining Rangers to pick a warrior out and when they saw him place his hand near his hat, they were to shoot their selected target.

According to the Ranger's version of the story, one of the Apache chiefs infuriated Woolsey when he demanded a blanket to sit on and some coffee and whiskey. Woolsey provided the blanket along with some pinole and jerked beef instead.

Woolsey later insisted this parley was only a subterfuge and the Apaches' true intent was to slaughter them. Soon he touched his hand to his hat and the Rangers opened fire, while Woolsey and his men shot and killed the six leaders. Though outnumbered, the whites had the advantage in that the Apaches had only bows and arrows. The fight was long and fierce with reinforcements arriving to support the Apaches.

The Rangers realized they'd better give up and escape. All of them survived the "battle" except a Mr. Allen who was thrust through his heart with a spear. Woolsey returned to his ranch with twenty-four scalps, a few lopped off ears and a young captive girl. Bloody Tanks, the once a popular gathering place for the Apaches, was shunned by them forever afterwards.

For years Woolsey and his Rangers told conflicting versions of the incident while the Apaches remembered it as another example of the white man's treachery. Their survivors claimed they had truly come in peace, and were not painted for war.

It is curious that Woolsey and his Rangers had the time and opportunity to take scalps and ears if engaged in such a "frenzied battle all day with reinforcements arriving for the Indians at every turn." Could Woolsey's version of the Battle of Bloody Tanks be a clear example of genocide? In one of his letters to General Carleton, Woolsey wrote: "I operate on the principle of extermination of the savages." This was a statement sure to please the crusty old general but also render Woolsey's explanations suspicious.

During this expedition, a 14 year-old girl by the name of Lucia Martinez managed to escape her Apache captors and ride to the safety of Woolsey's Agua Fria Ranch. Malnourished, dirty, naked and terrified, the miners took pity on her and gave her some empty flour sacks and a needle and thread from which Lucia created a serviceable dress. She spoke only Spanish, but was so helpful around the ranch the men affectionately called her Lucy.

After working for a Prescott couple as a servant for a while, the devastating effects of Lucy's captivity finally wore off. She learned to speak English and developed into an attractive young woman. Woolsey took her back to his ranch where she became his common law wife. He fathered her four children.

Then in 1869, following the birth of their second daughter, Woolsey arrived home with a housekeeper, Mary Taylor. Mary advanced from housekeeper to manager of Woolsey's Stanwix Stagecoach Station. After Lucy gave birth to their son Robert, Mary put her foot down and had Lucy and her three children banished to Yuma, never to return. In 1871, Woolsey and Mary became the first couple to marry in the newly formed Maricopa County.

The Woolseys prospered and soon he became one of the largest landowners in Phoenix. Apparently Woolsey did not completely abandon Lucy. She gave him one more son, Louis, two years after his marriage to Mary. But when Woolsey ran for a seat in the United States Congress in 1878, the Battle of Bloody Tanks, his abandonment of Lucy and his involvement in the Pinole Massacre were dredged up and exposed by his opponents. Once again, Woolsey attempted to put a gloss over the Pinole incident.

This incident took place in the summer of 1864. As Woolsey explained it, he and several men took three pack mules into the Bradshaw Mountains to examine his mining claims. According to Woolsey, somewhere past Wickenburg, a large party of Apaches attacked them. The situation appeared hopeless and their fight lasted until late in the afternoon. Two of their mules were killed and they found themselves cut off from water. The Indians knew they had only to wait them out before they would expose themselves. It was said of

Woolsey that when all other resources failed, he'd call for a "talk," and through these talks, make his escape. It's interesting that these Apache leaders always agreed to "talks" when they already had the upper hand.

Once again, the leader agreed to talk, or so Woolsey said. Before going, Woolsey placed a large sack of pinole on the remaining mule and hid it behind some rocks, knowing full well the Indians would steal it. He'd laced the pinole with strychnine, something he carried for his heart condition. Since they'd had nothing to eat all day, the Apaches quickly consumed the pinole. While Woolsey chatted with their leader, the poison began to take effect. As the warriors twitched and went into spasms, their companions who hadn't yet eaten the pinole, thought they'd been cursed by witches and fled. Woolsey and his men opened fire on the fleeing ones.

Several years later, Woolsey met up with the same leader and asked how many warriors he lost that day. "Many Indian can't fight no more till warriors grow up", he replied. The Yavapai later claimed they were the ones who suffered this depredation. They came in peace to Woolsey, they said, and once again he'd tricked them.

When the first territorial legislature met in Prescott on September 24, 1864, Woolsey won his seat by a landslide. He was 36 years old and one of the youngest members. He was appointed chairman of militia and Indian affairs, as well of as several other committees.

Despite a shortage of funds, the lawmakers that year appropriated $1487 to reimburse Woolsey, and the men who went on his expeditions, for the goods used while fighting Indians—adding their thanks to all those who under his guidance endured many hardships and privations and who contributed to the safety, knowledge and general welfare of the people.

Woolsey continued to earn voter approval for five more terms in office. When he ran as a delegate to the 46th U.S. Congress in 1878, he was defeated. His participation in the Battle of Bloody Tanks, the Pinole Massacre, and the abandonment of his family were issues raised by his opponents which came back to haunt him.

On June 30, 1879, King S. Woolsey died at his ranch of angina pectoris, a heart malfunction. Although he was not yet fifty years old at the time of his death, he left a substantial estate.

A sympathetic Yuma businessman, (probably George Martin, Woolsey's former partner) immediately began court proceedings on Lucy's behalf to gain a portion of Woolsey's estate for her children. Woolsey's wife, Mary, used slick legal maneuvers to block the action claiming that only the first two daughters were Woolsey's. She also falsely claimed that Lucy was an Indian and therefore under Territorial Law, the children had no rights of inheritance. The court ruled against the children and Mary inherited everything.

While Lucy and her children drifted into obscurity, Mary married two more times and by the year of her death in 1928, she was the wealthiest woman in Arizona. Governor Hunt ordered all the flags in the state to be flown at half-mast in her memory, the first woman so honored in Arizona.

Despite all of his accomplishments in helping settle the territory, King S. Woolsey was remembered most for his war with the Indians. Buried in the city cemetery in Phoenix, these words were carved on his tombstone: *HE BRAVED THE DANGERS AND HARDSHIPS OF FRONTIER LIFE FOR NINETEEN YEARS WITH SUCCESS AND WAS THE HERO OF MANY BATTLES WITH THE APACHES IN ARIZONA.*

* * * *

GENERAL GEORGE CROOK AND HIS SUCCESSFUL CAMPAIGN AGAINST THE INDIANS

Woolsey and other fighting citizens of his ilk were relieved of their responsibilities to protect the Territory against the Indians when the Secretary of War appointed General George Crook as Commander of the Department of Arizona in 1871. It took Crook less than two years to bring peace to Central Arizona.

General George Crook with Apache Scouts
—FVSP

Using tactics similar to those employed by Kit Carson when he defeated the Navahos in New Mexico, Crook added a highly successful, yet controversial plan of defense against the Apaches. He hired Indians to fight Indians. The advantage of his Indian Scouts' service proved invaluable.

Between 1872-74, fewer than 20 hostile Indians were killed or captured by the regular Army, which didn't use scouts. The Army units, who took advantage of the Indian Scout system, killed 275 hostiles and captured more than 300 during that same period.

The way General Crook persuaded Indians to become scouts against their own people was by telling them: "I expect good men to help me run down bad ones. This is the way white people do it. If there are bad men in neighborhoods, all law-abiding citizens turn out to assist the officers of the law in arresting and punishing those who will not behave themselves. I hope you will see it is your duty to do the same."

There was a stronger and more practical incentive for Indians to join this service however. They were fed, clothed and put on the Army payroll. More important, the government policy at that time was genocide. The Scout service was the safest place to be if you were an Indian.

Besides, scouting was an easy job for them, particularly when assigned to tracking old tribal rivals. The Indians had been doing that for centuries.

The Indians named General George Crook, Nan-tan-Lupan (Chief Grey Wolf). Many recognized that his attitude towards them was different from that of his military predecessors. He had a better understanding of their problems, and a true compassion towards their plight.

As to his appearance, Captain John Bourke, who served under him, described him this way:

"His personal appearance was impressive, but without the slightest suggestion of the pompous and overdressed military man. He was plain as an old stick, and looked more like an honest country squire than the commander of a war-like expedition. He had blue-gray eyes, quick and penetrating in his glance, a finely chiseled roman nose, a firm yet kindly mouth, a well-arched head, a good brow and a general expression of indomitable resolution, honest purpose, sagacity and good intentions. He had an aversion to wearing a uniform, and to the glitter and filigree of the military profession. He was essentially a man of action, and spoke little, and to the point, but was fond of listening to the conversations of others. He was at all times accessible to the humblest soldier, or poorest prospector, without losing a certain dignity which repelled familiarity, but had no semblance of haughtiness. He never used profanity and indulged in no equivocal language."

General Crook graduated from West Point in 1852. In 1862, he was wounded during the Civil War, where he attained the rank of Major General before the war ended. Following the War, Crook continued his Army career as an Indian fighter.

He fought Indians in California, Idaho and Oregon before arriving in Arizona. As a result, he knew a great deal about Indians, and was soon to learn more.

He studied them intensely, until he knew the Indian better than they knew themselves. He insisted on honest treatment of them and never made a promise he could not honor.

His outdoorsmanship, stamina, and endurance became legendary among fellow soldiers and officers alike. He also studied all aspects of nature with intensity, was an avid hunter and fisherman, a crack shot, and an accomplished horseman. When in the field, however, he preferred to ride his mule, Apache.

When Crook arrived in Arizona in June of 1871, he toured the territory and took full measure of his adversary. The only way to peace, he concluded, was to soundly thrash the Apaches. The offensive he used against them remains one of the most brilliant and successful ever mounted against Indians anywhere.

In addition to establishing the Indian Scout Service, he developed mule trains to peak efficiency. Instead of cumbersome wagons carrying supplies, the pack mules provided greater mobility. He also gave the troops a confidence and determination unknown under their previous commanders.

"The trail must be stuck to and never lost," he admonished them. "No excuse will be accepted for leaving a trail: if horses play out, then follow the enemy on foot. No sacrifice should be left untried to make a campaign short, sharp and decisive."

Before his campaign began, Crook laid down his policy towards the Indians at his base of command at Fort Whipple:

"The commanding General, after making a thorough and exhaustive examination among the Indians…regrets to say that he finds among them a general feeling of distrust and want of confidence in the whites, especially the soldiers; and also that much dissatisfaction, dangerous to the peace of the country, exists among them. Officers and soldiers are reminded that one of the fundamental principles of the military character is justice to all…Indians as well as white men—and that a disregard of this policy is likely to bring about hostilities, and cause the deaths of the very people they are sent here to protect. In all their dealings with Indians, officers must be careful not only to observe the strictest fidelity, but to make no promise, not in their power to carry out; all grieving arising in their jurisdiction should be redressed, so then an accumulation of them may not be a cause of an outbreak."

Next, Crook ordered all squatters and unauthorized miners to remove themselves from the Camp Date Creek and Camp Verde reservations. He even started an investigation that resulted in the reorganization of the Indian Department, and the discharge of some of the agents and higher-up officials in these same departments.

Then he installed Crook's Trail, a fully maintained trail 175 miles long. It began at Fort Whipple in Prescott, traversed the Verde Valley, then cut through the pine wilderness and higher Terrain of the Mogollon Rim. Martha Summerhayes, the first white woman to travel by wagon along this trail, recalled the experience in her fascinating book *VANISHED ARIZONA*:

"I was a young Army wife accompanying my Lieutenant husband to Fort Apache. Camped along the trail that night, I could not free myself from the anxiety of an Apache attack. Everywhere I looked, I imagined a fierce Apache behind a dark tree trunk. Seeking assurance from my husband, he patted me lovingly and told me it was safe to go to sleep. 'The Apaches never attack at night', he said. Several minutes later I whispered, when do they attack? 'Just before dawn', he yawned."

Crook's Trail cut through a rough semi-circle formed by Camps Verde, McDowell, Grant, and Apache in north central Arizona. He fielded from these posts nine troop-strength commands of the First and Fifth Cavalry, each accompanied by a detachment of Indian Scouts. He planned to clear the country, inside and outside of this semicircle, of the roving bands of hostiles. The soldiers were determined to drive them into the Tonto Basin, where they would close in on them for the kill.

Crook chose November 15, 1871, to initiate his campaign. He knew this date would further enhance his chances for a successful campaign, because winter food was harder to come by, and campfires, which the Indians needed to warm themselves in the higher elevations, could be spotted easily.

Throughout the winter, Crook's commands scoured the Tonto Basin and its bordering mountains, the Mazatzals, the Sierra Ancha, and the Superstitions where the soldiers suffered almost as much as the Indians they pursued. Subjected to numerous privations, prolonged fatigue, and extremes of climate, their most debilitating moments came while trying to traverse the treacherous mountain ranges where winter snows were considered more punishing than any place in the West.

Led by the Indian Scouts, the soldiers successfully sought out the hostiles, destroyed their food supplies and kept them on the run. In some twenty actions during that winter, almost 200 Indians were killed.

One of Crook's greatest victories occurred at the Battle of Skull Cave in the Salt River Canyon. There on December 28, 1872, the Indian Scouts led troops, under the command of Captains William H. Brown and James Burns, to a shallow cave high in the canyon where 100 Yavapai men, women and children thought they were safely hidden. Instead, they were all but annihilated by ricocheting bullets and boulders dropped from above. It could hardly be called a battle since the surprised Indians were unable to offer much resistance. For the Yavapai, it was their most demoralizing defeat.

Along with Apaches, General Crook had enlisted Yavapais, Walapais, Pimas and Paiutes, among others, to join his scout service. Rarely did the scouts of these tribes help the soldiers find their own people. The Tonto Apache scouts, for example, were the ones who tracked down the Yavapai gathered at Skull Cave.

* * * *

AL SIEBER, CHIEF OF SCOUTS

Al Sieber, one of Crook's favorite and most renowned Chief of Scouts, preferred to lead the Tonto Apaches. He considered the Yavapai excellent scouts as well, but they required a four-day purifying ceremony following a successful foray if any killing took place. This, of course, slowed things down too much.

Al Sieber was born in Rhineland, Germany in 1844. His widowed mother brought her family to America when Sieber was still a boy. He grew into a powerfully built man, six feet tall, with penetrating blue eyes and short blond hair. He sported a mustache, popular during this period. An excellent shot, Sieber never hesitated to take aim and kill when necessary. He maintained a loyalty among his Indian scouts both through fear and honest dealings. He said: "I do not deceive them, but always tell them the truth. When I say I'm going to kill them, I do it. When I tell them I am their friend, they know it." There was rarely a deserter among Seiber's scouts.

After Al Sieber mustered out of the Civil War, he worked his way west doing odd jobs. He arrived in Central Arizona during the height of the gold rush when the Apache war was at its peak. By 1867, Prescott was an established gold camp with a population of 500. Just 25 years old, Sieber took a job riding guard for teamster Dan Hazzard.

It was a dangerous job bringing freight into Prescott through hostile territory. From behind every bush and rock, there was a constant threat of being attacked by marauding Indians, Mexican bandits, or plain old outlaws.

Eventually Sieber made friends with such Indian fighters as Dan O'Leary, John Townsend, and Ed Peck. Dan O'Leary was the most famous Indian fighter in the area up until 1868, when King S. Woolsey took away the title.

After Sieber became foreman of a large ranch near Prescott, he found himself fighting Indians on a regular basis. His friend Dan O'Leary taught him the rudiments of scouting. Sieber caught on quickly and developed a keen ability to hear, see and smell his enemy, as well as accumulate and evaluate evidence. Upon this basis, he made fast decisions about what was happening and what might happen. He was just the sort of man Crook went looking for to oversee his companies of Indian scouts.

Al Seiber
—FVSP

THE CAMPAIGN BEGINS—AND ENDS

Throughout the winter of 1871, soldiers and scouts attacked, burned, and destroyed Indian encampments, wiped out food supplies and killed off the Indian's half-starved pony herds. After the Superstition Mountains were cleared of hostiles, the war moved east and west of the Verde River.

On March 27, 1873, a column led by Capt. George M. Randall, Twenty-third Infantry, reached the top of Turret Peak, south of Camp Verde. There they surprised a rancheria of Apaches, who like the Yavapai at Skull Cave, thought they were safely hidden from the soldiers. Randall's charge killed twenty-three Indians, and finally broke their resistance. Within weeks, bands of Apaches and Yavapais started drifting into the agencies to surrender.

Crook met with a Yavapai leader, Chalipun, at Camp Verde on April 6, 1873. He had 300 Yavapais with him and was said to represent 2,000 more. He gave this speech to Crook:

"You had too many cartridges of copper. We had never been afraid of the Americans alone, but now that our own people are fighting against us, we did not know what to do. We could not go to sleep at night, because we feared we'd be surrounded before daybreak. We could not hunt, the noise of our guns would attract your troops; we could not cook mescal or anything else, because the flames and smoke would draw down your soldiers; we could not live in the valley, there were too many soldiers. We retreated to the mountains, thinking to hide in the snow until your soldiers went home, but your scouts found us, and your soldiers followed. We want to make peace and be at good terms of good will with the whites."

One of the last to surrender was the infamous leader of the Tonto Apaches, Delshay. Also known as Red Ant, Delshay was described as mean-tempered and as sadistic in his dealings with whites as his Apache counterpart, Geronimo. Much like Geronimo, Delshay skillfully avoided capture, even after Crook put a price on his actual head. Payment would be received only if Delshay's head was brought to him. Delshay's distinguishing feature was an earring he wore in his right ear.

Yavapai warrior with owl feather headdress
—FVSP

Three Tonto Apache Scouts were sent out for the proposed capture and decapitation of Delshay. Returning from their escapade, they claimed they killed Delshay on Turret Mountain and handed Crook a scalp with the ear and earring intact. On two more occasions, Delshay's head, with earring, were presented to Crook. Crook paid all three parties hoping that at least one was the true head of Delshay. It wasn't until the final surrender of the Tonto Apaches and Yavapai at Fort Verde on April 27, 1873, that Crook came face to face with Delshay—his head intact.

Delshay told Crook he had 125 followers, but now only 20 existed. He added:

"There was a time when we could escape the white-eyes, but now the very rocks have become soft. We could not put our feet anywhere. We could not sleep, for if a coyote or fox barks, or stone moves, we are up-the soldiers have come."

Under Crook's protection, more than 6,000 Apache and Yavapai people lived in relative peace on reservations in Central Arizona for the next several years. It was the first time ever that the citizens of the area, as well as the Indians, enjoyed a period of relative tranquility.

Most of the white scouts were discharged by the end of April. Archibald McIntosh and Al Sieber were retained to mop up the remaining renegades. Sieber was assigned to Fort Verde from 1873 to 1879.

He was kept plenty busy.

The Indians at the Rio Verde Reservation, 16 miles from Fort Verde, were of mixed tribes. Old feuds erupted regularly among these 2,000 people and it was common for some of them to bolt the reservation. It was up to Sieber to bring them back. Regardless of what the trouble was at the reservation, Sieber was convinced that Delshay was behind it.

On July 7, 1874, Delshay finally was killed by his own people. They were tired of being punished for his murderous behavior. Every time he fled the reservation, some white miner or settler was killed. His death was a relief to Sieber, who could finally find time to poke around for the yellow metal, the lure of gold never being far from his thoughts.

When the military telegraph reached Prescott in October of 1873, the first message brought word of Crook's promotion to Brigadier

General. It was an unprecedented Presidential honor which leap-frogged Crook over the ridged line of seniority of the time, outraging many of his senior officers. But no officer deserved it more.

Crook left Arizona believing his task completed.

It wasn't.

By 1882, he was recalled to Arizona to track down Geronimo who had escaped the San Carlos Reservation. The Cibeque Mutiny precipitated his escape. This was the first and only time Indian Scouts ever mutinied against the U.S. Army. Once again, the Indian war would be fanned into flames throughout Arizona. Part of that war would take place in Central Arizona in a remote canyon on the Mogollon Rim called Big Dry Wash.

* * * *

THE CIBECUE MUTINY AND THE BATTLE AT BIG DRY WASH

By 1881, all the reservation Indians in Central Arizona had been removed to the San Carlos Reservation. Located at the junction of the San Carlos and Gila Rivers, it was a desolate "hardship post" according to those stationed there. Not only was it bare of vegetation, but harsh dry winds continuously swept dust and gravel across the surface of the parched earth. Rainfall was so infrequent it was considered a miracle when it did come. To call it a miserable place would seriously understate the true conditions at San Carlos in 1881.

Intrigue and discontent festered among all its inhabitants; soldier and Indian alike. Old enmities flared between the various bands of Apache and Yavapai people. Boredom born of idleness, and access to tizwin, a potent corn liquor, created another potential for trouble. Interior Secretary Carl Schurz referred to the corrupt agents there as "a stench in the nostrils of honest men."

Agent J.C. Tiffany was typical. He cheated in issuing rations, stole cattle meant for the Indians, and held back stores of supplies, sold them to unscrupulous others and pocketed the money. It was enough to provoke the most docile Indians. When General Crook was recalled to Arizona in 1882, he was not in the least surprised that the "tigers of the human race" (his description of the Apaches) had been driven back on the warpath.

Agent Tiffany did far more damage than cheating the Indians. He provoked the conditions leading to the Cibecue mutiny, which in turn precipitated the renewal of the Indian Wars. He demanded that a beloved medicine man, Nakaidoklini, be arrested, or better yet, killed.

Nakaidoklini was a White Mountain Apache who, ten years earlier, had been on a peace mission to Washington, where he conferred with President Grant. Although only in his twenties at the time, he had influence among the Apaches even then, and was considered a man of peace. He also was one of the first Indians to join Crook's scout service during the 1872 war.

By 1881, Nakaidoklini had stirred up the Indians at San Carlos with his own version of the Ghost Dance. This new religion, initiated by a Paiute mystic named Wavoka, would sweep through the Plains tribes eight years later.

The doctrine of this new religion promised the resurrection of all ancestral Indians, dead warriors and their relatives, and the restoration of lands stolen from the Indians. Nakaidoklini envisioned the removal and death of all white people from their sacred lands by the time the corn grew tall. All they had to do was to dance the Ghost Dance. For the first time ever, traditional enemies set aside their differences and joined in this dance.

This new religion threw Agent Tiffany into a frenzy of fear. He convinced Bvt. Major General Orlando B. Wilcox, colonel of the Twelfth Infantry, who was in charge of San Carlos, of the deadly peril this new religion might provoke. Wilcox ordered Col. Eugene A. Carr, Sixth Cavalry, to go to Cibecue Creek and arrest Nakaidoklini.

Carr was reluctant, and voiced his concern that such an act was heavy with the risk of unnecessary violence, Wilcox didn't agree. So on August 30, 1881, Carr marched towards Nakaidoklini's village on Cibique Creek, thirty miles northwest of Fort Apache, with two troops of cavalry, eighty-five men, and a detachment of twenty-three White Mountain Apache scouts. There are two versions of what happened next, the soldier's version and the Indian's.

According to the Army, the medicine man agreed to come peacefully after considerable arguing and pleading on the part of the soldiers. The Indian version states that a Captain Hentig forced his way into Nakaidoklini's wikiup and dragged the young medicine man out by his hair. This enraged the assembled Indians—including the White Mountain Apache scouts. The revered mystic was then put under guard in a tent.

That night, after the troops and their entourage made camp, Sgt. Dead Shot, one of the White Mountain scouts, asked permission to move his scouts closer to the Indian campsite because there "were too many ants" in their designated area. As soon as they moved closer, Sgt. Dead Shot let out a war-whoop. To the surprise and horror of the soldiers, their once loyal Indian scouts opened fire on them. Captain Hentig, the one accused of humiliating the medicine man, was killed first—shot in the back. The guards near the mules and horses were killed next, and the herd driven off by the Indians.

When the fighting erupted, the Sergeant guarding Nakaidoklini promptly shot the medicine man in the head. The medicine man did not die, but tried to crawl out of the tent. This time the troop bugler, who saw him trying to escape, shot him in the head again. This shot was fatal. Another trooper grabbed an ax and chopped off his head.

The fighting continued until nightfall, after which the troopers buried their dead, five in number, and escaped into the night. The bodies of Nakaidoklini, his wife and 18 Indians, including six of the White Mountain scouts, were left lying on the ground.

The mutiny provoked a major uprising. Fort Apache lay under threat from outraged Apaches who fled the reservation and once again raided and killed settlers and soldiers alike. The reports reaching the Eastern newspapers claimed that Carr and his entire command had been massacred at Cibecue. Sensational headlines proclaimed a Custer-like disaster had happened again. It took several weeks before Carr was able to get a courier through with the corrected report. Nevertheless, when the news of the outbreak reached General Sherman, he immediately wired General McDowell in Arizona,

"I want this annual Apache stampede to end right now. And to effect that result, I will send every available man in the whole Army, if necessary."

Squadrons of soldiers arrived from every direction. This heavy build up of troops descending on San Carlos frightened most of the fugitives into surrendering. The most dangerous renegades however, remained at large. Among them were Geronimo, Chato, Nana, Loco and a White Mountain renegade named Nantiotish.

General Wilcox ordered activation of twelve troops of cavalry and two companies of Indian Scouts under the command of Al Sieber, to go after Nantiotish. He, with a band of 54 White Mountain Apaches, all from Cibecue and including Indian Scout deserters, had raided the San Carlos agency, killed the Indian police chief and seven other

Indian policemen, stolen supplies, horses, guns and ammunition and headed north into Central Arizona.

Fort Verde, which had been abandoned in 1880, was re-garrisoned by July of 1882. Troops from Fort Whipple, Fort Thomas, Fort McDowell, and Fort Apache also were called to duty. Fourteen troops of cavalry took to the field to go after Nantiotish.

The renegades hid out on an escarpment on the Mogollon Rim near a favorite watering hole known as General Springs. Hot on his trail was Captain A.R. Chafee's troop of the Sixth cavalry and Company E, Indian Scouts, led by Al Sieber.

Nantiotish and his warriors, hidden on a pine-covered perch on the Mogollon Rim, watched Chaffee's column of 40 white horses pass below. He thought it would be quite easy to ambush these easily spotted soldiers, so he set about devising a trap.

Major A.W. Evans, 3rd Cavalry, came upon the trail of Chafee, who was only a half-day's march ahead of him. Evans sent a patrol forward to bring Chaffee into conference. Chaffee related that the hostiles were only a half-day's ride ahead of him, and he knew they'd discovered the white horses ridden by his men. Major Evans instructed Chaffee to pursue the enemy and that he would follow with his four troops in support. He also advised Chaffee that he would place Lt. Converse's white horse troop in the lead of his column to possibly mislead the Indians into thinking only Chaffee's single troop was chasing them.

Nantiotish took the bait. He never realized he was being pursued by all of these different columns. He thought his only threat was the forty white horse contingent he planned to ambush. He delayed leaving his camp at General Springs until he could see the pursuing column of white horses advancing in the canyon below.

About eight miles north of General Springs, where Nantiotish planned his ambush, the trail descends 800 feet into the almost vertical canyon of Big Dry Wash. The Indians barricaded themselves behind rocks in order to guard the trail up from the wash. At that point, the canyon is barely 700 yards in width. Sieber and his scouts discovered the potential ambush and warned Chaffee in time to avoid disaster. Nevertheless, every foot of trail, going up or down the canyon was held by the Indians.

Chaffee dismounted his troops at the south rim of the canyon. At the same time, Lt Converse, with his white horse troops dismounted, began firing across the canyon. Nantiotish, thinking this group of forty was all he faced, was surprised to realize that the troops firing at him numbered more than 80 with more still to come.

Several hours later, Major Evans arrived with four more contingents of troops, who went undetected by the Indians. When Chaffee reported to his senior officer, he was amazed when Evans told him to continue his plan of attack. In essence, Evans relinquished his rank to Chaffee in favor of "you found them…it's your battle, proceed as planned." Evans then dismounted his troops some 300 yards from the canyon where he kept them hidden from the hostiles.

While Lt. Converse kept the Indians engaged, Chaffee ordered Lts. Cruse and Kramer, Troop E, plus his own Troop I with Lt. West commanding, to proceed in an easterly direction. He also ordered Al Sieber and his scouts to proceed east and to flank the enemy to the right.

In order to outflank the hostiles from the west, Chaffee sent Indian Scouts, under the leadership of Lt. Morgan, 3rd Cavalry, and Lts. Hardy and Johnson of the 3rd Cavalry, along with Captain Abbott and Lt. Hobson, Troop K, of the 6th Cavalry in the opposite direction. The Indians didn't realize at first that they were surrounded.

Lt. Cruse and Al Sieber and their scouts reached the north rim of Dry Creek Wash where they discovered the Indian's pony herd. At the same time, Lt. Abbott on the west flank opened fire.

Confusion reigned. The Indians didn't know which way to turn. They just wanted to escape. They rushed for their ponies and were met with a volley of fire from Sieber's contingent. In the middle of the fight that followed, one of Sieber's scouts recognized two of his brothers and his father among the hostiles. He threw down his gun and ran toward his kin. Sieber ordered him to stop, and when he didn't, Sieber shot him in the back of the head.

The day of slaughter finally came to an end after a raging storm swept out of the west and prevented further carnage. An Indian Scout called it the heaviest rain and hailstorm he'd ever seen. It was so miserable and paralyzing that Major Chaffee got so cold and wet, he actually stopped swearing.

Under the cover of the storm, the remaining hostiles, many of them severely wounded, made their escape. Troopers who arrived from Fort Verde the following day were 'much out of temper' because they had missed the fight.

Details of soldiers were sent out after the storm to look for bodies and the wounded. They counted 22 dead hostiles, including Nantiotish, with seven wounded. It was presumed others lay dead, concealed in rocks and crevices of the rocky formations. Many of the wounded, who had escaped, later died of their wounds on the reservation where they had fled.

One of the patrols led by Lt. Hobson heard groans during the night. While investigating the next morning, he and his troops were fired upon. Gun smoke rose from behind a large boulder, betraying the direction of the shots. The soldiers took cover and returned the fire. When there was no longer a response, they went to investigate. They discovered a young Indian woman lying prone on the ground, her body shielding her six-month old baby. She drew her knife and tried to attack the soldiers, who quickly overpowered her.

Her leg was shattered, so a makeshift stretcher was made and she was transported for two hours down the tedious descent of the canyon wall to the soldiers' camp. She must have suffered terribly, but never uttered a sound, nor did she cry out when the Army doctor amputated her leg without anesthesia.

The Battle of Big Dry Wash marked the end of hostilities with all Apaches except the Chiricahuas and the Warm Springs band who had escaped into Mexico. One week after Nantiotish began his raid into Central Arizona, General Crook was called back into service in Arizona to go after Geronimo and the others in the southern part of the territory.

* * * *

ON THE TRAIL OF GERONIMO

Crook left his base in San Bernardino, California, with a company of 30 civilian volunteers and 200 Yavapai and Tonto Apache scouts under the leadership of Al Sieber and Lt. Gatewood. He successfully negotiated with the governors of Sonora and Chihuahua, Mexico, to be allowed to cross over one another's border without consequences. He believed this would ensure a quick victory over the hostiles who roamed and raided freely from one nation to the other. He was right.

Once the Indians got word that Crook was on their trail, most surrendered peacefully, including Geronimo. Unfortunately, the first night after Geronimo and the others were returned to San Carlos, they got drunk and off they went again. This brought Crook under severe criticism from General Sheridan in Washington.

Crook tendered his resignation, and it was accepted.

General Nelson Miles was sent to replace him. Miles had no faith in the Indian Scout Service and dismissed them all. He replaced them with 5,000 troops. It took these 5,000 troops, without the initial aid of the Indian Scout Service, 15 months to capture Geronimo and his 38 followers.

Although Miles took full credit for the capture of Geronimo and his band, in actuality he had little to do with it. It was Lt. Gatewood, four reinstated Yavapai and Tonto Apache scouts, along with two Chiracahua interpreters, who located Geronimo in the Sierra Madre Mountains of Mexico and convinced him to surrender.

As their reward, Miles shipped the four scouts and the two interpreters off to a Florida prison, along with Geronimo and his followers.

In March of 1882, three White Mountain Apache Scouts: Sgt. Dead Shot, Skippy and Dandy Jim, were found guilty of treason and were publicly hanged at Fort Grant. Out of grief, Sgt. Dead Shot's wife hanged herself from a tree at San Carlos that same day.

The military command reprimanded Carr for using poor judgment in engaging White Mountain scouts to help him arrest the beloved medicine man.

Just before they were hanged, the doomed scouts placed a curse on the attending priest and commanding officer. Both died mysteriously of "natural causes" a short time later.

After serving two years in the Florida prison, Geronimo lived the remainder of his life in Fort Sill, Oklahoma, never to see Arizona again. He often collected money by posing for photographs, autographing picture post cards of himself, and carving bows and arrows for children. He was quoted as saying, "I'm no longer an Indian, I'm a white man."

He bragged to anyone who would listen that it took 5,000 soldiers 15 months to finally capture him and his 38 followers. On several occasions while drunk, Geronimo admitted remorse for tossing white infants in the air and spearing them with his dagger.

Geronimo died of pneumonia following a drunken stupor. He fell off the back of a wagon, where he lay for hours in a shallow pool of water, face down in the mud.

At last, the citizens of Arizona Territory breathed the air of peace. Under the banner of safety, settlers arrived in droves. And with them, a whole new era was ushered into Prescott and Yavapai County.

MILITARY POSTS AND BATTLE SITES

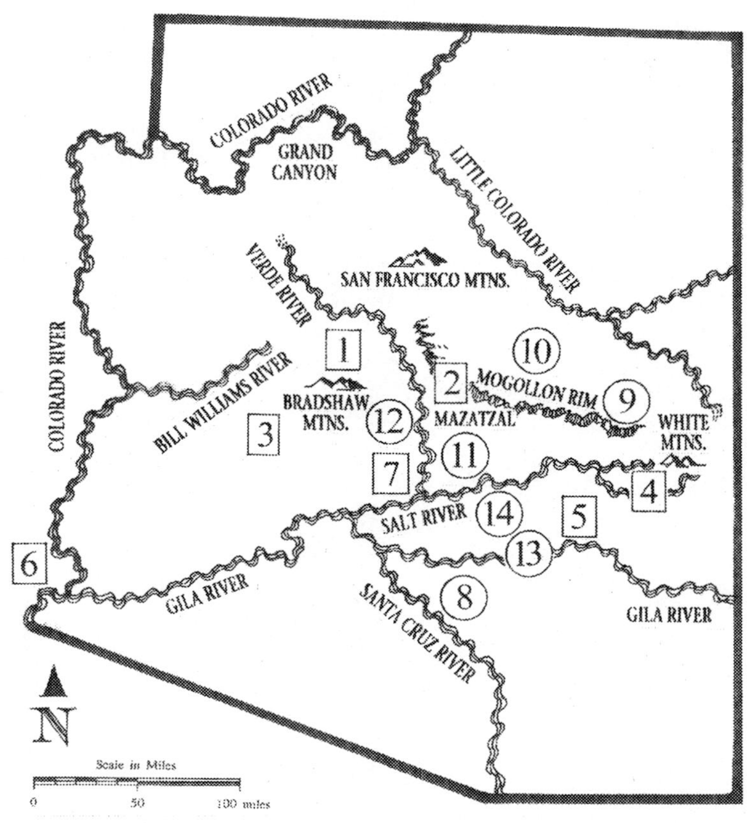

MILITARY POSTS

1. FORT WHIPPLE - 1864-1913
2. FORT VERDE - 1864-1890
3. CAMP DATE CREEK - 1867-1874
4. FORT APACHE - 1870-1890
5. CAMP SAN CARLOS - 1873-1900
6. FORT YUMA - 1849-1885
7. FORT McDOWELL - 1865-1890

BATTLE SITES

8. BATTLE OF PICACHO PASS - APRIL 1862
9. CIBICUE MUTINY - AUGUST 30, 1881
10. BATTLE AT BIG DRY WASH - JULY 17, 1882
11. SKULL CAVE MASSACRE - DECEMBER 28, 1872
12. BATTLE AT TURRET PEAK - MARCH 27, 1873
13. BATTLE AT BLOODY TANKS - JANUARY 1864
14. BATTLE AT PINAL MTNS - MARCH 8, 1874

"That's all Hell needs." Tecumseh Sherman in reply to "All Arizona needs is more water and a better class of people."

"Men and women thrive in that climate, but it is death to women." Martha Summerhayes, VANISHED ARIZONA

"When I was young I walked all over this country, east and west, and saw no other people than Apaches. After many summers I walked again and found another race of people came to take it." Cochise 1866

CHAPTER THREE
Whoopee, Let's Go Ma, Out Yon Whar the Injuns Be: Pioneering into Arizona Territory 1864-1872

"I counted the graves half lost in the grass, and more than once on many days, climbed off my pony to set some rotting headboard straight, or pile a little mound of stones over some grave more nearly lost." So wrote Sharlot Hall, who at the age of eleven, traveled by covered wagon with her family from Kansas, to Prescott, Arizona Territory.

For pioneer women, every single grave carried overpowering significance. Of all their hardships, privations and fears, pioneer women recorded the number of graves passed along the way with more precise attention than any other events.

"Child's grave…smallpox. Made 14 miles."

"Passed seven new-made graves. One had four bodies in it…cholera."

"Passed 21 new-made graves today. Made 22 miles."

The distinction between old graves, and new, was particularly important, because it told the pioneers how closely death stalked their own caravan.

"Passed where they were burying a man," Lodisa Frizzell wrote in her diary. "Scarce a day but someone is left on these plains. The heart has a thousand misgivings," she continued, "and the mind is tortured with anxiety, and often as I passed the fresh made graves, I have glanced at the side boards of our wagons, not knowing how soon they would serve as a coffin for some one of us."

Few women traveling west did so willingly. They went because their fathers, husbands and brothers decided they must go. Those were the days when patriarchy reigned supreme, and once their men folk made up their minds, there was little a woman could do about it. Refusal brought dire consequences, particularly abandonment, even when they had small children.

Yet the direst consequences were yet to come. Not a single pioneer was ever prepared for the unexpected hardships lying ahead. For all pioneers, physical stamina and an abundance of ingenuity were absolute requirements. It was not a trip for the fainthearted.

All the journeys began at what was referred to as one of the "jumping off places" along the Missouri River. Regardless of their destination, Independence, Missouri was the most popular starting point. The main trails from there were the Oregon, California, Santa Fe and Pony Express Trails. From Independence, wagon trains shared the same route for a time, traveling side by side until they reached Council Grove, Kansas. This was the last place to stock up.

After Council Grove, the wagon trains spread out on routes varying from one year to another, or even from month to month. Short cuts recommended one year might be forgotten the next. Deciding on the best trail was a capricious and confusing undertaking. Often, after the wagon trains separated, weeks or months might pass and they would find themselves mingling once again. Short cuts, or chosen trails were known to overlap.

The emigrants began arriving at their "jumping off place" in the spring to wait for relatives who might join them, and to buy livestock, wagons and provisions for the almost three-thousand-mile, six-month journey to the West.

For the emigrants traveling after 1856, the various trails had significantly improved. Where once confusing routes and vast, empty horizons lay ahead, now stagecoach stations and trading posts marked the way. Supplies were replenished at these places and help given. By 1861, telegraph poles stretched from one end of the country to the other. After 1856, Salt Lake City became another major stopping point, where everything the worn out wagon train needed was provided. This could include the luxury of a real bathtub, and a good shave. Despite these improvements, overland travel for women remained as dreary as ever.

Severe thunder and hailstorms could scatter terrified livestock and topple wagons, leaving supplies ruined. Unexpected mishaps befell every party before journey's end. Wood was usually non-existent on the prairie, so women gathered dried buffalo dung, or weeds to make their fires. They often cooked in wind, rain or hailstorms.

When high rising rivers needed crossing, women were expected to unload thousands of pounds of supplies and possessions from their wagons, reload them onto a raft, then repack everything in the wagons once across.

Men and boys maintained the herds of livestock, repaired wagons, searched for good camping spots, hunted wild game, and took turns standing watch at night. Few helped their women pitch the tents, or yoke and unyoke the oxen or mules pulling the wagon.

Added to this, women were responsible for attending disabled draft animals, searching for a lost child, nursing those who were injured or ill (usually from dysentery), enduring childbirth under the most primitive circumstances, washing clothes on river banks, walking miles a day in extreme heat or extreme cold, climbing steep mountains, and perpetually worrying whether their men would find adequate water, fresh game to replenish their dwindling food supplies, or locate sufficient forage for their exhausted livestock.

Women used many ingenious methods of food preparation along the trail.

Often they filled their Dutch oven with the ingredients for the evening meal, got it sizzling over the breakfast fire, then packed the Dutch oven in a wooden box lined top to bottom, and on all sides with thick bricks of straw. When they made camp that night, the slow cooked meal was ready to eat from their version of a "crock pot." If they owned milk cows, sheep or goats, they also filled their churn with cream in the morning, and hitched it to the front of their wagon. By evening, the jogging wagon had turned the cream into butter.

Remedies for illnesses were pitifully inadequate on the trail. A well-stocked medicine kit might consist of laudanum (tincture of opium), quinine for malaria, hartshorn for snakebites, citric acid for scurvy; a quart of castor oil, and plenty of rum.

Childbirth must have been a terrifying experience on the trail, yet it is rarely mentioned in diaries except as an announcement, or a death notice. Childbirth was often a deadly experience for women even under the best of circumstances. How these women felt about delivering their babies by the side of a road, in a wagon, or a tent, is rarely mentioned.

It was not unusual for a child to grow up with several stepmothers in succession; each one dying in childbirth. Death was the unseen partner in many a pioneer marriage.

In 1859, Lavinia Porter, age twenty, was traveling with her husband to Colorado. Like many young wives, she was pregnant before ever starting out on the trail. Late into the journey, Lavinia was overtaken with dysentery, a disease that usually struck everyone at some point along the way. Pregnancy, under that circumstance, made her suffering extreme. She later wrote in her diary:

"I became so weakened I could no longer climb in or out of the wagon and was compelled to keep to my bed. The jolting wagon soon became a torture to me, and at last became so unendurable that I implored my husband to take me out, make my bed on the sand, and let me die in peace."

The couple had not brought a medicine kit because "none of us had ever become ill. Lavinia's misery finally ended when an old prospector they met advised a big dose of castor oil. But there was no castor oil in their wagon. Then Lavinia remembered some hair tonic, "and I swallowed it down. It acted like a charm." Her cleverness won the day.

By 1856, there was also a greater threat of attack from the Indians.

The first wave of immigrants, particularly the 49ers, had introduced cholera, measles and small pox to the tribes, decimating their numbers. The buffalo and elk herds, which the Indians depended upon for sustenance, had also been reduced in number following the first wave of western migration. Native people now felt enough animosity, and fear towards this new onslaught of immigrants, that tribe after tribe decided to stop them. Helen Carpenter, a bride of four months who made the crossing in 1857 wrote:

"When the sun was just peeping over the top of the mountain, there was suddenly heard a shot and a blood curdling yell, and immediately the Indians we saw yesterday were seen riding full speed directly toward our horses…father put his gun to his shoulder as though to shoot…the Indians kept circling…and halooing…bullets came whizzing through the camp. None can know the horror of it."

Fortunately for Helen's party, the men of her group successfully used their Sharp rifles to scare off the Indians.

One month later their party found the nude and tortured body of a woman on the bank of a creek, her scalp gone, and a rope around her neck. Apparently she had been dragged behind a horse with that rope. "We gave the poor soul a Christian burial," Helen wrote.

Mary Perry Frost, also traveling after 1856, wrote that Indians were burning the grass along the trail in an effort to starve the livestock of the settlers. It forced their large wagon party to separate time and again in an effort to find sufficient forage. Finally, Mary's party was in a group of only four wagons. The Indians stopped their train, but appeared friendly. They asked for whiskey. When told there was none, the Indians opened fire, shooting their teamster, and Mary's father and uncle. Each man took several days to die of his wounds.

By comparison, Mary's group was lucky. When her group came upon the train ahead of them, they found all the men, women, and children tortured and burned, except for one fourteen year-old boy, who survived despite an arrow in his chest.

* * * *

WESTERING TO STRANGE AND DANGEROUS LANDS

What prompted entire families to pull up stakes and abandon their eastern homes to venture into strange, unknown and dangerous territories west of the Mississippi? Perhaps the most predominant reason was the spirit of Westering. Westering meant conquering, creating, building, and beginning anew. It fired their hopes and dreams that things would be better in the West.

Economic depressions in the east in 1837, 1841 and again in 1857, along with glowing descriptions of fertile lands in the Northwest, prompted the cries, "On to Oregon," during the 1840s. California Gold was the driving force behind the next major wave of pioneers from 1849 and throughout most of the 1850s, while the exaggerated rumors of gold discoveries in Colorado contributed to the rallying phrase "Pikes Peak or Bust" by 1858.

After the 1862 passage of the Homestead Act, signed into law by President Abraham Lincoln, free land, and the promise of new opportunities, signaled the next group of eager Western migrations.

All a homesteader had to do was be the head of a household, and at least 21 years old, to claim a 160 acre parcel of land. Settlers from all walks of life, including emigrants from other countries, farmers without land in the East, single women, and former slaves, flocked west in droves to take advantage of this astonishing policy. Their only requirement was to live on the land for five years, build a home, and make improvements. The cost was a mere $18 filing fee.

By 1864, gold discoveries in Arizona, along with the promise of free land, drew droves of hopeful emigrants. But hope soon turned to horror for the Arizona pioneers. Those who arrived in Central Arizona in the 1860s quickly discovered that the hardships of the trail paled in comparison to what awaited them at the end of this journey.

Throughout the 1860s, and most of the 1870s, Arizona, especially Central Arizona, was one of the most dangerous places in the West. Immigrants arriving in Arizona Territory during these turbulent times faced a carnival of blood. Their dreams of establishing homes and businesses were constantly dashed as they witnessed their neighbors being murdered, their homes destroyed, their livestock stolen, and their fields laid waste by the relentless native population determined to exterminate them. It was a determination that quickly turned mutual.

Only the most hardy stuck it out.

Throughout the country, newspapers echoed the popular cry for revenge. "Do away with the Indian reservations; fight the Apaches to the death."

Bitter hatred raged on both sides, until it fanned into a fever heat. Whites and Indians alike saw their friends and relatives butchered, and all sense of reason vanish. Peace seemed unimaginable, and the future appeared grim indeed. Despite finding themselves enmeshed in this horrific atmosphere, a few stayed, determined to endure and establish civilization, no matter what the consequences.

* * * *

THE PRESIDENT'S MEN

In September of 1863, the President's men gathered at Fort Leavenworth, Kansas Territory, to begin their trek to Arizona. Hand picked by President Abraham Lincoln, these men were mandated to impose federal law on an untamed land; define the territory; guide its growth from shacks to villages, and communities to cities; establish law and order, and prepare the new territory for eventual statehood.

The President's Men: seated (left to right) Joseph P. Allyn, John Goodwin, and Richard C. McCormick; standing (left to right) Henry W. Fleury, Milton B. Duffield, Almon P. Gage

Many were Lincoln's political cronies. Most had inflated egos and political ambitions. All came with a determination to get their hands on Arizona's gold.

They would last from several months to several years. A few stayed for the rest of their lives. Regardless of their personal goals, none was adequately prepared for the beast of violence looming ahead, waiting to pounce upon their every effort.

Enforcing the law and establishing a territorial government required the cooperation of all the officials. No one alone could enforce the law. It was absolutely necessary to work in tandem. Otherwise, their duties of collecting taxes, dealing with the Indians, protecting government property, and coping with any and all issues, would be ineffective if not impossible. Within a year after their arrival, the president's men found themselves in just such a dilemma. Arizona's U.S. Attorney Almon Gage expressed the exasperation of his fellow officials in a letter to U.S. Attorney General James Speed:

"This district has been judgeless and courtless for more than a year. Several judges, who westered out, stayed only a few days before returning to the states and the comforts of civilization. This flight and absence of officials from their post and duties appears to me to be somewhat of a swindle upon the government that pays them and a gross injustice to the people of this territory. I ask your help forthwith in sending back these renegade judges so courts can be held."

One such renegade judge was William T. Howell, appointed to the first judicial district of Arizona Territory. Immediately upon his arrival, Howell began work on a preliminary code of laws for the territory. He was well suited for the task, having been a noted Michigan legislator and attorney. With the assistance of Arizona's Attorney General, Coles Bashford, Howell adapted the laws of California, New York and other states. Within three months, he had constructed the "Howell Code of Laws" which the First Territorial Legislature accepted. Then Justice Howell took a leave of absence on the grounds that his wife was ill. He never returned, resigning his judgeship on March 8, 1865. Apparently U.S. Attorney Almon Gage's furor was directed primarily at Howell.

The one major oversight of the U.S. Government, when sending officials to new territories, was a lack of precise instructions on what their duties were. Hundreds of letters were sent to the U.S. Attorney

General's office throughout the 19th century, filled with questions from territorial officials, asking what to do.

The problem reached such a crisis that, on June 22, 1870, the government finally created the Department of Justice, to officially handle their concerns. In the meantime, the lack of formal rules and instructions opened the door to individual interpretation, and a temptation to take advantage of the situation for personal gain. Several of Arizona's officials fell prey to this situation.

Almon Gage, the territory's U.S. Attorney, was accused of extortion along with Surveyor General Levi Bashford, for selling government food and supplies to poor miners at exorbitant prices, to be paid in gold, rather than discounted greenbacks.

* * * *

ALMON GAGE

Almon Gage was 46 years old when he arrived in the territory with the governor's party. An ordained Universalist minister, born in New Hampshire in 1817, he had traveled throughout the South as an itinerate preacher for over 10 years. Before his appointment by Lincoln, he had briefly studied law.

Strongly anti-Southern, one of his first official acts was to file suits in Tucson against the property of six Confederate sympathizers. Due to Judge Howell's absence from the bench, nothing came of the suits until 1869, four years after the Civil War. The case was dismissed because of President Johnson's proclamation in 1868, granting a full pardon and amnesty for any offense of treason during the Civil War.

Except for a term of court in Tucson in May, 1864, all of Gage's service as U.S. Attorney was performed in Prescott, where he established a law practice, and was a sometimes prospector. He also served as Secretary of the First Legislative Assembly in 1864, and again during the Fourth Legislative Assembly in 1867. Three years later he resigned as U.S. Attorney and returned to New Hampshire for good.

THE BASHFORD BROTHERS

The Bashford Brothers, Coles and Levi, not only spent the rest of their lives in the Territory after their arrival in 1864, they contributed to its development and amassed a fortune for themselves and their heirs in the process.

Lincoln appointed Levi Bashford as Arizona's U.S. Surveyor General in 1863. He was 50 years old when he started on the arduous trek west with Governor Goodwin's party. His brother, Coles, was 47.

Both were born in Cold Spring, Putnam County, New York; Levi in 1813 and Coles in 1816. They both received formal educations at Wesleyan College. Levi became a merchant, and Coles studied law, passing the New York Bar in 1847.

When news came of the gold strikes in California, Levi joined the flocks of Argonauts who traveled by steamship, and overland, through South America to San Francisco. Although this was a faster way to get to the gold fields, (three months versus six months overland), it was a trip fraught with its own set of dangers. Overcrowded ships, poor food, dangerous ocean crossings in less than seaworthy vessels, threats from unscrupulous fellow passengers, and Yellow Fever were constant concerns for ocean travelers.

Levi's success in the gold fields of California is not known. When he returned to New York in 1853, he found that his brother, Coles, had moved to Oshkosh, Wisconsin. By then, Coles had married Frances Adams Foreman, who eventually bore him seven children.

Of the two brothers, Coles was the more politically ambitious. He had already served as the District Attorney of Wayne County, New York, and by the time Levi joined him in Oshkosh, Coles was serving in the state senate as a member of the Whig Party. In 1854, Coles helped organize the Republican Party in Wisconsin, and by the following year became that party's candidate for Governor of the state.

When the Democratic incumbent, William Barstow, won the election by 157 votes, Coles contested the results before the state supreme court. With the help of Barstow's enemies, and fortified with evidence of fraudulent returns from two counties, Coles forced the resignation of Barstow in favor of Lieutenant Governor Arthur

McArthur. Then, upon winning the court decision, he pushed McArthur aside, and took the office for himself.

During his short tenure as Governor (1856-1857), the legislature distributed two huge land grants awarded to Wisconsin by the U.S. Government for the purpose of building a railroad. Coles Bashford and his fellow legislators were soon accused of fraud in connection with land deals related to this property. Several Republican legislators had received bribes in proportion to the importance of their positions. The primary beneficiary was Governor Coles Bashford. He received $50,000 worth of bonds, which he later converted into $15,000 cash.

He had thus disgraced himself and his family, and he stepped down from the governorship. Coles and his family lived in relative obscurity for the next few years.

In the meantime, Levi served as director of the Chicago and Northwest Railroad in Oshkosh, when Lincoln selected him to be the Surveyor General of Arizona Territory. His task was to establish the boundaries of the new territory.

By then, Levi was newly married to Mary E. Foster and had one young son, Coles Allen, born in 1856. Despite the fact that both brothers had young families, Levi leaped at the chance to go to Arizona Territory, and his brother Coles, who hadn't been appointed to anything, leaped right along with him. They both were nearing 50, not young men anymore, yet traveling to the wild frontier of Arizona Territory seemed to fire them with a youthful energy, and offer them an entirely new outlook on life.

In the 1864 Arizona Territorial census, Levi gave his age as 41, ten years younger than he actually was. He claimed to be a trader with property valued at $200. Six years later, the 1870 census listed him as a merchant with property worth $30,000. During the six years between the two censuses, Levi completed his term as Surveyor General in 1866, after which President Johnson appointed him Collector of Internal Revenue for the territory. He served in that capacity until 1871. By then he had made substantial real estate investments, and initiated a mercantile company in Prescott called L. Bashford Mercantile. He advertised it as a "New York Cheap Store," carrying a variety of merchandise from groceries, to ladies dresses, to Henry's improved rifles. The merchandise arrived directly from

New York by rail or freight trains, thereby avoiding the huge tariffs usually levied by San Francisco merchants. His store was an enormous success.

His brother, Coles, appointed Attorney General of the Territory by Governor Goodwin shortly after his arrival in Arizona, became the first lawyer to be admitted to the Arizona Bar. Elected to the first Territorial government, he served as its president. Governor Goodwin reappointed him Attorney General in 1866.

During the Fourth Legislature in 1867, a complaint was filed against his serving as both Attorney General and legislator, earning a salary from both positions. The *Tucson Arizona Citizen* (owned by his friend Richard C. McCormick) defended him in an editorial:

"The power and duties of the Attorney General at that time, there being no District Attorneys, extended to all criminal cases in all of the territory, to all cases in which the territory or its officers were a party, or any of the counties of the Territory, or the officers thereof; and he was also the legal advisor of all Territorial officers, and of the Legislative Assembly.

"In what may be called the dangerous days, when the whole territory was alive with hostile Indians, Governor Bashford traveled with a degree of fearlessness that often surprised the most resolute pioneers. In 1864-5-6, he visited repeatedly the various counties, never missing a term of court, always traveling on horseback, and generally alone, armed with a revolver, knife and shotgun, and ready for any emergency."

In an Act of Congress approved in 1866, Coles was named one of the incorporators of the Atlantic and Pacific Railroad Company, and several months later, Arizonans elected him as a Delegate to Congress from Arizona.

Coles was back on top.

Coles served in Congress until 1869. Afterwards, President Grant appointed him Secretary of the Territory. The 1870 Census showed his property to be valued at $25,000. In his capacity as Secretary, he compiled in one volume all the laws of the Territory including the "Howell Code" which he had helped draft.

President Grant re-appointed him as Secretary in 1873. He resigned in 1876, disposed of his Wisconsin property interests, and finally brought his family to Arizona. In 1877, he built a fine home in

Prescott, and became associated in business with his brother Levi. One year later, he died at the age of 62. His estate consisted of real estate appraised at $17,000, and personal property, cash, notes and mortgages valued at $83,000.

Coles' son, William, and his daughter Margaret's husband, Robert H. Burmister, became partners in Levi's store in 1874, and the name changed to L. Bashford and Company. When Levi retired in 1886, the name became Bashford-Burmister. Levi died in Los Angeles in 1899 at the age of 86, leaving an estate appraised at around $200,000, equivalent to several million dollars in buying power by today's standards.

* * * *

MILTON B. DUFFIELD

Of all the President's men, Milton B. Duffield was by far the most colorful. Lincoln appointed him U.S. Marshal of the territory. Born in West Virginia in 1810, he stood well over six feet, was powerfully built, broad-shouldered and strong as a Texas bull. In time he earned the reputation as a gunfighter. He never left home without 13 or more weapons, from knives to pistols, on his person at all times.

His choice of attire would have put the lives of ordinary western men at risk. He was the only man in the territory, or probably the west, who wore black plug hats and silk ties. But Duffield was a man who dressed to suit himself, and woe to anyone who ventured a criticism.

He had made an impression on the President in the early days of the Civil War by displaying uncanny courage during the riots against recruitment in New York City. Apparently Duffield was a passerby when the riots broke out. A terrified black man ran past him with a mob of drunks in hot pursuit. They were swinging a rope, and shouting threats to hang the poor devil. Duffield pulled out his pistol, and without a blink of an eye, shot three of the mob dead, thus dispersing the crowd. Lincoln praised his action and declared him one of the crack shots of America. He considered Duffield a perfect choice for the job of Arizona's first U.S. Marshal.

For two years, Duffield took his job of marshal seriously. One of his duties was that of Mail Inspector. During his tenure, he suspected some thieving was going on at one of the postal stations and confronted the postmaster with these words:

"You see, there is so much stealing going on along this line, so that I'm gittin kind o' tired 'n must git th' whole bizz off mee mind; 'n ez I've looked into the whole thing and feel satisfied that yore the thief, I think you'd better be pilin' out o' here without anymore nonsense."

Within 12 hours, the postmaster was gone, and all thieving stopped along that line.

It was not unusual for some of the West's most vile desperados to come gunning for him. An incident in Tucson was typical. It caused a lot of excitement, and added to Duffield's tough reputation.

A cowboy by the name of Waco Bill called Duffield out one hot day in July. Waco Bill was thoroughly drunk and couldn't stop hiccoughing while shouting "Whar's Duffer? I want Duffer; he's my meat."

Duffield came right up to the drunk and introduced himself with a fist in the Texan's face. As Waco Bill sprawled on the ground, he reached for his pistol, a big mistake. Immediately he got a bullet in his groin. Duffield bowed gracefully over the prone man and said in the most gentlemanly manner; "My name's Duffield, Sir, and them 'ere's me visitin' card,"(pointing to the bullet hole in the man's groin). It was a true John Wayne moment. By 1866, Duffield had resigned his government appointment, and had turned to prospecting.

Unfortunately, it was a bullet that finally ended Duffield's own days. Joe Holmes shot and killed him in Tombstone in 1874, after a dispute over a mining claim. Joe was captured, but never punished. He escaped from jail and was not seen or heard from again.

* * * *

JOSEPH PRATT ALLYN

Joseph Pratt Allyn was one of the three associate justices appointed by Lincoln, along with Howell, and William F. Turner, all of whom traveled with the Governor's party. Allyn chronicled their journey west, and sent regular letters to the *Hartford Evening Press* about all the events that took place after they arrived.

Allyn, born in Hartford, Connecticut in 1833, came from a wealthy and prominent family whose English lineage in America dated back to 1632. Unlike his brother, Thomas, who graduated from Yale and Harvard Medical School, Joseph had little formal education. Since the age of 13, he had been so chronically ill with tuberculosis that his father took him out of school and put him to work as a clerk.

By the time he was 19, the doctors persuaded his father to send him to warmer climates. He spent one winter in New Orleans, and the next in Florida. Beginning in 1856, he enjoyed a long residence abroad. This sojourn seemed to restore his health, enough for him to accept an appointment as assistant clerk in the House of Representatives for the 37th and 39th Congress. He campaigned vigorously for Lincoln, writing speeches for him that 'commanded the closest attention'. Despite Joseph's lack of a formal education, Lincoln rewarded him by appointing him one of the territory's three chief justices.

Allyn, ecstatic with the appointment, considered himself superior in intellect to the other appointees. He assessed Governor Goodwin as "clever, limited and lazy." He, and Secretary Richard C. McCormick, took an instant dislike to one another, and in time would become vitriolic political foes.

Nevertheless, Allyn reveled in the trek west, riding his horse 'Swindle' the whole way. He shot his first buffalo, and slept on the ground in all kinds of weather without any reoccurrence of his tuberculosis. The West agreed with him.

Another appointed justice, William F. Turner, a native of Iowa, served in the Third Judicial District (Yavapai County) from 1864-1870. He shared Judge Allyn's disdain for Secretary McCormick. Both considered him a "carpetbagger who inflated his political reputation through his newspaper (*The Arizona Miner*), and used liquor to win votes by catering to a depraved class of saloon patrons for selfish ends."

None of the three justices stayed long in the territory. Howell left after only five months, due to his wife's illness. Turner fulfilled his term, and left shortly afterwards.

Allyn tendered his resignation to President Johnson in 1867, after suffering a severe setback in health. He had endured several months of travel throughout California and Nevada in dusty stagecoaches.

He was 36 years old when he died in Paris in May 1869, having returned to Europe in the hopes of restoring his health. The chronicles of his Arizona adventures provide an amazing insight about the people and places of Arizona's dangerous territorial years.

* * * *

RICHARD C. McCORMICK

President Abraham Lincoln appointed Richard Cunningham McCormick as Arizona's first territorial secretary. Prior to the Civil War, McCormick had campaigned for Lincoln's election, and became his friend.

McCormick was born in New York City, on May 23, 1832. His father's family emigrated from Ireland prior to 1735. The family was wealthy enough to provide private tutors for their frail and chronically ill son. As an adult, McCormick chose to be a traveling journalist rather than attend college. He wrote two travel books, edited the *Young Men's Magazine* and helped organize the YMCA.

At the age of 25, he served as a correspondent for the *New York Evening Post* during the Crimean War. After that war, he edited the Post until the Civil War erupted, and he became a correspondent again. He served with the Army of the Potomac recording the events of the war for the Post, and the *New York Commercial Advisor*.

As territorial secretary, McCormick designed the first Territorial Seal, which depicted a miner in front of a wheelbarrow with a pick and short-handled spade. Two mountains rose in the background, and it included the motto *Ditat Deus*-God Enriches. The images on the seal have changed several times throughout the decades, but the motto has remained.

The books McCormick brought with him to the new territory, in time, formed the core of the territorial library. He also brought the only printing press. When not putting out the semi-monthly news in the *Arizona Miner*, the press was used extensively to print the journals and acts of the new legislature. In 1870, he also established the *Tucson Arizona Citizen*, the first newspaper in that town.

McCormick married only once. It became the heartbreak of his life.

On a trip east by steamer, he met the lovely Margaret Griffiths Hunt of Rahway, New Jersey. It was love at first sight. They married a few months later on September 27, 1865.

McCormick escorted his bride by steamer and train as far as Los Angeles. From there they traveled overland to Prescott in the company of two ambulances, six government wagons, and two private baggage wagons. Apparently, according to her diary, Margaret found the trip exciting and pleasant. She often commented on how "very, very kind" her new husband was. What she wrote in her diary about her first impression of Prescott is not known. Those pages have not surfaced.

Margaret became "the first lady of Arizona Territory," in every sense. She was the first woman to live in the newly constructed Governor's Mansion (Governor Goodwin never brought his family to the territory). She embraced her new life with enthusiasm. She had a passion for gardening, and was an accomplished horsewoman. She always rode with her husband on his numerous trips throughout the new territory, enduring the dangers and hardships of each journey with the spirit of adventure.

Margaret opened her heart to the few first families in the territory, in particular Margaret Ehle's family. The two Margarets planned the first Christmas celebration to be held in the Governor's mansion. They met for weeks in the Ehle cabin making gifts and baking dozens of cakes and cookies.

The Territory's first official Christmas tree was set up in the parlor of the mansion. Captain Joseph Rutherford Walker was the honored guest during the celebration, which began with a prayer and a song, and was followed by a sumptuous buffet. Margaret McCormick presented one of her wedding handkerchiefs to each of the women of the territorial capital who'd helped with the party.

It was written of her that:

"Her hospitality was dispensed with an open and generous hand, a charming freedom and grace, which made her guests, whether in buckskins or broadcloth, at once at home and delighted."

Then in January of 1867, Margaret accompanied her husband (by then the Governor) on a four-month-long journey to San Francisco and back. Most of the 1,200 miles were over dangerous, rough roads, and through hostile Indian country. Margaret endured the difficult journey with her usual good spirit despite being pregnant with their first child.

The McCormicks returned to Prescott on April fourth. Margaret seemed well and happy, but three weeks later she went into premature labor. Her good friend Margaret Ehle, who was also a midwife, hurried to assist her friend.

It was a long and difficult labor. Shortly after giving birth to her stillborn child, Margaret McCormick died on April 30, 1867 at the age of 24. Her death plunged the territory into mourning.

Her obituary in the *Arizona Miner* included these words:

"The sudden and unexpected death of this estimable and beloved woman has cast a gloom over this community which language cannot describe. She came here in 1865, the companion of the governor. She has been the pride of the territory, and the demise of no other person could have created such a widespread sensation, or more universal and profound grief. As it is made known in the various settlements, in the mining and ranching camps and military posts, business will be suspended and stout hearted men who seldom mourn, will be excited to tears, for no one has had a stronger hold on the popular affection."

Margaret Ehle prepared her friend's body for burial with her stillborn child wrapped in her arms. Two days later, she was buried in the forest near the Governor's Mansion. Two years later, the Hunt family had her remains returned to them in Rahway, New Jersey, and reburied in the Hazelwood Cemetery there.

Her husband never remarried. Instead, Richard C. McCormick plunged himself into a variety of political activities for the rest of his life. He was never as beloved in Prescott as was his lovely wife.

President Johnson appointed him the second territorial governor in 1866. He served in that post until 1868 when he was elected as a delegate to the U.S. Congress. He would serve for three consecutive terms.

Prescott accused him of selling out to Tucson in order to win the congressional votes. When Tucson's Pima County, not Prescott's Yavapai County, garnered him the winning votes, the accusations appeared valid, especially after McCormick helped maneuver the territorial capital from Prescott to Tucson after being elected. This prompted angry Prescottonians to accuse him of fraud and bribery. In an enraged editorial, John Marion of the *Arizona Miner* referred to him as "His Littleness" and accused him of "flunkeyism" in order to win the election. McCormick soon moved to Tucson, where he started a rival newspaper, and enjoyed much greater popularity.

From 1872 to 1880, McCormick served as delegate to the National Republican conventions and was appointed commissioner to the Centennial exhibition from 1871-76.

After campaigning for Rutherford B. Hayes, the president appointed him Assistant Secretary of the U.S. Treasury, and Commissioner-General to the Paris Exposition.

McCormick continued to buy and sell mining stock in Arizona. Despite a lifetime of chronic ailments, he lived to the age of 70, and died in 1901, at his home in New York.

* * * *

JOHN NOBLE GOODWIN

After the Territorial Capital moved to Tucson in 1868, the territory's first governor. John Noble Goodwin, returned to the practice of law, this time in New York. He, too, left the territory under a cloud of suspicion and fraud.

John Noble Goodwin was born in South Berwick County, Maine on October 18, 1824. He graduated from Dartmouth College in 1844 and returned home to Maine to read law in the office of John Hubbard. He was admitted to the bar four years later. In 1854, he served in the Maine State Senate where he was appointed special commissioner to revise the laws of Maine.

He married Susan Howard Robinson at Augusta, Maine, on October 27, 1857, and by 1861, had been elected as a Republican from Maine to the 37th Congress under President Abraham Lincoln. In March of 1863, Lincoln appointed him Chief Justice of the United States Court for the Territory of Arizona. Following the sudden death of Lincoln's original appointee, Senator Gurley of Ohio, the U.S. Senate confirmed Goodwin's appointment as Governor, instead of Chief Justice.

In his first speech delivered to the joint session of the First Legislative Assembly Goodwin extolled the potential of Prescott's future and implied his advocacy of the Doctrine of Manifest Destiny. Among the words expressed in his speech that day he referenced the Apaches thusly:

"They respect no flag of truce, ask and give no quarter, and make a treaty only that under the guise of friendship they may rob and steal more extensively and with greater impunity. As to them one policy only can be adopted. A war must be prosecuted until they are compelled to submit and go to a reservation."

Goodwin lived in Arizona Territory for three years, and while Governor, also served as an elected delegate to the 39th Congress from 1865 to 1867. Two of his opponents in the congressional election, Charles Poston and Judge Joseph Pratt Allyn called him *"odious"* and charged that his Congressional election was fraught with irregularities:

"That soldiers, not citizens of the territory, voted; that a large majority of Mexicans and Indians had illegally voted; that polls had been placed illegally on Indian or military reservations; that Goodwin was never a resident of Arizona but remained a resident of Maine; and that Governor had in fact counted and certified his own votes and declared himself elected."

Accused also of unlawfully accepting both a Governor and congressman's salary at the same time, Goodwin never made restitution, despite repeated requests from the U.S. Government.

After Goodwin returned to his family in Maine, they moved to New York where he established his law firm. He died on April 29, 1887, at the age of 62 in Paraiso Springs, Monterey County, California, where he had retired to seek relief from the gout.

Once the old Governor's Mansion on Gurley Street was no longer in service as a government building, it became the residence of Judge Henry Fleury.

* * * *

HENRY W. FLEURY

Henry Waring Fleury, another of the territory's most colorful characters, came with Governor Goodwin serving as his secretary. From 1864 until his death in 1896, a night hardly went by that Judge Fleury didn't sleep beneath the roof of the old Governor's Mansion.

Elected Chaplain of the First Territorial Legislature over the Reverend Hiram Reed, the fact that Fleury was an avowed atheist did not seem to matter. The vote in his favor was decided after one of the members asked which of the two had the most whiskey. Fleury announced he had several five-gallon kegs, whereas Reed had none. Fleury won on a "pure whiskey platform."

Fleury served as Probate Judge for Yavapai County (1870-1874), and Justice of the Peace at Prescott, off and on until his death in 1896. His home at the Governor's Mansion became a rendezvous for hundreds of people over the years. It made no difference to Judge Fleury what a person's station in life might be, rich or poor, honest or otherwise, all were welcomed to his hospitality, a generosity that eventually ruined him financially.

At the time of his death, *The Prescott Weekly Courier* said this about him:

"He was a Hassayampa of Hassayampers, a pioneer of pioneers. He had no family and has no relatives in this section of the country. The log house where he lived from first to last is one of the historic landmarks of the territory and was the first building used as the territorial Capital.

"He died without state, having through his efforts to help friends, fallen into a high interest financial trap.

"He had donated a tract of land for a burying ground for the Masonic fraternity, and when the good old man's friends cast about for a place to lay his bones, the Masons came forward with a lot from the ground he had given them and his body now lies in the northeast corner of the Masonic Cemetery. His last request that no church people should conduct his funeral services.

"He was one of those adventurous still kindly spirits whose hardihood in hewing the way has enabled others to follow and build up a great commonwealth. This worthy man was allowed to live through all the troubled period to see the westward march of the Angle (sic) Saxon beat back the wild beast and the wilder man.

"He has for thirty odd years, like a patriarch of old, sat a judge among his people, and while not skilled in the lore of human lawgivers, the honest intent of all judgments rendered by him has ever gone unquestioned, for only justice dwelt in his heart."

The Governor's mansion, in which he had lived, was never used as a government headquarters again even though Prescott regained its Capital status in 1877.

Assembly Hall, also known as Curtis Hall, was used instead as the legislative headquarters. It served that purpose until 1889 when the Capital was moved permanently to Phoenix.

* * * *

THE FIRST CENSUS IN TIERRA INCOGNITA

In 1860, a year before the Civil War, the first census was taken in what was referred to as "Arizona County, Territory of New Mexico." The census reported the population of Arizona County to be 6,482, of whom 4,040 were listed as Indians. The largest city was Tucson. Other so-called cities with any population count were Gila City, Ft. Aravaipa, Casa Blanca and Ft. Buchanan, none of which exist today. The census of 1860 further showed that all land north of the Gila River, which included Central and Northern Arizona, was void of any Anglo or Mexican settlements. It was called *Tierra Incognita*, 'unknown land'. Four years later, the 1864 census showed a dramatic change.

By 1864, Arizona was no longer attached to New Mexico as a county. It was now a Territory with John Noble Goodwin presiding as the first Territorial governor. One of his first orders was to initiate a census, which was counted by the Rev. Hiram Reed, Arizona's first postmaster. Ironically, the county was named for the resident Yavapai Indians, who were excluded from the census.

Because of the influx of newcomers after the discovery of gold, the Anglo and Mexican population of Yavapai County leaped from zero in 1860, to the grand sum of 1088 by the spring of 1864.

The census showed that the population was made up almost entirely of men. They listed such occupations as miners (185); soldiers (256); laborers (136) and farmers (47). Merchants and traders numbered 36. Assorted other occupations included everything from Indian hunters and whiskey sellers to "whatevers." The "whatevers" outnumbered lawyers three to two.

Their place of birth could be pointed to from all over the globe. A little over half of them were born in the U.S. while Mexicans made up another 30 percent. The rest were from as far away as Russia and Africa, Germany and South America.

"When you open a rough, hard country, you don't do it with a lot of panty waists." Louis Dearborn L'Amour

"Westering is a whole bunch of people made into one big crawling beast. Every man wanted something for himself, but the big beast that was all of them wanted only westering…the chance to conquer, create, build, and begin anew. " John Steinbeck THE RED PONY

CHAPTER THREE - PART TWO
The Hassyampers
Yavapai County's First Citizens

They were referred to as the "Hassyampers," or "Hassyamps," named for the river near Wickenburg, which spilled its gold. They were the pioneers who came before the pioneers—the first to try and tame the wild wilderness of early central Arizona.

The miners, soldiers, legislators, businessmen and families who arrived between 1863 and 1872 were the original Hassyampers. It began with two mountain men, Pauline Weaver and Joseph Rutherford Walker, whose gold discoveries launched Arizona as a territory.

Pauline Weaver was the very first of the two according to historian Sharlot Hall. But according to his biographer Dr. James Byrkit, Pauline only was a member of the party that discovered the gold. Whatever the case, the Walker Party's discovery of gold preceded Pauline's party of miners and their discovery by two weeks.

Joe Walker and his entourage discovered the gold at Lynx Creek in the spring of 1863 that ushered in the Central Arizona gold rush, and set the stage for the founding of Prescott and Yavapai County.

At the time of the Lynx Creek discovery, Joe was 64 years old and nearly blind, yet still fit and powerfully built. He stood over six feet tall and weighed about 225 pounds. But stature alone was not what commanded awe and respect for this amazing man. By 1863, Joe Walker's name was known from New York to San Francisco, according to the Walker family archives.

Joe and Pauline knew each other well. In many ways, they led parallel lives. Beyond that, Pauline and Joe were about as alike as a bear and a woodchuck. Joseph P. Allyn, the territory's first Supreme Court Justice, knew them both and made this comparison:

"Captain Joseph Walker is a cool, reticent, courteous man, careful in what he says and is impatient with contradiction. Captain Pauline Weaver is the opposite of Walker in every respect; garrulous to a fault, tells tall stories until he has the reputation of a sort of Munchausen, is impulsive and with failing memory."

Before his arrival in Arizona Territory, Joe had been a fur trapper, explorer, trailblazer, military guide, cattleman, miner and sheriff. Famed historian Hubert Howe Bancroft described him as "one of the bravest and most skilled mountain men who ever lived." Among those who knew him well were John C. Fremont, Kit Carson, Bill Williams, Ewing Young and the Sublett brothers, among others. Without exception, all agreed that Captain Joe Walker had no superior.

His contemporaries described him as 'brave, truthful and kindly as a child'. His greatest fault, they said, was his modesty, something that was never said of Pauline.

Pauline had also been a fur trapper, explorer, military guide and miner, but unlike Joe, he'd not been very successful in those endeavors. Much of Pauline's life's story is relatively undocumented and subject to considerable speculation. He was illiterate, so he wrote down nothing about himself. Nevertheless, he too, was a legend during his own lifetime.

For most of that lifetime, he was known as Powell Weaver, but in the 1864 Arizona census, he gave his first name as Pauline. Purportedly his father was French American and his mother was a Cherokee Indian.

Both Joe and Pauline were born one year apart in Tennessee. Pauline in 1797 and Joe in 1798. They both entered the lucrative fur trading business during its heyday. But Joe would go on to become a renowned man of firsts: The first to help establish the Santa Fe Trail; to find a navigable route over the Sierra Nevada mountains to California; lead a wagon train of emigrants over that trail; the first white man to set eyes on the great Yosemite Valley; the first sheriff of Jackson County, Missouri; and of course the first to discover gold in Central Arizona. These were just a few of his astonishing accomplishments.

Pauline's only "first" was being with Henry Wickenberg's group when they discovered the first of several big gold strikes at Rich Hill near present day Octave, in 1863. Pauline and Joe's gold discoveries, which took place within weeks of one another, started the stampede into Tierra Incognita—the unknown territory of central Arizona.

Joe's first 30 years of life were illustrious enough to be well documented. Little to nothing is known about Pauline's first 30 years.

Pauline's name first turns up in 1829 as a member of an ill-fated and unsuccessful beaver trapping expedition destined for the Rocky Mountains under the leadership of Captain John Rogers. Of the group of 50 who started out on this expedition, only 15 made it safely back. Pauline was among them.

Beaver hats were the number one item worn by proper gentlemen throughout Europe and America from the early 17th Century, through the middle of the 19th Century, when they finally went out of style.

Fortunes were being made on beaver pelts. In 1760 alone, the Hudson's Bay Company exported enough beaver pelts for 576,000 hats. It took one pelt to make each hat. Beaver pelts were more valuable than gold in those days, and inspired as much of a "rush" to find them as gold ever did.

The best places to find these mammals were in the vast *Tierra Incognita* areas of the American West, where unexplored rivers and streams carried an abundance of them. It was the beaver that gave rise to America's Mountain Man Era, of which Pauline and Joe were active members until the 1850s. After 1850, when beaver hats fell out of style, most mountain men became guides for immigrant trains and army expeditions. Pauline was called upon to be one of those as well. He was never as skilled a guide as Joe.

Pauline's first appointment as guide was a dismal failure. After the United States Congress declared war on Mexico in 1846, Pauline was hired by the U.S military to guide Captain Philip St. George Cooke's Mormon Battalion to California to fight the Mexicans.

Under orders from their leader, Brigham Young, over 500 Mormon men joined this battalion. They saw it as their best opportunity to finance their migrations in the west in order to establish Mormon settlements.

The Mormon Battalion left Santa Fe for California on October 19, 1846. They were inadequately supplied and poorly clothed. Cooke wanted to follow the Rio Grande River southward. To his dismay, he learned Pauline not only knew nothing about this southern route, but he also was a very poor pathfinder. On top of that, he was often ill with respiratory problems. When Antoine Leroux turned up in their camp a month later, Cooke appointed him chief guide.

Although a better pathfinder, Leroux knew nothing of this southerly route either. Between Leroux and Pauline, the two led the Mormon Battalion into one disaster after another. Not only were they constantly lost but both had problems finding water, forage and enough food. Finally Baptiste Charbonneau, (son of Sacajawea) took the lead, found a short cut through uncharted gaps and passes, successfully hunted for food and water for them, and finally led them to the safety of their California destination.

Cooke complained bitterly in his diary about Pauline. When the Battalion did finally straggle into California, the war was already over. The Mormon Battalion was promptly discharged, along with Pauline and Leroux. Pauline had no use for Mormons from that point on.

Pauline became friends with Kit Carson. They met after Pauline joined an expedition headed by Ewing Young in the 1840s. It was Kit Carson's first try at trapping. Young took his expedition southeast from the Zuni pueblo, through Central Arizona, to the Gila River, and then to California. All early maps marked Central Arizona as Tierra Incognita, an unknown land of treacherous mountains and extremely hostile Indians. But Young, a veteran trapper and explorer, successfully led his men through this dangerous country. They were the first white men, since the Spanish explorers, to see the area. They didn't linger long, however, the Apaches were too threatening.

Around 1832, Pauline took a wife. A Catholic Church archival entry indicates he married a Maria Dolores Martin in 1832 in Taos. It is not known if she was Spanish or Indian. From this union came a son, Ben. Ben eventually followed his father to the Arizona gold fields in the 1860s where he was brutally murdered by the Yavapai Apaches.

Soon after the war with Mexico ended, Pauline took up ranching in Southern California, without his family. What he raised on the ranch, if anything, is unrecorded. Visitors passing through described his ranch as run down and dilapidated. When Doctor Isaac Smith and his family emigrated from Iowa to California in 1852, they also stopped at Pauline's ranch and found him deathly ill. The Smith family stayed on, nursed Pauline back to health, and adopted him into their family. In 1857, Pauline turned his ranch over to the Smith family and headed to Arizona.

He settled in Yuma and made his living trapping beaver for meat, which he sold to adventurers passing through. When the Civil War broke out, Pauline offered his services as a guide and scout for the Union Army.

After a contingent of Texas Rebels took over Tucson, declared it for the Confederacy and raised the Texas flag, Col. James Carleton and his California Volunteers were sent to contest the Rebel occupation. When Carleton arrived in Tucson, the Rebels had already fled. He wanted to track them down, but he needed guides. Pauline came highly recommended by Major Edwin Rigg who was stationed in Yuma. "He knows every foot of ground through the whole country, and is almost an Indian himself," wrote Rigg. Carleton promptly hired Pauline, and initially was pleased with his performance.

Pauline suggested the possible location of the Rebels near Picacho Pass, 50 miles northwest of Tucson. Carleton sent a detachment of advance riders there, and a brief skirmish ensued on April 15, 1862. It was the only Civil War battle to take place on Arizona soil. Three Union soldiers and two Rebel soldiers were killed. Still determined to track them down, Carleton used Pauline as a spy, since 'he knew the country so well'. This time, Pauline blew it.

Pauline and a Sgt. Wheeling were escorted by 40 soldiers of Company A, 1st Cavalry, California Volunteers part way into Tierra

Incognita (Central Arizona). Ten days later, Pauline and Sgt. Wheeling were back in Tucson saying they'd been unable to get through that unknown territory. Pauline was dismissed as a guide. He returned to Yuma. Carleton was no longer impressed. A soldier who knew Pauline during that time described him the way:

"He was pretty much an Indian himself and liked to scout far ahead of us. He has been so much alone that his speech was part English, part Spanish with a few Indian words thrown in for good measure. He wore his clothes until they fell off him and if he shook those long whiskers of his of a sudden, I'll bet woodchucks, gophers and trade rats would jump out.

"His mother may have washed him when he was little, but after he left home, he didn't believe in using water to wash in. After a hard march, we'd peel off our clothes and jump into the muddy Gila, but not Pauline. No Sir! He didn't believe in washing. Said it made him sick."

In truth, Pauline had been plagued with respiratory problems all of his life and probably attributed this to washing.

Authorities in Yuma called upon his services again, however, this time as a peacemaker. With gold discoveries popping up all along the Colorado River from La Paz to Ehrenberg, the Yuma and Maricopa Indians needed placating. Pauline succeeded in gathering the tribes together and making a peace treaty with them, but it was not a treaty sanctioned by the U.S. Government. The prospectors pouring into the country ignored it.

In an effort to protect the peaceful Indians, Pauline gave them a password to use when they encountered white men—"Paulino Tobacco." The prospectors either didn't know or didn't care about the password. They shot any Indian they saw. In those times most agreed with General Sheridan's public statement that 'the only good Indians were dead ones'.

By the spring of 1863, Abraham Harlow Peeples and Henry Wickenburg hired Pauline as a guide. Both of these dedicated prospectors were convinced Pauline could guide them into the forbidding Tierra Incognita of Central Arizona, where vast deposits of gold were rumored to exist. Wickenburg had seen gold himself there a year earlier, but didn't have the means to prospect it. Apparently this promise of gold inspired a new courage in Pauline he'd previously lacked.

With a party of 10 men, they traveled 110 miles from La Paz to the area Wickenburg remembered, an area now known as Octave and Stanton. Peeples killed three antelope there, and named the nearby mountain Antelope Mountain.

They found a little color in the creek the first day, but by the second, struck it rich. Using nothing more than butcher knives, the men dug out $1,800 worth of gold and named the area.

Rich Hill. Rich Hill was 30 miles south of what would become Prescott. Two weeks earlier, the Walker Party had already struck gold five miles south of the future site of Prescott. Between these two major strikes, the stampede for gold into Tierra Incognita was ignited, and the towns of Weaverville and Walker sprang to life.

Pauline emerged from the rush empty handed. He seemed to spend his gold as fast as he got it. He managed to buy a small ranch on the Hassayampa River in Walnut Grove, nine miles from Rich Hill.

Shortly afterwards, Pauline expressed a special concern for the Yavapai Indians whose lands were being invaded. He knew the tribe only wanted peace, yet prospectors were slaughtering them indiscriminately.

In a letter to Charles Poston, head of Arizona's Indian Affairs, Pauline wrote (with the aid of someone named R.J.R.) the following:

"It is hard to ceep hunkery Indians from stealing and almost as hard to ceep whites from making indescrimanade sloughter of them for stealing. I would like to here from you and know if anything can be done for these aboriginas that are inclined to be peasable." (sic)

But Pauline's attitude toward the Yavapais took a nasty turn after some Yavapai boys stole corn from his ranch. When Pauline complained to their elders, the elders only laughed, and did nothing to punish them. Enraged, Pauline gathered some soldiers and citizens together from Fort Whipple, divided them into two groups and led them to two Yavapai rancherias. In simultaneous surprise attacks, the two groups massacred the defenseless Indians, men, women and children, who had no firearms with which to protect themselves.

Pauline's son Ben was brutally murdered by Indians a short time afterwards, probably in retaliation. From then on, Pauline personally led soldiers on numerous raids that killed many Yavapai and Apache people indiscriminately. When the Indians retaliated further by constantly raiding his ranch, Pauline abandoned it for good, and spent the remainder of his life working as a guide at Forts Whipple and McDowell.

When Camp Lincoln was established on the Verde River, Pauline lived and worked there for two years. Always one to sleep outside, he camped near the sluggish Verde River, where he purportedly contracted malaria, and died on June 21, 1867. He was buried with full military honors.

Pauline Weaver's name is remembered with such Arizona place names as Weaver Mountain, Weaver Peak and Weaver Pass. Following Fort Verde's abandonment in 1891, Pauline's remains were moved, along with that of other military personnel, to the San Francisco National Cemetery.

Around 1927, Prescott attorney Alpheus H. Favour initiated a move to bring Pauline's remains back to Prescott after receiving permission from the United States War Department to do so.

Favour initiated a fund raising campaign among the county's school children, and the Yavapai-Mohave Council of Boy Scouts. Children were asked to contribute ten cents each to the cause. The entire cost of transporting his body back to Arizona, $150, was raised entirely by Yavapai County children.

On October 27, 1929, the Boy Scouts escorted Pauline's casket to the grounds of the Sharlot Hall Museum where a graveside ceremony took place. Many Prescott dignitaries were present. Sharlot Hall gave the eulogy which ended with these words: "The dust of Prescott's first citizen has come back to rest in an honored grave on Prescott's soil." Sharlot had it wrong. There were many people living in Prescott before Pauline ever settled near the area.

A few months later, the Arizona State Legislature authorized payment for a bronze memorial for his grave. The inscription on the monument called Pauline a pioneer, prospector, scout, guide, free trapper, fur trader, empire builder, patriot, and truly great man. "His greatest achievement," it said, "was as a peacemaker between races, understanding as few ever did the true hearts of two peoples."

* * * *

Unlike Pauline, Joe Walker was an excellent pathfinder, who also knew a thing or two about pioneering. He'd been born into a courageous pioneering family of Scottish descent who, from the early 1700s through 1850, continuously ventured westward again and again into untamed territory, and paved the way for others to follow.

His father Joseph, for whom he was named, married Susan Willis in 1789 in Virginia. Susan bore Joseph seven children. The first three were born in Virginia at the family compound, but the fourth, Joe Rutherford, was born in Roan City, Tennessee in 1798, where his family had migrated west again just before Joe was born. His father, Joseph, died twelve years later, leaving Susan with 12 year old Joe Rutherford, 13 year old Joel, John, 10, Sam 8, and Susan 6 years old. Their older sisters Lucinda and Jane were 20 and 19 at the time.

When Joe Rutherford was 14, he and his brother Joel, along with their teenaged cousin Sam Houston, ran off to fight in the War of 1812 under Andrew Jackson.

In 1818, when he was 20 years old, Joe Rutherford and his family immigrated to the far western frontier of Fort Osage, Missouri. Fort Osage was erected in 1808 under the direction of William Clark of the Lewis and Clark expedition. The main purpose was to protect the new territory, acquired in the Louisiana Purchase, and also to befriend the Osage Indians, house the soldiers, provide sanctuary for settlers desiring to go west, and establish a government trading post.

Here destiny awaited the arrival of Joe Rutherford Walker, and opened her arms to his adventurous spirit. It was from Fort Osage that his path towards greatness began.

Joe, his widowed mother Susan, and all her children and grandchildren, chose a site to homestead seven miles distant from Fort Osage, beyond the boundary of Louisiana Purchase lands. Following what had become a family tradition, they became the most westerly permanent settlers in the county.

Joe helped his family clear their new land, build a large cabin, plant corn, and the apple trees the family had brought with them from Tennessee, and set up a blacksmith shop.

The patriarch of the family now was Abraham McClellan, whose family had immigrated to America with Joe's great-grandparents in the early 1700s. Abraham, age 42, had married Joe's older sister Jane. Leaving the family in Abraham's capable hands, Joe and his older brother Joel, both in their early twenties, set off to explore the west.

At Fort Osage, they joined a group calling themselves the American Party. This group of young adventurers planned an illegal trading trip to Santa Fe. Santa Fe, in 1820, was under the control of the Spanish, who had outlawed all trade with Americans. Soon after they arrived in Santa Fe, the entire American Party was arrested and imprisoned.

During this time, the Spanish were having serious problems with the Pawnee Indians. When Joe learned of this, he negotiated with the Spanish to set his group free. In return they would help them fight the Indians.

His request was granted, and the American Party initiated a successful campaign against the Pawnees. The grateful Spanish granted them special trade privileges. The American Party, which soon evolved into the famous "Taos Trappers," trapped beaver on the upper Arkansas River and elsewhere in Spanish Territory. Joe alone netted an average of $30,000 worth of pelts each season. By 1825, he was back with his family in Missouri, but not for long.

Within months, an exciting new opportunity presented itself. President James Monroe was offering $30,000 to a group who would survey and establish the Santa Fe Trail. Joe, and his younger brother John, were hired as guides, along with Joe's good friend Bill Williams, a member of the original Taos Trappers. Williams was hired as an interpreter.

With the help of Bill Williams, Joe successfully negotiated a peace treaty with the Osage Indians. For the sum of $800, the Kansas and Osage tribes agreed to allow the survey party to pass, unmolested through, 150 miles of their lands.

With the Mexicans now in control of Santa Fe, (having declared their independence from Spain in 1821), the trailblazers led by Joe had little difficulty in mapping the approximately 775 miles of the Santa Fe Trail, from Fort Osage, Missouri, across present day Kansas, through corners of Colorado and the Oklahoma Panhandle, and into New Mexico.

* * * *

When he returned to Fort Osage, his name was now recognized throughout Missouri. The governor appointed him as the first sheriff of Jackson County. This newly formed county included the brand new town of Independence. The governor also appointed Joe's brother, Joel, as the county's first Justice of the Peace.

Independence, at that time, was made up of rough, feud prone citizens, but Joe had a knack for keeping the peace. There were no murders in Independence during the three years Joe served as sheriff.

One of his duties as sheriff was to keep watch for runaway slaves and escaping indentured servants. A 16 year-old indentured servant by the name of Kit Carson was just such a runaway. Joe took a liking to the lad. Rather than returning him to his master, who had offered a one-penny reward for his return, Joe put him in the care of his Taos trapper friend William Wolfskill, who in turn passed him into the hands of Ewing Young. Ewing Young and Joe were kinsmen. Young's sister had married Joe's brother, Joel.

Initially, Ewing Young hired Kit to take care of his horses, then eventually taught him to be a first rate trapper. Kit Carson, Ewing Young and Joe remained lifelong friends.

In the meantime, Joe, after serving two terms as sheriff in Jackson County, Missouri, realized he'd had enough of city life. He decided to become a freelance trapper and explorer once again, and rejoin the ranks of his Taos trapper friends. They included Jim Bridger, the Sublett brothers, Tom Fitzpatrick, Jed Smith and Bill Williams.

In 1830, his friend and kinsman, Sam Houston, contacted Joe and encouraged him to come to Fort Gibson, Oklahoma Territory, and bring horses. Houston wanted Joe to meet U.S. Army Captain Benjamin Louis Eulalie de Bonneville. Houston, a protégé of President Andrew Jackson, had been living at the fort for over a year with his Cherokee wife, and was privy to important happenings there. He hinted to Joe that Bonneville had been given an intriguing assignment by President Andrew Jackson, something he knew Joe would find interesting.

He did. Bonneville and Joe met and agreed on a joint venture that would connect their lives significantly for the next four years.

The "cover story" was that Bonneville's expedition was a major fur trading enterprise. Financed by such New York bigwigs as John Jacob Astor, the lavishly outfitted brigade of 110 men left Fort Osage in May of 1832. Each man was equipped with extra horses and mules, and the brigade was followed by 20 well-supplied wagons. Their real purpose was to find a navigable route across the Sierra Nevada Mountains to California, and assess the strength of the Spanish and Mexican armies stationed there.

For the next four years, Joe and his entourage endured incredible hardships including near starvation, Indian attacks, and treacherous descents and ascents through the freezing snow capped mountains of the Sierra Nevada.

Sighting Yosemite Valley, the first white men to do so, Joe's party took three days descending into this lush valley. They lost 24 of their horses in the process, 17 of which provided food for his starving followers. There is some indication that Pauline Weaver was on this expedition.

The group eventually made their way to Monterey, where the Spanish governor Don Juan Bautista Alvarado took a liking to Joe and offered him an enormous land grant, one which would make him wealthy. A man of integrity, Joe politely refused. He had no use for the Spanish who'd once imprisoned him.

Joe's party did not return the way they had come. Working their way south along the San Joaquin valley, they eventually discovered a low-lying pass through the mountains. The pass, known today as Walker Pass, would later become the major route for pioneers heading to California. In 1843, Joe guided the first successful wagon train through that pass.

From 1844-1846, Joe served as a guide for Charles Fremont's second and third expeditions to California. He was one of the most sought after guides for several other expeditions as well. By 1850, with California now in the hands of America following its war with Mexico, Joe settled down for a while and operated a large cattle and horse ranch in Monterey County.

Sometime during his employment with Bonneville, Joe had taken an Indian wife. Her name was Suisun, the daughter of a Ute Chief. Suisun bore him two children. No records exist as to what happened to them, but a bay and a city near Joe's California cattle ranch in Monterey County bear the unusual names of Suisun.

Nine months after Joe's remarkable gold discoveries at Lynx Creek, the newly appointed territorial officials arrived at Del Rio Springs. They hired both Joe and Pauline to guide them on an expedition to find a more suitable location for Fort Whipple, and the new Capital of Prescott, which they succeeded in doing.

In the 1864 territorial census of Yavapai County, Joseph Rutherford Walker listed his occupation as a mountaineer with property valued at $300. He remained in Yavapai County until 1867. Almost totally blind by then, he spent his remaining years with his nephew, James T. Walker, in Ygnacio Valley, Contra Costa County, California, where he died October 27, 1876, age 78. He is buried in Alhambra Cemetery, Martinez, California. His name survives today on Walker Pass, Walker Lake, Walker River, Walker Valley, Walker Gulch, Walker Canyon, Walker Creek, Walker Trail, Walker Peak, Walker Mining District, Walker, Arizona, and Walker, California.

* * * *

THE FIRST LADIES OF YAVAPAI COUNTY

Mary Catherine Leib, and Jennie Sara Wells, arrived with the First California Volunteers sent by General Carleton to establish a fort near the gold fields of Prescott and the Verde Valley. They became the first white women to set foot in the soon-to-be established county of Yavapai.

Mary Catherine Leib accompanied her husband Dr. Charles Leib, the acting assistant surgeon assigned to Fort Whipple. Jennie came as a single woman hired as a laundress for the troops. One of those troops, Wales Arnold, eventually married Jennie Sara Wells.

Although both women arrived under different circumstances, they proved to be equals when it came to courage, endurance, and surviving the hardships and deprivations of a wild frontier. Both would be remembered for contributing to the welfare and development of their communities; for living through the worst of the Indian depredations, and each for adopting and raising an Apache child as her own.

Born in 1836 near Bethlehem, Pennsylvania, Mary Catherine Smith came from an old and prominent Moravian family. The Moravians, one of the earliest protestant sects in the world, broke with the Roman Church 60 years before Martin Luther's denunciation of the Catholic Church in the 1400s. Their name is derived from their historic church's beginnings in ancient Bohemia and Moravia, in what is today the Czech Republic.

The Moravians settled in America in 1735, and by 1741, made their headquarters in Bethlehem, Pennsylvania, the area of Mary Catherine's birth. At a time when it was rare for women to be allowed a formal education, Mary Catherine enjoyed a fine education at her church seminary, where she advanced in music. This was an indication of her family's prominence as church leaders and citizens. Before meeting her first husband, Charles Leib, she had dedicated herself to a life of service in her church.

Mary Catherine married Charles Leib, also born in Pennsylvania, on January 6, 1852. The couple established their first home in Iowa, but by 1854 Dr. Leib was practicing medicine in a tent under a cottonwood tree in Leavenworth, Kansas Territory. When the first territorial governor, Andrew H. Reeder, arrived in the newly formed territory, Dr. Leib was selected to give the welcoming speech to this fellow Pennsylvanian.

There is considerable doubt that Dr. Leib ever received any formal medical training, which was not unusual during territorial days. Doctors were in such high demand in the territories that just about anyone with a stomach for it, could call himself "Doctor." Their credentials were rarely questioned.

It was an "on the job training" for most, even for those with a formal education. Many of the medical emergencies in the west differed from those in the east, the removal of arrowheads, and the treatment of rattlesnake bites, being most common.

By 1860, Dr. Leib was immersed in politics and had been for several years. Although a Democrat, he stoutly supported Abraham Lincoln. His adversaries described him as "shifty, mysterious—a scoundrel," and they blamed him for dividing the Democratic Party in favor of Lincoln.

His friendship with Lincoln garnered him the job as editor of the Rail Splitter, a Republican campaign sheet. When the Civil War broke out, Lincoln saw to it that Leib was appointed Quartermaster, serving the Union Army at Clarksburg, West Virginia from May 1861, to February 1862. After nine months, Leib was dismissed after being charged with a 1 million-dollar shortage in his accounts. Shortly afterwards, he and Mary Catherine headed for Santa Fe, New Mexico.

In Santa Fe, Leib founded the weekly *Santa Fe New Mexican* newspaper on January 23, 1863. Before the year ended, he sold his interest in the newspaper after General Carleton appointed him assistant surgeon to accompany troops to Arizona Territory under the command of Major Edward Willis. When Leib applied for this appointment, the exciting gold strikes in Arizona unquestionably inspired his interest.

With his devoted wife Mary Catherine accompanying him, they left Fort Union near Santa Fe on October 5, 1863. Their great caravan consisted of 200 troops, 60 mule teams, Army ambulances, droves of cattle and sheep and other supplies. They reached Del Rio Springs, the original site of the Fort Whipple, on December 20, 1863.

Three months later, Dr. Leib's contract with the Army was abruptly cancelled. The cause is not known, but in a letter from Inspector General Maj. Nelson Davis to General Carleton, the following statement was included: "The case of Dr. Leib was such an aggravated one, I acted upon it before your instructions in regard to him were received."

Dr. Leib and Mary Catherine moved into a rough log cabin on Granite Creek, and Leib promptly went from being a doctor, to being a full time prospector.

He also attempted to become a Union delegate to Congress at the first territorial election, but Charles Poston soundly defeated him. The *Santa Fe Gazette*, rival to Leib's New Mexican newspaper, crowed over his defeat calling him "an imposter, inconsistent, unscrupulous, cynical and without principal—a scoundrel." Six months later, Dr. Charles Leib was dead at the age of 39, cause unknown.

Leib's grave was one of the first in the Citizen's Cemetery in Prescott. At the time of his death he owned the Bonito, Washburn, Little Giant and Bullie Bueno mining claims, and interests in the Burro, Cadiz and Arizona quartz leads. However, once his estate was settled and debts paid, Mary Catherine found herself with what was left—the sum total of $50.

Mary Catherine's brother came to visit, and tried to persuade her to return with him to Pennsylvania, but she refused. She believed she was needed in this wild, untamed territory, and she was. With the help of two friends, Harriet Turner (wife of the territory's first chief justice), and Fannie Cave Stevens, she opened one of Prescott's first schools in her log cabin, using books the women had brought with them. They charged a minimal fee. Mary Catherine also faithfully visited the sick and befriended the few white women living in Prescott.

Two years after her husband's death, Mary Catherine married her neighbor, Judge Hezekiah Brooks, a beloved and respected pioneer. Throughout his long life, Judge Brooks was never referred to as a 'scoundrel'.

Born September 7, 1825, near Elyria, Lorraine County, Ohio, Judge Brooks went west by ship, via Panama, to seek his fortune during the California gold rush when he was 25 years old. From 1850 to 1863, he lived in various areas of California, and engaged in a variety of occupations. At first trying his luck at mining on the south fork of the American River, Brooks gave up after a year and turned to merchandising; served as a deputy sheriff, then postmaster, in Yreka, California; and by 1861 was engaged in contracting in San Francisco. When he met George Lount in San Francisco two years later, his life took its most significant and dramatic turn.

George Lount, a close personal friend of Joseph Rutherford Walker, traveled with the Walker Party when they discovered the gold at Lynx Creek in the spring of 1863. Several months after the discovery, Lount returned to San Francisco and organized another prospecting party. He returned to Lynx Creek with 12 men in October of 1863. Hezekiah Brooks was among them.

On May 30, 1864, territorial officials selected Brooks as one of the commissioners to lay out and dispose of lots in the proposed town site of Prescott. The following month, Governor Goodwin appointed him Probate Judge. He served in that capacity for the next seven years. His closest neighbor was Mary Catherine Leib.

On February 26, 1867, Judge Brooks married Mary Catherine with the Rev. Charles M. Blake reading the service. Besides teaching, Mary Catherine already had organized Prescott's first Sunday school, and was one of the original-founding members of the first church to be established in Prescott, the Methodist South. Her musical talents were used to organize the church's choir.

Two years after their marriage, Judge and Mrs. Brooks were picnicking on Independence Day with a group of friends, when they encountered a cavalry troop from Fort Whipple. The troop was returning from a raid on a band of Apaches. Their civilian guide, Ed Peck, had a bundle in his arms that turned out to be an orphaned Indian girl, about two years old. Peck had killed her mother during the skirmish. The Brooks eagerly accepted the little girl to raise as their own. They named her Bessie.

Bessie, now brought up in a loving home, learned all the manners of a proper Victorian lady. She attended school and church, and became adept in the various arts of homemaking. Everyone who met her spoke highly of her.

When Bessie was about 24 years old, Mary Catherine died suddenly of bronchial pneumonia. Earlier that year, Mary Catherine had sold some mining stocks, and along with an inheritance from her brother, initiated the building of her dream home. After she bought George Lount's ranch, she designed a large frame home with big rooms and fireplaces. New furniture and carpets had arrived from San Francisco. and been put in place, when Mary Catherine suddenly became ill.

Her new home did not long survive her. It burned to the ground within months after her death with all the new furniture, and a set of beautiful china, her brother's last gift, still unpacked. It was a double tragedy for Bessie and her father. They buried Mary Catherine in the Masonic Cemetery. Six years later, Bessie married James Edgar, a worthy and industrious citizen, in Mary Catherine's church, the Methodist South.

Initially, their engagement came to the attention of the press, due to the prevailing miscegenation laws, making it illegal for an Indian and a white to marry. But Judge Brooks quickly laid that issue to rest when he signed an affidavit that the bride-to-be was his legally adopted daughter, and therefore, by adoption, a white girl. Unfortunately, that affidavit disappeared ten years later, after the judge died without leaving a will.

In early 1907, Judge Brooks, then 81 years old, became gravely ill and decided to go to Cleveland, Ohio to seek treatment, while staying with relatives there. Before he left, he did a curious thing. He had Dr. Charles Leib's body removed from the Citizen's Cemetery, to the Masonic Cemetery, and laid to rest next to Mary Catherine. Then within a few months after arriving in Cleveland, Judge Brooks died there on May 30, 1907.

Before Bessie had an opportunity to recover from the shock and grief of losing her father, she received another shock. Judge Brook's cousin, Van H. Brooks, declared in an affidavit that he was the only next of kin to Judge Brooks living in Yavapai County. He asked the court to appoint him administrator of the Brook's estate, challenging all claims to the contrary by Bessie Brooks.

The judge's estate seemed hardly worth fighting over. Its total value, consisting of real estate and personal property, amounted to $3,400. Nevertheless, his relatives were determined not to allow Bessie to have any of it.

On the advice of her lawyer, LeRoy Johnson, Bessie moved into her father's home. That's when things turned ugly. The case became sensational and controversial throughout the territory, and the beleaguered Bessie was shot at and nearly killed while staying in her father's home. A man named Otis was arrested, but never prosecuted.

At the hearing held on June 21, 1907, Van Brook's attorney J.J. Hawkins presented several documents, all damaging to Bessie's case. Two were sworn statements from Judge Brook's sister and brother-in-law, Mattie and Dr. Theodore Breck, stating under oath that Judge Brooks had told them, on more than one occasion, that he had never legally adopted Bessie. The other was a handwritten letter, written by Judge Brooks five days before his death, granting his cousin, Van Brooks, Power of Attorney, and requesting that he sell his property known as the China wash house and lot in Prescott. The judge did not mention Bessie anywhere in the letter.

Despite testimony on her behalf by ten witnesses, Bessie's appeal for a share in her father's estate was soon denied on the grounds that Judge Brooks died without a will, and there were no documents that proved Bessie's legal adoption. The case went to the territorial superior court where Ed Peck, the civilian guide who saved her as a toddler from the battlefield, also testified on her behalf. But she lost again for the same reason.

Bessie did not go completely empty handed. She produced the title to a one-acre lot in Prescott, given to her and her family by Judge Brooks, shortly before he left for Cleveland.

Judge Brooks' family did not contest that claim. Afterwards, no one heard from Bessie Brooks Edgar or her family. They apparently moved to parts unknown after the trial.

* * * *

FIRST LADY OF CAMP VERDE

Jennie Sara Wells who, like Mary Catherine, traveled with the First California Infantry on their initial foray into Arizona Territory, came as a laundress for the troops.

Single women who wanted to go west, and had no other means of getting there, often signed on with the Army as laundresses. As such, they faced many of the same hardships as any other pioneer woman, but enjoyed more protection, plus a salary.

Jennie met her husband-to-be, Wales Arnold, a member of the First California Infantry, at some point along their way west. By

August 1864, Arnold was honorably discharged. Because he had gained considerable experience as an Indian fighter and scout before coming to Arizona Territory, he hired on as a civilian scout at Camp Lincoln, and became responsible for making improvements on many trails throughout the Verde Valley. He also served as the postmaster and Sutler (one who sold provisions to the troops) at Camp Lincoln for a while.

Jennie, in the meantime, continued working as a laundress at Camp Date Creek. Later she worked as a cook and housekeeper for the Nathan Bowers family who had settled on a tract of land that extended from present day Dewey to Humbolt. Wales Arnold courted her there for the next several years.

On October 24, 1869, Mary Catherine's husband Judge Hezekiah Brooks united them in marriage in Prescott. The salty publisher of the *Arizona Miner,* John H. Marion, acknowledged their marriage in his newspaper: "Although ourself a bachelor of ever so many years, it pleases us to record unions like this, especially when we know they spring from pure unadulterated love as has this one."

The Arnolds settled down in Camp Verde where their courage and hospitality made them one of the most beloved couples in their community. But homesteading in the Verde Valley was fraught with danger in those days. Indian depredations were at their peak.

In the spring of 1870, the Arnolds homesteaded a ranch at Montezuma Well where, with the help of their partner, Joe Burroughs, they built an adobe house with rifle portholes, but no windows. Their house was built over a well in the kitchen, and equipped with a trap door in case of siege by Indians. Soon after the house was completed, Indians killed their partner Joe Burroughs a few miles from their ranch. The *Arizona Miner* in an outburst of indignation, described the bloody event:

"Sunday the sixteenth of August, while savages were driving Mr. Arnold's animals toward the mountains; they met a white man named Joe Burroughs, who was returning home from a hunt for game, and it is scarcely necessary for us to say they made short work of him. Several days after the murder, the body was found about two miles from the Arnold's ranch and some six or seven miles from Camp Verde. When found, it was stripped naked, pierced in several places by arrows and bullets, and was also in a state of decomposition.

"Mr. Burroughs came here from Colorado in 1864; had worked ever since and was well thought of by all who knew him. His death is mourned by all who knew him and will be until the next victim of savage barbarity shall have been reported, which may be at any moment, as the savages are plentiful through this section of the country; but white avengers—citizens and soldiers—are on the trail of the red fiends and it may be that a just God will direct their steps to some Apache trysting place where punishment for their atrocious actions can be dispensed with unsparing hand."

Fortunately, the Arnolds never suffered such hideous deaths.

Jennie, known lovingly as 'Auntie Arnold' was looked upon as a ministering angel. Whenever anyone was sick or injured, she rode horseback to wherever they were in order to lend a helping hand. Whether at home washing dishes, feeding chickens, or on the trail to help a neighbor, Auntie Arnold never was without her pistol.

During the frequent Indian raids, the Arnolds' home became the place where neighbors sought refuge, sometimes having to stay for weeks until the danger passed. Even without danger, the Arnolds welcomed visitors. Regardless if they needed a place to stay, or a good meal, the Arnolds were always accommodating. Friends remembered Wales Arnold sitting down to an evening meal, facing the door, with his 50-caliber Bulldog pistol on the table within easy reach of his right hand.

Sometime around 1871, following an Indian skirmish in which the Indians were severely defeated, a little Indian girl of toddling age was found wandering among the dead. Soldiers brought her to Auntie Arnold. Never having had children of their own, the Arnolds adopted her and named her Lulu.

At first she was like a frightened wild animal, who had to be kept in a crate because she was inclined to spit and bite. But with infinite kindness and patience, Auntie Arnold tamed her wild ways and raised her as a white child. Auntie taught her to read, write and do arithmetic as well as many useful household chores. Upon coming of age, Lulu married Mr. Abe McKesson and bore him five or six children. One of them, Isabelle, spoke of her mother as a full-blooded Apache named Lulu Verde. Lulu died of consumption in Kingman, Arizona in 1897. The famous Apache Maid Ranch was named for Lulu.

Wales Arnold served as constable of the Verde Precinct from 1871-72. During General Crook's campaign against the Indians, he signed up once again as a scout. In 1878, he was appointed Justice of the Peace for the Beaver Creek Precinct.

In 1880, the Arnolds moved to the Flower Pot Ranch east of Squaw Peak and built another fortress of a home, complete with rifle gun ports. Here they lived for the next ten years. In 1890, they moved back to Camp Verde. Auntie Arnold operated the W.S. "Boss" Head boarding house, serving as its cook, while Wales hauled water by wagon and team.

In 1895, the Arnolds were homesteading what later became known as the Fain ranch. In 1909, Auntie Arnold died at their ranch following a long illness. Shortly after her death, Wales sold the ranch to O.A. Benedict and moved to Prescott. By then he was quite ill himself. He bought a home in Prescott and hired a nurse to look after him. After awhile he moved into the Pioneers' Home, but became unhappy there. He moved into the Old Soldier's Home in Sautelle, California, and decided he disliked it there even more, so he returned to Prescott where he died on May 21, 1913.

The cortège to his final resting place at the Clear Creek Cemetery was escorted by troops from Fort Whipple, and became the first in the Verde Valley to be accompanied by automobiles, eleven in all. Over four hundred people attended his funeral at the Clear Creek Church. He was buried next to his beloved Jennie at the Clear Creek Cemetery in Camp Verde.

Wale's gravestone reads:

CORPL. WALES ARNOLD
1 CAL. INF.

Auntie Arnold's stone is much larger and the tallest in the cemetery. It reads:

SARA J. ARNOLD
WIFE OF WALES ARNOLD
1846-1909
OLDEST WOMAN SETTLER IN THE VERDE VALLEY

And in much larger letters on the block it reads:

"AUNTIE ARNOLD"

* * * *

A CAPITAL IS BORN

Snow swirled in the icy wind as the First Infantry of California Volunteers and their entourage arrived at Del Rio Springs on December 20, 1863. Here the crude beginnings of Camp Whipple was started, 20 miles north of where the Territorial Capital would officially be located five months later. The group, which included Mary Catherine, her husband Dr. Leib, Jennie Wells and Wales Arnold, camped at Del Rio Springs for a month, and awaited the arrival of Governor Goodwin and the newly appointed officials for Arizona Territory.

Archbishop Lamy of the Roman Catholic Diocese for Arizona and New Mexico, had traveled with them. With Christmas only five days away, he decided to celebrate the Holy Sacrifice to honor Christ's birth. On December 25, twenty-five people knelt on the snow-covered ground before an altar created from the trunk of a tree. It was the first Christmas celebration in Arizona Territory.

One month later, Governor Goodwin arrived and soon realized that Del Rio Springs was not a suitable site for the new capital. It simply was too far from all the mining activity near Lynx and Granite Creeks.

Following a month long foray with Pauline Weaver and Joe Walker serving as guides, Goodwin chose a mesa east of Granite Creek for Fort Whipple. A couple of miles west of the fort's location, he chose the town site, yet to be named.

Miners were already calling the settlement Granite City, Granite Dells and Gimletville. After the Governor arrived, Goodwin City was also suggested. Richard C. McCormick, first Territorial Secretary, proposed the name Prescott in honor of the historian William Hickling Prescott.

McCormick arrived in the new territory with a printing press and a small library. His library included Prescott's *The History of The Conquest of Mexico*. This lengthy and scholarly book, published 20 years earlier, focused on the Spanish conquistador, Hernando Cortez and his subjugation of the Aztecs and their leader, Montezuma. In his book, the author expressed the view that the Aztecs came to Mexico from the Northwest. McCormick interpreted the "Northwest" to be Central Arizona.

McCormick wrote an editorial in his newly established newspaper, the *Arizona Miner*, that there were Aztec memorials everywhere existing in the region, which supported the notion that the Aztecs had once resided here. He also included the outstanding professional and personal qualities of the author, Prescott, and concluded; "We should be proud to have his name associated with a settlement for which we have faith to believe there is a prosperous future." William Hickling Prescott died in 1859. He never set foot in the west, nor knew about the honor that had been bestowed upon him.

With the site agreed upon and the town named, Governor Goodwin divided the territory into three judicial districts and initiated the first territorial census. He assigned Robert W. Groom the job of "laying out the town."

Groom, a devout Democrat and "convicted Confederate" was a puzzling choice for any kind of position in the new territory. Goodwin and all his fellow officials were dedicated Republicans, and totally anti-Confederate.

Apparently, they had no other choice at the time. Groom was the only surveyor around. An affable, loveable and entertaining character, Groom soon became close friends with the new governor and other members of his government.

Working at a table in a small log cabin (later known facetiously as "Fort Misery"), Groom built his own surveying equipment. Legend has it that he used a frying pan as one of his instruments. We do know for sure, he used an old fashioned spyglass and a tripod which he built himself.

Despite these primitive circumstances, Groom did an exceptional job of laying out the town of Prescott. He designed the streets to be 80 feet wide, perhaps the widest streets in the country. He created a town plaza that was twice the typical size of other town plazas, and insisted that the tall pines on the plaza grounds be left in place.

The original downtown streets were named for explorers Leroux and Aubrey; Army officers, Willis and Carleton; territorial officials, McCormick, Goodwin and Gurley, and pioneers, Sheldon, Walker and Lount. Three street names came from W.H. Prescott's book, *The History Of The Conquest Of Mexico*: Cortez, Montezuma and Marina. (Marina was Cortez' Mayan interpreter who eventually mothered his son, Martin Cortez). Aztec Street was added a few years later.

Robert William Groom was born in Kentucky in 1824. He studied surveying in Kentucky, and by 1845 was deputy County Surveyor for Trigg County, Kentucky. The California gold rush of 1849 fired his ambitions to strike it rich, an ambition that lasted throughout his lifetime.

From 1850 to 1860, Groom tried his hand at prospecting in California; operating trading posts; surveying the township of San Bernardino, from 1858 to 1860. When the Civil War broke out, Groom, a dedicated southerner, organized a company of 300 southern-minded frontiersmen, and headed east to join the Confederacy.

He was arrested as a Confederate spy in Santa Fe by General Carleton, made to wear a ball and chain, and marched to Fort Union where he feared he might be shot. With the help of a fellow inmate, arrested for drunkenness and released after a few days, Groom managed to get a message to his friend U.S. Senator James McDougal of California who managed to arrange his release.

Once again, Groom's likeability inspired a friendship with his jailor, General Carleton. Carleton hired him as a guide for the N.J. Pishon expedition sent to evaluate the validity of Joe Walker's gold claims in Arizona Territory. Groom not only found Walker and his party, but immediately joined the prospectors to locate the "Groom Lode" on Granite Creek along with a number other lodes in the area.

Whenever written about, Robert Groom's personality was always described as likeable. He had few if any enemies. A lover of whiskey, good or bad, he spent many hours in the Montezuma Street saloons when not out prospecting. During one of his drinking sprees, he got into an argument with a young officer from Ft. Whipple. The officer challenged Groom to a duel.

As the one being challenged, Groom was allowed to select the location and the choice of weapons. He chose a spot near Walnut Grove. When the smartly dressed challenger, and his fellow officers arrived at Walnut Grove, he was handed his weapon—a boat paddle.

Groom led the officer to a dead bull, all four of its feet up in the air, and in an advanced state of decomposition. Groom told the young officer they were to stand on either side of the putrefying bull, and whichever one of them could dig out the most guts, won the duel. With the stench so overpowering, the officer decided it was in the best interest of all concerned to call off the duel and return to Prescott for a drink, which they did. From that day forward, whenever the subject of a duel arose, the Groom story was told. It brought such laughter that the duel was always called off, and another drink called for.

Groom never married. He died in Wickenburg in 1899, at the age of 74. At the time of his death he owned mining properties in Maricopa and Yavapai Counties appraised at $34,500. Groom Peak in the Walapai Mountains in Mojave County, and Groom Creek in Yavapai County, are named for him

* * * *

CIVILIZATION TAKES A FOOTHOLD

On May 30, 1864, Robert Groom, Hezekiah Brooks and Van C. Smith were appointed commissioners to oversee the disposition of town lots. There were 1016 lots put up for auction, valued respectively at $7.50, $10, and $15. The first auction took place on June 4, 1864. Seventy-three lots sold that day for a total of $3,927. Their appraised value was $910. There was finally some money in the government coffers.

The first building raised on one of the new town lots was the office of the *Arizona Miner*. Issued semi-monthly, it became the first newspaper in the territory.

The first hotel and restaurant was the Juniper House operated by George Barnard, and opened in time for the Fourth of July festivities. He advertised fried venison and chili for breakfast, roast venison and chili for dinner, and chili for supper. All meals were served with bread, tea, and coffee with milk. Bernard being the "chef" put several assistants in charge of collecting money for the meals, and as a result, was soon out of business.

Tom Hodges opened the first saloon on Cortez selling "segars" and whiskey. He was known to take burros as payment for a drink.

The most pressing need, as far as Governor Goodwin was concerned, was a building to house the new government. Bids went out, but even the lowest bids that came back exceeded the amount the Governor felt authorized to spend. Finally, Van C. Smith came forward and offered to put up a structure for "business purposes" that would serve both branches of the legislature.

The result was a two-story structure built from hewn logs. It had a 50-foot frontage, a depth of 40 feet, and contained 11 rooms, at the cost of $6,000. Judge Joseph P. Allyn, one of the three territorial justices, said it looked more like a livery stable than a Governor's Mansion.

There was only a dirt floor, and the partitions dividing it into rooms, did not reach the ceiling. The furniture was of simple pine construction, the tables covered with fancy blankets, and an American flag hung on the wall. Still, it was a vast improvement over their temporary headquarters in a tent.

The Governor's Mansion
—ASLA

In January of 1864, Manuel Yseria, a merchant from New Mexico, built a two-room cabin that was later known as Fort Misery. Yseria arrived with the troops escorting the governor's party into Arizona. He was the first to bring merchandise to sell to the miners.

He set his store up in one room of the cabin, and lived in the other. It became the center of activity in Prescott, and was pressed into service as a courtroom, and also used for Protestant church services. When his goods sold out, Yseria returned to New Mexico, abandoning his crude cabin.

When the government moved into their new quarters at the Governor's Mansion, Fort Misery became a boarding house for miners presided over by Mary Decrow Ramos. Miners called her "Virgin Mary" because of her kindness to them. Mary charged $25 in gold per week—in advance. Two goats furnished milk for her boarders, a big attraction.

A man named Jackson established another boarding house soon afterwards, and cut the price to $16 per week. To offset Mary's goat milk, he offered occasional stewed apples.

Eventually Mary and her husband, Cornelius, moved to Lynx Creek, and Judge John Howard took Fort Misery over as his home and law office. He named it Fort Misery, not only because it was a miserable place to live but because he doled out miserable sentences there.

Howard had been a territorial judge in Colorado, and also had traveled with the Governor's party from Santa Fe. No one understands what the judge's attachment was to this crude little cabin. He had the means to live in a better home. Nevertheless, he had Fort Misery dismantled and moved to his lot on Montezuma Street. He replaced its mud roof with shingles, named it Fort Misery and proceeded to live and practice law there until 1892. During that time, he was appointed as territorial Fish Commissioner, and in the late 1880s, served as the mayor of Prescott.

Howard didn't leave Fort Misery until the age of 72, when he wed Miss Flora Darby, 28 years his junior. In 1934, historian Sharlot Hall rescued old Fort Misery from demolition, and had it moved to the grounds of the museum named in her honor.

* * * *

THE FIRST FAMILIES

Throughout the 1860s and early 70s, Prescott took on the appearance of a substantial town. The homes being built were unusual for the southwest because few were of adobe construction. Most were of an American design with peaked roofs and glass windows. Of all the cities in Arizona, Prescott was the most Eastern in appearance.

Yet during those early years, it remained a wild and barbarous place to live. There were more saloons than any other businesses, open night and day, including Sundays. Prices for everything were fearfully high—100 greenbacks for one sack of flour. News from the outside world took four to six weeks to reach them…and the Indians remained in control.

It was necessary to post guards night and day within the town limits. Folks were advised not to venture beyond those limits, unless in the company of a large and well armed group.

Despite its dangerous reputation, a few hardy and determined pioneers, the "Hassyampers" as these pioneers of pioneers were later called, took their chances and came anyway. By 1864, most were fleeing the ravages the Civil War was inflicting on their eastern and southern communities, and all were looking for new opportunities.

Following on the heels of the first miners, soldiers and legislators, the very first wagon train of brave pioneer families arrived two months after Prescott was declared the territorial capitol. Many of those families would remain for the rest of their lives, and contribute dramatically to the development of their new communities.

It was called the Wells and Osborn party, of which E.W. Wells was captain. John P. Osborn, James Swetnam, Joe Ehle, L.A. Stevens, E.A. Boblett and their families were among the members. Their wagon train arrived in Prescott on July 6, 1864. They were the area's first families.

Their wagon train emigrated from Colorado Territory, not the East. Initially most of them had followed the lure of the Pike's Peak gold rush of 1858. Most were merchants and tradesmen who had fallen on hard times during the Panic of 1857, which plunged the country, particularly the Midwest, into a depression, but as the

Colorado gold began to play out, these pioneers found themselves facing a greater threat to their livelihood: The Indian uprising following the Sand Creek Massacre.

Soldiers were no longer available to protect them from the uprising, having been pulled away to serve in the Civil War. And because of that war, the return to their former homes was not an option either. The lure of Arizona's gold strikes seemed their only hope. Unfortunately, unbeknownst to them, they were traveling from the proverbial frying pan, into the proverbial fire.

Of all the families on that wagon train, none would suffer more from Indian depredations than the Osborn family.

John Preston Osborn, a native of Clairborne, Tennessee, was born in 1815, and was 49 years old when he arrived in Prescott. His wife, Perlina Elizabeth Swetnam, and seven of his 11 children, accompanied him. He'd long been a prosperous merchant in the east, and believed great opportunities awaited him when he arrived with a small herd of Durham cattle, and three ox teams loaded with needed goods.

He promptly built one of Prescott's first hotels, the Osborn House, a two-story frame structure which was by no means ornate. All meals offered there each day were the same, pork and beans with coffee and bread, one dollar each. The Osborn House boarded members of the First Arizona Legislature when they met in September of that year. Osborn generously refused pay for their board and room.

Osborn also cultivated a tract of land north of Prescott and built a home. From March of 1865, until January of 1870, Osborn and his family endured relentless attacks of one kind or another from the Apaches.

In 1865 the Indians stole eight milk cows and a prized horse worth $100. When he moved his herd to the Verde Valley that same year, and joined it to his son's herd on a farm near Camp Verde, 30 head were stolen, including a Durham bull worth $500.

In 1866, his $1000 home was burned to the ground by the Indians. The following year, another valuable horse was stolen from him, along with most of his crops from the 60 acres he'd cultivated. In 1869, the Indians once again burned down his home worth $1000, along with his barn, which stored 10 tons of corn worth $600, farm implements, furniture worth $400, and three valuable horses.

By then, the Osborns had had enough, and the family moved to the Salt River Valley, where once again he built a home on 160 acres of patented land; became a member of the Salt River Town Association; took a leading part in selecting and surveying the town of Phoenix; was a member of the First Board of Trustees for the Phoenix School District; and in 1874, was elected Chairman of the Phoenix Town site Commission. John Preston Osborn died in Phoenix in 1900 at the age of 84, and is buried in the Pioneer Cemetery of Phoenix. His wife Perlina survived him by 12 years.

A grandson, Sidney Preston Osborn, son of Neri, would one day become the first Secretary of State for Arizona. In 1940, he was elected Governor of the state; was re-elected, and served until 1948, dying in office of Lou Gehrig's disease.

* * * *

THE FOUNDING OF CAMP VERDE

John Preston Osborn's nephew, James M. Swetnam, and his son, William Lewis Osborn, both in their early 20s when they came west with him in 1864, helped found Camp Verde, the first white settlement in Central Arizona's Verde Valley.

In January of 1865, after living in Prescott for six months, James M. Swetnam decided to join a party of nine men, who were determined to explore the Verde Valley for the purpose of establishing a farming community there. They set out on foot with one packhorse loaded with sufficient provisions to last ten days. They were well armed because they knew they were traveling under extremely dangerous circumstances. They chose to ignore the severe warnings of the military leaders at Ft. Whipple, who by then had only 24 soldiers left (out of the original 180), to protect the area.

"Gold fever," had stripped their ranks.

The military warned these potential settlers that native people of the area, the Yavapai and Tonto Apaches, had well-established villages and settlements in the Verde Valley. How, the military argued, will your handful of men ever stand a chance against them?

Swetnam, and the other men were a determined bunch, however. They set out on a trail leading them 25 miles east of Prescott, detoured along the Chavez military trail to the head of Copper Canyon, and then followed an old Indian trail to the Verde River.

Their journey took three days. When the men reached the riverbank, they were relieved to find that the reports they'd heard about the area were true. There were already traces of spring in the valley, contrasted to the deep snows of Prescott, and there was an abundance of Arizona's scarcest commodity—water—its primary attraction. Five of the territory's ever-flowing streams existed there, which later would be named Sycamore, Oak, Beaver, and two Clear Creeks. Fossil and Cherry Creeks also flowed part of the year. All were tributaries of the Verde River.

At the time of their arrival, the Verde River was known as the San Francisco, named by King S. Woolsey who was a member of the original Walker Party. In 1865, it was a sluggish river full of moss, only fifty feet wide and two feet deep.

Nevertheless, it was exhilarating to find such an abundance of water in the middle of a territory known for its dry, dusty desert terrain. They also delighted in the abundance of nourishing grama grass as high as their waists, plentiful game, fuel, lumber and moccasin tracks everywhere.

But it was just too much of a Utopia to allow a group of cranky natives to deter them.

They returned to Prescott filled with enthusiasm, and ready to return to the Verde Valley with other eager settlers, who included Swetnam's cousin William Osborn, Thomas E. Ruff, Ed Boblett, H.L.D Morse, Joe Melvin, C.M. Ralston, Mac Foster, John Lang and Joe Ramstein, and ten head of oxen. They set to work establishing a settlement at the junction of the Verde River and Clear Creek, five miles below the present site of Camp Verde.

Using stones from a pre-historic site, they built a fort with seven-foot high wall, which surrounded an enclosure 60 by 40 feet. A cabin was erected in each corner of the fort and a well was dug for water in case of seizure. They also dug a canal from the waters of Clear Creek to irrigate 200 acres outside the fort. All was accomplished in less than six weeks. They returned to Prescott to collect Edward A. Boblett's wife, when four more joined their venture: Boblett's in-laws, Mr. and

Mrs. Whitcomb, Charles Yates and John Culbertson. It didn't take long before the military's dire predictions about Indian hostilities proved true.

Before the year ended, the Apaches had stolen all their horses, and left them with only seven of the 60 head of cattle they had brought with them. Their corn and barley crops were decimated by the Indians, and Jacob Ramstein was shot and severely wounded. The only other casuality was John Culbertson, who was shot in the hand.

Nevertheless, the settlers later bragged they'd killed a number of Apaches while defending their lives and property. Fort Whipple answered their urgent call for help by sending sixteen men under Lt. Baty, who soon proved to be a coward, and was relieved.

Finally, a bedraggled troop of soldiers arrived to help. Sent from the southern part of Arizona on a forced march through the harsh desert, 94 men of Company E, and 35 men of Company A of the Arizona Volunteers under Captain Hiram H. Washburn, arrived with orders to establish Fort Lincoln on the Verde River near the present site of Camp Verde.

The arrival of these 129 men, almost entirely Mexican recruits, may have evoked more shock than relief. Instead of a mighty marching army, the settlers looked upon men who straggled in exhausted. Their clothing was tattered, shoes worn through, and they were completely out of supplies. Perhaps even more alarming, most were unseasoned, raw recruits. The settlers likely wondered if these soldiers might be more dependent on them then the other way around. With most of their crops and livestock nearly wiped out, the settlers must have questioned whether the arrival of these soldiers was truly a blessing after all.

To everyone's surprise, however, these ragged troops turned out to be fierce fighters. They managed to successfully suppress numerous Indian attacks, and on one occasion, seized a large store of plunder following a battle in which 32 Indians were killed. The soldiers' most prized acquisition following this foray was a large supply of buckskin, which the men fashioned into greatly needed footwear.

In the meantime, the small group of settlers did what they could to supply the needs of the soldiers, but by mid-summer of 1866, conditions on both sides had reached a deplorable state.

The soldiers struck for clothing, food and back pay. Their leader, Captain Washburn, later reported, he could not blame them. His recruits had served in the Verde Valley almost a full year and had yet to be paid. There was no question that they were underfed and poorly clothed. By the end of August, most of the men received their discharges, which left only Captain Washburn and five enlisted men at Fort Lincoln. One month later, three of these five were also discharged.

Washburn had no choice but to plead with the small band of settlers to join him, and the two remaining soldiers, in guarding the fort. The Verde pioneers agreed, and successfully helped protect the fort for several weeks until reinforcements arrived under Captain Downie and his 14th Infantry.

Swetnam stayed only a short while in the Verde Valley. He returned East and taught school for a while in Kirksville, Missouri where he also edited a newspaper. He married three times between 1871 and 1887. Each successive wife died after only a few years, leaving him with two daughters from two of those unions.

He studied medicine at the University of Michigan, and enjoyed a successful medical practice in Kansas and Nebraska. By 1894, he'd returned to Arizona for health reasons, and continued his medical practice in Phoenix. Held in high esteem by the citizens of Phoenix, Swetnam became a Mason, and later served as the Grand Commander, Knights Templar of Arizona from 1914-15. He died in Phoenix on February 4, 1921 at the age of 79.

The Bobletts, who originally came west in the Wells and Osborn party with Swetnam, and later joined him in the Verde Valley settlement, grubstaked themselves for that venture by becoming Prescott's first restaurateurs. They set up tables under a canvas cover tied to a jagged old juniper tree, where they dispensed the same meal three times a day; bacon, bread and venison—one dollar a plate.

After suffering serious losses of cattle, crops and depredations by the Indians in the Verde Valley, the Bobletts returned to Prescott and operated a tollgate on the Hardyville Road with their in-laws, the Whitcombs—who also were disgusted with trying to settle in the Verde Valley.

From 1867 to 1869, the Bobletts and Whitcombs endured continuous Indian attacks there as well, often reported by the *Prescott Arizona Miner:*

October 19, 1867: Indians at Tollgate.

"The Copper-skins are becoming unpleasantly familiar in the vicinity of the Tollgate on the Hardyville Road. Mr. Boblett, while out on the cienega about four miles from his house, was shot at by three well-armed Indians. Mr. Whitcomb, Boblett's partner says there are several rancherias in that vicinity and that if General Gregg will send out a party of troops that stomach for a fight, he will guarantee to find them one mess of Indians at least. The General has been duly informed of this matter."

By 1869, the Whitcombs and Bobletts had had their fill of Indians and trying to settle in Arizona Territory. They pulled up stakes and sailed away in a 'prairie schooner' for Puget Sound. They settled in Blaine, Washington where they lived peacefully for the remainder of their lives.

One of the first families who remained in Central Arizona until their deaths was the Joseph Ehle family. Joseph Ehle was born at Mohawk Village, Herkimer County, New York on March 16, 1814. He ran away from home at the age of ten and drifted into Canada, where he became an apprentice to a millwright. At the age of 20, he followed an immigrant party to Iowa where he met his future wife Margaret Williams. They were married in Iowa in 1841. For the next ten years, he and Margaret raised a family of seven children, one boy, John Henry, and six girls. When John Henry was only ten, his father Joseph left the family with relatives and headed for the gold fields of California. He would be gone for eight years.

In 1859, Joseph returned to Iowa and a year later the family immigrated to Colorado, where they remained for four years. They joined the Wells and Osborn wagon train, traveling over the historic Santa Fe Trail to Prescott.

Joseph drove a herd of 100 cows with the hope of establishing a dairy farm in the new territory. Ambushed by Apaches along the trail, Joseph was left with only three of his original herd. Several of his chickens did survive the trip, and with these, he embarked in the poultry business, which proved successful, since eggs sold for $2.50 a dozen.

His wife, Margaret, brought the first sewing machine into the territory, and helped territorial women in dressmaking. She caused a sensation by arriving with a yellow housecat, the first of its race to reach the area. The Ehles also were the first settlers to have honeybees. Within months after their arrival, Joseph, and his only son John, located the Thud and New York lodes in the Walker Mining District.

In 1865, Joseph erected the first gristmill in the territory and with his own hands built the first commodious home in the city, a log residence of five rooms. It stood on the corner of Goodwin and Marina streets for many years. He and Margaret were also proprietors of the Montezuma Hotel located, on Montezuma Street. The family prospered.

Joseph's oldest daughter Mary Jane married John Dickson, one of the original members of the Walker Party, in November of 1864. It was the first marriage in the territory, and was performed by the governor himself, John Goodwin. All his other daughters married well, too, except the beautiful young Maggie.

Maggie was six when she arrived in Prescott with her pioneering family. In 1877, at the age of 19, she eloped with William Foster Jr. by stagecoach. He apparently was a man the family did not approve of, because when word of their elopement reached the family, they hurried to Wickenburg just in time to pull them off the stagecoach. That very evening, a marriage was hastily arranged. The couple then proceeded to California. But after two and a half months, the distraught and miserable Maggie was back with her family. She lived only a short time afterwards, dying at the age of 20 of typhoid and pneumonia.

Her mother, Margaret Ehle was the mid-wife who attended the birth and burial of her dear friend Margaret McCormick, the young wife of Governor Richard McCormick, who died tragically in childbirth.

In 1880, the *Arizona Miner* referred to Margaret as "one of God's best women, one of the first ladies to settle in Prescott." Margaret Ehle lived to the ripe old age of 88, dying of pneumonia in Prescott on November 5, 1905. Sharlot Hall wrote her obituary and called her:

"A pioneer of pioneers who bore her full part. Past the toil and struggle of the early days, she lived to a serene and stately old age and was a benediction to all who knew her."

Joseph lived seven years longer than his wife, dying a few months short of his 100th birthday. At the time of his death, he was reputed to be the oldest living Mason in the world, having joined the Order in 1838 in Iowa. The *Arizona Miner* described the history of the Ehle family and concluded with these glowing words;

"Of remarkable vitality, this aged man attracted the admiration and attention of many, so well was it known throughout the nation that his long race on this earth has been attended with a distinction few if any has attained. He was a man of that sterling integrity and patriotic zeal that brought to his side friends by the score, and to his memory the tribute of his upright dealings with his fellow men will be a beautiful chapter to close his earthly career."

By far, the most remarkable fact is that both Ehles endured extreme hardships as all pioneers did, yet were hardy enough to live well past the age which carried most other pioneers to much earlier graves.

Fannie Cave Stevens, who came with her husband Lewis in the 1864 Wells and Osborn party, was by far the most accomplished, educated and remarkable young woman to arrive in the territory. Her father, a professor at Oxford University, England provided her with an extensive education. She helped Mary Catherine Leib, and Harriet Turner, organize the first private school for Prescott children in the fall of 1864. Fannie kept the school going long after her friends moved on to other endeavors. Besides being a dignified and accomplished lady, she had plenty of grit.

In 1867, while her husband was attending a session of the legislature in Prescott, 20 Apaches attacked their ranch at Point of Rocks, four miles outside Prescott. Only Fannie and a hired man were at home at the time.

When Fannie spotted the Indians emerging from behind some rocks and heading towards her horse corral, Fannie ran for her rifle. She and her hired man opened fire upon the thieves who returned the fire. The engagement lasted several hours. Fannie succeeded in driving the Indians away without losing a single horse.

Her neighbor, Mr. Johns, had heard the firing and came to the rescue with several men, but the Indians had already disappeared. Fannie asked Johns to ride into town, find her husband, and tell him he needn't come home, just send back more buckshot. The story was written up in the *Arizona Miner* with these words included:

"Many a man placed in that position would have taken to his heels and run for dear life, but she stood her ground and fought them like the true heroine she is. A little more shot, Mrs. Stevens? Bully for Mrs. Stevens. She is our favorite candidate for Commander of the District of Arizona."

Another of the most outstanding members of the Wells and Osborn wagon train was Edmund W. Wells, Jr. In time he would prosper, achieve considerable prominence and make history in the new territory.

Born on a farm in Lancaster, Ohio, in 1846, he was the son of the wagon master of the Wells and Osborn party, Edmund Wells, Sr. Edmund, Jr., was only 18 years old when he drove the team belonging to his father from Colorado to Prescott in 1864.

When he was six, his family moved from Ohio to Iowa, where his father became a prosperous merchant. The Depression of 1857 hit the family hard, and after his wife, Mary, died in 1862, father and son decided to heed the call to "Pikes Peak or Bust." For the next two years they engaged in mining and other endeavors in Colorado, until the gold ran out and the Indians became too threatening. It was at that time that Wells Sr. agreed to lead the wagon train from Colorado to Prescott, Arizona Territory.

Industrious and driven to achieve, Edmund Wells, Jr. would live out his life in Arizona becoming prosperous and notable in mining, ranching, stock raising, banking and government circles.

Within months after arriving in Prescott, young Wells made enough of an impression on the territorial legislators to be appointed Assistant Secretary of the Council, during the First Territorial Legislature, when they met in September of 1864. It was the beginning of numerous government appointments that continued throughout his lifetime.

After serving three years as Clerk in the Quartermaster and Commissary Department at both Forts Whipple and Lincoln, he was appointed Clerk of the U.S. District Court for Yavapai County. He was 21 years old at the time, and remained in that position for eight years. During those eight years, he also was appointed Recorder for Yavapai County, and studied law under Chief Justice William F. Turner. Wells was admitted to the Bar in 1875, at the age of 29.

When his term as Recorder ended, Wells formed a law partnership with Judge John A. Rush. During his 14-year association with Judge Rush, Wells enjoyed some of his greatest achievements.

From 1875 through 1889, Wells was elected District Attorney for Yavapai County; was Assistant U.S. Attorney for Arizona; served in the upper house of the territory; helped review, revise and codify the territorial statutes; and was appointed by President Harrison to the U.S. District Court of Arizona. In 1882, he became associated with the first organized bank in the territory, the Bank of Arizona, eventually becoming president.

When Arizona achieved statehood in 1912, Judge Wells was selected as the new state's Republican candidate for governor. Because the state was overwhelmingly Democratic at the time, he lost the election to his Democratic opponent, George W.P. Hunt.

Edmund Wells married Rosalind Banghart in 1869. One year later, the couple built one of the most beautiful homes in Prescott at 303 South Cortez Street. Their home, designed in the Victorian Italianate style, became the center of many social activities for the town.

Rosalind, or Rose as she was known, was 16 years old when she married Wells, 13 years her senior. Thirteen year-old Rose had arrived with her pioneering family in Prescott in 1866. She was one of the four daughters of Mary Ann and George Washington Banghart, and like her sisters, was considered a true beauty.

The Bangharts were one of three families who booked passage from the Colorado River to Prescott on Samuel C. Miller's Pullman wagon in 1866. Sam had been one of the youngest members of the Walker party when they discovered gold at Lynx Creek. Now, he and his brother, Jacob, operated a prosperous freighting and transport business. On this particular trip, however, he unwittingly introduced the Banghart family to the dangers of traveling through country dominated by Indians.

The route lay through Hualapai country. When the train reached Beale Springs and set up camp for the night, the area suddenly became alive with Indians. "I was skeered up somewhat," said Samuel Miller later. "It seemed the entire tribe was in action."

When the chief, Wauba Yuma rode up and demanded all the horses, mules and flour that they had, Sam Miller sent a bullet through the chief's lungs that left a hole as big as a fist. Instead of attacking their wagon train, the Hualapai warriors suddenly left. For years afterwards, Mr. Miller enjoyed displaying his Hawkins rifle at every opportunity, and telling how that rifle "did its business." Unfortunately the incident provoked the Hualapai to join in the war against the "white eyes," and caused charges to be brought against Sam Miller in Federal Court.

It was reported to the Department of the Interior at Washington, D.C., that a friendly Indian had been murdered. The Indians were under the War Department at the time. The War Department demanded that Sam Miller be arrested, and ordered the military authorities at Fort Whipple to take him into custody. One hundred citizens from Yavapai County came forward to post his bail, and he was released.

Mr. George Banghart, who with his wife and four daughters had observed the incident, was the most influential witness on Miller's behalf. After the trial was over, Sam Miller was discharged and given a unanimous vote of thanks by the Grand Jury.

* * * *

THE MILLER BROTHERS

Sam, his brother Jacob, and their father, John Jacob Miller, were noted Indian fighters. No story of early Prescott pioneers would be complete without the inclusion of the Miller family, for whom Miller Valley is named.

Sam's father, John Jacob Miller, owned a farm in Princeville, Illinois, but he was no farmer. He left the farming to his wife, Docia, and their nine children.

Dressed in the buckskin garb of the frontiersmen of his day, John Jacob roamed the west hunting buffalo, or searching for gold. He prospected in Oregon, California and Colorado, or wherever the spirit of adventure, and the lure of gold, might carry him. He would be gone for years at a time, something that didn't seem to bother his wife Docia.

Uncle Jack, as younger men called him, wore a wide leather belt under his buckskin clothing, in which he carried his money. He loved to tell the story of the time he came back to the farm, after being gone some years, and found Docia entertaining some ladies at tea. "Docia,

I'm lousy," he announced. "I need to take a bath." The ladies left in a hurry. Then he said, "Yes, I'm lousy, lousy with gold." He had sewed a substantial amount of gold into his wide leather belt.

Uncle Jack's homecomings were grand occasions. All their friends and family gathered around to hear him tell of his exciting adventures and Indian fights in the West. No one was more fascinated with these tales than one of Uncle Jack's youngest sons, Sam. He was the first of Jack's children to yearn to share in his father's great adventures.

When Sam was 16, he begged to go west with Jack, but Docia would not hear of it. Sam persisted. Docia finally agreed on the condition that her second oldest son, Jacob, accompany him. For some reason, she didn't seem to trust her husband to look out for her young son.

Jacob Leroy Miller (Jake) did not want to go. He was happily married to Jane Maria Reeves, and had three young children. Their only son, Roll, was seven at the time, and the oldest. His two younger sisters were Serilda and Cynthia.

Coerced into the trip by his mother and Sam, Jacob was not sure he'd ever see his family again. He willed 100 acres of his farm, and his house, to seven-year-old Roll, and 80 acres each to his young daughters. He bought enough food to last his family for two years, and paid his brother-in-law two year's wages in advance, to look after his family and the farm. Jane's mother agreed to live with the family until he returned.

If Jake's mother Docia had known the consequences that lay ahead for her son and his wife Jane, she never would have insisted that he go. The consequences would be the result of a contrived, deceitful and selfish act on the part of young Sam a few years later.

Jake, young Sam and one of their uncles set out on their journey on April 4, 1859. Their father was already in Oregon by the time they left, but their destination was not Oregon. It was Pike's Peak and the Colorado gold rush.

As Sam would write in a letter to his cousin some years later, "We found out there were more miners than gold at Pike's Peak. We met thousands of gold hunters who already had tried their luck and were headed home with "Busted" printed on the side of their wagons."

This discouraged their uncle who headed back home. The Miller brothers continued on to California. From there they went to Virginia City, Nevada, where their father eventually joined them. By 1862, they had joined the Walker Party, and in May 1863, their party was in Arizona on the Hassyampa River prospecting for gold. Sam, the youngest member of the Walker Party, would be the first to find the famous gold.

As Sam told the story years later, the prospectors had fanned out along the river and creeks in search for gold. He and his brother Jake were alone and realized they were out of meat, so Sam went hunting:

"I was hunting deer and saw one. I was crawling to get a good shot, and saw following the deer, a pretty spotted fawn, and I saw slipping behind them a very large lynx. I shot the lynx just in time to save the fawn.

"The lynx dropped and the deer ran off. I went to the lynx and stood over him and he jumped and caught me by the wrist, his teeth cutting sharply and his claws scratching. Had it not been for my buckskin clothes, he would have wounded me badly. I shot him three times in the head before he let go.

"I then went to camp without any meat. Brother said he would go kill some meat and for me to stay and doctor my arm. The day was long and I was alone and was tired of sitting around. Seeing a nice gravel bank on the edge of the creek, which still holds its name, Lynx Creek, I took a pan of gravel and washed it and got $4.85. By the time my brother returned to camp that evening, I had washed out another $17 with my crippled arm.

"There was a little excitement. We notified the balance of the party who were some ten miles away. We all located and staked claims and named the place Lynx Creek. Brother and I took out $6,000 over our yearly expenses that year."

With the proceeds from their mining venture, Sam located a large ranch in what was to become known as Miller Valley, located one mile from Prescott.

"There were no white men there," recalled Sam, "but plenty of redskins, as we soon found out. I have lived here and had a home here ever since."

Sam and Jacob realized the greatest need for the area was supplies, and in 1865, they started a very prosperous freighting business. They bought goods in Los Angeles and hauled them to Wickenburg, at times with as many as 22 teams, 12 mules to a team, and two wagons to each team. They received from 15 to 25 cents per pound, earning as much as $10,000 on each trip. Although they fought off numerous attacks by Indians while freighting and ranching, the brothers prospered.

With their freighting business well established, Jake decided it was time to go home to Jane and his children. But Sam needed him, so he contrived an elaborate and cold-hearted scheme to keep his brother in Arizona.

Jake received a letter with papers that indicated his wife had divorced him. A letter was sent at the same time to Jane informing her that Jake was dead, killed by Indians. Neither learned the truth of Sam's betrayal until many years later. By then, Jane had remarried.

Jake remained single, and died in Prescott on April 7, 1899, calling for Jane as he died. The next day, the family learned that Jane had died on April 8th, one day later. It was reported that with her last breath, she called out Jake's name.

Sam Miller married Mary Sanders, daughter of one of Prescott's earliest families. They had eight children. Mary died in 1908, and Sam followed her in death one year later, on October 12, 1909. He was 69 years old, and his funeral was a grand and impressive one, with hundreds of people in attendance. He was the last of the famous Walker Party to die.

* * * *

THE BANGHARTS

The Banghart family, who were with Sam Miller when he shot and killed the Hualapai chief Wauba Yuma, initially came to Prescott to settle on land that had been purchased by Mary Ann Banghart's brother, Edmund G. Peck of the Peck Mine fame. But the land, located in Chino Valley near the old site of Fort Whipple, was too dangerous to cultivate at the time. Until the Indian wars ended, the Banghart family lived in Prescott, where George ran a livery stable.

Eventually, the Bangharts developed a dairy herd and cattle ranch on their property in Chino Valley, and operated a stage station, which in later years became the stopping point for the Prescott and Central Arizona Railway.

The Banghart's hospitality was widely known and appreciated throughout the territory. They were particularly famous for hosting their annual New Year's Ball at their ranch, which helped create a needed sense of community in the early days.

Their daughter, Rose, and her prosperous husband, Judge Edmund Wells, gave the Bangharts six of their grandchildren. One of those grandchildren, Edith Wells, died in 1878. It was the first in a series of tragedies occurring that year, which made it the most devastating year of their lives.

Following on the heels of Edith's death, their ranch house burned to the ground. Two weeks later, another grandchild, Eddie Marion died. Several months after that, their 15 year-old son Georgie was struck and killed by lightening while out gathering the dairy herd in the hills. In the fall, a prized colt became crippled, and needed to be shot. Then George was robbed by a man he had helped.

"Seemingly he has fallen on bad luck that sticks to him like bark on a tree," reported the *Arizona Miner*.

The tragic year took its toll on the lovely Mary Ann. After suffering for over a year of ill health, she died on May 12, 1881 at the age of 48. Three of her four beautiful daughters married exceptionally well; Rose to Judge Edmund Wells, Nellie to prominent attorney N.O. Murphy, who eventually was appointed 10th and later 14th Territorial Governor, and Flora who married the flamboyant and controversial editor of the *Arizona Miner*, John H. Marion.

* * * *

THE WAR HORSE OF THE PRESS

John Huguenot Marion, described as a man with a great force of character, also was described as an ignoramus, liar, a coward and often compared to a "chained coyote." Although praised as the most vigorous and talented of pioneer editors, he also was at the same time being disparaged as a "slandering reptile." Everyone did agree on two things: He wrote with fire in his pen…and, he was the homeliest man they'd ever seen.

Three years after Prescott became the territorial capital, Marion purchased the *Arizona Miner* in 1867 from ex-Governor Richard C. McCormick. In a community made up mostly of Union Republicans,

Marion proudly proclaimed his Democratic allegiance to the Confederacy in his first editorial:

"In accordance with time-honored and necessary custom, we today address the readers of the Miner, for the purpose of informing them what they are entitled to know. That is: What shall be the future course of this paper? To which we answer, in all truth and earnestness, that, while under our control, it will fearlessly, but in respectful and dignified manner, advocate the ancient and time-honored principles of the grand, liberty-defending Democratic Party. Believing honestly, that the practices of the party in power have been and are subversive of that freedom which is the birthright of every free, white American citizen, we shall labor, with whatever our Maker has vouchsafed us, to cripple the monster that has grown fat on the misfortunes of our country.

"Its leaders, in conjunction with a few mad caps of the South, created, nursed and fanned into hellish flame an unnatural civil war, in which millions of Americans fell victim and drenched their native soil with precious blood, leaving behind wives, mothers, fathers, sisters, and brothers to lament their violent and unnecessary action.

"And for what good purpose has all this been done? What wrongs to right? What vital tenants to defend? Echo answers, none! It was a war for blood, for plunder, and for exaltation of the black, monkey-faced Ethiopian over the poor white men of both sections of the country. Besides which, it has saddled on the country a load of debt that fairly makes the bones of taxpayers crack under the pressure of the greenback, bondholding, black anaconda which has coiled itself around this nation."

Although off to a roaring bad start. Marion's worth to Arizona grew with the years, and in time he became an influential fixture in the development of the future state, he truly loved.

Born in Louisiana around 1835, Marion learned printing in his home state before heading, at the age of 16, to the California gold fields. There he worked for a time as a "printer's devil" on newspapers in Oroville, Butte County and Marysville. He gained additional experience on a St. Louis newspaper.

By 1864, the gold bonanzas heralded in Arizona Territory encouraged him to join a prospecting party led by Theodore Boggs. The party set up their prospecting ventures in Big Bug, Yavapai County, located 25 miles east of Prescott. Eventually Boggs prospered by discovering some of the richest mines in the Big Bug area. Marion's mining success seemed considerably modest by comparison.

Ever the journalist, Marion began sending in news items from Big Bug to the *Miner* office on a regular basis. For the next three years, Marion prospected successfully enough to purchase a ranch in Chino Valley and buy an interest in the *Arizona Miner* with his partner, Ben Weaver (no relation to mountain man Pauline).

Marion's employees described him as short in stature; slow in speech; inclined to drawl out his words; painfully shy in social situations; but a good man, honorable, and generous to a fault. They all agreed he was the most homely man they'd ever seen.

In little over a year after purchasing the *Miner*, Marion was leveling a vitriolic attack on the former *Miner* owner, Richard C. McCormick. By that time, McCormick owned a rival newspaper, the *Tucson Arizonian*. Marion began by ridiculing its editor, Judge Sidney DeLong:

"His head and face indicate that he belongs to the Caucasian type of man; his forehead is well suited for flattening tortillas; his nose projects some distance from his face, and is, we think, large enough to smell mice. His mouth appears to have been well cut with some dull instrument, either a crevice spoon or a shovel, and eyes—those glorious 'yorbs' look like empty egg shells."

Marion's next attack on McCormick followed McCormick's election to Congress in 1870:

"Another calamity has befallen our unfortunate Territory, the will of those whose citizens has just been defeated at the ballot box…Mr. McCormick the vile, and his backers—contractors, Federal office-holders, monopolists and their retainers—have again stuffed the ballot boxes with fraudulent votes."

Fortunately for Marion, this was not the era of libel suits.

Besides attacking Republicans, who displeased him, Marion's other great obsession involved the condemnation of Apaches. On January 22, 1870, Marion published a list of 300 people who had been killed by the Apaches in Yavapai County alone, including names, dates and places where they had been killed. Many people had already fled the territory by then, because of the Apaches.

When Vincent Colyer, Commissioner of Indian Affairs, came in 1871 to conclude peace treaties with all Indian tribes in Arizona, and place them on reservations, Marion lashed out:

"We ought, in justice to our murdered dead, dump the old devil (Colyer) into the shaft of some mine, and pile rocks upon him till he's dead. A rascal who comes here to thwart the efforts of military and citizens to conquer peace from our savage foe, deserves to be stoned to death like the treacherous black-hearted dog that he is."

Finally by 1873, after General George Crook's successful campaign against the hostile Indians brought relative peace to the Territory, Marion took a wife and enthusiastically named their first son, George Crook Marion.

Perhaps the most pressing question on everyone's mind at the time was, how did John H. Marion, considered one of the homeliest men in the Territory, manage to capture the heart of Flora Banghart, one of the most beautiful ladies in the county?

Obviously Marion adored Flora. He announced their pending marriage in a September 16, 1873 editorial:

"Quartz claims, placer claims, auxiliary claims had we in abundance, but all these did not satisfy us. Now, however, we have struck our claim on Miss Flora and said claim is not for sale. With her we hope to glide down life's rugged path in a pleasant way."

The path became more rugged than Marion dreamed. Their marriage lasted only 11 years.

Flora gave him three sons, one, Eddie, died in 1878. In 1884, Flora ran off with District Attorney Charles Rush, both abandoning their families. Rush was Marion's best friend, a fellow Democrat, and someone Marion helped win the office of District Attorney. The scandal shocked the community. Disclosure of Rush's books and official records proved him to be a political scoundrel as well.

John H. Marion and Flora Banghart Marion
—SHM

In an editorial written in a rival newspaper on November 19, 1884, Rush was royally chastised:

"District Attorney C.B Rush, whose official record was recently shown up as anything but an enviable light by the Journal, and who was paraded before the citizens of this county by the Democratic paper as a model of purity, virtue and integrity, has left for parts unknown, deserting his family, consisting of a wife and two children.

"He was accompanied in his flight by the wife of the man who was so enthusiastic in his defense during the last campaign. Malice, however, forms no part of our personal character, and we can as truly sympathize now with the man who has been thusly betrayed as if he were our best friend.

"For the poor misguided woman, in common with the entire community, we have only words of sorrow. For the semblance of a man, who paraded his virtues before the community, while plotting the destruction of two families; who so outrageously betrayed the confidence and hospitality of the best friend he ever had—a friend who stood up in his defense through good report and evil report—a friend to whom he owed his success in this community—we cannot find words in our vocabulary to express our condemnation.

"Judas Iscariot, or Benedict Arnold are models of human virtues when compared to this nefarious wretch. A man so lost to all honor and manly principle as Chas. B. Rush has shown himself within the past week to be, should have the brand of Cain stamped on his forehead and should be shunned as a creature too base, too low and entirely too contemptible for their notice."

Flora and Rush's betrayal devastated Marion. He became reclusive, and his pen lost its usual fire. He filed for divorce in 1887, having waited three years in the hopes that Flora would return to him. One year later, he married the handsome and stylish Miss Ida Jones who had been his typesetter at the *Prescott Courier*.

During their three years of marriage, Marion became calmer and less flamboyant. Ida bore him another son, John. But John never got to know his father. He was only two years old when his father suddenly died of a heart attack on July 27, 1891, at the age of 55. Marion's funeral was the largest and grandest Prescott had ever seen.

Throughout the town, flags flew at half-mast, and courts and businesses closed for the day. The procession that gathered at the Goldwater Store on Cortez Street included the Ninth Infantry Band from Ft. Whipple; the Prescott Fire Department in full dress uniform; three companies of volunteer firemen; printers from the Courier; the Aztlan Lodge of Free and Accepted Masons; Arizona pioneers on foot, members of the Prescott Bar Association, and a long procession of citizens on horseback, or in carriages.

The eulogies, tributes and speeches about him lasted for hours, as numerous citizens recalled his many accomplishments and efforts on behalf of the territory. They referred to the three newspapers he owned beginning with the *Arizona Miner* from 1867 to 1878; *The Enterprise* from 1878 until 1882, after which he started the *Prescott Daily and Weekly Courier* which exists to this day.

Also remembered was his success in helping wrench the territorial capital from Tucson in 1878 and returning it to Prescott; in successfully campaigning for electric lights; a telegraph; and for helping organize a company that built a railroad, The Prescott and Arizona Central, which linked Prescott to the Atlantic and Pacific Railroad in 1886. At the grand celebration of the railroad's completion, Marion was remembered as saying in his speech that day:

"I was here when two men right across Granite Creek were killed by Indians, and when it took a lady's stocking full of gold dust to buy a sack of flour. They tried to get my scalp, both the Indians and the white men, but damn 'em, I'm still here."

Remembered too, was his election in 1887 as County Treasurer, "always filling the office to the entire satisfaction of his constituents without the least misappropriation of a cent of the people's money." Also recalled was his answer in 1891 when he was mentioned as a possible territorial governor, "I am too old a fogey for the job," he'd said.

His stubbornness was not forgotten either, nor his willingness to divide his last dollar. His pallbearers were Sam Miller, Guilford Hathaway, Robert Connell, Fred Brecht, Louis Alters, and W.H. Williscraft. A lengthy description of his funeral in the *Courier* concluded with these words:

"So light was the rain and so sad were those upon whom it fell that it seemed the guardian spirits of our mountain home had assembled in mid air and sent down tears to moisten the grave of the bravest and best adopted son of this sun-kissed land."

These were not the last words to be written about John H. Marion, nor his family.

One year after his death, Ida was forced to sell their home and all its furnishings at a public auction. That same year, Marion's son Lewis died, and in 1947, John, his son by Ida, jumped off the San Francisco Bridge at the age of 52.

The *San Francisco Examiner*, after describing the illustrious accomplishments of his father, told the sad story of his son:

"For the past several days the battered body of a middle-aged man had lain, unidentified and un-mourned, at the morgue on Merchant Alley. It was just another John Doe from the Bay, another member of that strange, esoteric fraternity of bridge jumpers...until Joe McDonough, who manages an apartment house on Bush Street, came in, looked under the sheet, and told them they had John Marion under that sheet.

"When the deputy coroners made their routine examination of Mr. Marion's little apartment, they found very little that would tell them about the lonely life of this mousy little bachelor and architect. There were many souvenirs of his eminent father though; yellowed clippings and darkened photographs of the patriarch of Prescott, for whose funeral all the businesses in town closed. And there was a somber souvenir of his mother, the attractive little widow who turned her back on tragedy that day so many years ago.

It was a letter signed: Mrs. I. Marion: 'To whom it may concern. This is a plain case of suicide. I am sorry I have to go this way, but the law stands in the way of an easier death. Please roll me in a sheet just as I am. I don't know why I have given all this space to the foregoing. It has no pay-off, no punchline, no unusual twist. Just a short order of a quiet kind of tragedy that abounds in every big city. Maybe the reader himself can do something with it. Write a caption, or draw a moral, or forget the whole thing entirely'."

Did Ida commit suicide, too? So it appears.

In the end, George Crook Marion was the last survivor of his family. He died in 1949 in Denver, Colorado, at the age of 65. His obituary had little to say about him other than he was a member of the Sheet Metal Workers' Union and was survived by his wife Gertie.

* * * *

PEACE AND PROSPERITY
THE EMPIRE DAYS
1870s

General George Crook's successful campaign against the hostile Indians ushered in a new era for Prescott and the Verde Valley. By 1873, firearms were put aside as citizens set to work transforming their camps into villages, and their villages into towns. Mining continued as a major industry; cattle and sheep ranches flourished; farming finally became profitable; and enterprising men established successful businesses and built fashionable homes. Time was even found to organize theatrical events, and baseball teams. Most early social events centered on Fort Whipple, which by 1872, had replaced its original buildings with more permanent and attractive frame structures. When General August V. Kautz succeeded General Crook as Commander of the Army in 1874, his energetic wife, Fannie, decided to initiate lively social events. Each week at Whipple her "Wednesday Hops" became a Prescott institution. By 1877, she had organized the Fort Whipple Theater. Although ladies made up most of her casts, she did manage to lure a few officers to participate.

She produced Shakespearean dramas as well as zany epics with titles like "Dead Shot" and "Regular Fix." As the Sisters of Charity established Prescott's first civilian hospital, Fannie put on a charity performance for them entitled "The Two Orphans." Although she brought fun and gaiety to the area, citizens of Tucson sniped at her "frivolity." When the General and his wife departed the territory in 1878, the *Tucson Citizen* sarcastically referred to their departure as that of the "Fort Whipple theatrical troupe."

Churches, not considered a priority until more women arrived in the territory, finally found a home when the first place of worship was erected on 127 N. Marina. The building provided a place of worship for Catholics, Presbyterians, Congregationalists, Episcopalians, Baptists and Southern Methodists for the next 15 years.

Businesses surrounding Prescott's main plaza in the 1870's boasted 20 saloons, four livery stables, eight blacksmith shops, three breweries, two newspapers, and 14 mercantile establishments. The largest and most prestigious in the territory by far was L. Bashford and Company Mercantile.

By 1876, Levi Bashford's company had expanded into a three-story building. It boasted five warehouses, a lumberyard, and 15 "courteous and obliging" clerks. After Levi invited Robert H. Burmister to become his partner, the business flourished even more.

A native of Germany, Burmister, born in Mecklenburg on August 17, 1847, was the fourth of eight children, and only three years old when his family immigrated to America in 1850. At the age of 15, Burmister struck out on his own, leaving the family farm in Waupun,

Wisconsin, and moving to Oshkosh, Wisconsin, in 1864, where he went to work for the Clark and Forbes store. His paltry salary in the beginning, increased over time until he became the company's highest paid clerk. In Oshkosh, he met his future wife, Maggie Bashford. Her father Coles, the former Governor of Wisconsin, now served as Secretary of Arizona Territory.

In 1874, two years after his marriage to Maggie, the couple moved to Prescott where Burmister bought an interest in the L. Bashford Company, owned by Maggie's uncle Levi.

At the time of his partnership with Levi, the annual income of the business was about $35,000 per year. After ten years, it reached the annual sum of $347,200 with capital stock worth $150,000.

Robert Burmister didn't just relegate himself to success in the mercantile business. With his brother-in-law, William, also a partner in the mercantile store, the two owned the Jersey Lily gold mine, plus the Tiger, Old Reliable and Silver Belle mines among others. In addition, he became a prominent cattleman, owned considerable Prescott real estate, and helped establish the Prescott National Bank. He served as president of the Board of Trade; school trustee, and sat on the Prescott City Council.

In 1879, Morris Goldwater opened his mercantile store and became L. Bashford and Company's biggest rival. Despite their business rivalry, Robert Burmister, William Bashford, and Morris Goldwater became close friends.

Morris was the oldest son of Michael and Sara Goldwater. His father, affectionately known as "Big Mike" emigrated from London, England in 1852, the year of Morris' birth. Big Mike's brother Joe convinced him that a fortune could be made in the California gold rush.

One can only imagine what Sara Goldwater thought as her husband sailed away for America, leaving her with baby Morris, and his sister Carolyn. Would she ever see him again? And what was he thinking—leaving behind a prosperous tailoring business in London to chase a crazy dream? History confirms she was not the first wife to ask that questions.

Sara finally joined her husband several years later. To her horror, she discovered the brothers now operated a saloon and house of ill repute in the gold mining town of Sonora, California. Apparently the gold had eluded them.

A proper Victorian lady, devoted to her Jewish faith, Sara and her children moved to San Francisco, where she remained for the rest of her life. She must have had other means of support, because it would be ten years before Big Mike had any success in his endeavors.

The brothers were broke when they left Sonora. In 1859, they followed the next gold strike to Gila City, Arizona, where they borrowed enough money to outfit a freight train. When that boom ended, they were broke again.

La Paz lured them next after gold was discovered there. This time Big Mike took a job as a clerk in one of Bernard Cohen's mercantile stores. Cohen eventually made Big Mike a partner. Big Mike continued to help his brother, Joe, with his freighting business, even after it nearly cost him his life.

In 1872, while carrying a load of freight between Ehrenburg and Prescott, 30 Apaches ambushed them. They managed to escape, but not before Joe was shot in the back. Fortunately, a doctor happened to be traveling with them, and helped Joe to eventually recover.

Finally in 1876, Big Mike set up his own mercantile business in Prescott and brought his 24 year-old son, Morris, from San Francisco to help him run it. It wasn't the first time Morris had worked for his father. After a few years, Big Mike retired to San Francisco, and Sara finally reclaimed her husband.

Morris became a popular civic leader in Prescott, serving as a member in three legislative sessions. Elected mayor repeatedly over a 22-year period, he served without pay. With his friend Robert Burmister, he founded the Prescott National Bank, and together they promoted the Prescott and Arizona Central Railroad.

To avoid the rowdy annual 4th of July celebrations, and put an end to cowboys shooting up the town, Morris, Robert Burmister and William Bashford raised funds to initiate a "Cowboy Tournament." It evolved into America's first rodeo that remains to this day an annual celebration in Prescott every 4th of July.

During Prescott's Centennial celebration in 1964, Morris Goldwater was selected Man of the Century (although he had died in 1939). That same year, his nephew Senator Barry Goldwater was Arizona's unsuccessful Republican candidate for U.S. President.

* * * *

JOHN C. FREMONT
A GOVERNOR IN NAME ONLY

By the end of the 1870s, Prescott had built its first graded school, the Prescott Free Academy, with four classrooms on the ground floor, and the territorial office on the second. One of the first governors to occupy the second floor was John Charles Fremont, by far the territory's worst, and least effective governor to date.

When the citizens of Arizona Territory learned that one of America's most famous and popular explorers had been appointed their governor, they were ecstatic. No previous governor had a more stunning background, or national reputation. Citizens became wild with the hope that he could deal with their growing mining and transportation problems, and perhaps even bring them into statehood.

The year before he arrived, the seat of government had been returned to Prescott, where it remained for 12 years. By then, over 7,000 new mines had been recorded in Yavapai County alone. Money was needed to develop these mines. Railroads had yet to penetrate the territory's borders, and freighting costs, from gold to lemons, remained outrageously exorbitant. Citizens hoped Fremont would use his influence with eastern capitalists and politicians to remedy their problems.

No one realized that John C. Fremont's influence in the east no longer existed. He and his family had been destitute for years, barely subsisting on the writings of his wife, Jesse Fremont. President Rutherford B. Hayes, a longtime admirer, appointed Fremont territorial governor out of sympathy for his plight. The Fremont family looked at Arizona as their last hope to regain their own lost fortune.

John C. Fremont, the illegitimate son of a prominent woman of Virginia society and a penniless French refugee, was born in 1813. Due to the circumstances of his birth, he grew into an ambitious, self-promoting social climber. Throughout his life, he successfully sought patronage from among the most powerful.

John C. Fremont
—ASLA

Joel Poinsett, his first important patron and a diplomat, helped develop the U.S. Army Corps of Topographical Engineers. This prestigious organization of mapmakers and surveyors paved the way for western expansion.

Their first major project in 1838 included the exploration and mapping of the country between the upper Mississippi and Missouri Rivers. Fremont, named to this project, came under the tutelage of the expedition's leader, Joseph Nicolett. Nicolett took a liking to the personable Fremont and taught him his trade.

The dashing and charismatic Fremont, often invited into the social whirl of Washington D.C., eventually met Jesse Benton, the daughter of the powerful Senator Thomas Hart Benton. Benton, a Democratic Party leader for over 30 years, didn't like Fremont.

But Jesse was smitten. Usually an obedient and devoted daughter, she rebelled when her father objected to the "illegitimate" Fremont, and eloped with him. Her father was furious, but fury soon evolved into appreciation. With his new son-in-law making a name for himself as a member of the prestigious U. S. Army Corps of Topographical Engineers, Benton realized Fremont could be a political asset.

Senator Benton, an expansionist and a firm believer in Manifest Destiny, believed that the North American continent should belong only to the white citizens of the United States. His philosophy became a crusade. Benton pushed through Congress appropriations of money to be used for surveys of the Oregon Trail (1842), Oregon Territory (1844) and the Great Basin and Sierra Mountains to California (1845). Through his power and influence, he saw to it that Fremont lead all of those surveys.

Unofficially, Fremont's job was to write glowing descriptions of the West. Benton wanted Americans in the east to be inspired with enough imagination and desire to want to settle there. In this, Fremont proved to be a master promoter. With Jesse's help, Fremont published descriptions of his expeditions that were glowing, poetic and often exaggerated. His books and maps became wildly popular, and successfully advanced the cause of Manifest Destiny. He soon became known as "The Pathfinder."

His later years were not as successful.

The Fremont family enjoyed a few years of vast wealth, after the discovery of gold on land they owned in California during the gold rush days. However, by 1870, they lost everything due to litigation over mining rights, and an investment in a failed railroad. Fremont also had been an unsuccessful candidate for President in 1856. During the Civil War, President Lincoln stripped him of his command after he tried to free slaves in Missouri without presidential authorization.

Fremont arrived in Prescott on October 6, 1878. His wife Jesse, their daughter, 38 year-old Lily; 22 year-old son Frank; Mary McGrath, a maid; their Chinese cook, Au Chung; and dog, Thor, accompanied him. Left behind was Charles Fremont, Jr., a Naval officer, whose wife Sally had just lost a baby to premature birth.

The governor's salary at the time was $2,600 a year. Of the approximately $210 a month, the Fremont's monthly expenses included $90 for their rented home, $40 for their cook, and an unspecified amount for their maid.

Fremont wasted little time plunging into mining speculation with his partner, Judge Charles Silent. The two took options on mines in Yavapai, Mohave and Yuma counties. Fremont spent most of his time in the east promoting their mines, and even formed a syndicate of wealthy eastern investors. He and the judge received a percentage of the money that was actually invested. Lily often wrote in her diary that the family constantly looked for money to arrive for the purchase of mines. When a purchase didn't go through, the whole family became depressed.

Lily, plain, practical, well-bred and educated, spoke several languages. She had a slight stutter, a tendency towards stoutness, and frequent headaches. She never married. Instead she dedicated her life to tending the hearth of her illustrious parents.

With her parents off in the east promoting their mines, Lily was left alone to run their home and entertain the prominent ladies of Prescott. She complained in her diary that so many petty grievances existed among the society wives of Prescott, that "planning a dinner party was as confusing as an egg dance."

Although Fremont proposed many reforms for the territory, the only legislation he accomplished was removing the tax on mining products. It didn't take long for Arizona's citizens to see through him and brand him a carpetbagger. The family soon lost rapport with the people of Prescott as well. The *Arizona Miner* in 1881, described Fremont as "being a governor in name only and of no earthly use to the territory."

Fremont resigned in 1881. He never regained his wealth, and died in New York City nine years later, of a ruptured appendix. Jesse was left with only a small government pension to live on. The epitaph on John C. Fremont's gravestone reads: "From the ashes of his campfires have sprung cities."

* * * *

PRESCOTT'S WOMAN OF PASSION: MISS SHARLOT HALL
1880s

Prescott, incorporated as a city in 1883, now boasted five churches, two public schools, a theater, a concert hall, a new brick city hall, three newspapers, two banks, 18 saloons, and a strict set of ordinances.

Over 1,800 citizens called the territorial capital home. Behavior no longer tolerated included opium smoking, cross-dressing, public nudity and lewd behavior. Public fighting, obscene language and slingshots were prohibited. Owners of dogs, hogs, sheep, goats, cattle and horses were ordered to keep their animals contained, or incur steep fines. Licensing fees were imposed on every business, from real estate agents and peddlers, to street musicians. Fees were doubled for astrologers, seers, fortunetellers and clairvoyants.

The city seemed quite civilized.

To 12 year-old Sharlot Hall, an intelligent and impressionable new arrival, Prescott rendered her awestruck. In time, she wrote 10 books and over 500 articles extolling her love for Prescott and Arizona Territory, and one day would establish a museum in Prescott to house the territory's precious history and artifacts.

A dreamer, a romantic, and an intrepid historian, Sharlot Hall was born in 1870 on the Kansas prairie in a crude log cabin. Her mother Adeline, whom she adored, taught her to read by the time she turned three. An educated and refined woman, Adeline Hall, for some unknown reason, married a rough, crude, and uneducated man by the name of James Knox Polk Hall.

Hall, a tobacco-chewing frontiersman with a nasty attitude, ridiculed every good quality his wife possessed, her education in particular. If he heard any family member speaking proper English, he accused them of trying to sound too "high toned."

Sharlot witnessed her mother's spirit wither, and all hope of a better life die, as she endured decades of Jim Hall's iron fist and endless mockery. Unfortunately his attitude was not uncommon for his time, enough for the ever-observant Sharlot to vow never to marry. In her forties she wrote:

"Seriously and sadly—the average husband is a tough proposition out of which to get any satisfactory emotional life. I am a woman a full ten years beyond thirty. I am not married. I don't expect to be married. I don't want to be married. I am happier than any married woman I've ever known. My emotional life is fuller in every direction than that of any wife of my acquaintance. Unless an unmarried woman is a hopeless lump of stupidity she has a hundred times wider opportunity for an emotional life full to overflowing than it is possible for an ordinary married woman to have."

As harsh as those words may sound, Sharlot did love several men during her lifetime. If circumstances had permitted, she might have married one of them.

The first to capture her heart was Samuel Porter Putnam. Five years older than her own father, Putnam, described as short, chubby, red-faced and spry as a cat, arrived in Prescott in 1895 on a lecture tour advocating the popular Free Thought movement.

The American Secular Union and Free Thought Federation, founded by Robert Ingersol, appealed to intellectual liberals throughout the world. They embraced Ingersol's belief that reason and experience were the best guides for living, and not blind acceptance of the Bible's "divine revelations." The movement's greatest appeal to 22 year-old Sharlot was its advocacy of equality for women, and an easing of the marriage laws that discriminated against them. Putnam rose through the ranks of this movement, eventually succeeding Ingersol as President in 1892.

The Hall family attended all of Putnam's lectures in the winter of 1895, even inviting him to stay at their Orchard Ranch in Lonesome Valley, 15 miles outside Prescott. Putnam and Sharlot established a close friendship. Later she wrote to friends that she considered him her "soul mate."

Putnam's fiery oratory garnered 100 new members for the Free Thought Movement in Prescott. Sharlot, selected as one of their vice presidents, also became a lecturer on behalf of the movement after Putnam left. Putnam's final lecture before leaving Prescott for San Francisco was entitled Christianity And Women:

"The treatment of women by Christianity is one of the most horrific pages in human history. It makes the blood boil to think of the indignities that have been poured upon the daughters of Eve simply because woman was the first to begin the upward path of learning and progress while Adam was a sneak and a coward."

Putnam considered his campaign in Prescott a huge success. and in his January 28th report to the Truth Seeker, the official publication of the movement, he also extolled the virtues of Sharlot Hall.

"She was born into Freethought with every fiber of her being and has never had to fight any ghosts to get rid of them. She is a healthful representative of the abounding life of this great western land. She is entering upon a literary career of bright promise; is a contributor to many journals east and west on various subjects, especially the pre-historic relics of Arizona. We can be proud of this fearless and gifted exponent of Freethought who has such a brilliant future in the ranks of Western authors."

Putnam, apparently as smitten with Sharlot as she was with him, left a number of his books with her, all inscribed with lengthy and affectionate sentiments. The two stayed in contact throughout the year, and Sharlot grew to adore Putnam without reservation. Then came the great shock.

The *Chicago Tribune* reported the sudden and scandalous death of Putnam on December 11, 1896:

"In a richly furnished flat of a stylish apartment hotel on St. Botolph Street (in Boston) a double tragedy was enacted this morning…the victims…were Mary L. Collins, a pretty brunette, twenty years old, and Samuel P. Putnam.

When the occupants of the house smelled gas this morning and the door was broken in the bodies, fully dressed, lay upon the floor. That of Miss Collins was across that of Putnam. A half-filled bottle of wine and another of Benedictine stood on the table."

The lengthy article described how they had met, adding Miss Collins had been his traveling companion. It took Sharlot seven years to get over the shock of Putnam's death. In a letter to friends she wrote:

"For a few months it was my privilege to know and love one of the grandest men who ever lived. Perhaps our companionship was too perfect, our hopes and plans and happiness too great to be realized on earth. At last he was taken away, but life has seemed sanctified since then."

Despite her grief, Sharlot continued to write while enduring excruciating chronic back pain exacerbated by the tasking labor of ranch life. As a child she had suffered a spinal injury in a fall from her horse during the family's trek to Arizona.

No one appreciated her poetry and articles more than Charles Lummis, publisher of *Land of Sunshine*. This magazine later evolved into the acclaimed *Outwest Magazine* based in California.

While on assignment for Lummis in Northern Arizona in 1905, Sharlot learned of President Theodore Roosevelt's proposal to merge Arizona and New Mexico into one state and call it "Arizona the

Great." Her regional pride flared to a white-hot intensity. She grew so indignant with the thought that, upon arriving back at the ranch, she set to work composing the lengthy poem, Arizona, a defiant assertion of Arizona's claim for statehood. It ended with these words:

"We will wait outside your sullen door
Till the stars that you wear grow dim
As the pale dawn-stars that swim and
Fade o'er our mighty canyon's rim;
We will lift no hand for the bays ye
Wear, nor covet your robes of state—
But, ah! By the skies above us we will
Shame ye while we wait!"

The general consensus of most Arizona's citizens was, if the United States didn't want Arizona, then to hell with them. Time was on Arizona's side. Nothing captured that sentiment more than Sharlot's passionate poem.

Territorial governor Joseph Kibbey printed Arizona as a broadside and had it placed on the desk of every U.S. Senator and Representative. Reciting the poem on the House floor, Marcus Aurelius Smith persuaded Congress to permit the two territories to hold referenda on the proposed 'shotgun' marriage. New Mexicans approved the merger, but Arizonans, preferring a humble "Arizona" to "Arizona the Great," voted it down.

Arizona eventually entered the Union seven years later on Valentine's Day, 1912.

By then, Sharlot had traveled the territory collecting pioneer stories and historical artifacts as the territory's official historian. Appointed in 1909, she was the first woman to hold a territorial office.

Sharlot resigned her post as historian in 1912, returning to the Orchard Ranch to care for her long suffering, dying mother, and cantankerous, ailing father. Adeline Hall died in August of 1912, leaving Sharlot in a state of numbed disbelief. Later she wrote her friend Alice Hewins:

"I could not shed a tear—would not have dared to call her back into that worn and weary body—I had the overwhelming knowledge that she was free—out of bondage. The dear face was too peaceful and the soul of her seemed to enfold me with such joyous assurance of well being."

The next 13 years of Sharlot's life became bleak, painful and burdened with the toil and hardships of ranch life. She had no choice but to care for her impossible father, who grew more difficult with each passing day. She only wrote to a few close friends during this time, D.M. (Matt) Riordan being one of them.

Riordan, an engineer and mining superintendent for the copper mining interests of General Electric in Northern California, adored Sharlot. A ten-page letter written to her in 1905 ended with these sentiments:

"I often think of you in many, in fact most of the experiences I have and enjoy and wish you were here with me to share them. Your faithful, though sadly neglected, admirer, D.M. Riordan."

The two had met through their mutual friend, publisher Charles Lummis.

Sharlot spent a month with Riordan in 1908, researching an article on the gold rush for Outwest Magazine. Riordan wrote Charles Lummis during Sharlot's visit:

"I will mention in passing that Miss Hall is here holding down a large portion of the Bully Hill Mine to our great joy. I will let her tell you about it when she gets back, which she never will if we can help it, so there."

A letter Sharlot wrote to Riordan one year later included these sentiments:

"It rests me to think of you, the one man on earth in whom I have perfect faith, you're so strong and wise and tender, so clean and true. I thank God for you, as, next to mother, the best gift of my life."

Sharlot Hall
—ASLA

Unfortunately, Riordan was married. Although estranged from his wife for many years, his Catholic background eliminated divorce as an option. How different things might have been for Sharlot had that not been the case. Nevertheless, they maintained a close friendship until his death in 1928.

During her bleak years between 1912 and 1927, Sharlot wrote very little. She entered public life briefly in 1924, when she was chosen to hand-carry the state's vote for Calvin Coolidge to Washington D.C. She wore a specially designed gown of copper. Three years later, her father died, and Sharlot was free at last. She sold the Orchard Ranch, and devoted the rest of her life and savings to restoring the old Governor's mansion and turning it into a museum. The state bought the mansion in 1917, but it remained neglected until Prescott leased it, for life, to Sharlot Hall in 1927. There she lived and worked until her death on April 9, 1943 at the age of 77.

* * * *

THE WAR OF THE RAILROADS

In 1882, the year Sharlot Hall arrived in Arizona Territory, the Atlantic and Pacific Railroad (A&P) finally crossed through northern Arizona along the 35th parallel. At last the mountain town of Prescott, and surrounding mining communities, saw an end to their isolation. One major problem existed, however. The A&P had no funds to extend a link to the city.

Its rails passed through Prescott Junction (now Seligman), 72 miles north of Prescott. Area mines, opening up almost daily, desperately needed this link. The cost to ship machinery into the mines, and ores out to the smelters by wagon, were exorbitant. Throughout the area, everyone acknowledged the financial benefit of a railroad link to Prescott. Two powerful factions arose which recognized this need, and a long and bitter feud for control of Central Arizona interests began.

Thomas Bullock, a New Yorker with a background in railroad and streetcar building, led one group known as the New York Syndicate. He was blessed with charm and a gift for gab. He promised investors he could build the rail line on a shoestring budget and finish the link in a matter of months.

Frank Murphy represented the Congress Mine Group. Murphy's proposal showed a more expensive, practical and realistic approach.

These rival groups presented their vastly different visions on how the project should be handled to every venue they could find, from newspapers to town meetings, and to the territorial legislature. The stakes were high and the battle fierce for control and development of the needed railroad link to Prescott.

Bullock's group had a distinct advantage. They had enthusiastic support from Frederick A. Tritle, the territory's governor. His popularity and influence proved very advantageous to Bullock's group.

Tritle, who followed John C. Fremont into office, was not like some previous governors. He actually lived in Arizona when appointed. He never left the territory during his term of office, and appeared dedicated to the interests of the territory over personal gain. The territory's citizens were happy not to be supporting another "carpetbagger."

In the meantime, the A&P wanted the rival factions to cease their dispute and get on with the project. The new line, south from its main line, would generate revenues for them as well.

Wanting the two factions to consolidate their efforts, company officials from the A&P told Bullock that he would have their full support, if he mended fences with Murphy's group. The two groups did merge on July 16, 1885 and together formed the Prescott and Arizona Central Railway Company. Immediately after consolidation, a bitter battle for control followed, and lasted four months. By November of 1885, Bullock had forced three of Murphy's officials to resign including Murphy's brother, N.O. Murphy. The company promptly elected three new replacements, now ex-governor Frederick A. Tritle being one of them. Bullock would live to regret making an enemy of Frank Murphy.

Bullock finally had almost exclusive control of the company. He quickly secured financial assistance from the A&P, and from Yavapai County. The A&P owned much of the stock, and provided most of the materials for construction, at a greatly reduced rate.

Yavapai County issued bonds at a rate of $4,000 per mile. A caveat was attached to the funds from the county, however. Bullock had to agree that the first ten miles of the line would be completed by May 1, 1886, and the entire line into Prescott ready for service no later than midnight, December 31, 1886. Also, if the line was ever extended south of Prescott, it had to follow the Hassayampa route southwest rather than the Black Canyon route to the southeast.

Local insistence on the Hassayampa route stemmed from the fact that many of the potential local investors owned interest in mines along this route. Anxious to get on with the project, Bullock agreed to all terms.

The county bonded itself for $300,000. Bullock had less than a year to meet the deadline and accomplish it on a tight budget. If not ready for service by midnight of December 31, 1886, Bullock would forfeit $1,000 per mile, or $72,000.

From its inception until its demise seven years later, the whole enterprise became a fiasco. Work was well under way in the spring of 1886, and progressed at a rapid rate through Big Chino Valley. Only the most minimal of grading was done, just enough to allow the ties to be leveled and tamped down. The A&P, anxious to have the connection to Prescott, loaned Bullock anything he needed, from tools, to flat cars, to rails. With the added help of Mexican pick and shovel workers, teams of mules and some scrapers, Bullock worked feverishly to meet his deadline. While work was underway, he managed to acquire two old pigmy engines, a secondhand passenger coach, and several used box and flat cars.

In the meantime, the betting was heavy as to whether Bullock would meet his deadline. In order to hedge their bets, considerable vandalizing took place, from setting fire to a trestle, to removing sections of track.

Others "out to get Bullock" vandalized the company's two locomotives only a few days before the road was completed. No. 2 engine, The Tritle, had her pipes blown out, and No. 1, The Hassayampa, was set on fire. Bullock quickly leased an engine from the A&P. By late in the afternoon of the December 31st deadline, a half-mile of track still needed to be laid.

Finished by torchlight a few minutes before midnight, the jubilant Tom Bullock and his crew met the deadline just in time, and Bullock received his $72,000 bonus.

Bullock became the hero of the day. Hundreds gathered to celebrate the coming of the railroad. Speeches and cheers went on for hours. Attorney General Clark Churchill, solicitor for the railroad, spoke of the great opportunities ahead and the prospects of uninterrupted prosperity for Prescott. General J.S. Mason, commander at Whipple Barracks, recalled arriving in the territory 22 years earlier when the thought of even a stage line seemed far into the future.

Bullock reminded the audience that without the aid and influence of ex-governor Tritle, at the time lying sick in a New York hospital, the project might not have been consummated. Three more cheers were given for Tritle.

T.R. Gabel, general manager of the A&P railroad, telegraphed his company's congratulations to Bullock and added that he hoped this would be just one of many rail lines someday would crisscross the territory.

Train service started almost immediately. Each day the train left Prescott at 5 P.M, and Prescott Junction at 8 A.M. Its main stop, coming and going, was at the Banghart Ranch in Chino Valley.

For a fee of $75 a month, George Banghart provided water for the steam engine when it stopped at his ranch. If George didn't get paid on time each month, he refused to provide the water, causing delays in the schedule. Delays at the Banghart station occurred for other reasons as well. Old George, no longer under the influence of his deceased wife and four beautiful daughters, served alcohol and allowed gambling at his ranch. Passengers and crew often spent several hours at the Banghart station enjoying a crap game, a few beers and old George's hospitality.

The train, which was never on time, also stopped along the way whenever antelope were seen roaming nearby, allowing the crew and interested passengers an opportunity to target practice.

Not only did the constant delays cost the company money, but passengers soon learned they got a cheaper fair when they purchased their tickets directly from the conductor (the money possibly staying in his pocket). On top of all this, the little engines had no place to turn around when they reached Prescott. So the engines pushed their cars into Prescott, and pulled them back to Prescott Junction. Even after a wye, or turntable, was established in Prescott, the company's problems continued to increase.

The hastily laid tracks washed out with any adverse weather. Everything from rails, to grades, to the second-hand equipment needed constant repair. Timetables were not followed, and shipments were regularly late. Bullock promised the problems would be rectified, but they were not taken care of in a timely manner.

Three years after the railroad's inception, Bullock raised the rates, complaining he was operating at a loss. What remained of his local support ended with his rate-hike. Everyone from mine owners, to businessmen, to fraternal organizations felt betrayed. They decided to punish Bullock by boycotting the railroad for six months and shipping their goods by wagon instead.

Bullock countered by threatening to reduce daily service to two times a week, raise passenger fees, and open businesses of his own in Prescott that would support his railroad. A compromise was eventually reached between the railway and merchants, but the honeymoon was over with more trouble lying ahead.

The once ousted Frank Murphy and company stood poised and ready to take advantage of Bullock's company's deteriorating situation. By 1893, Frank Murphy had the financial and political clout to drive the Prescott and Arizona & Central Railroad into bankruptcy, and he did.

On August 5, 1893, Tom Bullock's railroad company was sold for $12,161.91 for back taxes. By 1896, all rails were removed and the rolling stock sold.

Frank Murphy became the prime mover behind the construction of the Santa Fe, Prescott and Phoenix Railway (SF, P&P). His new line ran south from Ash Fork to Prescott in 1893, and by 1895, it reached Phoenix. This shorter route charged lower freight rates, maintained a more efficient schedule, used better equipment, and became affectionately known as the "Peavine."

It had been an expensive undertaking, however. During the four years while under construction, the company was fraught with mishaps, setbacks, lawsuits and several deaths, as crews blasted their way through boulders and rugged terrain, building several hundred trestles along the way. The national economic panic of 1893 almost brought the construction to a permanent halt. But the SF, P&P met all obstacles and survived. When finally completed after four years of effort, the construction costs had reached $5,000,000.

Frank Murphy became president of the company in 1893. Under his leadership the SF, P&P became a multimillion-dollar enterprise, forming the backbone of economic development in Arizona Territory. Murphy went on to build connecting lines to the mining areas of central Arizona. Within 15 years, he owned or controlled a bank, five railroads, two newspapers, several mining companies, a development company and a number of valuable parcels of land. His brother, N.O. Murphy, was appointed Territorial Governor twice; first in 1892 by President Harrison, and six years later by President McKinley.

As for Thomas Bullock, he survived his failure in Arizona, moved to California, invested in a large lumber enterprise, a luxury hotel, and the Sierra Railroad. This railroad served both Calaveras, and Tuolumne Counties in northern California, carrying freight, lumber, ore, cattle and passengers.

When the romantic era of the steam engine ended, the motion picture industry rescued the Sierra Railroad from extinction and it became famous as the Movie Railroad. From 1919 until today, the

Sierra has been featured in over 200 television programs, advertisements, and motion pictures including High Noon and Back to the Future III.

CHAPTER THREE - PART THREE
Renegades, Rustlers, and Hoofed Locusts
The Rise and Fall of the Cattle Industry

In the early 1880s, the Cline family drove 1,700 head of cattle from southern California to Northern Arizona. As they neared the area where they planned to establish their cattle ranch, they came upon a shocking sight, the mutilated, nude body of a white man lashed to a tree, his penis amputated and stuffed into his mouth.

It was the Apache's sinister way of saying…Welcome to Arizona Territory.

The Clines stayed, eventually establishing one of Arizona's largest cattle ranches, but it was not easy. Along with other hopeful ranchers, they struggled to exist in Arizona Territory until long after 1885. Prior to that date, Indians made off with every hoofed creature that entered the territory as fast as they arrived, and murdered hundreds of ranchers in the process. Even after General George Crook successfully took to the field against the Indians in 1871, and concentrated most of them on reservations, there were still renegades and rustlers, and lackadaisical lawmen, who did little to help the situation. Cattle ranching remained a dangerous enterprise until well after 1900.

* * * *

THE BIG BOVINE SWITCH AND THE BEGINNING OF THE CATTLE INDUSTRY IN THE SOUTHWEST

The start of cattle ranching in the Southwest began with the coming of the Spanish in the 1600s. The Franciscan friars, who arrived with them, established missions from California to Texas. They were skilled both at breeding cattle, and in converting Indians. By the time Mexico declared its independence from Spain in 1821, the Franciscans were powerful and wealthy cattle barons. The Mexican government tried to claim some of that wealth by secularizing the missions. The priests would have none of it, and revolted.

In California, priests slaughtered thousands of their cattle and sold the hides. In Texas and New Mexico, they simply walked away from their 50-plus missions and turned their cattle loose to fend for themselves. These feral cattle flourished for three decades. By the eve of the Civil War, they had increased in the wilds of Texas alone from one hundred thousand to over 3.5 million.

By then, the Texas long horned cattle had evolved into adept scavengers. If there was no grass to feed on, they ate prickly pear cactus, or tree shoots and bushes. They could smell water 40 miles away. Always moving, they depleted the wild grasses and other flora of the Western frontier. After the Civil War, they became the basis for vast wealth among enterprising Texas cattle barons.

But the immense herds of Texas cattle were not enough to meet the growing country's insatiable demand for beef. Before the plains of the west could be converted to pasture lands for cattle, General Nelson Miles believed the Indians and the buffalo needed to be exterminated. In 1876, he predicted, "when we get rid of the Indians and buffalo, the cattle will fill this country."

Cattlemen joined ranks with eastern bankers, the railroads, and the U.S. Army to exterminate the buffalo, and thereby cut off the Indian's primary source of survival. The task proved to be enormous.

For 15,000 years, the buffalo herds had blackened the prairies of the West. In a few short years, all that remained of them were rotting carcasses strewn for miles across those same prairies. It is estimated that over four million had been slain. Fortunes were made on their hides and bones. By the end of the 1870s, the steer had replaced the buffalo, and the cowboy had displaced the Indian.

General Philip Sheridan, commander of the Armies of the West, summed up the situation to the Texas legislature in the late 1870s: "These men (the buffalo hunters) have done more to settle the vexed Indian question than the entire regular army has done in the last thirty years."

Having killed off the buffalo and squeezed the Indians on to reservations, ranchers then turned around and sold beef to the government to feed the hungry Indians. This was how many western ranchers made their initial fortunes. Often conspiring with corrupt Indian agents, they artificially hiked the prices on beef contracts destined for reservations, while manipulating the quantities and quality of the beef actually being delivered. The demand for cattle, both here and abroad, and the enormous profits they derived attracted groups of eastern investors. One such group formed the Aztec Land and Cattle Company, perhaps the largest cattle operation Arizona has ever known.

* * * *

THE AZTEC LAND AND CATTLE COMPANY
AND THEIR HASHKNIFE BOYS

The Aztec Land and Cattle Company came into existence because of the deteriorating range conditions in western Texas during the mid-1880s. Cattlemen there had overstocked their ranges. A drought, and falling cattle prices, including a complete crash of the cattle market in 1885, brought about the demise of the cattle industry there. As thousands of starving and thirsty cattle began to die off, frantic cattlemen tried to find someplace to relocate what cattle they had left. One group of Texans sold out to the Aztec Company, who already had discovered the lush grasslands of Northern Arizona.

With acreage available for a pittance, the Aztec Company bought the cattle and Hashknife brand from the Continental Cattle Company of Texas. The Atlantic and Pacific Railroad sold them land for 50 cents an acre. The company promptly shipped and distributed 40,000 starving, drought-stricken Texas cattle onto their two million acres in Northern Arizona. The herds quickly increased to 60,000. Their two-million-acre range, which extended from Flagstaff to the New Mexico border, made them second only to the King Ranch of Texas, as the largest cattle ranch in the country. They were known for their famous brand, the Hashknife (a cutting tool used by cooks). Each fall, this huge cattle operation sent thousands of their cattle by rail to eastern markets.

It would take several years before their absentee Boston owners realized that many of their cowboys were actually outlaws and cattle rustlers. Meanwhile, these nefarious hirelings profited greatly from their owner's extended absences. The art of cattle rustling reached a peak of perfection during their term of employment.

Cowboys, who engaged in such tactics, were said to "throw a long loop." They used many creative ways to steal cattle and get away with it.

Cowboys were expected to carry running irons and brand on the range whenever they found an unbranded calf. The Hashknife brand was placed on the right ribs. Each calf was marked with a crop on the right ear.

The Hashknife brand was difficult to alter, so a popular method of stealing was called "sleepering" the calves. The thief would put the Hashknife mark on the calf's ear, but not brand its ribs. During spring roundup, when thousands of head of cattle were being culled out for branding, if a cowboy saw a cropped ear, he assumed the calf already had been range-branded. After the roundup, the thief returned to gather the unbranded Hashknife calves, change the earmarks and put his own brand on them.

A Hashknife cook by the name of Tom South was so proficient at this, he stole enough Hashknife cattle to drive to Colorado and sell for a substantial profit. He bought a saloon in Denver that eventually failed. Tom returned to Arizona and was hired again by the unsuspecting Aztec Company. He was not alone. Many Hashknife cowboys started their own ranches with their employer's cattle.

The Hashknife boys were notorious for more than cattle rustling. Many of the more violent ones intimidated settlers by pistol-whipping them. and stealing their stock when any accidentally roamed on to Aztec lands.

The little railroad town of Holbrook grew to be important as the main shipping and distribution center for the Southwest. It also became the place where the Hashknife cowboys came to drink and gamble. The town took on all the vices of the "Wild West" complete with a popular saloon named the Bucket of Blood, and a large population of painted ladies.

Law enforcement there was non-existent. Drunken cowboys regularly shot up the town causing injuries and often death. In 1886 alone, 26 shooting victims were buried in the town's cemetery, many of them killed by the Hashknife boys. They also were accused of numerous stagecoach robberies, and at least two train robberies. They earned their reputation as the "thievinist, fightinest bunch of cowboys in the U.S."

The Aztec owners finally woke up to the fact that their lack of profit was the direct result of being robbed by their own men. They hired Burt Mossman, a future captain of the Arizona Rangers, to take over the management of their Arizona outfit.

Mossman arrived in Holbrook in January 1898, wearing a derby hat and city clothes. He had just sat down for a cup of coffee when he was informed that three cow thieves were heading for the town of Snowflake with Hashknife cattle.

Mossman didn't hesitate. Despite sub-zero temperatures, he was on his horse heading for Snowflake at a fast gallop. He caught the thieves red-handed, and turned them over to the local sheriff. From that day forward, Mossman put the fear of God into the cattle rustlers. Out of the 84 men on the Aztec's payroll, he fired 52. This reduced the winter crew to 32 men. Then he went after all other rustlers with an equal vengeance.

By the summer of 1898, 200 head of cattle a day were being branded for the Aztec company, 16,000 in all. Four thousand of them were shipped to market. For the first time, the Aztec Land and Cattle Company showed a profit.

It was too late to save the company, however. The winter of 1899 saw a blizzard considered one of the worst in history. Thousands of cattle died. When cattle prices dropped the following spring, it was all over for the Aztec Land and Cattle Company.

The directors ordered Mossman to liquidate their stock and sell their land. Area ranchers and farmers rejoiced at the news.

Unfortunately, the Aztec company itself had caused more damage than all its "bad" cowboys combined. It had allowed the destruction of Northern Arizona's richest grazing lands.

Successive droughts, repeated economic crises, rustlers, and declining cattle prices during the 1890s produced, once again, the cumulative effect of an overstocked range, and dead cattle. It was history repeating itself, just as in Texas. The blizzard of 1899 cast the final blow to the company's resources.

The effect on local farmers and ranchers also had been severe. For 16 years, not only had they been excluded from using the range owned by the company but after the company went bankrupt in the early 1900's, the grazing lands were so devastated, they were of little use to anyone. One old pioneer summed up the situation very well:

"When we came to Arizona in 1876, the hills and plains were covered with high grass and the country was not cut up with ravines and gullies as it is now. This has been brought about by the overstocking of the ranges. On the Little Colorado, we could cut hay for miles and miles in every direction. The Aztec Cattle Company brought tens of thousands of cattle into the country, claimed every other section, overstocked the range and fed out all the grass. Then the water, not being held back, followed the cattle trails and cut the country up. Later tens of thousands of cattle died because of drought, lack of feed and disease. The riverbeds were covered with dead carcasses."

Although there were no other cattle ranches in Yavapai County that would ever compare in scope to the Aztec company, a few spreads were large enough to command attention.

Improved roads, and the coming of the railroads had dramatically changed the face of Yavapai County by the late 1800s. Many farmers, whose livelihood depended for years upon selling fruits and vegetables to miners and soldiers, now turned their land into pasture for small herds of cattle or sheep. There were no fences to discourage the wide-ranging livestock from feeding on the luxuriant and abundant grama grass that grew as high as a horse's belly. Wild horses still roamed the land, and their capture and breaking provided extra income for both cowboys and ranchers alike. Lamb and beef were in great demand back east and in European markets. The price for this meat, sold by the pound, made ranching a profitable enterprise.

But those 'good old days' were about to end.

Unfortunately, efforts by the United States Government to initiate a more efficient range management did not occur until after 1930. Until then, the once lush grasslands of Arizona began to drastically diminish. Serious conflict arose among ranchers who coveted these grasslands for their own stock.

High in the mountains of Yavapai County's Tonto Basin, one of the worst of these conflicts began as a feud that soon erupted into war. Two families, the Grahams and the Tewksburys, started it. Eventually, numerous other families, who lived in the area, were enmeshed in their deadly conflict.

* * * *

THE PLEASANT VALLEY WAR
AN EYE FOR AN EYE

During the late 1870s and 80s, great herds of cattle and sheep ate up wherever grass and water was available. By the late 1880s, these livestock had far surpassed the carrying capacity of the range. There were no fences until 1915, and range management was unknown until after 1930. Periodic droughts stripped the land of its grasses even more.

In the meantime, the sheep industry flourished as much as the cattle industry. Sheep herds had increased in northern Arizona from 803 head in 1870, to 698,404 head in 1890, thereby contributing to the overgrazing problem.

Generally, the cattle and sheep men of Arizona did not indulge in the vicious range disputes that marred other areas of the west. However, by 1886, this all changed when the Pleasant Valley feud exploded. It was big enough and bad enough to command national attention, and resulted in convincing our nation that Arizona Territory was too uncivilized for statehood.

Deep in the heart of the Tonto Basin, Pleasant Valley (now called Young) is located 30 miles east of Payson, and 115 miles east of Prescott. During territorial days, Pleasant Valley was a place where people took possession of any unclaimed land they wanted. Everyone carried a gun, and because lawmen were few or far between, vigilante justice was not uncommon. This valley's sparse population allowed their grasslands to endure longer than in other areas of Arizona.

James Dunning Tewksbury (J.D.), age 55, arrived in Prescott around 1877 with a brood of motherless children. His four sons and one daughter were handsome half-breeds. They arrived from California after the death of his wife, and their mother, a full-blooded Shoshone woman. Known as a legendary beauty, it was reputed she had been educated in the east where J.D. Tewksbury had met her.

By 1879, J.D. married Lydia Ann Shults, a widow with three children, and a herd of cattle. The large Tewksbury clan settled in Pleasant Valley where J.D. and his sons raised racehorses, cattle and hogs. Lydia gave birth to two more sons for J.D., while her daughter Marcy Ann married J.D.'s oldest son, John.

It was a tight knit, prosperous family.

Every year, the Tewksburys sponsored a fiesta at their ranch, inviting all their neighbors. A large beef was barbequed, neighboring wives brought their best, covered dishes, and everyone camped out for days betting on horse races, drinking, dancing and having a memorable good time. The Tewksburys quickly became a popular family among the Pleasant Valley ranchers, with the exception of one, James Stinson.

Stinson brought one of the first cattle herds into Pleasant Valley in the 1870s. By the time the Tewksburys arrived and settled near his ranch, Stinson's herd had multiplied extensively. He was the most prominent and wealthy among his fellow ranchers.

Stinson rarely lived at his high country ranch, living part time in Phoenix in order for his son to attend school. He put John C. Gilleland, a cowboy with a checkered past, in charge of his Pleasant Valley ranch.

Stinson used an unregistered brand, the unembellished block letter 'T'. It was applied to the left side of his livestock with two easy stamps of a hot iron. The shear simplicity of it made it an open invitation for cattle rustlers.

Lydia Tewksbury, J.D's wife, registered her brand in Prescott: Block letters, 'L T'. Her stepson, Ed Tewksbury, registered the brand

'JK' while his father sponsored a brand that combined the old man's initials, 'JDT'. All these brands easily could be transferred onto Stinson's cattle, altering his brand with little detection—or so Stinson suspected. Large numbers of his cattle started disappearing soon after the Tewksbury clan arrived.

Ed Tewksbury, J.D.'s second oldest son, took occasional weekends in Holbrook, Prescott or Globe. Astonishingly handsome, Ed always showed up in town dressed to the nines, wearing gloves, starched shirts and tiepins. One weekend in Globe, he met a tall, handsome young man named John Graham. They took an instant liking to one another, and when Ed learned John was looking for land to pasture his small herd of cattle, Ed invited him to his home in Pleasant Valley. John Graham hit it off with all the Tewksbury clan, and after staying with them for several days, promised to return with his brother, Tom, and his small herd of cattle.

The Graham brothers settled on land a mile and a half from the Tewksburys, who helped the Grahams build a cabin, and advised them on raising stock. A warm friendship developed between the two families. The Grahams spent time at the Tewksbury compound whenever they could, helping them build corrals and extra cabins for the Tewksbury's growing clan.

Then one fateful cold day on January 12, 1883, while the Grahams were, as usual, helping the Tewksburys with chores, James Stinson's foreman, John C. Gilleland rode up. Accompanying him was his 16 year-old cousin Elisha, and a Mexican cowhand named Potash.

Ed Tewksbury strode out to meet them. Words were exchanged, when suddenly, a gunfight broke out. The versions of what provoked that encounter are as varied as the numerous people who witnessed it; from J.D's wife Lydia, to Gilleland's 16 year-old cousin Elisha.

The most likely version was that Gilleland accused Tewksbury of rustling Stinson cattle. When Gilleland reached for his gun, his horse suddenly turned, allowing Ed to shoot him first. At least 12 shots were fired back and forth before the shootout ended. By then, John C. Gilleland lay dead on the ground, and young Elisha lay mortally wounded. Potash somehow managed to escape, unharmed.

Word of the shooting spread like wildfire throughout Pleasant Valley. A posse was formed, but it was unnecessary. Ed Tewksbury rode to Prescott and turned himself in.

During the subsequent trial, John and Tom Graham testified on behalf of their friend, Ed, that Gilleland pulled his gun first. All charges were dropped, and the matter should have ended then and there.

It did not.

Nine months later, the Grahams entered into a secret agreement with cattle baron James Stinson to report any rustling of his cattle. In return, the Grahams cattle herd would be increased substantially from Stinson's stock. Stinson did not hide the fact that he was out to get the Tewksburys. The agreement was legalized and witnessed by Prescott's Judge Fleury.

It was tantamount to an all out double cross.

Graham and Company spent the next few months sleuthing for Stinson. On March 29, 1884, district attorney Charles Rush accepted a felony complaint brought by the Graham brothers against John, Ed and James Tewksbury, charging them with altering the brand on James Stinson's cattle. They also accused three of Tewksbury's friends, George Blaine, William Richards, and H.H. Bishop. After the complaint was filed, 200 head of cattle were delivered to the Graham brother's ranch.

All the defendants turned themselves in at Prescott, and each was released on $800 bond. During the trial, numerous witnesses testified on behalf of the popular Tewsburys. When the legalized, secret agreement between Stinson and the Grahams was presented by the defense attorney, (probably released by Judge Fleury), an immediate acquittal was announced by Judge Howard. He then demanded charges of perjury be brought against the Graham brothers. John Stinson somehow managed to get the charges dropped, and the Grahams were released. But the lines were now drawn, and the initial feud quickly turned Pleasant Valley into an all out war zone.

It would last for 15 years.

1. Young Cemetery   2. Ruins of Graham Ranch
3. Perkins Store; Site of John Graham and Charlie Blevins
killings   4. Where Ute sheepherder was murdered   5. John
Tweksbury cabin   6. James Tweksbury, Sr. cabin site
7. John Tweksbury and William Jacob gravesite   8. Middleton
Ranch (aka. Newton Ranch-site of Hamp Blevins and John
Payne killings   9. Young library.

Pleasant Valley War
—illustration by Ron Henry

Angry confrontations and shootouts became commonplace between those who supported the Grahams, and those who supported the Tewksburys. Meanwhile, the Graham herd increased substantially. By 1886, the Grahams owned one the largest cattle herds in Pleasant Valley.

When the grasslands of the Pleasant Valley region began to show decline from overgrazing, violence between cattle and sheep interests soon turned deadly.

The Grahams and Tewksburys were smack in the middle of it.

The Aztec Land and Cattle Company owned sections of land in the area and had employed a Hashknife enforcer named John Payne to run all sheepherders off their land. Payne delighted in harassing sheepherders by shooting up their campsites, stampeding their flocks, pistol whipping them, shooting their sheep dogs, and burning their cabins. The Grahams brothers did much of the same, except they also hauled sheepherders into court on a regular basis for trespassing.

James Stinson took the most drastic step. He offered a $500 reward for the head of any sheepherder who dared push across his boundaries.

Into the fray came the Daggs brothers.

These highly respected brothers were the largest wool shippers in Arizona. Based in Flagstaff, they too, were running out of range for their vast sheep herds. In the spring of 1886, the Daggs brothers listened to a proposition from the Tewksbury brothers. The Tewksburys would take flocks of the Daggs' sheep to their land on the Mogollon Rim and let them graze on their prime range, (right along side the free-roaming cattle belonging to the Grahams).

Knowing the Tewksburys to be smart stockmen, the Daggs agreed. It was pure spite on the part of the Tewksburys, who knew they would infuriate the Grahams.

Oh, did it ever.

Not long after the Daggs' sheep arrived in Pleasant Valley, over 100 of the Daggs' prized bucks were found clubbed to death, and several hundred ewes were stampeded over a high cliff.

Their herders were allowed to escape with orders to warn the Tewksburys to take the sheep back to Flagstaff.

The warning was ignored. A few months later, the Tweksburys' Ute sheepherder was found headless and riddled with bullets, his sheep shot to death.

The Grahams retaliated by hiring an outlaw named Andy Cooper (a member of the Blevins family) to ride out to all Pleasant Valley ranchers with a contract to sign ("or else"), agreeing to pay $50 for every Tewksbury scalp brought to any of them. Many signed under duress, several signed, and fled the valley.

Word soon filtered back to the Tewksburys that the Grahams were hiring strangers to kill them. Rather than taking back their sheep and staying out of the feud, the Daggs brothers chose to support the Tewksburys by supplying them with the newest Winchester rifles and plenty of ammunition. The feud would eventually cost the Daggs brothers $90,000 in lost stock, and copious regrets.

On August 9, 1887, six months after the murder of the Ute sheepherder, the Tewksbury brothers were staying at a ranch owned by their friend George Newton, when eight armed riders approached them. One of the riders, Hashknife cowboy John Payne, spotted Ed Tewksbury, shouted an insult, and pulled his gun. The heavily armed Tewksburys opened fire, immediately killing Payne and Hamp Belivens, brother to outlaw Andy Cooper (hired by Grahams to kill Tewksburys). Two more of the riders were wounded, but escaped along with the rest of the gang.

Yavapia County Sheriff Mulvenon immediately formed a posse with arrest warrants for the Tewksburys. Two weeks after the shootout, he arrived at the Newton ranch, found all the buildings burned to the ground, and the two fresh graves of Payne and Blevins nearby. It was the work of the Grahams, who when interviewed later by the sheriff, threatened to take matters into their own hands further, if Mulvenon didn't arrest the Tewksburys. But the Tewksbury brothers had disappeared into the mountains, and the sheriff finally gave up the search.

Shortly after he left, a small herd of Graham horses were stolen. The Graham's youngest brother, Billy, went looking for them, was ambushed and shot through the belly. Holding his guts in his hands, the stricken teenager managed to get back to his ranch. His family washed his guts and sewed them back into his body, but poor Billy died in agony. The Grahams swore oaths over Billy's grave.

What followed next was perhaps the worst episode in the entire Pleasant Valley war.

One month after the killing of Billy Graham, the Tewksburys' compound was surrounded, before dawn, by armed men, led by John and Tom Graham. They hid behind rocks, waiting for any Tewksbury to emerge from their home.

Staying in the home were old man Tewksbury, his wife Lydia, their two small sons, John Tewksbury, and his pregnant wife, Marcy Ann, family friends Bill Jacobs and John Rhodes, and a visiting schoolteacher named Mrs. Crouch.

Mrs. Couch had planned to return home that day. John Tewksbury, and his friend Bill Jacobs, went out the door early in the morning to harness horses for her trip. Once well out in the yard, the waiting Graham gang opened fire. Both Tewksbury and Jacobs were hit in the back. Jacobs, hit three times, staggered a few feet and fell dead.

John Tewksbury was hit in the back of his neck. After collapsing in screaming agony, Andy Cooper walked over to him, shot him three more times, and then bashed his head in with a large rock. Marcy Ann, large with child, ran towards the body of her husband, followed by Mrs. Crouch. They were driven back into the house by gunfire.

For the next three days, the Tewksbury house was peppered with gunshots. The women tried repeatedly to retrieve the dead men's bodies, but were not allowed. When hogs began eating at the bodies, the women pleaded with Tom Graham to let them bury the dead men. Graham refused. Outlaw Andy Cooper wanted to burn down the house, but Graham said no, because of the presence of too many women and young children.

No longer able to tolerate what the hogs were doing to her husband's body, Marcy Ann bravely walked out amidst the hail of bullets with a shovel, and covered the bodies as best she could. For that brief time, the shooting stopped.

The Grahams finally rode off. Eleven days later, the justice of the peace from Payson arrived and helped bury what was left of the mutilated and half-eaten bodies. The remaining Tewksbury brothers swore a vengeance, again, against the Grahams.

Throughout the valley, no one's life was safe. Strangers were shot, suspected Graham supporters were hung by vigilantes who were sympathetic with the Tewksburys. Bushwhacking and vigilante hangings became commonplace on both sides.

By now, the entire nation was aware of the horrific atrocities taking place in Pleasant Valley.

Once again, Sheriff Mulvenon was on his way to Pleasant Valley, this time to arrest the Grahams. While he was en route, the Tewksburys were camped near their Cherry Creek ranches.

The Grahams, with a contingent of hired gunmen, crept up upon their camp, but were spotted in time. A shootout followed. When the smoke cleared, only a few Graham men were left. George Newton and James Tewksbury were slightly injured.

When Sheriff Mulvenon reached Payson, he added a number of Tewksbury clansmen to his posse including Ed Tewksbury, Ed's good friend Jim Roberts (who would later serve as deputy sheriff of Yavapai County), and George Newton (who had been with the Tewksburys from the beginning.)

The posse surrounded the Perkins' store in Pleasant Valley, having learned the Grahams were nearby. Soon, John Graham rode in accompanied by Charley Blevins, (another brother of outlaw Andy Cooper). The sheriff stepped out the door of the store and told them they were under arrest. John Graham pulled a gun, but the sheriff shot his horse out from under him before he could take aim. The sheriff quickly turned his gun on Blevins and shot him just as he drew his rifle from its scabbard. As John Graham scrambled from beneath his fallen horse, a rifle ball ripped through him, and soon he was dead, too.

Tom Graham fled to Phoenix where he surrendered to Sheriff Mulvenon one month later. A few weeks previous to his arrest, he had married Annie Melton, six months pregnant with his child.

Sheriff Mulvenon took Tom to Prescott and jailed him. His arrest touched off a general abandonment of his suspected sympathizers, many skipping the country. After languishing in jail for several weeks, Tom Graham was released on a $3,000 bond. Eighteen months later, after all complaints and inquiries were examined by the Grand Jury, both Tom Graham and James Tewksbury were declared innocent and released. Apparently the Grand Jury could find no one who would testify against either one—everyone had had enough.

It still wasn't over.

Both parties emerged from the legal proceedings with intensified anger and a vengeful spirit. Tom left his Pleasant Valley ranch in the hands of a foreman, and moved to Tempe, Arizona outside of Phoenix. Things simmered down for five years, allowing time for Tom to became a prosperous farmer and devoted family man.

On August 2, 1892, Tom Graham was assassinated in broad daylight. He lived long enough to kiss Annie and his young daughter goodbye, and name Ed Tewksbury and his brother-in-law, John Rhodes, as his assassins. Rhodes had since married Marcy Ann Tewksbury after the murder of her husband John.

Tewksbury and Rhodes were arrested. After several trials and mistrials, they eventually walked out of Tempe courtrooms, free men. Ed Tewksbury died in 1904 of consumption. Two of his brothers had preceded him in death from the same disease. There were no Graham or Tewksbury brothers left.

The Pleasant Valley War ended at last.

No other feuds took place in Yavapai County, which continued to be peppered with ranching enterprises formed by brothers. Cooperation was the standard among most of them.

Some of those ranches exist to this day.

* * * *

THE APACHE MAID RANCH

Established in the early 1880s by the Marr brothers, the Apache Maid Ranch flourished for nearly 100 years, and was at one time the largest cattle ranch in the Verde Valley. Located at the base of the Apache Maid Mountain 20 miles north of Camp Verde, it became the Verde Valley's primary employer (outside the mines of Jerome). The Apache Maid brand was the T bar S, and the thousands of cattle that bore that brand ranged freely from the Verde River on the west, all the way north to Mormon Lake near Flagstaff.

Josiah Libby Marr, and his brother Dennis J. Marr, were nearing the age of 50 when they decided to give up mining and raise cattle. Born in Wales, Lincoln County, Maine, they were not born into cattle ranching.

In their early years, they were seamen. But while docked in San Francisco in the early 1850s, they caught the gold fever. They followed the gold strikes from California to Arizona, arriving in Prescott in 1864.

The Marr brothers staked claims in the Walker Mining District and Big Bug District. Both took on odd jobs when necessary, Joe as a storekeeper, and Dennis as an amalgamator. By 1878, Dennis also took a wife, Joan Pratt of Beaver Creek, who mothered his four daughters and one son.

When the railroad arrived in Northern Arizona, many pioneers saw an opportunity not conceivable before, a convenient location from which to ship cattle. Small cattle operations sprang up everywhere, and the Marr brothers decided to pool their savings and buy a large herd of cheap Texas longhorns. They had heard that this tough breed of cattle could withstand any kind of weather or grazing obstacles. Since the brothers knew nothing about cattle ranching, this was important information. They hoped their cattle would multiply quickly in Arizona's rich grasslands, and they did.

For the next twenty years, the brothers prospered. Their herd increased into the thousands. Both became respected cattlemen who took pride in their Puritan heritage and identified themselves with the pioneers who stood for civilization and the honest development of the country. Then in 1902, Dennis became gravely ill, and the now aging brothers decided to sell their ranch.

Dennis moved to Downey, California where he died on December 26, 1903, at age 67. Josiah retired to Portland, Maine, living with his sister until his death on September 7, 1912. The Apache Maid's new owners, the S.S. Akers, made substantial improvements to the ranch, and prospered even more.

The Akers family added a large log home, a barn, a blacksmith shop, and a roomy bunkhouse for the numerous cowboys, horse breakers, cooks, and general ranch help.

Thousands of Apache Maid cattle were branded in the spring and fall. The hospitable Akers accommodated many of the smaller ranching families who camped at the Apache Maid Ranch on their way to and from their summer and winter grazing ranges.

Typical of the cowboys hired by the Apache Maid was a memorable character named Dan Weaver. A Texan, and an accomplished horse wrangler, Dan's only family was his iron gray horse Princy, and his mongrel dog, Badger.

Badger helped Dan drive stock. The only time Dan lost his temper was after a roundup cook reprimanded Badger for wetting on his bedroll. The cook shouted that he would "knock Badger's head off if he ever did it again." Dan rode up to the cook, dismounted, and looked him sternly in the eye. His only words were, *"I don't know so much about that."* This quieted the cook, and everyone else within hearing distance. Dan remounted his horse and rode away, Badger running arrogantly behind.

Then during one spring roundup in 1917, Dan failed to bring in his horse herd for the night. He had always been prompt before, so the trail Boss suspected something was wrong. He sent some cowboys out to look for Dan. They found his horse herd scattered, and the still saddled Princey, moving among them. They finally located Dan, flat on his back, a deep gash in the side of his head from having been kicked by his horse. Badger fiercely stood guard over him. It took some coaxing before Badger was pulled away from his master.

Dr. John Taylor in Camp Verde nursed Dan back to health and within weeks, he and Badger were back herding horses. Dan's final years herding horses were possible only because of Badger. As he grew older, Dan became nearly blind, and relied entirely upon Badger to help him keep his job. When Dan was found dead in his tent one day, Badger was there standing guard, as usual.

The Babbitt Brothers of Flagstaff eventually became owners of the Apache Maid Ranch and added it to the number of other cattle operations they already owned including the old Hashknife cattle. Over the years, the ranch exchanged hands several more times. In the 1970s, it came under the stewardship of the U.S. Forest Service, ending a century of being a working ranch.

CATTLE RANCHES AND BRANDS

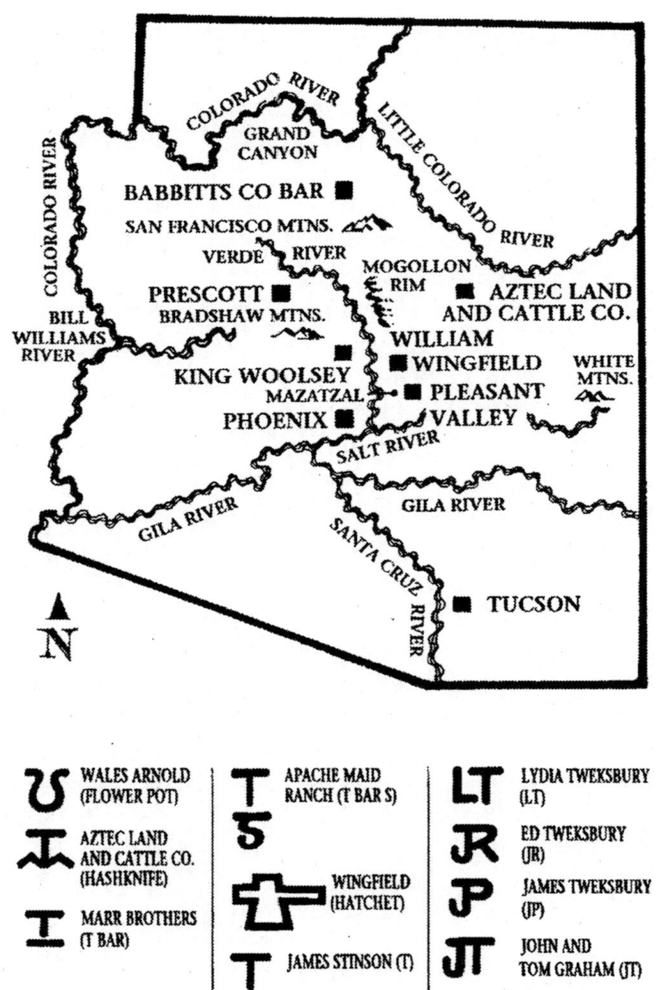

Cattle Ranches and Brands
—illustration by Ron Henry

* * * *

LOST GOLD: THE CASNER FAMILY SAGA

For most women, basic life in territorial Arizona remained backbreaking and grim. A memoir written by 80-year-old Rebecca Jane Casner for Pioneer Stories Of The Verde Valley, is particularly poignant and interesting. It involves another consortium of ranching brothers.

Rebecca met her husband Riley Casner in California in the early 1870s. Riley recently had lost his wife Nancy, and two of his four children to a fever. By 1875, Riley and his two small sons were on their way to Arizona with his new wife, Rebecca, already pregnant with their first child.

Riley's mother, Jencie Jane Casner, and three of his brothers, William, Daniel and Mose, had preceded Riley to Arizona, and were established and prosperous sheep ranchers in the Flagstaff area. Riley, however, considered himself a farmer, and had no interest in joining the family's ranching business.

During their first four years in Arizona, Riley dragged his family from one location to another, looking for just the right place to farm. All the while, Rebecca continued to have babies (she eventually had 11 children). She and her growing family lived in a tent during these years. She cooked all their meals over open fires, and washed the family's clothes in creeks and rivers.

Finally in 1879, Riley homesteaded the last place on Beaver Creek, now known as Southwest Academy. He planted fruit trees, in time owning 2,000 of them, which made him the first successful orchardist in the Verde Valley.

For the next six years, Rebecca continued to live in tents and have babies while waiting for their fruit trees to mature. During this time, she was given the added burden of caring for her 100 year-old mother-in-law, Jencie Jane, now bedridden and mourning the murder of her two sons.

The Casner family never trusted banks, and tended to bury their money in secret places. In the summer of 1876, William, Mose and Daniel Casner were paid $6,300 in 20-dollar gold pieces for a large shipment of lambs. William buried the money and believed it to be secure, not knowing that a ranch hand named Clancy was watching.

The next day, Clancy claimed illness and did not accompany William to check on the sheep. As soon as William left, Clancy dug up the treasure, secured the heavy buckskin bag of it to the back of his saddle, and took off. One of William's Navajo sheepherders saw Clancy steal the gold and ran to tell William. The brothers soon were in hot pursuit.

During the course of his escape, however, the heavy bag fell off Clancy's horse into some deep brush. Clancy tried to mark the area in his mind where the bag fell. When the Casner brothers finally caught up with him, they put a noose around his neck and proceeded to hang him unless he told where the gold had dropped. Clancy honestly couldn't remember, so they hanged him, almost.

Just as he was about to take his last breath, Mose rescued him and took him to the sheriff. The story hit the newspapers, and everyone who read it now knew that the Casner brothers buried their gold.

In the meantime, Clancy never went to prison because the Casner brothers forgot to show up to testify against him. The case was dismissed. Afterwards, Clancy tried unsuccessfully for years to find the lost gold, and so did others.

Unfortunately, thieves waited a year for the Casner brothers to be paid again for their next shipment of lambs. When they were, the thieves followed William and Daniel into the hills, killed them and stole their gold. They were never caught.

Once Riley's first successful fruit trees matured, their harvest provided the family with enough money to build a substantial log house. As wonderful as that was for Rebecca, her next dream of true luxury was to own a wood-burning stove. For the next few years she scrimped and saved her butter and egg money, and finally bought one. It did not last long. Without consulting Rebecca, Riley traded her new stove for a horse, which he considered more important. Rebecca never got over it, and talked about 'what he done' until her dying day.

Then about 1881, a young Mormon sheepherder named, Locy, found the lost Casner gold scattered in the brush on Mormon Mountain. Locy had heard about the lost Casner gold, and feared he might be murdered for it, just as the Casner brothers had been. Locy buried the treasure and slept over it. Beset with bad dreams, Locy finally confided his find to his trusted friend, Hube Burk, swearing him to secrecy. He asked Burk to ride to Beaver Creek and inform the two remaining Casner brothers, Mose and Riley, to come and reclaim their gold. Riley and Mose were so dumbfounded by the young man's honesty, Riley's whole family later converted to Mormonism. With the found money, we can only hope, Riley had the good sense to buy Rebecca another wood-burning stove.

Mose used his portion of the money to buy a ranch in Beaver Creek near his brother's farm. He also continued to bury his money.

Known far and wide as a grasping miser, Mose, it was rumored, buried his cash in coffee cans from Beaver Creek to Sycamore Canyon. He rarely spent a nickel on his family, or himself. Relatives recalled that whenever they went to visit, Mose would not allow his wife to serve eggs for breakfast, because they fetched too good a price in town.

Mose's miserly ways nearly cost him his life. A pair of bandits held him up at gunpoint one day, and demanded that he tell the location of his money. Mose refused, so the bandits built a fire and made him stand barefoot in it. Mose still refused to tell. The bandits finally gave up and left. Afterwards, poor Mose found walking a torture for the rest of his life.

In his old age, as he lay dying, Mose's sent for his son Lucky. Mose said that he would tell only Lucky where to find his caches of gold. But Lucky was not so lucky. He didn't arrive in time to learn the locations of his father's treasure. To this day, folks continue to look for Old Mose Casner's hidden gold throughout the Verde Valley.

* * * *

THE WINGFIELD FAMILY

Old Mose Casner limped out onto the porch of his Verde Valley ranch in 1877, and greeted a stranger named William Gilmore (W.G.) Wingfield. After the two shared pleasantries, and a hot meal, W.G. and Old Mose struck a deal that would make the Casner ranch the home and ranchland for a remarkable clan of pioneers, whose family members continue to live in, and contribute to, the development and history of the Verde Valley to this day.

Born in Charlottesville, Virginia on July 17, 1843, W.G. Wingfield traced his family's origins in America back to colonial times. His colonial ancestor was Captain Edward Maria Wingfield, the founding father of Jamestown, Virginia in 1607. Captain Wingfield is credited with recruiting 40 % of the colony's original settlers; for paying off the debts of the expedition; building a fort; planting the first crops, and bartering with the local Indians. A large marble memorial is dedicated to him in Jamestown.

Throughout the British Isles there are more than 100 churches and cathedrals that contain memorials to various prominent Wingfield family members that date back to the 1300s. In America, the Wingfield men were deeply involved in the politics and growth of their struggling commonwealth. They fought in the Revolutionary War, and the War of 1812.

W.G., at the age of 18, ran away from his Arkansas home at the outbreak of the Civil War to join the Union Army. His family encouraged him to go. They abhorred slavery and had little sympathy with the Southern cause. W.G. enlisted in Missouri as a sharpshooter under General Blount, and fought throughout the war. His only injury resulted from a saber cut at the Battle of Rio Ridge.

At war's end, he returned home to find his mother, Frances Gilmore, dead and his once robust father, Edward, severely crippled with rheumatism. Despite these adversities, W.G.'s three younger brothers, Thomas Yates, James Henry, and Francis (Tobe), had managed to keep their Arkansas farm going.

W.G. went into the mercantile business with his former captain, John A. Dienst, in Fayetteville, Arkansas. During the next two years, he also courted a pretty French girl, Margaret Ann Pleasants. They met during the war when he came across her while she was herding cows. Knowing an enemy foraging party was near, he helped her hide the cows. In return, Margaret gave W.G. safe refuge until the danger passed. They married in 1866.

That same year, he decided to sell his interest in the mercantile business to his partner, Captain Dienst. Reconstruction in the south made life impossible, as far as W.G. was concerned, and the lure of westward expansion had captured his interest. In 1869, two years after his first son Charles was born on July 29, 1867, W.G., his father Edward, brother Tobe, Margaret, and young son Charles, joined a wagon train to Oregon. His two other brothers stayed behind on the farm.

The family's wagon train followed the same route to Oregon established by John C. Fremont in 1842. The long journey proved arduous. They endured most of the typical hardships of the trail, from crossing flooded rivers, bogging down in quicksand, nearly freezing to death in winter storms, and fending off marauding Indians. Along the way, 17-year-old Tobe decided to part from the family at the California cut-off, and seek his fortune in the gold fields of Nevada.

Finally, by the winter of 1868, the weary Wingfields settled in Goose Lake, an area near Salem, Oregon. During the next nine years, they farmed successfully. Margaret gave birth to two daughters during this time, Frances Virginia, and Ida May. By 1872, James Henry, now married to his childhood sweetheart, Sara England, and his two young children, Clinton DeWitt, and Matilda Louise, had joined W.G.'s family in Oregon.

Sara England and James Henry met at a spelling bee in Fort Smith, Arkansas where they both attended high school. They married on February 10, 1869. Before the year ended, their first child, Frances Elizabeth was born, and died nine days later. She would be the first of their 10 children to die. Sara and James Henry would bury six more of their children before their three surviving children eventually buried them.

Once in Oregon, Sara gave birth to their fourth child, Matilda Louise, on March 28, 1874. Two years later, both families sold their property and prepared to leave for Arizona Territory. Their elderly father, Edward's, rheumatism had worsened in the damp Oregon climate, and none of the family liked the coastal storms, and long, snowy winters in Goose Lake. The climate had taken its toll on them all, and the decision was made to seek a more temperate area. The Wingfield brothers decided to reunite in Nevada at their brother Tobe's ranch before traveling on to Arizona Territory.

With money from the sale of their Oregon farm, the brothers bought 200 (some estimates say 400 head) of cattle and the two families set out on another arduous journey to Nevada. After a happy reunion in Nevada, the brothers decided to leave the cattle in the care of Tobe, while they continued on to Arizona with their families.

John Henry and Sara Wingfield
—Courtesy Babs Wingfield Monroe(BWM)

They reached Fort Walapai just as winter set in. There they remained until spring. Leaving their families under the fort's protection, W.G. and James Henry returned to Carson City to get their cattle.

On their return to Fort Walapai, the brothers suffered a substantial financial blow. While crossing the Colorado River near Lee's Ferry, a large number of their cattle became hopelessly mired in quicksand and died. It was a devastating setback, yet the family remained strong. They were determined to go on.

From Fort Walapai, the family traveled as far as Walnut Canyon, seven miles east of Flagstaff. Here they set up camp and stayed while W.G. went scouting for their new home.

After several days of rough travel, W.G. arrived in the small community of Camp Verde. Caught in a drenching thunderstorm, W.G. headed to the Sutlers' store (a mercantile store situated near forts to supply the needs of soldiers and their families), which at the time was owned and operated by a handsome but eccentric Englishman named "Boss" Head. W.G. could not know it at the time, but this same Sutlers' store would one day bring both terrible sorrow, and great joy, to members of his family, and "Boss" Head would become a trusted, life-long friend.

When "Boss" Head learned W.G. was looking for a ranch to buy, he recommended old Mose Casner's place. Located where the town of Cottonwood is today, not only did the Casner ranch already have a cabin on it but acres of bottomland were already cleared. The grazing land above flowed with abundant wild grass for their cattle. Cottonwood trees provided ample shade around the small cabin and along the Rio Verde. The land, so lush and beautiful, was exactly what the family had been looking for. Casner and W.G. struck a satisfactory deal, and W.G. hurried back to gather his family from Walnut Canyon. James Henry's family soon settled across the river from his brother, and not long afterwards, their fourth child, William Frances (Frank), was born on October 8, 1876.

The Wingfield brothers formed a cooperative, and dug the first workable irrigation ditch in the Verde Valley. They brought water from the river to their fields by following an ancient and crumbling ditch, originally dug by prehistoric Indians. The ditch allowed them to grow more vegetables than anyone else in the valley, and the family graciously shared these with their neighbors. They also built the first school in the area.

By 1878, W.G. had built a large home for his family. Neighbors came from miles around to celebrate a house warming, enjoy a feast and dance, while admiring one-year-old William Gilmore, Jr., their fifth child.

Soon the Wingfield ranches expanded to include wild horses. Usually they had more than 100 wild horses broken and branded each year. The government contractors at the nearby forts were their eager customers. The Hatchet brand, which marked all their livestock, was registered in W.G.'s name and became known far and wide.

With wild game in abundance to supplement their diet of beef and mutton, the Wingfields enjoyed the produce of their land. During these prosperous years, the family's moved back and forth with their livestock, from Cottonwood in the winter, to the Mogollon Rim's summer range. Unfortunately, this prosperity was not to last. By 1880, they had sold their holdings and moved.

Their precious land along the Rio Verde was a breeding ground for mosquitoes. Everyone in the family suffered attacks of malaria. Quinine, the only remedy, was hard to obtain. With someone in the family always sick, and doctors rare, their decision to move was heartbreaking, yet they felt they had no choice.

James Henry's family moved to Beaver Creek where Sara gave birth to their fourth and fifth children, Freddy on September 18, 1879, and Walter, on September 18, 1882. Walter was born at the home and fortress of Aunty and Wales Arnold, where they fled for protection from an Indian outbreak.

W.G. resolved to try his luck in California, leaving his herd of cattle with James Henry. In California, W.G. bought 300 acres of choice farmland near Signal Hill in Los Angeles County, planted barley, and once again prospered. Robert Wilson, their sixth child, was born there on March 28, 1881. One year later, the homesick family returned to Arizona.

Not long after their return, the last Indian uprising in central Arizona threw the Wingfields, and other citizens in the area, into a panic. An Apache renegade named Nan-tio-tish had fled the reservation at San Carlos with 80 warriors. They headed straight for the Verde Valley, burning homes, killing families, and stealing stock along the way.

"Boss" Head sent a rider to warn the area's families. They were encouraged to take refuge at the home of Wales and Auntie Arnold at Montezuma Well. For weeks, the fleeing families remained within the Arnold fortress. Finally, a soldier rode in to announce that the uprising had been suppressed.

Everyone left except the family of W.G. Wingfield. Six months prior to the uprising, W.G. had purchased the west half of the

Arnold's Montezuma Well ranch and moved his cattle there. After the uprising, the Arnolds moved to Cienga Creek and built a new fortress, while the Wingfields moved into the Arnold's old fortress home. They didn't remain long. The ever-restless W.G. uprooted his family once more, and moved back to California.

James Henry and Sara returned to their ranch at Beaver Creek with their new baby. One year later, that baby, and their next youngest son, contracted a deadly fever in 1883, and died within days of one another. They are buried in a small cemetery near Stoneman Lake.

Sara must have needed the comfort of Margaret Ann after burying her small boys. In response to her grief, James Henry sold their property, and took their family by train to California. There they met up with his still restless brother. The two families outfitted themselves with horse drawn wagons, and traveled up and down the California coast trying to figure out what to do with them selves. This must have been exasperating for both Margaret Ann and Sara, and all their children, but at least the two women found comfort in one another's company.

After several months of wandering up and down the California coast, the two families took a vote. They unanimously voted to return to Arizona—this time to stay.

W.G. purchased a ranch on Clear Creek from Robert Steadman in 1884. He promised Margaret Ann this would be their last move; and it was. He bought a herd of Texas longhorns from "Boss" Head, planted crops, and developed an orchard. The last two of their eight children were born on this ranch, John Henry (Hank), on May 10, 1885, and Minnie, born December 30, 1887. Their Clear Creek Ranch, located on what is known as Wingfield Mesa, became a show place, and their Hatchet brand became famous again.

Margaret Wingfield with Minnie and Hank
—Courtesy of BWM

The early years on their Clear Creek ranch were happy ones for W.G. and Margaret Ann. They painted their beautiful home white, the first painted house in the valley. Everyone referred to it as the "White House." W.G. figured out how to pump water into their home. He bought Margaret Ann her first sewing machine, and several of the newly invented coal oil lamps, as well.

From dances, to picnics, to church socials, the Wingfield family helped organize the many festivities that regularly took place in Camp Verde. Good times prevailed, until disaster struck again.

In 1892, a devastating flood wiped out W.G.'s fine orchard, uprooting most of his fruit trees. The swirling waters reached the barn, where surplus crops were stored, and finally swept against the foundation of the White House, totally demolishing it, and all their belongings. It was more than Margaret Ann could bear. After years of hardship, travel, backbreaking work, and giving birth to eight children, Margaret Ann Wingfield passed away not long afterwards, at the age of 44. W.G. never remarried. He rebuilt his ranch on higher ground, and continued to farm and run cattle until 1931. When he was 88 year's old, he was a passenger in an automobile returning from a pioneer's picnic in Page Springs, when the automobile crashed. Mortally wounded, W.G. Wingfield died a few days later at the hospital in Jerome.

Fate would deal an even crueler hand to Sara and James Henry after they returned from California in 1884. At first, they did not know where they wanted to settle down again. For two years, James Henry dragged Sara and the family up and down the Rio Verde. For awhile, they lived at Beaver Head Station, where their son, David, was born on July 3, 1884. Flagstaff came next, in order for the children to attend school. By 1886, they chose the little community of Strawberry, 40 miles east of Camp Verde, as home.

There they lived for nine years. James Henry farmed, raised cattle, and helped start Strawberry's first school. The little schoolhouse still stands, and is listed on the National Historic Register.

Sara served as postmistress in Strawberry, and gave birth to twin boys on December 1, 1888: John Wesley and Jim Henry. John Wesley survived only five months and was buried in Strawberry. Two years later, Sara gave birth to her tenth and last child, Margaret, born on December 7, 1890.

When Margaret turned five, her oldest sister, Matilda, married C.C. Calloway, a close family friend. That same year, Margaret's father, James Henry, bought the Shield Ranch in the Verde Valley. The Wingfield families were reunited once again.

In 1898, "Boss" Head sold his Sutlers' store in Camp Verde to Sara and James Henry's oldest son, Clinton Dewitt, and his partner, Mack

Rodgers. Mr. Head, heavily involved in local politics, was ready to retire from the mercantile business after 27 years. He knew the two young men would make a success of it.

And they did, until they were murdered.

Clint and Mack kept the Sutlers' store open seven days a week, from early morning until late at night. In the evenings, the store was a popular gathering place for the men of the community. Here they socialized, played cards, and "bellied up to the bar" for a few drinks.

One Sunday evening on July 2, 1899, the town was quiet. Most folks were home with their families. The only men still at the store were Clint and Mack; Lou Turner, an employee; Captain Boyd, a retired prospector; and a Mr. Hopkins, the mail rider. The men sat out on the front porch smoking their pipes and discussing the upcoming Fourth of July celebration, while Clint worked in the store's back room.

Finally, Mack got up to stretch his legs. He walked to the end of the porch to watch the sun set, when he sensed someone crouching in the shadows nearby. He called out, "you down there-you all right?" "Yep," came the answer, "just restin' a bit." Mack informed the stranger the store would be closing soon, and asked if he needed anything. The answer was, no, so Mack returned to his chair and companions.

Suddenly, Clint was startled by shots. He rushed from the back room, and through the darkened store towards the entrance, unaware that his partner, Mack, already lay dead inside. The murderer shot Clint in the stomach, severing his spine, then ran off.

Since the murderer did not attempt a robbery, it was speculated that he knew Mack, and was settling some old grievance. Clint's father, James Henry, and his brothers were notified in time to be with him just before he died a few hours later.

A manhunt, led by Sheriff Munds was instigated, with Clint's brothers joining the posse. After several months, an outlaw by the name of Black Jack Ketchum was caught after holding up a train. He refused to admit to Clint's murder. He was tried and convicted of robbing a train in New Mexico, a capital offence, and was subsequently hanged there.

Clint's father, James Henry, bought Mack Rodger's interest in the Sutlers' store from his widow, and with the help of his remaining sons, ran it for the next nine years. Unfortunately, Clint's murder was not the final tragedy for this family, there were more to come.

Sara, deeply despondent over the murder of Clint, took her daughter Margaret, now nine, on a train trip to visit her family in Arkansas. But the trip that was designed to raise her spirits, ended in more heartbreak. Margaret contracted measles on the train and died. Her mother buried her in Arkansas. Two years to the day after Clint was murdered, Matilda, their oldest daughter, also became ill and passed away on July 2. 1901. She left behind two small daughters and a grieving young husband. Sara, summoning what was left of her emotional strength, took charge of her granddaughters, but finally it all was too much. Sara died a few years later at the age of 56.

Finally, Robert, son of W.G., traded some of his father's cattle for the Sutlers' store, allowing James Henry to return full time to ranching. By then, James Henry had already married Hattie Loy Munds, now the stepmother of his three remaining sons: Frank, Dave and Jim. In 1908, James Henry purchased the Sunnyside Ranch from his long time friend, "Boss" Head, and ran cattle there until his death in 1926, at the age of 78.

With his nephew, Robert, now in charge of the Sutlers' store, it expanded and grew with the community. Not only did it supply dry goods and groceries, but Robert also installed the first refrigerated meat market, a post office, the first bank, and a drug store within its walls. The store prospered, and various family members enjoyed a total of 72 years of ownership. It has since become a beautiful shopping mall named in their honor.

Today, the Wingfield descendants can be found throughout Arizona in every walk of life. They owned and operated many of the prominent ranches in the Verde Valley for decades. A Wingfield relative once remarked, "there are more Wingfields around here (the Verde Valley) than Johnson grass." And if that is true, all of them can trace their lineage back to the courageous pioneering families of two brothers, William Gilmore (W.G.), and James Henry Wingfield.

* * * *

THE ARIZONA RANGERS AND THE BATTLE FOR STATEHOOD

By 1900, Arizona territory was plagued by unbridled lawlessness, and the people of the territory knew that statehood would continue to elude them unless they dealt with it.

The Graham-Tewksbury feud had shocked the nation. Tombstone's notorious gunfights, including the shoot-out between the Clantons and Earps at the OK Corral, fed national headlines for months. Geronimo and Nan-tio-tish, fleeing the reservation and wreaking fear and havoc, caused widespread alarm beyond Arizona's borders. The pens of pulp fiction writers immortalized the exploits of such nefarious Arizona outlaws as the Apache Kid, Pearl Hart and Johnny Ringo, which only exacerbated Arizona's reputation for lawlessness.

The coming of the railroads brought prosperity to the territory, and had inspired large-scale ranching enterprises, but they also unwittingly buoyed widespread cattle rustling and train robberies. Territorial prosecutors had not won a single conviction for cattle rustlers in 14 years, primarily because so many smaller operations were engaging in the crime. Many sheriffs looked the other way, rather than lose the votes of their cattle rustling constituents.

It was cattle rustling, in particular, that inspired the formation of the Arizona Rangers in 1901. Prescott's Nathan Oakes Murphy, who was serving his second appointment as territorial governor in 1901, proposed the idea of the Arizona Rangers to the legislature. Anxious to do anything to quell the territory's lawless reputation, the legislature readily agreed to the idea, and the Arizona Rangers finally came to prominence.

Nathan Oakes Murphy
—ASLA

Patterned after the Texas Rangers, Arizona's Rangers were not restricted by county lines, or country borders. In contrast, county sheriffs could only chase an outlaw as far as the county line, within his own jurisdiction, and rarely was there cooperation among sheriffs to apprehend criminals. For decades, outlaws knew this and took full advantage of the situation.

Particularly vulnerable was the territory's southern border, where outlaws easily slipped back and forth into Mexico. Some of the biggest gangs of cattle rustlers hid out in the canyons along the Arizona-Mexico border, stealing Mexican cattle and selling them to

Arizona ranchers. Most ranchers did not realize they were buying stolen cattle, but many did, and didn't care. Or, they were outlaws themselves, such as Ike Clanton's infamous gang of rustlers.

The Arizona Rangers were governed by the rules and regulations of the U.S. Army, and answered only to the authority of territorial officials. Five cents from every $100 of taxable property was assessed and placed into the 'Ranger Fund' to pay their expenses.

Initially, each member had to furnish his own horse, pistol and camping equipment. Packhorses were supplied for them, and their horses were replaced if they were killed or injured. The territory paid the Ranger's medical expenses if they were wounded on the job.

Their initial pay was $120 a month for their captain, $75 for his sergeant, and $55 a month for their recruits. They were given an allotment of $1.50 a day for their room and board.

Governor Murphy appointed his good friend Burt Mossman to organize and lead the first group of Rangers. Mossman's amazing performance in ridding central Arizona of cattle rustlers for the Aztec Land and Cattle Company in the 1890s, already had earned him the respect of the territory. A bulldog of a man, Mossman was of Scotch-Irish decent, spoke fluent Spanish, and was a gifted storyteller. Prior to his appointment, he'd been a farmer and cattle rancher in central Arizona. After breaking up the Hashknife rustlers, he served courageously with the famous Arizona Rough Riders during the Spanish-American War.

Mossman recruited 14 men, many former Texas Rangers, and fellow Rough Riders. All were good shots and seasoned frontiersmen. Their average age was 33.

Astonishingly, this handful of men was obligated to cover 11,406 square miles of territory, 8,000 square miles per man. Undaunted, they quickly gained a reputation of being tough and pitiless.

Under Mossman, the Rangers hid their badges, dressed like common cowboys and hired out to cattle ranchers, keeping their occupation a secret until making an arrest. During his tenure, the Rangers made 125 arrests of actual criminals, who either went to prison, or were sent back to other states to face earlier crimes.

Mossman's most celebrated arrest was of Mexico's notorious murderer named Augustine Chacon. Chacon bragged that he had killed 15 Americans and 37 Mexicans, including the brutal ax murder of a Morenci storekeeper. Captured and sentenced to hang, Chacon escaped after his girlfriend sneaked a hacksaw blade into his jail cell, concealed in the spine of a Bible.

Mossman went after him with a vengeance. Disguised as an outlaw, Mossman snuck across the Mexican border (in violation of international law), and caught Chacon unawares. After a bloody barroom fight, Mossman took Chacon to Solomonville, Arizona where he was hanged shortly afterwards.

Burt Mossman
—ASLA

After serving one year, Mossman resigned when his friend Governor Murphy left office. He bought a ranch in New Mexico, where he lived out his life, dying in 1956 at the age of 99. His successor was Thomas Rynning.

Born in Norway in 1866, Rynning came to the United States at the age of two. When he turned nineteen, he joined the frontier army and served under General Phil Sheridan during his campaigns against the Southern Cheyenne. Between 1885 and 1887, Rynning rode with General Nelson Miles against the Chiricahua Apaches and was present during Geronimo's final surrender. Upon his honorable discharge from the frontier army, he had a record of participating in 17 battles against Indians.

During the Spanish American War in the late 1890s, Rynning served as a second Lieutenant of "B" troop under Teddy Roosevelt's Rough Riders, and took part in all engagements leading to the Spanish surrender at Santiago, Cuba. By the time he took over the leadership of the Arizona Rangers, he was a 36-year-old, tough and seasoned veteran.

Rynning started a thorough training program for the Rangers, increased their number to 26, and helped get them a pay boost to $100 a month. During the five years he was captain of the Rangers, the Rangers became particularly noteworthy when they broke strikes by miners at the Morinci and Bisbee copper mines.

Under Rynning, the Rangers stationed themselves in the new town of Douglas, located on Arizona's southern border, which had become a gathering place for some of the worst outlaws in the southwestern United States. Shortly after settling there, Rynning learned about a notorious cattle-rustling family named Taylor.

Rynning roped 13 calves belonging to a rancher from whom the Taylors regularly had been stealing, made a small slit in each of their gullets, and inserted a Mexican coin inside. He waited a few months before checking the Taylor's cattle. When he spotted the 13 calves on their ranch, he promptly arrested the Taylors. During their trial, Rynning gathered the jury outside around the corralled calves, and opened their gullets. The Taylors were found guilty and the judge gave them 24 hours to clear out of the territory.

Thomas Rynning resigned as captain on March 21, 1907 in order to become the superintendent of the new territorial prison in Florence.

The third and last Captain of the Rangers was Harry C. Wheeler. Wheeler had attended military school, but later was rejected by the Army for being too short in stature; something that embarrassed him terribly. After joining the Rangers in 1903 under the leadership of Rynning, he quickly moved up the ranks from private, to lieutenant, to captain. Wheeler proved to be a forceful adversary against territorial outlaws.

One late night in Tucson, a bandit named Joe Bostwick was in the process of holding up the patrons of the Palace Saloon. Wheeler was in town and heard that the holdup was taking place. Through the saloon window, Wheeler could see the bandit, his face covered in a red bandana with slits for his eyes. He had all the patrons backed against the wall, and was just moving toward the money on the crap table, when Wheeler stepped inside the saloon. Both men fired, but Bostwick was no match for the sharp-shooting Wheeler. Bostwick died the next day.

Wheeler's only comment: "I'm sorry this happened, but it was either his life or mine."

Shortly after Wheeler took over the helm of the Rangers, both New Mexico and Arizona's territorial legislatures moved to crack down on gambling and prostitution. Not only was gambling forbidden, and females banned from saloons but the saloon-licensing fee shot up in Arizona to twice the former amount. It was one more effort to convince the nation that frontier evils were being dealt with, and that statehood should be the reward.

Wheeler applauded the new legislation. In his report to the governor in 1908, he noted that there had been an eighteen-percent decline in arrests over the previous year, and he attributed this primarily to the anti-gambling legislation.

The Arizona Rangers were disbanded in 1909, ending Wheeler's two-year term as captain. The reason was strictly political. The Rangers had been formed and supported by Republicans. Democrats were now in office.

Wheeler was elected sheriff of Cochise County in 1912. His calm in the face of danger made him a legend among Arizona's lawmen. During Wheeler's term, Pancho Villa was shooting it out with the federales near the border town of Naco, Arizona. Stray bullets were killing the residents of the town. Sheriff Wheeler rode between the warring factions carrying a white flag, and persuaded both sides to relocate. The two armies apologized, and moved their battle elsewhere.

The combined daring and ingenuity of Wheeler, Rynning and Mossman, and their Rangers reduced lawlessness from a flood to a puddle. During their seven years of operation, 107 men served in the Arizona Rangers. They brought about 4,000 arrests. Two years after they disbanded, Arizona became the 48th state on February 14, 1912, thanks in large part to their proud record.

The First Arizona State Legislature, under Democrat Governor George W.P. Hunt, gave women in Arizona the right to vote, eight years before suffrage was obtained nationally. Copper and cotton were the new state's primary industries, while the cattle industry followed a distant third.

Proud of their statehood status, frontier-hardened Arizonans marched off to World War I with patriotic zeal in 1914, contributing more soldiers, sailors and Marines per capita than any other state. Arizona's National Guard, the 158th Infantry Regiment, distinguished themselves with such valor during the "War to end all Wars" that President Woodrow Wilson chose them as his special honor guard during the Paris Peace Conference.

At last the courageous pioneer men and women, who had struggled and given their lives for the cause of Arizona statehood, could rest proudly in peace.

"I'll be in hell before you start breakfast, boys." Black Jack Ketchum's last words to the hangman.

"Lawlessness like wildness is attractive, and we conceive the last remaining home of both to be the West."
Wallace Stegner, author.

CHAPTER FOUR
Outlaws, Lawmen and Ladies of the Night

The wave of lawlessness following the Civil War perpetuated a dynasty of outlaws that lasted a half-century. Romanticized versions of their lives reached mythical proportions. Typically the outlaws of the Old West were unschooled youths, often illiterate and restless spirits who yearned for adventure. Many fled the post war turmoil of reconstruction in the east and south, or because they wanted to avoid the brutal hardships of their family farm.

These young men followed the railroads as they sliced their steel paths across the west, drawing them to the mining and cattle towns as they mushroomed into existence. The young men became cowboys adept with horse and gun, who battled Indians, rustlers, and wild animals. Later they might use that same gun to hold up a stagecoach, a train, rob a bank, or steal cattle.

It was an era of unspeakable hardships that bred hard men and women. The cowboy rode into towns consisting of clapboard shacks with muddy, rutted streets, where saloons and bordellos outnumbered churches and schools. Typically, the women of these towns were prostitutes, bawdy characters who masked their identity with colorful nicknames like 'Big Nose Kate' and 'Juicy Lucy'.

It was a man's world, and those who prospered did so because they knew how to shoot or could afford to hire gunmen to protect their interests. Fearless and capable of taking care of themselves, western men of that era are still romanticized today regardless of which side of the law they were on.

It was easy to become a bad man. Lawlessness was a way of life then and lawmen were few and far between. Bad men were boldest when working in gangs, a fact that has been true throughout history. Outlaw gangs of the Old West often were made up of brothers. As gang members, those brothers led notorious raids against banks and railroads.

The gunfighters who hired out as assassins, usually for greedy cattle barons, preferred to kill by ambush. It was a rare gunfighter who challenged his victim face-to-face. Those who did were considered to be so egotistical, they bordered on insanity. The western lawman who faced the outlaws needed to be as courageous as the outlaw was scheming.

Most lawmen were sons of pioneers, and were born into the hardships of the frontier. Their histories indicate strong family backgrounds, often raised by both a mother and a father who taught them the moral necessity of upholding the law.

In contrast, most of the worst outlaws were orphans, or grew up with only one parent, often a brutal father.

Between 1850 and 1900, when this heyday of lawlessness spawned most of our myths about outlaws, only a few good men had the courage to don a badge and take them on.

There were no schools to train them in law enforcement. Instead, these lawmen relied upon their own raw courage, gut instinct and relentless determination to catch their man.

It is the lawmen of the Old West who truly merit our romantic accolades. They not only stood for justice, but they are the ones who finally triumphed over one of most anarchistic eras in American history.

Some of Arizona's best western lawmen and worst outlaws came from Yavapai County.

* * * *

SHERIFF EDWARD FRANKLIN BOWERS (1874-1878)

Shortly after Edward Franklin Bowers was sworn into office, two strangers—reputed to be bad men from Texas—encountered a cowboy headed for Prescott.

"We've killed every sheriff we've come across and we're going to kill yours," they told the cowboy. "Tell your sheriff to come on out here, if he's got any backbone."

Sheriff Bowers and his men got the message and set off to find the troublemakers. After riding about three miles, they caught sight of the outlaws who immediately opened fire on the sheriff, shooting his horse out from under him. As the sheriff tried to crawl out from under his horse, another bullet hit him in the chest. Fortunately a receipt book in his vest pocket deflected the bullet and the sheriff was unharmed. He returned the fire and killed one of the outlaws on the spot. When the smoke cleared the other outlaw was mortally wounded. He died in Prescott a few hours later.

Sheriff Edward Bowers was 37 years old and a family man when he took on those outlaws in 1874. Six years earlier he had married 18 year-old Olive Ehle, daughter of Joseph and Margaret Ehle, one of Prescott's first families. Sheriff Bowers and his brothers were early pioneers, as well.

Born at Greenfield, Hillsboro County, New Hampshire, on June 27, 1838, Edward left home at the age of 19 to seek his fortune in the gold fields of Colorado and later California. In 1865 he accompanied his brothers (Herbert and George) to Arizona.

Herbert, already an established businessman in Prescott, had purchased the Sutlers store at Fort Whipple in 1864 with another brother, Nathan. The three Bowers brothers became prominent, respected and prosperous in the mining, ranching, and mercantile circles of Yavapai County.

Initially, Edward worked for his brothers (Herbert and Nathan) freighting goods for their store. When these same brothers bought the huge King Woolsey ranch in Lonesome Valley, Edward worked there as well herding cattle and fighting Indians. The Bowers brothers lost thousands of dollars worth of livestock during Arizona's Indian wars. They also lost their 21 year-old nephew, George, son of Dexter

Bowers, another brother who lived in California. Named after his uncle, George Washington Bowers, young George was killed by Apaches shortly after he arrived in Prescott.

After Edward married Olive Ehle, he entered into the mercantile business with his brother-in-law, D.J. Cook, opening the Adobe Store located on the corner of Granite and Gurley Streets. The business flourished under the name Cook and Bowers allowing Edward to indulge in his first love, mining.

In partnership with C.C. Bean and A.B. Wells, Edward started working hydraulic claims on Lynx Creek in the Walker Mining District. By 1871, he had enough money to buy a cattle ranch in Skull Valley, where he continued to defend his livestock against Indian raids. In 1872 he was appointed postmaster of Skull Valley.

By 1874 he won the office of sheriff on the Independent ticket and was elected again in 1876. By then he and Olive had four children, George Alfred (1871-1892), Stella (1873-1940), Charles Herbert (1875-1944), and Edward Franklin, Jr. (1877-1921).

Shortly after his near death encounter with the Texas bad men, Edward performed the first legal hanging in Yavapai County.

Unfortunately, the man was innocent.

A young Mexican named Manuel Aviles was accused, tried, and pronounced guilty of killing a ranch hand in the Verde settlement. The personal testimony by the defendant was without support of any kind, merely that he was riding past on his way to Prescott when he saw a man lying in a ditch. He got off his horse to investigate and found the man dead. Then seeing a shovel lying nearby, he picked it up and was examining it when two men rode up and promptly arrested him for murder.

On the day of his execution the jail yard was crowded. The priest in attendance, as a last gesture, asked Aviles if there was anything he wanted before "taking off."

With the rope lying slack around his neck and the black cap resting upon his head ready to be pulled down, the condemned man looked out over the crowd and said, "My father was a revolutionist in Mexico, struggling for the freedom of my people. He too had bad luck and was shot. When he died, he had a cigarette on his lips. Will some friend give me a cigarette?"

Every man in the crowd jerked out his makings and feverishly began rolling cigarettes. While this went on the young Mexican continued. "I have told you that I did not know this man who was killed. Why should I kill a man I did not know? Someday, perhaps, you will find he was killed by someone else, but it will be too late for me. You will know, however, I do not lie."

At that point cigarettes flew like snow flakes upon the scaffold. The priest reached down and chose one to light. He placed it in Aviles' mouth. Aviles said thanks, inhaled a lungful, then nodded to Sheriff Bowers. The black hood was pulled over his face and the man dropped through the trap door dying almost instantly.

Sixty years later, long after Sheriff Bowers and just about everyone else who attended the young Mexican's hanging, were dead, a neighbor of the victim confessed on his deathbed that he had done the killing. He said they had gotten into a fight over water rights.

Throughout the 1870s, stagecoach robberies were rampant, particularly between Prescott and Wickenburg. Stagecoaches carried more than passengers. They carried everything from the payrolls for the mines, to mail containing valuable government stocks and bonds. Two notable stagecoach robberies occurred during Sheriff Bowers' term of office.

The U.S. Postal Service finally hired a detective named John Mantle to investigate these Yavapai County robberies. Mantle liked working in secret, so he did not inform Sheriff Bowers of what he was up to.

Mantle had been successful in the past because he pretended to be an outlaw himself, and as such, was able to infiltrate the outlaw gangs. By the spring of 1877, Mantle infiltrated a band of robbers who planned to hold up the stagecoach near Wickenburg. Unbeknownst to Mantle, Sheriff Bowers was traveling on that same stage when it was stopped. Bowers was relieved of $450 by the robbers, who included Mantle. Besides money and jewelry taken from the passengers, the robbers got away with a considerable amount of payroll money and government bonds.

Not long after the robbery, Sheriff Bowers was in hot pursuit of the outlaws. When he caught up with them he shot the arm off one, wounded another and was aiming at Mantle when Mantle put up his hands and revealed his true identity. Bowers took all three to Prescott, and threw them in jail. After a few days, Mantle was ordered released by the U.S. Attorney General. Later, Mantle was called to task during the Grand Jury proceedings. The Grand Jury issued a statement that condemned his tactics as "a criminal lack of common sense."

Mantle's behavior was unusual. Unless a sheriff was suspected of being corrupt, (which Bowers was not), government officials, private detectives, and U.S. Marshals preferred to work closely with local sheriffs. Each respected his own separate sphere of law enforcement and decried any infringement.

However, Sheriff Bowers faced another infringement when deputy U.S. Marshal Joseph W. Evans took possession of two suspected mail robbers from his jail in Yavapai County while Bowers was away. Evans convinced the deputy in charge that he held proper United States commissioner's warrants for their arrest. These prisoners included pioneer Arizonan Jack Swilling.

Swilling founded Phoenix and co-founded Prescott. He purportedly led the Walker Party to Lynx Creek, where they discovered the gold bonanza that initiated Arizona as a territory.

Swilling, born in Anderson County, South Carolina in 1830 served as a Lieutenant in the Confederate Army during the Civil War. After the war he became an Indian scout, farmer, rancher, prospector, and entrepreneur.

Observing the old Hohokam canals that crisscrossed the Salt River Valley, he formed an irrigation company, re-dug the ancient canals and planted crops. A small community of farmers established themselves in the valley near those canals, and from the ashes of the ancient ones, Phoenix was officially born on May 4, 1868 with Jack Swilling as the first postmaster.

Swilling, known to be a kind and generous man, also had a dark side. He was addicted to alcohol and morphine. By 1873 he had moved to the Agua Fria River area where he prospected and soon partnered in a gold and silver mine named the Tip Top.

But by 1878, he had been accused of a stagecoach robbery that he did not commit. Nor was he even near the area when the robbery took place.

While drinking in a saloon a few days after the robbery, he made a joke to a friend that he might have to rob a stage to get some ready cash. A Wells Fargo detective, who was looking for the culprits, heard about the remark and arrested Swilling and his friend.

After Deputy Marshal Evans took Swilling from the Prescott jail to the Yuma prison, jail officials there would not allow Swilling to have his morphine. Swilling wrote letters declaring his innocence and predicted he would die from suffering if he could not have his "medicine". At the age of 47 he was found dead in his cell on August 12, 1878. The men who were the actual robbers were finally caught and they confessed. Swilling's friend was released from prison and later took up a collection for Swilling's wife and five children.

The only time Sheriff Bowers' behavior raised eyebrows was when he hired James S. Giles as his clerk, a man with a criminal record. While serving as Prescott's postmaster Giles had absconded with postal receipts but was captured in Utah. While Giles was serving time in Prescott's jail, Sheriff Bowers got to know him.

One of the most important appointments a sheriff made was that of clerk. In those days sheriffs were also tax collectors. Records had to be meticulously kept because the sheriff would be liable for any discrepancies. There weren't many people to draw from for the clerk's office. The majority of the population was illiterate.

Sheriff Bowers insisted that Giles had been rehabilitated and indeed Giles honored the sheriff's trust. When Sheriff Bowers' term ended all taxes, licensing fees and poll taxes were accounted for.

Sheriff Edward Bowers died in 1879 at the age of 43. His older brother George Washington Bowers, who had made a fortune in mining, erected a monument to him at the Masonic cemetery in Prescott. In 1921 Sheriff Bowers' son and namesake was shot and killed in the line of duty while serving as under-sheriff of Yavapai County. He was 44 years old at the time of his death and like his father left behind a wife and four children.

* * * *

SHERIFF JOSEPH RUTHERFORD WALKER (1879-1882)

Joseph Rutherford Walker succeeded Edward Bowers as sheriff in 1879. Walker, named after his famous path-finding uncle, was born in Fort Osage Township, Jackson County, Missouri, on April 30, 1832. His parents were Samuel and Barbara (Toomey) Walker.

As a teenager he was with the Walker Party when they located the gold bonanza on Lynx Creek that initiated the founding of Prescott. In the 1864 territorial census, he listed his occupation as a miner with property valued at $70. The 1870 census listed him as a laborer. Walker was 47 years old when he was elected Sheriff of Yavapai

County. His one term in office was notable only because during his watch two of Arizona's most nefarious con men were operating in the county. One was derisively referred to as the "Irish Lord". The other claimed to be a Spanish Baron, later known as the "Red Baron of Arizona".

James Addison Reavis opened a real estate business in St. Louis after serving in the Confederate Army. He pandered to a shady clientele who paid him sizable commissions to forge authentic looking property titles. He was very good at forging but when authorities became suspicious he left St. Louis in the dark of night and turned up in Santa Fe.

There he found a job in the records division of a government agency. His job was to handle the claims of Spanish and Mexican residents whose lands were ceded to the U.S. at the close of the Mexican-American War. The U.S. government was obligated, by the terms of the 1848 Treaty of *Guadalupe Hidalgo*, to restore land to the owners and to honor all legitimate claims. It didn't take Reavis long to figure out how to forge Mexican and Spanish land documents but it did take him a few years to put it all together.

He studied the kind of parchment paper used by scribes hundreds of years earlier, whittled the type of pen they used, and mixed up a similar type of ink. He decided to go after the Peralta Land grant in Yavapai County among others. He invented a name for himself, Miguel de Peralta, the half brother of Juan de Peralta, who, he would claim had purchased vast lands in Arizona. He also would claim that he and his non-existent half-brother were direct descendants of King Ferdinand of Spain.

Reavis then traveled to Guadalajara, Lisbon, Madrid, Seville and Mexico City, placing his forged documents including wills, deeds and mortgages, in all the important monasteries, libraries, and archives—exactly where any suspicious lawyers might look for them.

He arrived in Arizona with his beautifully forged documents and placed notices in all the newspapers in the territory (which included not only Prescott, but Globe, Silver King, Florence, Tempe and Casa Grande) that anyone living on his various properties owed him taxes. Even the Southern Pacific Railroad and the Silver King Mine were included.

A battery of lawyers hired primarily by the mine and railroad owners searched through the Torrens records and the ancient land grants only to discover that Reavis' claims appeared valid. Overnight Reavis became one of the wealthiest land entrepreneurs in Arizona Territory.

To add even more legitimacy to his claims, he plucked a Mexican girl off the streets in Prescott, sent her to finishing school and married her. He told everyone she was a direct descendant of the Peralta royal line. The couple had twin boys who were educated by private tutors. They lived in an assortment of mansions throughout the country and the "Baron" even traveled with his family to Spain, where King Alfonso cordially received them.

The charade came to an unceremonious end in 1890 when a document expert took a more thorough look at the forged papers. Using a variety of methods including chemical analysis he exposed the infamous Red Baron of Arizona. Mr. Reavis was tried and convicted. After serving six years in the Arizona penitentiary, Reavis spent his remaining years begging for spare change on the streets of Santa Fe.

In the meantime in the mining camps throughout the Bradshaw Mountains and along the Hassayampa River lawlessness had reached epic proportions. The little town of Weaver, approximately 50 miles south of Prescott, had a particularly unsavory reputation.

Located at the base of Rich Hill where Harlow Peeples and explorer Pauline Weaver had discovered one of the richest placer discoveries in Arizona history, the community of Weaver grew in size and prosperity. After the major gold deposits began to play out the town was taken over by thieves and cutthroats. The most notorious gang of outlaws the Vega gang (also known as the Valenzuela gang) used Weaver as their headquarters.

For years this gang of homicidal desperados terrorized everyone who lived in the region. They preyed upon miners in particular, robbed them and did not hesitate to kill them if they resisted. Lawmen including Sheriff Walker had tried unsuccessfully to track them down.

Then a shrewd, avaricious and conniving Irishman moved into the area by the name of Charles P. Stanton. At first he landed a job as assayer at the Vulture mill near Wickenburg. While there he somehow managed to acquire half-interest in the Leviathan mine at Rich Hill. When the mill shut down Stanton moved near his mine in a community called Antelope Creek. He built a cabin and opened a store.

At first his store was the main purveyor of food and supplies for the local miners. He bought their gold and acted as a banker for those who wanted a safe place to stash their money. In time the miners nicknamed him the 'Irish Lord' because of his haughty and unpleasant attitude. His customers didn't like him.

Before long Stanton found he was losing too much business to two competitors. One was Yaqui Wilson, who also operated the stage station at his store. About one half mile from Wilson's store, another store was operated by an old Englishman named Partridge. Partridge and Wilson did not like each other and Stanton decided to take advantage of their enmity. Stanton plotted to get rid of both competitors by creating a feud between them.

By then Stanton had become friendly with Francisco Vega, a cold-blooded murderer and the leader of the infamous Vega gang. With the help of this gang hogs belonging to Yaqui Wilson were rounded up and moved into Partridge's cabin while he was away. The hogs ate most of the food stored there and did considerable damage to the cabin. When the old Englishman returned home he managed to chase the hogs away with a barrage of rocks.

Wilson had no idea how his hogs had done this but said in front of witnesses that he would pay Partridge for any damage his hogs had caused. Before Wilson could make amends however Stanton sent a member of the Vega gang to tell Partridge that Wilson was hopping mad and was out to get him.

Poor Partridge fell for this lie, loaded his rifle and waited. When Wilson arrived to pay Partridge the old man shot and killed him. Partridge was tried and convicted for murder and spent his remaining years in the territorial prison in Yuma.

Stanton gleefully moved Wilson's stage stop to his headquarters renamed Antelope Creek, Stanton, in honor of himself, became its first postmaster and enjoyed running the town with an iron fist.

Unbeknownst to Stanton Partridge owed money to some people. In order to recoup their losses they sold Partridge's store to an unsuspecting young man named Barney Martin. Martin moved into the Partridge cabin with his wife and four children. A quiet, unassuming man, Martin's store soon became popular and prosperous, to the chagrin of Stanton.

Soon Martin received warnings from his customers that his life might be in danger. Martin knew of no enemies and told people he was not easily scared thereby brushing away the warnings. Years went by and Martin continued to prosper becoming a prominent and wealthy miner, as well as a prosperous merchant. Then in 1886 the Martin family disappeared on their way to Phoenix. By that time Walker was no longer sheriff. It became the responsibility of Sheriff Billy Mulvenon, who followed him in office in 1885, to find out what happened to them.

Sheriff Walker chose not to seek a second term of office. He bought a ranch on Beaver Creek in the Verde Valley where he ran a small herd of cattle. He never married. When he died on February 26, 1897, he was 64 years old. The hall in Prescott where his memorial service took place was filled to capacity. Friends and neighbors traveled long distances to pay their last respects to a man, who everyone agreed, had been universally liked throughout the county.

* * * *

SHERIFF WILLIAM J. MULVENON (1885-1888)

A man with one of the most exemplary records of sheriff in Yavapai County was William (Billy) J. Mulvenon. Best known for helping end the Graham-Tewksbury feud in Pleasant Valley, Mulvenon also tracked two murderers through three states on another occasion. In addition he pursued and captured the desperado who had murdered his deputy. In fact, Mulvenon had more desperate outlaws to deal with during his term of office than any other sheriff of Yavapai County.

The oldest of thirteen children born to Hugh and Ann King Mulvenon, (both Irish immigrants) "Billy" Mulvenon was born on October 25, 1851 in Belchertown, Massachusetts. In 1858 his family immigrated to the Leavenworth settlement in Kansas Territory. Over the years his hard working father listed several occupations during his long life from laborer, to teamster, to railroad worker. Billy came from a loving, close-knit family.

Billy left home at the age of 17 to seek his fortune in the west. He spent a few years prospecting in Colorado Territory. By 1871 he was in Silver City, New Mexico, where he served as a Deputy Sheriff for the next four years. He arrived in Prescott at the age of 24. Still fascinated with mining he prospected in the Bradshaw Mountains settling for a while at the Peck mine encampment. In the 1880 census he listed his occupation as a stable keeper at the Peck mine where he enjoyed some success with his mining investments.

People who knew him described Mulvenon as having a pleasant yet no-nonsense type personality. He got his blood up over injustice, they said, and "he was good with a gun." After he was appointed Deputy Sheriff of Yavapai County he moved to Prescott where he lived for the rest of his life.

Shortly after Mulvenon won the office of sheriff in 1885 Judge Fleury issued a warrant for the arrest of D.W. Dilda, charging him with misdemeanor larceny. No one knew how dangerous Dilda actually was. Had Sheriff Mulvenon known he would not have sent his young deputy, John Murphy, to Walnut Creek to make the arrest. He would have gone himself.

Dennis Dilda was a hard man who was known to have brutalized his wife and two small children. Around 1885 Dilda leased a ranch in Walnut Creek from W.H. Williscraft. A hired man named James Jenkins went with the lease. Williscraft left some of his personal belongings in a locked room at the ranch and asked Dilda if that was O.K. It was.

Soon Dilda's neighbors began noticing groceries were missing from their homes and calves were disappearing as well. None of this had happened before. The neighbors became suspicious of Mr. Dilda.

After several months passed, Williscraft returned to the ranch he had leased to Dilda and discovered his locked room had been broken into, its contents missing. There was no sign of Dilda or the hired man, Jenkins. Mrs. Dilda, a frail, terrified-looking woman, insisted she knew nothing about her husband's whereabouts or what had happened to the contents of the locked room.

Williscraft returned to Prescott and filed a complaint.

Deputy Murphy traveled to Walnut Creek to arrest Dilda but could not find him either. He returned again a few weeks later and was never seen alive again.

A search party was formed, led by Sheriff Mulvenon. Along the way they stopped at a nearby ranch owned by W.T. Shook and asked some questions. Mrs. Shook said she had heard gunshots coming from the Dilda's house a few days past. The posse found Deputy Murphy's horse tied to the gate at Dilda's home with footprints and wheelbarrow tracks leading to a nearby field. In the field the posse found patches of blood and soon saw handyman Jenkins' body partially buried in the dirt. More searching led them to the discovery of Deputy Murphy's body stuffed in a grain sack in Dilda's celler. Mrs. Dilda, cowering in the ranch house hugging her two small, ragamuffin youngsters, cried and finally admitted her husband had shot and killed Murphy as he approached their home. The Sheriff sent Dilda's wife and children back to Prescott with one of his deputies and then went immediately after Dilda.

The sheriff and his posse tracked Dilda to Ashfork where he had hidden near the railroad tracks in the hopes of hopping a train. The posse surrounded him and soon a large crowd gathered, threatening to lynch Dilda on the spot. Mulvenon assured the crowd that Dilda would hang for his crimes.

While the posse ate breakfast that morning Mulvenon slipped Dilda out the back door and got him to Prescott before the still angry crowd could get their hands on him. Within two months Dilda had been tried, convicted and was standing on the scaffold in Prescott with a rope around his neck. The only unusual incident that occurred during the hanging was when Buckey O'Neill, (who would become sheriff after Mulvenon), fainted after Dilda's body dropped through the trap door. The incident caused O'Neill constant embarrassment for the rest of his life.

One year after the Dilda hanging Sheriff Mulvenon received word that George Martin and his family had disappeared while on their way to Phoenix. Their friend, Captain Calderwood, had organized a rescue party. When the rescue party learned that the Vega gang had followed the Martins out of the town of Stanton—the home of the wily Irish Lord—they became genuinely alarmed. Calderwood knew that the Martins were planning a vacation back east to visit relatives and that Martin was carrying $4,000 in gold coins.

Maricopa lawmen were called in and more rescue parties were formed. They met a teamster who had seen the Martin family twenty days before at the Agua Fria River crossing. One search party led by Charles Genung found the Martin family, or what was left of them. Their wagon had been forced off the road near the crossing. Tracks led to the charred remains of the family. Their murderers also had cut the throat of one of their horses and made off with the rest. Of course there was no sign of the $4,000 worth of gold coins.

Since the bodies were found in Yavapai County, Sheriff Mulvenon was called in. A reward was raised of $2,500 for the identity and capture of the murderers.

The trail was cold but Mulvenon formed a posse and set out to find the killers. It didn't take him long to suspect that Charles Stanton, the Irish Lord, was behind the murders.

Stanton was known to have arranged a number of mysterious deaths and disappearances over the years and that he employed the infamous Vega gang to do his dirty work. Mulvenon arrested him on the charge of complicity in the murders of the Martin family. Later, Stanton was released for lack of evidence.

However Justice did catch up with him a few months later. A member of the Vega gang, Christo Lucero, shot and killed him in a fit of anger. Two versions of why he did it were given. One was that Stanton had not shared the loot from the Martin murders. The second version seems more likely. Stanton had made unwanted moves on Lucero's sister. Lucero was never found, and most folks didn't care. They were happy to see Stanton dead. The crime rate dropped considerably in the area of Stanton and Weaver after the Irish Lord's death.

Mulvenon hardly had time to rest up after the Martin murders before he received a telegram from a deputy on the Arizona Strip near the border of Utah.

Two cowboys working the range near House Rock on the Arizona Strip had discovered the shallow graves of a pioneer couple. Animals had dug them up exposing their bodies. The man's throat had been slit from ear to ear. The cowboys also found a burned out camp near the bodies, and the charred remains of a light wagon.

Mulvenon immediately took the stage to House Rock. It was a 250-mile journey to this Mormon settlement, the northern most town in Yavapai County. He arrived on October 26, 1886, and spent several days in town making inquiries. By then rumors were flying like autumn leaves.

Witnesses informed Mulvenon that the couple had stopped in town five months earlier. They were traveling with two wagons and their 17 year-old daughter was with them. Two men also accompanied them, driving their light wagon. No one remembered their names but one storekeeper said they had mentioned they were from Ft. Thomas (near Globe) and were on their way to Spokane, Washington.

Mulvenon purchased a small rake, borrowed a horse and headed out to the crime scene with the two cowboys who had found the bodies. Sifting through the ashes of the charred wagon with his rake, the sheriff found three items: A watch fob with the initials S.C. (but no watch), an ax handle, and an unusual hunting knife with an ornately carved handle. All were encrusted with dried blood. Mulvenon decided the knife was his best clue. The carved knife handle was unusual and rare enough to be traced.

Three hundred yards from the murder scene the sheriff found a campsite and some waded up newspapers from Globe. The name and mailing address printed on them was that of F.O. Weinlass, Thatcher, Arizona. Thatcher was a small town outside of Globe.

Before leaving the Arizona Strip, Mulvenon learned that a long forgotten message had turned up at the deputy sheriff's office in Kanab for a Mr. and Mrs. Samuel Clevenger (S.C). It was from their daughter Jessie. Apparently the two Clevenger wagons had become separated according to the message, and Jessie wrote that they (the two men and herself) would meet up with her parents in Salt Lake City. Now the sheriff had the names of the victims. The locals also informed him that the Clevengers never did come through Kanab.

Wires were sent to the newspaper in Globe inquiring about Weinlass, and to the postmaster at Ft. Thomas inquiring about the Clevengers. The inquiries produced quick results. The Globe newspaper reported that Weinlass had recently changed his address to Prescott. So the sheriff wired his deputy in Prescott to find Weinlass and keep an eye on him until he returned. The wire from the postmaster at Ft. Thomas was full of useful information.

According to the postmaster, the Clevengers had owned a small ranch in the area and were prosperous, but eventually tired of the desert heat. They had sold their ranch and left town with a large sum of money accompanied by their daughter and two hired men. Their friends did receive several letters from them up until April but had heard nothing from them since.

The sheriff returned to Prescott. His under-sheriff Joe Waddell had tracked Weinlass to a nearby ranch where he was working as a ranch hand. Waddell had learned that Weinlass called himself a prospector, but actually was a notorious gambler suspected of several robberies and had served time in jail for attacking a Ft. Thomas soldier with a knife.

Sheriff Mulvenon was sure he'd found his man and wasted no time riding out to the ranch where Weinlass worked. He found Weinlass mending fences. He showed him the knife and said he wanted to return it to him. The tall, gangly cowboy insisted it was not his knife but he'd seen ones like it in Ft. Thomas. He told the sheriff some Army men from back east had a dozen of them and were selling them to the soldiers at the fort.

Weinlass admitted he'd camped out near House Rock in the spring but never saw anyone. He produced an I.O.U. he'd received in a poker game in Williams (200 miles from House Rock) dated about the time of the murders. Mulvenon checked out Weinlass' story and learned it was true. The cowboy was not his man after all. Mulvenon then headed for Ft. Thomas.

There he met with some of the Clevenger's friends. They told the sheriff that the Clevengers had hired two men to help drive one of their wagons. One was a Texas cowboy named Frank Wilson and the other was a recently discharged soldier from Ft. Thomas named Johnny Johnson. Further inquiries indicated Johnson had bought one of the unusual knives like the one found at the murder scene.

Wires went out to all the sheriffs in Utah and Nevada to look out for Johnson, Wilson, and Jessie Clevenger. When Mulvenon received a wire from a Nevada sheriff that the three were spotted in a village named Duckworth in Nye County, Nevada, Mulvenon was immediately on the stage to Duckworth, Nevada. There he found Johnny Johnson gambling in a local saloon. He dropped the knife on the table in front of Johnson and asked, "this yours"?

Trembling, Johnson denied the knife was his. Mulvenon told him it was used in a murder and that he knew it was Johnson's. Finally, Johnson did admit the knife belonged to him, but insisted he had not committed the murders. He said Wilson was the killer.

Johnson explained that Wilson wanted Jessie and had made several attempts to seduce her. She'd resisted causing her father and Wilson to get into a big fight. Wilson killed the Clevengers, burned their wagon and divided the Clevenger's money with him (Johnson). They parted company in Duckworth. The last Johnson knew they were headed for Oakley, Idaho, where friends of Wilson owned a ranch.

Mulvenon arrested Johnson and sent him back to Prescott with his deputy. He then caught the next stage to Oakley, Idaho, where it took him no time at all to find Wilson and Jessie Clevenger. They were working on a ranch under the names of Mr. and Mrs. Frank Wilson.

Wilson denied everything at first but after the sheriff took Jessie aside, it quickly became apparent she was not with Wilson of her own free will. She was terrified of him. After interviewing her alone, the truth came out. She confirmed most of what Johnson had said about the murders. She told the sheriff that Wilson had been after her since the family left Ft. Thomas. It finally came to a head near House Rock when her father ordered Wilson to leave. The night of the murders Jessie awoke to her mother's screams. She ran to their tent and saw Johnson standing over her father who lay in a pool of blood. Wilson ordered Johnson to drag Jessie out of the tent, which he did. Jessie heard her mother scream again—then silence.

Wilson ran out of the tent, grabbed Johnson's hunting knife, and returned to the tent.

The next thing Jessie knew Wilson and Johnson were burying her parents and setting their wagon on fire. After dividing the $2,000 taken from her parent's tent, Wilson beat her, threatening to kill her too if she gave them any trouble. She virtually became Wilson's prisoner. The message she left for her parents in Kanab was meant to throw the sheriff off their trail. She said Johnson and Wilson parted company in Duckworth.

During their trial in Prescott Wilson confirmed that Johnson was not involved in the murders. The jury did not believe him. The two were convicted and sentenced to hang.

As they stood together on the scaffold, a messenger rode up with a reprieve for Johnson from Governor Zulick, thanks to the efforts of Johnson's attorney.

As Johnson was led off the scaffold to be taken to Yuma Prison, he glanced back at his friend. By then Wilson's body was jerking spasmodically at the end of the hangman's rope.

The last and most famous of Sheriff Mulvenon's accomplishments was the shootout at the Perkins' store in Pleasant Valley that put an end to the infamous Graham-Tewksbury feud. It was written of him afterwards that: "Sheriff Billy's fighting blood was up and his shotgun roared, bringing to a climax one of the most frightful episodes in Arizona history."

After Sheriff William Mulvenon retired as sheriff he organized the first ice plant in Prescott and was one of the organizers and primary stockholders of Arizona Brewing Company. Along with other family members he owned and operated a bar and rooming house on the corner of Gurley and Granite Streets. He also served two terms in the territorial legislature. In 1894 he was married for the first time to a woman named Ella, 16 years his junior. They had no children.

Mulvenon died on May 26, 1915 of Bright's Disease, a deadly inflammation of the kidneys. He was 64 years old at the time.

* * * *

SHERIFF WILLIAM OWEN "BUCKEY" O'NEILL (1889-1890)
"He had more friends than any peace officer has ever had," recalled an old timer who knew him well. "That Irish wit made you like him the first time you laid eyes on him.

He was full of fun, fight and fearlessness. Soft hearted as a baby when dealing with women or an orphaned child. Let some bully start putting the screws on a helpless widow, or a fella down on his luck, that bully better turn tail and run, or he'd be skinned alive by Buckey O'Neill."

Tall, handsome and dark complexioned, with a neatly trimmed mustache that curled around the edges of his full mouth, Buckey O'Neill cut a dashing figure whether strolling the streets of Phoenix, Tombstone or Prescott. Of all the famous and admired Sheriffs who ever donned a badge in Yavapai County, Buckey O'Neill was by far the most legendary.

William "Buckey O'Neill
—ASLA

William Owen O'Neill was the first child born to John Owen and Mary McMenimem O'Neill in St. Louis, Missouri on February 2, 1860. While he was still at his mother's breast his father marched off to the Civil War, soon becoming a member of Thomas Francis Meager's famous Irish Brigade. This brigade proved themselves gloriously on the battlefields time and time again, from the Battle of Bull Run to the Battle of Fredericksburg.

In that last battle, John O'Neill fell gravely wounded. A ball penetrated his right shoulder and passed through his right lung. No one expected him to live. But John O'Neill was a strong willed and tough young Irishman, who had survived the devastating potato famine in his homeland before immigrating to America. He did endure and lived to be 64, fathered three more children, educated himself and worked as a clerk in several offices for the United States government. His first born, William, inherited many of his father's courageous traits.

In Washington, D.C., where his family moved after the war, William was educated in public schools where he learned legal shorthand and typesetting. He grew to manhood filled with self-confidence, a ready wit, a craving for adventure and a nervous, restless spirit.

At the age of 18, he read a series of articles in the *Washington Star* by Charles C. Fremont, who had recently been appointed governor of Arizona Territory. Fremont wrote glowingly of the potential in Arizona for any ambitious hardworking young man. One year later William answered an ad in that same paper describing a company forming for the purpose of settling in Arizona. Before the group left for Arizona Territory, William received notice that he had a job waiting for him in Phoenix as a typesetter for the *Phoenix Herald*. A letter he had written to Governor Fremont had paid off.

The letter William wrote included this compelling and very articulate paragraph: "I am a young lawyer, also a practical printer, and am desirous to reap whatever advantage that may accrue by taking the advice of Horace Greeley and seeking a new home and better fortune in the land of the setting sun." There is conflicting data as to whether William ever attended law school but in those days credentials were rarely checked.

From 1879, when he first arrived in Phoenix, until 1889 when he won the election of Sheriff of Yavapai County, William Owen O'Neill wore more hats and experienced more exciting adventures during those ten years than any three men combined.

Working for the *Herald* provided him some hard cash, but the job did nothing to fulfill his restless need for adventure. With gambling rampant throughout the territory, William took to it like a grizzly bear to salmon; so much so, it became his life long addiction.

Faro was his favorite game of chance and in less than a year, because he so casually placed his bets and went for broke, he earned the gutsy nickname of "Buckey." Gambling hall regulars had a name for his kind of betting: Bucking the tiger, hence his nickname. William liked it, too. From then on, whenever signing letters to family and friends, he always signed his name Buckey.

O'Neill also signed on as a deputy for Phoenix Marshall Henry Garfias. Phoenix had more than its share of stage robbers, gunmen, cattle thieves and claim jumpers. Even legal grand necktie parties, in which the sheriff hanged six men at the same time, didn't slow the lawlessness down.

The job of deputy provided some excitement for O'Neill, but apparently not enough. He also volunteered to join a troop of rangers organized by Major C.H. Vail to go after hostile Indians. In the meantime, the McNeil brothers started a new weekly in Phoenix, the *Arizona Gazette* and invited O'Neill to be their first editor. This he accepted. It did not last long, however. One year later he was in the territory's most lawless town of all, Tombstone, working as a reporter for John Clum's infamous newspaper the *Tombstone Epitaph.*

O'Neill found plenty to write about in Tombstone. He was there when the feud between the Clantons and the Earps started racing toward its deadly conclusion at the O.K. Corral. He gambled often in the Earp brothers' Oriental Saloon where he played poker with Doc Holliday and Bat Masterson. Other notorious characters with whom he became acquainted were Doc Holliday's girlfriend, Big Nose Kate Elder, Curley Bill Brocius, and Johnny Ringo. O'Neill, however, was in Prescott working for *The Arizona Miner*, when the feud between the Earps and the Clanton gang reached its deadly climax.

When O'Neill arrived in Prescott in 1882, the town's population had reached 5,000. It was a saloon town with gambling running day and night. Democrat John H. Marion no longer owned *The Arizona Miner* where O'Neill went to work as editor. It now was a daily with Republican leanings owned by Charles Beach. Beach proved to be just as controversial and cantankerous as Marion ever was. Besides being a newspaperman, Beach also owned a ranch and speculated in railroads. He attracted trouble wherever he went.

In Prescott O'Neill immersed himself in the delightful attractions offered by the gambling establishments along Prescott's notorious Whiskey Row. It wasn't long before his devil-may-care way of gambling made him one of the Row's most popular regulars.

Before long O'Neill took on a second job probably to maintain his gambling addiction. He became the court stenographer for the Yavapai County District Court. Two months after taking the job he found himself caught up in one of the bloodiest episodes in courtroom history. His *Arizona Miner* boss, Charles Beach, was smack in the middle of it.

Water disputes dominated the hearings and trials in the district court in those days. Usually they were lengthy affairs filled with boring legalities. Nevertheless, securing water rights could mean the life or death of a ranch or farm. The case of Kelsey versus McAteer came up during O'Neill's term of employment. The case had been pending for five years and it seethed with hatred.

Mrs. Kelsey, a widow, was suing Patrick McAteer for half the rights to the water in Kirkland Creek, which bordered both of their ranching properties. Mrs. Kelsey's son-in-law was Charles Beach. Beach had been looking after Mrs. Kelsey's interests ever since her husband died. Over the years, he and McAteer had been face to face in one altercation after another. McAteer, known as a dark and brooding man with a fiery temper, had threatened Beach on numerous occasions. It had reached the point that Beach started carrying a gun to protect himself.

On the third day of the trial, December 3, 1883, the courtroom filled early with spectators. Uncle Jimmy Moore and Moses Langley, two other ranchers along Kirkland Creek, were in court that day to testify on behalf of Mrs. Kelsey. District Attorney Charles Rush represented McAteer and Attorney General Clark Churchill represented Mrs. Kelsey.

While O'Neill recorded the proceedings, Rush and Churchill suddenly got into a shouting match during the testimony of Moses Langley. Judge French banged away on his gavel in an attempt to stop them but he was ignored. Then Churchill called Rush a liar. Enraged and beyond control, Rush seized an inkstand and hurled it at Churchill, then leaped over the table separating them and grabbed Churchill by the throat. The courtroom abruptly exploded into a free-for-all with fists, papers and chairs flying everywhere.

O'Neill abandoned his chair and lunged after Rush trying to pull him away from Churchill. Meanwhile, McAteer arose from his chair, pulled out a large hunting knife and marched into the melee. He first thrust his knife into the arm of Uncle Jimmy Moore, severing an artery and penetrating his chest. McAteer's next target was Charles Beach.

Beach barely dodged McAteer's slashing knife, receiving a gash on his neck. In the process Beach fell backwards over a railing.

McAteer's next target was Buckey O'Neill, who looked up just in time to see him coming. O'Neill shoved McAteer backwards and received a slice on his hand in the process. As McAteer started to fall backwards, Charles Beach rose up from the floor, pulled out his .38 Colt revolver, and shot McAteer in the back.

The shot resounding throughout the courtroom brought the bloody pandemonium to an abrupt halt. All the injured participants were rushed to the hospital, or nearby doctor's offices. Uncle Jimmy Moore survived, but lost his arm a few weeks later. McAteer lived only one month completely paralyzed. Beach later was exonerated in the killing of McAteer. The two opposing attorneys who had started it all were fined $500 each.

Two years later Charles Beach bought McAteer's ranch and all of his holdings then adjoined it to his mother-in-law's property. Five years after the infamous courtroom fracas Charles Beach was shot and killed by a man named George Young who accused Beach of having an affair with his wife.

In 1885, O'Neill started his own publication, the *Hoof and Horn*, a medium dedicated to the cattlemen of Yavapai County. That same year, he also fell in love for the first time. Following a whirlwind courtship, he married 20 year-old Pauline Marie Schindler. Soon afterwards he filled the front page of the *Hoof and Horn* with an exalted tribute to his beautiful new wife and to the institution of marriage calling it "unalloyed bliss."

Between 1887 and 1889, O'Neill ran for and won the office of probate judge. During his two terms in office he efficiently cleared a backlog of cases that had been languishing on the books for years. He also invested in the Buckeye Canal System in Phoenix, promoted the territory as a health spa and retirement center, and wrote stories about the West for William Randolph Hearst's new newspaper, the *San Francisco Examiner*. During this time he and Pauline also lost their first child to a premature birth.

In 1889 the popular and prosperous O'Neill decided to throw his hat in the ring for sheriff. He stomped through the mining camps with barrels of whiskey and promises that, if he were elected, he'd tax the powerful railroad interests and make them pay their fair share. This promise was highly appealing to land owners in particular. At that time they were paying $1.52 per acre in taxes while the railroad companies only paid thirty cents per acre on their right-of-ways and land grants. It was an appealing campaign promise, even though no one seemed to realize that sheriffs had no authority to raise anyone's taxes.

When Election Day came the railroads shipped in hundreds of their employees to vote against O'Neill. It did no good. Buckey O'Neill won the office in a landslide.

Two months later he was in hot pursuit of four men who staged one of the most notorious train robberies in Arizona history.

On March 20, 1889 four Hashknife cowboys, who worked for the Aztec Land and Cattle Company, became bored while waiting for the spring roundup. They decided on a lark to rob the Atlantic & Pacific train when it made its regular stop at Diablo Canyon Station to replenish its wood box. The station, located 28 miles east of Winslow, consisted only of a lonely station and a trading post.

It was 11 P.M. on a cold and snowy night when the passenger train pulled into the station. The fireman jumped down first. He bent over to check something beneath the engine when a hand on his shoulder startled him. A pistol poked him in the ribs and a low voice told him to put up his hands. Two of the outlaws, John Halford and J.J. Smith, marched him towards the express car where the other two outlaws, William Sterin and Danial Haverick, were waiting with the engineer already in custody. The engineer was ordered to tell the express messenger to open the door of the express car. When he did he saw four guns pointing at him. Three of the outlaws climbed inside while Halford stood guard over the fireman and engineer.

Inside the express car were two safes, a large metal box and some big mailbags. The express man told the outlaws that one of the safes was time locked. It couldn't be opened. He did open the other safe and the outlaws quickly stuffed empty mailbags with all the loot they could, including the contents of the metal box. By the time they climbed down from the express car, the conductor and a number of passengers had disembarked out of curiosity to see why the train was so delayed. When a volley of bullets was fired over their heads they scurried back inside the train.

Using the fireman, engineer and express man as hostages, the outlaws pushed them toward their waiting horses. After securing the heavy bags onto their mounts the outlaws rode off into the night.

*The Diablo Canyon Posse: (left to Right) Carl Holton,
Jim Black, Sheriff Buckey O'Neil and Ed St. Clair
—ASLA*

News of the robbery did not reach Sheriff O'Neill until the following morning. Immediately he formed a small but capable posse consisting of Jim Black, Carl Holton and Ed St. Clair. The railroad provided transportation for the posse and their mounts to Diablo Canyon. Five miles from the Diablo Canyon Station the posse found the remains of a recent campfire and tracks leading in two directions. Sheriff O'Neill deduced that the outlaws had separated to throw them off their trail but very likely they were headed north for the Arizona Strip. There he knew the outlaws could cross into the badlands of southern Utah and easily be lost in its labyrinth of canyons. As it turned out, he was right.

As the posse thundered toward the Arizona Strip the word quickly spread that they were after four outlaws with a $2,000 reward offered for each of them. Faster than lightening the news of the fabulous reward reached the ears of many. By the time the posse arrived at Lee's Ferry on the Colorado River most of the polygamous communities hidden throughout the canyons of Arizona and Utah had heard the news.

The Johnson family who ran the ferry declared they had not seen nor taken the outlaws across the river. Unbeknownst to them the four outlaws already had secretly crossed the river in the dead of night while the family slept.

The exhausted posse spent the night at the ferry crossing. In the predawn hours they were awakened by a young rider from Cannonville, Utah Territory. He proclaimed that the people from his town had all four outlaws surrounded and for the sheriff to come quickly and bring them their $8,000 reward.

When the posse arrived in Cannonville later that day they found an embarrassed group of townspeople. The outlaws had turned the tables on them and escaped, shooting up their small community as they rode away.

For the next five days the posse tracked the outlaws into Glen Canyon, traveling through its confusing twists and turns and running into numerous dead ends. Finally on March 31st, eleven days and 600 miles of travel after the train robbery, they spotted the outlaws encamped in a deep canyon called Wahweep. The only way out of the canyon would be right past them. Realizing they had the advantage, O'Neill admonished his posse not to kill the outlaws. He wanted them alive. Shoot their horses instead if necessary he told them. O'Neill suspected the outlaws had buried much of their loot. It was too big a haul to travel with in a hurry. He knew if they killed the outlaws they would never find out where the stolen loot was hidden. As it turned out, he was right again.

O'Neill stepped boldly into the open and told the surprised outlaws they were under arrest. Gunfire erupted immediately. Two of the outlaws, Smith and Havrick, scrambled up a canyon wall and disappeared down the other side as bullets flew all around them. The other two surrendered.

For the next two days Smith and Havrick eluded their pursuers. Starved, thirsty and walking barefoot on swollen feet, Smith and Havrick reached a water tank not far from Lee's Ferry. Drinking their fill, they hid themselves among some boulders and collapsed into an exhausted sleep. It was there that the posse found and captured them but not before another brief gunfight.

Realizing that taking their prisoners back the way they had come would be too much of a risk, O'Neill decided to take them to Melford, Utah and from there board a train for Salt Lake City. They would return the long way round to Prescott. From Salt Lake City they planned to ride the train to Denver, then to Albuquerque, and on to Prescott. The posse had no idea that their troubles were far from over.

Newspapers throughout the West carried the exciting news of the daring capture of the four outlaws by Sheriff Buckey O'Neill and his courageous posse. While the four outlaws rested behind bars in Salt Lake City, O'Neill and his men were wined and dined and hailed as heroes. More celebrations awaited them in Denver. By the time they boarded the train for Albuquerque O'Neill and his men had hangovers.

They rode in their own private car. The handcuffed and shackled prisoners sat facing one another. O'Neill allowed their handcuffs to be removed as the train pulled out of Denver. It was a big mistake. Exhausted, the posse members drew lots to determine who would stand guard over the prisoners first while the others slept. Hours later as the train began its chugging assent up Raton Pass around midnight all four members of the posse were fast asleep.

J.J. Smith, the smallest of the outlaws, had been wiggling his foot around in his boot for hours. He realized he could pull his foot out of his shackled boot. He waited patiently until all the posse members started snoring and then he did just that. His fellow prisoners tried to do the same but to no avail. They helped Smith quietly raise the window and watched enviously as he jumped out into the darkness. The cold blast of air from the window soon awakened the posse.

O'Neill pulled the cord to stop the train. For the next hour everyone searched the area for Smith but he was long gone. Soon after the train arrived in Albuquerque, O'Neill organized another posse led by Holton and St. Clair while he and Black continued on to Prescott with the rest of the gang. After two weeks of futile searching Holton and St. Clair gave up and returned to Prescott.

Smith in the meantime staggered through the cold night dragging the shackled right foot. Apparently the shackle was too tight for him to free his other foot.

After a few days of walking Smith came across two hobbled horses. He helped himself to one of them. That night a late spring blizzard caught him unawares. As he plodded along through the storm he came across a young schoolteacher lost and staggering about in the snow. He gave her a ride to the farm where she was boarding. As the door opened and the grateful farmer ran out with a lantern to greet them, the lantern light fell upon Smith's shackled boot. Although this sparked some suspicion the grateful teacher and farmer offered Smith a meal and bed by the fire. He politely declined and galloped off into the darkness.

The next morning a party of riders arrived searching for their stolen horse. Upon hearing about the bareback riding cowboy with a shackled foot the riders took off after Smith. They tracked him all the way to the Texas line. The riders appealed to the authorities in Texas for assistance and within days Smith was captured and soon returned to Prescott. But, the story does not end there.

The big question during the Grand Jury hearings and subsequent trial was what happened to the loot? And how much did these cowboys actually get away with? There was only $1,300 among them when they were captured.

Wells Fargo had insured the shipment and downplayed the amount. They claimed the $1,300 was all there was. Further testimony from the express man, railroad and bank officials, and a Phoenix jeweler proved otherwise. The four Hashknife cowboys had gotten away with $100,000 in cash, $40,000 in gold coins, $2,500 in silver coins and considerable jewelry and loose diamonds.

The cowboys insisted they knew nothing about that much loot but no one believed them.

Train robbery carried the death penalty in Arizona but the Wells Fargo officials wrangled a deal and the outlaws were sentenced instead to 25 years in Yuma Prison. Somehow the outlaws knew they'd be getting out a lot sooner than that.

After four years Smith received a pardon and was released first. As he rode out of Yuma a Wells Fargo detective kept him secret company. Instead of streaking north into the area of the robbery Smith went south and signed on as a cowboy for a ranch near Tucson. There he remained for several years.

Havrick was released next. He was stalked to Los Angeles where he also remained for years working odd jobs. When it didn't appear that either of those two would lead them to the loot, the Wells Fargo Company arranged for Halford's pardon. He died shortly afterwards in El Paso, Texas from consumption contracted while in prison.

That left only Sterin to pursue. He proved to be equally disappointing. He went to work on a cattle ranch near Prescott and never ventured north of there.

By 1903 Wells Fargo gave up their surveillance and all hope of recovering the loot from one of the biggest, and most successful train robberies in Arizona history.

Smith eventually married and ran a small cattle ranch near Douglas, Arizona. For years he could barely make ends meet. Then around 1904, a year after the Wells Fargo Company had given up, Smith kissed his wife and two small children goodbye. He told them he had business to attend to and would see them in about a month. When he returned home a month later he was driving a herd of 300 prime Hereford cattle. He built his family a fine home and soon expanded his herd until he owned one of the largest spreads in southern Arizona.

In the meantime Havrick, still living in Los Angeles, no longer was working odd jobs. He, too, seemed to have come into unexplained wealth after 1903 and was now living extravagantly in that city.

Sterin did not live long enough to out wait the Wells Fargo detectives. He joined Buckey O'Neill's Arizona Rough Riders in 1898 and was killed during the Spanish American War.

In 1915 a cache of Wells Fargo money sacks was dug up near Canyon Diablo. They contained thousands of dollars and a considerable amount of gold and silver coins. But this accounted for only one quarter of the missing loot. To this day folks are still looking for the rest of it.

After serving one very successful term as Sheriff, Buckey ran unsuccessfully as a candidate for the U.S. Congress on the Populist ticket in both the 1894 and 1896 elections. His affiliation with the unpopular Populist Party however did not interfere with his winning the office of Prescott mayor in 1897.

The following year, the U.S.S. Battleship Maine was blown up in Cuba's Havana harbor on February 15, 1898. Two months later on April 25, the United States declared war on Spain. O' Neill's wife, Pauline, recalled his reaction to the news:

"When the Maine blew up and the whole nation was discussing the question of the war that might follow, Mr. O'Neill felt that his country would demand his services. A meeting was held here in Prescott on the evening following receipt of the news. Mr. O'Neill again declared that he was ready and willing to shed his heart's last drop for his flag and his country. He had said 'Who would not die for a new star on the flag'?

O'Neill practically suspended all city business to prepare for the coming conflict.

With approval of Governor McCord O'Neill became the force behind and the most energetic champion of the organization known as the Arizona Rough Riders. In the end he also became their principal hero.

On April 26th, one day after war was declared, O'Neill enlisted as a volunteer, the first in the country to do so. One day later he traveled to Phoenix to receive his commission as Captain of the Arizona Rough Riders. Pauline later recalled:

"Until he received his commission, I would not believe he was in earnest. He laughed and joked about going, and I thought the idea that he was needed had left him. On April 28, he was mustered in—the first volunteer in the whole United States to offer his services."

O'Neill believed it his destiny to volunteer for the Spanish American War and he was right. It was his destiny with death.

After Captain O'Neill resigned as mayor he flung himself into the preparations for war with the same zeal that had sent him like a hurricane after the four Atlantic and Pacific train robbers. On the fourth day of May, 1898, with bands playing and flags waving, the entire population of Prescott gathered at Whipple Barracks to see Captain O'Neill and his Rough Rider regiment board a train and ride off to war. Sixty-seven days later he would lie dead on the battlefield near San Juan Hill.

One of Buckey's great admirers was Lt. Col. Theodore Roosevelt. On numerous occasions the future president mentioned O'Neill in his memoirs and book about the Spanish American War:

"As we looked out over the mangled dead following the battle at Guasimas, Captain O'Neill turned to me and said, 'Colonel, isn't it Walt Whitman who says of the vultures, they pluck out the eyes of princes and tear the flesh of Kings'? Just a week later, we were shielding his body from the birds of prey."

Many conflicting stories were told of Buckey's last hour. The one most often repeated is: "As the Spanish fired volleys at them from atop San Juan Hill Buckey, thinking only of the comfort and safety of his men, walked up and down the trenches smoking a cigarette while encouraging his men. They urged him to get down out of danger but he told them that there wasn't a Spanish bullet that could kill him. At that instant, a bullet entered his mouth and exited out the back of his head." He later was buried in Arlington Cemetery not far from the grave of his heroic father. The marble stone marking his grave has this inscription:

William Owen O'Neill
Mayor of Prescott, Arizona
Captain of Troop A, First U.S.
Volunteer Cavalry, Rough Riders
Brvt. Major
Born Feb. 2, 1860. Killed July 2. 1898
At San Juan Hill, Cuba
"Who Would Not Die for a New Star on the Flag."

The Spanish American War ended on December 10, 1898 five months after Buckey's death. As a result of losing the war, Spain lost its control over the remains of its overseas empire—Cuba, Puerto Rico, the Philippine Islands, Guam, and other islands.

* * * *

SHERIFF GEORGE C. RUFFNER (1895-98) (1923-24) (1927-1933)
He was the oldest and longest serving lawman in Arizona history. Standing over six feet, four inches tall, Sheriff Ruffner possessed nerves of steel and a calm demeanor in the face of danger. Outlaws were terrified of him, but his friends and family adored him and considered him loyal, congenial—"a delightful and amusing companion."
In the 1700s, the Ruffner family immigrated to America from Switzerland and settled in Virginia. They prospered as farmers until the Civil War, a war that divided the family. George's father and his three brothers did not agree on the conflict. With the war practically at their doorsteps, the four brothers went their separate ways. Some

joined the Confederate side and some the Union. After the war there was no farm to return to. George's father moved his family to Mason, Illinois, and once again took up farming. George was born there on November 5, 1862. When he turned 18, he was ready for adventure. He left home, traveled to Minnesota, and hired out as a lumberjack driving logging teams.

In the meantime George's uncle, Morris Andrew (Andy), had walked all the way to Arizona after the war. He arrived on the Verde River in 1867. In partnership with two brothers, Angus and Rod McKinnon, Andy staked several claims on Cleopatra Hill where the town of Jerome would eventually be located. But Andy's wife Sara complained bitterly about the hardscrabble life they were living and finally convinced him to return to farming.

Andy and his partners sold their claims on Cleopatra hill to James Douglas for $15,000. The Douglas properties became the Phelps Dodge Company and the Ruffner claims, along with others, evolved into the United Verde mine where $600 million worth of ore was taken out before the mine shut down in 1953.

After paying off debts, Andy took his share of money ($3,500) and moved to the Salt River Valley. Farming there was now prosperous thanks to Jack Swilling's reclamation of the vast irrigation canals once used by the ancient Hohokam people.

Andy wrote to George's father in Madison, Illinois asking if his nephew wanted to join him in Arizona Territory. George left his freighting job and arrived by train at Maricopa Wells where Andy met him. In a matter of months, George knew that farming was not for him.

George traveled north to Prescott, arriving there in 1883. Now 21 years old, he decided to become a cowboy. Cattle ranching was in its heyday then. He already knew horses and how to care for them. He figured that being a cowboy would come naturally to him, and it did.

He went to work for Jake Miller (of the Walker Party and Miller Valley fame) on his ranch in the Big Bug country near Mayer. There he met his first Arizona friend, Jim Parker. Although a top hand, good natured, likable and excellent with horses, Parker also possessed a restless spirit. He loved gambling, heavy drinking, wild women and he was a magnet for trouble. Parker had already served time in a California penitentiary for cattle rustling.

Parker was born in Visalia, California. His mother died when he was eleven leaving a family of three girls and Parker. Parker's despondent father committed suicide shortly after his wife's death leaving his 13 year-old sister, Sadie in charge of her siblings. Sadie married at the age of 15, but Parker and Sadie's husband did not get along. At the young age of 14, Parker lit out to be on his own. He always seemed to find work, and the wrong companions. "I fell in with bad company," he once said. "I lernt to drink, smoke, gamble and run with fast ladies."

Despite the fact that the Parker and Ruffner were polar opposites, this did not deter them from remaining good buddies. Even years later, after Parker turned outlaw and Ruffner became sheriff, Ruffner compassionately shared Parker's last hour with him.

It was Parker who introduced Ruffner to the wild life of Prescott's Whiskey Row and the lure of the gambling tables. Of all the vices Parker introduced Ruffner to, gambling stuck. Much like his predecessor, Buckey O'Neil, Ruffner loved faro and he played with the same cavalier attitude as Buckey once did. On one occasion he lost $1,700 at the faro table. But he must have had his share of good luck, too. Fifteen years after arriving in Prescott, Ruffner owned and operated a 60-team freighting company, a livery stable, a ranch and had already served as a deputy for Sheriff Jim Lowry. He also found himself the new owner of an undertaking business in 1903, which he won in a poker game.

In 1891, Ruffner married Molly Birchett. The *Miner* described the bride as: "*One of the most beloved and successful teachers in the public schools of the county.*" Three years later, Ruffner won his first term as Sheriff by a landslide vote. He soon earned the reputation as a sheriff who fought without a gun whenever possible.

Sheriff Ruffner went after Bugger Bennett, unarmed. Bennett had shot a local doctor with whom he had a grudge. Ruffner tracked Bennett into the Bradshaw Mountains. Standing behind a boulder, Ruffner talked Bennett into surrendering. He told Bennett the doctor wasn't even harmed. A gold pocket watch had defected the bullet. Bennett was so relieved he gave himself up immediately.

Another time, Ruffner went after a notorious highwayman, Lark Pierce. He trailed Pierce for a week but couldn't quite lay his hands on him. Finally Ruffner decided to masquerade as a broken down old prospector. Pierce made no attempt to hide from the dejected looking man passing by. Suddenly Ruffner was behind him, tapping him on the shoulder and swiftly putting him in handcuffs.

Between 1897 and 1900, three events took place in Ruffner's life that launched him into the annals of Arizona's legendary characters.

The first involved his old friend Jim Parker. Parker and Jim Williams held up the Santa Fe Railroad near Peach Springs on February 8, 1897. It was a crime that went terribly wrong. Williams was shot and killed in the robbery attempt. All Parker found in the mail car was $5.00 in cash. They had robbed the wrong car. It had been a lot of trouble for nothing, and Parker knew Sheriff Ruffner would soon be after him. Fourteen days later, Ruffner caught Parker hiding out in Diamond Canyon near Peach Springs and took him back to Prescott for trial.

Parker probably would have gotten off with a light sentence due to the circumstances of the case. But his restless nature got the better of him and he planned an escape with his two cellmates, L.C. Miller, and Cornelio Sarata. They overpowered the jailer, got his keys, and let themselves out. As he passed through the Sheriff's office, Parker picked up a sawed-off shotgun. He was almost out the door when the assistant county attorney Lee Norris spotted them and shouted for help. Parker promptly shot Norris to death.

The trio dashed across the street to Ruffner's livery stable to steal some horses. They held Ed Ruffner, George's brother, at bay while selecting their get-away horses. Parker chose Sure Shot, the Sheriff's prized gelding. The other two outlaws were so scared and in such a hurry, they both climbed on one horse and together, loped hurriedly out of town.

Sheriff Ruffner received word of the escape by telegraph in Congress Junction where he'd gone to investigate a cattle-rustling incident. Commandeering a locomotive, the sheriff rushed back to Prescott to organize a posse. He found the townspeople enraged and ready to form a lynching party. After calming them down, he tried to calm himself. It infuriated him that 28 year-old Norris was killed, and that Parker had had the audacity to steal Sure Shot.

The sheriffs of neighboring counties were notified, Indian trackers and bloodhounds were brought in, and the all-out manhunt for Parker was under way. Parker, riding Sure Shot, managed to outsmart all of them, particularly after he re-shod Sure Shot. He put the horseshoes on backwards.

This confused the trackers for a while but Ruffner soon figured out what Parker had done. Everyone had to start all over again. Parker eluded them for weeks until everyone finally gave up and went home. Ruffner returned to Prescott to rest, too, but he had not given up the chase. By this time, there was a $4,000 reward on Parker's head. Posters, with Parker's picture, went up throughout Yavapai and all neighboring counties.

One such poster ended up at a general store in Tuba City on the Navaho reservation. Two Navahos saw the poster, studied it for awhile, then informed the store keeper that they had seen Parker that morning and knew where he was hiding.

The storekeeper notified Sheriff Ralph Cameron of Coconino County and he notified Ruffner. Parker soon was surrounded and returned to Prescott under heavy guard, along with Miller, his fellow escapee. Miller had already been captured sometime earlier in Jerome and was being held in Flagstaff. The third escapee, Serata, simply disappeared, probably into Mexico.

Parker and Miller had a speedy trial. Miller was sentenced to life imprisonment but was paroled after ten years. Parker was sentenced to death. After all of his appeals had failed, Parker was scheduled to hang on June 8, 1898.

Ruffner often visited his old friend in jail. Parker never seemed bitter or remorseful. He'd gambled and lost, that was his attitude. The night before his death, Ruffner asked Parker what his last wish was. "Well, I don't want any damn last meal," he answered. "I'd like one of my girl friends on Whiskey Row to visit me." Ruffner granted his wish.

Parker had another wish. He wanted Ruffner to do the hanging. "I want to die like a man, and I want a man I respect to pull the lever." Ruffner obliged him.

Sure Shot, Ruffner's beloved horse, was never the same after his ordeal. He was too lame to be ridden again. Rather than put him down, Sheriff Ruffner arranged for him to be pastured in the Salt River Valley on land now owned by the Arizona Biltmore Hotel. There Sure Shot enjoyed a lush life, and when he died, he was buried there. Lester Ruffner, George's younger brother, loved to quip; "well, he's the only Ruffner buried at a swanky resort hotel."

In the summer of 1897, one year before the hanging of Jim Parker, Sheriff Ruffner entered a steer roping and tying contest in Phoenix. The sheriff had helped Prescott's city fathers organize the first "cowboy tournament" in 1888. It became America's first rodeo, and so popular an idea, that it spread throughout the Southwest.

Ruffner was 35 years old when he entered the Phoenix rodeo. He threw his rope at the stampeding steer but missed. The steer charged toward the grandstand filled with people. Ruffner's quick thinking stopped the ferocious beast from rampaging through the crowd. He spurred his horse up alongside the steer, leaped off his horse, grabbed the steer by the horns, twisted its neck and forced him to the ground.

The crowd went wild with delight and relief. A pot of $100 was collected in appreciation, and with the money, a beautiful silver inlaid bridle was purchased and presented to Ruffner. The "bulldogging" that George Ruffner initiated that day provided such excitement it has been a featured event in rodeos ever since.

The third event that sealed Ruffner's reputation as a man of heroic proportions was the great Prescott fire on July 14, 1900.

Apparently a miner overturned an oil lamp at the O.K. Lodging House on Montezuma and Goodwin Streets. The fire could have stopped there with a few buckets of water, but there was no water. The pumping plant one block away was under repair, the pump disconnected and all water shut off. Quickly, the fire raged out of control, threatening the entire business district.

Ruffner leaped into action. He organized dynamiting parties, and removed a burning fuse from a powder charge that was set to blow the entire stock of a powder in a supply store, and all of Prescott, to kingdom come. As the fire swept up Whiskey Row, bar owners, patrons and girls from the Row removed several pianos and as much whiskey as possible. Bars were soon set up across the street in the Courthouse Plaza. Whiskey was served throughout the night while the Whiskey Row girls cheered the fire fighters on by singing, *"There's a Hot Time in the Old Town Tonight."*

Most of the buildings along Montezuma, Gurley, Cortez and Goodwin Streets were destroyed before the fire was finally stopped. Ruffner organized a tent city on the Courthouse Plaza grounds and soon tents and pine shacks were doing a brisk business. He also set up a banking operation on the Plaza's bandstand in order to accommodate the burned out merchants. Damage was estimated at more than one million dollars. Few if any merchants carried insurance. Nevertheless, rebuilding started immediately, all with brick and stone. No more wood. And it was the people of the town who raised the money necessary to rebuild it.

A new water system was established by the following year. More than a half a million gallons a day was pumped into Prescott's new municipal reservoir from Del Rio Springs, 19 miles away. Prescott would not be caught without water again.

Prohibition was in full swing when Sheriff Ruffner took office for a second time in 1923. He hated having to catch moonshiners and pour out their whiskey, but it was the law. He tended to look the other way if widows were making moonshine but sometimes he had to arrest them, too, and it nearly broke his heart.

Sheriff George Ruffner
—ASLA

It was common for 'do gooders' to come running into his office to report someone moonshining. Ruffner tended to respond with, "is that a fact?" If they kept insisting, he promised them he'd take care of it. Then he would load two saddle horses into his homemade trailer, hitch it to his Buick car, and drive around the Plaza area three times. This gave the moonshiners plenty of notice to pack up and clear out. Ruffner believed in "live and let live."

Finally it reached the point where, if a do-gooder ran into his office saying, "I know where there's a still," Ruffner's typical response became: "Do you? Well, I know where there are twenty. Run along, now."

When he was 65 years old, Ruffner was elected sheriff for a third and last time in 1927. Five years later, while still in office, he contracted pneumonia after chasing a kidnapper for weeks. The kidnapper escaped to Wisconsin where he was finally captured and held. Soon after Ruffner returned from Wisconsin with his prisoner, he died on July 26, 1933.

His funeral was one of the largest in anyone's memory. People from all walks of life came to pay their respects, from high government officials, to miners and farmers from throughout Yavapai County.

In 1958, twenty-five years after his death, Sheriff George C. Ruffner was inducted into the newly created National Cowboy Hall of Fame in Oklahoma City. His name was added to a roster of men who included Lewis and Clark, Buffalo Bill Cody, and President Teddy Roosevelt.

* * * *

SHERIFF JOHN L. MUNDS (1899-1902)

John L. Munds' appearance belied his toughness. He looked younger than his years so everyone called him Johnny. Once he entered law enforcement he quickly gained a reputation for pursuing outlaws with the resolve of a bloodhound. While serving as Sheriff George C. Ruffner's deputy, Munds earned his reputation for toughness and was enthusiastically endorsed to replace Ruffner as sheriff in 1899.

Before being elected sheriff Munds had been trained in business. He managed his own and his father's livestock and made investments in mining. Several northern Arizona landmarks bear his family's name: Munds' Trail, Munds' Park and Munds' Mountain.

John L. Munds was born in 1868, the youngest of three children born to William and Sara Munds in Rosebud, Oregon. When John was seven years old his family loaded up two covered wagons, gathered their herd of 110 cattle and 15 horses, and headed to Arizona Territory. By the spring of 1876 they had established a ranch in Spring Creek in the Verde Valley. Several years later John's father went into partnership with the four Willard brothers who owned a large herd of cattle and horses in the upper Verde Valley. The Willard brothers also helped their widowed mother Mary care for her substantial homesteaded farm near the future town of Cottonwood. By 1885 the Willard brothers' youngest sister Frances (who had graduated from the Maine Central Institute in Pittsfield, Maine) had returned to Arizona to be with her mother.

Frances loved western life. An accomplished horsewoman, she received a beautiful gray horse from her brothers when she returned home. She named him Fred. Her brothers also had a sidesaddle made for her. Proper ladies never rode astride in those days. Frances often rode the range with her brothers who remained in partnership with the Munds family for several years. When Frances first met John Munds on the range one day sparks flew and neither of their lives would ever be the same again. The summer of 1885 became one of the happiest ever for the two young lovers. They knew from the moment they met they would spend the rest of their lives together.

They had to wait five years to tie the knot, however. John's father insisted he attend business school in Stockton, California. Frances promised to wait for him and while he was away she became a pioneer schoolteacher in Pine, Stoddard, Mayer and Jerome. Finally on March 5, 1890 the two were scheduled to marry in Frances' mother's beautiful newly-built home in Cottonwood. However several mishaps occurred that nearly put off their wedding day.

Shortly before the wedding day Frances and John set off in a buckboard for Prescott to get their marriage license and buy wedding rings. They had to cross the Agua Fria River near Cherry Creek that a few days before had flooded and now was a muddy morass. John thought nothing of plunging into the deep water with his two-horse team. Frances was terrified but concealed her fright. Just as they were about across one of the horses stepped into a hole and went down, his head barely above water. John immediately jumped onto the other horse's back, leaped over his head to the bank and grabbed the downed horse by the bridle. With the help of the other horse he pulled the first horse to his feet and onto the muddy bank. Then John climbed over the horses' backs again, leaped into the wagon and grabbed a shovel. He pulled off his shirt cuffs handing them to Frances before climbing over the horses' backs once more to dig their way through the mud to safety. Frances was so terrified she dropped the cuffs in the river and hardly noticed them float away with John's gold cuff links still attached. When they were finally on their way again John looked at his future bride and realized she was on the verge of hysteria. 'Gee, honey', he said. 'I didn't know you were so scared'.

On their wedding day everyone was present except the minister. After a long wait Wallace Willard (Frances' cousin) mounted his horse promising to bring the preacher back — 'dead or alive'. When he reached the Middle Verde River the river was in flood stage. The Reverend Windes lived across the river and had been too frightened to attempt the crossing. Wallace, completely undeterred, swam his horse across the raging waters and ordered the Reverend Windes to mount his horse promising to get him safely through.

Wallace tied their two horses together and told the reverend to hang on tight. Chalky white and trembling with fear, the reverend did as he was told. Wallace got them through safely but after reaching the other side the poor preacher was in such a state of shock, he nearly collapsed. Wallace wrapped him in a blanket and they rode swiftly back to the wedding party. Finally, decked out in borrowed, dry clothes, the reverend performed the wedding at 8:00 p.m. Everyone enjoyed a delicious banquet and a good time, including Reverend Windes. John Munds didn't know it at the time, but he had just married a woman who one day was destined to write a brilliant page in Arizona history, just as he would.

When Sheriff Ruffner appointed John Deputy Sheriff in 1885, John sold his cattle and some of his horses and moved his family to Prescott. The family now included their first-born son, William

Harold. They would have two more children, Sara and Mary Frances. John served Sheriff Ruffner as deputy for the next three years.

Shortly after his appointment, Ruffner sent John to investigate a murder in Seligman. The perpetrator was William Faught (the press insisted on calling him Bill Fott), who had shot and killed A.N. Carter in the back for no apparent reason. Carter worked for the railroad and was a well-liked family man with three children. When Munds arrived in Seligman two days later he found Faught in the hands of an angry mob ready to lynch him. The mob paid little heed to the youthful looking deputy and already had the hangman's rope slung over a tree limb. It took raw courage and grim determination on Munds' part to face down the mob and save Fought's life, which he did. Faught was tried, convicted and sentenced to life in Yuma Prison. He got out seven years later. Shortly after his release he was shot and killed by unknown assailants believed to be friends of the murdered Carter.

Munds continued to show his grit time and time again and he never let up when going after a criminal. When everyone else gave up on the pursuit of Ruffner's outlaw friend Jim Parker, Munds stuck it out until Parker was finally apprehended. He showed the same relentless determination after he was elected sheriff in 1899.

In the summer of 1899, only months after his election, Munds found himself involved in one of the longest manhunts in Arizona history. On July 2, 1899 two of Camp Verde's most respected young men were shot and killed by a "mysterious stranger." R.M. 'Mack' Rodgers and Clint Wingfield owned the Camp Verde Military Provisions Store, also called the Sutlers Store.

The murders took place on a warm July night. Mack Rogers was sitting on the porch of the store chatting with two friends. The mysterious stranger moved on to the porch. There was a casual exchange of chit-chat, when Mack suddenly seemed to recognize the stranger. He jumped up and ran to get his gun from inside the store with the stranger hot on his heels. Once inside the store the stranger shot Mack in the back and killed him.

Wingfield, working in the back room, rushed out to see what the shooting was about and found himself face to face with the killer. The killer promptly shot Wingfield in the stomach, severing his spine. It was a mortal wound and two hours later, Clint Wingfield was dead, killer unknown.

Clint Wingfield and Mack Rogers
—Courtesy of BWM

It later was learned there had been threats on Mack Rodgers' life. A few months before the shooting, Mack had given evidence against an outlaw named Oscar Wade in a horse stealing trial. Wade was a member of an outlaw gang and even though he was acquitted, he swore vengeance against Mack Rodgers. Wade did not fit the description of the killer, but a member of his gang did. Months later this gang member was identified as the notorious Black Jack Ketchum.

The Black Jack gang rivaled any other group of outlaws for brazenness, brutality, robbing, and killing with impunity. Jack Christianson, (AKA: Black Jack) was the original leader of the gang but after he was shot and killed, Tom Ketchum (a member of his gang) took over the leadership and the name, Black Jack.

Tom Ketchum was born in San Saba County, Texas in 1866 and raised in New Mexico. He and his outlaw brother Sam ran away from their brutal father's farm at an early age and became cowboys. It apparently was Tom's love life that turned him into an outlaw and left him 'unhinged' for the rest of his life. A young woman named Cora had been two-timing him. She wrote him a cruel letter ridiculing him and announcing she had run off and married someone else.

Tom read the letter to his cowboy friends, then took his six-gun and began beating himself on the head with the butt of it until blood ran down his face. The whole time, he admonished himself for being so foolish as to ever trust a woman. In front of his dumbfounded cowboy friends, he continued to beat himself until he was unconscious. Shortly thereafter he launched into his vindictive, criminal career, specializing in robbing stagecoaches and trains. His one virtue was his loyalty to his gang members hence his carrying out Oscar Wade's vendetta against Mack Rogers. At the time of the Camp Verde murders no one knew any of this.

Camp Verde had no telephones at the time so Harvey Hance saddled Clint Wingfield's horse and rode to Prescott to notify Sheriff Munds. The Sheriff hurried to Camp Verde and gathered a posse together including Indian trackers and members of the Wingfield family. They quickly realized they were following a killer on an unshod horse. Munds measured the size of the killer's boots from prints near the store. He also knew the measurements of his horse's hooves. Plus, he had a full description of the killer from witnesses at the store the night of the killing.

For more than a month the posse tracked the suspect in an area bounded on the west by Camp Verde, the north by Flagstaff, the south by Payson and the east by the territorial line at New Mexico. The posse was never sure if they were after the right man or even the same man. The search continued for almost two months.

Finally Munds sent notices to every newspaper in Arizona and New Mexico Territory:

"$2750 reward for the arrest or capture of the murderer of Mack Rodgers and Clint Wingfield of Camp Verde, Yavapai County, Arizona, July 2, 1899. The following is a description of the murderer, his wearing apparel and outfit:

"Age–32-36 years old. Weight—about 175 pounds. Height—5 feet 10 inches—Well built—Dark complexioned—Dark brown hair and eyes, mustache and beard—quick nervous actions. Wears black hat, brown shirt, dark pants and cut-away coat. Wears canvas belt with double row of cartridges. Colt .45 in right front pocket of pants without scabbard, wears spurs with a long shank made of a file. Carries a .30-.40 rifle in a scabbard on saddle, has a double cinch, with hand cinch off. Limber bit bridle with rope reins. Carries a gallon canteen and large field glasses. If arrested, I will go and get him from any jail in the United States or Mexico."

Signed, Johnny L. Munds—Prescott, Arizona. Sheriff of Yavapai County.

After having searched unnumbered canyons, mesas and hiding places for almost two months, the posse had dwindled to only a few. The horses were exhausted and their riders even more. Munds dismissed them and boarded a stagecoach to Luna Valley, New Mexico Territory.

At the border he took a train to Albuquerque, and from there, sent telegrams to his family and his deputy in Prescott, telling his whereabouts. Johnny Munds was not ready to give up the search.

John's deputy wired him back immediately that a man answering the murderer's description had attempted to rob a train near Folsom, New Mexico. His right arm, almost shot off during the robbery attempt, had been amputated. The outlaw was recovering in Santa Fe's Penitentiary Hospital. He had gangrene and was not expected to live. He already had admitted that he was the outlaw Black Jack Ketchum.

Munds immediately wired Governor N.O. Murphy for extradition papers, and received them. But U.S. Marshall Foracker refused to accept them. Munds visited Black Jack and asked him if he had committed the murders in Camp Verde. Although he said no, Munds didn't believe him. Black Jack matched the description of the murderer too perfectly.

Munds returned to Prescott and again requested extradition papers. Before he was able to serve them, he received word that Mr. Ketchum had already been convicted of train robbery, a capital offence, and had been hanged in Clayton, New Mexico, on April 25, 1901. His shocking hanging would go down in the history of Western outlawry.

The night before he was to die, Black Jack had fried chicken and apple pie for dinner. He asked for a fiddler to play for him as he mounted the scaffold. As he stood on the scaffold facing the crowd, he had two things to say: "I'll be in hell before you have breakfast, boys, and—let 'er rip."

Sheriff Garcia, who had had a few belts of whiskey that morning, swung the hatchet to cut the rope to the trap door, but missed it. His second attempt succeeded but not as everyone expected.

The trap door opened and Black Jack plummeted through, landing on the ground below. There was a collective gasp as everyone surged forward, confused. Why wasn't Black Jack's body swinging in the air? They could see lots of blood spurting through his black hood. When the doctor pulled off the hood, a shock wave rippled through the crowd. Black Jack's head had come completely off.

In order to bury him in one piece, the doctor sewed his head back on. So ended the career of outlaw Black Jack Ketchum, remembered more for his death than for his life.

Johnny Munds did not run for the office of sheriff again. He returned to cattle ranching, became the owner of a mine in Chloride in 1912 and later operated another mine in Oatman, Arizona.

In the meantime, Frances was cutting a wide swath as a major leader for women's suffrage in Arizona. She served as state chairman of the Arizona's Women's Suffrage Organization. She led the campaign that resulted in the Nineteenth Amendment being approved in Arizona giving women the right to vote in 1912. In 1914 she was elected State Senator, the first woman in Arizona to be elected as such, and the second woman in the United States to serve in an elected office.

In 1942 the Sheriff's Magazine named Buckey O'Neil, Johnny Munds, George Ruffner and Billy Mulvenon the most outstanding sheriffs in the history of Yavapai County, Arizona.

After 1909, the term 'Outlaw' became obsolete.

CHAPTER FOUR - PART TWO
Ladies of the Night

"They ride around in fancy carriages, dressed in high fashion, and go to expensive restaurants. Someone does their washing and cleaning, while I...I work and slave day and night, and have one baby after another," so observed many a "good" woman on the Western frontier.

Of course there would be envy and resentfulness toward the apparent high life of the 'sporting ladies'. A good woman had few choices in life then, particularly if she was single. She could take in laundry, clean houses, sew for others, wait tables or, if she had an education, teach...for half the pay of male teachers.

The settling of the West was an outdoor adventure that excluded females economically. Prostitution brought wealth to a few, but for most it was a miserable career choice under wretched circumstances, dictated by the lack of opportunity. For every high-living sporting gal, there were thousands of miserable girls who lived in squalor and despair, selling their diseased and drug addicted bodies for pennies on the streets, or from the doorways along crib row.

Despite this, prostitutes played an important role in taming the West. They served a need in the rough, raw camps that sprouted into cattle, mining and railroad towns. Like everyone else coming West, these women hoped for something better than what they had. Almost all were poor and young. The reasons that propelled them into this life included poverty, bad marriages, boredom, and desperation.

Prostitutes on the frontier were as status conscious as people anywhere, with 'parlor houses' occupying the top rung of their ladder. Courtesans there could spend more time talking, drinking, eating, and gambling than 'working'. Next down the ladder was the brothel, a much smaller operation where the madam prided herself on having clean linens and towels and frilly curtains on her windows. After that a woman could work in dance halls, saloons, or lower class "hurdy-gurdies." From there it fell to the lowest of low, the dismal 'cribs' lining the red light districts of most frontier towns and cities. No matter how high on the ladder a prostitute may have started, most eventually ended up in the cribs, or worse, as streetwalkers.

The most enterprising woman went where the action—and gold— was. They reinvented themselves and lived pretty much as they pleased, unrestricted. They saved enough to open their own parlor houses and made a fortune having other women working for them, while selling liquor and food at exorbitant prices. As madams, they paid taxes, gave money to local charities, put kids through college, bought and sold real estate and played major economic roles in building frontier towns. They may have been classified as bad women but often they did a lot of good. Most madams earned the respect and admiration of the men who paid for their services because those services included fine food and drinks and entertainment in luxurious surroundings, along with elegant female company. Unfortunately whenever these madams decided to take on a lover or a husband, they did not always choose wisely.

* * * *

BELGIAN JENNIE

Belgian Jennie of Jerome was one such madam. Also known as Jennie Banters, she was a smart businesswoman and at one time was reputed to be the richest woman in Arizona.

She arrived in Jerome in the 1890s and built three parlor houses. After being burned out twice during Jerome's frequent fires, her parlor house was saved the third time after Jennie rushed to the firehouse and promised the volunteer firemen 'free passes' to her house if they saved her place of business first. The firemen rose to superhuman efforts and Jennie's house was saved.

Once Jennie's Jerome parlor house was thriving, she decided to open another one in Goldroad, a mining community south of Kingman. In 1899, Jose Jerez stumbled on a gold crop there while tracking his burros. Goldroad became a prosperous boomtown and by 1931, more than $7,000,000 worth of gold had been mined there. It was just the sort of place to attract an enterprising businesswoman like Jennie.

After opening her new establishment, she met a charming gambler named C.C. Leigh. For several years Mr. Leigh lived with Jennie. Unfortunately he was addicted to opium. After several years of putting up with his opium habit, Jennie kicked him out.

One Sunday morning in 1905, Leigh was hanging round a saloon owned by Jennie. He'd been drinking all night, and announced to the few patrons at the bar that Jennie owed him money and he intended to get it.

He stomped upstairs to Jennie's room and kicked in her door. He was armed and walked in firing his gun. As Jennie ran screaming and begging for her life, Leigh followed her out to the street still firing. Jennie was hit three times in the back before falling to the ground. Leigh went back inside the saloon to reload his gun. By then all the terrified spectators were hiding under anything they could find.

Leigh marched back out to the street where he noticed Jennie stirring. He went right up to her and fired again at her head. He then placed the gun to his own breast, and after selecting the right spot, shot himself producing a slight wound. Next he stretched out on the street beside Jennie and put his hat over his face in order to block the sun. Constable Fred Brown soon was on the scene. He yanked Leigh up off the ground and threw him in jail. Mr. Leigh was hanged the following year for his dastardly crime.

* * * *

SAMMIE DEAN

The murder of Marie Juanita (Sammie) Dean sent shock waves through Jerome in 1931. Born in Texas in 1901, Sammie was a divorced woman who became a popular courtesan in Jerome. Sammie wrote to her family in Texas that she had been dating the Mayor's son, ten years her junior. She said he wanted to marry her but she turned him down. This infuriated him, she wrote, and he had threatened her.

According to the death certificate, an unknown assailant had strangled Sammie some time between 8:30 A.M. and 2:P.M. on July 7, 1931. Before her body was removed, members of the coroner's panel met that night at the scene of the crime. According to the police report, no fingerprints or other evidence was taken because "everyone already knew who did it"—Wes Owens, the mayor's son.

Wes worked in one of the copper mines and while considered a nice fellow, he could be mean when drunk. His family was prominent and among Jerome's early pioneers. There would be no justice for Sammie—she was a prostitute. Wes Owens was told to get out of town and shortly afterwards he went to Ajo, Arizona where he worked in the copper mines. The case was branded 'unsolved'—then closed.

* * * *

JEROME'S OWN JACK THE RIPPER

The story of Jerome's own 'Jack the Ripper' filled headlines in 1904. L.W. Watson, an employee of the United Verde smelter, went to the Tenderloin District of Jerome one night and took up with Fannie Howard. After visiting several saloons that night they went to her room around 2:A.M. Fannie awoke at 6:A.M. with Watson's hand around her throat, and his other hand flourishing a knife.

His first cut was from her ear to her chin. He continued to slash at her while she fought for her life. She finally pushed him to the floor and begged for him to call the doctor. In response to her pleading, he demanded she return the five dollars he had given her then he went after her again, laying open her cheeks and exposing her teeth. The fact that she was very 'fleshy' was all that saved her.

Watson then ran from her house and was tracked by Officer Fred Hawkins to the Montana Hotel. While Hawkins was describing the assailant to the desk clerk, Watson walked up and asked for his bill. Hawkins promptly arrested him. Watson seemed surprised and asked why he was being arrested.

After checking his room at the hotel, they found the water in his slop jar cloudy with blood. When Watson was stripped, his underclothing was found to be soaked in blood.

He was taken to the hospital where Fannie positively identified him as her assailant. Despite suffering 91 slashes, Fannie survived her ordeal. Watson's crime, as it turned out, was similar to ones that had been inflicted upon other women of easy virtue in Tucson, Phoenix, and Los Angeles before coming to Jerome. Several of his victims in those cities identified Watson's photograph as well. Miraculously, no one had died from their wounds. Watson was sentenced to life in prison where he eventually died.

* * * *

TWO PRESCOTT MURDERS

Prescott had its share of murder and mayhem surrounding its denizens of the red light district, too. In 1870 Mary Anschutz was shot and killed by William Gertrude after sharing a night of debauchery. In the middle of the night Mr. Girtrude pulled a gun on her and demanded his ten dollars back, which she refused. A scuffle followed and Mary screamed for help. Her neighbor, G.W. Bernard, had just gone to bed when he heard Mary's screams and ran to her house. He found Mr. Girtrude sitting on her bed holding a revolver and Mary sprawled on the floor. Bernard ordered Mr. Gertrude to go home and sleep it off. Instead, Mr. Girtrude took up his demand for money again. When Mary refused once more, he shot her dead—in the presence of Mr. Bernard. Girtrude was quickly apprehended and later sentenced to death.

His victim, Mary, had been one of five women who in 1870 unabashedly told the census taker in Prescott that they were "sporting women." All were around 18 years of age at the time. Mary and Ellen "Nellie" Stackhouse were both murdered before the year ended. A third, Mollie Shepard, was one of only two survivors of the infamous Wickenburg Stage Massacre.

The murders of Mary and Nellie so incensed John H. Marion, the flamboyant editor/owner of the *Arizona Miner*, that he admitted he was ready to help organize a lynching party for the first and only time in his life. There are no records of what happened to the other two sporting ladies, Maggie Taylor and Jennie McKennie.

* * * *

GABRIELL DOLLIE WILEY

Denver historians can boast all they want to about their colorful frontier madams, Jennie Rogers and Mattie Silks, or Dodge City, Kansas can brag about their colorful madam, Squirrel Tooth Alice. But Prescott had a madam who topped them all: Gabriell Dollie Wiley.

'Gabe', as she was known the first half of her life (and 'Dollie' in her later years) is known to have married four men and purportedly, murdered each one of them. Her nephew, Gil Layral, a retired food service worker in California believed there were probably twice that many. "It's hard to say how many there were (murdered)," he said in a phone interview after her death in 1962. "Probably eight. Rat poison—that was her preferred method."

Gabe was born in France in 1890. When asked about her past, she claimed to have lost her mother in the great San Francisco earthquake of 1906, which left her alone to fend for herself at the age of 15. She managed to get herself to the gold fields of Nevada where she tried to make her living working in hash houses. Then, she said, she started turning tricks at night to make ends meet and found she was good at it. Being pretty, petite and having a French accent quickly made her very popular. She was smart enough to save her money and find her first husband, a prizefighter name Kid Curry.

The couple arrived in Prescott in 1909. Although only 19 at the time, Gabe soon was operating her first parlor house and making enough money to own fur coats and stash away a fortune in diamonds. Her husband, a gambling man, got into a dispute over a $20 gambling debt and was shot and killed in broad daylight on the streets of Prescott.

Her next paramour was a man named Leonard Topp. By 1915 Topp had run off with one of Gabe's sporting girls. The two also had robbed Gabe of her diamonds.

Gabe hired detectives who tracked Topp to Los Angeles where he had bought a liquor store. Dressed in her finest furs and silks, and carting a fur muff with a pistol concealed inside, Gabe entered the liquor store, came up behind Topp and purred, "Hello Leonard." As the startled man turned, Gabe shot him in the chest—the pistol never leaving her muff. Leonard lived long enough to knock her to the floor where he banged her head on the floor a few times before a strange look crossed his face and he said: "Well, I guess I'm about through for good." At that, he fell across her prone body and died.

Her murder trial was so sensational it filled the headlines of newspapers throughout the West. "I killed him because I loved him," Gabe tearfully testified at her trial. One of Gabe's sporting girls ("a substantial blond" according to the newspapers), named Pearl Valley, described the terrible abuse that Topp had heaped upon Gabe while living with her. "One of his favorite pastimes was to scuff his boots against her," declared Pearl dramatically. This so outraged the all male jury, they took a total of eight minutes to declare Gabe "not guilty."

A famous California reporter named Adela Rogers St. Johns had covered the trial from the beginning. After Gabe's not guilty verdict was announced, she wrote: "The jury understood that with men like Leonard Topp, homicide was not only justifiable, but obligatory."

Four years later Gabe married again this time to Bernard Melvin. She left him after six months and divorced him four years later, but not before having him arrested for embezzlement. Melvin insisted Gabe had given him the $2,000 but the jury didn't believe him. He was found guilty and served time in jail. He became a broken, reclusive man who earned his living as the caretaker at the Prescott dump. One night several unknown assailants jumped him and nearly beat him to death. The $800 he had hidden in his shack was stolen. No one was ever arrested but most suspected Gabe was behind the attack. Melvin died shortly afterwards of pneumonia.

About the same year of Melvin's death in 1928, Gabe attended a silent movie at Prescott's Elk's Theater entitled *The Red Kimono*, touted as the true story of a notorious prostitute and murderer. To her complete shock and surprise, the movie was about her—and they even used her real name. Gabe was outraged. She sued the producer, Dorothy Davenport Reid, the widow of Wallace Reid one of Paramount's leading silent stars. The lawsuit was unprecedented and drew coverage from coast to coast. Gabe demanded $50,000. She relentlessly dragged the case through the courts until it was finally settled five years later. As a result, Dorothy Reid, lost everything she owned including her West Hollywood mansion.

Gabe Wiley
—SHM

Throughout the 1930s, Gabe continued to operate her high-class parlor house on the second floor of Prescott's Rex Arms Hotel (now the Bank One building). Every night, she escorted her girls around the corner to the Palace Saloon for a nightcap. The late Mary Swartz, whose husband managed the Palace in those days, remembered her well. "She wasn't a floozy," said Mary. "She was plump, pretty and usually wore nice business suits. She had a different shade of red hair each time I saw her, which didn't look too good, but she did take good care of her girls." Mary also stated that Gabe put several of her girls through a business college after they retired from prostitution. "She did a lot for people around here", said Mary. "Everyone liked her, except the Sunday school people."

Between the ages of 50 and 60, Gabe married two more times, both husbands died under strange circumstances. Her next husband was a barber named Everett Fritz. He went completely mad after a few months of marriage to Gabe and ended up in the Arizona State Asylum raving about his gold mine near Prescott, a mine that existed only in his mind. He died a month later at the asylum of what the records described as "general paralysis of the insane."

Gabe's last husband was George Wiley, an ex-bootlegger with a face that "looked like a tomato." On January 23, 1940 George got into a fight with one of Gabe's girls, Mae Grisson. When he lunged at her, she fell off her stool and hit her head on a water cooler. She died two weeks later...a few hours after Gabe visited her in the hospital. George was charged with murder, and released in the custody of Gabe. His trial was set for January.

Apparently Gabe was furious with both of them because a few weeks before Wiley's trial, he also was found dead in their home. He had swallowed a glass of rat poison.

The coroner's jury suspected, given her past, that Gabe purposely had left the glass of rat poison on the kitchen counter but they couldn't prove it. They ruled Wiley's death a suicide, and Mae, it was determined, had died of natural causes.

By the 1940s, Prescott began seriously cracking down on prostitution. Gabe retired and moved to the town of Salome where she opened a café. On Christmas day in 1962 Gabe fell and broke her hip. She was admitted to the Wickenburg hospital where pneumonia was added to her diagnosis. She knew the end was near. She telephoned her old friend Lester Ruffner, a Prescott funeral home operator, and asked if he'd come and bring the Episcopal minister to administer last rights. They arrived in time to help Gabe make peace with her Maker. She died shortly afterwards at the age of 72, was cremated, and her ashes were buried in Prescott beside E.L. Fritz, the husband who went mad.

After World War II the term 'sporting girl' lost its lurid definition. Sporting girls thereafter commonly referred to women who were adept at golf, tennis, and other sports.

Another era had ended.

And so has this book.

RESOURCES

CHAPTER ONE: BEFORE WHITE CONTACT

NORTHEASTERN AND WESTERN YAVAPAI by E.W. Gifford, U. of California Publications in American Archaeology and Ethnology, 1936, Vol. 34

YAVAPAI OF FORT MCDOWELL, U.S. Dept. of Urban Development, Sigrid Khera, editor, Washington, D.C. 1978

JOURNAL OF AMRICAN FOLKLORE, Northeastern and Western Yavapai Myths, by E.W. Gifford, Vol. 36, 1933

1877: ARIZONA AS IT WAS by Hiram C. Hodge, The Rio Grande Press, 1967

THE PHOTOHISTORIC PERIOD IN THE NORTH AMERICAN SOUTHWEST, AD 1450-1700, A review of Yavapai Archaeology by Peter J. Pillis, Jr., Arizona State University, Anthropological Research Papers No. 24, 1981

THE SOCIAL ORGANIZATION OF THE WESTRN APACHE by Grenville Goodman, U. of Arizona Press, Tucson, Arizona

THE YAVAPAI: People of the Red Rocks, People of the Sun by Kate Ruland-Thorne, Thorne Enterprises Publications, Sedona, Arizona, fourth printing, 2001

INTERVIEWS:

David Sine—Yavapai-Apache, Camp Verde, AZ. 1989-90

Mabel Dogka, Yavapai-Apache, Kachina Point Nursing Home, Sedona, Az. 1990

Louis Hood, Bernie Boyd, Sniffen Dickens, Fort McDowell Indian Reservation, Fountain Hills, AZ. 1990

The Elders of the Tribe, Yavapai-Apache Reservation, Clarkdale, AZ. 1989,1990

Nancy Quid, Yavapai Apache Tribe, Prescott, AZ. 1990

Vincent Randall, Tonto Apache historian and educator, Clarkdale, AZ. 1990

Ted Vaughn, Yavapai historian and educator, Prescott, AZ. 1990

CHAPTER TWO: THE INDIAN WARS

COMPLETE WORKS OF ABRAHAM LINCOLN, v 5, New York, Frances D.Tandy Company, 1897

ONCE THEY MOVED LIKE THE WIND, David Roberts, Simon and Schuster, N.Y., 1975

WORKS OF HUBERT HOWE BANCROFT, v 17, History of Arizona and New Mexico, 1530-1888

TERRITORIAL VERDE VALLEY MANUSCRIPT—by Bob Munson, Supt. Of Fort Verde State Park—1992

BURY MY HEART AT WOUNDED KNEE—by Dee Brown, Bantam Books, N.Y. 1972

CAMP RENO:OUTPOST IN APACHERIA, 1867-1870—by Jim Schreier, Arizona Historical Society—1992

KING S. WOOLSEY—by John S. Goff, Black Mountain Press, Cave Creek, AZ. 1981

WIVES OF KING S. WOOLSEY: LUCY'S LOVE STORY, Al Bates, Days Past, Sharlot Hall Museum, Prescott Daily Courier, 2006

FRONTIER REGULARS, The United States Army and the Indian 1866-1891—by Robert M. Utley, Macmillan Publishing Co., N.Y. 1975

THE INDIAN FRONTIER OF THE AMERICAN WEST 1846-1890—by Robert M. Utley, University of New Mexico Press, 1984

THE APACHES, Eagles of the Southwest—by Donald E. Worcester, University of Arizona Press, 1979

ON THE BORDER WITH CROOK—by John Bourke, University of Nebraska Press, 1891, 1976

FORTY MILES A DAY ON BEANS AND HAY—by Don Rickey, Jr. University of Oklahoma Press, 1963, 1972

DEATH IN THE DESERT—by Paul Wellman, University of Nebraska Press, 1935

FORT VERDE STATE PARK LIBRARY AND MUSEUM, General Crook in Indian Country by John Bourke, The Filer Press, Colorado, 1891

BOARD OF ENGAGEMENTS WITH HOSTILE INDIANS 1868-1882, Washington Government Printing Office

SCOUT WITH BUFFALO SOLDIERS—by Fredrick Remington. The Filer Press, Colorado 1974

FIGHTING INDIANS OF THE WEST by Dee Brown with Martin Schmitt, Ballantine Books, New York, 1975

ARIZONA ADVENTURES by Marshall Trimble, Golden West Publishers, 1982

THE INDIAN WARS OF THE WEST by Paul Wellman, Doubleday & Company, New York, 1963

THE TROOPERS—by S.E. Whitman, Hastings House Publishers. N.Y. 1963

INDIAN WARS OF THE U.S. ARMY—by Fairfax Downey, Doubleday & CO.,N.Y., 1963

FOLLOWING THE INDIAN WARS—by Oliver Knight, University of Oklahoma Press, Norman, 1960

CAMPAIGNING WITH CROOK—by Capt. Charles King, University of Oklahoma Press, Norman 1964

VANISHED ARIZONA—by Martha Summrehayes, University of Nebraska Press—1977

AL SIEBER, CHIEF OF SCOUTS—by Dan Thrapp, University of Oklahoma Press, Norman, 1964

DEPARTMENT OF ARIZONA CAMPAIGN REPORT TO ASSISTANT ADJUTANT GENERAL—Camp Verde, A.T, G.M. Brayton, Capt. 8th Infantry 1877

PIONEER STORIES OF ARIZONA'S VERDE VALLEY—by Verde Valley Pioneer's Association, 1954

THE PAPERS OF THE ORDER OF INDIAN WARS—by John Carroll, Old Army Press, Fort Collins, Co. 1975

SCOTTSDALE DAILY PROGRESS—"Cibecue Creek, Apache Battle Site Located," April 30, 1971

THE FIGHT AT CIBECUE, August 30, 1881—by Fred Coxens, Research Papers at Fort Verde State Park

THE TRUTH ABOUT GERONIMO—by Britton Davis, Chapter 2, The Fight At Big Dry Wash." Fort Verde State Park

HEADQUARTERS DEPARTMENT OF ARIZONA, Whipple Barracks, Prescott, July 31, 1882. General Orders #37

COUNCIL OF ABANDONED MILITARY POSTS USA, "Battle of Big Dry Wash," Fort Verde State Park

ARIZONA REPUBLIC—"Big Dry Wash Battle Ended Apache Resistance," by James E. Cook July 16, 1987

THE BATTLE OF CIBECUE AND ITS AFTERMATH, A White Mountain Apache's Account—by William Kessel, University of Arizona Ethnohistory, Spring 1974, Courtesy of Ruth Kessel, Sedona, Arizona

CHAPTER THREE: THE PIONEERS

PRESCOTT: A Pictorial History by Melissa Ruffner, Primrose Press, Prescott, AZ. 1981

WORKS OF HUBERT HOWE BANGCROFT, VOL. 17, HISTORY OF ARIZONA & NEW MEXICO, 1530-1888

WOMEN'S DIARIES OF THE WESTWARD JOURNEY by Lillian Schlessel, Shockton Books, N.Y., 1982

WIVES OF KING S. WOOLSEY; Lucy's Love Story by Alan Bates, Days Past, Sharlot Hall Museum, Prescott Daily Courier, 2006

THE ARIZONA OF JOSEPH PRATT ALLYN, 1863-1866, edited by John Nicolson, University of Arizona Press, Tucson, AZ. 1974

B. SACKS, PROCLAMATION IN THE WILDERNESS: The salary clause in the Territorial Act, with a note on the illegal payments to Governor Goodwin, 1867

A CONCISE HISTORY OF THE MORMON BATTALIAN IN THE MEXICAN WAR, 1846-47, by Sergeant Daniel Taylor, Rio Grande Press, 1881

DEATH IN HIS SADDLEBAGS, Charles B. Genung Arizona Pioneer, by Dan Genung, Sunflower University Press, Manhattan, Kansas, 1992

THE STORY OF PAULINE WEAVER, ARIZONA'S FORMOST MOUNTAIN MAN by Jim Byrkit and Bruce Hooper, Sierra Azul Productions, 1993

ARIZONA DIARY OF LILY FREMONT 1878-1881, edited by Mary Lee Spence, University of Arizona Press, 1997

A PASSION FOR FREEDOM; The Life of Sharlot Hall by Margaret F. Maxwell, University of Arizona Press, 1982

SHARLOT HERSELF, edited by Nancy K. Wright, Sharlot Hall Museum, 1992

FIND DEATH TOGETHER: S.P. Putnam and Mary L. Collins Asphyxiated, Chicago Tribune, 1896

PROBATE COURT OF YAVAPAI COUNTY, ARIZONA TERRI-TORY, In the matter of Hezekiah Brooks, Van H. Brooks—Plaintiff vs. Bessie Brooks—Defendant, June 6, 1907

ARIZONA JOURNAL MINER, Sam Miller, 10-7, 1909, p. 9, sc. 1; 10-8, 1909, p.4, sec. 3

PRESCOTT COURIER, Supplement, "Pioneer Families," 7-2, 1980, p.18

Biography of Wales and Jennie Sara Arnold compiled by Bob Munson, Fort Verde State Historic Association, Camp Verde, AZ.

William J. Mulvenon, Arizona Nineteenth Legislature by Jas. H. McClintock, Phoenix, 1897

"MURDER ON THE ARIZONA STRIP," by Bill Roberts, The Traveler, July 1994

"THE DIABLO CANYON HOLDUP AND THE GREAT CHASE," by A.J. Patane, Wild West Magazine, April 2002

"ARIZONA'S GREAT TRAIN ROBBERY," by Maurice Kildare, Yavapaico Magazine, 1889

ARIZONA'S BLOODIEST DAY IN COURT," by Editor, Tombstone Epitaph, National Edition, March 1982

ROUGH RIDER BUCKEY O'NEILL OF ARIZONA, by Dale L. Walker, Bison Books, U. of Nebraska Press, 1975

THE ARIZONA ROUGH RIDER MONUMENT AND CAPTAIN W.O. O'NEILL, by Sharlot Hall, 1928

THE SANTA FE, PRESCOTT & PHOENIX RAILROAD by John Sayre, Pruitt Publishing, 1990

TELLS OF EARLY RAILROADS HERE, Jack Aitkin, Prescott Courier, June 15, 1935

ARIZONA, A CAVALCADE OF HISTORY by Marshall Trimble, Treasure Chest Publications, 1989

VANISHED BULLOCK RAIL LINE WAS FREE AND EASY by Roscoe Willson, Weekly Gazette, June 26, 1949

THE FIRST RAILROAD AND THE BATTLE FOR PRESCOTT by Eleanor Gilly, Days Past, Sharlot Hall Museum, Prescott Courier, 1999

TIMELESS HERITAGE: A HISTORY OF THE FOREST SERVICE IN THE SOUTHWEST, Chap. 3, The Land and its People

BEYOND BEEF; THE RISE AND FALL OF THE CATTLE INDUSTRY by Jeremy Rifkin, Penguin Books, N.Y. 1992

HOLBROOK HISTORY, www.route66.com/Holbrook/history.html

THE SOCIAL AND ECONOMIC CONSEQUENCES OF EARLY CATTLE RANCHING IN NORTHEASTERN ARIZONA by W.S. Abruzzi, Human Ecology 23, 1995

A LITTLE WAR OF OUR OWN by Don Dedera, Northern Publishing, Flagstaff, 1988

WINGFIELD FAMILY SOCIETY WEBSITE

ON THE BANKS OF BEAVER CREEK by Til Lightbourn and Mary Lyons, Private Publication, 1991

ARIZONA PAGENT by Madeline Ferrin Pare, Arizona Historical Foundation, Tempe 1967

PIONEER STORIES OF THE VERDE VALLEY by the Verde Valley Pioneers Association, 1954

ECHOES OF THE PAST; Tales of Old Yavapai Vol. 1-2, by Yavapai Cowbelles of Arizona 1964

ANCESTORY .COM, OBITUARY AND CENSUS FILES

SHARLOT HALL MUSEUM ARCHIEVES

CHAPTER FOUR: OUTLAWS, LAWMEN AND LADIES OF THE NIGHT

THE LAWMEN: United States Marshals and their Deputies, 1789-1989, by Frederick S. Calhoun, Penguin Books, N.Y, 1991

HISTORY OF VALUABLE PIONEERS OF THE STATE OF ARIZONA, by Sally Munds Williams, Private printing, 1987

ENCYCLOPEDIA OF WESTERN LAWMEN AND OUTLAWS, by Jay Robert Nash, DeCapo Press, N.Y. 1994

FAMOUS SHERIFFS AND WESTERN OUTLAWS, by William MacLeod Raine, Doubleday, Doran & Company, Inc. Garden City, N.Y., 1929

DESERT LAWMEN: The High Sheriffs of New Mexico and Arizona 1846-1912, Larry D. Ball, University of New Mexico Press, Albuquerque, 1992

OUTLAWS AND GUNFIGHTERS OF THE OLD WEST, by Phillip W. Steele, Pelican Publishing Company, Inc. Gretna, LA., 1991

A DYNASTY OF WESTERN OUTLAWS, Paul Wellman, University of Nebraska Press, Lincoln and London, 1986

THE TRAIN ROBBERY ERA: An Encyclopedic History, by Richard Patterson, Pruett Publishing, Boulder, Colorado, 1991

THE FAMOUS CHARACTERS OF THE WILD WEST, by Richard Garrett, Saint Martins Press, N.Y., 1975

EXPERIENCE JEROME AND THE VERDE VALLEY LEGENDS AND LEGACIES, by Kate Ruland-Thorne, Thorne Enterprises, Sedona, AZ. 1991

JEROME TRAVELER: Sheriff Ruffner, Yavapai County's Pioneer Lawman, by Bill Roberts, May 1990

GEORGE C. RUFFNER: Frontier Sheriff, Yavapai County, by Toni and Robert McInnes, Sheriff Magazine, August 1950

STORY OF GEORGE RUFFNER, by Lester W. "Budge" Ruffner (nephew), Sharlot Hall Museum Archives, 1982

PRESCOTT'S GREAT FIRE, July 14, 1900, by Richard Gorby, DAYS PAST, Sharlot Hall Museum, Prescott Courier, 1998

FLEMING PARKER: "I Will Steal Before I Will Bum," by Sue Abbey, DAYS PAST, Sharlot Hall Museum, Prescott Courier, 1998

WOMEN'S VOICES FROM THE WESTERN FRONTIER, by Susan G. Butruille, Tamarack Books, Inc. Boise, ID. 1995

PISTOLS AND PETTICOATS, by Bob and Virginia L'Aloge, Flying Eagle-Thunderhawk Enterprises, New Mexico, 1995

A QUILT OF WORDS: Women's Diaries, Letters, and Original Accounts of Life in the Southwest 1860-1960, by Sharon Niederman, Johnson Books, Boulder, Colorado, 1988

MORE THAN PETTICOATS: Remarkable Arizona Women, by Wynne Brown, Twodot Press, Guilford, Connecticut, 2003

DAUGHTERS OF THE WEST, by Anne Seagraves, Wesanne Publications, Hayden, ID. 1996

INQUEST HELD UPON THE BODY OF SAMMY DEAN, Clyde B. Jones, Justice of the Peace and Ex-officio Coroner for Jerome Precinct, Yavapai County, State of Arizona at 2:00 P.M., July 8th, 1931

"FACE OF FANNIE HOWARD HORRIBLY SLASHED," Editor, Jerome Chronicle, Feb. 18, 1904

PISTOL PACKIN' MADAMS, True Stories of Notorious Women of the Old West, by Chris Enss, Twodot Press, Guilford, Connecticut, 2006

LADIES OF THE LAMPLIGHT, by Kay Reynolds Blair, Western Reflections Publishing Company, Montrose, Colorado, 2004

CELESTIALS AND SOILED DOVES: The Archaeology and History of Lots 4-9, Block 13 of Historic Prescott's Original Townsite, Cultural Resources Report No. 03-386, 2004

PRESCOTT PROSTITUTE FOUND SORTED LIFE MADE FODDER FOR FILM, by Leo Banks (a two part series), DAYS PAST, Sharlot Hall Museum, Prescott Courier, 2004

INDEX

K.
Kakakas—23
Kautz, Gen. August V.—141
          Fannie—141
Ketchum, Black Jack—199, 240-243
          Tom—240
          Sam—241
Kibbey, Joseph—151
Komwidapakwia—16
Kwevikabya—18

L.
Lamy, Archbishop—112
Land of Sunshine—150
Lees Ferry—185,
Leib, Dr. Chas.—102-105
          Mary Catherine—102-107, 126
Leigh, C.C.—246-247
Leroux, Antoine—93, 114
Lincoln, Abraham—11, 25, 36, 74, 80, 82, 83, 86, 104, 146
"Long Knives"—27-28
Lount, George—105-106, 114
Lucero, Christo—212
Lummis, Chas.—150, 152

M.
Mangus Coloradas—32-34
Mantle, John—203-204
Manifest Destiny—26, 37, 86, 146
          Marion, John H.—41, 42, 85, 133-140, 249
          George Crook—136, 140
          John—138-140
          Flora Banghart—136-138
          Ida Mae—138, 140
Martin, George—45, 50
          Andrew—46
Martin, George Barney—208-209, 211-212
Marr Brothers—175-176

Contents

PREFACE

About two centuries ago the German poet, writer and philosopher J.W. Goethe noted that Nature is not only a great artist but also a skillful master. The contemporary generation of scientists who work in the fields of molecular biology, biochemistry and biophysics can appreciate to the fullest extent not only the internal beauty of natural molecular structures but also with what consummate skill these structures have been created. One of the wonderful creations of Nature, biological catalysis, appears as a challenging problem to chemists of the 21th century. The unique catalytic properties of enzyme, which are their precise specificity, selectivity, high rate of chemical reaction, and regulatory capacity occupy a great deal of attention. Classical and modern physical chemistry, chemical kinetics, organic, inorganic and quantum-chemistry provide an arsenal of physical methods and establish a basis for the investigation of structure and action mechanism of enzymes. The general properties of enzymes, the "ideal" chemical catalysts, are the formation of intermediates, smooth thermodynamic relief along the reaction coordinate, fulfillment of all selection rules for chemical reactions, the ability to proceed and to stop temporarily and spatially, and compatibility with the ambient media. These properties are possible by multifunctional active centers, by the unique structure of protein globules, possessing both rigidity and flexibility, and the formation of catalytic ensembles. Biochemistry returns to chemistry a plethora of knowledge about nearly "ideal" catalysts and opens the way for chemical modeling of enzyme reactions.

This book is a view of enzyme catalysis by a physico-chemist with long-term experience in the investigation of structure and action mechanism of biological catalysts. This book is not intended to provide an exhaustive survey of each topic but rather a discussion of their theoretical and experimental background, and recent developments. The literature of enzyme catalysis is so vast and many scientists have made important contribution in the area, that it is impossible in the space allowed for this book to give a representative set of references. The author has tried to use reviews, and general principles of articles. He apologizes to those he has not been able to include.

The first chapter of the present monograph expound upon new approaches and twists to traditional physical and kinetic methods of investigation of structure and action mechanism. The second chapter is a brief outline of current ideas on the general mechanisms of separate stages of enzyme catalytic processes. In the subsequent chapters, the author's attention focuses on an analysis of structure and action mechanism of "tough" enzymatic processes which can not yet be effectively realized by chemists in ambient conditions: reduction of nitrogen, hydroxylation of alkans, conversion of light energy, photosynthetic water oxidation; etc. The present status of the knowledge of protein molecular dynamics (fluctuation dynamics of protein) and its paramount role in enzyme functions will be reviewed. Areas related to enzyme catalysis such as antibody catalysis, enzymes in organic solvents, enzymes in synthetic chemistry and enzyme design are outlined. In concluding chapter, a progress in chemical mimicking of "tough" enzymatic reactions is considered.

The monograph is intended for scientists working on enzyme catalysis and adjacent areas such as chemical modeling of biological processes, homogeneous catalysis, biomedical research and biotechnology. The book can be use as a subsidiary manual for instructors, graduate and undergraduate students of university biochemistry and chemistry departments.

The author is very grateful to his students and his colleagues from the Laboratory of Chemical Physics of Enzyme Catalysis, the N.N. Semenov Institute of Chemical Physics, Russian Academy of Science and from the Laboratory of Chemical Biophysics, Department of Chemistry, Ben-Gurion University of the Negev, who have shared the bad and good times over many years in investigations in the field of enzyme catalysis. I acknowledge with gratitude and affection the generous help and encouragement I have received from Professor Rufus Lumry. Finally, the author is deeply indebted to the PhD students Pavel Parkhomyuk-Ben Arye, Nataly Medvedeva, and Evgenia Lozynsky for their help in the preparation of the manuscript.

CHAPTER 1

METHODS OF INVESTIGATION OF THE STRUCTURE AND ACTION MECHANISMS OF ACTIVE SITES OF ENZYMES

1.1. Physical methods

1.1.1. X-RAY STRUCTURAL ANALYSIS

The traditional approach to the investigation of intermediates of an enzymatic reaction involves the X-ray structural analysis of enzyme complexes and substrate analogs. Recently three different crystallographic techniques to trap enzyme bound intermediates in a crystal lattice have been proposed. The first technique uses ultrafast kinetics methods to obtain complete data sets on the enzymatic time scale (Bolduc et al., 1995; Stoddard, 1996). One successful strategy is flash-photolysis inducing the homogeneous synchronization cycle in an enzyme crystal with a photoactive substrate analog. As a result the enzyme-substrate complex is formed. As an another strategy, site-directed mutagenesis of key catalytic residues creates a kinetic bottleneck at specific steps which can be used to determine the structure of distinct intermediates. These methods have been used to determine the structure of intermediates in isocitrate dehydrogenase.

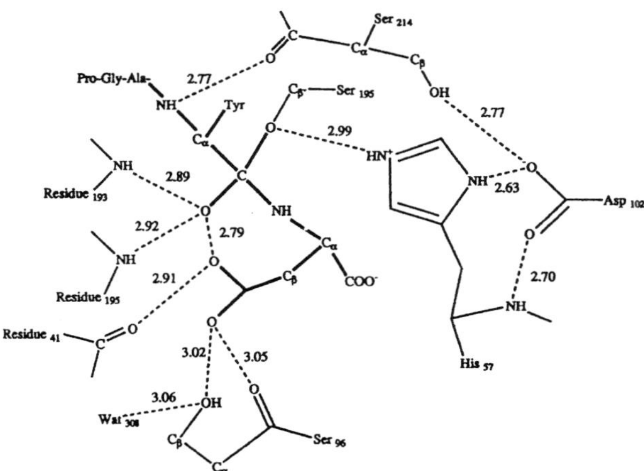

Figure 1.1. The active site of the first tetrahedral intermediate of chymotrypsin (Farber, 1999). Reproduced with permission.

The third approach to solving this problem (Farber, 1999) involves the preparation of an enzyme-intermediate complex at high substrate concentration for X-ray data collection. Under such a condition active sites in the crystal lattice will be filled with intermediates. Using a combination of flow cell experiments and equilibrium experiments, it is possible to obtain the structure of important intermediates in an enzyme reaction (Bolduc et al., 1995). It was also discovered that some enzyme crystals can be transformed from their aqueous crystallization buffer to nonaqueous solvents without cross-linking the crystals before the transfer (Yennawar et. al., 1995). It is then possible to regulate the water concentration in the active site. The structure of the first tetrahedral intermediate, tetrapeptide –Pro-Gly-Ala-Tyr- in the γ-chymotrypsin active site obtained by this method is shown in Fig. 1.1.

1.1.2. INFRARED, RAMAN AND LIGHT ABSORPTION SPECTROSCOPY

Infrared spectra are related to changes of nuclear vibrational energy under absorption of electromagnetic radiation. In polyatomic molecules, the complex vibrational process may be resolved into a combination of n-collective normal harmonic vibrations. If the parallel vibrations differ substantially in frequency, they may be regarded as independent. If the frequencies of two normal modes with frequency v_n are equal and a sufficiently strong dipolar interaction occurs between the modes of vibration, then, as a result of the resonance quantum-mechanical effect (the Fermi resonance), this degenerate vibration splits into two modes with frequencies less and greater than v_n. The stronger the interaction, the magnitude of splitting the higher.

The vibrational processes in molecules are also reflected in the Raman spectra (Spiro, 1987, 1988). When the substance is irradiated at a frequency far from the frequency of its absorption, additional (satellite) lines may appear in the scattering light. The origin of such lines is accounted for by the fact that during the interaction of electromagnetic radiation, the molecule part of the radiant energy is transferred to the excited vibrational levels and part of the energy is released from the excited levels. In metalloenzymes and in substrate-enzyme and inhibitor-enzyme complexes the active sites incorporate only a small part of the macromolecular atoms.

The considerably more selective method is resonance Raman scattering (RRS). The selectivity of the method is due to the fact that the spectra display only vibrations associated with the electronic excitation of the chromophore being studied. After irradiation of the substance with monochromatic light of frequency v_0 in its absorption band, in the scattering light narrow RRS bands are observed with frequencies shifted relative to v_0. The origin of these bands is ascribed to the electronic transition from the excited level to the first vibrational level of the ground state.

Vibrational spectroscopy is a powerful tool for the study of molecular structure and dynamics. The typical vibrational frequency range of this spectroscopy is 100-4000 cm^{-1} which corresponds to the energy range 0.3-12 kcal/mole. Because the resolution of vibrational spectroscopy is on the order of 5 cm^{-1}, the band shift on this order corresponds to a 0.02 kcal/mole. The empirical Badger-Bauer relationship allows for the estimation of energy differences of the hydrogen-bonding interaction between molecules in different conditions using the experimental values of the band shift. For a given chemical bond, it is directly related to its bond length (Deng and Callender, 1999). Therefore, vibrational spectroscopy is well suited to the studies of chemical bond distortion during enzymatic catalysis.

The conventional methods of investigating nuclear vibrational properties of proteins, namely spontaneous infrared, Raman resonance spectroscopy, have serious limitations, because many vibrational modes contribute to the spectrum of a protein at any given frequency. To overcome these limitations, new experimental approaches have been developed during the last decade. Among such approaches are differential and time resolved IR and Raman spectroscopy, coherent anti-Stockes Raman scattering (CARS), Fourier transform infrared spectroscopy (FTIR), multidimentional IR and RR spectroscopy, two-dimentional infrared echo and Raman echo (Hamaguchi and Gustafson, 1994; Deng and Callender 1999; Asplund et al., 2000; Uchida et al., 2000; Mukamel, 2000; Fourkas, 2001; and references herein).

In Raman differential spectroscopy, a conventional Raman spectrometer was adapted to measure small differences in the Raman spectra (Deng and Callender 1999). The spectrometer system permits detection with an accuracy of 0.1%. Laser light is focused on a specially fabricated split cell from underneath. The Raman-scattering light at v_L is frequency shifted from the incoming laser light by v_0, the frequency of a vibrational mode. Scattered light is collected from one side of the split cell. The cell is translated and the scattered light is collected from the cell's second side. The two spectra are then subtracted in a computer to form the difference spectrum.

Raman differential spectroscopy was applied to the investigation of enzyme-substrate complexes. The protein phosphoglucomutase (PGM) catalyzes the interconversion of glucose 1-phosphate to glucose 6-phosphate. It was shown that the difference in the spectra of enzyme complexes with the substrate samples, the phosphate group of which was enriched with ^{18}O and ^{16}O correspondingly, belong to the P-O symmetric stretch with a frequency of 977 cm^{-1}. The differential Raman spectra of complexes of lactate dehydrogenase with cofactors NAD and NADH and substrates lactate and pyruvate were detected. These techniques in combination with site-directed mutagenase and isotope editing of pyruvate's C=O, COO$^-$, carboxamid group and the C-4-H fragment of the NAD, allowed the establishment of the correct geometry of the reactive complex.

Time-resolved anti-Stokes Raman spectroscopy is used for monitoring vibrational relaxation dynamics in solution and provides information about specific modes in molecules under investigation (Nakabayashi et al., 1997; Uchida et al. 2000). The experimental setup of a picosecond time-resolved Raman spectrometer is schematically shown in Fig. 1.2. A pump pulse excites a molecule, and the anti-Stokes Raman spectrum of vibrationally excited S_0 state of the molecule is obtained by a probe pulse following the pump pulse after the delay time. The method was used for the investigation of Fe-ligand interactions, an active site of carbonmonoxy CooA hemoprotein (Uchida et al., 2000). This protein acts as a transcriptional activator for the expression of CO oxidation system in bacteria. To identify the axial ligand of CO-bound CoooA, the protein samples, with and without imidazol ligand, were photodissociated by a picosecond laser pulse, and vibrations of the transiently formed five-coordinate species were monitored by the subsequent picosecond probe pulse. It is shown that His77 is the axial ligand and CO binding induces dissociation of another trans-ligand and triggers the activation of CooA via the conformational changes.

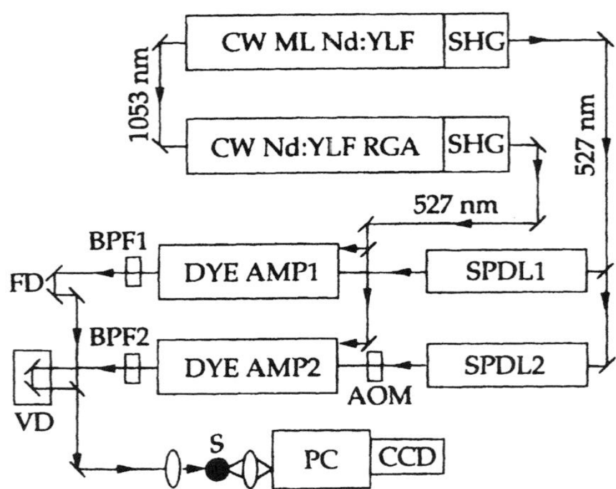

Figure 1.2. Block diagram of a time resolved Raman spectrometer. (See details in reference Nakabayashi et al., 1997). Reproduced with permission.

In CARS two ultrashort pulses of laser light (from femtoseconds to picoseconds in duration) arrive simultaneously at the sample of interest (Mukamel, 2000; Fourkas, 2001 and references herein). The difference between the frequencies ($w_1 - w_2$) matches the frequency of a Raman active vibrational mode in the sample. A "probe" pulse (w_3) emits a signal pulse of frequency $w_1 - w_2 + w_3$ in a unique special direction. By scanning the delay time between the pump and "probe" pulses, the delay of the vibrational coherence can be measured. The distinct advantage of CARS is that it is a background free technique, since the signal propagates in a unique direction.

To overcome the problem of separating homogeneous and nonhomogeneous contributions to the line shape, the special technique, called the photon echo, has been developed (Fourkas, 2001 and references therein). The principle idea of this method is similar to fundamentals of spin-echo techniques in NMR and ESR (Sections 1.1.5 and 1.1.6). The photon spin echo technique generally involves five laser pulses of at least two different colors. Two time-coincident pulses of light create a Raman coherence at frequency w_g that is allowed to involve for longer time τ_1, after which the response for a single vibrational frequency occurs. At this point, another pulse pair is focused upon the sample. Each pulse in these pairs interacts with the system twice, reversing the coherence so that it is frequency w_g'. This coherence is allowed to involve for time τ_2, second delay, after which the response for a single vibrational frequency takes place.

The ability to rephase inhomogeneity in Raman-active intermolecular vibrations was increased with the use of five-order spectroscopic technique (Tanamura and Mukamel, 1993; Mukamel, 2000; Fourkas, 2001). Five-order spectroscopy relies on the existence of some sorts of nonlinearity, either in the coordinate dependence of polarizability or in the vibrational potential, and involves a three vibrational energy level. In this technique, the 2D response is obtained when the system is subjected to pairs of excitation pulses followed by the probe pulse. This technique provides the capacity for probing ultrafast intramolecular and intermolecular dynamical processes including charge transfer and chemical reactions.

Multidimentional nonlinear infrared spectroscopy is used for identification of dynamic structures in liquids and conformational dynamics of molecules, peptides and, in principle, small proteins in solution (Asplund et al., 2000 and references herein). This spectroscopy incorporates the ability to control the responses of particular vibrational transitions depending on their couplings to one another. Two and three–pulse IR photon echo techniques were used to eliminate the inhomogeneous broadening in the IR spectrum. In the third-order IR echo methods, three phase-locked IR pulses with wave vectors k_1, k_2, and k_3 are focused on the sample at time intervals. The IR photon echo eventually emitted and the complex 2D IR spectrum is obtained with the use of Fourier transformation. The method was applied to the examination of vibrational properties of N-methyl acetamid and a dipeptide, acyl-proline-NH_2.in D_2O. The 2D IR spectrum showed peaks at 1,610 and 1, 670 cm^{-1}, the two frequencies of the acyl-proline dipeptide. Geometry and time-ordering of the incoming pulse sequence in fifth-order 2D spectroscopy is shown in Fig. 1.3.

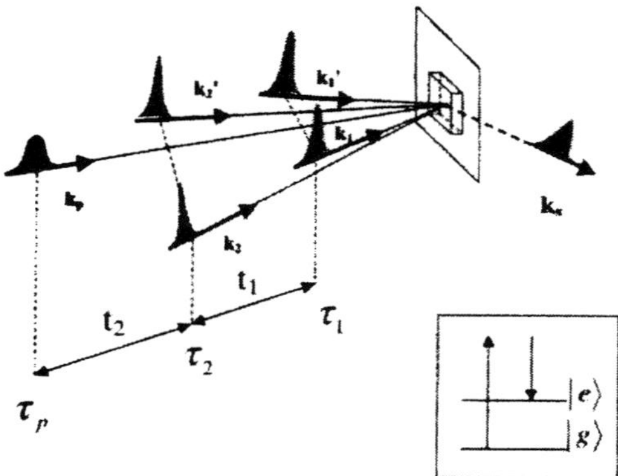

Figure 1..3. Geometry and time-ordering of the incoming pulse sequence in fifth-order 2D spectroscopy. Δk_1 c k_1-k_1', $\Delta k_2 \equiv k_2$-k_2'. Only one of the nine possible signal pulses in the direction $k_s = \Delta k_1 + k_p$ is shown. Inset shows the elementary Raman process (Mukamel et al., 1999). Reproduced with permission.

Femtosecond linear dichroism
Circular dichroism is associated with the difference in the extinction coefficient between the left- (eL) and right-hand (eR) polarized light :

$$Q_v = \alpha_{CD}(\varepsilon_L - \varepsilon_R) = \beta_{CD} m_0 \mu_0 f_{CD}(v) \qquad (1.1)$$

where α_{CD} and β_{CD} are coefficients, m_0 and μ_0 are the matrix elements of the dipolar electronic transition moment and dipolar magnetic transition moment, respectively, and $f_{CD}(v)$ is the function of the line shape.

In the femtosecond liner dichroism (FLD) experiments (Önfelt et al., 2000) the output of a femtosecond laser system is split into pump and probe pulses with independent wavelength tunability. The pump pulse passes through an optical delay line and a polarizer, and crosses the probe beam on the sample cell at a small angle. The probe beam passes through a polarizer that is adjusted to produce a linear polarization at the pump beam. After traversing the sample, the probe pulse is passed through a polarizer for the separation of light polarized parallel and perpendicular to the pump beam. The ratio between normalized transmitted probe energies in the presence and absence of excitation of the sample by the pump pulse formed the basis of the polarization-resolved ΔA transition, recorded as a function of the time delay t between passages of the pump and probe pulses. The measured transients are analyzed by applying them to a sum of exponential terms of amplitude A and lifetime τ_i. The FLD technique was used for the study of solvation and charge separation of {Ru(1,10-pheantrolin)2dipyrido[3,2-a:2'-3'-c]phenazin} incorporated into DNA.

1.1.3. FLUORESCENCE AND PHOSPHORESCENCE

Because of their high sensitivity, fluorescence and phosphorescence techniques are especially suited for solving many problems of structure and dynamics of the biological molecular system. The main luminescence parameters traditionally measured, are the frequency of maximal intensity v_{max}, intensity I, the quantum yield, ϕ, the lifetime of the exited state τ, polarization and excited state energy migration (Lacovicz, 1985). The usefulness of the fluorescence methods is greatly enhanced by the developments of new experimental techniques such as nano-, pico- and femtosecond time-resolved spectroscopy, single-molecule detection, cofocal microscopy and two-photon correlation spectroscopy.

Time –resolved fluorescence spectroscopy
The excitation of a chromophore group is accompanied by a change in the electron dipole moment of the molecule. This involves a change in the interaction energy with the surrounding molecules, which manifests itself by a shift of the time-dependent frequency maximum of the fluorescence spectra, (relaxation shift) (Bakhshiev, 1972):

$$\Delta v_{max} = v_{max}(t) - v_{max}(\infty) = \left[v_{max}(0) - v_{max}(\infty)\exp\left(-\frac{t}{\tau_r}\right) \right] \qquad (1.2)$$

where the indices t and 0 are related to the nmax of the time -resolved emission spectrum at a given moment, $t \to \infty$, and $t \to 0$, respectively, and τ_r is the characteristic time of reorganization of the dipoles in the medium around the fluorophore. The value of

τ_r can also be independently derived from the analysis of the temperature (T) dependencies of the relaxation shift using the following equation:

$$\Delta v_{max}(T) = \frac{\left[v_{max}(0) - v_{max}(\infty)\right]\tau_f}{\left[\tau_f + \tau_r(T)\right]} \qquad (1.3)$$

where Δv_{max} *(T)* is the relaxation shift in the steady-state fluorescence spectra and τ_f is the fluorescence life time. Gradual increase of temperature results in the gradual decrease of the τ_r. The experimental Δv_{max} *(T)*-T dependence can be used for the estimation of $\tau_r(T)$ in each temperature if τ_f is known. In real systems (viscose liquids, polymers, proteins, membranes, etc.) there is, as a rule, a set of τ_r values, relaxation energy and entropy activation, and other parameters. Analysis of relaxation shifts in such systems requires special approaches. For instance, if one assumes a Gaussian distribution over the free activation energies of the reorientation of surrounding particles $(\Delta F^{\#})$, it is possible to find an expression to relate the energy activation of relaxation in the distribution maximum (E_{max}) to the second moment of the distribution curve (ΔF_0^2)

$$E_{app}(T) = E_{max} - \frac{\Delta F_0^2}{RT} \qquad (1.4)$$

where E_{app} (T) is the experimental value of apparent energy activation derived from the Arrhenius plot, log Δv_{max} (T) -1/T. Eq. 1.4 allows the estimation of E_{max} and (ΔF_0^2) plotting E_{app} (T) versus 1/T.

Nano- and picosecond time resolved fluorescence technique is used for monitoring the dynamic Stokes shift of a tryptophane, Trp31, in cytidine monophosphate kinase from *E. coli* in a water-glycerol mixture at temperatures, ranging from 293 to 230 K (Vincent at al., 2000). This residue is located at the opposite site of the nucleotide-binding sites, in a partially hydrophobic region, but not very far from the protein surface. It is shown that the emission maximum of the fluorophore fluorescence is shifted to 320 nm by decreasing the temperature to 230-240 K with the time constant about 100 ps. In the temperature range 293-232 K, the relaxation shift kinetics exhibit multiphase behavior with time constants ranging from 100 ps to several nanoseconds with a total amplitude between 130 and 340 cm^{-1}.

The dynamics of the fluorescence relaxation shift of the dual fluorescence-nitroxide probe

incorporated into the hydrophobic binding site of human serum albumin (HAS) was monitored indirectly (Rubtsova et. al., 1993, Fogel et al., 1994; Likhtenshtein et al.,

2000) by the measurement of the temperature dependent relaxation shift (Eq. 1.3) and directly using the picosecond fluorescent time resolved technique (Likhtenshtein et al., 2000).

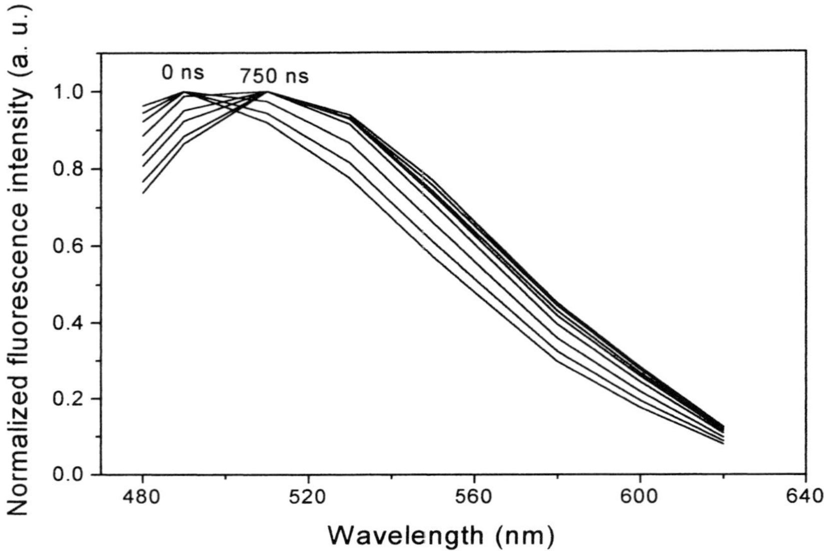

Figure 1.4. Time resolved fluorescent spectra of a dual dansyl-nitroxide probe 1 incorporated in bovine serum albumin (Likhtenshtein et al., 2000a). Reproduced with permission.

Both methods showed that the relaxation of the protein groups in the vicinity of the dansyl moiety of the FNP in the excited state occurs, upon the ambient temperature, with a rate constant of about one ns.

Recently, the femtosecond fluorescence polarization technique was employed for studies of the dynamics of a proton-transfer fluorescence probe, 2-(2'-hydrophenyl)-4-methyloxazol (HPMO), incorporated into the hydrophobic binding site of human serum albumin, HSA (Zhong, 2000). In the non-polar solvent, p-dioxan, the minor component (26%) was found to decay with a time constant of 5.3 ps, whereas the rest of the anisotropy decayed with time constant 45 ps. The latter is attributed to a photoinduced intermolecular proton transfer. During the last decay in the HSA binding site, the probe anisotropy has a slight drop (8%) with a life time 93 ps and major component (92%) which stays with no decay at a large constant value of 0.304. The rotational relaxation of HAS in water is the time scale of tens of nanoseconds. Therefore, the HPMO high amplitude orientational motion and intramolecular proton transfer are strongly restricted by the hydrophobic phase of the structure at least for hundreds of picoseconds. The solvent effect (decay of the blue and rise of the red) was also not observed within a time period. This means that the reorientation of dipoles of proteins and water in the vicinity of the probe occurs with time constants longer than a hundred picoseconds.

A novel pump-damp-probe method (PDPM), which allows the characterization of solvation dynamics of a fluorescence probe not only in excited but also in the ground states has been recently developed (Changenet-Barret, 2000 and references therein). In PDPM , a pump produces a nonequilibrium population of the probe excited, which, after media relaxation, is simulated back to the ground states. The solvent relaxation of the nonequlibrium ground state is probed by monitoring with absorption technique. The inramolecular protein dynamics in a solvent-inaccessible region of calmodulin labeled with coumarin 343 peptide was examined by PDPM. In the pump-dump-probe experiments, part of a series of laser output pulses was frequency-doubled and softer beams were used as the probe. The delay of the probe with respect to the pump was fixed at 500 ps.

Single molecule and two photon fluorescence spectroscopy
Recent developments in fluorescence spectroscopy and microscopy have made it possible to detect and image single molecules (Denk et al., 1990; Xue and Yeung, 1995; Craig et al., 1996; Edman et al., 1996; Xie et al., 1998; Heinze et al., 2000; and references therein). These techniques allow the conducting of spectroscopic measurements for studying chemical and biological species and their interaction with the environment. Single molecular measurement (SMM) offers time resolution to monitor dynamic processes such as translation, orientation and enzymatic reactions on a time scale from milli-seconds to ten- seconds. Confocal fluorescence methodologies are based on the detection of laser-induced fluorescence of single molecules in a very small focal volume of approximately 1 fl. At present, molecules with an extinction coefficient larger than 10^4 and a fluorescent quantum efficiency greater than 0.1 can be studied with SMM. The techniques which have evolved to the level of single molecule sensitivity at room temperature are as follows: flow cytometry, confocal fluorescence correlation spectroscopy, and micro-droplet technique.

The single-molecule fluorescence technique was used for the study of differences in the chemical reactivity of individual molecules of enzymes. The kinetics of producing fluorescent NADH from lactate and NAD^+ catalyzed by lactate dehydrogenase has been monitored by this technique (Xue and Yeung, 1995). The enzyme molecules are presented at very low concentration $(7.6 \times 10^{-17} - 1.5 \times 10^{-16}$ M) in a narrow capillary and each discrete molecule produces a discrete zone of the fluorescent NADH. The activity of individual enzyme molecules was found to be variable up to a factor of four. The kinetics of synthesis of a fluorescent product, 2'-(2-benzothiazol)-6'-hydrobenzthiazol, produced by single alkaline phosphotase molecule has been investigated (Craig et al., 1996). Single enzyme molecules show a range of activity from 1 to 10. The experimental values of activation energy of the enzymatic reaction vary more than a factor of 2. Some of the above mentioned results may be explained by a partial adsorption of enzyme molecules on the capillary walls' surface which exhibit different activity as compared with molecules in bulk. This problem can be solved by comparing parameters of the enzyme kinetics in the single-molecules regime and in "regular" conditions with high concentrations of enzymes. The single-molecule fluorescence technique has been useful in the study of conformational transition of biopolymers (Edman et al. 1996). It has been shown that single DNA molecules labeled with a fluorescence probe exhibit different fluorescence properties related to open and closed conformations of biopolymers.

Two-photon molecular excitation is performed by very high local intensity provided by tight focusing in a laser scanning microscopy (LSM) (Denk et al., 1990; Heinze et al., 2000). This technique is combined with the temporal concentration of femtosecond pulsed lasers that produce a stream of pulses with a pulse duration of about 100 fs at a repetition rate of about 80 MHz. An average incident laser power which can saturate the fluorescence output has been estimated as about 50 mV (about 10^{31} photones/cm^2). Advantages of the two-photon laser spectroscopy are as follows: high resolution, tolerance of infrared light by biological objects, different selection rule and vibronic coupling. The latter feature allows the accomplishment of simultaneous two- photon and one-photon excitation.

A dual-color cross-correlation fluorescence spectroscopy (DCCFS) appears to be a variant of SMM that is the most suitable for direct monitoring of enzymatic reactions (Winkler et al., 1999; Heinze et al., 2000). In DCCFS experiments, a sample, containing two fluorophores with different emissions in each molecule, is irradiated with two lasers (or with one laser) to perform simultaneous excitation of the fluorophores. The DCCFS in combination with the confocal laser microscopy allows the separation of microcopic volume with two different fluorophores from volume with only one of them and, therefore, the monitoring of dissociation of the dual-labeled molecules or association of two single-labeled molecules. The confocal fluorescence coincidence analysis has been employed for a rapid homogeneous assay for restriction endonuclease EcoRI (Winkler et al., 1999). This methodology has been improved by the application of two-photon excited dual-color cross-correlation spectroscopy on the level of single diffusing molecules (Heinze et al., 2000). A double-strand of DNA was labeled with Rhodamin green and Texas red. The kinetics of the enzymatic cleavage of the labeled DNA by restriction endonuclease was monitored by this new technique.

Two-photon laser fluorescence
In confocal spectroscopy, the exciting laser beam is focused to a diffraction- limited sport by illumination of a high numerical aperture objective. A pinhole in the image plane serves as a field diagram and discriminates against out-of-focus fluorescence. The optically defined detection volume is usually of the order of 10^{-16} liters. The high resolution of technique in the single–particle regime allows the investigation of molecular objects at nanomolar concentrations. Fluorescence correlation spectroscopy is an effective tool for measurement of local concentrations, investigation of partile diffusion, intramolecular dynamics, association and dissociation rates and enzymatic activity (Denk et al., 1990; Winkler et al., 1990; Schwille et al., 2000; Elson and Rigler, 2000; Heinze et al., 2000).

Two-photon excitation of a fluorescent within the cross section of the day molecule about 10^{-16} cm^2, is an induced probe for time about 10^{-15} s by laser light in the visible or near UV spectral range (Denk et. al., 1990). Such an excitation requires instaneous photon flux densities of the order of 10^{31} photons/cm^2.

1.1.4. FLUORESCENCE - PHOTOCHROME LABELING TECHNIQUES

Theoretical grounds

The photoisomerisation of stilbenes is found to be a simple and convenient model for the detailed study of factors affecting unimolecular photoreaction dynamics. Saltiel and co-workers first proposed a detailed mechanism for light- induced *trans-cis* photoisomerisation of *trans*-stilbene (Saltiel, and D'Agostino, 1972; Saltiel et al.,1992, Waldeck,1996; Papper et.al, 1997, 1998; Papper and Likhtenshtein, 2001).

The measurements of direct and sensitized *trans-cis and cis-trans* photoisomerisation allow the investigation of rotational and translational diffusions of the stilbene labels in biomembranes and labeled proteins in a wide temporal region (Mekler and Likhtenshtein, 1986; Mekler and Umarova, 1988; Likhtenshtein et al., 1992; Likhtenshtein, 1993; Likhtenshtein et al., 1996; Papper et al., 1999, 2000; Papper and Likhtenshtein, 2001). The cascade photochemical system based on the combination of the stilbene, triplet and nitroxide-spin probes have kept their own regular facilities as fluorescence probes and have gained an additional advantage in measurements of the rate constant of the triplet state quenching and in estimation of the local concentration of stable radicals.

The light-induced reversible *trans-cis* photoisomerisation of *trans*-stilbene molecule in condensed media includes at least four macroscopic stages: excitation of the stilbene chromophore, radiative deactivation of the excited state with the rate constant k_r, medium relaxation around the excited stilbene molecule with the rate constant k_m (to provide space for torsional distortion during the photoisomerisation process) and eventually, twisting transition with the rate constant k_{t-c}.

If the rate-limiting stage in an overall photoisomerisation process of the excited stilbene molecule in a viscous medium is the medium relaxation ($k_r \gg k_m$) and the isomerization after the relaxation proceeds faster than the excited-state fluorescence decay ($k_{t-c} \gg k_r$), the apparent steady-state rate constant of the overall *trans-cis* photoisomerisation process may be expressed as follows (Likhtenshtein et al., 1992, 1996; Likhtenshtein, 1993; Papper and Likhtenshtein, 2001):

$$k_{app} = \sigma \phi_{fl} I_{ex} k_m \qquad (1.5)$$

Here, σ, ϕ_{fl} and I_{ex} are the absorption cross-section, fluoresence quantum yield and the intensity of the incident light, correspondingly.

Actually, the apparent rate constant of the photoisomerisation in a viscous media, like biological membranes, was found to be dependent upon the medium relaxation rate. Hence, it is possible to study the dynamics of proteins and biological membranes in the vicinity of the incorporated stilbene probe by monitoring the steady-state fluorescence decay of the stilbene probe with the conventional constant-illumination spectrofluorimeter. The experimental values of $\sigma \phi_{fl} I_{ex}$ can be measured independently or can be omitted by comparison with photoisomerisation kinetics of the same probe and similar conditions in a medium with known macro- and microviscosity. A combined analysis of the *trans-cis* photoisomerisation kinetics of a stilbene probe and its polarization allows the establishment of the mechanism and the estimation of the frequency and amplitude of the probe motion in an organized medium (Likhtenshtein et al., 1996).

The traditional fluorescence and electron-spin resonance methods for recording molecular collisions do not allow the study of translational diffusion and rare encounters of molecules in a viscous media because of the short characteristic times of these methods. To measure the rate constants of rare encounters between macromolecules and to investigate the translation diffusion of labelled proteins and probes in a medium of high viscosity (like biomembranes), a new triplet-photochrome labeling technique has been developed (Mekler and Likhtenshtein, 1986; Mekler and Umarova, 1988; Likhtenshtein, 1993; Papper and Likhtenshtein, 2001).

The stilbene photoisomerisation through the triplet potential surface can be sensitized by a donor molecule excited to their triplet state, which is close energetically to the stilbene excited triplet level T_1 (Hammond et al., 1962). The sensitizers (donors) with triplet energies of at least 255 kJ/mole (in a case of unsubstituted stilbene) transfer their energies to both *trans* and *cis* isomers of the stilbene molecule in the ground state in a diffusion-controlled process. The reaction proceeds from an initial donor-acceptor encounter complex, which generates the stilbene excited triplet states without change of spin. From the excited triplet states of stilbene molecule, a relaxation process takes place on the triplet potential energy surface, leading to the deactivation transition occurrence. Finally, the triplet-triplet energy transfer drives the stilbene photoisomerisation through the triplet pathway (Fig. 1.5).

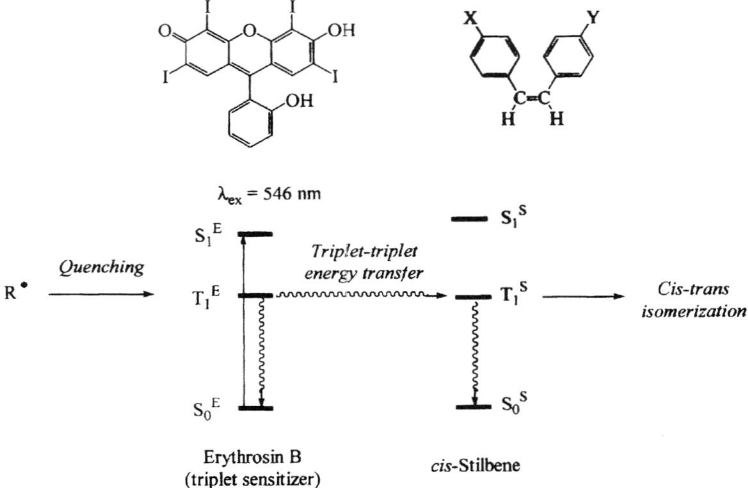

Figure 1..5. Schematic presentation of the cascade reaction between Erythrosin B and cis-DMAAS (Papper and Likhtenshtein, 2001). Reproduced with permission.

The triplet-photochrome method is based on the above mentioned cascade scheme. Starting from *cis*-stilbene, which is not fluorescent at the steady-state conditions of our experiment, and measuring the rate of increase of emitted fluorescence, it has been possible to monitor the process of the sensitised *cis-trans* photoisomerisation (Mekler and Likhtenshtein, 1986). The *cis*-stilbene concentration, which is proportional to fluorescence intensity, approaches the photostationary level exponentially with the rate constant

$$k = \left(k_t^{\,T} \zeta_t + k_c^{\,T} \zeta_c \right) \times \sigma I_{ex} \tau_{ph} \Phi_{ph} \qquad (1.6)$$

where $k_t^{\,T}$ and $k_c^{\,T}$ – the rate constants for the triplet-triplet energy transfer from a sensitiser to *trans* and *cis*-stilbenes respectively, ξ_t and ξ_c – the fractions of the *trans* and *cis*-stilbene molecules respectively that undergo the photoisomerisation after encounters with the triplet sensitiser and τ_{ph} and Φ_{ph}– the sensitiser's triplet lifetime and phosphorescence quantum yield respectively. Eq. (1.6) permits the calculation of the experimental rate constant $k_{exp} = (k_t^{\,T} \xi_t + k_c^{\,T} \xi_c)$ with the use of regular fluorescence technique if all other constants from this equation are measured independently or calibrated in a model system with these known values.

Due to the relatively long lifetime of the sensitiser triplet state and the possibility of integrating data on the stilbene photoisomerisation, the apparent characteristic time of the method can reach hundreds of seconds. This unique property of the cascade system and, therefor triplet-photochrome technique, allows the investigation of slow diffusion processes, including encounters of proteins in membranes using very low concentrations of both the triplet and photochrome probes.

An additional step in the cascade reaction scheme is the quenching of the sensitizer triplet state with relatively low-concentration radicals (Fig. 1.5) (Papper et al., 1999, 2000; Papper and Likhtenshtein, 2001). The entire investigated reaction that is shown in Fig. 1.5 is the sequence of the four kinetic processes and serves as a basis for the spin-triplet-photochrome labeling technique. This technique combines the three types of biophysical probes: stilbene photochrome probe, triplet probe and stable nitroxide-radical spin probe, which depresses the sensitiser exited triplet state.

Solving the kinetics equation based on the total cascade reaction with the consequent quenching by radicals, and taking into account the steady-state approximations, one can calculate a product of the quenching rate constant kq and the sensitizer excited triplet state life time τ_{ph} and the kq value if τ_{ph} is known. The quenching radical concentration in the vicinity of the probes can be determined using appropriate calibration.

Eventually, this method allows quantitative measuring of the translational diffusion of proteins modified with these three labels in solution and in biomembranes. The minimal approximate volume of a sample available for the fluorescence measurement (using a regular commercial spectrofluorimeter) in this method is about 10^{-3} µl when the total concentration of fluorophores is close to 0.01 µM and the local concentration of radicals is about 10 µM.

Experimental data
The fluorescence-photochrome technique was first applied to studying molecular dynamics of a stilbene fluorescence-photochrome molecule, SITC, attached covalently

to the terminal amino group of sperm-whale myoglobin (Likhtenshtein et. al., 1993). The same myoglobin residue was also labeled with a spin label, 4-iodoacetamide-TEMPO. Kinetics of the stilbene *trans-cis* photoisomerisation (k_{app}) and the rotational diffusion frequency of nitroxide radicals (v_c) were monitored by fluorescence and ESR techniques, respectively. These data on the probes in a bound state were compared with data obtained in 60%-ethylene glycol/water solution. The values of k_{app} and v_c for labels bound to myoglobin were found several times less than those values for the free labels indicating that microviscosity in the vicinity of the labels attached to myoglobin is higher than that in the bulk solution.

The triplet-photochrome labeling method has been used to study very rare encounters in a system containing the Erythrosin B sensitiser and SITC photochrome probe (Mekler and Likhtenshtein, 1986). Both types of the molecules were covalently bound to α-chymotrypsin. The photoisomerisation kinetics was monitored by fluorescence decay of the *trans*-SITS. The rate constants of the triplet-triplet energy transfer between Erythrosin B and SITS (at room temperature and pH 7) were found $k_t^T = 2 \times 10^7$ M^{-1}s^{-1} and $k_t^T = 10^7$ M^{-1}s^{-1}. It should be emphasized that the concentration of the triplet sensitiser attached to the protein did not exceed 10^{-7} M in those experiments, and the collision frequencies were close to 10 s^{-1} which are 8-9 orders of magnitude less than those measured with the regular luminescence or ESR techniques.

The triplet-photochrome labeling technique was first used to follow the protein-protein dynamic contacts in biomembranes (Mekler and Umarova, 1988). SITS and Erythrosin-NCS (ERITC) were bound covalently to Na$^+$, K$^+$ ATPase. Triplet-triplet energy transfer from the light-excited triplet ERITC to SITS initiated the *cis-trans* photoisomerisation of *cis*-SITS. The photoisomerisation kinetics of SITS was recorded with a regular spectrofluorimeter. The apparent rate constant of triplet-triplet energy transfer from ERITC to *cis*-SITS was found to be $k_{app} = 0.43 \times 10^3$ M^{-1}s^{-1} (at 25 °C). The k_{app} value of the triplet-triplet energy transfer between unbound ERITC and SITS was measured in solution to be 7×10^7 M^{-1} s^{-1}. The drop of k_{app} in the case of labels bound to ATPase is a result of the increased media viscosity and steric factors.

1.1.5. ELECTRON SPIN RESONANCE (ESR)

In the past 18 years new electron spin resonance technology similar to that of nuclear magnetic resonance (NMR) has been developed (Freed, 2000; Eaton and Eaton, 2000). These technologies include two-dimensional Furier transform ESR (2D FT ESR), multiple quantum ESR, high-frequency (high-field) ESR, and low frequency ESR imaging. Such developments have significantly improved method application in investigation molecular structure and dynamics of biological objects.

High-field-high-frequency ESR.
Accordingly, the electron magnetic resonance condition is:

$$hv = g\beta_B H_0 \tag{1.7}$$

where g is a g-factor, β_B is the Bohr magneton, and ν and H_0 are the resonance frequency and magnetic field, respectively. At conventional X-band ESR spectroscopy (9.5 GHz, 3 cm), small g-factor differences of different paramagnetic species and small g-factor anisotropy of anisotropic paramagnetics lead to strongly overlapping ESR lines. Based on the pioneering works of professor Y. S. Lebedev and his colleagues, who developed 148 GHz - 2 mm ESR technique, (Grinberg et al. 1979) these problems have been solved by the use of the high-field ESR spectroscopy. From 1980-1990, the 2 mm spectroscopy was applied to the investigation of spin-labeled proteins and enzymes (Krinichnyi, 1991, 1994; Krinichnyi et. al., 1985, 1987a, b, 1989, 1991; Belonogova et al. 1983, 1997; Likhtenshtein, 1993). The increased magnetic field leads to a separation of spectral features belonging to different principle values of g-tensor, increasing spectral sensitivity to motion dynamics sensitivity in a slow-motion regime (Möbeus, 1998).

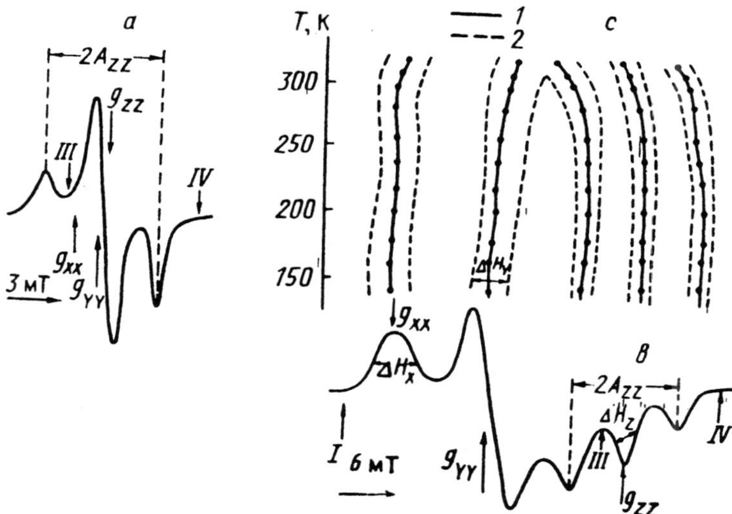

Figure1.6. Temperature dependencies of the parameters of the 2-mm band ESR spectrum of spin-labeled lysozyme; (a) 3-cm band spectrum, 150 K; (b) 3-mm band spectrum,150 K; (c) effect of temperature (Krinichny et al., 1987). Reproduced with permission.

In high-frequency ESR spectroscopy which generates strong magnetic fields (up to 9 T), the cryogenic systems based on superconducting solenoid and standard microwave technology at high frequencies are used. Recently, significant progress in HFHF ESR has been achieved with the use of millimeter-wave quasi-optic technique, permitting the construction of a 9-T, 250-GHz (1.2 mm) spectrometer (Freed, 2000, Budl et al. 1990).

Fig. 1.6 demonstrates advantages of the 2 mm HFHF ESR spectrometer in the separation of spin-probe ESR spectra over the traditional X-band 30 mm ESR spectrometer (Krinichny et al., 1987). Temperature dependences of g- and A-tensors of the 2-mm band ESR spectrum of spin-labeled lysozyme are presented in Fig. 1.6. As is seen in the Figure, the HFHF ESR spectroscopy not only determined the spectral parameters but also followed their temperature dependencies in a wide range of temperatures.

Two-dimentional electron spin resonance (2D ESR)
The 2D ESR technique was developed by Freed and his co-workers (Freed, 2000; Gorcester et al., 1990; Freed and Möbius, 1992) by the analogy of the well-known NMR two-dimentional spectroscopy, correlation spectroscopy (COSY) and spin-echo correlation spectroscopy (SECSY) (Wütrich, 1986 and references tsherein).
In modern NMR, in order to obtain data on through-bond, scalar connectivities or through-space, dipolar connectivities between individual spins, double or multiple irradiation experiments are used. These rely on selective irradiation of a particular resonance line with a radio frequency field and observation of the resulting effects in the rest of the spectrum. With 2D ESR techniques as well as with 2D NMR techniques, limitations of one-dimentional methods connected with overlapping resonance have been overcome (Fig. 1.7).
    Modern 2D ESR methods provide a 2D display of the homogeneous linescape across an inhomogeneous ESR spectrum. This approach allows direct study of dynamic processes (rotational and translational diffusion, electron transfer) and static dipole and exchange spin-spin interactions. The possibility of the two-dimentional approach has been significantly extended with the use Fourier transform (2D FT ESR) and electron spin-echo (2 D SEXSY) techniques. In the 2D FT ESR spectroscopy it has become possible to obtain a 2D display of peaks whose intensities relate directly to cross-relaxation phenomena as spin exchange and dipole-dipole spin-spin interactions. The ability to cover the entire spectral range of a spectrum, leads to a complete 2D mapping of the transition rates between all points in the spectrum (two-dimentional electron-electron double resonance, 2D ELDOR). The 2D SEXSY experiments provide a similar map of the homogeneous transverse spin relaxation rate $(1/T_2)$ and additional information from nuclear modulation of the echo envelope.
Multiple-quantum ESR recently developed for measuring distances between spins (r) longer than 12 Å is based upon double quantum coherence (DQC) pulsed ESR methods (Freed, 2000; Borbat and Freed, 2000). Introducing an extensive cycling of four-pulse sequence allowed the selection of the only coherence pathway related to dipole-dipole splitting in the homogeneous ESR spectrum. The latter is directly connected to the r value

Distance estimation
In solving problems of enzyme catalysis, molecular biophysics of proteins, biomembranes and molecular biology it is necessary to know the spatial disposition of individual parts. One must also know the depth of immersion of paramagnetic centers in a biological matrix, i.e. the availability of enzyme sites to substrates, distance of electron tunneling between a donor and an acceptor group, position of a spin-label in a membrane and in a protein globule, distribution of the electrostatic field around the PC, etc.

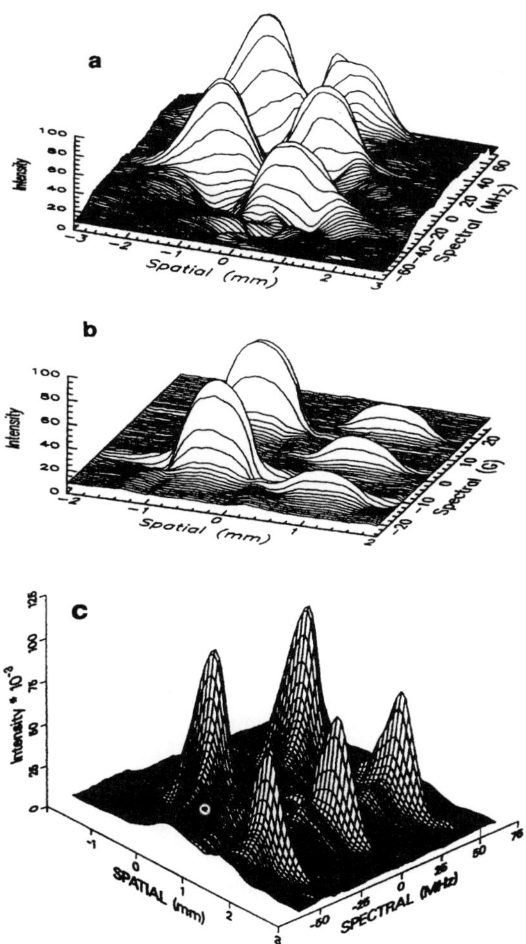

Figure 1.7. Surface plots of the spectral-spatial experiments. (a) Pulsed spectral-spatial frequency encoded experiment, (b) cw analogue of (a), (c) Pulsed spectral-spatial phase encoded image. (Ewert et al., 1991). Reproduced with permission.

Distances between unpaired electrons ranging from 5 to 80 Å and depth of immersion of a paramagnetic center up to 40 Å can be measured by a combination of continuous wave (CW) and pulsed EPR techniques.

Structural studies of systems that cannot be obtained as pure single crystals are beset with serious difficulties. This problem can be solved with the use of ESR techniques if the lineshape or spin-relaxation parameters of the ESR signals from a paramagnetic center respond suitably to the approach of another paramagnetic center. Two types of spin-spin interactions can be distinguished: (1) dipole-dipole interaction arises because the magnetic dipole of one paramagnetic center induces a local magnetic field at the site of another paramagnetic group; (2) exchange interaction is caused by overlap of the orbitals occupied by unpaired electrons as the particles approach each other.

The first applications of dipole-dipole spin-spin interactions to the investigation of protein surface topography were based on changes in the line shape of nitroxide radical ESR spectra arising from dipole-dipole interaction with a second nitroxide radical or paramagnetic ions (Likhtenshtein 1968, Likhtenshtein and Bobodzhanov, 1968; Taylor et al., 1969; Kulikov et al. 1972; Kokorin et al. 1972). Later the greater sensitivity of power saturation curves of a radical to interactions between the radical and paramagnetic ions was demonstrated (Kotel'nikov et al., 1974; Kulikov, 1976; Kulikov and Likhtenshtein, 1977; Case and Leigh, 1976). Dynamic spin exchange interaction during an encounter between radicals and paramagnetic ions diffusing freely in solution (spin label-spin probe technique) was employed to study the dynamics and microstructure of biological objects in the vicinity of added labels (Likhtenstein, 1976, 1977, 1988a,b; 1990, 1993; Likhtenshtein et al., 1970, 1972, 1986a; Hyde et al., 1979; Zamaraev et al., 1977, 1981)

The magnitude of the spin exchange integral J_{SE} characterizes the degree of overlap of molecular orbitals containing the unpaired electrons. J_{SE} is about 10^{14} s^{-1} at Van der Waals distance and decreases exponentially with increasing distance between spins in a vacuum or in homogeneous media (Zamaraev et al., 1981). The exchange interaction can be strengthened by "conductive" (for example, covalent bonds, conjugated structures, etc.) bridges via so called indirect exchange.

Experimental data on the dependence of exchange parameters (the rate of triplet-triplet energy transfer (k_{TT}) or the spin exchange integral (J_{SE})) on the distance (r) between interacting centers are approximated by the following equation (Likhtenshtein 1988(a,b), 1993,1995; Likhtenshtein et al. 1982; Kotel'nikov et al. 1981)

$$k_{TT}, J_{SE} \sim 10^{14} \exp\left[-\beta(r - r_v)\right] \tag{1.8}$$

where r_V is the distance at the Van der Waals contact. For system in which the centers that do not belong to one single molecule are separated by homogeneous "non-conducting" medium (for example, in solvents consisting of molecules with saturated chemical bonds), the dependence of k_{TT} on r is characterized approximately by $\beta_{TT} = 2.6$ Å. For a system in which the radical centers are linked by "conducting" conjugated bonds the dependence of J_{SE} on r followed Eq. (5) with $\beta_{SE} = 0.3$ Å^{-1} (Kotel'nikov et al.,1981; Likhtenshtein 1988a,b, 1995, 1993). To first approximation, spin exchange involves two orbitals with unpaired electrons and in the triplet energy transfer process four orbitals are involved (orbitals of the donor in the ground and exited states, and the acceptor in the ground and excited state). Taking this into consideration we can estimate β_{SE} for "non-conducting" media as $\beta_{SE} = 1.3$ Å^{-1}. In "non-conducting" media J_{SE} is damped by factor of about 4 for one Å increase in r (Eq. 1.8.) The Eq. 1.8 with $\beta_{SE} = 1.3$ Å^{-1} was used for distance estimation between centers involved in spin exchange (Likhtenshtein et al., 1981, Likhtenshtein, 1988b). Since the smallest value of J_{SE} that can be determined experimentally is about 10^6 s^{-1}, the longest distance that can be derived by measuring J_{SE} is <10 Å for "non-conducting" systems.

CW ESR spectroscopy, which is a commonly employed method in many chemical and biochemical laboratories, has been still intensively using in structural investigation for two last decades. Among new tendencies in CW ESR applications the following ones can be pointed out: 1) site directed spin labeling (Feix and Klug, 1998; Hustedt and Beth, 2000; Mchaourab and Perozo, 2000), 2) rigid incorporation of a spin label in proteins backbone alpha carbons (McNulty and Millhauser, 2000); 3) using fast Fourier transform deconvolution (Xiao and Shin, 2000; Steinhoff et al., 1997), 4) electron nucler double resonance (ENDOR) of labeled enzyme active centers (Makinen, Mustafi, and Kasa, 1998), 5) pairwise interaction spin-spin interaction on a solely-tumbling macromolecul, 6) and measurements of depth of immersion and location of paramagnetic centers (Likhtenshtein, 2000; Kulikov et al, 1989).

Recently many modifications of pulse ESR have been designed that allow to improve the distances measurement accuracy and to expand range of distance available for ESR spectroscopy (Eaton et al., 2000; Eaton et al., 2000; Freed, 2000; (Milov et al., 1998) Maret, 1993; and references herein). The principle advances of such the pulse methods is the direct determination of spin-relaxation parameters which, in turn, directly related to spin-spin interactions depending on distances.

Several pulse methods were developed for estimation distances between two slowly-relaxing spins. In a pulse electron-electron double resonance (PELDOR) technique a spin echo is created by a two-pulse sequence at one microwave frequency. The timing of a pulse at a second microwave frequency is varied (Milov et al., 1998). This method is suitable for analysis of weak dipolar interactions. 3-pulse PELDOR with all three pulses at the same microwave frequency ("2 + 1" sequence) was proposed by Raitsimling and his co-workers (2000). A specific feature of the "2 + 1" technique is suppression of dipolar interaction of randomly distributed spins, which allows the selection of a dipolar interaction between radicals. Using a 4- pulse experiments it was possible to eliminate an inherent dead experimental deadtime that limits the magnitude of the dipolar interaction in 2 + 1 sequence and in 3-pulse ELDOR experiments (Pannier et al., 2000).

Pulse methods were used also for measurements of distances between a slowly-relaxing spin (SLS) and rapidly-relaxing spin (RLS). Among them are spin echo dephasing (Eaton and Eaton, 2000), methods based on the enhancements of the SLS in the presence of (RLS) (Eaton and Eaton, 2000; Lakshmi and Brudvig, 2000), and selective hole burning (Dzuba and Kawamori, 1996). In the latter technique a low-power selective 180° pulse is used to burn a hole of a slowly-relaxing spin. The rate of the hole broadening which in certain condition depends on interspin distansc, is monitored by the free induction decay and two-pulse echo. This technique allows to measure distances from 25 to 50 Å. The spin-spin interaction can causes modulation in the out-of-phase echo generated in experiments with spin-polarized radical pairs (Salikhov et al. 1971, 1992; Tang et al., 1994; Dzuba and Hoff, 2000). This method is especially suitable for estimation distance (25-40 A) between ion-radical pairs created in photosystems. Examination of the effect of distances and orientation distribution can be done with the use the "2 + 1", DEER ESE, and double-quantum coherence techniques (Astashkin et al., 1998; Milov et al., 1998; Borbat and Freed, 2000; Steinhoff. et al., 1997).

Depth of immersion of paramagnetic centers
<u>Dynamic exchange interaction in solution.</u> In solutions of low viscosity electron spin-spin dipolar interactions between paramagnetics are averaged by fast rotation of molecules and the short lifetime of the encounter complex and therefore are very weak. When a "radical" in solution encounters another paramagnetic species the broadening of the Lorentian line of the radical is related to the rate constant of the exchange relaxation (k_{ex}).   The value of k_{ex} also can be determined from the change in the rates of the spin-spin ($1/T_{2s}$) and spin-lattice ($1/T_{1s}$) relaxation of a radical in the presence of a paramagnetic species:

$$\Delta\left(\frac{1}{T_{1s}}\right) = k_{ex}C \tag{1.9}$$

Since $1/T_{1s}$ usually is more sensitive to spin-spin interaction than $1/T_{2s}$, especially in the region of slow rotation and in solids, this method widens the accessible range of k_{ex} values (Likhtenshtein and Kulikov, 1977 Kulikov et al. 1983a; Hyde and Subczinski, 1989).

According to Salikhov et al. (1971)

$$k_{ex} = P_{ex}k_d = \frac{f_g f_{ns} k_d J^2 \tau^2{}_c}{\left(1 + J^2\tau^2{}_c\right)} \tag{1.10}$$

where k_d is the rate constant of encounters in solution, P_{ex} is the probability of spin exchange in the course of life time (τ_c) of the encounter complex, f_g is the geometric steric factor, f_{ns} is the nuclear statistical factor and J is the exchange integral of interaction in the encounter complex at the direct contact between the particles. Eq. 16 is valid if $J \gg \delta$ (the differences between the resonance frequencies of the spins), $\delta\tau_c \gg 1$, and the ion spin $S_f = \frac{1}{2}$.

If $J^2 \tau_c^2 \gg 1$, k_{ex} is independent of J (strong exchange) and

$$k_{ex} = f_g f_{ns}\, k_d \tag{1.11}$$

In the case of weak exchange $J^2\tau_c^2 \ll 1$ and

$$k_{ex} = f_g f_{ns}\, k_d\, J^2\tau_c^2 \tag{1.12}$$

Substituting the definition of J from Eq. (1.8), with $\beta=1.3$ Å^{-1} into Eq. (1.12) gives

$$k_{ex} = f_g f_{ns} k_d \tau_c^2 10^{28} \exp 2\left[-1.3(R_0 - r_v)\right] \tag{1.13}$$

This equation can be used for estimation of the distance of closest approach (or depth of the paramagnetic center immersion), R_0, if other factors in the equation are known. For example, in water solution a typical value of $f_g\, f_{ns}\, k_d = 2\times10^{-9}$ $M^{-1}s^{-1}$ for interaction between a nitroxide radical and a paramagnetic species and and $\tau_d = 5\times10^{-11}$ s. For an object with a buried paramagnetic center, if the experimental $k_{ex} = 10^{-7}$ $M^{-1}s^{-1}$, the value of $(R_0\text{-}r_v) = 10$ Å, based on Eq. 1.13.

A more general theory has been developed for exchange relaxation during encounters between paramagnetic particles in solution. According the theory the probabilities of spin relaxation of paramagnetics during encounters depend in general case on a number of parameters such as the exchange integral, the spin-lattice relaxation time, the duration of the encounters, and the differences between the resonance frequencies of the spins (δ) (Salikhov et al., 1971; Likhtenshtein, 1993). A method for the determination of an excited fluorophore depth of immersion, based on the experimental measurement of the exchange interaction with nitroxides, has been recently developed (Strashnikova at al., 2001)

1.1.6. NUCLEAR MAGNETIC RESONANCE

Overview
Nuclear magnetic resonance is proven to be a powerful method for studies of structure, dynamics and conformational transition in proteins and enzymes (Wütrich, 1986; Turner, 1989; Saito and Ando, 1989; Kay et al., 1989, 1998; Palmer et al., 1996; Palmer, 2001; in references therein). As a structural approach, NMR is complimentary to X-ray crystallography. The method allows the investigation of noncrystalline samples in different solution conditions (e.g. temperature, pH, ionic strength, etc.) and in solid nonmonocrystal states. The principle advantage of NMR over X-ray crystallography is the possibility of measuring internal dynamics of biomolecules in a wide range of correlation frequencies, from picosecond to seconds. NMR's method serious limitation is that it cannot be applied to proteins of high molecular mass.

The main parameters of NMR connected to structural and dynamical properties of the object under investigation, are chemical shift (δ), NMR line intensity, scalar spin-coupling constant (J), the nuclear Overhauser effect (NOE) related to dipolar interaction between nuclei, spin-lattice, longitudinal (T_1) and spin-spin transverse (T_2) relaxation times.Among "routine" applications of the method in chemistry is the determination of the concentration of molecules and sequence-specific ^{1}H resonance assignments in solution (Rozek et al., 1998; Wishart and Nip, 1998; Song and Nip, 1998; Slupsky et al., 1998). In the NMR spectra of complex molecules, mutually overlapping resonances are limited by the use of an one-dimensional (1D) NMR. Investigation of structure and molecular dynamics of biological macromolecules, proteins in particular, in solution and solid state, has caused the development of special advantage techniques such as high resolution NMR spectroscopy, Fourier transform technique, pulse two- and multidimensional spectroscopy, and solid state NMR (SSNMR).

A 1D NMR experiment provides information on the chemical shift and spin-spin coupling fine structure of the individual resonances in the spectrum. Double or multiple pulse irradiation experiments provide additional data on through bond *scalar* connectivities or through space *dipolar* connectivities, which relate to resonance assignments, conformational state and dynamics of the molecules under investigation.

The pulse methods rely on selective irradiation of a particular resonance line with a radio frequency (rf) and observation of the resulting effects in the rest of the spectrum. Among commonly employed methods are 2D correlated spectroscopy (COSY), 2D spin-echo correlated spectroscopy (SECSY), 2D nuclear Overhauser and exchange spectroscopy (NOESY), 2D J-resolved spectroscopy (2D-J), and relayed coherence-transfer spectroscopy (RELAYED-COSY) (Wütrich, 1986).

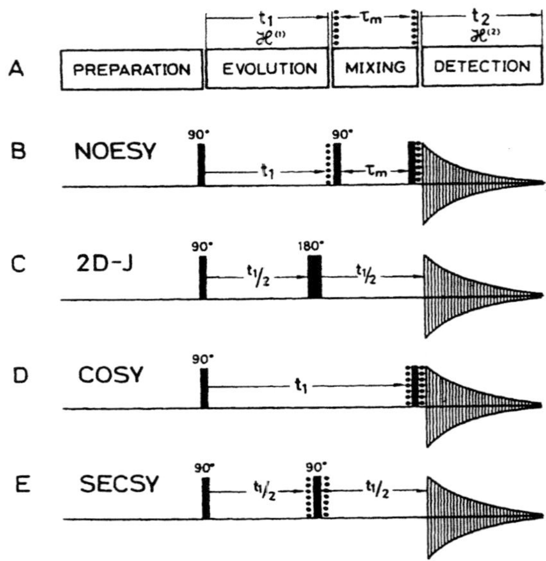

Figure 1.8. Scheme for homonuclear 2D NMR. The dotted lines indicate the bounds of the mixing period (or mixing pulse) in different experiments. D-J spectroscopy has no mixing period (Wütrich, 1986). Reproduced with permission.

In two-dimensional techniques, prior to the observation pulse with the detection period τ_2, an rf pulse is applied with the evolution period χ between the two pulses. A second time dimension (COSY) is created by repeating the same experiment with the incrementation of τ_1. For each value of t_1 a free induction decay (FID) is recorded and, after 2D Fourier transformation, the desired 2D frequency spectrum $S(w_1, w_2)$ is obtained. In the NOESY spectroscopy, the mixing period consisting of two 90° pulses separated by the mixing time τ_m is used. The general experimental scheme for homonuclear 2D NMR (^1H, ^{13}C, ^{15}N and ^{31}P, for example) is shown in Fig. 1.8.

In combination, the 2D NMR spectroscopy allows the determination of resonance frequency (w_i), chemical shift (δ), relaxation times (T_1 and T_2) for each NMR active atoms, coupling constant (J) between adjacent atoms, and parameters of Overhauser enhancement experiments (NOE). These data make a basis for establishing chemical structure and measurement of dynamics of the molecules under investigation. The main trends in recent NMR research on protein and enzymes involve the development and employment of the following methods: 1) NMR spectroscopy with maximal high resolution; 2) high resolution solid state NMR; 3) multidimensional spectroscopy; (4) NMR studies of protein dynamics; (5) heteronuclear NMR; 6) quadrupolar ^{2}H and metal ion NMR; and (7) NMR of paramagnetic molecules.

NMR studies of proten dynamics
In the frame of capacities of the NMR method, motional processes are commonly categorized as (1) fast motion in the nanosecond and picosecond range, which are detected through relaxation rates; (2) intermediate motion in micro- and submicrosecond range, which are probed primarily through shape analysis, rotating frame relaxation rate, and selective inversion recovery method; and (3) slow motion from millisecond to seconds time scale manifesting itself in change of NMR spectrum as a result of averaging of picks position (spin exchange) in the hole-burning experiments, and T_2 anisotropy spectra. (Palmer et al., 1996; Palmer, 2001; Turner, 1998; Kay et al., 1989; Buck et al., 1995; Ekiel et al., 1998; Hammond et al., 1998; Kannelis et al., 1998; Kotovich et al., 1998; Hill et al., 2000; and references therein).

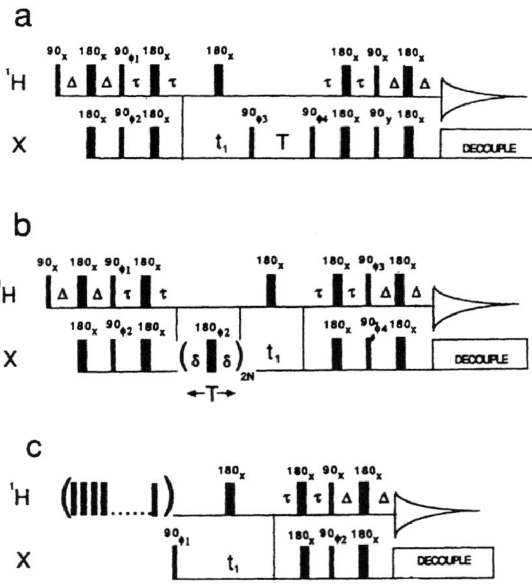

Figure 1.9. Schemes for measurements of ^{15}N spin T_1 (a) and T_2 (b), and ^{1}H NOE values with ^{1}H detection (Kay et al., 1989). Reproduced with permission.

According to the theory of Lipardi and Szabo (1982), values of the spin-lattice $(1/T_1)$ and spin-spin $(1/T_2)$ relaxation rates are dependent on three important structural and dynamic parameters. The first parameter d is proportional to $\mu_i\mu_j/r^3$, where μ_i and μ_j are magnetic moments of nuclei interacting through space, and r is the distance between the nuclei. The second parameter c is proportional to the anisotropy of the nuclear chemical shift. In the spin-lattice relaxation case, the third parameter is the spectral density function:

$$J(w) = \frac{2}{5}\left[\frac{S^2\tau_M}{1+w^2\tau_M{}^2} + \frac{(1-S^2)\tau}{1+w^2\tau_{c^2}}\right] \tag{1.14}$$

where w is the resonance frequency, τ_M and τ_c are the correlation times of the macromolecule overall tumbling   and overall motion of a given nucleus, respectively; and S is the order parameter which indicates the extent of the restriction of internal motion. τ_c is the sum of τ_M and the internal correlation time τ_e. Measuring dependencies of $1/T_1$ on temperature and frequency (with the use of NMR spectrometers of different frequencies) allow the calculation of dynamic parameters τ_e, τ_M and S for a given nucleus.

The nuclei ^{13}C and ^{15}N have been found to be the most suitable for dynamic investigation since the relaxation of these nuclei is governed predominantly by dipolar interaction with directly bound protons and to a much smaller extent, by the chemical shift anisotropy (Kay, 1989; Buck et al., 1995; Shaw et al., 1995; Palmer et al., 1996; Hill et al., 2001; and references herein). Deuterium NMR is also convenient for such a purpose because the spectrum is dominated by a single interaction, the anisotropic quadrupolar interaction of order 200 kHz (Palmer, 1996; Aramani and Vogel, 1998). Schemes of Figure 1.9 illustrates the multi-pulse sequences developed to record ^{1}H-^{15}N correlation spectra for measuring $1/T_1$ and $1/T_2$ relaxation rates of ^{15}N and NOEs for ^{1}H-^{15}N.

Solid-state high resolution NMR
Motivation for the use of the SSNMR for investigation of proteins is arising due to very complicated NMR spectra of macromolecules as a result of dipolar interactions between nuclei, the poor solubility of many proteins, and inefficiency of high resolution NMR spectroscopy in the case of proteins immobilized in membranes or on surfaces, and in suspensions. The first step toward overcoming these principle limitations came in the pioneering work of Schaefer and Stejkal (1976) in an example of the carbon-13 nuclear magnetic resonance of polymers. Using a combination of the magic angle spinning (MAS) and cross-polarization (CP), these authors demonstrated the ability of the CP-MAS NMR methodology to characterize the primary and secondary structures and dynamic features of macromolecules in solid. A sample rotation on the magic angle with a frequency close to dipolar interaction between nuclei, expressed in frequency units, results in a partial or full damping of this interaction and, therefore, simplifies the NMR spectra of objects under investigation.

In dynamic investigations, the dipolar interactions in pairs ^{1}H-^{15}N, ^{1}H-^{13}C, ^{13}C-^{2}H-^{15}N-^{2}H are commonly utilized (Saito and Ando, 1989; Shaw et al., 1995; Palmer et al., 1996; Simanovich, 1998; Wu, 1998; Prosser et al., 1998; Garbutt et al., 1998; Palmer, 2001; and references therein). For example, in the deuterium SSNMR, the anisotropic quadrupolar interact-ion (AQI) contributes an offset from the Larmore frequency (w_o), which is given by

$$w - w_0 = \left(\pm \frac{w_q}{2} \right) \left\{ \left[3(\cos \beta)^2 - 1 \right] + \left[k (\sin \beta)^2 (\cos \gamma)^2 \right] \right\} \qquad (1.15)$$

where w_q is proportional to the quadrupole coupling constant, β is the polar angle relating the bond vector to the applied field, γ is the azimuthal angle relating the quadrupole principle axes to the laboratory frame, and κ is the asymmetry factor for the electric field gradient tensor. The magic angle spinning can dampen AQI and annihilate the spectral overlap. The parametric values of individual nuclei such as resonance frequency, chemical shift, relaxation rates and NOE relating to chemical structure, conformation, and intra molecular dynamics can be obtained through the methods described in the previous subsection.

Electron nuclear double resonace
In the ENDOR methods, the spin system is irradiated by a microwave field to partially saturate the EPR transition while simultaneously sweeping the sample with radiofrequency radiation through nuclear resonance transitions (Makinen, 1998; Makinen et al. 1998). ENDOR provides a means of precisely measuring the hyperfine interaction (A_{hf}) between electron and nuclear spins. Within the strong-field approximation, the observed A_{hf} is given by Eq. 1.16:

$$A_{hf} = \left(\frac{g_e \beta_e g_n \beta_n}{hr^3} \right) \times \left(3 \cos^2 \alpha - 1 \right) + A_{iso} \qquad (1.16)$$

where r is the modulus of the electron-nucleus position vector $\mathbf{r}$ and α is the angle between the magnetic field H_0 and r. Direct structural information about a paramagnetic molecule orientation and conformation can be achieved in single-crystal EPR and ENDOR studies. Nevertheless, the theoretical analysis of ENDOR spectra allows the calculation of r and α of polycrystalline or frozen glassy samples.

Another method that is important for structure assignment is the electron-nuclear-nuclear triple resonance (TRIPLE) spectroscopy (Endeward et al., 1998; Makinen et al., 1998), which is an extension of the ENDOR method. In the general TRIPLE experiment, transitions of different nuclei are driven simultaneously. One ENDOR transition is irradiated saturating rf power at a constant frequency, while the entire ENDOR frequency range is swept to obtain the TRIPLE spectrum.

Nitroxide spin molecules are convenient probes for the ENDOR application for solving some problems of enzyme catalysis. From ENDOR studies of molecular structures and conformations, several spin-labeled amino acid derivatives incorporated into enzyme-active sites have been reported (Makinen et al., 1998). For instance, the spin-labeled transition-state analog in the α-chymotripsin reaction, N-(2,2,5,5-tetramethyl-1-oxypyrrolinyl0-L-phenylalaninal, has been synthesized. The stereoview of this molecule into the active site of α-chymotripsin is shown in Fig. 1.10. The conformation of the acyl moiety of the substrate analog in the active site of the reaction intermediate differs significantly from that of the free substrate in solution. This is strong evidence that torsional alterations are induced in the substrate by binding to enzymes to form a catalytically active productive pretransition state. (Section 2. 8)

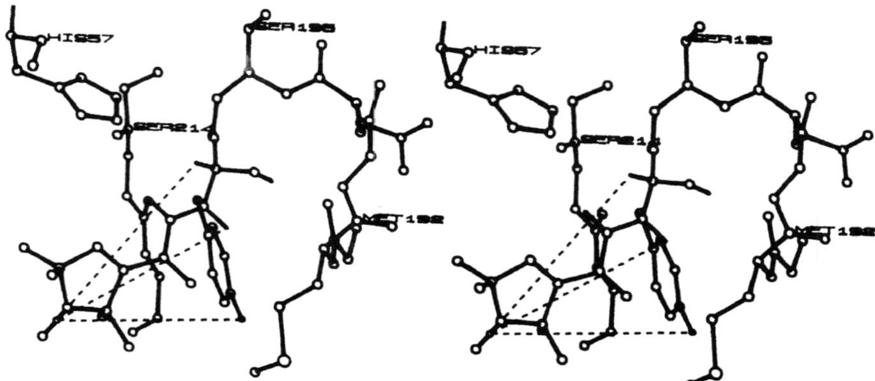

Figure1.10.   Stereo diagram of the acyl moiet of the spin-labeled tryptophanyl-acylenzyme reaction intermediate of α-chymotrypsin. Active site residues close to the acyl moiety are labeled (Makinen et al., 1998). Reproduced with permission.

1.1.7. MASS-SPECTROSCOPY (MS)

In the traditional mass spectroscopic technique, a volatile sample is introduced to the vacuum region of the mass spectrometer and subsequent ionization can be accomplished with an electron beam. Previously, the volatile samples were routinely separated with the use of gas chromatography. For the analysis of nonvolatile biological species special methods for sample introductions and ionization have been developed. These methods together with Fourier transform (FT), cyclotron resonance (ICR) and mass spectrometry provide highly efficienct modern MS analysis of complex biological systems (Cole, 1977; Spiro, 1997; Burlingam, 1999; Hendickson and Emmett, 1999; Gerber et al., 1999; and references herein).

Electrospray ionization (ESI) is a widely accepted MS interface for the introduction of nonvolatile samples to the mass spectrometer at atmospheric pressure. The basic process involves flow of the analate solution through a capillary that is held at a potential. At the end of the capillary, because of the large change in potential, the solution is dispersed into finely droplets. These charged droplets are drawn into the source through a heated passage by a pressure gradient towards the analyzer. Under the combined effect of the pressure drop and temperature, the droplets are desolvated and ion charges on the analate ions. The maximum number of charges can usually be predicted from the primary sequences of the molecule (Hendrickson and Emmett, 1999). For instance, for ion analysis of peptides and proteins, the positive charges are normally associated with basic amino acids of the molecules and amino terminus.

All variations of the ESI use the pressure gradient, countercurrent gas with glass capillary, heated capillary (or heated chamber) and previous high-pressure liquid chromatography (HPLC). Several ionization methods have been developed. In an ionspray method, nebulization (formation of droplets) is performed in the presence of an applied potential. Atmospheric pressure chemical ionization (APCI) is a nebulizer for formation of droplets at high-flow rates and an additional electrode that provides an ionizing corona discharge. Recently developed low-flow ESI has several advantages which provide increased sampling efficiency, better desolvation, reduction of the gas load to the vacuum system, and less analate (Hendrickson and Emmett, 1999 and references therein).

The high field ESI FT-ICR mass spectrometry permits routine analysis for proteins as large as 67 kDa and with the highest mass 112 kDa. The favorable ration mass/charge for the method detection is $500 < m/z < 2500$ with the mass accuracy about 100 ppb. The ESI FT-ICR MS is used for the investigation of the hydrogen/deuterium exchange, conformational analysis, complex mixture analysis, and for establishing elemental composition from isotopic fine structure.

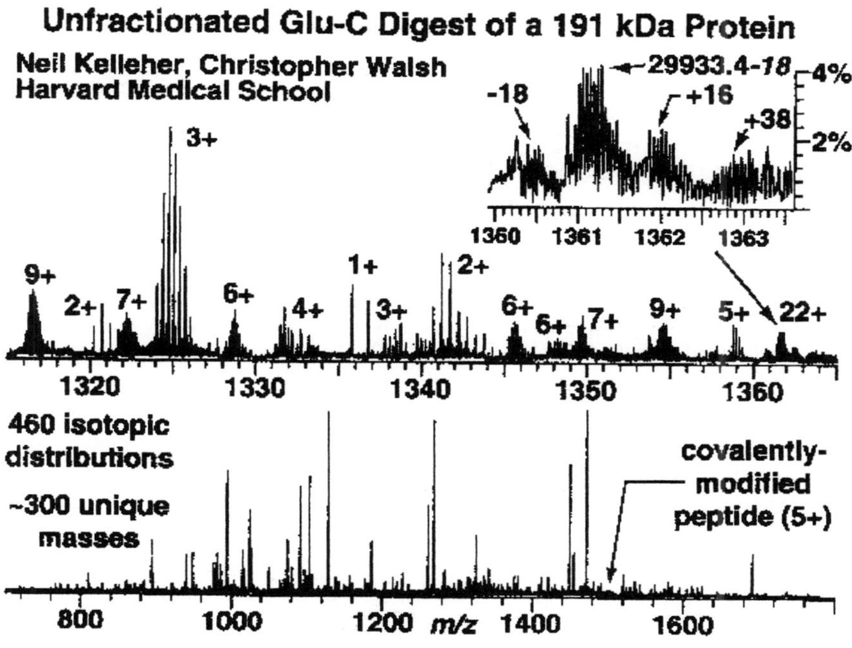

Figure 1.11. Electrospray ionization Fourier transform ion cyclotron resonance mass spectrum of a glu-c-digested 191-kDa protein, collected on the NHMFL 9.4-T system. (Inset) A resolved 30-kDa fragment. Data kindly provided by N. Kelleher.

The ESI-MS is used for simultaneous detection of enzymatic products and chemically identical standards, which are distinguished by the deuterium labeling (Gerbert et al., 1999). The method starts with the design of a synthetic conjugate molecule that contains a target substrate for the desired enzyme. The conjugate molecule is covalently attached to a link , which in turn is attached to a molecular handle. The linker and handle are designed to facilitate ionization by ESI, to allow highly selective capture from a biological fluid for facile purification, and to block action of other enzymes. The method is used for the simultaneous assay lysosomal β-galactosidase and N-acetyl-a-D glucosaminidase. Biotin is served as a molecular handle which is coupled to sarcosine. Sarcosine provides an N-methylated amide linkage to biotin to block the enzyme biotinase. Biotin in turn allows the specific capture of the substrate conjugate to steptavidin immobilized on an agarose matrix.

Mass spectroscopy, in combination with other physico-chemical and biochemical methods, promises to be an effective tool for fruitful study of the structure and action mechanism of enzymes.

1.2. Kinetic methods

Various kinetic methods in the enzyme catalysis has been described elsewhere (Likhtenshtein, 1988a; Gates, 1991; Bugg, 1997; Cornish-Bowden, 1995, 2001; Varfolomeev and Gurevich, 1998); Fersht,1999; Gutfreund,. 1995; Hammes, 2000; Leninger et al.1993;). In this section we concentrate on recent developments in methods of the kinetic isotope effect, transition state analoges, and nanosecond temperature jump techniques.

1.2.1. KINETIC ISOTOPE EFFECT

Methods of kinetic isotope effects (KIE) permit experimental access to the transition-state (TS) structure of chemical and enzymatic reactions (Swain et al., 1958; Marcus, 1968; Levich et. al., 1970; Warshel et. al., 1992; Hwang and Warshel, 1996; Bruno and Bialik, 1992; Kresge and Silverman, 1999; Cleland and Northrop, 1999; Schramm, 1999; Berti, 1999; Northrop and Cho, 2000; Alhambra et al., 2000: and references therein). The method include the following steps: (1) chemical or enzymatic synthesis of substrates with specific and stereospecific isotopes; (2) experimental measurement of KIE; (3) measurement of binding isotope effects and their influence on observed KIE; (4) use of KIE information for suggestions about TS structure; and (5) application of TS information for the design of TS analogs, inhibitors of the enzyme reactions.

Quantitative analysis has become possible due to technical advances in synthesis of complex molecules with isotopic labels at any one of many specific position and measurements of KIE determined accurately and precisely by mass-spectrometry and radioactive methods.   The most informative method for elucidation of the enzyme reaction limiting step and nature of transition-state is the competitive labeled method (Schramm, 1999). This method is based on the use of two labeled preparations of the same substrate, one with the labeled atom at a site expected to experience bonding changes at the TS and a second preparation with a different labeled atom at a site remote from the bond-breaking site. Many molecules of interest can be specifically labeled with radioactive atoms T or ^{14}C and can be incorporated into substrates that also contain stable isotopes D, ^{15}N and ^{18}O.

A theory of KIE for multistep enzymatic reactions was developed by Cleland and Northrop (1999). It is obvious that when the barrier of the chemical reaction step is at least several kcal/mole above all others, the step is essentially step- limiting. The isotope in this step is fully expressed in the experimental ratio V/K , where V and K are the reaction maximum rate and Michaelis constant, respectively. If the chemical step does not have the highest barrier, the isotope effect can be partially or fully suppressed. For the mechanism:

$$E + S \; \underset{k_2}{\overset{k_1}{\leftrightarrow}} \; ES \underset{k_4}{\overset{k_3}{\leftrightarrow}} ES^* \underset{k_6}{\overset{k_5}{\leftrightarrow}} EP^* \underset{k_8}{\overset{k_7}{\leftrightarrow}} EP \overset{k_9}{\rightarrow} E + P$$

where $ES^* \leftrightarrow EP^*$ is the isotope sensitive chemical step, the isotope effect on V/K at the substitution of a light atom X for a heaver atom Y is given by

$$\alpha_{X,Y} = \frac{V^X K^Y}{K^X V^Y} = \frac{\left[\left(\frac{k_5^X}{k_5^Y} \right) + c_f + \left(\frac{K^X}{K^Y} \right) c_r \right]}{1 + c_f + c_r} \tag{1.17}$$

where c_f and c_r are combinations of rate constants of different steps (so called commitments). The forward commitment

$$c_f = \left(\frac{k_5}{k_4} \right)\left(1 + \frac{k_3}{k_2} \right) \tag{1.18}$$

whereas the reverse commitment

$$c_r = \left(\frac{k_6}{k_7} \right)\left(1 + \frac{k_8}{k_9} \right) \tag{1.19}$$

When c_f and c_r are very small $(\alpha_{X,Y} = k_5^X/k_5^Y)$ and experimental KIE is directly related to the limiting chemical step. If c_f is very large, the KIE will be completely suppressed.

Analysis of experimental data on KIE indicate certain interesting conclusions about the detail mechanism of rate-limiting chemical reaction step and TS structure. In general, atoms that become vibrationally less constrained in the TS give normal KIE ($k_{light}/k_{heavy} > 1$). Conversely, atoms more constrained at the TS course give inverse KIE. Fig. 1.12 summarized the primary ^{14}C and secondary T KIE's expected for different reaction mechanisms. As is seen from the Figure, the pattern of these two KIF is sufficient to distinguish the mechanisms. Analysis of the KIE magnitudes is capable of providing quantitative information on broken bonds order in transition state for each type of reaction.

In the framework of this approach, the theoretical magnitude of kinetic isotope effect is given by:

$$KIE = MMI \times ZPE \times EXC \qquad (1.20)$$

where *MMI*, *ZPI*, and *EXP* are related to the moment of inertia, zero point energy, and excited states energy, respectively. The input required for BEBOVA analysis is (1) the structure of the initial and final states; (2) the substrate spring force constants for each internal coordinate; (3) the list of atomic masses; and (4) the reaction coordinate.

The method was applied to nucleophilic substitution on NAD^+, including hydrolysis and ADP-ribolization reactions of peptide substrates. It was shown that in these systems the hydrolytic TS's follow S_N2 mechanisms with highly dissociative structure. In the TSs the ADP-ribosyl bond is completely broken with low but significant bonding to the water nucleophile.

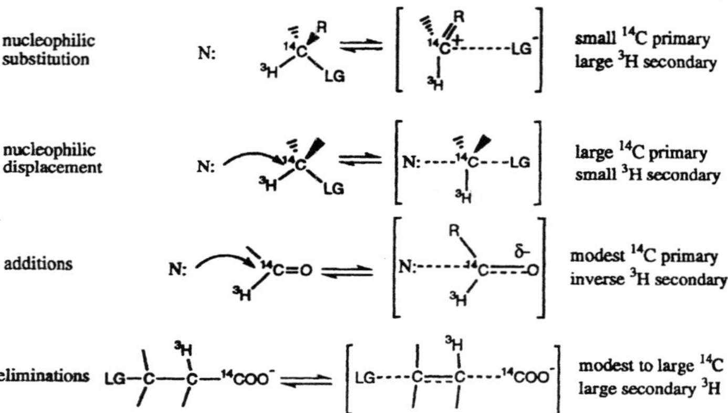

Figure 1.12. The KIE expected for the primary ^{14}C and a secondary ^{3}H isotopic label are indicated (Schramm, 1999). Reproduced with permission.

The analysis of experimental KIEs via the structure interpolation approach to bond energy/ bond order vibrational analysis (BEBOVA) makes it possible to quantitatively determine TS's (Berti, 1999 and references therein).

Solvent isotope effects are complicated by the fact that primary, secondary and medium effects are multiplied together and

$$\left(\frac{k_{H_2O}}{k_{D_2O}}\right) = \left(\frac{k_H}{k_D}\right)_{prim} \times \left(\frac{k_H}{k_D}\right)_{sec} \times \left(\frac{k_{H_2O}}{k_{D_2O}}\right)_{medium} \qquad (1.21)$$

In proton inventory technique, solvent isotope effects are plotted against atomic fractions of deuterium in mixed isotopes of water. A linear plot represents a contribution from a single origin, whereas nonlinear plots may be generated from multiple origins.

Interpretation of experimental data on the proton inventory technique is difficult because of the products of multiple effects, but also because of the uncertain of influence of solvent isotope composition on pKa of enzyme functional groups and on electrostatic interactions between charges. Changes of the vibrational properties of water molecules inside enzyme globules and the complexity of multistep mechanisms can also complicate an unequivocal interpretation. To avoid these difficulties, high pressure was proposed as a perturbant (Northrop and Cho, 2000). It is suggested that high pressure simply changes distribution within preexisting equilibrium, and pressure effects can separate multiple isotopes effects from each other. When applied in conjunction with substrate isotope effects, a primary kinetic assignment can distinguish between concerted and stepwise chemical mechanisms of enzymatic catalysis.

Effects of high pressure on the kinetic parameter V/K are given by Eq. 1.22:

$$\left(\frac{V}{K}\right)_p = \left\{\frac{k_1}{1 + K_{\frac{G}{E}}\,\exp{-\frac{\Delta V_{\frac{G}{E}}}{RT}}\,p}\right\} \times \left\{\frac{R_0\,\exp{-\dfrac{\Delta V^{\neq}p}{RT}}}{1 + c_f\,\exp\left(\dfrac{-\Delta V^{\neq}p}{RT}\right) + c_f\,\exp{-\left(\dfrac{\Delta V^{\neq} - \Delta V_{eq}}{RT}\right)}p}\right\} \quad (1.22)$$

where p is the pressure, R_0 is the product ratio of forward and reverse enzymatic constant, $K_{G/E}$ is the equilibrium constant for transition between two non-active and active enzyme conformations, c_f is the forward commitment (Eq. 1.18); ΔV_{eq}, $\Delta V^{\neq}$, and $\Delta V_{G/E}$ is the difference in volume at the formation of the enzyme-substrate complex, the transition state, and the G $\rightarrow$ E conformational transition, respectively. Eq. 1.22 predicts at least biphasic dependence of (V/K)p on pressure originating from the changes of the volume at limiting chemical steps and at the enzyme conformational transition.

This method was used for investigating the mechanism of oxidation of benzyl alcohol by yeast alcohol dehydrogenase (YADH). In this reaction an intrinsic tritium effect k_T is fully expressed in V/K. At pressure up to approximately 1.5 kbar, changes in (V/K)p or the substrate binding were directly proportional to pressure, probably because of the increase of the rate constant for hybrid transfer due to its negative activation volume. The subsequent decrease in binding at higher pressure was shown to be due to a positive volume change in conformational transition of E-NAD$^+$ complex. Such a transition involves considerable solvent reorganization and, therefore, leads to a solvent isotope effect. The experimental ratio (V/K)$_{D2O}$/(V/K)$_{H2O}$ first increased as pressure increased up to 1.5 kbar and, then decreased. Thus, the pressure effect on the reaction is stronger in D$_2$O than that in H$_2$O. The extremely small sum of commitments c_f + c_r = 10^{-17} shows that the hydrid transfer is the reaction limiting step.

1.2..2. TRANSITION STATE ANALOGS METHODS

In 1946 Pauling introduced idea that lowering of the activation energy in enzyme catalysis stems from the enzyme's affinity for the transition state exceeding it's affinity for the substrate. This idea was supported by the finding of effective inhibitors called "transition state analogs" Transition state theory for enzymatic reactions proposes that the rate enhancement imposed by enzymes is due to the tight binding or stabilization of the activated complex relative to initial reagents. Knowledge of the TS can provide information to design stable TS analogs. Such an approach has three important aspects: (1) hinting to chemists about the plausible structure of specific inhibitors for synthesis, (2) using these inhibitors to test working hypothesizes about TS structures, and (3) using these inhibitors for the regulation of enzymatic processes in vitro and in vivo.

A computational method of the structure prediction of an inhibitor is based on an analysis of the quantitative structure-activity relationship (QSAR) (Ariens, 1989: Martin et al, 1996). In this method, quantities such as volume, hydrophobicity or a number of specific groups are experimentally derived. QSAR for a given TS is a polynomial equation with n terms. Each of these terms corresponds to the number of aforementioned regions of a particular molecule under investigation. In the framework of this approach, it is necessary to define, prior to synthesis and testing, a functional relationship between molecular structure and molecular action. Then the polynomial equation can be used to predict the inhibition constant of molecules that have been not tested experimentally.

Braunheim and Schwartz (1999) used *ab initio* quantum mechanics to investigate molecules in transition states. Molecules in enzyme active sites are described as coincidently oriented van der Waals surfaces that vary in geometry and electrostatic potential. The theory takes into consideration that the energy of ionic interactions and hydrogen bonds drops off with $1/r$ and van der Waals interactions drop of with $1/r^{12}$. As a result, the relative geometric position of groups is important for the task of simulating molecular recognition. The authors stressed that analysis of the quantum mechanical wave function in the system is important for this recognition because the molecular interactions are sensitive to subtle variations caused by intra- and intermolecular polarization. Polarization across conjugated bonds and of large atoms such as Br and I can have profound effects on binding.

The quantum description of molecules was created in the following way (Braunheim and Schwartz, 1999): 1) the molecular structures were energy minimized using semiempirical methods; (2) the wave function for the molecule was calculated; (3) from this wave function, the electrostatic potential was calculated at all points around and within the molecule: (4) the electron density, the square of the wave function, was calculated; (5) with this information the electrostatic potential (EP) at the van der Waals surface was generated. Regions with EP close to zero, a partial EP positive or negative EP, and even greater potentials, may be involved in the van der Waals, hydrogen bonds or in coulombic interactions, respectively.

The theoretically predicted values of ligand-binding free energy $\Delta G_{theor}/RT$ for cytodine deaminase agreed with the values from experimental $\Delta G_{exp}/RT$. Thus, for the citidine transition state $\Delta G_{theor}/RT = -30$ and $\Delta G_{exp}/RT = -36$, for a strong inhibitor hydrated pyrimidine-2-one ribonucleoside $\Delta G_{theor}/R = -27$ and $\Delta G_{exp}/RT = -27$; and for a weak inhibitor uridine $\Delta G_{theor}/RT = -6.1$ and $\Delta G_{exp}/RT = -6.0$. Fig. 1.13 shows the structures of the AMP nucleosidase transition state and of inhibitor structures, which were theoretically predicted. The equilibrium constant of AMP was estimated as $K_{TS} = 2\times10^{-17}M$. The strongest inhibitor, formycin 5'-PO_4 has the inhibitor constant $K_I =$

4.3x10^{-8} M, whereas the Michaelis constant for the substrate AMP was found to be K_M = 1.2x10^{-4} M.

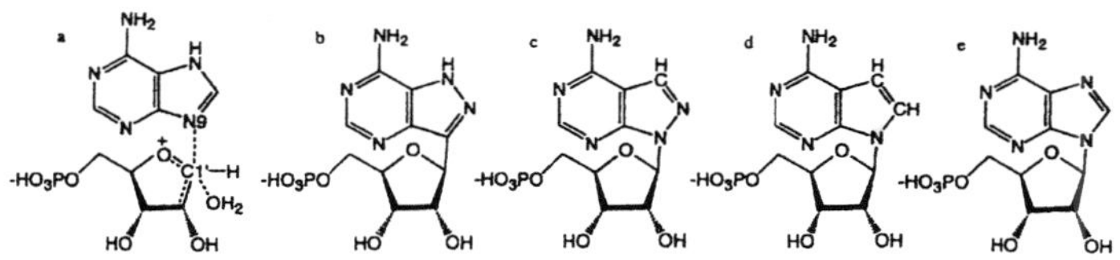

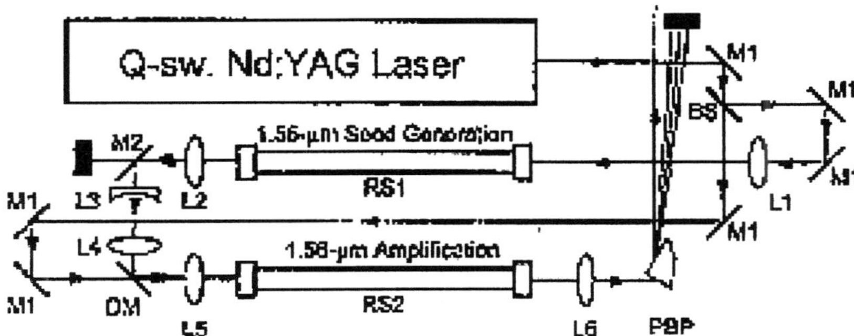

Figure 1.13. Structures of AMP transition state (a) and inhibitors of the nucleosidase reactions (b-e) (Braunheim and Schwartz, 1989). Produced with permission.

Theories that do not invoke tight binding of the TS complex have also been proposed (Cannon et al., 1996 and references therein)

1.2.3. NANOSECOND TEMPERATURE JUMP

A nanosecond temperature jump is induced by an illumination of a sample with the laser heat pump. For instance, in the work of Yamamoto et al. (2000) the 1.56-μm heat pulse 9 ns width at 10 Hz was obtained through the two-step stimulating Raman scattering in D$_2$ gas.

Figure 1.14. Schematic diagram of the 1.56-μm pulse-generation system with the stimulated Raman seeding and amplification technique (Yamamoto et al., 2000). Reproduced with permission.

The temperature rise (DT) was determined by the anti-Stokes (I_{as}) to Stokes (I_s) intensity ratios of the 317 and 897 cm^{-1} bands of MoO_4^{-2} in an aqueous solution. These intensities were exited with another laser for variable times (Δt) after the illumination of the 1.56 μm pulse. The ΔT value was calculated from the equation:

$$\ln\left(\frac{I_{as}}{I_s}\right)_{T_0+\Delta T} - \ln\left(\frac{I_{as}}{I_s}\right)_{T_0} = -\left(\frac{hc\nu_o}{k_B}\right)\left[\frac{1}{(T_0+\Delta T)} - \frac{1}{T_0}\right] \qquad (1.23)$$

where T_0 is the initial temperature and ν_0 is the molecular vibration wavenumber. The NTP technique in combination with the time-resolved Raman method was used to study the unfolding of bovine pancreatic ribonuclease. After a T-jump as large as 9°C in 10 ns, the time resolved Raman spectra excited at 532 nm were monitored. A schematic diagram of the 1.56-µm pulse-generation system with the stimulated Raman seeding and amplification technique is presented in Fig. 1.14.

CHAPTER 2

MECHANISMS OF ENZYMATIC REACTIONS

2.1. General principles of enzymatic catalysis

Creating enzymes in the processes of biological evolution, Nature used a whole arsenal of mechanisms of chemical reactions including covalent catalysis, general acid/base catalysis, electrostatic catalysis, desolvation, strain or distortion, short- and long-distance electron transfer, proton and hydride transfer, multielectron transfer, synchronous reactions, and donor-acceptor catalysis. Specific forces maintaining the enzyme's native structure and providing its interaction with substrates and inhibitors are similar to those we meet in chemistry. They are covalent bonds, ionic (electrostatic) interactions, ion-dipoles and dipole-dipole interactions, hydrogen bonds, charge transfer complexes, hydrophobic interactions, and van der Waals Forces.

A large group of scientists, including the author, believe that a chemical catalytic process, as well as an enzymatic reaction contains a certain sequence of elementary chemical steps. Each of these steps proceeds by "ordinary" laws of chemical kinetics. The accelerating action of a catalyst is accounted for by the fact that its active centers become involved in such chemical reactions with substrate molecules, which lead to an increase in the velocity of the process as a whole. Within the framework of this concept, enzymes are characterized by a set of certain specific properties, which have been "polished off "in the course of biological evolution.

According to modern concepts, the occurrence of a catalytic reaction proceeds at a sufficient rate provided the following factors ("selection" rules) are operating in concert:

1. <u>The Thermodynamic Feasibility of the Process as a Whole.</u> The change of the positive standard Gibbs energy (ΔG_0) in an each step must not be greater than about 20-30 kJ/mole.

2. <u>Proximity and Orientation Effects of the Substrate Molecules and the Catalytic Site.</u> The preliminary approach of two reacting particles during a complex catalyst-substrate formation, resulting from the interaction of the groups that do not participate directly in subsequent chemical reactions (binding groups), increases the rate constant of the reaction by about 10^2 times. The precise orientation of the substrate relative to catalytic groups may provide an additional acceleration of 10^2 to 10^6 times, depending on the type of reactions. For reactions involving three and more molecules, the acceleration due to these effects may be considerably greater. The proximity and precise orientation prevents a loss of entropy converting a multimolecular reaction to a monomolecular one.

3. <u>Low Energy Activation in Each Step.</u> In certain cases, the rule is, the better the thermodynamic of the step, the lower the energy activation (Polanyi-Semenov, Bronsted equations, for example).

Among the factors determining low energy activation of elementary chemical steps are concerted and multi-electron mechanisms, mechanical stress on substrate and catalytic groups and optimum polarity of the active site cavity.

4. <u>Favorable Quantum-Mechanical Factors.</u> The rate constants of an elementary step of a chemical process (k) depend significantly on the value of resonance integral V which is proportional to the overlap integral S. The latter characterizes the degree of positive overlap of the electron wave functions. If the overlap is, as a rule, very significant, then frequencies of electronic motion exceed the frequencies of nuclear motion with characteristic times t = 10^{-12} to 10^{-13} s. In this case, adiabatic approximation is valid and k does not depend on V. If the overlap is slight, i. e. the centers are separated by a large distance or electronic transitions are symmetrically forbidden, then k is proportional to V^2. Another quantum-mechanical selection rule, the principle of the total spin conservation follows from the low of momentum conservation.

5. <u>Effective Synchronization of Nuclei in a Chemical Concerted Reaction.</u> In a concerted process the transition from initial state to transition states occurs upon the motion of nuclei (taking about 10^{-13} s) in a certain direction, which is the only possible path that can lead to reaction products. Obviously, the statistic thermal nature of chemical processes limits the number of nuclei, which can be involved in a signal elementary step. In such cases, the value of synchronization factor (α_{syn}) can be markedly less then 1.

6. <u>Formation of Catalytic Ensembles. Regulatory Capacity.</u> Formation of ordered catalytic ensembles can greatly facilitate the accessibility of substrates in consecutive chemical and enzyme reactions. Capacity of catalysts to be or not to be active in proper space and proper time is of great importance especially in biological cells. A catalyst's capacity for switching activity in the appropriate space and time is very important, especially in biological cells.

2.2. Electron Transfer

Electron transfer is one of the most ubiquitous and fundamental phenomena in chemistry, physics and biology (Jortnter and Bixon, 1999a, b; Marcus, 1968, 1999; Sutin, 1999; Marcus and Sutin, 1985). Non-radiative and radiative ET are found to be a key elementary step in many important processes involving isolated molecules and super molecules, ions and excess electrons in solution, condensed phase, surfaces and interfaces, electrochemical systems and biology. A combination of X-ray crystallographic and physicochemical experiments on isolated proteins and enzymes and kinetics investigations produces detailed picture of initial events in those systems under investigation. Some of the most critical steps in the functioning of photosynthetic reaction centers, mitochondrial enzymes, nitrogenase, copper, heme and non-heme iron and molybdenum- containing enzymes and proteins are the long-range electron transfer reactions (Marcus, 1999; Sutin 1999; Marcus and Sutin 1986; Likhtenshtein, 1988a; Moser and Dutton, 1992: Farver and Pecht, 1999; Jourtner and Bixon, 1999a; Bixon, 1992; Bixon and Jortner, 1999; Gray and Winkler, 1996; Gray and Ellis, 1994; MacLendon et al., 1999; Machonkin et al., 2000; and references therein)

2.2.1. THEORETICAL MODELS

Two states models

As a light microscopic particle, an electron easily tunnels through a potential barrier. Therefore the process is governed by the general tunneling law formulated by Gamov (1926). The principle theoretical cornerstone for condensed-phase ET was laid by Franck and Libby (1949-1952) who asserted that the Frank-Condon principle is applicable not only to the vertical radiative processes but also to non-radiative horizontal electron transfer. The next decisive step in the field was done by Marcus, Zwolinski, Eyring and Weiss (1954) and then by Marcus (1956-1960) for the ET in solution. These authors articulated the need for readjustment of the coordination shells of reactants in self-exchange reactions and of the surrounding solvent to the electron transfer. They also showed that the electronic interaction of the reactants gives rise to the splitting at the intersection of the potential surfaces, which leads to a decrease of the energy barrier.

Let us now consider the situation involving the transition of a system from one state to another using the concept of energy terms. With a certain value of the coordinate Q_{tr} the energy of the initial (i) and final (f) states is the same and the law of energy conservation permits the term-term transition (Fig. 2.1). Generally, the rate constant of the transition in the crossing area is dependent on the height of the energetic barrier (activation energy, E_a), the frequency of reaching of the crossing area (υ) and the transition coefficient (κ):

$$k_{tr} = \kappa\nu\exp\left(- E_a\right) \tag{2.1}$$

The transition coefficient κ is related to the probability of the transition in the crossing area (P) and is described by the Landau-Zener equation (Landau, 1932, Zener, 1933)

$$k = \frac{2P}{(1+P)} \tag{2.2}$$

where

$$P = 1 - \exp\left[\frac{-4\pi^2 v^2}{hv(S_i - S_f)}\right] \tag{2.3}$$

V is the electronic coupling factor (the resonance integral), v is the velocity of nuclear motion, and S_i and S_f are the slopes of the initial and final terms in the Q_{tr} region. If the exponent of the exponential function is small, then

$$P = \frac{4\pi^2 v^2}{hv(S_i - S_f)} \tag{2.4}$$

and the process is non-adiabatic. Thus, the probability of non-adiabatic transfer is higher, the smaller the magnitude of the resonance integral, the lower the velocity of nuclear motion and the smaller the difference in the curvature of the terms. At P = 1 the process is adiabatic and treated by classical Arhenius or Eyring equations.

The theory predicts a key role by electronic interaction, which is quantitatively characterized by the value of resonance integral V in forming energetic barrier. If this value is sufficiently high, the terms are split with a decreasing activation barrier and the process occurs adiabatically. In another non-adiabatic extreme, where the interaction in the region of the coordinate Q_{tr} is close to zero, the terms practically do not split, and the probability of transition i $\rightarrow$ f is very low.

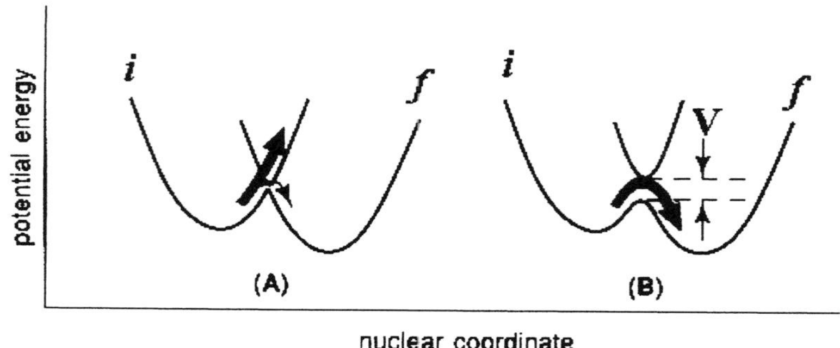

Figure 2.1. Variation in the energy of the system along the reaction coordinate: a diabatic terms of the reactant (1) and products (2): b adiabatic terms of the ground state (I) and excited state (II): V is the resonance integral.

Marcus model. Reorganization energy
According to the Marcus model (Marcus, 1968, 1999; Marcus and Sutin 1985), the distortion of the reactants, products and solvent from their equilibrium configuration is described by identical parabolas, shifted related to each other according to the driving force of the value of the process, standard Gibbs free energy ΔG_0 (Fig. 2.2). Within the adiabatic regime (strong electronic coupling, the resonance integral V > 200 cm^{-1}), the value of the electron transfer rate constant is

$$k_{ET} = \left(\frac{hv}{k_B T}\right) \exp -\left[\frac{(\lambda + \Delta G_o)^2}{4\lambda k_B T}\right]$$

(2.5)

and the Gibbs energy of activation is:

$$\Delta G^\# = \frac{(\lambda + \Delta G_0)^2}{4\lambda k_B T}$$

(2.6)

where λ is the reorganization energy defined as energy for the vertical electron transfer without replacement of the nuclear frame. The formula 2.2 predicts the log k_{ET} - ΔG_0 relationships depending on the relative magnitudes of λ and ΔG_0 (Fig. 2.3): (1) $\lambda > \Delta G_0$, when log k increases if ΔG_0 decreases (normal Marcus region), (2) $\lambda = \Delta G_0$, the reaction becomes barrierless, and (3) $\lambda < \Delta G_0$, when log k decreases with increasing driving force.

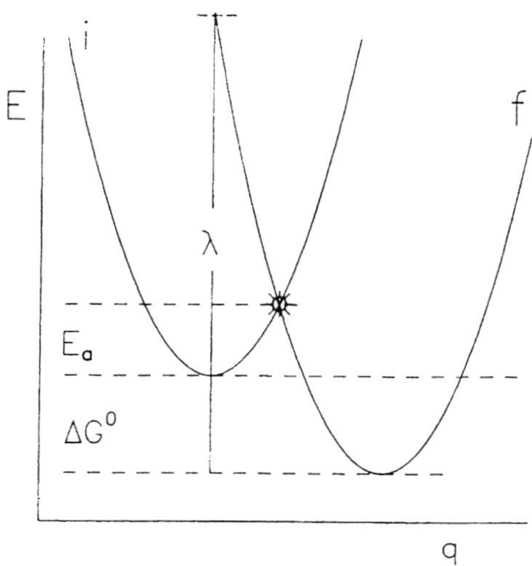

Figure 2.2. The free energy of initial (i) and final (f) terms as a function of generalized classical coordinates. ΔG_0 and l are the Gibbs and reorganization energy respectively (the Marcus model).

The Marcus theory also predicts the Bronsted slope magnitude in the normal Marcus region:

$$\alpha_B = \frac{d\Delta G^{\#}}{d\Delta G_0} = \frac{1}{2}\left(1 + \frac{\Delta G_0}{\lambda}\right) \qquad (2.7)$$

The processes driving force (ΔG_0) can be measured experimentally or calculated theoretically. For example, when solvation after the process of producing photo-initiated charge pairing is rapid, ΔG_0 can be approximately estimated by the following equation:

$$\Delta G_0 = E_{D/D^+} - (E_{A/A^+} + E_{D^*}) - \frac{e^2}{\varepsilon}(r_{D^+} + r_{A^-}) \qquad (2.8)$$

where $E_{D/D+}$ and $E_{A+/A}$ are the standard redox potential of the donor and acceptor, respectively, E_{D^*} is the energy of the donor exited state, r_{D+} and r_{A-} are the radii of the donor and acceptor, respectively, and ε is the medium dielectric constant.

The values of λ can be roughly estimated within the framework of a simplified model suggesting electrostatic interactions of oxidized donor (D^+), and reduced acceptor (A^-) of radii r_{D+} and r_{A-} separated by the distance R_{DA} with media of dielectric constant e_0 and refraction index n:

$$\lambda = \frac{e^2}{2}\left(\frac{1}{n^2} - \frac{1}{e_0}\right)\left(\frac{1}{r_{D^+}} + \frac{1}{r_{A^-}} - \frac{2}{R_{DA}}\right) \tag{2.9}$$

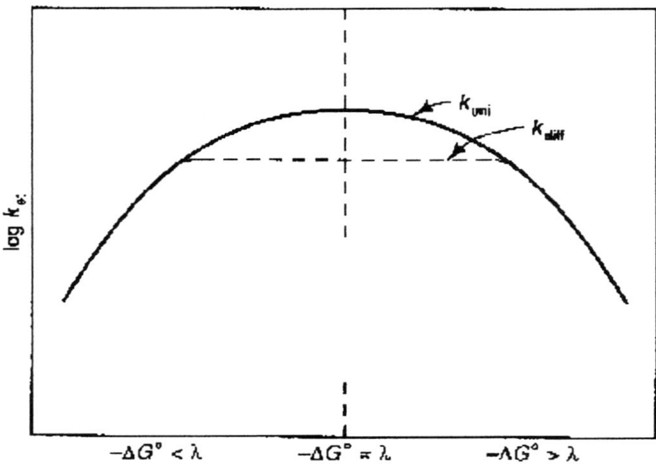

Figure 2.3. Variation of the logarithm of the rate constant of electron transfer with the driving force for the reaction after Marcus.

Taking into account the volume of reagents, the theory gives the following Eq. 2.10 (Kharkats, 1976).

$$\lambda = \frac{e^2}{2}\left(\frac{1}{n^2} - \frac{1}{e_0}\right)\left(\frac{1}{r_{D^+}} + \frac{1}{r_{A^-}} - \frac{2}{R_{DA}} + \frac{\left[r_{D^+}^3 + r_{A^-}^3\right]}{2R_{DA}^4}\right) \tag{2.10}$$

Further development of theory of reorganization energy consists in taking to consideration the properties of medium and manner in which it interfaces with the solute (Newton, 1999). These properties must include both size and shape of the solute and solvent molecules, distribution of electron density in reagents and products and the frequency domain appropriate to medium reorganization.

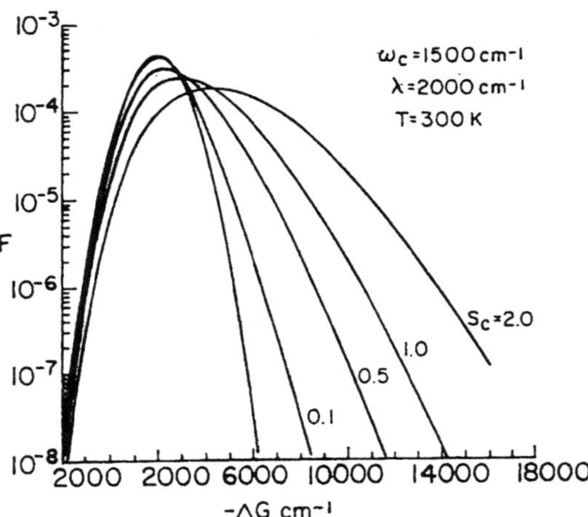

Figure 2.4. The energy-gap dependence of the nuclear Franck-Condon factor, which incorporates the role of the high-frequency intramolecular modes. $S_c = \Delta/2$ is the dimensionless electron-vibration coupling, given in terms which reduce replacement (Δ) between the minimum of the nuclear potential surfaces of the initial and final electronic states. (Bixon and Jortner, 1999) Reproduced with permission.

When the symmetry of donor and acceptor is equivalent, reorganization energy can be generalized as:

$$\lambda = C\Delta g_{eff}(e^2)(\frac{1}{r_{eff}} - \frac{1}{R_{DA}}) \qquad (2.11)$$

where C = 0.5 is a coefficient, Δg_{eff} is the effective charge and r_{eff} is the effective radius of charge separated centers. More general theory of the reorganization energy (Miyashita and Go, 2000) takes the difference between energies of the reactant state and product state, U_R and U_P, with the same nuclear coordinates q, as the reaction coordinate:

$$\Delta e(q) = U_P(q) - U_R(q) \qquad (2.12)$$

Within this theory, the reorganization energy is related to the equilibrium mean-square fluctuation of the reaction coordinate as

$$L = \frac{1}{2}(\beta < \Delta e - < \Delta e >)^2 \qquad (2.13)$$

The atoms in the systems are divided into four groups: donor (D) and acceptor (A) sites of a reaction complex (as in protein), non-redox site atoms and water atoms as the environment. The following calculation determines each component's contribution to Δe and, therefore, to the reorganization energy.

Electronic and nuclear quantum -mechanical effects
The nonadiabatic electron transfer between donor (D) and acceptor (A) centers is treated by the Fermi Golden Rule

$$k_{ET} = \frac{2\pi V^2 FC}{h} \tag{2.14}$$

where FC is the Franck-Condon factor related to the probability of reaching the terms crossing area for account of nuclear motion and V is an electronic coupling term (resonance integral) depending on the overlap of electronic wave functions in initial and final states of the process.

The theory of non-adiabatic electron transfer was developed by Levich, Dogonadze and Kuznetsov (Levich and Dogonadze, 1959; Levich et al. 1970). These authors, utilizing the Landau-Zener theory for the intersection area crossing suggesting harmonic one-dimensional potential surface, proposed a formula for non-adiabatic ET

$$k_{ET} = \frac{2\pi V^2}{h\sqrt{4\pi\lambda k_B T}} \exp\left[-\frac{(\lambda + \Delta G_0)^2}{4\lambda k_B T}\right] \tag{2.15}$$

Therefore, the maximum rate of ET at $\lambda = \Delta G_0$ is given by

$$k_{ET(max)} = \frac{2\pi V^2}{h\sqrt{4\pi\lambda k_B T}} \tag{2.16}$$

Involvement of intramolecular high-frequency vibrational modes in electron transfer was considered (Efrima and Bixon, 1974; Nitzan et al., 1972; Neil et al., 1974, Jortner and Bixon, 1999b; Hopfield, 1974; Grigorov and Chernyavsky, 1972; Miyashita et al.,, 2000). As an example, when the high-frequency mode ($h\nu_v$) is in the low-temperature limit and solvent dynamic behavior can be treated classically (Jortner and Bixon, 1999 and references therein), the rate constant for non-adiabatic ET in the case of parabolic terms is given by

$$k_{ET} = \frac{\sum_j 2\pi F_j V^2}{h\lambda k_B T} \exp\left[-\frac{(jh\nu + \lambda_s + \Delta G_0)^2}{4\lambda k_B T}\right] \tag{2.17}$$

where j is the number of high-frequency modes, $F_j = e^{-S}/j!$, $S = \lambda_v/h\upsilon$ and λ_v and λ_s are the reorganization energy inside the molecule and solvent, respectively.

In the case of thermal excitation of the local molecular and medium high frequency modes, before mesntioned theories predicted the classical Marcus relation in the normal Marcus region. While in the inverted region, significant deviation on the parabolic energy-gap dependence is expected. The inverted Marcus region cannot be experimentally observed if the stabilization of the first electron transfer product for the accounting of the high-frequency vibrational mode occurs faster than the equilibrium of the solvent polarization with the momentary charge distribution can be established. Another source of the deviation is the non-parabolic shape of the activation barrier. The Marcus inverted region can not be observed experimentally when term-to-term transition in the crossing region is not limiting step of the process as a whole. When ET reaction is very fast in the region of maximum rate, the process can be controlled by diffusion and, therefore, is not dependent on λ, V^2 and ΔG_0. (Burshtein, 2000).

Role of medium dynamics
Media molecular dynamics is important to the formation of the energetic profile of the electron transfer. When ET occurs faster then the medium relaxation, the process is governed by the medium dynamics with the medium relaxation time τ_s. In such a case the pre-exponential factor in non-adiabatic equation is described by equation (Bixon, 1992)

$$k_0 = \frac{1}{\tau_s}\sqrt{\pi\lambda^3 k_B T} \qquad (2.18)$$

and the ET rate constant becomes independent of the electronic coupling and the process driving force.

When the initial state distribution remains in thermal equilibrium throughout the ET process, the process driving force is related to the standard Gibbs energy (ΔG_0). A different situation takes place if the elementary act of ET occurs before the formation of conformational and solvatational states of the medium. In fact, two consecutive stages take place: ET for the accounting of fast vibration translation modes of the system and the media relaxation. In such a case, the thermodynamic standard energy for the elementary act (ΔG_0^{neq}) appears to be less than that involved in the case of the equilibrium dielectric stabilization of redox centers ΔG_0 (Likhtenshtein, 1996). It can be concluded, therefore, that the elementary steps of ET in these systems are not accompanied by significant shifts in the position of the medium nuclear frame nor are they governed by such shifts.

It can be concluded that the initial and final energy terms in the non-equilibrium case will be positioned closer to each other in space and energy than in equilibrium (Fig. 2.5). Consequently, in the inverted Marcus region, the value of the reorganization, Gibbs and activation energy are expected to be markedly lower than that in the equilibrium case. In the normal Marcus region we predict a larger activation energy and slower ET rate for non-equilibrium processes than for equilibrium processes when differences in their standard Gibbs energy would be larger than that in the reorganization energy. In general, the situation would be dependent on the interplay of both parameters of the Marcus model.

The second property expected for non-equilibrium processes is the lack of dependence (Fig. 2.6, curve 1) or weak dependence (curve 2) of the experimental rate constant of ET in both Marcus regions (inverted and non-inverted), compared to that predicted by the classic Marcus expression (curve 3).

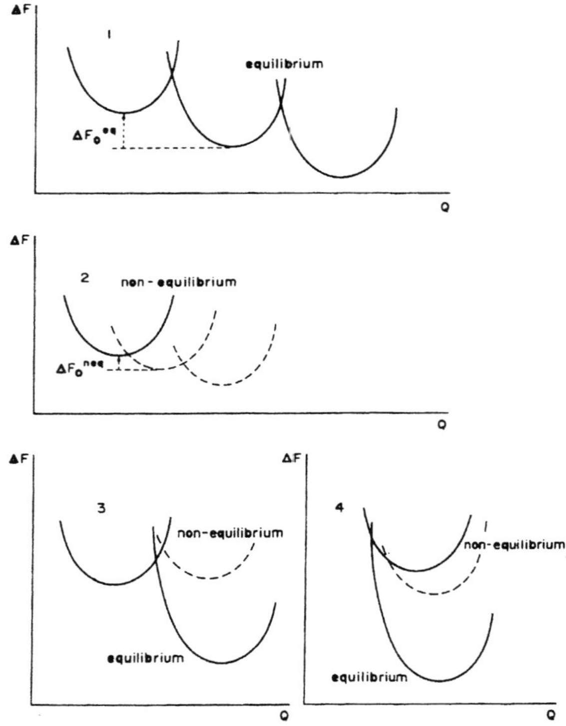

Figure 2.5. Schematic representation of electronic potential energy surfaces: 1, consecutive conformational and solvatational equilibrium processes with the essential change in the nuclear coordinates Q and the standard Gibbs energy ΔG_0; 2, consecutive non-equilibrium processes with small changes in Q and ΔG_0; 3, 4, equilibrium (full line) and non-equilibrium (broken line) processes in the normal and inverted Marcus regions respectively. (Likhtenshtein, 1996) Reproduced in permission.

Another approach to solvent fluctuation control of reactions in solution based on the Kramer model (Kramer, 1940; Sumi, 1999 and references therein). According to this model a transition over a double-well potential $W_{(Q)}$ occurs as a result of zigzag diffusion. An important parameter of the theory is the relaxation time of the average motion of the medium

$$\tau = \frac{k_B T}{\omega_0^2 D} \tag{2.19}$$

where ω^2 is the potential surface curvature and D is the diffusion coefficient. In the higher viscosity region the Kramer model gives the rate constant

$$k_{KR} = \frac{w_b}{\tau 2\pi\omega_0} \exp\left[\frac{-W_{(b)}}{k_B T}\right]$$

(2.20)

where w_b is the square root of curvature in the area of the top of the potential barrier. In high viscose media the τ values are dependent on the media viscosity (Sumi, 1999) and

$$k_{KR} \propto \tau^{-\alpha} \propto k^{-\alpha} \quad 0 < \alpha < 1$$

(2.21)

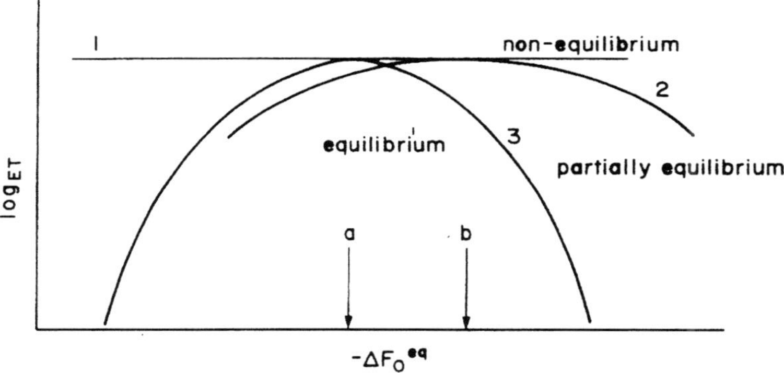

Figure 2.6. Schematic representation of the dependence of the ET constants logarithm on the equilibrium Gibbs energy ΔG_0: 1, non-equilibrium conformational and solvational processes; 2, partial non-equilibrium processes, λ^{neq} and ΔG_0^{neq} are slightly dependent on ΔG_0; 3, equilibrium processes. Arrows a and b are conditions for the maximum $\lambda = \Delta G_0$ and $\lambda^{neq} = \Delta G_0^{neq}$ respectively. (Likhtenshtein, 1996). Reproduced in permission.

Long-range electron transfer (LRET)
LRET between donor (D) and acceptor (A) centers can occur by three mechanisms: 1) direct transfer which involves direct overlap between electron orbitals of the donor and acceptor, 2) consecutive electron jumps via chemical intermediates with a fixed structure, and (3) superexchange via intermediate orbitals.

In direct LRET the direct electronic coupling between D and A is negligible and this mechanism is not practically realized in condensed media being non-competitive with the consecutive and superexchange processes. In theoretical consideration of the consecutive LRET a relevant theory of ET in two-term systems can be applied.

Of considerable interest is the superexchange process (Beratan et al. 1990; Beratan and Onuchic, 1987; Beth et al., 1992; Gehlen et al., 1996; Likhtenshtein, 1993, 1996; Tanaka and Marcus, 1997; Stuchebrukov and Marcus, 1995; Siddarth and Marcus, 1993a, b, c; Scourotis and Beratan, 1999; Balabin and Onuchic, 2000).

According to the Fermi Golden Rule, the non-adiabatic ET rate constant is strongly dependent on electronic coupling between the donor state D and acceptor state A connected by a bridge (V_{AB}) which is given by an expression derived from the weak perturbation theory

$$V_{AB} = \frac{\sum V_{A\alpha} V_{\alpha B}}{\Delta E_\alpha} \qquad (2.22)$$

where $V_{A\alpha}$ and $V_{\alpha B}$ are the couplings between bridge orbitals and acceptor and donor orbitals, respectively, and ΔE_α is the energy of the bridge orbitals relative to the energy of the donor orbital. The summation over α includes both occupied and unoccupied orbitals of the bridge. This approach was extended to a more general case, where D is connected to A by a number of atomic orbitals. A special, so-called "artificial intelligence", search procedure was devised to select the most important amino acid residues, which mediate long-range transfer (Siddarth and Marcus, 1993a)

According to the approach of Beratan and colleagues (1990), for a pathway between bridged donor and acceptor groups the coupling element can be written

$$V_{AB} = V_0 \prod_i^N \varepsilon_i \qquad (2.23)$$

where V_0 is the coupling between the donor and donor and the first bond of the pathway and ε_i is a decay factor associated with the decay of electron density from one bond to another. The ε_B, ε_H and ε_s values are related to superexchange through two covalent bonds sharing a common atom, an H-bond, and space, respectively. The decay factor is approximated by equation

$$\varepsilon_i = \varepsilon_i^0 \exp\left[\beta_i (R - R_i^0)\right] \qquad (2.24)$$

where R_i^0 is the equilibrium length bond or Van der Waals distance, β_i is some factor, specific to the distance R, which depends on the orbital interactions and ε_i^0 is the value of ε_i for $R = R_i^0$, which is proportional to factor σ related to the interaction orientation. The values of $\varepsilon_B = 0.4 - 0.6$, $\sigma_H = \sigma_B = 1.0$ and $\beta_s = 1.7$ Å were taken for the calculation of V_{AB}. According to this theory the increase in connectivity for the electron transfer is about 0.24 per atom.

A semi-empirical approach for the quantitative estimation of the effect bridging the group on LRET was developed by Likhtenshtein (1993, 1995). The basic idea underlying this approach is an analogy between superexchange in electron transfer and such electron exchange processes as triplet-triplet energy transfer (TTET) and spin-exchange (SE). The ET rate constant is proportional to the square of the resonance integral V_{ET}. The rate constant of TTET

$$k_{TT} = \frac{2\pi}{h} J_{TT} FC \tag{2.25}$$

where J_{TT} is the TT exchange integral. The Hamiltonian of the exchange interaction (HSE) between spins with operators S_1 and S_2 is described by the equation

$$H_{SE} = -2J_{SE} S_1 S_2 \tag{2.26}$$

where J_{SE} is the SE exchange integral.

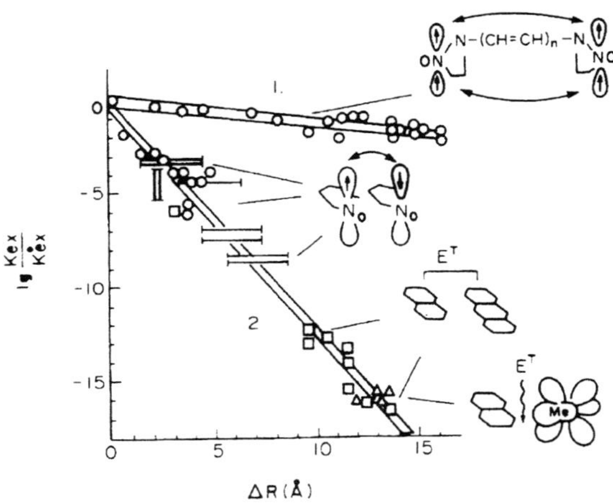

Figure 2.7. Dependence of the logarithm of relative parameters of the exchange interaction on the distance between the interacting centers (ΔR). k_{TT} is the rate constant of triplet-triplet electron transfer, and JSE is the spin-exchange integral. Index 0 is related to van der Waals contact. (Likhtenshtein, 1996) Reproduced in permission.

All three integrals V_{ET}^2, J_{SE} and J_{TT} are related to the overlap integral (S_i), which quantitatively characterizes the degree of overlap of orbitals involved in these processes. Thus

$$V_{ET}^2, J_{SE}, J_{TT} \propto S_i^n \propto \exp(-\beta_i R_i) \tag{2.27}$$

where R_i is the distance between the interacting centers and β_i is a coefficient which characterizes the degree of the integral decay. In the first approximation $n = 2$ for the ET and SE processes with the overlap of two orbitals and $n = 4$ for the TT process in which four orbitals overlap (of ground and triplet states of the donor and ground and triplet states of the acceptor). The spin exchange and TT phenomena may be considered an idealized model of ET without or with only a slight) replacement of the nuclear frame. Thus, the experimental dependence of exchange parameters k_{TT} and J_{SE} on the distance between the exchangeable centers and the chemical nature of the bridge connecting the centers may be used for evaluating such dependences for the resonance integral in the ET equations (Eq. 2.27).

A vast literature is connected with the quantitative investigation of exchange processes (see, for example, Zamaraev et al., 1981; Ermolaev, et al., 1997; Likhtenshtein, 1995; and references therein). As it seen in Fig. 2.7, experimental data on the dependence of k_{TT} and J_{SE} on the distance between the centers (ΔR) lies on two curves, which are approximated by the following equation (Likhteshtein, 1996)

$$k_{TT}, J_{SE} \propto \exp(-\beta\Delta R) \qquad (2.28)$$

For systems in which the centers are separated by a "non-conductive" medium (molecules or groups with saturated chemicals bond) β_{TT} equal 2.6 Å^{-1}. For systems in which the radical centers are linked by "conducting" conjugated bonds, β_{SE} is 0.3 Å^{-1}.

We can consider the ratios

$$\gamma_{TT}(\Delta R) = \frac{k_{TT}^0}{k_{TT}} \quad \text{and} \quad \gamma_{SE} = \frac{J_{SE}^0}{J_{SE}}(\Delta R) \qquad (2.29)$$

as parameters of attenuation of the exchange interaction of TTET and SE through the given medium. Taking into account Eqs. 2.27 and 2.28 with values n = 4 for TTET and n = 2 for SE and ET, and Eq. 2.29, we have an expression for the dependence of the attenuation parameters for SE and ET on the distance between remote donor and acceptor centers $D_R D_A$

$$\gamma_{ET} = \gamma_{SE} = \exp(-\beta_i \Delta R) \qquad (2.30)$$

with β_{ET} (nc) = 0.5β_{TT} = 1.3 Å^{-1} for a "non-conducting" medium and β_{ET} (c) = 0.3 Å^{-1} for a "conducting" bridge. The value of β_{ET} (1.3 Å^{-1}) is found to be close to that obtained by analysis of k_{ET} on the distance ΔR in model and biological systems Fig. 2.7.

An examination of the empirical data on the exchange integral values (J_{ET}) for the spin-spin interactions in systems with known structure, e.g. biradicals, transition metal complexes with paramagnetic ligands and monocrystals of nitroxide radicals, allows the value of the attenuation parameter γ_X for the exchange interaction through a given group X to be estimated. By our definition, the γ_X is

$$\gamma_X = \frac{J_{RYZP}}{J_{RYXZP}} \qquad (2.31)$$

where R is a nitroxide or organic radical, P is a paramagnetic complex or radical and X, Y, and Z are chemical groups in the bridge between R and P.

TABLE 2.1. Values of the attenuation parameter of individual groups (γ_X), van der Waals contact (γ_v) and hydrogen bond (γ_{hb}) for spin exchange in biradicals and paramagnetic complexes of transition metals with nitroxide ligands (see text) (Likhtenshtein 1996) Reproduced with permission.

Group, X	γ_x	Group, X	γ_x
C_6H_4	6.00 ± 0.03		
C=C	1.7	-NH-CO-	55 [a]
C=O			
C	8.4 ± 0.4	γ_v	50
NH	6.5	γ_{hb}	10
O	5	H	12
S=O	2.1	SO_2	2.2
	3.5	RP=O	2.40 ± 0.03 [b]

[a] Calculated by equation $\gamma_x = \gamma_{CO}\gamma_{NH}$
[b] $R \equiv$ Ph-, CH_2=CH-, Ph-CH=CH-, Ph-CCl=CH-.

Table 2.1. shows the results of the calculation parameter γ_x from empirical data by Eq. 2.31 (Likhtenshtein, 1993, 1995). The table of values for X, C=O, S=O, P=O and C=C, calculated from independent experimental data, are similar. Data presented in Table 2.1 and Eq. 2.31 may be used for the analysis of alternative electron transfer pathways in biological systems.

2.2.2. EXPERIMENTAL DATA

Remarkable progress has been made in the elucidation processes of electron transfer in biological and model systems. This progress has been achieved through massive and concentrated applications of the entire arsenal of modern chemical, biochemical and physical methods. Biochemistry and biophysics provide isolated and functionally well-characterized samples of electron transfer in biological objects. Synthetic chemistry and genetic engineering allowed purposeful modification of biological and model molecules. Structural methods including X-ray analysis and all kinds of spectroscopy from Gamma-resonance to nuclear magnetic resonance reveal the detailed chemical structure of proteins with natural and artificial donor and acceptor sites. The most advanced theories of electron transfer have been used to analyze the experimental data.

The present section is a brief survey of experimental data on electron transfer rate and its theoretical treatment being focused on (a) the Franc-Condon (FC) factor and (b) electronic coupling (resonance integral) V. Role of the media molecular dynamics on ET is discussed in Sections 3.5.1 and 4.1.7

Franc-Condon factor
According to the Marcus (Eqs. 2.9-2.10), the FC value is strongly dependent on medium polarity. For example, for electron transfer between centers with radius about 4 A the following values of the energy reorganization were estimated in eV: 0.052 (benzene), 0.12 (acetonitryl) and methanol (0.35). For an aqueous solution a value was estimated within λ = 1.0 – 1.3 eV for the centers with radius 3 – 4 Å. Suggesting a dielectric constant of

media inside protein globules, the rough estimation gave $\lambda = 0.0 - 0.1$ eV for the dielectric constant $\varepsilon = 2 - 4$.

Concerning proteins, the λ value is strongly dependent on local polarity, which differs in different portions of such a mosaic structure as a protein globule. Positions of the donor and acceptor centers relative to the protein-water interface, chemical nature and mobility of adjacent groups can drastically affect λ values. Thus, the precise calculation of real λ in biological objects requires special theoretical approaches.

An effective approach to the systematic studies that are required to explore the fundamental aspects of ET in proteins, involves measurements of ET in proteins modified by artificial donor and acceptor centers. By varying redox properties and position of the centers, it has been possible to elucidate the factors affected the rate of long-range electron transfer reactions in proteins. A particularly significant contribution in this area has been made by H. B. Gray and his colleagues using redox metalloproteins that have been surface-labeled with redox-active ruthenium complexes (Gray and Ellis, 1994; Gray and Winkler, 1996; Tezcan et al., 2001; Ponce et al., 2000; Winlker et al., 1999).

Ru^{+2} complexes readily react with surface histidine residues to form stable derivatives. Photochemical methods were used to inject an electron into the Ru^{3+} site followed by monitoring kinetics of ET from Ru^{2+} to the metalloprotein active site.

The $Ru^{3+/2+}$ reduction potential can be varied from <0.0 to > 1.5 eV. The λ values can be estimated by the analysis of experimental dependences log k_{ET} - ΔG_0. According to the Marcus 2.5, the maximum of this dependence is related to the equality $\lambda = \Delta G_0$. Such an analysis was performed by Gray and Winkler (1996) using data on the driving-force dependence of long-range electron-transfer rates in Fe-cytochrome c and Zn-substitutes cytochrome c modified by Ru complexes with different ligands effected on ΔG_0. The estimated λ values were found to be different for different complexes that highlight the important role of interaction of complexes with water. The bulky bipyridine ligands shield the charged metal center from the polar aqueous solution reducing the solvent reorganization ($\lambda = 0.8$) as compared to less bulky ligands ($\lambda = 1.2$ eV). These experiments also demonstrated that centers located in the aqueous phase contribute more significantly than groups, buried in protein globule.

According to Miyashita and Go, 2000 the main contribution to λ in electron transfer in cytochrome c, modified by the $Ru(NH_3)_2$ complex, originates from the interaction of donor and acceptor with protein groups and water, whereas the contribution of high-frequency vibration modes inside of the donor and acceptor centers is very small (about 1%). Nevertheless, high-vibration modes of protein and water add about 30% to the system fluctuation energy. This calculation also revealed the strong correlation between protein and water and, therefore the division of reorganization energies between protein and water in a simple way is not appropriated. The reorganization energy can be also estimated from experimental Gibbs energy activation (Eq.2.6) (Fogel et al., 1994) when ΔG_0 is known.

A problem of the experimental measurement of local polarity in the vicinity of donor and acceptor centers incorporated into a protein (bovine serum albumin, BSA) was solved with the use of the dual fluorescence-nitroxide probe (Bystryak et al., 1986; Rubtsova et al., 1993; Fogel et al., 1994; Likhtenshtein, 1993, 1996; Likhtenshtein et al., 2001). In such a hybrid molecule, the photoactive chromophore fragment in the excited singlet state can serve as an electron donor (D*) and the nitroxide fragment as an acceptor (A). The same group allows the estimation of the local apparent dielectric constant of the medium (ε_{loc}) near the donor by the measurement of the relaxation shift of the D fluorescence spectra and of the medium near the acceptor by the analysis of the nitroxide ESR spectra. It was shown (Rubtsova et al., 1994) that $\varepsilon_{loc} = 11$ for the chromophore fragment imbedded in hydrophobic portion of BSA and $\varepsilon_{loc} = 65$ for the nitroxide fragment protruded in 50% water-ethylene glycol solution. On this basis the values of Gibbs energy ($\Delta G_0 = 1.75$ eV) and reorganization energy ($\lambda = 0.9$ eV) for ET in the DA pairs were estimated with the use Eqs. 2.8 and 2.9 respectively. Using Eq. 2.6 and the aforementioned value of ΔG_0, $\lambda = 0.8$ eV was found.

Though rational estimations of the reorganization energy in protein and other complicated biological objects were done, the precise calculation of λ remains a challenging problem.

Electronic coupling (resonance integral)
The non-adiabatic long-range electron transfer (LRET) has been proven to be one of the key stages of many processes in enzymes, proteins and model systems. Therefore, theoretical calculation and experimental determination of the resonance integral (V) and its dependence on the distance between donor and acceptor centers appears to be a fundamental problem.

Information garnered from studies with simple homogeneous media and artificial systems in which these centers are tethered by a bridge of appropriate chemical nature in comparison to natural objects provides insight into what occurs mechanistically in both systems (Gust and Moor, 1992, Sessler, 1992, Wasielewski, 1992, 2002; Wesielwski et al., 2000; Ponce et al., 2000; Tezcan et al., 2001; Likhtenshtein, 1993,1996; and references therein).

The theoretical and experimental results in non-biological objects can be briefly summarized as follows:

1. In systems in which the donor and acceptor centers are in direct contact with each other or connected by a "conducting" bridge (conjugated bonds), electron transfer rates are very fast ($k_{ET} = 10^{-13} - 10^{-12}$ s^{-1}). The transition occurs markedly slower when the donor-acceptor mutual orientation is not favorable for positive orbital overlap and, therefore, the electron coupling V is small.

2. Separation of D and A centers by "non-conducting" media resulted in the strong dependence of the ET rate on distance between D and A and the marked effect of the chemical nature of saturated molecules and bonds between the pair. This dependence can be quantitatively characterized be the decay factor, β, (Eq. 2.27). The following values of β (in Å^{-1}) were found: 3-4 (vacuum), 1.6 – 1.75 (water), 1.2 (organic solvents) and 1.08 – 1.2 (synthetic D-bridge-A molecules). The effects of distance and the number of intermediate saturated groups (n) on photoinduced electron transfer between a donor and acceptor are discussed in (Verhoeven, 1999).

Fig. 2.8 shows that the logarithm of maximum rates (Eq. 2.16) spanning 12 order of magnitude for intraprotein ET reaction as a function of the edge-to edge distance generates an approximate linear relationship with $\beta = 1.4$ Å-1 (Moser and Dutton, 1992). A similar relationship with β = 1.3 Å-1 was demonstrated for the experimental rate constant in reaction centers (RCs) of purple bacteria and the green plants photosystem I (PSI) (Fig. 2.29) (Likhtenshtein 1995). The value β = 1.4 Å-1 was predicted in the classical work of Hopfield (1974). It should be stressed that this β value corresponds to the similar slope for dependence of the spin exchange attenuation coefficient (γSE, Eq. 2.30) vs. distance between centers involved in the spin exchange (βSE = 1.3 Å-1). Since βSE is related to the shortest distance tunneling through "homogeneous" media, we can consider any deviation from this relationship as a result of involving some specific effects in a given process. For example, for the first step of ET from (a) the excited primary donor (bacteriochlorophyll dimer, Bchl$_2$, P) to the intermediate bacteriopheophytin acceptor (Bph, H) in the bacteria RC and (b) from P700 to pheophytin intermediate acceptor in PSI (circles 8 and 9 in Fig. 2.9), the experimental rate constants are considerably larger than those expected from "regular" dependence shown in Figs. 2.8 and 2.9. Such deviation can be explained by the superexchange promotion of conducting bacteriopheophytin chromophore, which is located between P and H. As a result, this fast ET process may occur in the adiabatic regime.

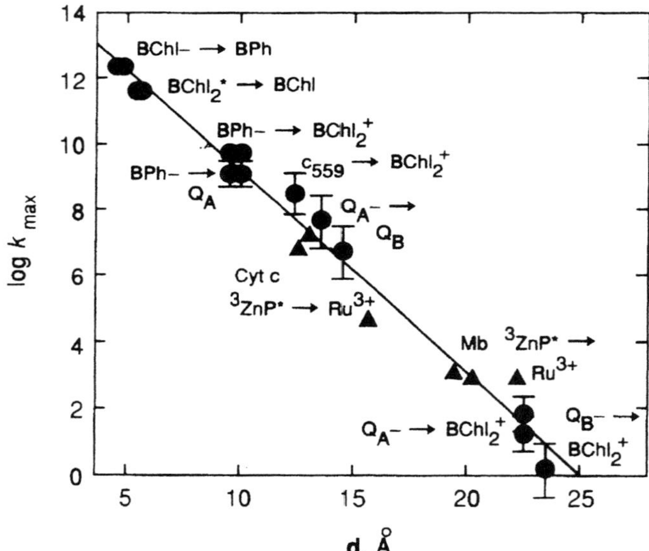

Figure 2.8. The Gibbs energy optimized ET rate vs. edge-to-edge distance relationship for intraprotein electron transfer. The bacteria RC rate constants are shown as circles and excited heme-ruthenium ET in modified myoglobin and cytochrome c are shown as triangles (Moser and Dutton, 1992). Reproduced with permission.

Another deviation (circle 10) is related to ET from that reduced primary quinone acceptor Q$_A$ to the secondary quinone acceptor Q$_B$. The process takes place at an edge-edge distance of about 14 Å, but these centers are bridged with two hydrogen bonds and Fe atoms coordinated with two "conducting" imidazol groups (Rees et al., 1989). The estimation of the resonance integral for the process using Eq. 2.30 with the values of the attenuation parameters presented in table Y, gives the integral value $V_{QAQB} \approx 5 \times 10^{-1}$ eV, that exceeds the limit for adiabatic processes $V_{ad} > 2.5 \times 10^{-2}$ eV at room temperature. This implies that this process runs adiabatically but relatively slowly due to the large energy of media reorganization around the quinine anion-radicals.

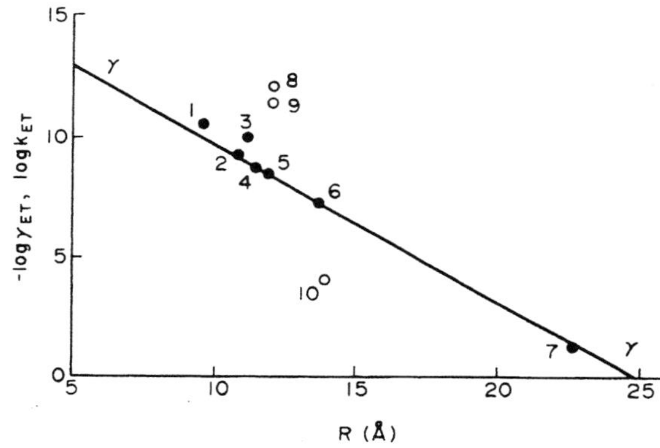

Figure 2.9. Dependence of maximum rate constant of ET on the edge-to-edge distance in photosynthetic RCs of bacteria and plant PSI: 1, $A_0^- - A_1$; 2, $H^- - Q_A$; 3, A_1-F_X; $H^- - P^+$; 5, C559 –P^+; 6, $F_X - F_A$; 7, $Q_A^- - P^+$; 8, P^- - Bcl; 9, P700* - A_0; 10, $Q_A^- - Q_B$; P700 is the chlorophyll dimer, A_0 is chlorophyll, A_1 is phylloquinone and F_X and F_A are the 4 Fe-4S clusters. The straight line is related to the dependence of the attenuation parameter for spin exchange (γ_{SE}) in homogeneous "non-conducting" media. Filled circles correspond to a "regular" dependence, open circles to a "deviation" (Likhtenshtein, 1996). Reproduced with permission.

As was shown in large series works, (Gray and Ellis, 1994; Gray and Winkler, 1996; Tezcan et al., 2001; Ponce et al., 2000; Winlker et al., 1999) by varying the position of the ruthenium complexes relative to metalloproteins redox-active sites, it has been possible to estimate experimentally the coupling factor and its dependence on the distance between the redox centers and the chemical nature of the intermediate medium. An electron tunneling time table of proteins with imidazol residues modified by Ru-complexes is presented in Fig. 2.10 (Tezcan et al., 2001). As seen in the figure, electron transfer in the modified proteins occurs significantly faster than it would in a vacuum or aqueous medium. The coupling decay constant β for the donor-acceptor pairs falls in the 1.0 to 1.58 Å-1 range and for most of them in the 1.0 to 1.2 Å $^{-1}$ range with an average β of 1.1 Å^{-1}. The latter b value is about 15% less then $\beta_{SE} = 1.3$ Å^{-1} for spin exchange derived from dependence of the attenuation coefficient γ_{SE} vs. the distance between centers involved in the spin exchange and related to homogeneous "non-conducting" media (Likhtenshtein, 1995). Therefore, the ET reactions in the most investigated protein take place faster than it is expected for homogeneous media. The most probable explanation of this fact is the presence of more "conductive" ET pathways including aromatic groups and σ-bonds. Specifically, according to Gray and Winkler, 1996, different protein secondary structures mediated electronic coupling with different efficiencies. Thus, the β-sheet zone, represents an efficient mediation of electronic coupling which is characterized $\beta= 0.9 - 1.15$ Å^{-1}. The α-helix zone describes systems with coupling decay constant between 1.25 and 1.6 Å^{-1}.

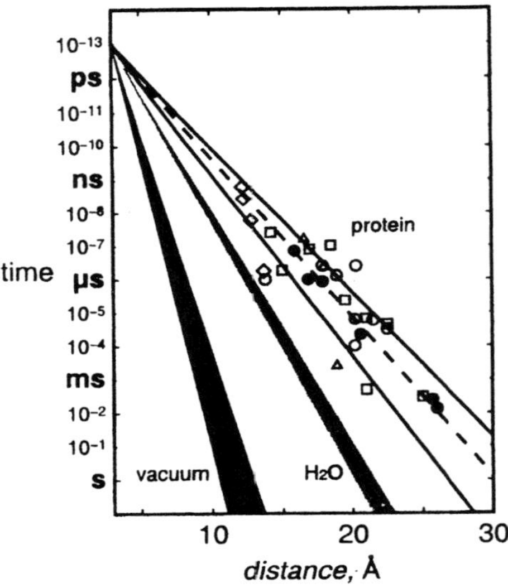

Figure 2.10. Correlation of theoretical and experimental maximum rate constants for Ru-modified cytochrome c derivatives. The numbers on the figure are related to the number of modified His groups. (Tezcan et al. 2001) Reproduced with permission.

Another reason for a deviation from relationships expected for a homogeneous "non-conducting" medium is the difference in reorganization energy for the same Ru-complexes located in the protein-water interface of different local dielectric constant and local electrostatic potentials.

A numerical algorithm (Beratan et al., 1990) was implemented to survey electron-tunneling pathways in tRu-modified myoglobin and cytochrome c. The calculation results concerning the optimum pathway for ET between ruthenated (His 48) and Fe in myoglobin taking $\beta= 1.0$ Å^{-1} and orientation parameter $\sigma_s = 0.1$ and $\prod_i \varepsilon_i = 4.65 \times 10^{-6}$ (Eqs. 2.23 and 2.24) agree with the experimental data.

The artificial intelligence-superexchange method in which the details of the electronic structure of the protein medium are taken into account was used for estimating the electronic coupling in the metalloproteins (Siddarth and Marcus, 1993a,b,c). Fig.2.11 demonstrates a correlation of experimental and calculated ET rate constants for cytochrome c derivatives, modified by Ru complexes. The influence of the special mutual orientation of the donor and acceptor orbitals in Ru(bpy)$_2$im HisX-cytochrome c on the rate of electron transfer was analyzed by the transition amplitude methods (Stuchebrukhov and Marcus, 1995). In this reaction the transferring electron in the initial and the final states occupies the 3d shell of the Fe atom and the 4d shell of Ru, respectively. It was shown that the electron is localized on t_{2g} subshells of the metal ions. Due to the near-octahedral symmetry of the complexes, the orbitals d_{xy}, d_{xz} and d_{yz} of the t_{2g} subshell interact mainly with π orbitals of ligands. Meanwhile, the networks, which start as a σ-path will not participate much in the superexchange coupling under this consideration.

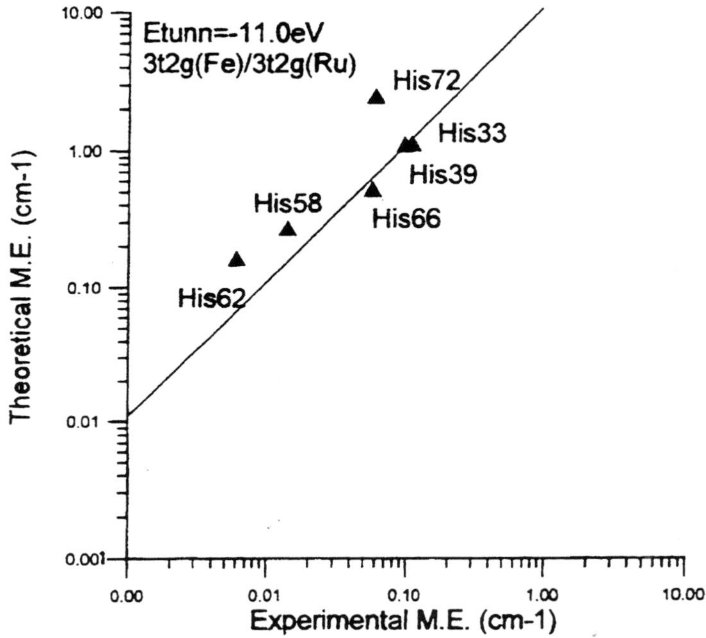

Figure 2.11. Comparison of experimental and theoretical values of matrix element for ET in Ru-modified cytochrome c. The calculation takes into account the $3t_{2g}$ orbitals of Fe and $3t_{2g}$ of Ru wich are involved in the ET process (Stuchebrukhov and Marcus, 1995). Reproduced with permission

The Fig.2.11 shows, that good correlation between theoretical and experimental electron coupling matrix elements takes place when $3t_{2g}$ orbitals of Fe and $3t_{2g}$ orbitals of Ru are involved in the ET process. The general tendency is to have coupling markedly stronger for His39 than for His62, although the distance between the donor and acceptor is approximately the same. When effective s-orbitals are localized on metals and, therefore, mostly s-paths contribute in the coupling, a drastic difference between theoretical and experimental values of electronic coupling has been found. This observation clearly demonstrates the importance of symmetry and stereochemical effects in long-range electron transfer.

2.3. Hydrogen transfer

Many enzymatic reactions involve transfer protons, hydrides or hydrogen atoms (Alhambra et al., 2000; Allison, 1998;; Backgren et al., 2000; Blum et al., 2001; Cha et al.,

1989; Bruno and Bialek, 1992; Hwang and Warshel, 1996;s Isaev and Scheiner, 2001; Musser and Theg, 2000; Sjoergen et al., 2000; Swain et al., 1958; Tripp and Ferry, 2000; Likhtenshtein and Shilov, 1976; Likhtenshtein, 1988a).

2.3.1. THEORETICAL GROUNDS

The classical theory of kinetic isotope effect (KIE) treats the vibrational ground state quantum-mechanically and motion across the top of the barrier classically. The theory asserts that KIF arises from the larger quantum zero-point energy of the larger isotope and

$$\ln KIE = \ln \frac{k_{ml}}{k_{m0}} = \left[\sqrt{\frac{m_0}{m_1}} - 1 \right] \frac{hw_0}{4\pi k_B T} \tag{2.32}$$

where m_1 and m_0 are the masses of two isotopes and w_0 is the vibration frequency of the lighter isotope. For example, for a process with participation of the C-H bond, the theory predicts at room temperature the approximate magnitude of KIE = 22 and 2.6 for hydrogen/tritium and deuterium/tritium respectively.
The ratio (the so-called the Schaad-Swain exponent)

$$\frac{\ln\left(\dfrac{H}{T} KIE \right)}{\ln\left(\dfrac{D}{T} KIE \right)} = 3.26 \tag{2.33}$$

is considered as a criterion for a process to run "classically".
In the framework of Marcus theory (Marcus, 1968), the difference between Gibbs energy activation for hydrogen and deuterium transfer is given by the equation

$$\Delta G_T^{\#} - \Delta G_D^{\#} = \frac{1}{4}\left(\lambda_H - \lambda_D\right)\left[1 - \left(1 - \frac{\Delta G_0}{\lambda_H} \right)^2 \right] \tag{2.34}$$

Application of Marcus rate theory to proton transfer in enzyme-catalyzed reactions was discussed by Kresge and Silverman, 1999. Relationships of log KIE and kinetics of the enzyme catalysis (k_{cat}) and parameters of the reaction driving force were found to be in agreement with the Marcus model.
The first theory of hydrogen transfer wich takes into account the nuclear tunneling was developed by Levich et al., (1970). The authors calculated the transfer probability, Wif, using the general formula of the perturbation theory:

$$Wif = \frac{4\pi^2}{h} I < \Psi_f \, IV_{pB} \, I\Psi_i > I^2 \rho_f \qquad (2.35)$$

where Ψ_f and Ψ_i are the wave functions of the final and initial states, V_{pB} is the potential of interaction of proton, bound to a proton donor, with a proton acceptor; and ρ_f is the level density of the final state.

The effect of isotopes substitution on fast nuclear vibrations and, therefore, nuclear tunneling and KIE can be derived from Marcus-Jortner Eq. 2.17. As seen from Eq. 2.17, both energy activation and preexponential factors are dependent on the vibration frequency.

In the absence of fluctuation, the probability of nuclear tunneling through a static barrier (Bruno and Bialik, 1992) is given as

$$P_{tun} = \exp\left[-2\int_a^b \sqrt{2m[N(x) - E]}\,dx \right] \qquad (2.36)$$

Here $N(x)$ is the potential energy barrier between reactant and product state of the hydrogen and E is the particle energy. For a static square barrier the theory predicts a huge non-realistic isotope effect and its non-sensitivity to temperature. The thermal fluctuations produce a thermal distribution of the transfer distance, l. For a rectangular barrier and low frequency vibration of substrate and medium and harmonic behavior of l:

$$P_{tun} = \exp\left[-2\int_a^b \sqrt{2mV_{eff}}\,dx \right] \qquad (2.37)$$

where V_{eff} is the barrier height. In such a case

$$\ln KIE = \left(1 - \left(\frac{m_2}{m_2}\right)^2 \sqrt{2m_0 V_{eff}}\,\frac{l_{eq}}{h} - \left(m_0 - m_1\right)\frac{4V_{eff}k_B T}{h^2 \kappa}\right) \qquad (2.38)$$

where κ is the stiffness which resists changes in l. Eq. 2.38 implies dependence of KIE on temperature.

When the critical configuration in which the distance l favorable for tunneling is reached more slowly than the rate of tunneling, the overall rate of the process becomes independent of the tunneling probability and therefore independent entirely or partially of isotope substitution. A quantum mechanical model for proteinase- catalyzed peptide, amide and ester hydrolysis was proposed in (Sumi and Ulstrup, 1988). The model rests on electron and atom transfer theory, but incorporates the dynamics of conformational nuclear modes. It is suggested that the mobility of a catalytic group (His-57 in serine proteinase, for example) can bring the proton donor and proton acceptor groups within suitable reach.

The quantitized classical path approach (Hwang and Warshel, 1996) was applied to the analysis of quantum mechanical nuclear motion in enzyme catalysis. According to this approach the rate constant of the process

$$k_q = F \frac{k_B T}{h} \exp\left(- \frac{\Delta G_q^{\#}}{k_B T} \right)$$ (2.39)

where F is the transmission factor and, $\Delta G_q^{\#}$ is the quantum mechanical activation free energy. The main quantum mechanical effects are associated with the exponential factors. According to the modified Marcus relationship (Warshel et. al., 1992)

$$\Delta G_q^{\#} = \frac{\Delta G_0 + \lambda}{4\lambda} - H_{12} + \frac{H_{12}^2}{\Delta G_0 + \lambda}$$ (2.40)

Here H_{12} is the nuclear off-diagonal matrix element

$$H_{12} = A_{12} \exp\left(\mu_{12} r_0\right)$$ (2.41)

where r_0 is the distance between the proton donor and acceptor groups. In the initial proton-transfer step in the carbonic anhydrase reaction, $A_{12} = 54$ kcal/mole and $\mu_{12} = 0.4$ A-1 for the oxygen – oxygen distance.

Quantum dynamics effects for hydride transfer in enzyme catalysis have been analyzed by Alhambra et. al., 2000. This process is simulated using canonically variational transition-states for overbarrier dynamics and optimized multidimensional paths for tunneling. A system is divided into a primary zone (substrate-enzyme-coenzyme), which is embedded in a secondary zone (substrate-enzyme-coenzyme-solvent). The potential energy surface of the first zone is treated by quantum mechanical electronic structure methods, and protein, coenzyme, and solvent atoms by molecular mechanical force fields. The theory allows the calculation of Schaad-Swain exponents for primary (α_{prim}) and secondary (α_{sec}) KIE

$$\alpha_{prim} = \frac{\ln\left(\dfrac{k_H^H}{k_H^T} \right)}{\ln\left(\dfrac{k_D^D}{k_D^T} \right)}$$ (2.42)

$$\alpha_{src} = \frac{\ln\left(\dfrac{k_H^H}{k_H^T}\right)}{\ln\left(\dfrac{k_D^D}{k_D^T}\right)} \qquad (2.43)$$

Ab-initio and density functional theory are used to calculate the probability of proton conduction via a chain of water molecules from Zn^+ to its residue in the active site of carbonic anhydrase (Isaev and Scheiner, 2001). They conclude that proton conduction occurs as a concerted process and includes the shortening of each H-bonds as the proton donor and acceptor move towards one other.

2.3.2. EXPERIMENTAL DATA

Besides obvious participation of protons, hydrids and hydrogen atoms in a chemical reaction in enzymes active sites, two main criteria are used for discrimination of particle involvement in the reaction limiting stage: site-directed substitution of chosen enzyme groups and kinetic isotope effects (KIE).

A structure-function study of a proton pathway in the γ-class carbonic anhydrase from *Methanosarcina thermophila* was conducted in the work of Tripp and Ferry (2000). Four enzyme glutamate residues were characterized by site-directed mutagenesis. It was shown that Glu 84 and an active site residue, Glu 89, are important for CO_2 hydration activity, while external loop residues, Glu 88 and Glu 89 are less important. Glu 84 can be substituted for other ionizable residues with similar pKa values and, therefore, participates in the enzyme catalysis not as a chemical reagent but as a proton shuttle.

Enzyme cytochrome c oxidase catalyzes the respiratory reduction of O_2 coupled to proton translocation across the mitichondrial or bacterial membranes. Proton translocation by cytochrome c oxidase was investigated with the use of site-directed mutagenesis and molecular dynamic simulations (Backgren et al., 2000). The substitution of conserved glutamic acid, Glu 278, in subunit I of the enzyme from *Paracoccus denitrificans* for a nonacidic residue, resulted in the drastic decrease of its catalytic activity and proton translocation. When a phenylalanin in subunit I that lies close to the structure was changed to tyrosine, the activity increased more than 100-fold and the proton translocation was restored. The molecular dynamic simulation showed that water molecules in the active site cavity can within a few picoseconds reorganize to form a hydrogen-bonded chain. Proton transfer is thus limited by the dynamics of production and removal of water molecules within the cavity. According to authors' suggestion, the Glu 278 divides the proton conduction path between the D-channel and the bimetallic site into two short water chains. Therefore, it may have a proton-shuttling function for the two water chains, functioning as a true proton donor and acceptor.

For many enzymatic reactions involving hydrogen transfer, experimental data on KIF and its temperature dependence are roughly consistent with a classical (nontunneling) theory (Eq. 2.32) (Bruno and Bialik, 1992 and references therein). Nevertheless, anomalies in the relationship between hydrogen/tritium and deuterium/tritium KIEs (Schaad-Swain exponents, Eqs. 2.42-2.43), which could not be explained by classic kinetics have been reported (Cha et al., 1989; Grant and Klinman, 1989).

The Bruno and Bialik, (1992) theory which takes into account nuclear tunneling (Section 4.2.1), was applied to an analysis of "anomalous" Schaad-Swain exponents in a reaction catalyzed by bovine serum amine oxidase, BSAO (Grant and Klinman, 1989). The isotope effect in this reaction is found to be markedly larger than one, expected classically. Theoretical values of H/T and D/T KIFs and its temperature dependence match Grant and Klinman's experimental data.

According to Hwang and Warshel (1996), Tripp and Ferry (2000) and references therein, the rate limiting step in the reaction of CO_2 hydration catalyzed by carbonic anhydrase is proton transfer from a zinc bound water to His 64 through water molecules. Hwang and Warshel employed the quantized classical path approach to evaluate the quantum mechanical activation free energy and the isotope effects on the proton–transfer step in the catalytic reaction of carbonic anhydrase. Both parameters are in good agreement with the appropriate experimental data. It was also shown that taking into account the quantum mechanical nuclear tunneling effects resulted in reducing the theoretical free activation energy by approximately one kcal/mole.

Experimental data on primary and secondary kinetic isotope effects in the hydride–transfer step in liver alcohol dehydrogenase, LADH, were analyzed using canonical variational transition theory (CVT) for overbarrier dynamics and the optimized multidimentional path (OMT) for the nuclear tunneling (Alhambra et al., 2000 and references therein). This work demonstrates somewhat better agreement of theoretical values of primary and secondary Schaad- Swein exponents calculated by combining CVT/OMT methods with the experimental values instead of CVT and classical transition states (TST).

2.4. Electron-proton coupling. Mechanism of ATPase reactions in energy-conversion systems

At present, much attention is devoted to enzymes that utilize the energy of ATP hydrolysis for realization of energy-rich mechanics (myosin), transport (Na^+,K^+-ATPase, Ca^{2+}-ATPase, chemical processes (nitrogenase), polymerases, topoisomerases, GTPases, and for creation of electrochemical gradients in biomembranes (H^+-ATPase, ATP synthase). In this section we focus on the latter process. The coupling mechanism in the nitrogenase reaction is discussed in Section 3.1.

The idea that oxidative phosphorylation and photophosphorylation systems are coupled with the transfer of a proton through the membrane was introduced by Mitchell (1966) and is now widely accepted. H^+-ATPase (ATP synthase, F_1F_0-ATPase) catalyzes ATP synthesis coupled to an electrochemical gradient and ATP hydrolysis driven by proton translocation in mitochondrial or bacterial membranes. (Boyer, 2001; Babcock and Wikstroem, 1992; Abraham et al., 1994; Allison, 1998; Ogilvie et al. 1997; Musser and Theg, 2000; Backgren et al., 2000; Arechada and Jones, 2001; Gibbsons et. al., 2000; and references therein). The enzyme from *Escherichia coli* consists of two parts, a water-soluble F_1 part, composed of five different subunits α (3), β (3), γ, δ, ϵ and the membrane bilayer integrated F_0 part made up of three different subunits a, b (2), and c (11). There are six nucleotide-binding sites on the enzyme: three catalytic sites, located on b-subunits, and three noncatalytic sites, located on a-subunits.

According to the binding change model proposed by Boyer (2001 and references therein) the ATP synthesis proceeds in the following stages: (1) condensation of ADP with phosphate (Pi) that occurs inside the enzyme without energy input from proton translocation, (2) sequential operation of three catalytic sites of F1, which have tight, loose, and open conformation and undergo binding, interconversion and release steps of the process, respectively, and (3) binding of ADP and Pi to a low –affinity catalytic site that promote release of ATP bound to a high-affinity catalytic site for the expense of energy provided by proton translocation. Boyer postulated also that the enzyme operates by a rotational mechanism in which proton translocation in the F_0 portion drives an internal rotation of γ–subunit of F_1, causing sequential conformational change in the β-subunits.

Elucidation of the crystal structure of the bovine heart mitochondrial F_1-ATPase (Abraham et al., 1994, Gibbons et. al., 2000) focused attention on rotational catalysis in coupling ATP synthesis and hydrolysis with the proton translocation. Electron microscopy and X-ray structural analysis studies have shown that the F_1 part of the enzyme is separated from the F_0 by a narrow stalk of around 45 Å.

In a series of elegant biochemical and chemical engineering works, direct evidence for rotation of c-ring ang γ-subunit relative to β-subunits during catalysis were presented. A mutation allowed Duncan et al., (1995) to induce formation of a specific disulfide bond between β and γC87 in soluble F_1 from *E. coli*. Formation of the crosslink inactivated the enzyme, and reduction restored full activity. In contrast, fixing δ-subunit to α-subunit by cross-linking does not greatly impair either the ATPase activity or coupling proton translocation Counterclockwise rotation of a fluorescently-labeled actin filament attached to the γ-subunit of F_1-ATPase driven by ATP hydrolysis was directly demonstrated with the use of a fluorescence microscope (Noji et al., 2001 and references therein).

Investigation of kinetics of the catalytic process revealed drastic differences in the k_{cat} values for reaction in the presence of substoichiometric concentrations of substrate, MgATP, occurring in 10^5-10^6-fold lower than that in saturating conditions (Allison, 1998). This result clearly indicates strong positive cooperativity of the process. The Allison models for the minimal steps of ATP hydrolysis and synthesis under saturating conditions suggest that catalytic site F_1 adopt only two stable conformations, rather than three postulated by Boyer.

Recently new models were proposed and animated to demonstrate how each of $3\alpha\beta$ subunit pairs can be stabilized against rotation of the γ-subunit while also maintaining the chemical equivalency of the three $\alpha\beta$ pairs (Blum et al., 2000).

For elucidation of chemical mechanisms of ATP hydrolysis and synthesis and proton translocation positions of the enzyme groups in the vicinity of the binding substrate, MgAMP-PNP (AMN-PNP is 5'-adenylyl-imidodiphosphate) and MgADP, are of special interest (Abrahams et al., 1994, Allison, 1998). In the liganding catalytic sites the adenine of bound MgAMP-PNP, β_T, and MgADP, β_D, is present in a hydrophobic pocket contributed by two Phe, Tyr and Val. In this state, σ-ammonium of βLys162 interacts electrostatically with γ-phosphate of AMP-PNP. The hydroxyl oxygen of β-Thr, and oxygens of β- and γ-phosphates of bound MgAMP-PNP are directly liganded to the Mg^{2+} ion. Carboxylate oxygens βGlu192 and βAsp256 interact with Mg^{2+} through water molecules. The γ-carboxylate of βGlu188 probably plays a key role in the catalysis. This group locates 4.4 Å from the γ-phosphate of MgAMP-PNP, where it is hydrogen bonding to a water molecule. Modification of βGlu188 by dicyclohexylcarbodiimid accompanied inactivation of F_1ATPase). According to the suggestion of Abraham et al., (1994), this group functions as a general base that activates the water molecule for an attack on the γ-phosphorus during ATP hydrolysis, while the guanidinum of αArg373 might stabilizes a pentavalent phosphorus transition state during catalysis.

The following pathway having a large H-bonds polarization in hydrated F_0 subunits has been proposed (Zundel, 2000): carboxylate Ala79, Tyr10 (c-subunit), Glu219, His245 (a), Asp61(c), Arg41 (c) and Arg 210 (a). A proton conducts by the mechanism of concerted proton tunneling within less than picosecond. Chemical modification and mutagenesis studies implicate that ε-ammonium of β-Lys162 is involved in the catalysis, most probably indirectly (Weber and Senior, 1997).

It has been proposed (Likhtenshtein and Shilov, 1976; Likhtenshtein, 1988a) that the first result of ATP hydrolysis in the active site of energy-converting enzymes may be the forced protonation of one of the functional groups of the active site X followed by the formation of the protonated energy-reach intermediate XH^+. The energy of XH^+, which is not in equilibrium with the environment, may be then utilized for performance of chemical, mechanical or electrical work. Such a mechanism will be efficient if this intermediate is shielded from the water environment long enough for the performance of work. A similar idea was exposed by Williams (1982) who suggested that protons are generated in the vicinity of the ATP-synthetase by oxidative or photon-energy flow through the ATP-synthase site without equilibrating with the bulk phases.

As far as concern the mechanism of ATP hydrolysis, the nucleophilic capacity of the βGlu188 group ($pK_a = 5.9$) is not sufficient for fast cleavage of the γ-phosphorus bond of ATP. A more realistic explanation of the process is that the attack of water molecule on the bond results in the force protonation of this carboxylic group accounting for the energy released in the ATP hydrolysis. Protonation annihilates the carboxylate negative charge. The formation of such an nonequilibrium intermediate violates the electrostatic balance in the active site and can induce conformational transition favorable for a series of proton jumps from the energetically nonequilibrium βGlu188 group along the translocation channel.

Recently a mechanism that links conformational coupling of energetics of two chemical reactions through conformational change during a catalyst reaction cycle was proposed (Leyh, 1999). ATP sulfurylase from *E. coli* catalyzes and energetically links the hydrolysis of GTP and the synthesis of activated sulfate, APS (adenosine-5'-phosphosulfate) by reaction between ATP and sulfate. Experiments showed that the enzyme undergoes a conformational change in the GTP-binding reaction and the rate-limiting conformational step precedes the GTP hydrolysis. Formation of active signaling conformation promotes synthesis of APS. Active conformation is transformed to inactive during the release of Pi and $Mg^{2+.}$ Existing structural data don't contradict the aforementioned hypothesis, which suggests that the forced protonation of a functional group accounts for the GTP phosphate bond hydrolysis: the hydrolytic water is positioned by the γ-phosphate.

2.5. Concerted reactions

2.5.1. SYNCHRONIZATION FACTOR

In order to explain the high efficiency of many chemical and enzymatic processes, wide use is made of the concepts of energetically favorable, concerted mechanisms. In a concerted reaction a substrate is simultaneously attacked by different active reagents with acid and basic groups, nucleophyle and electrophyle, or reducing and oxidizing agents. It may however be presumed, that certain kinetic limitations exists on the realization of reactions which are accompanied by a change in the configuration of a large number of nuclei (Bordwell, 1970, Likhtenshtein, 1974, 1976a, 1977a,b, 1988a; Bernasconi, 1992).

According a simplified theory (Alexandrov, 1976), a concerted reaction occurs as a result of the simultaneous transition (taking approximately 10^{-13} s) of a system of independent oscillators, with the mean displacement of nuclei φ_0, from the ground state, to the activated state in which this displacement exceeds for each nuclei a certain critical value (φ_{cr}). If $\varphi_{cr} .> \varphi_0$ and the activation energy of the concerted process $E_{syn} > nRT$, the theory gives the following expression for the synchronization factor which is the ratio of the pre-exponential factors of the synchronous and simple processes:

$$\alpha_{syn} = \frac{n}{2^{n-1}}\left(\frac{nRT}{\pi E_{syn}}\right)^{\frac{n-1}{2}} \tag{2.44}$$

where n is the number of vibrational degrees of freedom of the nuclei participating in the concerted transition.

At $\varphi_{cr} < \varphi_0$ and $E_{syn} < nRT$,

$$\alpha_{syn} = \frac{n}{2^{n-1}} \tag{2.45}$$

In fact, in the frame of the Alexandrov model, when the average thermal energy of the system ($E_{av} = nRT$) exceeds the energy of the activation barrier, the process can be considered as activationless. Analysis of Eqs. 2.44 and 2.45 provides a clear idea of the scale of the synchronization factor, and the dependence of this factor on the number of n and therefore on the number of broken bonds and the energy activation (Fig. 2.12). For example, at moderate energy activation 20-40 kJ/mole, typical for enzymatic reactions, the incorporation of each new nucleus into the transition state can lead to a ten-fold decrease in the rate of the process.

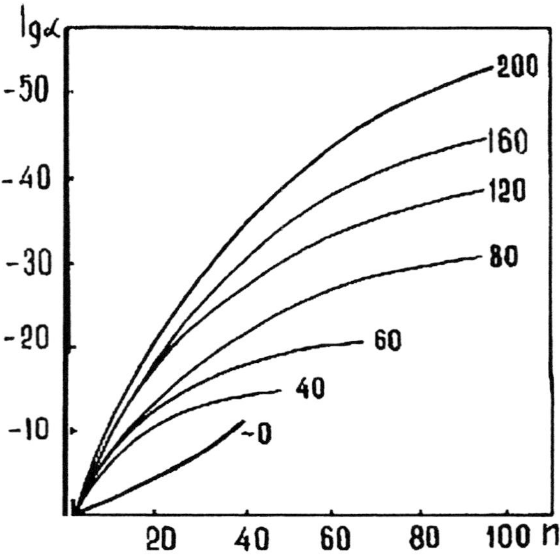

Figure 2.12 Theoretical dependences of the synchronization factor (asyn) on the number of degrees of freedom (n) of the nuclei involved in a concerted reaction. The curves have been constructed in accordance with Eqs 2.44 and 2.45. (Likhtenshtein, 1988a). Reproduced with permission

Therefore, in the case of an effective concerted mechanism, the decrease of the synchronization probability (α_{syn}) with increasing n must be compensated for by an appreciable decrease in the activation energy.

The transformation in complex molecules, which is accompanied by an appreciable rearrangement of the structure, by a change in nuclear distances and bonds angles, and by rearrangement of ligands or solvent molecules, can be approximately described with the aid of the concept of normal modes of vibration. In general the number of such modes (n_1) in molecule of m atoms is equal to 3m-6. For instance, the transition of a system consisting of a central atom in an octahedral environment of six ligands to a state with an increased distance between the central atoms and the ligands corresponds to a normal, totally symmetric mode. The value of the statistical weight of this is equal to $n_1 = 1/15$.

The models of concerted processes discussed above are only a crude approximation of the motion of a complex system of nuclei along the reaction coordinate. However, such an approximation apparently permits one to choose between the possible reaction mechanisms. The reliability of such a choice increases through a comparative examination of alternative reaction coordinates.

2.5.2. THE PRINCIPLE OF "OPTIMUM MOTION" IN ELEMENTARY ACTS OF CHEMICAL AND ENZYMATIC PROSESSES.

From the point of view of general concepts of chemical reactions, the less nuclei change their position in the course of an elementary step, the lower reorganization the energy and, therefore, the energy of the activation of the step (principle of "minimum motion"). On the hand, involving several acid-base, donor-acceptor and redox groups in concerted reaction can markedly decrease the reaction activation energy. These considerations have led to the formulation of the principle of "optimum motion" (Likhtenshtein, 1974, 1976a, 1977a,b, 1988a; Likhtenshtein and Mullokandov, 1977). According to this principle, the number of nuclei whose configuration is changed in the elementary act of a chemical reaction must be sufficiently large to provide favourable energetics for the step and, at the same time, sufficiently small for the maintenance of a high value of the synchronization probability during motion along the reaction pathway to the reaction products.

The condition preferring the concerted reaction as opposite to the direct with a rate constant k_{dir} and energy of activation E_{dir} is the inequality

$$\frac{k_{syn}}{k_{dir}} > \alpha_{syn} \exp\left(\frac{E_{dir} - E_{syn}}{RT}\right) \tag{2.46}$$

Though the estimates that illustrate the principle of "optimal motion" are based on simplified models and approximation formulas (2.44 – 2.46), they have, nevertheless, made it possible to drew some conclusions which are apparently useful in taking into account the treatment of complex elementary acts of chemical and biochemical processes (Likhtenshtein, 1988a).

In transition state theory, the rate of an adiabatic chemical reaction depends only on the difference between free energy in initial and transition states. From point of view of thermodynamics, formation of an intermediate complex can not give any preference to the process as compared with a collision complex. Nevertheless, the formation of a preliminary (pretransition) structure on the reaction coordinate can constrain the system of nuclear motions that do not lead to reaction products and, therefore, accelerate the process. It is necessary to stress that this acceleration is not caused by entropy reason, but by the optimization of the synchronization factor.

In liquid-phase chemical and enzymatic processes accompanied by a change in the state of an assemble of solvent particles or conformations of protein groups outside of the reaction complex, the simultaneous reorganization of more than four or five particles is hardly probable. The actual mechanism of the reorganization is a series of consecutive and parallel simple transitions, which precede processes within the reaction complex.

Enzymatic reactions, despite the obvious energy preference of certain concerted mechanisms, may be inefficient because of a too low synchronization factor. In such cases, the sequential transformation of the system through a number of steps is favorable. Here, the role of a multi-functional catalyst, in reaching a pretransition state is to provide favorable energy and synchronization factors through the optical use of the corresponding functional groups at each step of the process.

In the multinuclear clusters of transition metal with high degree of electron delocalization, an addition or subtraction of one or two electrons does not cause a significant rearrangement of the nuclear frame. Thus, this molecule can serve as an effective electron donor and acceptor.

2.6 Multi-electron mechanisms of redox reactions. Switching molecular devices

There are a considerable number of reactions in which the products contain two electrons, more than the starting compounds, and the consecutive two-step one-electron electron transfer process proves to be energetically unfavorable. In such cases, it is presumed that the two-electron process occurs in one elementary two-electron step. An example of a two-electron process is the hydride transfer, when two electrons are transported together with a proton. BH_4^-, hydroquinones and reduced nicotinamides are typical hydrid donors. A specific feature of quinones is the capacity to accept and then to reversibly release electrons one by one or two electrons as a hydride. Therefore, quinones can serve as a molecular device, which can switch consecutive one-electron process to single two-electron process.

Another possible two-electron mechanism involves the direct transport of two electrons from a mononuclear transition metal complex to a substrate (S). Such a transport alters sharply the electrostatic states of the systems and obviously requires a substantial rearrangement of the nuclear configuration of ligands and polar solvent molecules. For instance, the estimation of the synchronization factor (α_{syn}) for an octahedral complex, with Eq. 2.44 shows a very low value of $\alpha_{syn} = 10^{-7}$ to 10^{-8} and, therefore, a very low rate of reaction. The probability of two-electron processes, however, increases sharply if they take place in the coordination sphere of a transition metal, where the reverse compensating electronic shift from the substrate to metal occurs. Involvement of bi- and, especially, polynuclear transition metal complexes and clusters and synchronous proton transfer in the redox processes may essentially decrease the environment reorganization, and, therefore, provide a high rate for the two- electron reactions.

The reduction of molecular nitrogen to ammonium and water oxidation to molecular oxygen causes six- and four-electron transfer to occur eventually in these reactions, respectively. Such processes obviously cannot occur in a single step. Analysis of the thermodynamics of plausible intermediates rules out one- and two-electron transfers for both reactions and only four-electron mechanisms are energetically allowed (Section 3.1). Evidently, the direct transport of four electrons from (or to) a mononuclear or even binuclear transition metal complex appears to be ruled out. Practically the only possible variant of the four-electron mechanism is the conversion in the coordination sphere of a transition metal polynuclear complex. The multi-electron nature of the process does not impose any new, additional restriction on its velocity. The substrate-metal interactions in such complexes occur via multi-orbital binding with high degree of orbital overlap and the electron transfer resonance integral V is high enough to maintain fast velocity of the process. The electron transfer from (or to) d-orbitals of the metal to the substrate orbitals is accompanied by the simultaneous shift of electron clouds to the reverse direction. Such an electron transport may cause significant changing of local charges and, therefore, does not violate significantly the reaction complex nuclear frame.

The multi-electron nature of the energetically favorable process does not evidently impose any new, additional restriction on its velocity. Within a coordination sphere the orbital overlap is effective and, therefore the resonance integral V is high. The strong delocalization of electrons in clusters, polynuclear complexes in clusters and polynuclear complexes reduces to a minimum the reconstitution of the nuclear system during electronic transitions and, therefore, provides a high value for the synchronization factor.

An important feature of polynuclear transition metal complexes in redox enzymes and its chemical models is their ability to evolve inert molecules, such as N_2, O_2, and H_2O into inner-sphere chemical conversion under ambient condition to N_2O_4, H_2O_2 and O_2, correspondingly. According to thermodynamic estimations the formation of N_2H_2, $HO_2^{\cdot}$ and $HO^{\cdot}$ as intermediates in the above mentioned processes is energetically strongly unfavorable. Therefore, these reactions include multi-electron elementary steps. It is necessary to stress that realization of elementary four-electron redox reaction is provided by a simultaneous transport of additional number electrons from the nearest electron donating or electron-accepting centers, that is to say, metal clusters or polynuclear complexes.

As an example, a four-electron transfer from two M^{+n} metal atoms in a binuclear complex may be visualized:

$$[2M^{+n} + S] \rightleftharpoons [M^{+n+\delta} \underset{\longleftarrow}{\longrightarrow} S \rightleftharpoons M^{+n+\delta}] \xrightarrow{\;4H^+\;} [2M^{+n+2} + SH_4]$$

Here, the longer arrow indicates the direction of the preferred electron transfer from the metal to the substrate (S), and the shorter arrow indicates the direction of the reverse transfer. It is obvious that four protons accompanied by the water molecule rearrangement cannot be transferred in one synchronous step. Owing to the high degree of electron delocalization in the polynuclear metal complexes, these complexes are more suitable for multi-electron processes.

In real situations (Sections 3.1 and 3.5) sequential one-electron transfers precede the formation of electron-rich or electron deficient multi-electron catalytic complexes. Thus, such systems may be considered as devices for switching processes from the multistep one-electron mechanism to the multi-electron mechanism.

2.7. Stabilization of enzyme reactions transition states

The fundamental concept of the transition state stabilization was introduced to Linus Pauling in 1948 who said: "I think that enzymes are molecules that are complementary in structure to the activated complex of the reactions that they catalyze, that is, the molecular configuration that is intermediate between the reacting substances and the product of the reaction". This concept was widely accepted and used for the interpretation of experimental structural and kinetics data on enzyme catalysis, for the design of new substrates and inhibitors and for chemical mimicking of enzyme reactions. Decisive contributions in this area have been made by structural physical methods, X-ray analysis, in particular, and site-directed mutagenesis.

The basic idea underlying modern approaches to enzyme transition states is that finding a substrate molecule in the transition state in an enzyme active is connected with protein by multiple bonds. At a relatively modest energy of an individual bond, the energy from multiple bonds of only 2-3 kcal/mole can generate energy of 20 –30 kcal/mole in the transition state (Cleland and Northrope, 1999 and references therein). Such control of a strong interaction by the cooperation of many weak bonds has been called the "Lilliput principle" (Lumry, 2002). Because energy of different interactions such as van der Waals contacts, electrostatic ion-ion, ion-dipole and dipole-dipole, and hydrogen bonds are strongly dependent on media polarity, the transition of an interacting pair from water to a less polar medium is accompanied by drastic increases in the interaction energy and, therefore, by a change in the group's reactivity.

Values of local dielectric constants in proteins and enzyme active centers are estimated within the range of ε_{loc}= 4–12 (Marcus and Sutin, 1985; Fogel et al. 1994; Likhtenshtein, 1996; Honig and Nicolls, 1995; Cleland and Northrop, 1999) and, therefore, electrostatic interactions in these media are essentially more favorable as compared to a aqueous solution. Hydrogen bonds in aqueous solution are relatively weak, with energy formation ΔH =3-5 kcal/mole and l_H >2.8 Å in length. In nonprotic solvents of lower dielectric constant, hydrogen bonds become stronger (ΔH = 20-25 kcal/mole) and shorter (l_H = 2.4 between two oxygen atoms). As the bonds shorten, the barriers between two positions decrease and the possibility of nuclear tunneling increases. Such a bond is called a "low barrier hydrogen bonds" (LBHB).

In low dielectric organic solvents and enzyme active sites a number of hydrogen bonds between groups with similar pKa exhibit highly deshielded 1H NMR peaks (>16 ppm), low isotopic fraction factors and relatively short H-bonds (data on neutron and x-ray diffraction analysis (Gerlt and Gassman, 1992; Zundel , 2000; Cleland and Northrop, 1999).

Fig. 2.13 illustrates the electrostatic effects in transition state in enolase reaction (Larson et al., 1996). During this reaction a proton is removed by Lys-345 from C-2 of 2-phosphoglycerate to give an enolyzed, charged intermediate. This intermediate is stabilized by electrostatic interaction with five positive charges supplied by two Mg^{+2} ions and a protonated lysine. The 10-11 electrostatic interactions were found in the transition state of formate dehydrogenase and carbamoyl synthetase (Bruice and Benkovic, 2000) Another example of multifunctional interactions during enzymatic reactions in intermediate is the X-ray structure of tetrahedral intermediate in the chymotrypsin active site (Fig. 1.1).

One of the most important factors providing acceleration of enzymatic reactions as compared to chemical reactions is drastic changes of chemical reactivity catalytic groups inside and outside the enzyme protein globule. Drawing the charges of metal ions, carboxylate and protonated residues into the protein interior is accompanied by essential alternation of its acid-base and redox properties. This effect can be illustrated by the reaction of cleavage and formation of an α-C-H bond in enzymatic reactions of racemization, transamination, and isomerization (Ha et al., 2000 and references therein).

In these reactions a proton is abstracted from a carbon adjacent to carbonyl, carboxylic acid, or the carboxylate anion group by active cite residues. In water the pK_a of α-protones of most aldehydes, ketons, thioesters, and carboxylate anions lies between16-32, whereas pK_a of most carboxylate bases is usually < 7. Thus, the thermodynamic barrier for the proton extraction from α-CH bond is 12-34 kcal/mole. A 'kinetic" acidity of the α-proton may be increased by a concerted formation of either hydrogen-bonded or metal-coordinated enolates by the general acid catalysis (Gerlt, 1999; Gerlt and Gassman, 1992).

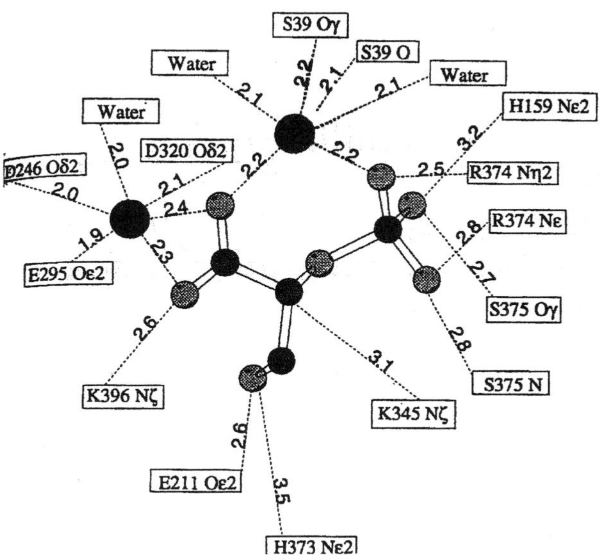

Figure 2.13. Schematic diagram of the enolase active site residue interactions with the $(Mg^{2+})_2$ substrate/product complex (Larsen et al., 1996). Reproduced with permission

An essential contribution to lowering the activation barrier is proposed by the formation of a low barrier hydrogen bond (LBHB) with short distance between the proton donors and acceptors as demonstrated in the Δ^5-3-ketosteroid isomerase (KSI) reaction (Ha et al., 2000). This enzyme catalyzes cleavage and formation of the substrate C-H bond at a diffusion-controlled limit. The crystallographic and NMR investigations of KSI with its competitive inhibitors (equilenin and androsteron) showed a large perturbation of pKa values of both inhibitors and a key catalytic residue at the active site. NMR spectroscopic investigation evidenced "unusual" ionization of a hydroxyl group (pK_a =11,5) of an inhibitor with a catalytic residue Tyr14 (pK_a =11.5) at pH =6.7. The protonation of the catalytic residue Asp38 (pK_a = 4.5) in the interaction with a carboxylate group of an inhibitor also takes place. The pKa differences between catalytic groups and substrates can be significantly reduced in the active site environment and thereby eliminate a large fraction of thermodynamic and activation barriers in general acid/base reactions. Similar effects have been found in glutamate, triose-P, mandelate racemiases, aconitase and citraite synthase (Gerlt and Gassman, 1992; Cleland and Northrop, 1999; and references therein)

In serine proteases the hydrogen bonds between Asp and the His of the catalytic triad is normally weak. At the substrate presence the histidine becomes "unusually" protonated and a LBHB forms between Asp and His. The LBHB formation is proven by the low field proton NMR signal and fractionation factor of its protons in stable adduct fluorinated methyl ketone inhibitor with serine proteases (Cassidy et al. 1997; Cleland and Northrop, 1999). The increased strength of the hydrogen bond lowers the activation barrier for formation of the tetrahedral intermediate and thus facilitates catalysis of the reaction.

Lactate dehydrogenase accelerates the hydride transfer rate between NADH and pyruvate by a factor of 10^{14} over the rate found in solution. As it was judged by the narrowing of Raman bands of NADH and carbonyl of pyruvate, about 1.4 kcal arises from elimination of nonproductive conformations on binding of the substrate (Deng and Callender, 1999). A most significant factor for the transition state stabilization is the strong electrostatic interaction between polarized carbonyl oxygen (+C-O-) and His-195 in the enzyme active site. This stabilization can provide at least 6 orders of rate enhancement of the enzymatic reaction.

2.8. Pretransition states

In 1953 Eyring, Lumry and Spikes concluded that the high efficiency demonstrated by enzymes must be a mechanical consequence of conformational changes. Accordingly, interactions of a substrate with an enzyme active site raise the potential energy of the pre-transition state with high efficiency using the force vector. From this point of view, a better explanation for enzyme reaction acceleration is the similarity of the transition state (TS) to the pretransition state (PTS) (Lumry and Eyring, 1954; Jencks, 1981; Bruice and Lightstone, 1998; Bruice and Benkovic, 2000; Wolfenden and Snider, 2001). If so, very effective inhibitors resemble PTS rather than TS. Within the last half a century this concept has been sustained by more and more theoretical and experimental investigations.

Full support for that hypothesis came with information concerning the position of atoms in enzymes, their complexes with substrates and inhibitors, and the values of so called B-factors that relate to the average amplitude of atoms displacement. Structural investigations with the use of such physical methods as NMR and Raman resonance spectroscopy, theoretical calculations, in particular, also produce evidence in favour of this concept.

Bruice and his colleagues (Bruice and Lightstone, 1998; Bruice and Benkovic, 2000) introduced the term near attack conformation (NAC) to define the requirement of conformation for juxtaposed reactants to enter the transition state. The greater the mole fraction of reactant NAC conformation in the pretransition state, the greater the reaction rate constant. It was demonstrated that in intramolecular enzyme catalysis, changes of the enthalpy activation $\Delta H^{\#}$ as compare with chemical analoges, essentially predominate over entropic contribution, which was estimated to be $T\Delta S^{\#} = -4\text{-}6$ kcal mole.

Examination of the molecular dynamics (MD) simulation dehydrogenases with substrate and NAD(P)H at the active site shows that only one of the possible quasi-boat conformations exists (Bruice and Lightstone, 1998). The NAC structure in the lactate dehydrogenase active site is associated with the formation of the quasi-boat conformation. In this configuration the distance between the transferring hydride and pyruvate carbonyl is about 1 Å shorter when the dihydropyridin ring is in the boat form than in the planar conformation. The closeness of the approach of the reactants in this pretransition state, and the lessened bond energy of C(4)-axial-H as compared to C(4)-equatorial-H can provide a kinetic advantage to hydride transfer.

According to (Bruice and Benkovic, 2000 and references therin) multiple electrostatic interactions between the formate and nicotinamide of NAD^+ in the formate degydrogenase pretransition state (PTS) persist in the TS. These two states differ only by a lengthening of the hydrogen bond between the positively charged guanidine group of Arg284 and the negative formate oxygen by 0.4 Å, and a shortening of the hydrogen bond between the nicotinamide amide carbonyl oxygen and the imidazole of His332 by 0.5 Å in TS as compared to PTS. The MD simulations showed a similarity between TS and PTS in catecholate O-methyltransferase, haloalkane dehydrogenase and other enzymes (Bruice and Benkovic, 2000; and references therein).

Recently the investigation of the structure, molecular dynamics and action mechanism of enzymes revealed that protein globules of many enzymes consist of two tightly packed knots (matrix, domains, blocks) tethered with a relatively flexible spacer. (Lumry, 1995a,b, 2002; and references herein) (See also Section 4.1). The enzyme active sites are most commonly located in a cleft between these domains. Binding of substrates and inhibitors depends on the extend of matrix contraction (Fersht, 1999).

For example, the absolute value of negative entropy of parent substrate N-acetyl-L-tryptophan binding to chymotrypsin (-25 cal/moleK) was found to be markedly less than that for inhibitors indole and N-acetyl-D-tryptophan (-60 and −135 cal/moleK, respectively) It was proposed that the excess free energy (10 -12 kcal/mole) in the enzyme-subsrate complex is converted to energy of the substrate compression from the protein matrix contraction. An artificial substrate siltone, having a five-membered ring with strain energy 23 kcal/mole, forms acetyl derivative with opening of the ring in the chymotrypsin active site. Because an equilibrium-binding constant is close to unity, the ring energy compensates presumably the matrix contraction at binding of "regular" substrates and inhibitors. The several methods for measuring matrix contraction, including analysis of B-factors and protein dynamics data, indicate a correlation between aforementioned thermodynamic estimations and the enzyme matrix state.

During last decades the domains C-2 symmetry (the dyad rotation symmetry) of low-B palindrome was established in many enzymes (chymotrypsin, trypsin, aspartyl proteinases, HIV-1 protease, carboxypeptidase A, phospholipase A-2 ribonuclease, etc.) (Lumry, 2002; and references therein). It is proposed that the pair domain closure causes constrain of pretransition state complex that activates cleavage or formation of chemical bonds. Thus control of strong bonds by the cooperation of many matrix or knots bonds takes place. As an example, in the active site of carboxypeptidase A the zinc ion is attached to one of the catalytic domains by histidine 69 and glutamine 72 and connected by hystidine 196 to the second domain. Similar structures were found in the chymotrypsin and pepsin active sites where protons are driven under compression of the domains closure.

2.9. Principle of "optimum motion" and mechanisms of enzymes reactions

From point of view of considerations, which led to the formulation of POM, the formation of pretransition states have to be preceded by a number elementary steps optimally combining enthalpy, entropy and synchronization factors. This principle allows discussion of altrernative mechanisms of transformation of the pretransition state to the transition state. Beneath some chosen enzymatic systems will be analyzed.

The reaction catalyzed by enzyme lactate dehydrogenase is a good example of a catalytic reaction with a "simple" elementary act of the hydride transfer. Nevertheless, as it is seen from of the structure of the enzyme active site-substrate complex, of lactate dehydrogense (Fig. 2.14) (Deng and Callender, 1999) three atoms of substrate (conversion of pyruvate to lactate) and five atoms of the nicotine ring (conversion of NADH to NAD^+), and five atoms of the imidazole ring should change their position at formation of the transition state. According to Eq. 2.44 involving 13 heavy nuclei in the transition (marked by *) would "cost" a decrease of the process probability by the synchronization factor $\alpha_{syn} \approx 10^{-10}$. Taking experimental value of activation energy as about 10.0 kcal/mole and value of $T\Delta S^{\#} = - 4\text{-}6$ kcal mole, a value of ratio of rate constants for concerted and experimental reactions of the transformation can be estimated as $k_{syn}/k_{exp} \approx 10^{-8}$. Accordingly, the concerted mechanism has very low probability.

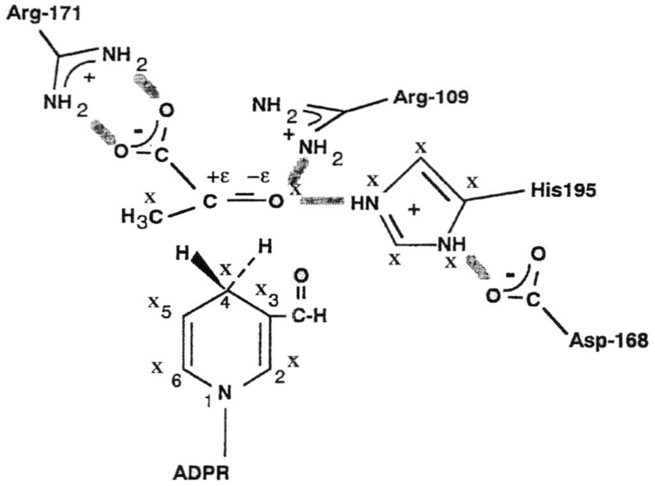

Figure 2.14. Modified scheme of lactate dehydrogenase reaction. Nuclei participating in the formation of the transition state are marked by * (Deng and Callender, 1999). Reproduced with permission .

Enolase catalyzes the reversible elimination of water from 2-phosphoglycerate to phosphopyruvate. According X-ray structural analysis (Larsen et al., 1996) the ε-amino group of Lys 345 is positioned to interact with the phosphopyruvate proton whereas the carboxylate of Clu 211 is positioned to interact with 3-OH group of the substrate (Fig. 2.13). It is necessary to stress that the former group can serve as a base, that to say be deprotonated, to abstract proton and latter as an acid (be protonated) to abstract OH⁻ only if their pKa are far away from the equilibrium pKa values at neutral pH. According to the schematic diagram of the enolase active site-substrate complex, in the case of a concerted reaction with simultaneous elimination of H^+ and OH^- from the substrate six nuclei of the phosphopyruvate, three nuclei of the Glu 211 carboxyl and three nuclei of amino group of Lys 345, and at least one atom of water have to move in the course of PTS-TS transformation. Estimation of the synchronization factor for a reaction with participation of 13 nuclei gives $\alpha_{syn} \approx 10^{-8}$ that is too small to provide fast reaction even if the activation barrier would be as low as 5.0 kcal/mole. The similar analysis showed that each of two steps in the sequential mechanism with formation of carboxylate dianion intermediate stabilized by two Mg^{+2} and protonated lysine group has more preferable synchronization and energetic factors. This mechanism has been proved experimentally (Larsen et al., 1996 and references herein)

Similar analysis of the reactioncatalyzed by formate dehydrogenase (Fig. 2.15 gives value of the synchronization factor $\alpha_{syn} \approx 10^{-8}$

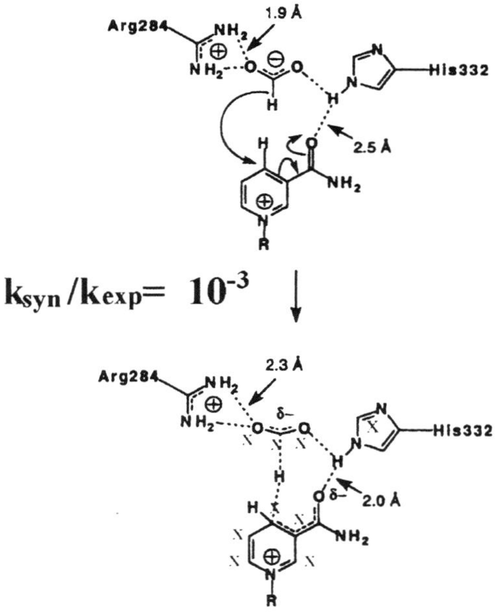

Figure 2.15. Modified scheme of the formate dehydrogenase reaction. Nuclei participating in the formation of the transition state are marked by *. (Bruice and Benkovic, 2000) Reproduced with permission.

S-adenosyl-L methionine (ADO-Met) dependent DNA methyl transferase catalyzed the transfer of a methyl group from AdoMet to a specific nucleotide within the DNA helix (Cheng et al., 1993). In a concerted reaction in the enzyme active site (Fig X) with a simultaneous addition of methyl residue of AdoMet to the cytosine ring and with an elimination of the ring proton by a water molecule requires involving seven heavy nuclei (two of Cys 81, four of AdoMet and one of water. An estimation with aid of Eq. 2.44 leads to value of the reaction synchronization factor $\alpha_{syn} \approx 10^{-4}$, that does not rule out the concerted mechanism, if the activation energy is less than 10 kcal/mole Nevertheless, a sequential mechanism in which the cysteine catalytic group attacks the ring to form an intermediate with the S-C covalent bond and the negative charge on the ring in a first step and with the proton elimination in the second step has been proven by structural and kinetic investigation and by molecular dynamics simulation (Cheng et al., 1993; Lau and Bruice, 1998. 2000).

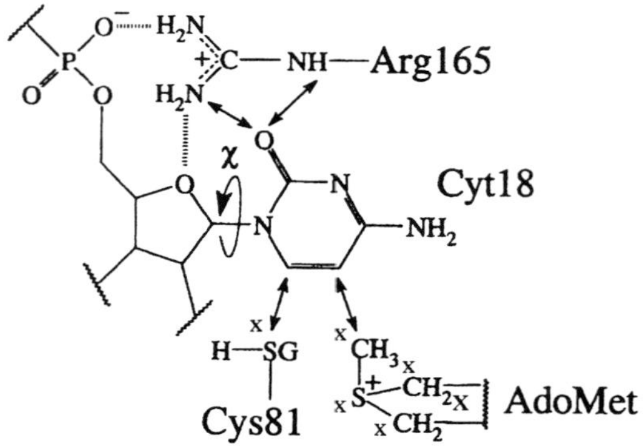

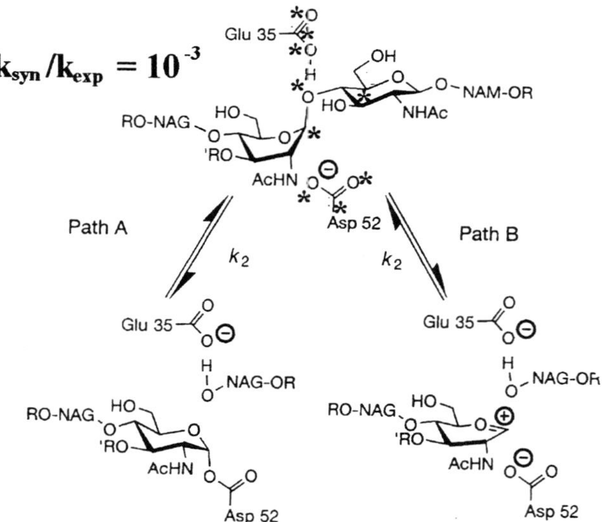

Figure 2.16. Modified scheme of the methyl transferase reaction. Nuclei participating in the formation of the transition state are marked by *. (Cheng et al., 1993) Reproduced with permission.

Fig. 2.17. Modified scheme of lyzozyme reaction. Nuclei participating in the formation of the transition state are marked by *. (Vocadlo et al., 2001) Reproduced with permission.

In 1977 the book author (Likhtenshtein, 1977b), analyzing possible mechanisms of hydrolysis of polyaminosaccharides catalyzed by lysozyme, had concluded that the concerted attack of carboxylate and carboxyl and water molecule on the substrate is characterized by very low theoretical value synchronization factor ($\alpha_{syn} \approx 10^{-9}$). Such a low probability of synchronous motion of nuclei along the reaction coordinate can not be compensated by low energy activation of concerted process. Recently, strong experimental evidence has been provided that the reaction occurs through the formation of covalent glycosyl-enzyme intermediate during catalytical cycle of hen egg-white lysozyme (Fig 2.17) (Vocado et al., 2001). The formation of the intermediate was proved using electrospray ionization mass spectrometry and X-ray diffraction. The proposed reaction mechanism includes substrate distortion, formation of a covalent intermediate. Nevertheless, the concerted elementary process required simultaneous motion of nine nuclei and estimated synchronization factor ($\alpha_{syn} \approx 10^{-6}$) and also is not possible.

Though the aforementioned estimates that illustrate the principle of "optimal motion" are based on simplified models and approximation formulas (2.44 – 2.46), they give independently indirect evidences in favor of, a similarity between transition and pretransition states of the enzymatic reactions.

2.10. Radical mechanisms of enzyme catalysis

In 1949 Chance in his classical work has constructed the following radical mechanism of substrate (DH_2) oxidation catalyzed by   peroxidase (E)

$$E + H_2O_2 \rightarrow E_1$$
$$E_1 + DH_2 \rightarrow E_I + DH_2^{\cdot+}$$
$$E_{II} + DH_2 \rightarrow E + DH_2^{\cdot+}$$

According to the Chance mechanism, the interaction of H_2O_2 with the enzyme gives "compound I " (E_I). The oxidation of the donor molecules leads to "compound II" (E_II) which oxidizes the second donor molecule. The radical intermediates were detected experimentally for such substrates as amines and phenols with relatively high reduction potential (Dunford and Stillman, 1976). The one-electron steps with the formation of free radicals at oxidation of amines and phenols have been proved in the ceruloplasmin, laccase and ascorbic oxidase reactions (Malsmstrom et al., 1975).

Recently enzymatic mechanisms that proceed by free radical chemistry initiated by the 5'deoxyadenosyl radical were discovered. (Frey, 2001). Three radicals were specroscopically characterized in reaction of the interconversion of L-lysin and L-□-lysin by lysine 2,3-aminomutase. The enzyme $[Fe_4S_4]^+$ center undergoes the chemical cleavage of S-adenosylmethionine (SAM) with the reversible formation of 5'-deoxyadenosyl radical. In other reactions with SAM, iron-sulfur proteins generate this radical which activate an enzyme to abstraction a hydrogen atom from an enzymatic glycyl residue to form a glycyl radical. 5'deoxyadenosyl radical also arises in adenosylcobalamin reaction as the result of hemolytic cleavage of the cobalt-carbon bonds. In the following reaction this radical initiates abstraction hydrogen atoms from substrates.

The radical rebound mechanism has been proposed and proved in several cases in reaction of hydroxylation catalyzed by cytochrome 450 and methane monooxigenase (Section 3.2)

2.11. Substrate channeling

Substrate channeling is a process by which two or more sequential enzymes in a pathway interact to transfer a metabolite (or intermediate) from one enzyme to another without allowing free diffusion of the metabolite into bulk solvent. (Ovadi, 1991; Srere, 1987; Anderson, 1999). The substrate tunneling is one of fundamental process of regulating enzymatic processes in cells. Glycolysis, biosynthesis of nucleic acids, aminoacids, and fatty acids are found to be among these processes.

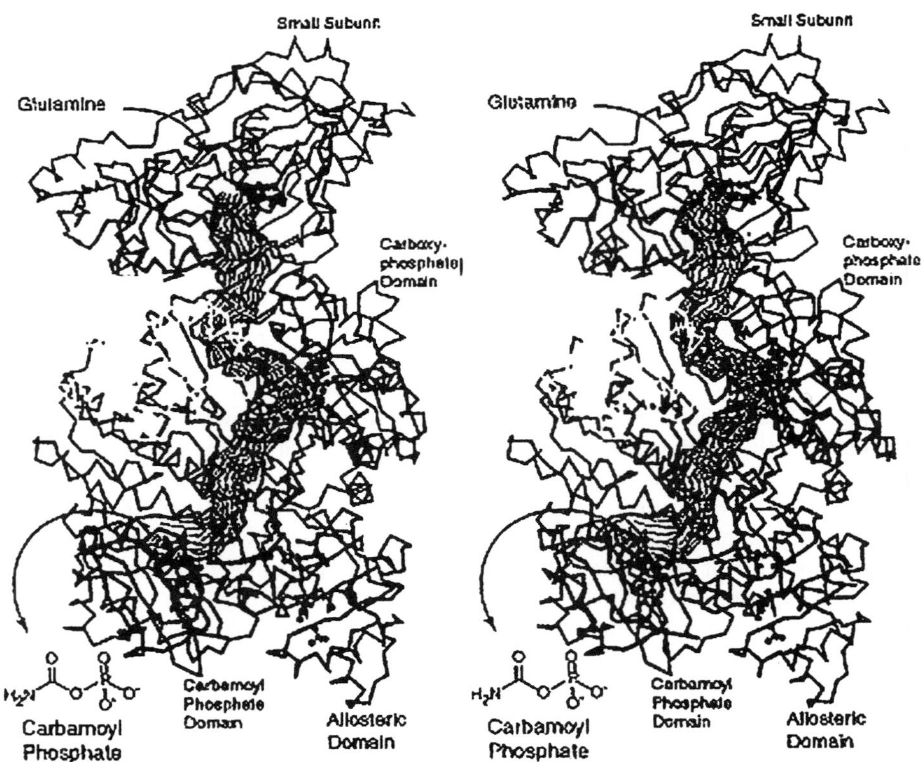

Figure 2.18. Putative channel connected three active sites in CPS (Thoden et al., 1997). Reproduced with permission.

Techniques for demonstrating channeling behavior include enzyme buffering, ligand exchange kinetics, isotope dilution, and estimation of the transition time. One of the most frequently used methods is the method of the transient time approximation. At the first experiment the steady state kinetics of reaction $B \rightarrow C$ was investigated, V_{max} and K_M were measured, and on this base a lag in attainment of steady state was calculated. In conversion three metabolites $A \rightarrow B \rightarrow C$, catalyzed by coupled enzyme complex E_1E_2, the transient time is expected to be shorter if the intermediate B did not freely diffuse in solution. A second steady state technique is the isotope dilution method. This method involved determining the rate of conversion of radiolabeled substrate ($A^* C^*$) in the presence of excess of unlabeled B for individual (E_1) and coupled (E_1E_2) enzyme reactions. In the case of channeling mechanism, the radioactive intermediate would not appear in solution in the course of the reaction.

More direct approach to the problem is based on measuring rapid presteady state kinetics with the use rapid chemical quench and stop-flow techniques (Johnson, 1995; Fierke and Hammes, 1995). These techniques allow monitoring individual rates of binding, conversion and dissociation of substrate. The most effective variant of such an approach is based on using a single turn over kinetics in which enzyme is taken in excess over radiolabeled substrate.

Carbamoyl phosphate synthetase (CPS), which catalyzes the synthesis of carbamoyl phosphate from bicarbonate, glutamine, and two molecules of MgATP (Fig. 2.18), can serve as an example of employment of the substrate channeling mechanism (Anderson, 1999). The CPS crystal structure in the presence of ligands has been solved, which provides a structural basis for substrate channeling (Fig. 2.18) (Thoden et al., 1997, 1999). Glutamine amidotransferase activity is associated with the small subunit whereas ATP-dependent phosphorylations of bicarbonate and carbamate occur on the large subunit. A linear distance of about 100 Å separates the glutamin-binding site in the small subunit and the site for carbamoyl phosphate synthesis in the large subunit. Fig. 2.14 shows a pathway of length of > 96 Å by which enzymatic intermediates may pass from the small subunit to the ultimate carbamoyl phosphate synthetase active site.

2.12. Relationships between the energy and entropy activation of enzymatic processes

The energy (E_a) and entropy ($\Delta S^{\#}$) activation of an enzymatic reaction are determined experimentally through the use of temperature dependencies of the rate constants of various macrosteps the process. Though most of the reactions catalyzed by enzymes differ from analogous non-enzymatic reactions by lower values of the apparent activation energy, these parameters are not related directly to experimentally observed acceleration of the reactions. The values of activation entropy for formally unimolecular enzymatic steps usually goes beyond the range of "normal" values typical for corresponding chemical reactions. The both activation parameters are often very sensitive to the structure of substrate (even when structural modification does not change the chemical active group reactivity), temperature regions, pH, solvent composition, etc. It is obvious that, for a chemical reaction in active sites of enzymes, the experimental values of E_a and $\Delta S^{\#}$ are apparent parameters, which jointly reflect the entire complexity of the process (presence of intermediate microsteps, involving accompanying conformational transitions and solvent molecule reorganizaton).

Materials on the activation parameters of enzymatic processes have been analyzed in review articles (Likhtenshtein, 1966; 1976a, 1979a,1988a; Lumry and Rajender, 1970; Lumry ans Biltonen, 1969; Lumry and Gregory, 1995). Cases were indicated, where for the same enzymes the change of the activation energy and entropy of the process caused by variation of chemical structure of substrates and other conditions, mentioned above, take place in parallel. The following linear dependences are approximately satisfied:

$$E_\alpha = \alpha_c + \beta_c \Delta S^\#$$
(2.47)

The dependences, such as Eq. 2.47, are known as compensation effect, and coefficient β_c is denoted as isokinetic temperature at which all reactions of given series have the same rate constant. An example of compensation effect for for catalytic rate constant of the *Sulfolobus solfataricus* β-glycosidase reaction with different substrates is shown in Fig. 2.19. Similar relationships were reported for many other prosesses, involving the binding ligands to hemoglobin, the oxidation of alcohols by catalase, the hydroxylation of substrates by cytochrome c, etc.

The compensation phenomena considered above are not only characterisic of enzyme reactions. The compensation relationships in protein denaturation are noted for enormous ranges of E_a values (from 0 to 120 kcal/mole) and $\Delta S^\#$ of (from 10 to 400 eu) (Likhtenshtein and Troshkina, 1968) . These quantities have been found to be highly sensitive to to external condidion (pH, additive, moisture content, etc.) and rotational diffusion of spin labels introduced into various portions of globular proteins. They have also been observed, though to a less extend, in various processes in the condenced phase (chemical reactions, diffusion, evaporation, electrical, conduction, electron transfer, etc. The main property of all these systems, which differ from simple gas reactions, is the cooperative behavior of particle assemblies surrounding the reaction centers.

The anomalies pointed out above, including compensation effects, may be accounted for in general bases of the assumption that the chemical elementary steps on the enzyme are accompanied by the arrangement of the conformational structure of protein globules and surrounding water molecules. The kinetic and thermodynamic parameters of such structural rearrangements make a contribution to the experimentally measured and whose reflect cooperative properties of the water-protein matrix.

Following this assumption, we can represent the apparent activation parameter in the form of following equations

$$E_a = E_r + n\Delta H_0 \text{ and } \Delta S^\# = \Delta S_r^\# + n\Delta S_0 + A$$
(2.48)

where E_r and $\Delta S^\# r$ are attributed to energy and entropy activation of the chemical step, respectively; n is the number of particles in the surrounding cooperative assemble; ΔH_0 and ΔS_0 are the standard enthalpy and entropy of the rearrangement of one elementary unit; and the value of A depends on the manner in which the particles are packed.

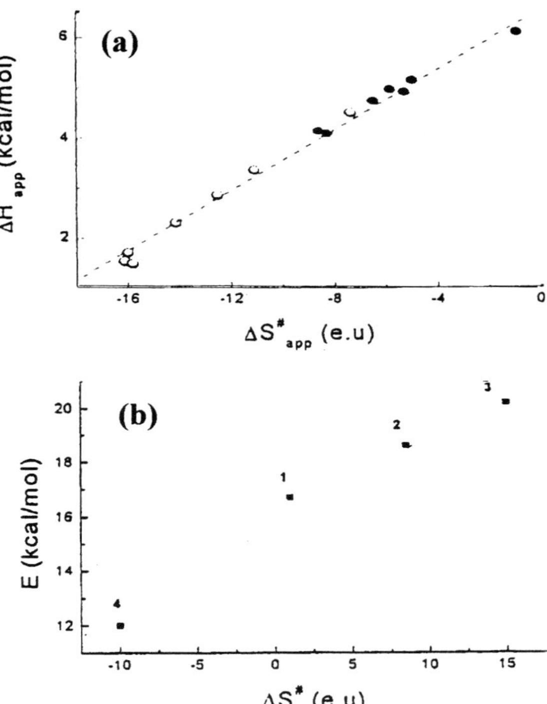

Fig.2.19. (a) Dependency of the apparent enthalpy activation $\Delta H^{\ddagger}$ on the apparent entropy activation ΔS_{app} for the rotational diffusion of the nitroxide labels attached to the enzyme, according to EPR data, low temperature region (T < 312 K) (open circles), high temperature region (T > 312 K) (closed circles) and (b) for catalytic rate constant of the *Sulfolobus solfataricus* β-glycosidase reaction with different substrates. 1) *p*-npGlu; 2) *o*-npGal, 3) laminaribiose, 4) Cellobiose. The activation parameters were calculated from kinetic data derived from (Likhtenshtein et al. 2000a) Reproduced with permission.

For series of reactions that mainly differ in the number of particles in a cooperative assemble, and have approximately equal other parameters of Eq. 2.48

$$\alpha_c = E_r - T\Delta S_r^{\#} \text{ and } \beta_c = \frac{\Delta H_0}{T_c} \qquad (2.49)$$

where T_c is the "melting" temperature of the cooperative assemble which is expected to be close to average temperature of the experiment. In a general case, the chemical reaction and the accompanying rearrangement cannot be regarded as independent events. If the quantities and are represented, to a first approximation, as linear function of n with the coefficients being, respectively, equal to a_1 and b_1, then the isokinetic temperature will be given by:

$$\beta_c = \frac{\Delta H + a_1}{\Delta S_0 + b_1} \tag{2.50}$$

Thus, the experimental value of β_c may significantly deviate from the "melting" temperature of the matrix, depending on the sign and magnitude of the coefficients a_1 and b_1.

The above treatment is based on the simplest model of the cooperative processes. In real cases, not all the portions of the cooperative assemble are identical and rate of elementary rearrangements are equal. Such cases require special consideration with the use modern theoretical methods. Nevertheless, equations of types 2.48-2.50 disclose, in principle, the physical meaning the physical meaning of experimentally determined activation parameters of enzymatic processes.

MECHANISMS OF CHOSEN ENZYME REACTIONS

3.1. Nitrogenase

3.1.1. OVERVIEW

Microbiological nitrogen fixation is the global large-scale process of the atmospheric nitrogen reduction to ammonia with the yield approximately 200,000 million tons per annum. The process occurs in anaerobic and aerobic bacteria such as *Azotobacter vinelandii, Clostridium pasterianum, Klebsiella pneumonia,* etc., and Rizobium from the root nodules of legumes. Since the publication of the pioneer works of the Bulen (Bulen and LeCompt, 1996) and Mortenson (Mortenson et al., 1997) groups, who reported the isolation of the first partially purified dinitrogen fixing complex (nitrogenase), the efforts of many biochemists have been concentrated on the preparation of individual components of nitrogenase and on the study of their structure and action mechanism.

The central enzyme of biological nitrogen fixation catalyzes in the nitrogen-fixing bacteria the reduction of molecular nitrogen to ammonia by biological (ferredoxin) and non-biological ($S_2O_4^{2-}$) reducing agents with the assistance of ATP hydrolysis hydrolysis (Bulen and LeCompt, 1996; Mortenson et al., 1967, Newton, 1996, 1997, 2000). 1996, 1997, 2000).

$$N_2 + 8H^+ \; 16MgATP \rightarrow 2NH_3 + H_2 + 16MgADP + 16\,Pi$$

The active form of nitrogenase is formed through the combined action of two components: a protein containing [Fe_4S_4] cluster (FeP) and iron-molybdenum protein (FeMoP) with two [Fe_8S_8] so called P-clusters and two iron-molybdenum cofactors (FeMoCo). The FeP consists of a γ_2 -dimer equivalent subunit with a total molecular weight of 64 kDa. FeMoP is an $\alpha_2\beta_2$ tetramer of molecular weight 250 kDA containing two molybdenum atoms and about 30 iron and acid labile sulfur atoms distributed into (FeMoP) and (FeMoCo). The Fe protein passes electrons from FeP to MoFe protein in a reaction, which requires hydrolysis of MgATP to MgADP.

Apart from N_2 and H^+, nitrogenase catalyzes reduction of many substrates (C_2H_2, C_2H_4, NO, HCN, HN_3, cyclopropene, etc), which are also inhibitors of nitrogen reductions. Besides well–characterized classical molybdenum nitrogenase, two genetically distinct nitrogenases were isolated from *Azotobacter vinelandii* (Bishop et al., 1980; Eady, 1996; Harvey et al., 1990). All three nitrogenase enzymes comprise two separable components, Fe-protein and proteins containing iron P-clusters, and cofactors iron-molybdenum, iron-vanadium or only iron clusters.

Since the time of Daniel Rutherford, who discovered molecular nitrogen about 200 years ago, this gas has served as an example of a very inert substance. Thus, the mechanism of the relatively fast reduction of N_2 in the nitrogenase active site with turnover about 0.2 s^{-1} appears as a mysterious and challenging problem not only for biochemists but for chemists as well.

Recent developments in this important field have been reviewed in the last decade (Burgess and Lowe, 1996; Howard and Rees, 1996; Seefeldt and Dean, 1997; Smith, 1994, 1999; Smith et al., 1995; Tikhonovich et al., 1995; Likhtenshtein and Therneley, 1995; Thikhonovich et al., 1995; Shilov, 1997; Therneley and Dean, 2000; Rees and Howard, 2000; Chiu et al., 2001; Elmerich, 2001; Syrtsova and Timofeeva, 2001).

3.1.2. STRUCTURE AND PHYSICO-CHEMICAL PROPERTIES OF THE NITROGENASE ACTIVE SITES.

The first indirect information about structure of nitrogense metal-containing active sites was obtained in the early 1970's employing spin and electron-density labeling (Syrtsova et al., 1971, Likhtenshtein et al. 1973, 1980), ESR and Mössbauer spectroscopy (Ohrme-Johnson et al., 1972, 1978; Münck et al., 1975). The replacement of iron atoms in FeP and FeMoP from *Azotobacter vinelandii* for para-chloromercury benzoate derivative of nitroxide spin labels has led to spin-labeled preparations whose ESR spectra showed strong exchange interaction similar to those for spin-labeled pea ferredoxin. The electron micrographs of nitrogenase preparations, in which Fe atoms were substituted for mercury atoms, revealed electron-scattering granules related to the formation of closely arranged ensembles with four to six mercury atoms in each. These factors indicate that FeP and FeMoP belong to the class of non-heme iron-sulphur proteins.

More detailed information about structure and spectral properties of the nitrogenase Fe-clusters were obtained by a combination of physical methods. The structure suggested at that time and variation of spectra parameters is presented in Fig. 3.1, which was plotted on the basis of the data obtained in the works of Ohrme-Johnson's and Münck's groups cited above. Subsequent investigations have confirmed the main parameters and added some important details.

The principle advances in the area has been made using x-ray structural analysis. Crystallographic data have been first produced for the nitrogenase complex of FeP (A2) and FeMoP (A1) from *Azotobacter vinelandii* (Kim and Rees, 1992) and for the corresponding complex of Cp2 and Cp1 from *Clostridium pasterianum* (Bolen et al., 1993),). A 1.6 Å resolution X-ray crystallographic structure of *Klebsiella pneumoniae* proteins has been recently reported (Mayer et al., 1999) It was shown that FeMoco sites in A1, Cp1, and Kp1 are 70 Å apart and FeMoco and P clusters are separated by about 19 Å. X-ray structures of the nitrogenase complex and the active site clusters are presented in (Figs. 3.2-3.4).

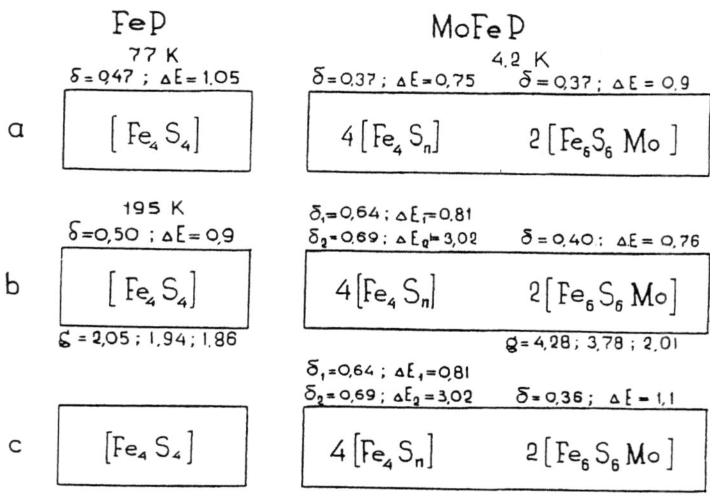

Figure 3.1. The values of the parameters of the EPR and Mossbauer spectra of various forms of nitrogenase: a) native form, b) reduction by dithionate and c) reduction in the presence of MgATP. The Mössbaur parameters, of the chemical shift (δ) and the quadrupole splitting (ΔE) are given in mm/s. (Likhtenshtein 1988a). Reproduced with permission.

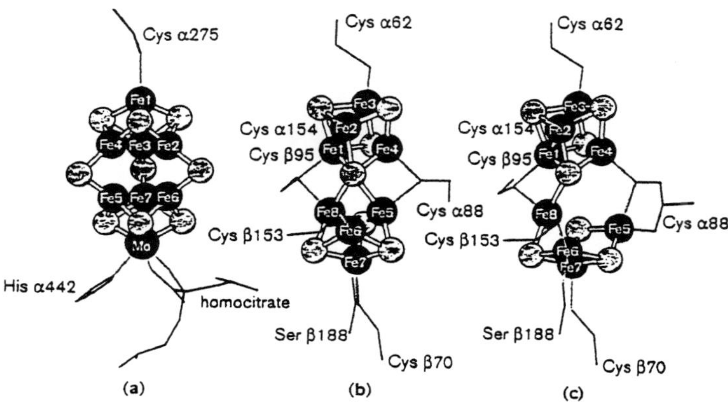

Figure 3.2. Structural models of FeMo cofactor (a), the dithionate reduced P-cluster (b), and oxidized P-cluster (c) (Rees and Howard, 2000). Reproduced with permission

In the presence of an excess of dithionite, the $[Fe_4S_4]$ cluster of FeP exists in the oxidation state 1+ and exhibits the ESR spectrum of a mixture of spin states $S = 1/2$ and $S = 3/2$ .The half-reduction potential E_0 in Av2 for $[Fe_4S_4]^{2+} \rightleftharpoons [Fe_4S_4]^{1+}$ and

$[Fe_4S_4]^{1+} \rightleftharpoons [Fe_4S_4]^{0}$ transitions is equal to -0.29 and -0.46 eV, respectively (Watt and Reddy, 1994; Yoo et al., 1999). It was shown in the case of Av2 mutant (L127Δ), $E_0 = -0.42$ eV for the $[4Fe_4{-}4S_4]^{2+} \rightleftharpoons [4Fe_4{-}4S_4]^{1+}$ transition in the Av 1 (Lanzilotta and Seefeldt, 1997; Lanzilotta et.al, 1997). The potential of Av1 in the Av2·Av1 complex in the absence of MgATP was found to be equal to -0.62 eV. In the presence of dithionate the second electron is not transferred without MgATP, but the state $[Fe_4 S_4]^{0}$ was observed using Ti (III) as a reductant (Nyborg et al., 2000).

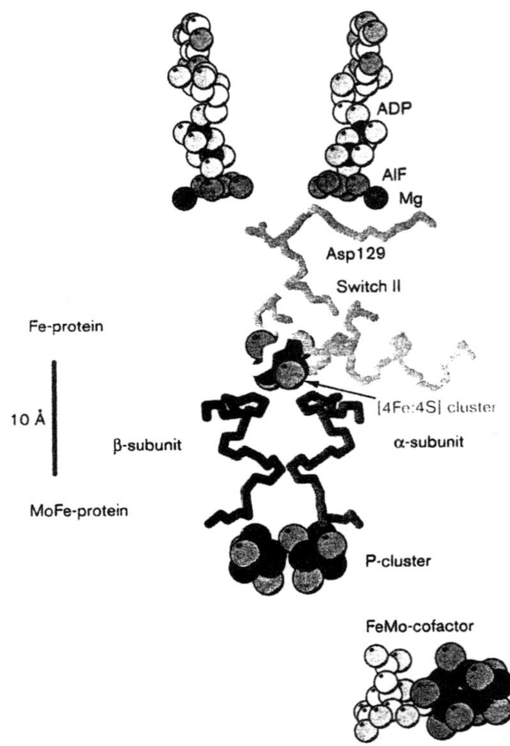

Figure 3..3. Relationship between ADP.AlF4⁻, [Fe₄,S₄] cluster, P-cluster, and FeMo-cofactor (Rees and Howard, 2000). Reproduced with permission.

In the oxidized state, the P cluster is a single cluster consisting of $[Fe_4S_4]$ and $[4Fe{-}3S]$ subclusters connected by the bridging S(1) sulfur (Fig. 3.3) (Rees and Howard, 2000). The cluster reduction is accompanied by a change in its structure. The ferro-iron cluster of FeMo-protein in the initially reduced state (p^N) can reversibly be oxidized to the paramagnetic states D^{1+}, D^{2+}, and D^{3+}. The potentials E_0 for the transitions $p^N \rightleftharpoons p^{2+}$, $D^N \rightleftharpoons D^{1+}$, $D^{1+} \rightleftharpoons D^{2+}$, and $D^{2+} \rightleftharpoons D^{3+}$ are equal to -0.307, -0.309, -0.309, and $+0.09$ V, respectively (Pierik et al., 1993). In the presence of dithionate, the FeMo-protein P-cluster (P^N) and D cluster are ESR silent. Oxidation of FeMo-protein P-clusters induced the ESR signal associated with S = 7/2. The ESR spectrum of the P^{2+} cluster exhibits the signal characteristic of S = 3. The ESR spectrum of the D^{1+} cluster contains the signals of the spin states S = 5/2 and S = 1/2.

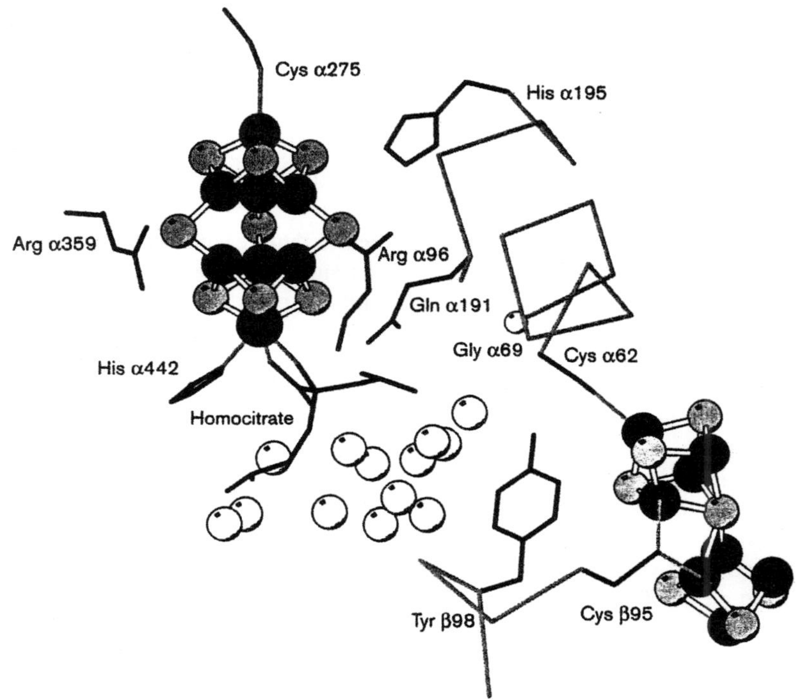

Figure 3.4. View of the protein environment between the FeMo-cofactor and P-cluster of the FeMo-protein (Rees and Howard, 2000). Reproduced with permission

As isolated in the presence of dithionate, the FeMoco exists in a semi-reduced state (M^N) with a plausible assignment of metal atoms to the state as Mo^{4+}, nine S^{2-}, six ferrous Fe^{2+}, and one ferric Fe^{3+}. The reduction center of the FeMoco substrates is a cluster of the new type containing both Mo and Fe. In this cluster each Fe—S—Fe group binds two 4Fe—3S and 1Mo—3Fe—3S subclusters as bridges and forms two 4Fe—4S faces. The Val-α70 residue is localized at a short distance from one of these faces (Fig. 3.3-3.4) (Rees and Howard, 2000; Christiansen et al., 2000). Site-directed substitutions allow the identification residues around the Fe-Mo-cofactor (Fig. 3.4) (Fisher et al., 2000; Christiansen, et al., 2000). As an example, after the replacement of proton donor Hisα195 with glutamine residues, the enzyme still reduces acetylene to ethylene but not dinitrogen though the latter is bound to FeMoco. The stopped-flow IR spectroscopy and ENDOR have demonstrated that CO, which is an inhibitor of the N_2 reduction, can bind to the cofactor (Newton et al., 1995; Christie et al., 1996; George et al., 1997).

In the presence of dithionate, FeMoco exposes the S= 3/2 ESR signal (Münck et al., 1975); Lee et al., 1997). The $FeMoco^N$ $\rightleftharpoons$ $FeMoco_{ox}$ transition requires the potential $E_0 = -0.042$ V (Pierick et al., 1993). The reduced P-cluster of Av2 transfers at least one electron to $FeMoco^N$ to form the ESR silent "super-reduced" FeMoco, $(FeMoco)^{-1}$. (Ohrme-Johnson et al., 1972; Münck et al., 1975). A combination of cyclic voltampermetry, potentiometry and ESR spectroscopy has allowed the observation in isolated FeMoco of two redox transitions with essentially different potentials, $E_0 = -0.3$ eV and $E_0 = -1.0$ eV (Newton et al., 1996). The first transition of FeMoco is from oxidize state to semireduced state of FeMoco and the second transition is related to the substrate-reducing state in FeMoco during the nitrogenase reaction turnover. Independently, for the redox pair $FeMoco^N$ $\rightleftharpoons$ $(*FeMoco)^{2-}$, the E_0 was estimated as about -1.0 V (Syrtsova and Timofeeva, 2001).

The X-ray structural model of FeMoco indicates that FeMoco is completely buried in the protein matrix approximately 10 Å from the surface, but a channel is formed at the interstice between two of the protein subunits. According to molecular modeling (Durrant, 2001), the Arg-b105 side–chain nitrogen in Kp1 and water molecules of the inner region act as a proton conductor from the bulk water to the homocitrate via the Grotthuss mechanism. Other possible ways for proton transfer to a sulfur ligand of the Kp1 FeMoco are via a chain of Tyr 279-H_2O-His 194 and His 360-His 272- H_2O-H_2O. Because the tyrosine acidity constant in proteins ($pK_a \sim 10$) is too high to transfer H^+ in the neutral pH, the hystidine channel looks more rational.

ESR, Mossbauer and X-ray absorbtion spectroscopy (K-edge EXAFS measurements) studies have shown that Mo and V in the FeMo and FeV proteins are present in analogous cofactor centers and have close ligand geometry (Harvey et al., 1990; Eady, 1996; Lei et al., 2000). The FeV- cofactor extracted from *A. chroococcum* was found to be similar but not identical to FeMoco. Indirect evidence from genetic data and some physical experiments suggests the structure of $[F_4S_4]$ and P-clusters in Fe nitrogenase, which contains only Fe centers, is also similar to those in Mo and V nitrogenases. (Eady, 1996;,Peters, 1999). ESR analysis shows the absence of signals related to S = 3/2 in Fe nitrogenase which is typical of FeMo- and FeV cofactors. Maximum specific activity (nmole of NH_3/mg of protein/min) of nitrogenases isolated from different microorganisms was found to be 1040, 660 and 350 units for FeMo-, FeV- and FeFe proteins, correspondingly (Eady, 1996).

3.1.3. KINETICS AND MECHANISM OF THE NITROGENASE REACTION

The basic mechanism of nitrogenase with the use of dithionate as an electron donor for the iron protein involves the following steps (Thorneley and Lowe, 1985; Likhtenshtein, 1988a; Burgess and Lowe, 1996; Smith, 1999; Seefeldt and Dean, 1997; Rees and Howard, 2000; Syrtsova and Timofeeva, 2001): 1) reduction of Fe-protein with flavodoxin or dithionate and attachment of two ATP molecules to the protein, 2) formation of a complex between the reduced FeP with two bound ATP molecules and FeMo-protein, 3) electron transfer between the reduced $[Fe_4S_4]$ cluster of FeP to the P-cluster of FeMoP coupled to the ATP hydrolysis, 4) electron transfer from P-cluster to

FeMoco, 5) dissociation of the FeP-FeMoP complex accompanied by re-reduction of FeP and exchange of ATP for ADP, and repetition of this circle until a sufficient number electrons and protons have been accumulated in FeMoco so that the available substrate can be reduced.

The results of studying the kinetics of electron transfer from the Fe protein to the Mo—Fe-protein with the artificial electron donor, dithionite (Thorneley and Lowe, 1985), are presented in Fig.3.5.

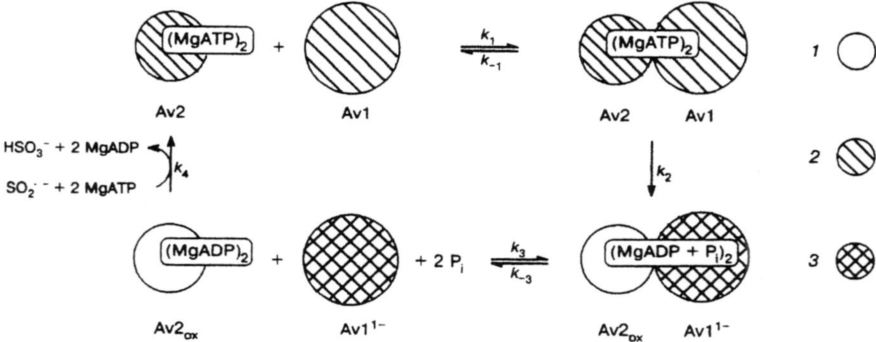

Figure 3.5. Kinetics of ET in the nitrogenase reaction. The smaller sphere is Av2, and the larger is Av1 in the oxidized (1), reduced (2), and super-reduced (3) states. $K_1 = 4.4 \cdot 10^6$ M^{-1}s^{-1}, $k_{-1} = 6.4$ s^{-1}, $k_2 = 200$ s^{-1}, $k_3 = 4.4 \cdot 10^6$ M^{-1}s^{-1}, $k_{-3} = 6.4$ s^{-1} and $k_4 = 3.0 \cdot 10^6$ M^{-1}s^{-1}. (Syrtsova and Timofeeva, 2001). Reproduced with permission.

With dithionate as an electron donor, the rate-determining stage is the dissociation of nitrogenase to components after the intramolecular transfer of an electron from Av2 to Av1 ($k_{-3} = 6.4$ s^{-1} at 23 C°). In this case, it is necessary for the Fe-protein to be reduced again after the dissociation. According to kinetic data (Thorneley and Lowe, 1985) and X-ray analysis (Schindelin al., 1997; Rees and Howard, 2000; Chiu et al., 2001), only one Fe-protein is bound to each half of the FeMo-protein. Nevertheless, an alternative cooperative model assumes two FePs interacting with a single FeMo active site (Johnson et al., 2000). This model is based on experiments in which ratio FeP:FeMoP was changed from 0.4 to 50. The sigmoidal behavior for low ratio (<0.4) and hyperbolic steady state kinetic for high values of FeP:FeMoP were observed.

According to recent data, the property of dithionite as an electron donor for nitrogenase is different from that of the natural donor flavodoxin (Burgess and Lowe, 1996). Flavodoxin from Azotobacter vinelandii has the redox potential equal to –0.515 V for the reversible transition between the semiquinone and hydroquinone forms of flavodoxin. Unlike dithionite, flavodoxin can reversibly reduce the [Fe$_4$S$_4$]$^{+1}$ cluster Av2 by one electron to the [Fe$_4$S$_4$]^0 state in which all iron ions exist in the ferrous form. It is assumed that, under natural conditions, two electrons can transfer from Av2 to Av1. Flavodoxin reduces both Av2 bound to Av1 and free Av2 in a solution. The apparent rate constants of these reactions are 400 s^{-1} and > 1000 s^{-1}, respectively (Duyvis et al. 1998).

A series of experiments on photoreduction of nitrogenase complex (Av2·Av1) and its component were performed (Druzhinin et al., 1993, 1995, 1996, 1989, 1998; Syrtsova et al., 1995, 1998, 2000; Syrtsova and Timofeeva, 2001). In the case of the photodonor eosin in the presence of NADH, the reducing agent for nitrogenase is the radical anion with E_0 for the transition photodonor $\rightleftharpoons$ photodonor radical anion equal to -0.58 V (Chan and Bolton, 1980), which is sufficient for reducing the $[4Fe-4S]^{+1}$ cluster of Av2 to the $[4Fe-4S]^0$ state in the successive transfer of two electrons. Stages of the transfer of the first and second electrons in nitrogenase were detected by kinetic laser spectroscopy using the photodonor system DBF—NADH in the presence of nitrogen (Syrtsova et al., 2000).

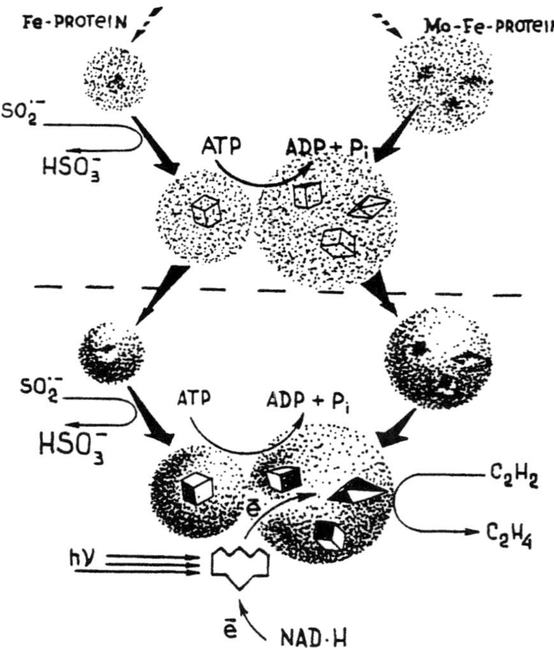

Figure 3.6. Schematic presentation of photoreduction of the nitrogenase complex (see details in text)

It has been established (Druzhinin et al., 1995) that, in the case of the photochemical eosin—NADH system and dithionite concentrations not higher than $4 \cdot 10^{-4}$ M, the Av1·Av2 complex (1:1) is enzymatically active. The slow process (0.1 s^{-1} $< k < 2.0 \cdot 10^2$ s^{-1} at 20 °C) of nitrogenase dissociation to the Av1 and Av2 components was not observed. The rate constant of a second order for the reduction of Av2 in the nitrogenase complex with the eosin—NADH photodonor was found to be equal to $1.1 \cdot 10^7$ M^{-1} s^{-1}.

The relative positions of the metalloclusters indicate that electron transfer from FeP to FeMoco procees through the P-clusters. The edge-edge distances between FeP and P-cluster and between P-cluster and FeMoco were found to be about 14 Å (Schindelin et al., 1997). Theoretical considerations and experimental data allow for rapid long-distance electron transfer between these donor-acceptor sites (Section 2.1). For instance, Eq. (Fig. 2.6) predicts that at this distance the maximum rate constants for long distance ET would be about 10^5 s^{-1}. The latter values are even higher than correspondent experimental rate constants of electron transfer from FeP to the P-cluster of FeMoP $k_1 =$ 400 s^{-1} (Burgess and Lowe, 1996).

The helix, which binds the ligand of the P cluster of Cys-α62 with Val-α70 in the region of FeMoco, is assumed to be the way for the transfer of an electron directly from the P cluster to FeMoco (Christiansen et al., 2000). When nitrogenase reduces N_2, the oxidation of D-clusters has been independently proved by the finding that, during the transfer of an electron from Av2 to Av1, changes in the absorption of Av1 occur before the transfer of an electron to FeMoco (Duyvis et al., 1997).

The P cluster undergoes redox-dependent structural rearrangement, which can be coupled with the transfer of an electron or a proton to FeMoco. (Peters et al., 1997). The oxidation of the P cluster is accompanied by the coordination of βSer188 and the amide nitrogen of αCys88 with the Fe atoms of the P cluster. Redox titration of P-cluster indicates that the redox potential of $P^{1+} \rightarrow P^{2+}$ transition is pH dependent (0.053 V/pH unit) (Lanzilotta et al., 1998). It was suggested that electron transfer from P-cluster to FeMoco at physiological pH values is accompanied by coupled proton transfer.

3.1.4. ATP CENTERS AND ATP HYDROLYSIS

The isolated Fe-protein can bind MgATP and MgADP at a stoichiometry of two nucleotides per dimer (Schindelin et al., 1997; Rees and Howard, 2000; Chiu et al., 2001). It was shown that an ATP analog, ADP·AlF$_4$, forms a stable and non-active complex with A2 component of nitrogenase (Av1-Av2), in which it is located between two domains at a distance about 15 Å from the [Fe$_4$S$_4$] cluster. The cluster and ADP·AlF$_4$ are separated by a region, which includes Asp125, Glu128, Asp129 and Cys132 (Fig. 3.3).

Although various biological systems of energy transformation (the system of oxidative phosphorylation, K^+, Na^+-ATPase, the actin—myosin complex, nitrogenase) have different structures and perform different biological functions, the main regularities of ATP hydrolysis in these enzymes are similar (Rees and Howard, 2000; Syrtsova and Timofeeva, 2001; and references therein). All ATPases hydrolyze ATP at the phosphoanhydride O—P$_\gamma$ bond, catalyze direct and intermediate [^{18}O] exchange, and have at least two regions of MgATP binding. One of the regions of conformational variability in FeP is a switch region, which includes Asp125, Glu128, Asp129 and Cys132.

In a complex with ADP.AlF4, which is considered to be the structural analog of ATP, Av2 undergoes a large conformational change relative to its structure in the nucleotide –free, autonomous state in the absence of A1 (Howard and Rees, 1994; Shindelin et al., 1997, Rees and Howard, 1999). The conformational change in A2 results in about a 13° rotation of each monomer toward the subunit interface and about a 4 Å closer approach of the A2 [Fe$_4$S$_4$]-cluster to the A1 P-cluster. Because electron transport between FeP to FeMoP occurs as a long-distance process, it was suggested that nucleotide hydrolysis may serve as a regulator of conformational switching. In contrast, only a small conformational change in A1 was detected. Experiments with mutant A2 deleted of residue Leu 127 indicated a key role of this group in supporting mechanically productive ATP hydrolysis. Binding of ATP or ADP to the Fe-protein stabilizes its oxidizing state and lowers the redox potential by -0.10 V (Watt et al., 1986).

The Asp39 group in Av2, which is located in the vicinity of γ-phosphate of ATP, was genetically replaced for asparagine and three forms of the proteins were isolated: wild-type homodimeric [Asp39/Asp39], mutated heterodimeric [Asp39/Asn 39], and homodimeric [Asn39/Asp39] forms (Chan et al., 2000). The assessment of the MgATP binding-induced conformational changes in Av2 indicated that the nucleotide effect weakens in succession: [Asp39/Asp39] > [Asp39/Asn 39] > [Asn39/Asp39]. In this expression, the relative substrate reduction activity of the protein forms was found to be $1: 10^{-2}: 10^{-4}$. Thus, present results reveal that carboxylic residues of the Asp39 groups in native Av2 play a key role in protein activity and only simultaneous action of both groups maintains the high rate of the substrate reduction.

It was shown that the product of ATP hydrolysis, MgADP, remains bound on the enzyme for the time necessary for the formation of $(*FeMoco)^{-1}$ (Syrtsova et al., 1988). The rate of MgADP elimination from the nitrogenase molecule at the stage of transfer of the first electron is low: the first MgADP molecule separates from nitrogenase with $k_{eff} \leq 0.2$ s^{-1}, and the second molecule does with $k_{eff} \geq 0.6$ s^{-1}. It has been established in stopped-flow calorimetry experiments at 60 °C and at pH 7.0 that a proton is released from the ATP-Kp1.Kp2 complex before the Kp2 $\rightarrow$ Kp1 electron transfer (Thorneley et al., 1989; Thorneley and Dean, 2000). P_i is found to be liberated after the intramolecular electron transfer during ATP hydrolysis by nitrogenase (Lowe et al., 1995).

In the case of Av2 mutant (Leu 127 deleted, L127Δ), the midpoint potential for the $[4Fe_4 - 4S_4]^{+2} \rightleftharpoons [4Fe_4 - 4S_4]^{+1}$ transition is changed from by -0.420 eV for the free protein to -0.620 eV for its complex with A1 (Lanzilotta and Seefeldt, 1997). Only a slight shift by -0.08 eV and no marked shift were observed in potentials of P-cluster and FeMoco, respectively. In the presence of dithionate, the second electron is not transferred to Av2 without MgATP, but the state $[Fe_4 S_4]^0$ was observed using Ti (III) as a reductant (Nyborg et al., 2000). The energetic profile of the nitrogenase reaction, presented in Fig. 3.7, indicates that formation of reaction plausible intermediates is thermodynamically forbidden without utilization energy of ATP hydrolysis (Likhtenshtein, 1979, 1988a; Likhtenshtein and Shilov, 1976; Syrtsova and Timofeeva, 2001).

Avaible experimental structural and kinetics data and energetic considerations indicate two plausible roles of ATP in the nitrogenase reduction: a) the triggering of electron transfer from iron protein to iron-molybdenum protein (Howard and Rees, 1994; Rees and Howard, 2000) and the strengthening reducing power of the enzyme catalytic redox centers (Likhtenshtein and Shilov, 1977, Likhenshtein 1988a, Syrtsova and Timofeeva, 2001; see also Section 6.1.4).

Taking into consideration the X-ray structural model of the Fe-protein complex with ADPAlF$_4$, we can discuss a possible mechanism for utilization of the ATP hydrolysis energy. According to our model, the protein undergoes substantial structural change at the complexation with ATP due to changes in interaction between Asp129 that presumably activates the nucleotide hydrolysis via a water molecule, which is located in the vicinity of the γ-phosphate (Rees and Howard, 2000).

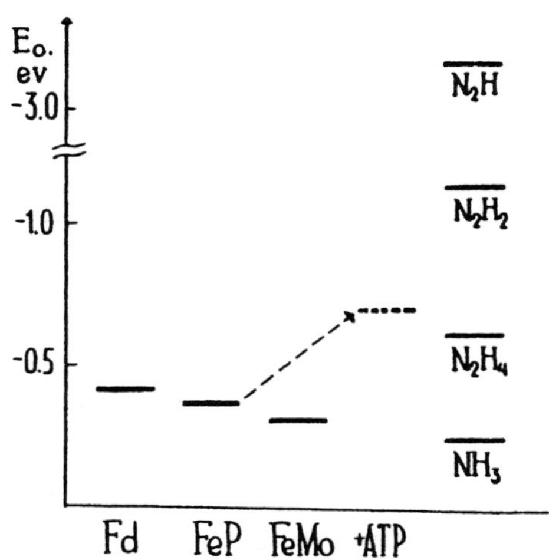

Figure 3.7. The energy profile of a nitrogenase reaction. E_0 is the standard redox potential of the reactants, intermediates and products of the reaction; Fd = ferredoxin; FeP = Fe protein; FeMo = FeMo protein. The arrow indicates the increase of the reduction potential upon ATP hydrolysis (Likhtenshtein 1988a). Reproduced with permission.

We can speculate that the first result of hydrolysis is the forced, compulsory protonation or phosphorylation of the carboxylic Asp groups, which drastically changes the electrostatic balance of the protein and eventually leads to a change in the redox potential of the [F$_4$S$_4$] cluster. This change may occur due to an increase in the cluster positive charge, and, as a result, transfer an additional electron and a release proton with the formation of a super-reduced state of the cluster. Such a mechanism can cause an increase in the reducing capacity of this redox center at least by 0.30 eV. The redox potential of this super-reduced center (about −1.0 eV) is sufficient to reduce dinitrogen to hydrazine derivative with potential −0, 75 eV.

3.1.5. DINITROGEN REDUCTION

Early concepts
For many decades chemists faced the problem of nitrogen fixation under mild conditions. The energy of electron detachment from the binding orbitals of dinitrogen or molecule excitation to the excited states is very high (369 and 143 kcal/mole,

respectively). Though reduction of dinitrogen to ammonia with dihydrogen, (whose redox potential is similar to those for native electron donors like ferredoxin and flavodoxin) is thermodynamically favorable, serious energetic obstacles are expected on the way. From the works of Pauling (1962), it follows that the energy of the first bond being broken is very high (560 kJmole^{-1}). Rupture of such a strong bond requires energetic compensation. Analysis of the thermodynamic profile of subsequent dinitrogen reduction indicates that the dinitrogen reduction in ambient conditions (room temperature, atmospheric pressure, and neutral pH) with the use of the native reducing agents couldn't be performed by traditional one- or two electron mechanisms.

In 1970 Likhtenshtein and Shilov advanced the supposition that the enzyme nitrogenase by-passed the above mentioned energy difficulties by realizing a reaction mechanism that provides the rupture of two bonds in N_2 with simultaneous compensation due to the formation of four new bonds with catalytic transition atoms. This supposition was based on the following thermodynamic grounds and kinetics considerations.

1. Though reduction of N_2 to NH_3 is thermodynamicaly favorable ($\Delta Go = -7.8$ kcal/mole, 1 atm, 298 K), the catalytic process in mild conditions faces a serious thermodynamic problem. Calculation of the enthalpy of dinitrogen reduction with dihydrogen using the semi-empirical method of estimation of dissociation energy allows the estimation of the thermodynamic profile of the multi-step non-catalytic process with a reducing agent of redox potential similar to those for dihydrogen (about -0.4 eV, at pH 7), ferredoxin for example. (Likhtenshtein and Shilov, 1970, Likhtenshtein, 1979a, 1988a). The values of standard redox potential (E_0) of plausible intermediate products N_2-H or N_2H_2, were estimated to be approximately equal to -3.2 and and -1.2 eV, respectively. Thus, for reduction of N_2 to these compounds, reagents with reducing power essentially higher than those of the natural electron donors ($E_0 = -0.4, -0.5$ eV) are required. In fact, these reactions are thermodynamically forbidden under mild conditions. The mechanism implicated in the formation of hydrazine ($E_0 = - 0,75$ eV), as the first intermediate, is thermodynamically more preferable, though requiring additional energy consumption. This mechanism was provisionally termed as the four-electron mechanism. Recent ab initio calculations of energy of N_2H_2 and related compounds (Pople, 1991 and references therein) have made some corrections in the data calculated with the above-mentioned semi-empirical method due to the difference between the value of the first nitrogen bond being broken estimated by Pauling (133 kcal/mole) and that value calculated ab initio (about 101 kcal/mole). Nevertheless, the conclusion that only the four- electron mechanism of dinitrogen reduction under mild conditions is still thermodynamically and, therefore, kinetically allowed has been confirmed (Fig. 3.7).

2. It was postulated that a better way for realizing such a mechanism is through involving complexes of transition metals as catalytic sites. The multi-orbital binding of nitrogen in a polynuclear complex (binuclear complex in the simplest case, makes it possible to donate electrons from d-orbitals of metals to anti-binding π^* orbitals of N_2 and to accept electrons from binding π-orbitals of N_2 to empty d-orbitals of the metal. Possible binding of nitrogen iron atoms in FeMoco is shown in Fig. 3.8.

3. In order to estimate the thermodynamics of a reaction that occurs in the coordination sphere of a metal (M), it is expedient to conditionally divide the reaction

into steps that represent the process taking place under certain idealized conditions (e.g. in the gas phase or a neutral solution) and the interaction of the reactants (A) and products (B) with the metal complex (M): It is obvious that $\Delta G_{AB}{}^{M} = \Delta G_{AB}{}^{0} - \Delta G_{MBA}$, where $\Delta G_{MBA} = \Delta G_{MB} + \Delta G_{MA}$. One of the fundamental principles of catalysis under mild conditions is that the catalyst should provide for a chemical process with smooth thermodynamic relief on each step along the reaction path without deep energy holes or high hills. It means that the Gibbs energy of the substrate A adsorption and product B desorption can not be very high by the absolute value, i.d. $|\Delta G_{MB}| = |\Delta G_{MA}| < 0.2 - 0.3$ eV.

$$M + A \xrightleftharpoons{\Delta G_{AB}{}^{D}} M + B$$

$$\Delta G_{MA} \updownarrow \qquad\qquad \updownarrow \Delta G_{MB}$$

$$M - - - A \xrightleftharpoons{} M - - - B$$
$$\Delta G_{AB}{}^{M}$$

Because ΔG_{MB} and ΔG_{MA} have different signs and, therefore, the difference between these values should be even less, we can take $\Delta G_{AB}{}^{M} = \Delta G_{AB}{}^{0} \pm 0.2$ eV. We conclude that the difference in the estimated energy of plausible intermediates of the dinitrogen reduction, which takes place in the coordinate sphere of transition metal, cannot be essentially higher than that in water solution. Therefore, the values of the reducing agents, redox potential which are required to reduce dinitrogen through the intermediates $\cdot N_2H$ or N_2H_2, can not be markedly different from those presented in Fig.3.5, and the conclusion of thermodynamic preference for the four-electron mechanism is still rational energy of plausible intermediates of the dinitrogen reduction, which takes place in the coordinate sphere of transition metal, cannot be essentially higher than that in water solution. Therefore, the values of the reducing agents, redox potential which are required to reduce dinitrogen through the intermediates $\cdot N_2H$ or N_2H_2, can not be markedly different from those presented in Fig.3.5, and the conclusion of thermodynamic preference for the four-electron mechanism is still rational.

4. In the four-electron process, in order to avoid a drastic change in the electrostatic status of the system and to minimize reorganization energy due to electron transfer, the following requirements should be fulfilled: a) multi-orbital binding of dinitrogen in a metalcluster when a transfer of electrons from the filled d-orbitals to the anti-binding of the ligand is accompanied by the reverse transfer of electrons from the binding orbitals of the ligand to empty d-orbitals of the metal, b) essential delocalization of the electrostatic charge among the electron donor atoms with only a slight change of local4. In the four-electron process, in order to avoid a drastic change in the electrostatic status

of the system and to minimize reorganization energy due to electron transfer, the following requirements should be fulfilled: a) multi-orbital binding of dinitrogen in a metalcluster when a transfer of electrons from the filled d-orbitals to the anti-binding of the ligand is accompanied by the reverse transfer of electrons from the binding orbitals of the ligand to empty d-orbitals of the metal, b) essential delocalization of the electrostatic charge among the electron donor atoms with only a slight change of local charge on each atom (only a polynuclear metalo-complex fits such requirements) and c) the decisive four-electron elementary steps of the nitrogen reduction to be preceded by consecutive accumulation of electrons in the catalytic cluster accompanied by proton transfer.

5. It was suggested (Likhtenshein and Shilov, 1976; Likhtenshtein et al., 1980; Likhtenshtein, 1988a) that the role of ATP hydrolysis might eventually consist of a forced non-equilibrium protonation of a protein group, which increases the iron- sulfur cluster positive charge. This increase contributes in turn to the transfer of an extra electron and, after removal of the proton to the consequent formation of a super-reduced form of the cluster. Thus, ATP hydrolysis energy may be consumed for producing a center with high reducing power.

6. According to the principle of dynamic adaptation (Likhtenshtein, 1976a), the multi-orbital interaction between a substrate and metal atoms in a bi- or polynuclear center and the consequent chemical conversion require a certain optimum flexibility of metal atoms involved in the catalytic process. Such flexibility would allow the space provision for each step of the consecutive chemical reaction, i.e. complexation, product formation and release.

Studies on model polynuclear catalytic systems have confirmed that for the catalytic reduction of dinitrogen under mild conditions, it is necessary to use a polynuclear transition metal complex capable of donating four electrons to form the hydrazine derivative.

Recent quantum mechanical calculations

A simplified model of FeMoco as $[HFe_4S(Fe_3MoH_3)]$ was theoretically examined by Deng and Hoffman (1993). An energy level diagram was calculated and on this basis various models of dinitrogen complex were considered. A model with N_2 bridged between two iron atoms inside the cluster was found to be best for electron occupation of π_g^* of dinitrogen and, therefore, for weakening the N-N bond and negatively charging the nitrogen atoms. This model is similar to those suggested earlier by Ohrme-Johnson (Ohrme-Johnson 1972, 1992; Ohrme-Johnson et al. 1972). This calculation has led to an important conclusion: to be activated, dinitrogen should accept at least three electrons and be protonated.

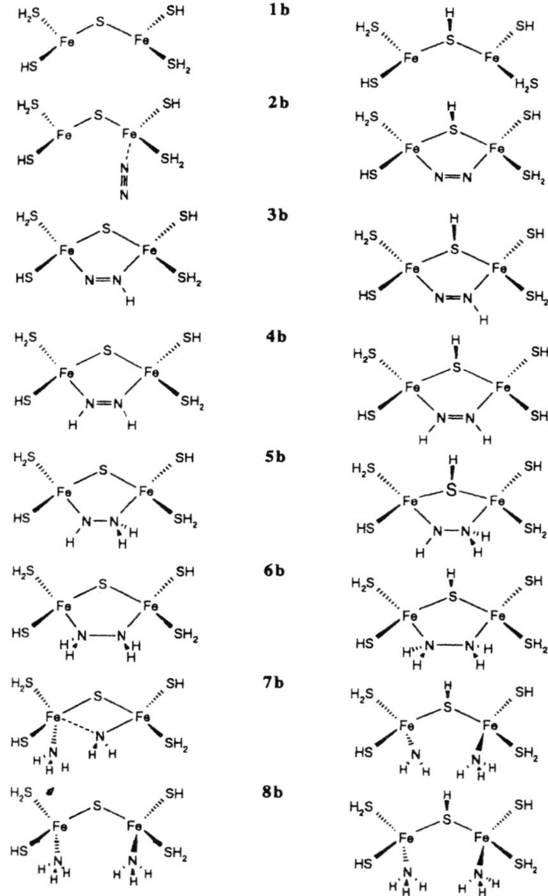

Figure 3.8. Structures obtained for the dimmer model. The **a** structures have a bridging, while the **b** structures have an additional hydrogen atom on this structure (Siegbahn et al., 1998) Reproduced with permission.

The first application of the density function theory to the FeMoco structure and action mechanism has produced the following conclusions (Dance, 1998): a) the cofactor core [Fe_7MoS_9 (cis)(his)(cit)] is flexibile in a free state and restrained to some extent by protein, b) the cofactor reduction and protonization influence its structure, c) terminal binding of N_2 to one of the atoms does not elongate N-N but binding both atoms to the Fe_4 face of the cluster increases the basicity of the S ligand allowing it to accept H^+ and to transfer it eventually to N_2. Possible N_2 binding is shown in Fig. 3.8.

According to the calculation of Siegbahn et al., (1998), the cofactor is built up from two incomplete F_4S_3 cubanes, each having a non-saturated coordination sphere. Three sulfur bridges link the cubanes. If N_2 is placed, bridging four iron atoms inside the cavity between the cubanes and simultaneous it placing one hydrogen atom on a sulfur atom bridging the cubanes, the molecule interaction with the cofactor is found to be attractive. The calculations (Rod and Norskov, 2000; Rod et al., 1999) were based on density function theory, with plane wave expansion of the Kohn-Sham wave functions and a generalized approximation for the exchange correlation term. Two different clusters to mimic the central part of the FeMoco have included the effect of the surrounding by invoking a proton donor in the vicinity of the cofactor. The authors have come to the following conclusions: 1) N_2 can adsorb in and end-on fashions, 2) N_2 binding is strongest during turn over: an electron needs to be transferred to the FeMoco and a proton to the vicinity in order for N_2 to spend an appropriate time in the adsorbed state, 3) NNH state is not stable and quickly decays, 4) If there are three H atoms on the cluster, the system can transfer into adsorbed hydrazine immediately and this state is irreversible. In fact, only the forth electron/proton transfer will make the reaction irreversible (Fig. 3.9).

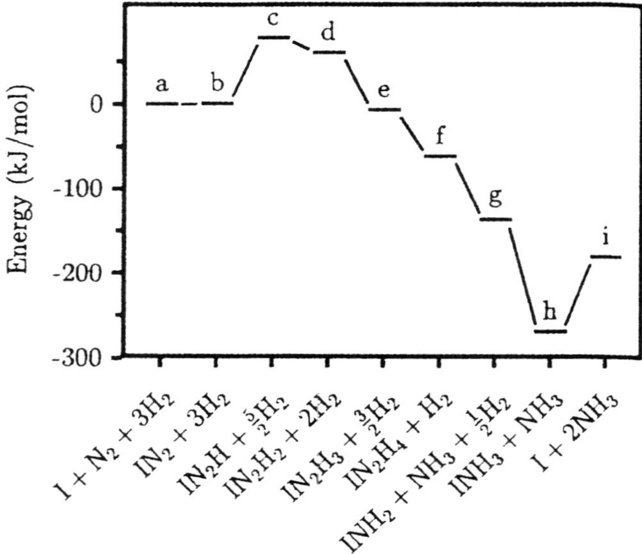

Figure 3.9. The calculated binding energies of the intermediates along the reaction path for hydrogenation of N_2 on model I are plotted (Rod, T. nd Norskov, 2000). Reproduced with permission.

This conclusion appears to agree fully with the concept of the aforementioned thermodynamically favorable four-electron mechanism of N_2 reduction (Likhtenshtein and Shilov, 1970) and with the evolution of free hydrazine at the acid or base treatment of nitrogenase during turn-over (Lowe et al., 1993), (5) Histidine is the only amino acid side chain capable of donating protons in neutral pH. The Fe atoms are not saturated. Though aforementioned theoretical calculations are based on simplified truncated models of FeMoco and use an approximate computational approach, they allow the revelation of several important structural and mechanistic features of this unique catalytic center.

1. The iron atoms in FeMoco have non-saturated coordination spheres to give the opportunity for dinitrogen molecules to interact with two or more iron atoms.

2. The dinitrogen coordination has to be suitable for the overlap of both filled binding and empty antibonding dinitrogen orbitals with d-orbitals of iron atoms.

3. Three-four electrons and three-four protons should be transferred to the dinitrogen to activate the molecule for subsequent reduction of the hydrazine derivative to ammonia.

4. The FeMoco structure has be flexible enough to provide a free space for dinitrogen to come into in the cofactor cavity, transformating and then coming out from the cofactor.

All these conclusions agree in principle with above-mentioned earlier considerations about the mechanism of nitrogen reduction under mild conditions. The dinitrogen reduction occurs in the polynuclear FeMo-cofactor. Available experimental and theoretical data allow us to conclude that the enzyme nitrogenase can overcome the high chemical inertness of dinitogen using the energetically favorable four-electron mechanism in which a hydrazine derivative appears to be the first intermediate product. The accumulation of reducing power, due to consecutive four one electron and one proton transfers, precedes the dinitrogen reduction.

3.2. Cytochrome P-450

3.2.1. OVERVIEW

Powerful enzyme hydroxylation systems of organic substrates, i.e. steroids, hydrocarbons, organic acids, alcohols and amines, are operatives in animal and plant tissues and bacteria (Coon et al., 1981; Guengerich and Mcdonald (1984); Weiner, 1986; Sono et al., 1996; Oriz de Montellano, 1995; Sono et al., 1996; Newcomb et al., 2000; Ogliaro et al., 2000, 2001; and references therein). These enzymes catalyze oxidation processes according to the following general scheme:

$$DH + RH + O_2 \rightarrow ROH + H_2O + D$$

where RH is the substrate and DH is the reducing agent (NADH or NADH with the use of the appropriate reductase). The action of these systems on compounds having unsaturated bonds may result in their epoxidation or demethylation with methylamines. They are involved in a number of vital processes including the biosynthesis of steroids, degradation of xenobiotics, drug metabolism, and carcinogenesis.

The hydroxylation reaction is directly effected by an enzyme-hemoprotein, monooxigenase, cytochrome P450 containing protocheme IX. The reduction of the enzyme involves flavin reductases and electron carriers, such as adrenodoxin, rubredoxin, and cytochrome b_5. Dioxygen, being a weak one-electron oxidant, is activated after the reduction in the enzyme heme coordination sphere. The various forms of cytochrome P450 from liver microsomes and from Pseudomonas putida have a molecular mass of about 49000. One of the subunits of the enzyme from mitochondria of the adrenal cortex has a molecular mass of 55000. There is one heme per protein macromolecule or subunit.

The protein globule of cytochrome P450 from the adrenal cortex consists of two fragments. The hydrophilic fragment F1 has a molecular mass of 27000 and contains a heme and an adrenodoxin-binding site. The hydrophobic fragment of molecular mass 22000 binds the enzyme to the biomemrane. The presence of extensive hydrophobic portions has also been detected in liver cytochrome.

In non-catalytic conditions, reactions catalyzed by cytochrome P450 require extremely high temperature and proceed nonspecifically. Therefore, structure and the action mechanism of the enzyme effectively operating under mild conditions attract special attention. An entire arsenal of modern physicochemical, biochemical and theoretical methods have concentrated on the solution these problems.

3.2.2. ENERGY OF THE HYDROXYLATION REACTION

Though hydroxylation of an organic substrate with dioxygen and biological reducing agents is thermodynamically favorable, serious energetic problems along the reaction pathway are expected. Dioxygen is a weak one-electron reductant (E_0 = -0.3 eV, Kobayashi et al., 1994) and the energy gain in formation of O_2-H bond is small. Therefore, dioxygen cannot abstract a hydrogen atom by from such inert molecules as saturated hydrocarbons in ambient conditions. In biological systems, the two one-electron transfers activate dioxygen in the coordination sphere of the cytochrome P450 heme group. Midpoint reduction potentials for native reducing agents (ferredoxin, flavin cofactors in NADPH-cytochrome P450 oxidoreductase) are determined as E_0 = -0.240 ÷ - 0.420 eV. Such potential is sufficient to reduce the cythochrome P450 heme iron Fe^{3+} to Fe^{+2} (E_0 = -0.410 eV), dioxygen to superoxide, and dioxygen to H_2O_2 (E_0 for the transition $O_2 + H^+ + 2e$ at pH 7 is equal 0. 282 eV). H_2O_2 is essentially a stronger two-electron oxidizing reagent than those dioxygen in a one-electron process. Oxidation of a hydrocarbon by H_2O_2 with the formation of a hydroxylated product and water is a highly exothermic process. For instance, in the reaction $H_2O_2 = H_2O + O$, the estimated lost of enthalpy is ΔH_0 = 35,7 kcal/mole, whereas the oxygen atom insertion across the R-H group of hydrocarbons gains about 190 kcal/mole. The next thermodynamically allowed step in the cytochrome P-450 reaction is a full or partial electron transfer from Fe^{+2} to H_2O_2 (the Fenton-like process) with the formation of a strong oxidant, whose center can be an analog of an OH radical. This radical has E_0 = 2.7 eV. Nevertheless, the appearance of such an active radical would immediately destroy chemical groups in the vicinity of an active site.

It was shown (Likhtenshtein, 1988a), that the redox potential of a center which can abstract hydrogen in compound RH with the dissociation energy D_{RH}, can be estimated by the following relationship:

$$E_0 \geq D_{RH}/23 - 2.38, \text{ eV} \tag{3.1}$$

According to Eq. 3.1, for the reaction to occur by the one-electron mechanism of hydrogen abstraction from an alkane in a free state (for instance, from a terminal methyl group of fatty acids, with energy dissociation $D_{RH} \sim 95$ kcal/mole) it is necessary that the redox center has the potential $E_0 \geq 1.7$ eV. It that appears that dioxygen can be activated in the coordination sphere of the cytochrome by two steps of electron transfer to be converted into peroxide or hydroxyl radical-like (radicalloid) derivatives. Both types of species have high oxidizing reactivity and the capability to hydroxylate and epoxidaze of numerous organic substrates including hydrocarbonates. This feature opens the way for miscellaneous energy-favorable mechanisms of oxidation of organic compounds.

3.2.3. STRUCTURE OF CYTOCHROME P450 ACTIVE SITE

Combined physico-chemical methods including optical and magnetic circular dichroism, Mössbauer, X-ray and Raman spectroscopies, EXAFS, NMR, ENDOR, spin-echo, and spin labeling permit the establishment of ligands, electronic structure and location relative to the substrate binding site of the cytochrome catalytic heme group (Sharrock et al., 1976; Chevion et al., 1977; Champion et al., 1982; Hahn et al., 1982; and references therein). These data indicate that the enzyme heme active site has structure and some features of the action mechanism similar but not identical to those of peroxidase and catalase. The main differences between the active site of cytochrome P450 and those of other heme-containing proteins and enzymes (except chloroproxidase) is the presence of sulfur ligands in the fifth position of the heme iron instead of histidine for the other heme–proteins.

It was shown that hydrogen peroxide, aliphatic and aromatic peroxides and peracids can replace the biological system of electron transport and oxygen activation in the coordination sphere of the cytochrome P450 heme. Thus, the active electrophilic oxidant in P450 has been assumed to be a high-valent iron-oxo species with structural similar to intermediates Compound I and Compound II in peroxidase (Fig. 3.8) (Groves, 2000;Groves and McClusky, 1976; Groves and Subramanian, 1984).

Starting from the pioneering work of Poulos et al., (1985), detailed information on the structure of cytochrome P450 from different sources has been obtained (Shlichting et al., 2000; Ji et al., 2000; Ravichandran et al., 1993; Jano et al., 2000; and references therein). Structurally, the enzyme with the best characteristics is $P450_{cam}$ from Pseudomonas putida, which catalyzes the regio- and stereospecific hydroxylation of camphor, the physiological substrate, to 5-exo-hydroxycamphor. According to the X-ray structural method (Poulos et al., 1985) the heme group is in a hydrophobic environment and is buried in the protein globule to the depth of about 8 Å and coordinated at the fifth position to the cysteine residue. The substrate molecule is located in the hydrophobic pocket in the distal region in such a manner that the substrate C-5 group can be attacked by the activated oxygen attached to the iron atom. The precise orientation of the substrate is favored by the formation of the hydrogen bond between the hydroxyl group of tyrosine 86 and the carbonyl oxygen of camphor.

Recent X-ray investigation (Schlichting et al., 2000), revealed important structural and dynamics details in the area of the $P450_{cam}$ active site. In the ferric P450-camphur complex, the heme group is covalently attached to the thiolate sulfur of Cys357. The heme is ruffled and the five-coordinate iron atom is out of the porphyrin plane by 0.3 Å. The camphor molecule is oriented by a single hydrogen bond between its carbonyl oxygen atom and the side-chain hydroxyl of Tyr96. Single electron reduction of Fe(III)-P450$_{cam}$ to the Fe(II) form does not markedly change the protein structure. Dioxygen is bound end-on to the heme iron. At the ligand binding, some displacement of camphor occurs and the substrate appears to be within the van der Waals contact of dioxygen. The second changes in the active sites upon oxygen binding are the appearance of an ordering water molecules (WAT901) close to dioxygen and the hydroxyl group of Thr252. These water molecules sit in the groove in the distal I helix, which forms the dioxygen-binding niche. The second water molecule (WAT902) is located next to the hydroxyl group of Thr252 and the carbonyl oxygen of Gly248.

The crystal structural analysis of cytochrome P450 14a-sterol demethylase from Mycobacterium tuberculosis indicated the presence of two different channels (Podust et al., 2001). According to the suggested dynamic scenario, when one of the channels is open, the second channel remains closed. This synchronization might provide a means for a substrate to enter one channel and a product to depart via another. Molecular dynamic investigation has indicated that the passage of a substrate, palmitoleic acid into active site of cytochrome P450BM-3 requires a large backbone motion (up to 4 Å), whereas for the passage of camphor through cytochrome P450cam only small backbone motion (less than 2.4 Å) in conjunction with side-chain rotations is needed (Ludeman et al., 2000).

3.2.4. MECHANISM OF THE CYTOCHROME P450 CATALYZED REACTIONS

Early concepts

According to a widely accepted consensus, the complexation of O_2 with heme followed by the two-step electron transition leads to the formation of the state $[Fe^{2+}O^{2-}]$, in which the dioxygen adopts an active form capable of hydroxylating the substrates, including saturated hydrocarbons (Coon et. al., 1981; Guengerich and Macdonald 1984). The complexation and the first electron transfer proceed rapidly and take place at atmospheric pressure of dioxygen from 10^{-2} to 10^{-3} s. The second electron transfer is a relatively slow reaction (for the enzyme from P. Putida, $k = 4$ s^{-1}), which commonly limits the entire process.

The activation of oxygen in the heme iron coordination sphere and reactions of the activated species with substrates are very rapid processes and can, in principle, occur by the following mechanisms.

1. <u>The oxenoid mechanism</u> implicates the insertion of an oxygen atom (oxenoid) across the C-H bond of the hydrocarbon (Hamilton et al., 1973). This mechanism is evidently energetically preferable, since it is accompanied by the formation of three bonds, two of which, O-H and C-O, are extremely strong and compensate the rupture of the relatively weak C-H and O-O bonds. The transition state, however, involves the formation of a three-membered ring with oxygen, whose formation is accompanied by a strain with an energy of about 30 kcal/mole. More over, the insertion of O to C-H or H-H bonds is a symmetrically forbidden process.

2. <u>Ferryl rebound mechanisms</u> suggests that the formation of the ferryl-oxene structure is similar to those for Compound I (Por·FeIV-O) in the peroxidase reaction (Fig. 3.8). This mechanism (Groves and McClusky, 1976; Groves and Subramanian,

1984) involves initial hydrogen abstraction from the alkane by (Por·FeIV-O) followed by the alkyl radical rebound on the ferryl-hydroxo intermediate with formation alcohol. Another possible reaction of the ferryl-oxene with the hydrocarbon is the oxenoid insertion. The "mixed" mechanism, involving the elementary reaction, starts with the partial abstraction of the hydrogen atom from the C-H group by the ferryl-oxene and ends with the insertion of an oxynen atom across the C-H bond (Shilov, 1997).

3. The <u>masked radical rebound mechanism</u> (Likhtenshtein, 1979 a, 1988 a) involves the reaction of a superoxide-like radical structure formed in the heme coordination sphere with the hydrocarbon followed by fast radical recombination:

$$\text{I} \qquad\qquad\qquad \text{II}$$
$$[Fe^{2+} O\text{-}O^{\cdot -} + HR] \rightarrow [Fe^{2+}O_2H + R\cdot] \rightarrow [Fe^{2+} O^- + ROH]$$

The reaction I is to a certain extent analogous to the reaction of hydrogen atom abstraction by the peroxide ot hydroperoxide radicals from the hydrocarbons:

$$HO\text{-}O^{\cdot -} + CH_3\text{-}R \rightarrow HO_2H + \cdot CH_2R$$

The heat effect of such a reaction in a non-polar solvent for linear hydrocarbons (e.g. decane) is equal to about 4 kcal/moles. The radical activity of superoxide is dampened by the molecule stabilization on account of the conjugation of unpaired electrons with the second oxygen electron pair. This activity can be strengthened by a competitive involving of the sulfur ligand orbitals in the interaction resulting in weakening the stabilization, and therefore, increasing the reactivity of superoxide in the heme coordination sphere. The reaction II is essentially exothermic with $\Delta H_0 \sim$ -50 kcal/mole and should run very fast.

Recent developments
One of the most intriguing reactions in the chytochrome P450 catalysis is the transfer of second electron and dioxygen activation, which appears to be a key step of the entire process. The chemical nature of reactive oxidizing species appears in the coordination sphere of heme iron and the mechanism of hydroxylation of organic compounds, saturated hydrocarbons in particular, is a much debated question in the field of the cytochrome P450 catalysis. To solve this problem, an entire arsenal of modern experimental and theoretical methods are employed. The catalytic pathway of cytochrome P450cam from *Pseudomonas putida* obtained on the basis of X-ray analysis at atomic resolution is presented in Fig. 3.10.

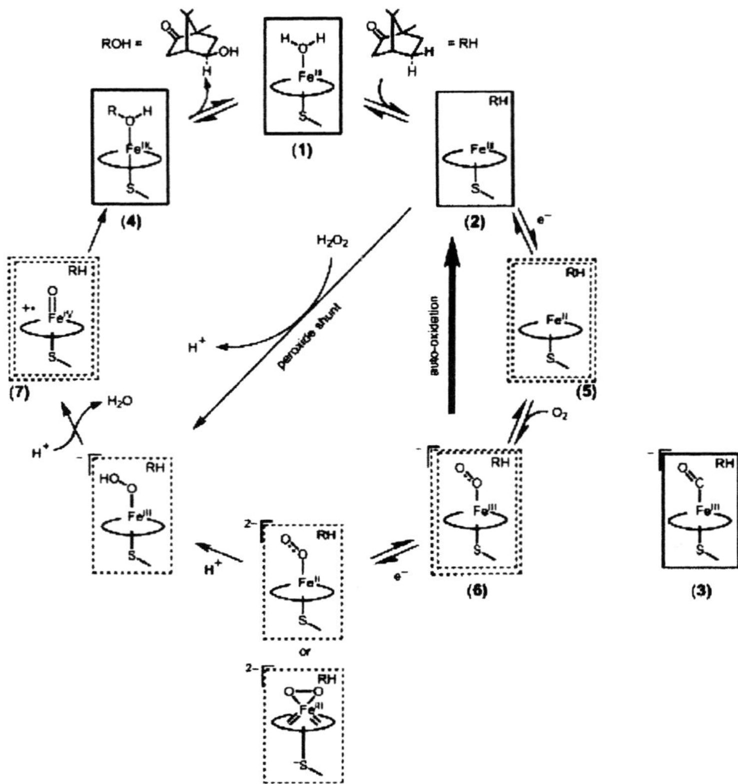

Figure 3.10. Reaction pathway of P450cam. The catalytic cycle of P450cam consists of reversible substrate binding, which converts the six-coordinate, low-spin met form [1(4)] of the protein to the five-coordinate, high–spin Fe(III) camphor complex [2(4)]; addition of the first electron, which reduces the enzyme to the five-coordinate Fe(II) camphor complex (5); binding of molecular oxygen to give the six–coordinate Fe(II)-O$_2$ dioxygen intermediate (6); addition of a second electron and two protons followed by cleavage of the oxygen-oxygen bond to produce a molecule of water and an oxidizing species, the so-called activated oxygen intermediate (7); and insertion of the iron-bond oxygen into the substrate to produce 5-exo-hydroxycamphor [4(4)] and product release. The unnumbered oxygen species shown in dotted boxes between 6 and 7 represent other possible species along the reaction pathway. Also shown is the previously determined complex of P450.camphor.CO (6) (Schlichting et al., 2000). Reproduced with permition.

The last two recent decades have been marked by attempts to directly detect directly and characterize reactive oxidizing species using physico-chemical methods. During the reaction of m-chloroperbenzoate with the low spin ferric form of cytochrome P450$_{cam}$, the formation of several transient intermediates was detected by employing rapid scan absorption spectroscopy (Egava et al., 1994). The first one appearing within 10 ms gave an adsorption spectrum similar to those of compound I of chloroperoxidase, another thiolate-heme protein. In contrast, Blake and Coon (1981) in their spectral and kinetic experiments on interaction of cytochrome P450LM2 with various peroxycompounds, did not detect intermediates which can be attributed to the compound II or I. In an attempt to observe the active oxidizing species of cytochrome P450cam, the reaction of superoxide with the enzyme ferrous form was monitored by employing the stop-flow spectral technique (Kobayashi et al., 1994). The intermediate spectrum was found to be quite different from charcteristic spectra of compound I of horseradish peroxidase, or intermediate products of reaction of ferric cytochrome P450cam with peracetic acid or iodobenzene.

The enzyme species of $P450_{cam}$ at temperature 100 K with the dioxygen, substrate and second electron were produced by x-ray radiolysis of water, which is one of the triggering methods in crystallographic enzyme kinetics, (Schlichtich and Goody1997). The X-ray analysis of the radiolysis product suggested that O-O bond cleavage had occurred, leaving a single atom on the heme iron (Schlichtich et al., 2000). This conversion is not complete. Nevertheless, the electron density in the species was found to be similar to that observed by the time-resolved x-ray diffraction studies of the compound I intermediate in cytochrome c peroxidase and catalase (Groves and Subramanian, 1984). Other changes which may be important for the enzyme catalytic mechanism are the move of the camphor molecule by about 0.2 Å towards the heme iron and the appearance of a new water molecule close to the oxyferryl oxygen which might be leaving water molecules produced after the O-O bond scission. After warming the radiolitically treated crystal, its electron density was found to be consistent with that for the product complex 5-exo-hydroxycamphor (Poulos et al., 1985).

The EPR and ENDOR spectroscopy was used for studies of catalytic intermediates in native and mutant cytochrome P450cam in cryogenic temperatures (6 and 77K) (Davydov et al., 2001). The ternary complex of camphor, dioxygen, and ferrous-enzyme was irradiated with γ-rays to inject the second electron. This process showed that the primary product upon reduction of the complex is the end –on intermediate. This species converts even at cryogenic temperatures to the hydroperoxo-ferriheme form and after brief annealing at a temperature around 200 K, causes camphor to convert to the product. In spite of conclusions derived from x-ray analysis (Schlichtich et al., 2000) no spectroscopic evidence for the buildup of a high-valance oxyferryl/porphyrin π-cation radical intermediate during the entire catalytic circle has been obtained.

Freeze-quenching technique in combination with ESR and Mossbauer spectroscopy was used for monitoring intermediates in the reaction of substrate free ^{57}Fe-$P450_{cam}$ with peroxy acetic acid (Schünemann et al., 2000). In such a condition, the oxidant oxidized the enzyme active site iron (III) to iron (VI) and Tyr 96 into tyrosine radical, 90% and 10% from the starting material, respectively. Thus the tyrosine residue may be involved in the catalytic process.

The kinetic methods and analysis of products can provide valuable information about mechanisms of the cytochrome P450 reactions. According to the pioneering works of the Groves group (Groves and McGlusky, 1976; Groves, 1985 and references therein) the observed kinetic isotope effect (KIE) is large: $k_H/k_D > 11$ for benzylic and aliphatic hydroxylation. This observation was confirmed in kinetics studies of various systems. In one instance a large intramolecular KIE was observed for flour derivative of camphor (Sono et al., 1986; and references therein). The experimental KIF was attributed to the Groves rebound mechanism in which the iron-oxo species abstracts an H atom from substrate to give an iron-hydroxo species and an alkyl radical, followed by recombination of the hydroxo-species and the alkyl radical. This mechanism was also supported by experimental results of stereochemistry and regiochemistry in some systems (Oritz de Montellano, 1995; Oritz de Montellano and Stearns, 1987; Sono et al., 1996; and references therein). Thus, stereochemical allylic transformation was demonstrated by Groves and Sabramanian (1984) using microsomal P450-2B4 as a substrate. The radical mechanism was also supported by the absence of skeleton-rearranged alcohol products, which were expected to be generated from a carbocation intermediate in hydroxylation of substrates as norcaran (Oritz de Montellano, 1995; Sono et al., 1996;).

Information about nature and redox properties of activated species in the cytochrome P450 active site was obtained via kinetic experiments with substrates of various redox potential. Oxidation of a series of substituted N,N-dimethylanylines which proceeds by mechanism of electron transfer followed by rapid deprotonation of nitrogen-centered radical cation intermecdiate and subsequent collapse, appeared to be suitable object for solving this problem. Hammet analysis of the rate of N-demethylation of the set of substituted N,N-dimethylanylines by P450 yields a negative ρ value, -0.61 and –0.74 for the O_2/NADPH series and iodozylbenzene, respectively. These data were interpreted in terms of a positively charged intermediate (Burka et al., 1985). The catalytic rate constant (k_{cat}) of N-demethylation of substituted N.N-dimethylanylines by rat liver cytochrome P450PB-B was determined using NADPH-P450 reductase/dioxigen system or iodozylbenzene (Macdonald et al., 1989). In both cases, the rate of the reaction decreases with enhancement of the substrate redox potential within a range from 0.74 to 1.27 eV (SCE). According to analysis made on the basis of the theory electron transfer, the value of redox potential of the active oxidizing species E_0 = 1.85 eV has been estimated. This value is significantly higher than those for Compound I (E_0 = 0.970 eV) and Compound II (E_0 = 0.950 eV) (Hayashi and Yamazaki, 1979), which appeared during the reaction catalyzed by horseradish peroxidase. It is necessary to stress that the demethylation rate constant for each substrate studied was approximately 20-fold faster in the iodosylbenzene-supported system than in the NADPH-P450 reductase/dioxigen system. The sensitivity of k_{cat} to the substrate redox potential of the former system was markedly higher than that of the latter system. It means that the oxidizing species in different systems are different.

Existence and life time of intermediate active particles in cytochrome P450 active site can be estimated using radical clock substrates (Griller and Ingold, 1980; Ortiz de Montellano et al., 1987; Sono et al., 1996; Newcomb et al., 2000). A carbon radical localized adjacent to a ring of a radical clock substrate (cyclopropane or bicyclopentane derivative, for instance) rearranges to another ring-open radical at a previously determined rate constant (k_r). Employing different substrates with different k_r, it is possible to estimate the rate constant (k_s) for the subsequent reaction of the "clock" radical species intermediate. Such an approach was used to estimate the rate constant of recombination of the carbon radical of bicyclo[2.1.0]pentane with a putative hydroxyl (k_s = 1.4x 10^{10}s^{-1}) for P450-2B1-catalyzed hydrocarbon hydroxylation.

Recently the ultrafast radical-clock technique (k_r = 5x10^{12} –10^{13} s^{-1}) has been developed (Newcomb et al., 2000 and references therein). Two probes, trans, trans-2-methoxy-3-phenylmethyl cyclopropane and methyl cubane were used to study the mechanism of the substrates oxidation catalyzed by six isozymes of hepatic P450 2B1. Two principle finding were observed: 1) ratios of the products related to putative "radical" and "non-radical" reaction pathways were found to be within a range 8-20 indicating only a small contribution of the former process, 2) the chemical nature of the products indicates at least two active species are involved in the substrate oxidation process. These experimental data were interpreted in the framework of the following description: 1) because the rate of rearrangement of the 'clock" carbon-centred radicals in a free state is very short (80-100 fs), formation of a majority of the products via radicals produced in the active site is excluded, 2) two electrophylic oxidants are produced in the natural course of P450 oxidation reaction, a peroxo-iron species and a hydroperoxo species and 3) hydroxylation by both species occurs by a mechanism which is similar to the Hamilton "oxenoid" mechanism, e.g. insertion of oxygen atoms across the substrate C-H bond, 4) in the case of the hydroperoxo species the insertion runs as a concerted process in which an oxygen atom attacks the substrate carbon with simultaneous protonation of the atom and rupture of the species O-O bond. The first product of the process is protonated alcohol. An analysis of products of epoxidation and hydroxylation of olefins by cytochrome P450 2B4 (Vaz et al., 1998) also supports the concept that two species with different electrophilic properties hydroxo-iron and oxi-iron, can affect epoxidation.

Apparently contradicting evidence for and against radical and non-radical mechanisms of hydroxylation and epoxidation caused by the thermodynamic allowance of different reaction pathways and the possible involvement of several active oxidizing species, aroused special interest in the theoretical analysis of putative mechanisms of these processes.

A theoretical model for the cytochrome P-450 hydroxylation of saturated cyclic hydrocarbons (quadricyclane, cyclopropane) suggested by Bach et al., (1995) implicates the formation of symmetrically bridged complex H_2O_2 in the coordination sphere of the heme ferric iron atom followed by its consequent transformation to an epoxide-like positively charged complex. After the hetrolytic O-O bond cleavage, the complex produces a cation OH^+, which inserts across the substrate C-H bond by a barrierless concerted mechanism. Two alternative mechanisms of hydroxylation catalyzed by cytochrome P450, synchronous insertion of oxygen atom across C-H bond and a synchronous two- step rebound process, were recently discussed (de Visser et al., 2001a,b.c). Density function calculations and the conservation of orbital symmetry analysis were performed to analyze energy and quantum mechanical factors affected by the reaction of the ferryl structure [HS-Por-Fe=O] with ethane. The barrier for the synchronous reaction was estimated to be at least 4 kcal/mole higher than one for the asynchronous process. The estimation also indicated that the barrier for asynchronous stepwise epoxidation of ethylene is about 11 cal/mole lower than for the synchronous insertion. It was also stressed that the addition of O to C_2H_4 (or H_2) is a symmetry forbidden process.

The first investigations of the cytochrome P450 by physicochemical methods unequivocally indicated that the enzyme heme iron could exist in low- and high-spin states, depending on reduction, binding of substrates, temperature, pH and chemical modification (Peisach etal.1972; Coon et al., 1981; and references therein). According to

Shaik and coworkers (Filatov et al., 1999; Ogliaro et al., 2000; Visser et al., 2001) the ferryl-hydroxo species in the enzyme may also exist in two electromeric forms, FeIII centered with a cation radical porphyrin and FeIV centered with a neutral porphyrin. The spin state of the complex may be low (S= 1), intermediate (S = 2) and high (S = 3). When porphyrin orbitals are involved in the substrate oxidizing process, closely lying states a_{1u} and a_{2u} with different symmetry may be taken into consideration (Fig. 3.11). A two-state reactivity (TSR) situation, which involves high-spin (HS) and low-spin (LS) states, has been suggested. Orbital diagrams showing the HS and LS rebound processes are presented in Fig. 3.11.

As one can see from the Figure 3.11, the "high-spin" pathway retains the values of the system spin constant (S = 3/2) and is accompanied by an electron transfer from the binding d_{xz} orbital to the d_{z2} orbital of iron involved in the formation of the σ-bond with the oxygen atom. Simultaneously, a_{2u} orbitals are filled. The $d_{xz} \rightarrow d_{z2}$ excitation causes the elongation of the Fe-S and Fe-O bond lengths and is manifested in the increase of the energy barrier for the recombination process. In contrast, in the "low-spin" pathway, the $d_{xz} \rightarrow d_{z2}$ transition does not occur.

Along this pathway, two additional effects are expected: 1) an electron transfer from the antibonding σ*C-O orbital to the porphyrin "hole" in the a_{2u} orbital, which strengthens the C-O linkage in the three-electron transition state and 2) strengthening the Fe-S bond as a result of interaction of the σ*(d^{z2}) orbital with the ps(S) orbital and stronger p-back bonding of thiolate to iron. As a result of all these effects, the recombination between carbon-centered radicals and ·OH radicals connected with iron can run practically barrierlessly. The aforementioned model predicted the high kinetic isotope effect for both TSR pathways and the dependence of the "radical clock" results on the donor ability of substrates. The two-state reactivity suggesting multiple electromer species has been also applied to the reaction of epoxidation of ethane in the chytochrome P450 active site (de Visser et al., 2001b). Two reaction pathways were considered: 1) addition of the Compound I- and Compound II-like species to the ethane double bond with formation of a radical intermediate and 2) concerted addition of the species oxygen atoms to the double bond.

Theoretical calculation of the kinetic isotope effect showed that for three systems in which methoxyl and tertiary butoxyl radicals and porphyirin-Fe0 (Por-Fe0) are involved in the reaction of a hydrogen abstraction from methane and toluene (Ogliaro et al., 2000). The approximate tunneling corrections were done. The calculation indicates large $KIE_{H/D}$ (8-15) for the reactions of alkoxy radicals and less $KIE_{H/D}$ (6-9) for the high- and low-spin pathways of Por-Fe0. It is significant that the $KIE_{H/D}$ values were found to be similar for the high-spin patway implicating formation of a long-living substrate radical and for the low-spin pathway with a short-living radical.

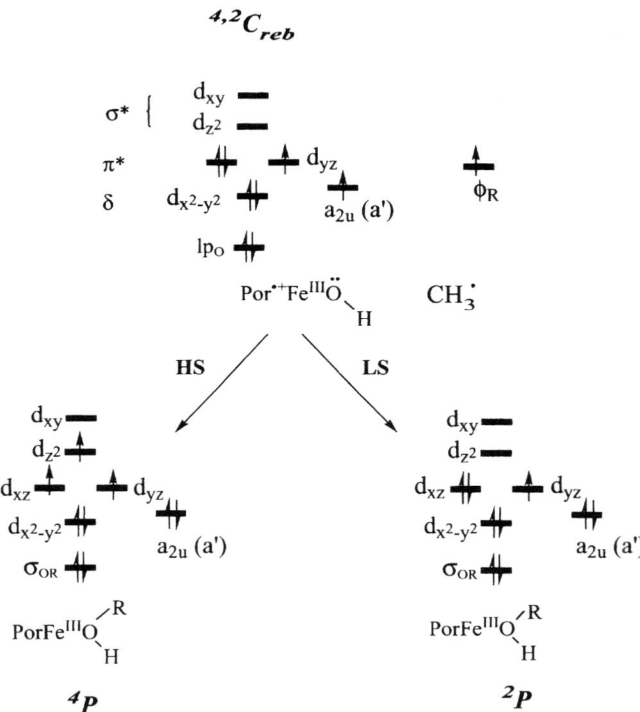

Figure 3.11. Orbital diagrams showing the high-spin (HS) and low-spin (LS) rebound processes to form the corresponding alcohols, [4]P and [2]P (Ogliaro et al., 2000). Reproduced with permission.

The rebound mechanism, though in a modified version, has been recently supported by theoretical calculations of KIF using the density functional theory (Yoshizawa et al., 2000). The calculations demonstrate that the transition state for the H-atom abstraction from ethane involves a linear [FeO….H…C] array; a resultant radical species with a spin density of nearly one is bound to an iron-hydroxy complex, followed by recombination and release of product ethanol. According to the calculation of the reaction energy profile, the carbon radical species is not a stable reaction intermediate with a finite lifetime. The calculated KIF at 300 K is in the range of 7-13 in accord with experimental data and is predicted to be significantly dependent on temperature and substituents. It was also shown from femtosecond dynamic calculations in the FeO^+/CH_4 system that the direct abstraction mechanism can occur in 100-200 fs.

The role of medium polarization in the vicinity of the model compound I-like the ferryl species, [Por (HS)-Fe (IV) O], and the effect of hydrogen bonding of the fifth sulfur ligand with the H-NH$_2$ group were discussed in (Ogliaro et al., 2000). As a result of theoretical calculations, two conclusions emerged: 1) the interactions in the protein pocket strengthens to the Fe-S bond and 2) the hydrogen bonding of the thiolate ligand (NH-S$^-$) stabilizes resonance structure of a compound I species [Por$\cdot^+$ (SR) Fe(IV)O].

300-picosecond molecular dynamics simulation of Compound I of cytochrome P450 with CH$_3$-S- fifth ligand and methane as a substrate revealed that the methyl radical is a product of the hydrogen abstraction (Hata et al., 2001). In another recent molecular dynamics calculation (Yoshizawa et al., 2001) the dynamic aspect of ethane hydroxylation mediated by Compound I was considered. The calculations have also supported the rebound mechanisms and added important details concerning the hydrogen atom abstraction transition state. These indicate that the molecular vibrations of the C-H bond being dissociated and the O-H bond being formed are significantly activated before and after the transition state, respectively. The porphyrin ring vibrational modes υ_3 and υ_4 are involved in Fe-N stretching motion and in energy transfer during the enzymatic process.

Thus, it is becoming increasingly evident that the rebound mechanism is the most probable mechanism of the hydroxylation. Nevertheless, direct proof of occurrence of the ferryl active intermediate is as yet incomplete. Above mentioned the masked radical rebound mechanism can not be excluded.

3.3. Methane Monooxigenase

3.3.1 OVERVIEW

In microorganisms utilizing methane, a methane-hydroxylating system, metan monooxigenase, (MMO) has been detected, which catalyzed the reaction:

$$CH_4 + O_2 + DH_2 \rightarrow CH_3OH + D + H_2O$$

The electron donor (DH$_2$) is NADH, which can be replaced by NADPH, and ascorbic acid (Wallar and Lipscomb, 1996). Methane is produced as a primary product of anaerobic metabolism by methanogenis bacteria and is assimilated as biomass, the energy source, by the methanothrophus. Rapid and specific hydroxylation of such an inert molecule as methane has attracted the special interest of biochemists, chemists and physico-chemists. The soluble preparations of MMO have been isolated from a number microorganisms. For the last two decades, the enzymes from *Methylococcus capsulatus* (Bath) and *Methylosynus trichosporium* OB3b have been intensively investigated with the entire arsenal of biochemical, kinetic and physical methods (Belova et al., 1976; Gvozdev et al., 1982; Rozenzwieg et al., 1993; DeRose et al., 1996; Waller and Lipscomb, 1996; Willems et al., 1998; Jin and Lipscomb. 2000; Austin et al., 2000; Stahl et al., 2001; Merkx et al., 2001; Guallar et al., 2002.).

The enzyme consists of three protein components: a 245 kDa hydroxylase (MOH), a 15 kDa protein (component B), and a 40 kD reductase (MMOR). The hydroxylase is a dimer, each half of which contains 3 types of subunits (α,β,γ) and two iron atoms. The enzyme does not possesses a high substrate specificity and catalyzes the reaction of dioxygen with C-H, C=C, N-H, and C=O bonds with the formation of alcohols, epoxides, hydroxyl amines and CO_2, respectively. Ethane, propane and other alkanes up to C_8 are oxidized in the metane monooxigenase reaction but at significantly lower rates than methane. Halogenated alkenes and alkanes, one two ring aromatics, hetrocycles, etc. are also involved in the oxidizing process. The MMO reaction has a number of specific features, which distinguish it from the "traditional" cytochrome P450 hydroxylating systems: (1) the value of binding constant, K_S, increases with increasing temperature, (2) carbon monoxide is both a substrate and a competitive inhibitor, (3) CF_4 does not inhibit the oxidation of methane, (4) hydrogen peroxide and organic peroxides are not active in the oxidation of methane and other substrates, (5) spectroscopic parameters of the MMO active site are drastically distinguished from those of the heme-containing hydoxylating system and indicate its non-heme nature.

3.3.2. STRUCTURE OF MMOH ACTIVE SITE

The hydoxylase fragment of methane monooxidase was extensively investigated with ESR, ENDOR, EXAFS, Mössbauer spectroscopy, circular dichroism and magnetic circular dichroism (Lee et. al., 1993; Waller and Lipscomb, 1996, Merkx et al., (2001); and references therein). A set of physical parameters has unequivocably indicated that each half part of MMOH contains a hydroxo-bridged diiron cluster. In the resting state the cluster has two high spin iron atoms with S =5/2 each. Owing to the antiferromagnetic spin coupling, the cluster [Fe(III)-Fe(III)] is diamagnetic. After the one-electron reduction, the experiments showed that the S = 5/2 and S = 2 mixed-valence antiferromagnetically coupled state [Fe(III)-Fe(II)] produces 1/2 spin species. The second electron transition converts the mixed-valence structure to the ferromagnetic form of each ferrous iron atom (S = 2) to give an S = 4 ground state [Fe(II)-Fe(II)] which is characterized by an unusual signal of high intensivity with a g-factor about 16. As a result of the large Jahn-Teller distortion, the Fe-O-Fe bridge is highly assymetric, giving the structure Fe(III)-O-Fe(V)=O high oxidizing reactivity.

ESR and Mössbauer studies indicated that oxygen bridged iron atoms are protonated. ENDOR revealed histidine groups and at least nine protons within a few angstroms of the cluster. This method has established the identity of the bridging ligand as a hydroxyl rather than an oxo atom (DeRose et al., 1996). Continuous wave and pulse ENDOR spectroscopy was used to examine ^{14,15}N, ^{1,2}H, ^{13}C and ^{57}Fe nuclei. The experiments indicated the presence of a bridging hydroxide and aqua ligands in the mixed-valence diiron complex. Acetate labeled with 13 at carboxylate carbon atom gives rise to ENDOR signals, whereas ^{13}C labeling and deuterating the methyl group did not affect the ENDOR signals (Willems et al., 1998). The latter results provide evidence that the acetate ion binds with its carboxylate group in the detection of the diiron center. According to CD/MCD data, the iron atom complex has distorted square-pyramidal ligation geometry.

The crystallographic structures of MMOH from both microorganisms, *Methylococcus capsulatus* (Bath) and *Methylosynus trichosporium* OB3b have been determined at various temperatures (18°, 4°, -18° and −160°) and redox states [Fe(III)-Fe(III)] and [Fe(II)-Fe(II)] (Rosenwieg et al., 1993; Waller and Lipscomb, 1996; and references therein). According to the crystallographic model (Fig.3.12), two iron atom are bridged with two protonated oxygen atoms ([Fe(III)-Fe(III)]) or oxygen atoms of two carboxylates [Fe(II)-Fe(II)]. Histidine, the carboxylate group and water ligands form the six-ligand coordination sphere of both atoms in the complex oxidized state and mixed six – five coordination in its reduced state.

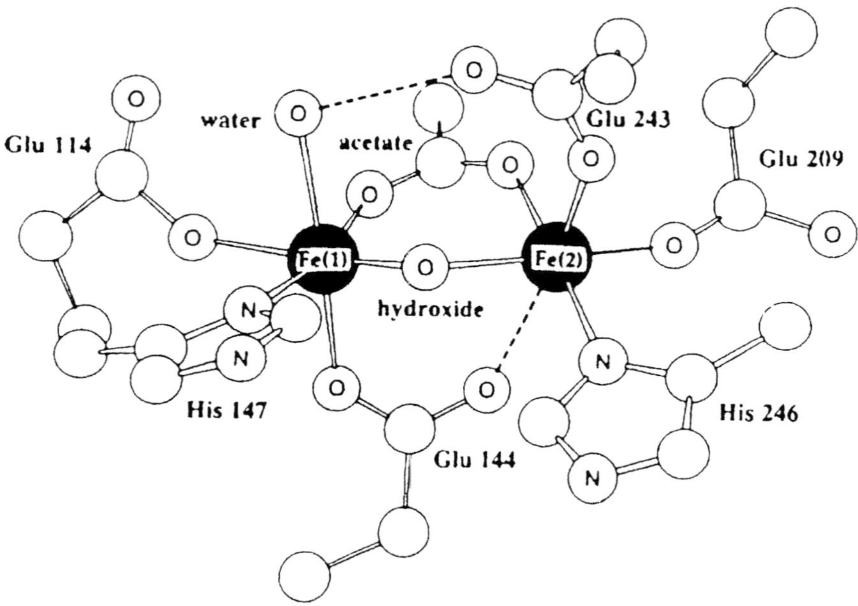

Figure 3.12. Structure of active center of MMO (Rosenzweig, et al., 1993). Reproduced with permission.

No obvious evidence concerning substrate entry to the diiron cluster have been revealed indicating that the entry channel may be opened due to the proteins spontaneous flexibility or may be created by binding MMOB or MMOR (Wallar and Lipscomb, 1996). Recent data on crystal structure of MMOH from M. capsulatus demonstrate the geometric variability of the enzyme active site (Whittington et al., 2001). It is shown, that ferrous atoms, adjacent α-helix, and the Asn214 group have a certain pliability, which enables small molecules to penetrate into the active site.

3.3.3. MECHANISM OF HYDROXYLATION CATALYZED BY THE MMO COMPLEX

Methane and other substrate hydroxylation by dioxygen occurs with the participation of all three components of the enzyme: MMOH, MMOR and MMOB (Feig and Lippard, 1994; Wallar and Lipscomb, 1996; and references therein). The redox potential of the transition [Fe(III)-Fe(III)] $\leftrightarrow$ [Fe(II)-Fe(II)] is $E_0 = 0.048$ V in the MMOH resting state and changes into -0.084, $+0.097$ and $+0.100$ V after the addition of MMOB, MMOR and (MMOB + MMOR), respectively (Waller and Lipscomb, 1996).

X-ray structural analysis indicates that the M. capsulatus MMOH reduction is accompanied by a shift of the E243 carboxylate ligand position. This finding has been confirmed by a density functional study (Torren et al., 2000), which indicated the flexibility of carboxylate ligands in MMO. The complete MMO reacts very quickly with dioxygen forming compound O (Fig. 3.13). The oxygen kinetic isotope effect (k_{16O}/k_{18O} = 1.0167 ± 0.0007) in the oxidation of substrate analog CH_3CN by MMO from M. capsulatus is similar to KIE for reversible dioxygen binding with myoglobin, hemoglobin and hemerythrin (Stahl et al., 2000). Compound O consequently converts at $4°C$ to compound P (presumably peroxoadduct) with the rate constant about 22 s^{-1} and, after protonation and water elimination, to compound Q (Fig. 3.13).

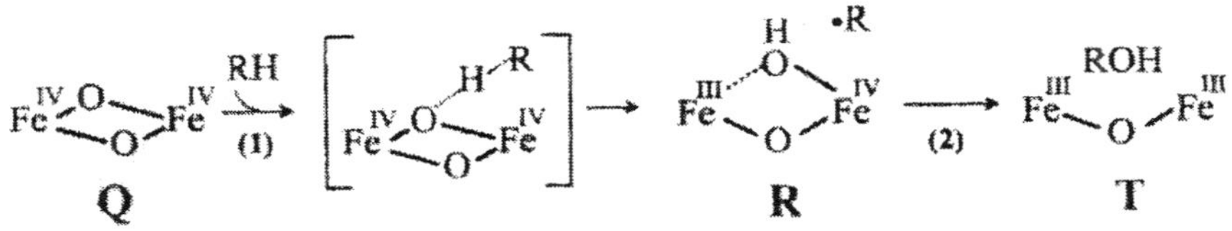

Figure 3.13. The proposed mechanism for Q to T conversion during the substrate oxidation process catalazed by MMO. The mechanism shown is analogous to the conventional "oxygen rebound" mechanism proposed for P450 (Jin and Lipcomb, et al., 2000). Reproduced with permission.

The latter compound attracts special interest because it forms more rapidly in the absence of substrates (k = 1.2 s^{-1}) than it autodecays (k = 0.05 s^{-1}) and, therefore, can be directly investigated by physicochemical methods. The Mössbauer spectrum of compound Q from *M. trichosporium* indicates that the diiron center consists of two high-spin antiferromagnetically-coupled iron atoms, each in the Fe(IV) state bridged by oxygen atom. Compound Q reacts very quickly with methane and other substrates with the formation of compound T. The latter releases a product and is transformed to diferric MMOH.

It has been suggested that the oxidizing reactivity of compound Q is similar to the reactivity of Compound I in peroxidase, catalase and cytochrome P450 (Wallar and Lipscomb, 1996; and references therein). This suggestion is supported by experiments with the use of radical clocks and chiral substrates. Similar to cytochrome P450 reactions, the MMO system from M. trichosporium (Ruzicka et. al., 1990) catalyzes the oxidation of a range of radical-clock reagents (norboran and cyclohexane derivatives) and produces a rearranged product corresponding to a mechanism based on hydrogen atom abstraction followed by recombination with the diiron cluster radical species and formation of the hydroxylated product (rebound mechanism). The formation of radical and carbocation intermediates is assumed on the basis of the formation of 1-methylcyclobutanol from the substrate (Ruzicka et al., 1990).

The rebound mechanism is not unequivocally supported by the radical clock investigation of MMO from *M. capsulatus* (Liu et al., 1993). The intramolecular kinetic isotope effect of $k_H/k_D = 5.0$ indicates the involvement of the substrate C-H bond in an elementary act of hydroxylation. Nevertheless, products, expected in the case of radical intermediate rearrangement with $k_r = 4 \times 10^{11}$ s^{-1}, have not been detected. In a recent investigation (Jin and Lipscomb, 2000), the rearrangement products were observed during oxidation of 1,1,2,2-tetramethylcyclopropene with the rate constant of the carbon centered radical rearrangement $k_r = 1.7\text{-}17.5 \times 10^{8}$s^{-1} at 30° but not for cis- or trans-1.2-dimethyl cyclopropene ($k_r = 1.2\text{-}6.4 \times 10^{8}$s^{-1}) or trans-2-phenylmethylcyclopropane ($k_r = 3,4 \times 10^{11}$ s^{-1}). The authors concluded that the bulky radical clocks have sterical obstacles to recombination and, therefore, can be rearranged before recombination. In contrast, more elegant substrates produce radicals able to reach the reduced diiron ferryl cluster. Carbon-centered radical intermediates were proved by the spin-trapping technique in reactions of MMO from *M. capsulatus* (Bath) (Deighton et al., 1991). Results of elegant experiments with chiral substrates (R)-and (S)-[^{12}H,^{13}H]ethane in reaction of the enzyme from M. trichosporium and M. capsulatus were reported (Priestly et al., 1992). According to ^{3}H-NMR data, both (R)-and (S)-[^{12}H,^{13}H] ethane underwent about 35% inversion of configuration. This means that a radical intermediate, ethyl radical, can rearrange its configuration in the active site before the formation of ethanol.

Strong evidence in favor of the rebound mechanism was obtained in experiments on the kinetic isotope effect (KIe). Upon hydroxylation of methane and ethane catalyzed by MMO in the steady-state kinetics condition, relatively low KIE ($k_H/k_D = 1.75 -5.0$) was observed (Belova et al., 1976)). A very high KIE (50-100) in the decay of compound Q in the presence of CH_4 and CD_4 was reported (Waller and Limscomb, 1996). The use of CH_3D, CH_2D_2 and CHD_3 showed a linear decrease of the decay rate constant. These results were interpreted as support for the rebound mechanism. The observed KIE is significantly high than the KIE detected in other hydrogen and proton transfer reactions (Section 1.2.1). Such high values of KIE can be explained in the framework of a "quasi-reversible" mechanism of the reaction in the active site (Waller and Lipscomb, 1996). According to this mechanism, the hydrogen abstraction reaction can be generated in an altered form of compound Q (Q'). This form is equilibrium in the compound Q-substrate complex and with compounds R^H-CH·$_3$ and R^D-CD·3, which make possible secondary processes.

The mixed-valent [Fe(II)Fe(III)] state of MMOH from has the ability to accommodate simultaneously several molecules (methanol, water and DMSO) as recently demonsrated by ENDOR spectroscopy (Willems et al., 1998). The structure of the binuclear iron-methanol complex and the detailed mechanism of the complex dissociation were investigated with the use of density function methods (Bash et al., 2001a.b).

Among other discussed concepts concerning the MMO substrate hydroxylation in the compound Q active site, the following suggested mechanisms should be mentioned.

1. Formation of a protein radical, for example Cys 151, RS, which promotes the synchronous insertion of oxygen atoms across the substrate C-H bond (Waller and Limscomb, 1996, Shilov, 1997). The absence of rearranged products of the radical clock substrates for MMOH isolated from M. capsulatus raises the possibility in principle, of such a mechanism.

2. Drawing a parallel of the compound Q to the cytochrome P450 Compound I (Newcomb et al., 2000), a nonsynchronous concerted mechanism in MMO was suggested . According to this mechanism, the difference in the bond vibration of C-H and Fe-O bonds causes the insertion of oxygen atoms across the C-H bond via a transition state in which the substrate possesses a radical character. Such an elementary process is possible in the approach of the substrate to the ferryl oxygen.

3. A concerted mechanism assuming the elecrophylic attack of one oxygen atom of the diiron ferryl to the C-H bond carbon with nucleophylic assistance of the second oxygen atom with the formation of a pentavalent carbon intermediate (Shteinman, 1996).

4. Using the analogy of model reactions of alkane oxidation in mixtures of Fe(II) and dioxygen in solvents, a mechanism invoking the formation of intermediate with an iron-carbon bond followed by interaction with soxygen was proposed (Waller and Limscomb, 1996; Shilov, 1997).

The mechanism of C-H bond activation was examined in recent theoretical work with the use of ab initio density functional methods (Dunietz et al., 2000; Gherman et al., 2001).

3.4. Nitric Oxide Synthase

Nitric oxide (NO) is a tiny molecule with enormous biological impact. NO mediates a large number of physiologic and pathophysiologic processes including vascular relaxation, inhibition of platelet aggregation, regulation of endothelial cell adhesivity, preservation of the normal vessel wall structure, etc. (Stuehr 1999; Stuehr and Ghosh, 2000); and references therein). NO is generated in an enzymatic process of oxidation of L-arginine (Arg) by dioxygen catalyzed nitric oxide synthase (NOS) in the presence of NADPH. The process involves stepwise oxidation of Arg to N-hydroxyl-L-arg, which is converted to cirulline and nitric oxide. Both reactions occur within the hydroxylase domain of NOS containing heme, the cofactor tetrahydrobiopterin (H_4B) and the Arg binding site. The second, the reductase domain, containing FMN, FAD and NADPH, provides electrons for the active site reduction. Two O_2 and 1.5 NADPH are consumed for each NO. The third component of the enzyme system is calmodulin (CaM), which lies between these two domains and promotes electron transfer from NADH to heme. CaM binds only at certain concentrations of Ca^{2+}. Three isomers of the enzyme are intensively investigated: neuronal (nNOS), endothelial (eNOS), and cytokine-inducable (iNOS).

A set of structural and kinetic investigations indicates that the heme active structure of NOS and the mechanism of Arg hydroxylation are similar to those for cytochrome P450 (Bec et al., 1998; Stuehr, 1999; Adak et al., 2001a,b; Abu-Saud et al., 2000; Wei et al., 2001; Wolthers, 2002; Lange et al., 2001). The mechanism involves the reduction of heme, O_2 binding and its activation by the second electron and proton transfer with the formation of oxoferryl structure [S-Fe(IV)=O] similar to those of peroxidase Compound I but with sulfur ligand instead of histidine (Fig. 3.14). According to the NOS crystallographic model (Crane et al., 1998; Raman, 1998; Fishmann; 1999), the guanidinium group of Arg is adjacent to the heme ring and can be directly attacted by the [S-Fe(IV)=O] center. In contrast, the H_4B cofactor is located at the opposite site of the heme ring. Kinetics of argenine hydroxylation catalyzed by NOS is shown in Fig. 3.14 (Wei et al., 2001)

Recent investigations have shed light on peculiarities of the NOS action mechanism: the role of the H_4B cofactor and CaM, and cooperativity in kinetic and thermodynamic properties of different components of the nitric oxide synthesis system. Stop flow experiments with eNOS (Abu-Soud et al., 2000) showed that calmodulin binding caused an increase in NADH-dependent flavin reduction from 0.13 to 86 s^{-1} at 10 °C. Under such conditions, in the presence of Arg, heme is reduced very slowly (0.005 s^{-1}). Heme complex formation requires a relatively high concentration of NO (>50 nM) and inhibits the entire process: NADH oxidation and citrulline synthesis decreases 3-fold and K_m increases 3-fold. NOS reactions were monitored at subzero temperatures in the presence of 50% ethylene glycol as an anti-freeze solvent (Bec et al., 1998).

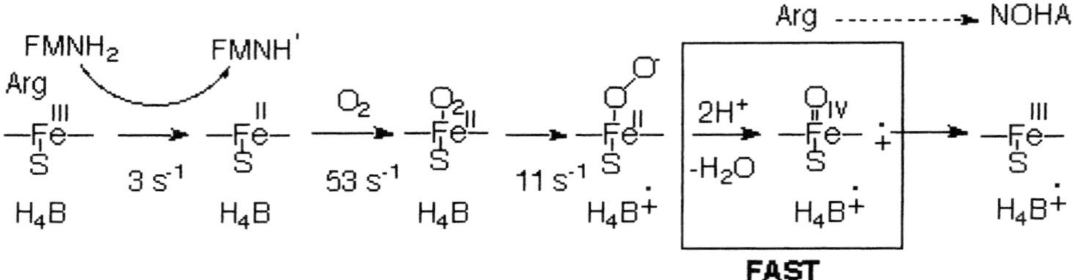

Figure 3.14. Kinetics of arg hydroxylation. In NADPH-driven reaction, shown step in the transfer of an electron from the reductase flavins (FMNH$_2$) to the ferric heme. Oxygen then binds to form the $Fe^{II}O_2$ speicie, which receives an electron from H_4B to form a heme-peroxo intermediate. Subsequent steps that lead to Arg hydroxylation are rapid and genetate ferric iNOSoxy contaning NOHA and the H_4B radical (Wei, et al., 2001). Reproduced with permission.

At 30°C in the absence of Arg, the ferrous-oxi complex transforms very slowly to the ferric state. In the presence of substrate and H_4B, a new species with the 12-nm shifted Sorey band is detected. A decay of this species is accompanied by the formation of N^ω-hydroxy-L-arginine. Because the presence of H_4B is necessary for these reactions, the main function of this compound is to be a reducing agent. This suggestion is supported by experiments on the stabilizing effect of ascorbic acid on the chemical stabilization of tetrahydropterin in the endothelial nitric oxide synthesis (Heller et al., 2001). At the same time, a significant increase in the half lifetime of H_4B in solution is demonstrated. As is shown (Wei et al., 2001), a ferrous-dioxy intermediate in iNOS forms for 53 s^{-1} and then is transformed to the [S-Fe(IV)=O] state. The rate of the [S-Fe(IV)=O] decay is equal to the rate of H_4B radical formation and the rate of Arg hydroxylation. In contrast, in the presence of dihydrobiopterin, the ferrous-dioxy decay occurs more slowly and is not associated with Arg hydroxylation. The authors have come to the reasonable conclusion that H_4B transfers electrons to the active site to form a center with strong oxidizing power.

A 10-step kinetic model has been developed (Santolini et al., 2001). Crystal structures of xyNOS show that a Tyr-409 indol nitrogen atom forms a strong hydrogen bond with the heme thiolate (Crane et al., 1988; Raman et al.1998; Fishmann et al., 1999). The Try-409 mutation suggests that the heme potential controls the NOS reactions (Adak et al. 2001). Suppression of this hydrogen bond through the mutation lowers the reduction potential of the heme, inhibits heme reduction and accelerates oxidation of the Fe(II) heme-NO complex. The Arg binding increases the reduction potential of the NOS heme.

3.5. Light energy conversion and water-oxidation systems in photosynthesis

The main outcome of photosynthesis is the oxidation of water and the synthesis of glucose from carbon dioxide at the expense of sunlight energy. The immensity of this process on the scale of the Earth is evident by the fact that annually about 50 billion tons of carbon from carbon dioxide is bound into forms that provide energy and structural material for all living organisms on Earth (Dismukes, 2001; Blankenship, 2001; Rutherford and Faller, 2001; Witt, 1996).

The problems of photosynthesis embrace practically all aspects of modern biochemistry, biophysics and molecular biology. Here, we shall briefly consider two aspects of fundamental importance not only for biology but for modern chemistry as well: (1) the structure and action mechanism of the system of conversion of light energy into chemical energy in the primary charge photoseparation in bacterial and plant photosynthesis and (2) the possible mechanisms of the participation of polynuclear manganese systems in the photooxidation of water. The first system is a remarkable example of the appearance of qualitatively new properties upon combination of active groups into an ordered structure. The second system accomplishes one of the most surprising reactions that occur in nature, the production of a strong reducing agent from water on account of the quanta of low energy.

3.5.1. REACTION CENTERS FROM PHOTOSYNTHETIC BACTERIA

The primary photochemical and photophysical processes in the donor-acceptor pair D-A lead to charge photoseparation, i.e. an appearance of the pair of two charges (D^+A^-), where (D^+) the cation-radical is a strong oxidant and $(A^-.)$ is the anion-radical is a strong reducing agent (Fyfe and Jones, 2000). Therefore, in the D-A pair, the light absorption energy is converted to chemical energy accumulated in the photoseparated pair. The most important problems are the structure and action mechanism of biological photosynthetis, which prevent fast recombination of D^+ and A^- centers of high chemical reactivity and provide relatively long lifetime for these centers. Involving it in subsequent chemical reactions eventually results in the formation of stable compounds such as ATP and NADPH.

Early results

The primary photochemical processes of photosynthesis take place within membrane bound complexes of pigments and protein, reaction centers (Shuvalov and Krasnovsky, 1981; Deisenhofer et al., 1986, Rees et al., 1989; Norris and Shiffer, 1990; Kirmaier and Holten, 1991; Feher et al., 1992; Stowell et al., 1997). One mole of a reaction center from different bacteria contains 4 moles of bacteriochlorophyl (Bchl), 2 moles of bacteriopheophytin (Bph), two moles of ubiquinone (Q) and a non-heme Fe atom. In RC from Rhodobacter speroides, a total of 11 hydrophobic α-helixes create a framework that organizes the cofactor and a hydrophobic band approximately 35 Å wide. RC from Rhodopseudomonus viridus has three polypeptides having pronounced hydrophobic properties. The molecular mass of the polypeptides are 37 571 (L), 35902 (M) and 28902 (H). The H subunit does not carry pigments but it is sufficient for the photochemical activity. The protein components of reaction centers from different-bacteria are similar.

A series of early studies based on the use of a whole arsenal of biochemical, physicochemical and physical methods including ESR, ENDOR, TRIPPLE, ESSEM, EXAFS, Mössbauer spectroscopy, optically detected magnetic resonance ODMAR, adsorption detected magnetic resonance (ADMAR), reaction yield detection magnetic resonance (RYDMER), magnetic field effect on reaction yield (MARY), as well as pico- and femtosecond optical spectroscopy have established the main features of the structure of RCs and the kinetics of electron transfer during photoseparation of charges Hoff, 1992; Hoff and Deisenhofer; 1997;Okamura et al., 2000; Deligiannakis and Rutherford, 2000; Yakovlev and Shuvalov, 2000; Yakovlev et al. 2001; and references therein).

The process starts with the accumulation of light quanta by the light-harvesting complex (LHC), the so-called antenna protein, which is a complex of 12 polypeptides with 12 Bchl molecules Hoff and Shertz, 1992 and references therein). The distances between chlorophyll molecules are sufficient for an effective energy transfer by the Forster mechanism. The singlet electronic excitation migrates along the LHC and enters the primary acceptor P_{870}, the dimer of bacteriocchlorophyl (D_A), which also passes over into the singlet state. This is followed by a chain of events (Fig. 3.15). During time of the order of a picosecond, an electron from the excited P_{870} is transferred to bacteriochlorophyl, DA 1 and then, in picoseconds, to bacteriopheophytin Bph and, in about 200 ps, to the primary acceptor ubiquinone (Q_A). The next electron transfer from Q_A to the secondary acceptor Q_B occurs at a rate in the millisecond range. During this time the electron from the secondary donor, e.g. type c chytochrome, has the chance to be transformed from reduced cytochrome c to P_{870}^{+}. As a result, the energy of a solar quantum is transformed into chemical energy of the reduced secondary acceptor, which can be involved in consequence reactions.

The author of this monograph has suggested that rapid electron transfer in reaction centers in the forward direction and significantly slower transfer in the reverse direction may account for the tunneling (long-distance) mechanism of the photoseparated charges (Likhtenshtein et al., 1975, 1979a,b; Likhtenshtein, 1988a). The concepts of tunneling mechanisms of electron transfer in photosynthetic systems were originally worked out in the classical works of Chance and De Vault (1967) for the electron-transfer reaction between oxidized chlorophyll and reduced cytochrome c in photosynthetic bacteria. But the new basic idea underlying the suggested mechanism is an assumption that the donor (D) and several acceptor (A_i) centers compose a cascade in an ordered structure, in which all these centers are placed at <u>an optimum distance</u> from each other and are separated by a <u>nonconducting</u> protein medium. Such a separation slows down the forward electron transfer between adjacent D-A_1 and A_i-A_{i+1} pairs as compared to electron transfer in a system with close contacts between the centers. Nevertheless, the transfer can be sufficiently fast, if the optimum distances do not exceed 6-10 Å (see Section 2.1). What is important is that the recombination of each D^+-A_i^- pair becomes slower and slower as A_i moves away from the donor. In the system of tightly packed centers the recombination rate is expected to be very fast.

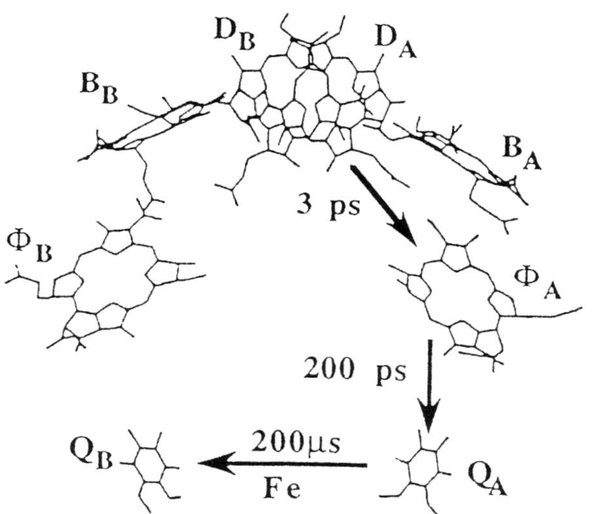

Figure 3.15. Structure of the cofactors of the RC from Rb. Sphaeroides. Phytyl and isoprenoid tails have been omi6tted for clarity. Electron transfer proceeds preferentially along the A branch as shown by the arrows with characteristic times as indicated (Rees et al., 1989). Reproduced with permission.

From this analysis, the main two conclusions are: (1) an effective fast conversion of light energy to energy of a chemical compound of high quantum yield can take place only in biological and model cascade photochemical systems in which photo- and chemically active centers (aromatic photochromes, transition metal clusters) are separated by "insulated" zones of 6-10 Å width, consisting of nonsaturated molecules and bonds, and (2) the electron transfer between the donor and acceptor centers has to occur by a long-range, most probably nonadiabatic mechanism.

The tunneling hypothesis has been supported in subsequent experiments. By the electron paramagnetic resonance measurements (Kulikov et al., 1979) the distances between $(Bchl)_2^+$ and Q_A^- in RC from Rhodopseudomonas spheroidos was shown to be 32-35 Å. This value was obtained employing the method based on measurement of the effect of Q_A^- on the spin-lattice relaxation time of $(Bchl)_2^+$. On the basis of this result and analysis of quantitative data on exchange interactions (exchange integral J values) between other RC components (Tiede et al., 1976; Shuvalov and Asadov, 1979; Schepler et al., 1975; Klevanik et al., 1980;) and the experimental dependence of the spin-exchange integral on the distance between paramagnetic centers (Section 2. ??, Fig. Xxxx), a scheme of the spatial localization of the electron donors and acceptors in reaction centers has been composed (Likhtenshtein et al., 1979,1981,1982). As one can see from Figs. 3.13-3.14, the RC model proposed on the basis of a physico-chemical investigation shows similar principle features just as a subsequent crystalographic model does, namely, that the pigments in the reaction center from R. viridis are located at distance of 7-11 Å and are separated by non-conducting protein media. The center-center distance between between $(Bchl)_2$ and Q_A is about 30 Å.

The linear dependence of the logarithm of the rate constant of the electron transfer in RCs of purple bacteria and plant photosystem I (log k_{ET}) on the edge-edge distance between the donor and acceptor centers (R) was observed (Fig. 2.9) (Likhtenshtein, 1996, 2000). The slope of the dependence corresponds to the slope predicted for long-distance spin superexchange orbital overlap through non-conducting media by the shortest pathway (Eqs. 2.6 with $\beta_{DA} = 1.3$ Å^{-1}). As one can see from Fig. 2 9, the values of k_{ET} for the transfer from $(Bchl)_2^+$ to Bph and from $P700^+$ to pheophytin acceptor (Ph) markedly deviate from the general log k_{ET} - R plot. Such deviation is explained by assuming the participation of intermediate acceptors located between $(Bchl)_2^+$ and Bph, and between $P700^+$ and (Ph) (Michel and Deisenhofer et al., 1985; Kirmaier et al., 1991; Yakovlev and Shuvalov, 2000). Another deviation is related to ET from the primary quinone acceptor Q_A to the secondary quinone acceptor Q_B. The process takes place at an edge-edge distance of about 14 Å, but the centers are connected with two hydrogen bonds and two aromatic imidazol groups. On the basis of estimation of the resonance integral of the energy reorganization, it was concluded that the process runs adiabatically and is controlled by media reorganization (Likhtenshtein, 1988a, 1996).

The first experimental evidences that electron transfer from Q_A^- to P^+ and from Q_A^- to Q_B in reaction centers are controlled by the protein conformational dynamics, was obtained in the late 1970's (Berg 1978a,b; Likhtenshtein et al., 1979 a, b) This conclusion was confirmed in subsequent experimental studies in which molecular dynamics of RC and the photsynthetic membrane were determined with a whole set of physical labels. (Kotelnikov et al., 1983, Kochetkov et al., 1984; Parak et al., 1983). It was shown that the electron transfer from reduced primary acceptor Q_A^- to secondary acceptor Q_B takes place only under conditions in which the labels record the mobility of the protein moiety in the membrane with the correlation frequency $\upsilon_c > 10^7$ s-^{1} (Fig. 3.16).

This fact was explained in the framework of two models. The first model is based on the concept of dynamic adaptation of a protein matrix in every step of an enzymatic reaction. Concerning the $Q_A^- \rightarrow Q_B$ transition, fast reversible conformational transitions can provide dipolar relaxation favourable for the media reorganization process (Likhtenshtein, 1976, 1979 a, 1988 a). Such reorganization is necessary to release electrons of Q_A^- from the stabilizing elecrostatic frame and to stabilize the Q_B^- anion. The second model (Petrov at al., 1977) suggested conformational gating as a mechanism for providing the shortest, most effective pathway for this transition. According to this model, at temperatures lower than 210-220 K, the position of protein groups between Q_A aand Q_B is not favorable for electron transfer due to weak superexchange conductivity. Such conductivity is essentially improved under physiological conditions when the intermediate group stands in a position favorable for electron transfer.

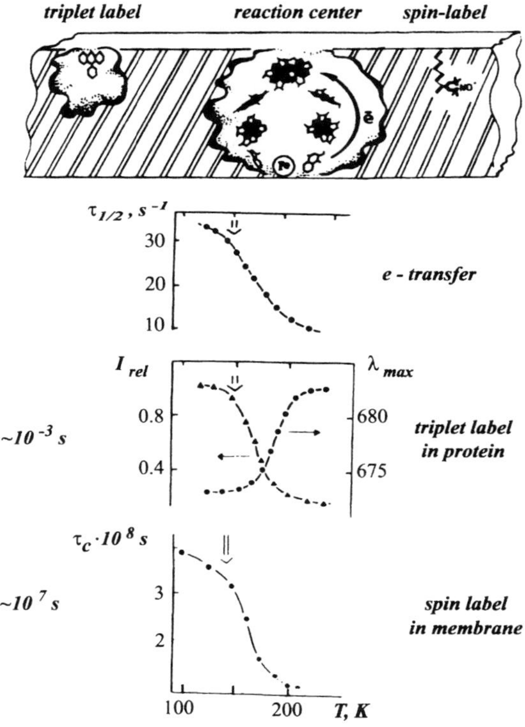

Figure 3.16. Temperature dependences of the parameters of physical labels on chromotophores from R. rubrum: (a) Shematic diagram of the locations of spin and triplet labels. (b) Experimental data: $\tau_{1/2}$ is the characteristic time of electron transfer from the reduced primary acceptor to the oxidized primary donor (Likhtenshtein, et al., 1996). Reproduced with permission.

The rate of another important process, the recombination of the primary product of the charge separation, i.e. the reduced primary acceptor (Q_A^-) and oxidised primary donor, bacteriochlorophyl dimer (P^+), falls from 10^3 to 10^2 s^{-1} when dynamic processes with $\upsilon_c = 10^3$ s^{-1} monitored by the triplet labelling method occur. Very fast electron transfer from P^+ to bacteriochlorophyl (Bchl) and from (Bchl)$^-$ to Q_A does not depend on media dynamics and occurs via conformationally non-equilibrium states (Fig. 3.16).

Recent developments

Three main tendencies have been underlined in recent studies of structure and action mechanism of bacterial photosynthetic reaction centers. The crystallographic structure of the reaction centers from Rps. viridis and Rb. spheroids was initially determined to be 2.8 and 3 Å resolutions (Michel and Deisenhofer et al., 1985; Allen et al., 1986). Resolution and refinement of these structures have been subsequently extended to 2.2, 2.3 and 2.6 Å. (Rees et al., 1989; Stowell et al., 1997, Fyfe and Johns, 2000; Rutherford and Faller, 2001). Investigations of the electronic structure of donor and acceptor centers in the ground and exited states by modern physical methods with a combination of pico- and femtosecond kinetic techniques have become more precise and elaborate. Extensive experimental and theoretical investigations on the role of orbital overlap and protein dynamics in the processes of electron and proton transfer have been done. All the above-mentioned research directions are accompanied by extensive use of methods of sit-directed mutagenesis and substitution of native pigments for artificial compounds of different redox potential.

The primary photophysical and photochemical events in reaction centers from RCs of Rh. sphaeroides (Rb.) and Chloroflexus aurantiacus have been interesting to researchers. Detailed analysis of kinetics and the thermodynamics of electron transfer from the excited primary donor P* to bacteriopheophytin (Bph) via bacteriochlotophyl (Bchl) have been performed (Bixon and Jortner, 1999 and references therein). Levels of energy for the primary charge separation in photosynthetic RC are presented in Fig. 3.17. Accordingly, the primary ET in RC takes place as a transition in Franck-Condon systems with two quasicontinua. Transfer P* (Bchl)(Bph) $\rightarrow$ P$^+$ (Bchl)(Bph)$^-$ can occur as a two-step process via an intermediate P$^+$(Bchl)$^-$ (Bph) or by a one-step process, in which (Bchl) provides a superexchange bridge for the direct P* (Bchl)(Bph) $\rightarrow$ P$^+$(Bchl)(Bph)$^-$ transfer. The possibility of superposition of both sequential and suprexchange mechanisms has been also advanced. According to Bixon and Jortner (1999), the P* (Bchl)(Bph) $\rightarrow$ P$^+$ (Bchl)(Bph)$^-$ transfer and electron transfer from (Bph)- to the primary quinone acceptor Q_A are activationless processes. The mean characteristic vibrational energy of the former process was estimated as $h\omega$ = 80-100 cm^{-1}, where ω corresponds to the vibrational mode of the dimer P. Other quantitative characteristics of the primary processes derived from the theoretical analysis are as follows: (1) the spread of the energy of the P$^+$ (Bchl)(Bph)$^-$ relative to P* is accounted for in terms of a Gaussian contribution with width-parameter $\sigma \approx$ 0.05 eV, (2) for the superexchange route, the reorganization energy $\lambda \approx$ 0.1 eV, (3) the energy gap between P* (Bchl)(Bph) and P$^+$ (Bchl)(Bph)$^-$ was estimated as $\Delta G_1 \approx$ 0.06 eV.

In a wide range of temperatures both processes occur significantly faster than the media relaxation (Fig. 3.18) and, therefore, the media around the intermediates (Bph)$^-$ and QA$^-$ exist in the conformationally nonequilibrium state (Likhtenshtein, 1996 and references therein). In such a condition, as was mentioned above, the energy gap ΔG_1 and the reorganization energy λ for primary ET are small. Hence, this activationless process is controlled by the orbital overlap factor but not by the Franck-Condon. The linear plot of log k_{ET} and the logarithm of the attenuation parameter for superexchange processes (γ_{ET}) versus the distances between the donor and acceptor centers (Fig. 3.18) support independently this conclusion.

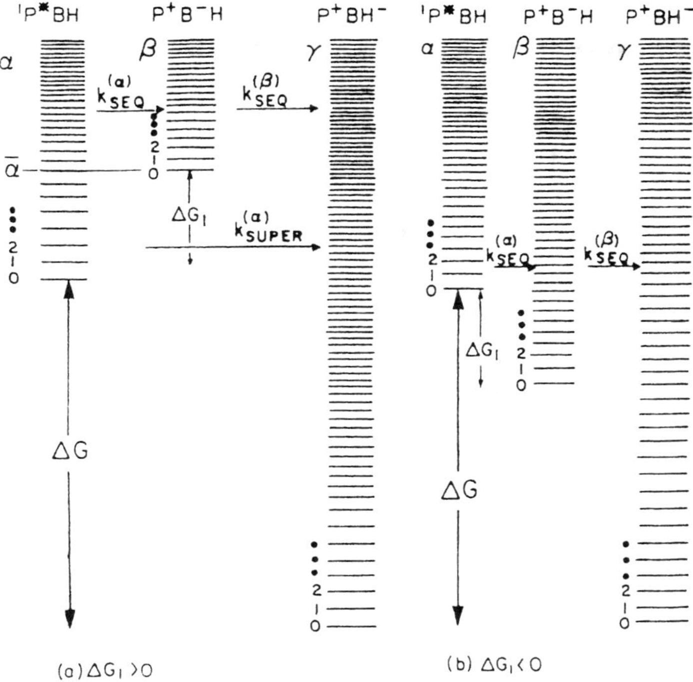

Figure 3.17. Level structure for the primary charge separation in photosynthetic reaction centers. (a) unistep superexchange dynamics; (b) two-step sequential dynamics (Bixon and Jortner, 1999) Reproduced with permission.

Primary photochemical events in reaction centers from the *Rb. sphaeroides* wild type and site directed mutant RCs, where the tyrosine at the M210 position was replaced by phenylalanine and leucine, were investigated by femtosecond time-resolved absorbance and ENDOR/TRIPLE spectroscopy techniques (Wachtveitl, et al., 1998). The results allowed the authors to suggest that primary electron transfer follows a stepwise mechanism and P^+Bcl^- state is the first electron transfer intermediate in these mutants. Independent evidence in favor of the anion radical Bchl·⁻ as the first material (but not "virtual") intermediate, was obtained (Yakovlev et al., 2000). It was demonstrated that in the porphyrin-modified RCs of Rb. spheroidas R-26, the femtosecond oscillations in the excited primary donor emission occur (Vos et al., 1994).

Primary photochemical events in two site-directed mutants YF(M208) and YL(M208) of RC from Blastochloris viridis, in which tyrosine at position M208 is replaced by phenylalanine and leucine, respectively, were investigated with the use of 1H-ENDOR as well as optical absorption spectroscopy (Mue et al., 2000). The residue at M208 is in close proximity to the primary electron donor, P, the (BChl), and the BPh. Analysis of the experimental data revealed two torsional isomers of the 3-acetyl group of

Bph. Enzymes in the $Bph^-Q_A^-$ state accumulates at 100 K and undergo an irreversible change between 100 K and 200 K. It was shown (Kotel'nikov et al., 1983b; Likhtenshtein, 1993) that within this temperature range the phosphorence probes detect animation of millisecond dynamics in the RC.

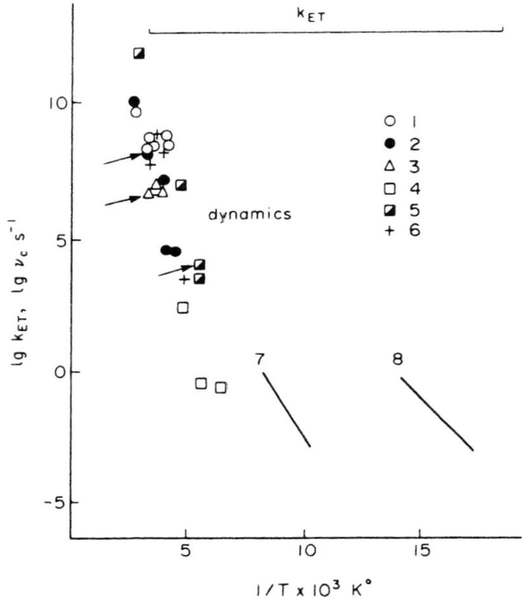

Figure 3.18. Data on the correlation frequency of the mobility of physical labels and their environment in bovine and human serum albumins and in the photosynthetic RC (I) and the rate constants of ET's primary donor (P) to the bacteriaophephytin acceptor (II) in the Arrhenius coordinates. (Likhtenshein, 1996). Reproduced with permission.

One of the enigmatic problems of photsynthesis is the drastic difference between the rate of photelectron transfer in the active (M) and inactive branches of bacterial reaction centers. The quantum mechanical calculation (Kolbasov and Scherz, 2000) showed that the square of electronic matrix element V_A^2 for the electron transfer from the excited primary donor, P*, to bacteriochlorophyl in the active brunch is larger by three order of magnitude than that in the inactive part V_B^2. Therefore, the electron transfer rate in the RC inactive L-brunch should be essentially slower than that in the M-brunch.

The X-ray crystal structure of a reaction centre from *Rhodobacter sphaeroides* with a mutation of tyrosine M210 to tryptophan (YM210W) has been determined to have a resolution of 2.5 Å (McAuley et al., 2000). It is shown that the main effect of the introduction of the bulkier tryptophan in place of the native tyrosine is a small tilt of the macrocycle of the $(Bchl)_L$. The effect of the redox potential of the electron acceptor (Bchl) in RC from Rb. spheroides on the initial electron transfer rate and on the $P^+(Bchl)^-$ population was investigated (Sporlein et al., 2000). Analysis of experimental data estimates the free energy as ($\Delta G^0 = 0.104$ eV), the energy of reorganization as ($\lambda = 0.065$ eV) and the coupling factor as ($V = 6.5 \times 10^{-3}$ eV) of this non-adiabatic process. The free energy difference between $P^+Q_A^-$ and P^+H^- (ΔG^0) is indirectly estimated by measuring the rate of the charge recombination ($P^+H^- \rightarrow PH$) via the uphill route ($P^+Q_A^- \leftrightarrow P^+H^-$). It is suggested that the rate of charge recombination by this pathway is proportional to the equilibrium constant between $P^+Q_A^-$ and P^+H^-. This suggestion is sustained by the fact that the recombination rate increases by a factor of 10 for each 0.060 eV increase of the difference of the redox potential of quinines replacing the native ubiquinone-10. The calculated values of ΔG^0 and $-T\Delta S^0$ increase monotonically with the temperature increase from 40 K to 200 K, while enthalpy ΔH_0 does not change in this temperature range. Within 200 –318 K, ΔG^0 and $-T\Delta S^0$ slightly decreased and ΔH^0 increased by a jump from 0.050 to 0.300 eV. The authors suggest that the observation of large entropy at temperature lowers than 210 K (for example $\Delta S^0 = + 23$ cal/molexK at 100 K) is caused by a formation of the $P^+Q_A^-$ which is trapped before media relaxation. The Gibbs energy of the trap state at 10 K is estimated as about 0.200 eV higher than relaxed form at room temperature

Another matter of recent interest is detailed mechanisms of electron transfers with participation of primary Q_A and secondary Q_B acceptors and the role of the coupling proton transfer in these processes. The chrystallographic structures of RC from R. spheroides at cryogenic temperature (90 K) in the dark and under illumination, at resolution 2.2 and 2.6 Å respectively, have been reported (Stowell et al., 1997). The main difference in the two structures was the charge-separated state within an area of the primary (Q_A) and secondary (Q_B) acceptor location. In the charge neutral state PQ_AQ_B, the distance between two ubiquinones is approximately 5 Å. In the "light" structure $PQ_AQ^-_B$ the Q_B has moved about 4.5 Å and undergone a 180propeller twist. It was proposed that a hydrogen bond of ubiquinone with HisL190 prompts the electron transfer from Q_A^- to Q_B and Q_BH^-. These results give evidence in favor of the gating model of the protein dynamic, which suggests that electron transfer occurs only in an active conformational state of the medium, promoting electron transfer (Petrov et al., 1977).

Recent theoretical studies have added important conclusions (Balabin and Onuchik 2000; Rabinshtein et al., 2000) and have confirmed above mentioned conclusions (that electron transfer between the two quinines Q_A and Q_B in the bacterial photosynthetic centers is coupled to conformational rearrangement. The pathway method (Beratan and Onuchik, 1987; Beratan et al., 1990; Onuchik et al., 1992) for estimation of the quantomechanical-coupling factor V_{DA} was assumes that the electron transfer involves multiple pathway tubes of different V_{DA}, the population of which is controlled by conformational and nuclear dynamics. The MD simulation performed for both the "dark" and the "light" structures indicates that dominant pathway tubes are similar for light and dark RC structures, except the position of Q_B. According to the calculation (Stowell et al., 1997), the transition from "dark" to "light" states is accompanied by the flipping and moving of Q_B which shortens the ET pathway by five covalent steps and replaces a through-space jump by a hydrogen bond. As a result of this transition, the ET rate increases by about three orders of magnitude.

In the high-resolution ESR (326 GHz) study of the biradical state $Q_A - Q_B -$ in the Rb. Spheroids, RC determines the exchange integral in the biradical (Jo = 10^9 s^{-1}) (Calvo et al., 2001). Because the rate constant of electron transfer from Q_A^- to Q_B is essentially less ($k_{ET} \approx 10^4$ s^{-1}) (Feher et al., 1992; Xu et al, 2000) than expected for an nonadiabatic activationless ET and the k_{ET} values considerably deviate from the dependence of the supperexchange attenuation parameter (γET) on the distance between donor and acceptor centers in RCs (Fig. XXX), we can conclude that the ET is adiabatic and requires thermal activation.

The $Q_A^- \rightarrow Q_B$ electron transfer of free energy in RC from Rb. spheroidas is calculated by applying an electrostatic model using the Poisson Boltzmann equation and Monte Carlo sampling (Rabinshtein et al., 2000). It is shown that the electron transfer is energetically uphill for the "dark" structure (ΔG^o = 0.157 eV) and downhill for the "light" structure (ΔG^o = -0.056 eV). Another interesting conclusion is that coupled groups GluL212 and L213 bind one proton in the $P^+Q_A^-Q_B$ structure and two protons in $P^+Q_AQ^-_B$. An important role of the hydrogen bond bridges in the long-range electron transfer between Q_A^- and Q_B^- in photosynthetic reaction centers has been suggested computationally (Peluso et al., 2000).

The effect of the replacement of native ubiquinone Q_A in RC from Rb. spheroids for naphtaquinones of different redox potential on the two-phase kinetics of the $Q_A^- \rightarrow Q_B$ transition is investigated using spectral technique (Li et al., 2000). The variation of the naphtoquinone free energy ΔG^o from -0.090 to -0.250 V leads to a decrease of characteristic time of the fast component τ_1 from 29 to 0.2 μs, yet no affect on the slow component kinetics with τ_2 =100 μs. The former fraction increased with increasing driving force and decreases as the Q_A isoprene tail is elongated from 2 to 10 units. The above-mentioned experimental data are rationalized in the framework of a model suggesting that the fast process is related to electron transfer from Q_A^- to Q_B with formation of $(Q_B^-)^*$ which is not in the conformational equilibrium with the medium. The energy difference between $(Q_B^-)^*$ and equilibrium state Q_B^- is estimated as 0. 09 V. The slow transition is assumed to be gated by a conformational change at $\approx$ 100 μs. Another kinetic model suggests a formation of conformationally excited primary acceptor $(Q_A^-)^*$ followed by fast ET to Q_B.

The electron transfer from the primary donor P to the secondary acceptor Q_B is coupled to two protons uptake followed by exchange of doubly reduced Q_BH_2 for Q_B from the cytoplasm (Witt, 1996). The high-resolution x-ray diffraction study revealed in the "dark" structure two water channels, P1 and P2 leading from the Q_B pocket to the surface of the protein on the cytoplasmic side of the RC. These channels have been assumed to deliver protons to photo reduced states Q_B and Q_BH^-. The GluH173 in the "light" structure, located along the P2 channel, is disordered compared to this group in the "dark" structure.

The pathway for proton transfer to Q_B is studied in the reaction center (RC) from Rb. sphaeroides using two approaches (Ädelroth et al., 2001): 1) the binding of Zn^{2+} or Cd^{2+} to the RC surface at His-H126, His-H128, and Asp-H124 and 2) the replacement of the histidines for Ala. In the double mutant RC at pH 8.5, the observed rates of proton uptake associated with both the first and the second proton-coupled electron-transfer reactions $k_{AB}^{(1)}$ [$Q_A^-Q_B$-Glu$^-$ + H$^+$ →$Q_A^{-\bullet}Q_B$-GluH →$Q_AQ_B^{-\bullet}$-GluH] and $k_{AB}^{(2)}$ [$Q_A^{-\bullet}$ $Q_B^{-\bullet}$ + H$^+$ →$Q_A^{-\bullet}$(Q_BH)

3.5.2. PLANT PHOTOSYNTHESIS

In oxygenic photosynthetic organisms, plant and green bacteria, the reaction centers of two systems PS I and PS II convert the absorbed light energy into energy of stable products, i.e. ferredoxin and dioxygen (Witt 1996 and references therin) PS I from plants and cyanobacteria mediates light-induced electron transfer from plastocyanin to ferredoxin (flavodoxin) at the stromal membrane side, while PS II is a photoenzyme that catalyzes oxidation of the water in a water-splitting Mn-containing system (Dismukes al., 2000). Subsequent absorption of four light quanta by PS I and PS II results in evaluation of dioxygen from a two water molecule. The overall process occurs by the following scheme:

$$4h\upsilon$$
$$2H_2O + 4 \text{ [ferredoxin (oxidized)]} \rightarrow O_2 + \text{[ferredoxin (reduced)]} + 4H^+$$

The key step of the process is the water splitting under absorption of light quanta of relative low energy. Here we will focus mainly on the latter process which appears to be one of the most enigmatic reactions in chemistry and photochemistry and will only briefly consider the light energy conversion reaction centers of PS I and PS II.

Reaction centers of PS I and PS II.
PS I from cyanobacteria consist of 11 protein subunits and several cofactors. After the photoexcitation of the primary donor, a dimer of chlorophyll a (Chla)$_2$, P700, an electron is transferred via a chlorophyll (A$_0$) to a phylloquinone (A$_1$) and then to the iron sulfur clusters, F$_x$, F$_A$ and F$_B$. (Witt, 1996;Itoh et al., 2000)).

Data on chrystallographic models PS I from cyanobacteria have been reported (Jordan et. al., 2001). PS I from S. elongates contains nine protein subunits featuring transmembrane α-helices and three stromal sububits. The organic cofactors are arranged in two branches along the pseudo-C2 axis. The distances between adjacent donor and acceptor centers of the system vary from 8.2 to 14.9 Å for the "right" brunch (A) and from 8.6 to 22 Å for the "left" brunch (B). Therefore, "non-conducting" zones similar to those in the bacterial RC separate the centers.

The time scale of different steps of electron transfer along the PS I cascade system is also similar to those of the electron jump in bacterial RCs. The primary transfer from the excited chlorophyll dimer, primary donor P*, to A$_0$ takes place with a time constant of about 25 ps. The next step from A$_0$ to a secondary acceptor occurs in 200-600 ps. The recombination time constants of P$^+$ with reduced intermediate acceptors increase as the electron moves along the chain, and range from nanoseconds for transition A$_0^-$ → P$^+$ to millseconds for transition reduce FX to P$^+$ (Shuvalov and Krasnovsky, 1981; Schloder et al., 1998; Shmidt et al., 2000; Shmidt et al., Guergova-Kuras et. al., 2001; Setif et al., 2001; Vassiliev et all., 2001; Gobets et al., 2001 and references therein). Kinetic and spectral inhomogenity of samples of PS I has been reported (Shmidt et al., 2000;

Melkozernov et al., 2001). According to kinetic investigation (Guergova-Kuras et al., 2001), electron transfer in PS I involves both brunches with different rate constants of 35×10^6 s^{-1} (brunch B) and 4.4×10^6 s^{-1} (brunch A) for the ET from each phylloquinone to the iron-sulfur cluster F_X.

The FS I primary donor has very high positive redox potential of about 1.17 V in contrast to 0.4 –O.6 V for other oxidized primary donors in photosynthesis and in solution. Values of enthalpy ($\Delta H^0 \approx$ -0.33 ev) and entropy ($\Delta S^0 \approx$ + 0.4 e.u.) for the formation of ion pair P700$^+$F$_{AB}^-$ in the intact cells of Synechocystiss PCC 6803 and in vitro are determined using pulsed, time resolved photoacoustics (Boichenko et al., 2001). The electronic structure of the PS I donor and acceptor centers is investigated by the whole set of modern physical methods, including ESR, ENDOR, FT-IS, etc. (Nogushi et. al., 1999; Rigbi et. al., 2000; Kim et. al., 2001; and references therein). The orientation of the primary donor cation radical (P700$^{\cdot +}$) in the single crystals of photosystem I from the thermophylic cyanobacterium *Synechococcus elongates* is investigated by ESR and ENDOR techniques (Käss et al., 2001). The orientation is found to be similar to those in the purple bacteria. The similarity of direction of the principle axes of the P700$^{\cdot +}$ g-tensor in single crystals of PS I and in bacterial reaction centers is demonstrated by X$^-$, Q$^-$, and W-band ESR spectroscopy (Zech et al., 2000).

The dependence of the logarithm of the rate constants of electron transfer (log k$_{ET}$) between the donor (D) and acceptor (A) centers on the D-A distances is similar to the correspondent dependence for the superexchange attenuation coefficient (log γ_{ET}) (Fig.2.6). Therefore, we can conclude that, similar to primary events in RCs from bacteria, the primary fast electron transfers take place as nonadiabatic and conformationally nonequilibrium processes.

Investigations of structure, protein sequence and kinetics of the photosynthetic centers from photosystem II and from purple bacteria have confirmed relevance to both structures (Fig.3.18) (Michel and Deisenhofer, 1988; Noguchi et al., 1999; Mino et al. 2000; Gerken et al, 1988; Gibasievich et al., 2001; Boichenko et al., 2001; Rhee, 2001; and references therein). The FS II RC is a complex consisting of perepheryl and integral thylakoid proteins including chlorophyll A dimer (P680), two pheophytin A (Ph$_A$) molecules, two plastoquinones molecules (Q$_{AP}$ and Q$_{BP}$), and one atom non-heme iron atom. (Fig. 3.19). In addition, FS II also includes four Mn-containing water-oxidizing complexes (WOC).

The charge separation photoelectron pathway across the membrane, P680$^* \rightarrow$ Ph$_A \rightarrow$ Q$_{AP} \rightarrow$ Q$_{BP}$, is similar to those in the bacterial RCs. The Q$_{BP}$, after receiving two electrons and two protons, is replaced by a plasma plastoquinone. The most important function of the FSII reaction center is the oxidation of a water splitting manganese cluster with photooxidized P680$^+$. This process runs via an intermediate, redox active tyrosine (D1 Tyr 161). P680*. The P680$^* \rightarrow$ Ph$_A$ transfer occurs for about 10 ps, followed by the transfer from Ph$_A^-$ to Q$_{AP}$ (300 ps) (Witt, 1996). P68* is reduced by tyrosine (D1 Tyr 161) for the time constant within nano- and microsecond regions (Shuvalov and Krasnovsky, 1981; Gerken et al., 1988; Anderson, 2001; and references therein). The existence of a specific channel connecting the water molecules bound to WOS and the tylakoid membrane surface has been suggested (Anderson, 2001).

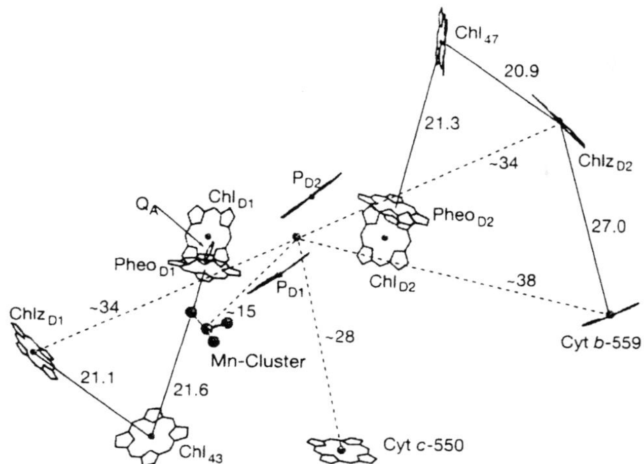

Figure 3.19. Crystal structure of photo system II from(Synechoccus elongatus)(Zouni, et al., 2001). Reproduced with permission.

Water splitting Mn-containing system

Manganese has long been assumed to play a role in the photosynthetic decomposition of water by plants. In the classical work of Koch and subsequent investigations (Koch et al., 1970; Widrzynski and Sauer, 1980; Covindjee et al., 1985; Shutilova, 2000; Yagi and Kaneko, 2001; Dismukes, 2001; Dismukes et al., 2000; Carrell et al., 2002) the key role of Mn has been confirmed. It was shown that for O_2 to be evolved four light flashes are required. In the currently adopted terminology, the redox state of the O_2 evolution system is designated as S_0, S_1, S_2, S_3, S_4 in accordance with the number of electrons transferred from the complex. After prolonged dark adaptation the complex is found in the S_1 state. The evolution of O_2 is realized in the presence inorganic ligands Cl^- and Ca^{2+}.

Photosystem II containes four Mn atoms in the complex attached to a protein. The cluster nature of the complex has been convincingly demonstrated by a whole arsenal of physical and biochemical methods. As an example, in the work of Kulikov et al., (1983), manganese was first removed from a preparation of FS II; then Mn was gradually introduced. The magnetic state of the Mn complex was traced by the extent of saturation of the ESR signal of the anion radical of pheophytin. The incorporation of one Mn atom into the system sharply charges the saturation curve parameters of the ESR signal; the introduction of the second Mn atom removes this effect. A third Mn atom again affects on the saturated curve, while the incorporation of further Mn atoms into the medium has no effect the ESR spectrum. Multiple evidence for strong magnetic interaction within four-nuclear Mn cluster were reported in 1970's and 1980's by the ESR method (Evans et a., 2000, 1977; Yocum et al., 1981; De Paula et al. 1986; Hoff, 1986; Dismukes, 1986; Govingee et al., 1985) and was confirmed in recent investigations (Matsukava et al, 1999; Hanley et al., 2000; Ioannidis and Petrouleas, 2000; Yagi and Kaneko, 2001; and references therein).

The S_0 state is ESR silent but methanol is required to observe the multiline ESR spectrum (Evans et al., 2000). The S_1 state is characterized by ESR signal at $g = 4.8$ and a multilane signal at $g = 12$. The S_2 state exposes the $S = \frac{1}{2}$ multilane signal at $g = 2$ and $S \geq 3/2$ at $g = 4.1$ (Onado et. al., 2000; Boussac and Rutherford, 2000). At near IR (T > 60 K) illumination the $S = 1/2$ signal is reversibly converted to the $g = 4.1$ signal via intermediate $S \geq 5/2$ state with $g = 10$ and 6. Strongly anisotropic low-field ESR signals $S = 1$ at $g = 6.7 - 12$ are attributed to the S_3 state (Ioannidis and Petrouleas, 2000). The authors detect these signals after illumination of FS II membranes, in which the non-heme iron is chemically preoxidized. During iIllumination of the low-field the S_3 state with near infrared light at temperature 50 K produces the in appearance of a broad radical-type signal at $g = 2$.

A combination of physical methods such as ESR, ESEEM, EXAFS, XAS, FTIR, Resonace Raman spectroscopy and UV-absorbance spectroscopy indicates that the oxygen-evolving complex (OEC) consists of a pair of di-μ-oxo bridged Mn dimers. The use of the EXAFS method has indicated that the Mn-Mn distance is about 2,7 Å (Meinke et al., 2000 and references therein). At room-temperature, distances between Mn and ligands of 3.10 and 3.65 Å are found by EXAFS The tetranuclear manganese complex is investigated by X-ray absorption spectroscopy on PS II particles at 18 and 296 K in the dark stable state S_1, seemingly $Mn(III)_2Mn(IV)_2$. At both temperatures the same Mn-Mn distance of 2.71-2.72 Å is measured. Such a distance is typical for model Mn_2 di-μ-oxo Mn-(m-oxo)-Mn compounds. In these compounds Mn-(μ-oxo)-Mn vibrations have an intensive and characteristic FTIR absorpton around 600-700 cm^{-1}. The 606 cm-1 vibrational mode was detected in the partially degraduated PS II samples in the S_2 state has been attributed to the Mn-(μ-oxo)-Mn structure (Chu et al., 2000). It was shown that the bridged oxygen atom in the cluster is exchangeable and accessible by water. An ESR signal ($g = 2$, line width of 1600 G is trapped by treatment of the FS II with NO at -30 °C (Hanley et al., 2000). The orientation dependence of the ESR spectrum with respect to the thylakoid membrane was studied. The results suggest that the Mn -(μ-oxo)- Mn plane makes an angle$\approx 20°$ with the membrane plane and the axis connecting the bridging oxygens parallel to the plane.

It is suggested that the four Mn atoms of WOC consist of a pair of di-μ-oxo bridged manganese clusters linked by a mono-μ-oxo bridge, one calcium atom, and one chlor atom (Yachandra et al., 1993). Nevertheless, analazing data on spin densities derived from ^{55}Mn hyperfine structure in the S_3 state ESR spectrum and XAS, together with data on the evolution of O_2, Dismukes and his colleagues (Carrell et al., 2002) have suggested two feasible models for the reactive S_4, a calcium-capped "cuboidal" core and a calcium-capped "funnel" core.

The photooxidized PS II primary donor P700$^+$ is re-reduced with time constant > 10 ms, a change of the UV-difference spectrum at 260 nm and 310 nm and an appearance of ESR signal at $g = 2$ and $S = \frac{1}{2}$ (Gerken et al., 1988 and references therein). This state was attributed to a neutral radical of Tyr-160, which is an intermediate acceptor for the Mn-custer oxidation. The tyrosyl radical and the plastoquinone ananion radical, Q_{AP}^- were shown to have different vibrational lines in the difference FTIR spectrum, a positive 1478 cm^{-1} line and positive (1482 cm^{-1} and 1469 cm^{-1}) for the former and latter species, respectively (Kim, et al., 2001).

High-frequency ESR spectroscopy at 94 GHz is used to study the dark-stable tyrosine radical YD· in single crystals of photosystem II isolated from the thermophilic cyanobacterium *Synechococcus elongates* (Hofbauer, et al., 2001). Magnitude and orientation of the g tensor of YD· and related information on several proton hyperfine tensors are deduced from analysis of angular-dependent EPR spectra. The flash-induced Fourier transform IR (FTIR) difference spectrum of the oxygen-evolving Mn cluster upon S_1-to-S_2 transition indicates that in FS II from Synechocystis 6803 a tyrosine residue specifically labeled with ^{13}C at the ring-4 position, is coupled to the Mn cluster, and the vibrational modes of this tyrosine are affected upon S_2 formation (Noguchi and Tang, 1997). It is suggested that the Mn cluster and a tyrosine are linked via chemical and/or hydrogen bonds and the structural changes of the Mn cluster are transmitted to the tyrosine through these bonds.

Experiments on the binding of Mn^{2+} to manganese-depleted photosystem II and electron donation from the bound Mn^{2+} to an oxidized tyrosine have showed that only one tightly bound manganese is essential for electron transfer. Pulsed ESR studies in the oriented Ca^{2+} depleted FS II membranes (Mino et al., 2000) indicate that an angle between the vector connecting the tyrosin radical YD with a center, which exposes a doublet ESR signal, and the plane of the tylakoid membrane, is about 8°. A functional role for tyrosine-D in the assembly of the inorganic core of the water oxidation complex of photosystem II and the kinetics of water oxidation was discussed by Ananyev et al., (2002).

Efforts have been undertaken to evolve both state and dynamics of water molecules in the Mn-cluster. Biphasic rapid isotope exchange beween bulk water and substrate water in the S_3 state of spinach Photosystem II has been detected (Hiller et al., 1998). Two first order exchange rate constants are determined from measurement of $^{18}O_2$ release after injection of $H_2^{18}O$ at 10 °C, fast ($k_1 = 38$ s^{-1}) and slow ($k_2 = 2.2$ s^{-1}). The activation energies of the fast and slow processes are estimated as 9.3 and 18.6 kcal/mole, correspondingly. These results are considered as evidence that two water molecules bind at two separate binding sites. Evidence for the presence of a component of the Mn complex of the Photsystem II which has been exposed to water in the S_2 state of the water oxidation complex, has been obtained by the ESEEM method (Evans et al., 2000). The experiments indicated that water protons locate within 3-5 Å of part of the Mn complex. The use of Fourier transform infrared (FTIR) spectroscopy with a combination of replacement $H_2^{16}O$ by $H_2^{18}O$ and D_2O allows the detection O-H stretching vibrations of a water molecule coupled to the Mn-cluster in the S_1 and S_2 states (Noguchi and Sugiura, 2000). It is shown that one of the molecules of the O-H group is weakly H-bond and other is strongly H-bonded. This H-bonding asymmetry becomes more prominent upon the S_1-to-S_2 transition. The authors suggest that such structural change might facilitate the proton release reaction by lowering the potential barrier.

In Photsystem II, the water oxidation with evolution of dioxygen occurs under the action of a relatively mild oxidant: the cation of chlorophyll which is the product of one-electron oxidation with redox potential $E_0 = 1.1$ eV (Anderson, 2001). The potentials of the oxidation of water by one-, two- and four electron mechanisms are equal to 2.7 V (hydroxyl radical), 1.36 V (hydrogen proxide), and 0.81 (dioxygen). Enclosed in paranthesis are the products evolved in the most endothermic step of the oxidation process. It is evident that under the condition of biological photosynthesis, the thermodynamically favorable pathway (the smoothest thermodynamic profile of the reaction) can be provided only by a four-electron mechanism (Section 2.5), in which dioxygen is evolved from two water molecules in one elementary act (Semenov et al., 1975; Likhtenshtein et al., 1979; Likhtenshtein, 1988). It was predicted that such a mechanism could be realized under mild conditions only by the involvement of a cluster of transition metals, which would be able to accumulate, step by step, four oxidizing equivalents and to accept four electrons from two deprotonated water molecules. Therefore, the evolution the O_2 from water in the Photosystem II manganese may be described as sequences of steps: four one-electron steps of oxidation of the Mn-cluster and one four-electron step of O_2 evolution.

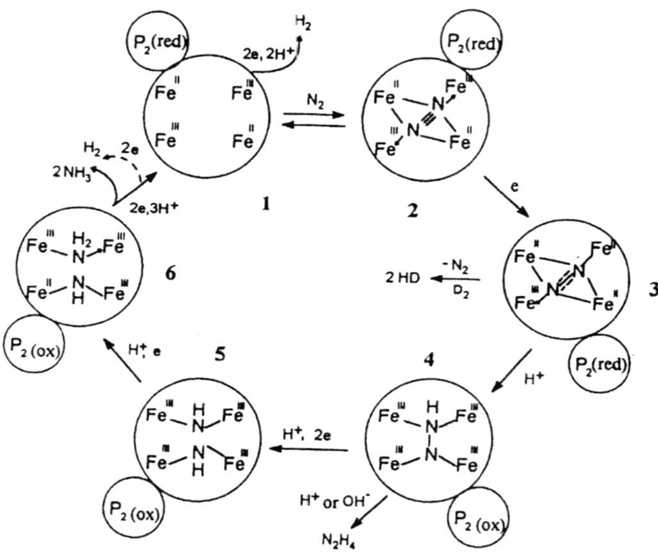

Figure 3.20. Suggested model of primary reactions of oxygenic photosynthesis (Witt, 1996) Reproduced with permission.

According to the suggested simplified scheme (Likhtenshtein, 1988a), one-electron steps are accompanied by the evolution of a proton that contributes to the preservation of the total charge of the complex and considerably simplifies the last, key step of the process. Participation of all four Mn atoms in the four electron transfer from ligand to the cluster provides minimum reorganization energy in this thermodynamically allowed process and, therefore, contributes of the fast running process. Recently suggested model of the quaternary water-oxidizing S-state cycle and its coupling with light-induced electron transfer from P 680 to Q_A is presented in Fig. 3.20.

According to Dismukes and coauthors (Carrel et. al., 2002) the state S_2 has states attributed to $Mn_4(3III,IV)$ structure. Thus, we can consider the structure of the dioxygen evolving state S_3 as $Mn_4(IV)$. It has been suggested that Ca^{2+} binding increases the Mn-ligand covalency by increasing electron transfer from shared ligands to Mn. The coordination of two water molecules to two different manganese atoms cannot be excluded (Hiller et al., 1998).

CHAPTER 4

SOME PROTEIN PROPERTIES IMPORTANT FOR ENZYME CATALYSIS

4.1. Intramolecular dynamics and conformational transition in enzymes

4.1.1. OVERVIEW

The present conception of the intramolecular dynamics of proteins is based on a hypothesis put forward in the 1950's and 1960's. First, Lumry and Eyring (1954) assumed that substrate-enzyme interaction was accompanied by a certain structural distortion of both substrate and enzyme. Later, this concept developed into the theory of "complementarity" of the free energy of the chemical reaction in the enzyme-active centre and the enzyme conformational free energy (Lumry and Biltonen, 1969). In this theory, energy redistribution occurs in such a way that the energy profile of the process as a whole is eventually flattened. Another basis for the modern concept of protein molecular dynamics is the Linderstrom-Lang hypothesis regarding the structural fluctuation of the protein macromolecule, which is visible in the ability of inner peptide groups to exchange hydrogen atoms for water protons (Linderstrom-Lang and Schellmann, 1959). According to the Koshland induced-fit theory (Koshland, 1959) the conformational structure of the enzyme can be induced to fit the structure of the substrate during their interaction.

At a later stage, the concepts of protein dynamics were supplemented by the principle of the dynamic adaptation of the enzyme conformational structure to the substrate configuration in consecutive reactions to the enzyme. Such an adaptation promotes both the first step of precise orientation and the subsequent chemical steps, without allowing cleavage of the contacts needed for the chemical mechanism (Likhtenshtein, 1976, 1988a).

In the 1960's and 1970's, much indirect evidence was obtained in favour of protein intramolecular mobility, i.e. the entropy and energy specificity of enzyme catalysis (Likhtenshtein, 1966, 1976a, b, 1979, 1988; Lumry and Rajender, 1970; Lumry and Gregory, 1986). The first observations made concerned the transglobular conformational transition during substrate-protein interaction (Likhtenshtein, 1976), the reactivity of functional groups inside the protein globule, and proteolysis.

From the late 1960's to the early 1970's, more direct approaches to the investigation of protein dynamics were intensively developed. Such investigations featured the application of physical methods, such as physical labeling, NMR, optical spectroscopy, fluorescence, differential scanning calorimetry, and X-ray and neutron scattering. The purposeful application of the approaches made it possible to obtain detailed information on the mobility of different parts of protein globules and to compare this mobility with both the functional characteristics and stability of proteins, and with results of the theoretical calculation of protein dynamics.

Besides indirect kinetic methods of hydrogen exchange, proteolysis and the availability of buried functional groups and analysis of the activation parameters mentioned above, a wide range of physical methods are used for the study of the intramolecular dynamics and adjacent solvent molecules (Table 4.1). The joint application of these methods makes it possible to study intramolecular mobility over an extensive range of characteristic correlation frequencies ($\tau_c^{-1} = 10^{-3} - 10^{14}$ s^{-1}) and over a wide range of amplitudes (A = 0.01 - 15 Å). A general limitation of the above-mentioned methods is that they commonly allow information to be obtained on the average dynamical parameters of the system being studied.

In addition to the direct methods of studying molecular dynamics, several physical methods, indirect but nonetheless providing valuable complementary information, are applied to the solving of dynamical problems. Among them are such methods as X-ray diffraction (Frauenfelder, and McMahon 2001; Frauenfelder et al., 1991, 2001), thermal broadening of chromophore absorption (Di Pace et al., 1992), and heat capacity (Lumry and Gregory, 1986).

The essential contribution when tackling the problem, especially at the early stages of the study of protein dynamics, was the development and use of biophysical labelling methods (McConnel and McFarland, 1970; Park and Trommer, 1989; Trommer and Vogel 1992; Likhtenshtein, 1876a, b, 1978, 1979, 1988, 1993; Seiter et al. 1996; Likhtenshtein et al., 2000; Berliner, 1976, 1979; Waggoner, 1986; Lakowicz, 1981; Palm et al. 2001; Vogel, 2000; Hammerström et al., 2001). The basic idea underlying the physical labelling approach is the modification of the chosen sites of the object in question by specific compounds, which are bound covalently (labels) and/or non-covalently (probes), whose properties make it possible to trace the state of the surrounding biological matrix by appropriate physical methods. The following main types of compounds are used as labels and probes to monitor the dynamic parameters of proteins: (1) centers with unpaired electrons (stable nitroxide radicals, radical pairs and paramagnetic complexes) which exhibit electron spin resonance (ESR), (2) luminescent fluorescence and phosphorescence chromophores, and (3) Mössbauer atoms (e.g. ^{57}Fe) which yield the nuclear γ-resonance (NGR) spectra.

The principle advantage of the physical labeling method is the possibility of receiving direct information about the structure, mobility and local micropolarity of certain parts of a molecular object of any molecular mass. Developments in synthetic chemistry, biochemistry and site-directed mutagenesis have provided researchers with a wide assortment of labels and probes, and have paved the way for the specific modification of protein function groups, including enzyme active sites.

Biophysical labeling methods provide a unique possibility for monitoring local intermolecular dynamics properties in a wide range of correlation times ($\tau_c = 10^2 - 10^{-10}$ s). They enable the investigation of the dynamics of different parts of protein globules in the vicinity of the spin, fluorescence, phosphorescence and Mössbauer labels under various conditions (temperatures 30 -330 K, water content, viscosity, substrates and inhibitor additions, etc.). The experiments revealed the following tendency: appropriate physical methods detect the mobility of labels starting from the temperature of liquid nitrogen; the lower the value of the characteristic frequency of the method, the lower the temperature at which the label mobility can be recorded. Thus, the mobility recorded results from a gradual softening of the protein-water matrix, rather than from an individual phase transition. At physiological ambient conditions, all labeling methods indicate the mobility of labels and surrounding media in the nanosecond temporal region.

Since the late 1970's, molecular dynamics simulation (MDS) has been proven a powerful tool for the study of protein intermolecular dynamics (McCommon et al., 1977,; McCommon and Harvey, 1987; Brooks et al., 1988; Karplus and McCammon, 1986; Karplus and Petsko, 1990; and references therein).

TABLE 4.1. A brief characterization of physical methods used to investigate protein dynamics. (Likhtenshtein et al., 2000a). Reproduced with permission.

Method	Parameters measured	Information obtained[a]
IR and Raman spectroscopy	Spectra	$v_c = 10^{12}\text{-}10^{14}\ s^{-1}$
Fluorescence	Depolarization	$\tau_c^{-1} = 10^8\text{-}10^9\ s^{-1}$
	Radiation autocorrelation	$\tau_c^{-1} = 10^8\text{-}10^9\ s^{-1}$
	Relaxational shift	$\tau_c^{-1} = 10^8\text{-}10^9\ s^{-1}$
	Quenching by reagents	$k_{tran} = 10^8\text{-}10^{10}\ M^{-1}\ s^{-1}$
Phosphorescence	Depolarization	$\tau_c^{-1} = 10^{-1}\text{-}10^6\ s^{-1}$
	Relaxational shift	$\tau_c^{-1} = 10^{-1}\text{-}10^6\ s^{-1}$
	Quenching by the exchange mechanism	$\tau_c^{-1} = 10^8\text{-}10^9\ s^{-1}$
Rayleigh scattering	Doppler shift of frequency	$\tau_c^{-1} = 10^9\text{-}10^{10}\ s^{-1}$
	Line broadening	$\tau_c^{-1} = 10\text{-}10^7\ s^{-1}$
Newton non-elastic scattering		$\tau_c^{-1} = 10^{10}\text{-}10^{13}\ s^{-1}$
Spin labeling	Shape of absorption lines	$\tau_c^{-1} = 10^7\text{-}10^{10}\ s^{-1}$
	Saturation transfer parameters	$\tau_c^{-1} = 10^4\text{-}10^6\ s^{-1}$
	Quenching by paramagnetics	$k_{tran} = 10^6\text{-}10^{10}\ M^{-1}\ s^{-1}$
Recombination-kinetic method	Kinetics of radical recombination	$k_{tran} = 10\text{-}10^8\ M^{-1}\ s^{-1}$
Mossbauer labels	Recoil-less absorption	$\tau_c^{-1} = 10^7\ s^{-1}$
	Diffusion line broadening	$\tau_c^{-1} = 10^7\ s^{-1}$
Dielectric measurement	Absorption and dispersion of electromagnetic radiation	$\tau_c^{-1} = 10^3\text{-}10^{10}\ s^{-1}$
Ultrasonic methods	Sound absorption and dispersion	$\tau_c^{-1} = 10^5\text{-}10^9\ s^{-1}$
NMR	Line splitting in high resolution spectra	$\tau_c^{-1} = 10\text{-}10^3\ s^{-1}$
	Frequency and temperature dependencies T_1 and T_2	$\tau_c^{-1} = 10^4\text{-}10^{10}\ s^{-1}$
	Relaxation in the magnetic field gradient	$\tau_c^{-1} = 10^7\text{-}10^{10}\ s^{-1}$
	Narrowing of broad line	$\tau_c^{-1} = 10\text{-}10^4\ s^{-1}$

[a] τ_c^{-1} is the correlation frequency; k_{tran} is the rate constant of collisions; τ_{tran}^{-1} is the translational jump time.

4.1.2 LOW TEMPERATURE PROTEIN DYNAMICS

Molecular-dynamical processes at sub-zero temperatures appear interesting for a number of reasons: 1) some biological reactions including electron transfer were found to occur at low temperatures; 2) cryoprotection of proteins and enzymes against denaturation and deactivation is an important method in biotechnology and in the investigation of enzymatic mechanisms; and 3) comparison of data of molecular dynamics and enzymic functions at sub-zero and ambient temperatures paves the way for elucidating which dynamical modes can be responsible for the enzymatic activity and stability of the object under investigation.

The first direct experimental evidence of the intramolecular mobility of a protein matrix at low temperatures was obtained using spin and Mössbauer labels and probes in the 1970's (Likhtenshtein et al., 1969, 1974, 1976a, b, 1979a, b; Frolov et al., 1973, 1974, 1977; Belonogova et al., 1978, 1979). Thus, a hydrophobic aromatic derivative of a nitroxide radical was embedded in the human serum albumin binding site and the mobility of the spin probe was traced by ESR spectroscopy. This conclusion was further supported by the investigation of the mobility of Mössbauer atoms ^{57}Fe, which were attached as a metal-complex to the surface of an HSA globule and incorporated as a polynuclear serum-iron cluster within the globule. The experiment performed in the temperature range 77-300 K showed a sharp decrease in NGR spectra intensity (f) at temperatures exceeding 210 K. Such a change is caused by an anharmonic vibration of the Mössbauer atom whose correlation frequency is about 10^7 s^{-1} and whose amplitude is A > 0.4 Å at T > 210 K.

Subsequent systematic studies of the intramolecular mobility of bovine (BSA) and human (HSA) serum albumins, lysozyme, myoglobin, α-chymotrypsin, ferredoxin and bacterial photosynthetic reactions over a wide temperature range (20-300 K) by the combined use of biophysical labeling methods (radical-pair, spin, fluorescence, phosphorescence, Mössbauer labeling) and NMR allowing the motion to be studied at a frequency of $\upsilon_c = 10^{-2} - 10^{10}$ s^{-1} has revealed a general picture of the dynamic effects in these proteins (Likhtenshtein, 1985; 1988a, b, 1993a, b; Likhtenshtein and Kotelnikov, 1983; Likhtenshtein et al., 1983, 1986, 2000). Starting from 40 K, the broadening of the width ($\Delta H_{1/2}$) of the ESR signal from the spin label attached to the HSA surface was observed, showing an intensification of vibrational processes. At increasing temperatures, the general tendency is as follows: the lower the value of the characteristic frequency of the method, the lower the temperature at which the label mobility can be monitored. In a wide temperature range (130-300 K), the experimental data for surface labels follow an Arrhenius straight line, with E_{app} = 16 kcal/mole and $\Delta S^{\#}_{app}$ = 38 e.u. Thus, the recorded mobility stems from a gradual softening of the water-protein interface, rather than from an individual phase transition. Dynamical effects in serum albumins studied by biophysical labeling techniques are illustrated in Fig. 3.18. (see Section 3.5.1.). The mobility of the hydrophobic aromatic spin probe in the hydrophobic binding site of HSA was described by the following parameters: E_{app} = 4.8 kcal/mole and $\Delta S^{\#}_{app}$ = 5.5 e.u. in the temperature range 80 -280 K. The spin, fluorescence and Mössbauer label mobility at $\upsilon_c > 10^7$ s^{-1} increases from approximately 200 K upwards and reaches nanosecond range in physiological temperatures. This fact was independently confirmed later by the data for the Rayleigh scattering of the Mössbauer radiation. According to this data, the intensity of the scattering increases dramatically at T > 200 K.

Recent studies have confirmed the basic inferences highlighted in the works cited earlier (Krupyanskii et al,, 1980; Parak et al., 1982; Krinichnyi, 1991, 1994; Krinichnyi at al., 1985; Smith et al., 1989; Doster et al., 1989; Likhtenshtein, 1993, 1996; Likhtenshtein et al., 2000; Shaw et al, 1995; Nishimoto et al., 1998; Miyzakiet al., 2000; Dvorsky et al., 2000; Vincentm et al., 2000; Vitkup et al., 2000; Leo et al., 2000; Tsai et al., 2000; Terek et al., 2000; Palmer, 2001; Palmer et al., 1989, 2001; Rozovscy, and McDermott 2001). These results agree with the mean displacement values obtained for separate myoglobin atoms $<\Delta x>_{cs}$, which were calculated on the basis of the X-ray diffraction data and relate to the conformational substrates. Fig. 6a and b demonstrate a correlation between the temperature dependencies of non-harmonic parameters of Mössbauer atoms in heme, the heme spectra Soret band Gaussian broadening, non-elastic neutron scattering, and molecular dynamics simulation in myoglobin. According to these data, the anharmonic intramolecular mobility of proteins increases dramatically at $T > 200$ K. This conclusion was confirmed by low-temperature experiments with the use of the fluorescence dynamic Stokes shift, neutron scattering and molecular dynamics simulation in other proteins, superoxide dismutase, lysozyme, elastase, bacterriorodopsin, and Rnase (Smith et al., 1989; Doster et al., 1989; Zhou et al. 1998; Dvorsky et al., 2000; Vincentm et al., 2000; Vitkup et al., 2000; Leo et al., 2000; Tsai et al., 2000; Tarek et al., 2000; Diaz et.al., 2001; and references therein).

It is necessary to stress that the anharmonic nanosecond dynamics of the proteins recorded with labeling methods only appear if the water content of the sample being studied exceeds a critical value by about $10 - 25$ %. The critical degree of hydration depends on the protein's nature and temperature and on the nature of the solvent, in the presence of cryoprotectors in particular (Likhtenshtein, 1976a, b, 1979a, b, 1988, 1993; Likhtenshtein and Kotelnikov, 1983; Likhtenshtein et al., 2000; Frolov et al., 1973, 1977; Belonogova et al., 1978;). A study of neutron scattering within the molecular dynamics of solid-state lysozyme showed a significant effect of glycerol and water on dynamic transition temperatures (T_d) (Tsai et al., 2000). T_d was not detected in the dehydrated protein but was found to be equal to 210 and 270 K in samples containing 30% D_2O 50% glycerol, respectively. At subzero temperatures the intramolecular dynamics of enzyme xylase in the picosecond time scale was studied by neutron scattering and computer simulation methods (Reat et al., 2000). It was shown that the normalized integrated elastic intensity dropped drastically at 220 K in rigid solution (D_2O and mixtures CD_3OD/D_2O, and $DMSO/D2$) but not in dry samples. The importance of solvent mobility for protein dynamics at temperatures above 180 K was demonstrated by molecular dynamics simulation (Vitkup et al., 2000).

4.1.3. PROTEIN DYNAMICS AT AMBIENT TEMPERATURE

In 1950, while analysing data on the binding of organic molecules to bovine serum albumin (BSA), Karush reached a conclusion on the flexibility of the protein binding site structure. It was later discovered that the binding of a substrate in the binding site of albumins causes a change in the conformation of the protein globule. By way of example, a change was observed in the rotational mobility of the spin labels located at a distance greater than 16 Å from the binding site, into which steroid molecules were introduced (Sergeev et al., 1976). This was accompanied by a change of spin dipole-dipole interaction of the labels with water protons, which was monitored by the rate of the proton spin relaxation by NMR.

The direct experimental evidence of the nanosecond intramolecular mobility of a protein matrix at ambient temperatures was obtained using spin and Mössbauer labels and probes (Likhtenshtein, 1976a, b, 1979a, b; Likhenshtein et al., 1969; Frolov et al., 1973, 1974, 1977; Belonogova et al., 1978), employing the phenomenon of fluorescence quenching of the buried tryptophane residues (Lackovicz and Weber, 1973; Munro et al., 1979), and NMR (Wutrich, 1986). To illustrate, a hydrophobic aromatic derivative of a nitroxide radical was embedded in the human serum albumin binding site and the mobility of the spin probe was traced by ESR spectroscopy. The apparent correlation frequency ($\upsilon_c = 10^8$ s^{-1}) of the probe, which is essentially faster than macromolecular tumbling, was not found to be dependent on viscosity and, therefore, was attributed to the local mobility of the label. The apparent energy ($E_{app} = 2.5$ kcal/mole) and entropy ($\Delta S^{\#}_{app} = 15.0$ e.u.) activation were determined. Thus, it was concluded that probe mobility follows the mobility of the flexible walls of the protein binding site with a similar frequency.

This conclusion was strongly supported by the investigation of the mobility of Mössbauer atoms ^{57}Fe, which were attached as a metal-complex to the surface of an HSA globule and incorporated as a polynuclear serum-iron cluster within the globule. The experiment showed a sharp decrease in NGR spectra intensity (f) at temperatures exceeding 210 K. Such a change is caused by an anharmonic vibration of the Mössbauer atom whose correlation frequency is higher than 10^7 s^{-1} and whose amplitude is A > 0.4 Å at T > 210 K. The serum albumin intramolecular mobility in a nanosecond temporary region at ambient temperatures was confirmed later by a series of independent dynamical methods such as spin and fluorescence labeling, tryptophane fluorescence and proton NMR (Likhtenshtein and Kotelnikov, 1983; Krynichny et al., 1985; Likhtenshtein, 1988a, b, 1993; Likhtenshtein et al., 1993; Vogel et al., 1994; Likhtenshtein et al., 2000)

Recently, the dynamics of the HSA binding site around the dansyl moiety of the dual fluorophore-nitroxide probe was monitored indirectly by the temperature dependent relaxation shift $\Delta\lambda^{fl}_{max}$ (T) and directly using the picosecond fluorescent time-resolved technique (see Fig. 1.4. in Section 1.1.3.) (Rubtsova et al., 1993; Fogel et al., 1994; Lozinsky et al., 2000; 2002; Likhtenshtein, et al., 2000). Both methods showed that the relaxation of the protein groups in the vicinity of the excited chromophore occurs with a rate constant of approximately 10^9 s^{-1}. Polarization fluorescence technique experiments showed rotational mobility of the probe fluorophore fragment with the correlation frequency $\approx 10^9$ s^{-1}. 2-(2'-Hydroxyphenyl)-methloxazole (PMO), a proton-transfer fluoresecent dye was used as a probe for the study of HAS hydrophobic binding site dynamics (Zhong et al., 2000). The observed dynamics indicated that the binding structure is rigid and the local motions of the probe are nearly "frozen" in the femtosecond-to-nanosecond time scale. The probe intramolecular twisting of the two heterocycles rings was slowed down in the protein hydrophobic pocket. Measurement of the fluorescence dynamic Stokes shift in single tryptophane of cytidine monophosphate kinase, located in the protein hydrophobic pocket, showed multiphase dynamic processes with time constants ranging from 0.1 to several nanoseconds with the total amplitude between 130 and 340 nm (0.4 – 1.0 kcal/mole).

The first direct evidence of the intramolecular mobility of hemeprotein globules was obtained by the spin and Mössbauer labeling methods (Frolov et al., 1977; Belonogova et al., 1978; Park et al., 1981, 1982; Myo et al., 1983; Likhtenshtein and Kotelnikov, 1983). The experiments were carried out on dry and moistened powders, which excluded any motion by the macromolecule as a whole. The ^{57}Fe atoms were incorporated into the heme group in myoglobin and hemoglobin. Given that the rigid heme ring is bound to the protein by numerous contacts, it is evident that anharmonic motion of heme above 200 K is related to the intramolecular mobility of the protein globule. This mobility appears only at a critical degree value of hydration samples. The increase of mobility recorded by NGR-spectroscopy correlates with the data for isotopic H-D whose relatively higher amplitude must be accompanied by the displacement of the helical polypeptide chain. Such an unharmonic nanosecond motion with $<\Delta x>_{nh} > 0.2$ Å also was recorded at temperature T > 210 K in myoglobin using spin and fluorescence labeling methods (Likhtenshtein and Kotelnikov, 1983; Likhtenshtein, 1988; and references therein). The flexibility of the cavity of the myoglobin active site is evidenced by the mobility of a spin probe, a derivative of isocyanate attached to the heme group in the single crystal. At room temperature the mobility parameters are that υ_c is about 10^8, $E_{app} = 2.8$ kcal/mole and $\Delta S_{app} = 14$ e.u.

NMR relaxation studies can provide detailed information pertaining to the internal dynamics in proteins on a time scale from milliseconds to picoseconds (Section 1.6.2.). The ^{15}N, ^{13}C and ^{2}H spin-lattice relaxation rate $(1/T_1)$ and heteronuclear NOE's are sensitive to high frequency motion $(10^8\text{-}10^{12}$ s$^{-1})$, while the spin-spin relaxation rate $(1/T_2)$ is a function of much slower processes.

The NMR relaxation technique was used to investigate the backbone dynamics of staphylococcal nuclease (S. Nase) complexed with a ligand and Ca^{2+} and labeled uniformly with ^{15}N (Kay et al., 1989). The relaxation parameters and NOE's were obtained for over 100 assigned backbones amid nitrogen in the proteins. Information on internal motions was extracted from experimental data using the model-free approach (Lipardi and Szabo, 1982). High values of the order parameters (S≈ 0.8), characterizing the extent of rapid ^{1}H-^{15}N bond motion and the correlation time of protein intramolecular daynamics (τ_e) were determined for α- and β-helices, turns and loops. These values as well as the spin-lattice relaxation rate of ^{15}N did not correlate with the temperature B-factor calculated from the X-ray analysis. The authors explained this discrepancy by suggesting different timescales for the different methods. In fact, the B-factor characterizes not only dynamic processes but also a disordering owing to the presence of a large number of nearly isoenergetic conformational substrates (Frauenfeldr, 2001; Frauenfelder et al., 1991). No correlation between rapid small amplitude motions and secondary structure for S.Nase was found. In contrast, ^{15}N line widths suggest a possible correlation between secondary structure and motions on the millisecond time scale monitoring by the measurement spin-spin realaxation rate. The loop region between residues 42 and 56 appears to be considerably more flexible on the slow time scale than the rest of the protein. The solid state and solution state ^{15}N NMR studies of the rapid and highly restricted backbone dynamics of *Staphylococcal* nuclease indicated the coincidence of the solution and crystalline chemical shifts for all ^{1}H-^{15}N bonds except His 46 and Val 56 located in a loop of the active site of the enzyme. The spin relaxation rate of the ^{1}H-^{15}N bonds of His 46 and Val 56 residues exhibit a wide range of values, which correspond to correlation times from 10 ps to 0.1 ns. These data correlate with B-values derived from X-ray structural analysis (Cole et al., 1991).

A similar approach was employed to study the backbone dynamics of uniformly ^{15}N-labeled chymotrypsin inhibitor 2 and of the complex formed by the association of two fragments of the protein (Shaw *et al.*, 1995). It was shown that most of the backbone NH groups is highly constrained ($S^2 \approx 0.9$) with the exception of residues in the binding loop with a parameter of slightly lower order. The cleavage of covalent bonds between Met59 and Glu60 leads to a large increase in the mobility of residues in the loop region. It was suggested that the NH_2 group of protein inhibits the attack of water on acyl-protease and is optimally placed for reversing the formation of the acyl enzyme.

Structural determination of hen egg white lysozyme dynamics was carried out through the analysis of ^{15}N relaxation measurement for the main chain NH group and arginine and tryptophane side ^{15}N nuclei (Buck et al., 1995). The 2D and 3D NMR experiments indicated that the majority of main-chain amids undergoes only small amplitude librational motion on the fast time scale ($S^2 > 0.8$). Increased main-chain motion ($0.5 \leq S^2 \leq 0.8$) is observed for 19 residues located at the C-terminus, in loop and turn regions, and in the first strand of the main β-sheet. Tryptophane residues closely packed in the protein core also have a high order parameter, while the S^2 values for side chains and arginine residues are characterized by S^2 ranging from 0.05 to 0.9. The order parameter for side-chains of asparagines and glutamine residues ranges from 0.2 to 0.8. It is interesting to know that many main-chain and side-chain groups with low order parameters have higher than average temperature factors in X-ray crystal structures.

The role of intramolecular conformational dynamics and folding kinetics in *de novo* designed dimeric protein α_{2D}, labeled with ^{13}C at the C^α position, was investigated using NMR spin relaxation methods (Hill et al., 2000). The protein backbone mobility was found to be typical of natural proteins. The folding and unfolding rate constants determined by analysis of the chemical exchange line broadening of leucine ^{13}C spins were determined as 4.7×10^6 $M^{-1}s^{-1}$ and 15 s^{-1}, respectively. In contrast, NMR spectroscopy experiments showed low order parameters for a variety of NH groups in a dihydrofolate reductase binary complex. Among such groups involving large-amlpitude motion on the fast time scale are residues in the adenosine binding site, hinge residues Lys 38 and Val 88, residues in βA-αB loop, and residues in the βF-βG loops. These regions are implicated in the transition state stabilization and ligand-dependent conformational changes (Palmer et al., 1996).

4.1.4. DYNAMICS OF ENZYMES ACTIVE SITES

The mobility of a single deuterated tryptophane located in a loop of the active site of triosephosphate isommerase has been investigated by solidstate deuterium NMR and solution state ^{19}F NMR. The rate of the loop's opening and closing was detected using samples of the enzyme in the presence and in the absence of a substrate analogue DL-glycerol 3-phosphate at temperatures ranging from −15 to +45°C. It was shown that the rate of the loop's opening and closing is of order $10^4 s^{-1}$. In contrast, NMR spectroscopy experiments showed low order parameters for various NH groups (Kay et al., 1989;Kay 1998) ^{15}N NMR dynamics experiments indicated that residues in the adenosine binding site of dihydrofolate reductase such as Lys 38, Val 88 of a hinge, and residues of the βA-αB and βF-βG loops involve large-amlpitude motion on the fast time scale (Palmer et al., 1996). These regions are implicated in the transition state stabilization and ligand-dependent conformational changes.

According to experimental data on Mössbauer spectroscopy, at ambient temperatures the myoglobin heme group exhibits the unharmonic nanosecond motion with $<\Delta x>_{nh} >$ 0.2 Å (Frolov et al., 1977; Belonogova et al., 1978; Parak et al., 1982). The flexibility of the cavity of the myoglobin active site is evidenced by the mobility of a spin probe, a derivative of isocyanate attached to the heme group in the single crystal. At room temperature the mobility parameters were found as follows: correlation frequency τ_c is about 10^8, $E_{app} = 2.8$ kcal/mole $\Delta S_{app} = 14$ e.u. (Likhtenshtein and Kotelnikov, 1983; Likhtenshtein, 1988a).

The influence of solvent viscosity on the surface and the structural dynamics of the heme group in the myoglobin active site was studied using the ultrafast infrared vibrational echo method. (Rector et al. 2001) It was shown that pure dephasing of the A1 CO stretching mode of myoglobin-CO is markedly dampened in the presence of ethylene glycol and trehalose and with a temperature increase. The authors concluded that when the solvent viscosity and temperature are lowered, the increased rate of fluctuation of the protein surface allows more rapid internal protein dynamics including the area of the protein active site.

4.1.5. SIMULATION OF PROTEIN MOLECULAR DYNAMICS

Availability of supercomputers and development of elegant molecular methods of dynamics simulation have been made a basis for the employment of explosive methods and a wide range of successful applications (Karplus and Petsko, 1990). The computer simulation produces individual particle motions as a function of time followed by the examination of specific contributions to the process.

Dynamic simulation for a protein includes the following steps:

1) Establishment of potential energy functions for interaction between atoms. Usually only empirical energy functions can be used for calculations for proteins. These functions are generally composed of bonding terms representing bond length, bond angles, torsional angles, Van der Waals interactions and electrostatic contributions.

2) A set of atomic coordinates is obtained from X-ray crystallographic or NMR structure data, or by model building. The structure is first refined to relieve local stresses due to overlaps of non-bonded atoms, bond-length and angles distortions, etc.

3) Using the classic Newton's law $F_i = m_i x a_i$ (F_i, m_i and a_i are the force on the atom, its mass, and its acceleration, respectively) and taking into consideration a Maxwellian distribution for a given temperature, a simulation of the atoms velocities is performed for a few picoseconds.

4) For relatively small proteins, like myoglobin, about 1,000 water molecules can be included in the calculation. For large proteins, simplified treatments are used. A set of

atoms close to the site of interest, an enzyme active site for example, is restricted for the computation and other atoms are treated as stochastic particles or eliminated.

Mean deviations of the nuclear positions in cytochrome c at ambient temperatures have been calculated 0.7 Å for a-carbon atoms of the main chains, 0.85 Å for other heavy atoms, and 0, 51 Å for the heme group (Karplus and McCommon, 1986). These values agree with data on Mössbauer spectroscopy (Belonogova et al., 1978). According to a 300 ps molecular dynamics simulation of myoglobin, different conformational minima are accessed every tenth of a picosecond. Backbone dynamics occur via changes in the relative orientations of the nearly rigid a-helices (hinge-like loop displacements). The mechanism of ligands O_2 and CO migrating into and out of the fluctuating active site of myoglobin was also examined. The simulation indicates that atoms surrounding the heme group move enough out of the way to allow the ligands to come into the active site pocket and to escape from it. It was shown that the helix fluctuations correlate with the motion of side chains and the rearrangements of loops. The maximum dynamical displacements in the simulation were found to be larger than those observed in the X-ray structure of protein.

Molecular dynamic simulation of lysozyme revealed two types of protein dynamical behavior: 1) anharmonic nanosecond fluctuations related to only less than 1% of general degree of freedom and occurring via a hinge-like motion mechanism, and 2) constrained motion with a narrow Gaussian contribution (Amadei et al., 1993). The first type of motion is relevant to such protein functions as opening and closing of domains enclosing the active site, while the second type seems to be irrelevant to local fluctuations, which are inherent in rigid polymers.

Conformational gating as a mechanism for enzyme specificity was also confirmed by molecular dynamics simulation of different proteins. The theoretical study of anisotropy fluctuation dynamics of proteins with an elastic network model indicated enhanced flexibility in the entry to the ligand binding site of the retinal-binding protein (Atilgan et al., 2001). The nanosecond molecular dynamics of the active-site structure of catechole O-methyltransferase containing cathechole, also known as catecholate in the ground and transition states, was studied by the MDS method. This method was also employed for comparing differences in the active-site dynamics of the wild-type and W137F mutant enzymes of 4-chlorobenzoyl-CoA dehalogenase (Lau and Bruice, 2000). In both simulations, water molecules are able to diffuse into active sites of the enzymes, but only in the wild-type enzyme are conformations relevant for interaction of the catalytic Asp 145 and 4-chlorobenzoyl-CoA shown to be available. The MDS of the Michaelis complex formed between zinc-β-lactamase and benzylpenicillin revealed the dynamical effects in the enzyme active site induced by the substrate binding (Diaz et al., 2001).

To provide an understanding of the importance of solvent mobility and the intrinsic protein energy surface, an MDS of proteins and surrounding solvent molecules at different temperatures has been performed. The simulation of myoglobin dynamics showed that solvent mobility is the dominant factor in determining protein atomic fluctuations above 180 K (Vitkup et al., 2000). The drastic effects of water molecule dynamics on the intramolecular motion of RNase and xylase was demonstrated in recent computer simulation studies (Reat et al., 2000; Tarek et al., 2000). Extensive simulations were carried out to identify the time-scale of water attachment to lysozyme (Steprone et al., 2001). The buried water molecules in hydrophobic pores and in superficial clefts are measured on a nanosecond time scale, while sub-nanosecond correlation time is characteristic of surface hydration water.

All theoretical results for protein and solvent dynamics mentioned above agree with experimental data obtained earlier by physical methods and biophysical labeling methods, in particular).

4.1.6. MECHANISMS OF PROTEINS MOLECULAR DYNAMICS

Data on the intramolecular dynamics of proteins obtained by the physical labeling approach combined with other dynamical and complementary theoretical and experimental methods may be briefly summarized as follows.

1. At low temperatures and in dry samples, protein macromolecules exhibit high frequency low amplitude harmonic nuclear vibrations with $\upsilon_c = 10^{12} - 10^{14}$ s^{-1} and amplitude A = 0.01 - 0.05 Å. This type of motion, directly detected by the methods of IR, Raman, Mössbauer, NMR and ESR spectroscopy, takes place in all proteins, at all temperatures and degrees of humidity, and apparently is not directly related to their functions and stability.

2. Anharmonic low frequency ($\upsilon_c = 10^{7} - 10^{9}$ s^{-1}) and relatively high amplitude motions (0.2 Å.and more) appear at certain critical temperatures, 180 - 210 K, and degree hydration (10- 30%) depending on protein structure. Protein conformational flexibility in the nanosecond and subnanosecond time scale was revealed in experiments on the fluorescence quenching of the buried tryptophane residues (Lakowicz and Weber, 1973; Munro et al., 1979), time-resolved tryptophane fluorescence by time- resolved fluorescence (Nishimoto et al., 1998), and spin, fluorescence and Mössbauer labelling (Likhtenshtein, 1976a, b, 1979, 1988, 1993; Likhtenshtein et al., 2000; Parak et al., 1982; Vogel et al., 1994), neutron and γ-ray scattering (Tsai et al., 2000; Tarek et al., 2000), NMR (Kay, 1989; Buck et al., 1995; Shaw et al., 1995; Palmer et al., 1996; Hill et al., 2001) and in theoretical molecular dynamics simulation (Karplus and McCammon, 1986; Karplus and Petsko, 1990; Zhou et al., 1998; Smith et al., 1998). These motions are governed by dynamics of media which provide necessary free volume (Lumry and Rajender, 1970; Lumry and Gregory, 1974, Likhtenhtein, 1969; 1976a, b, 1988).

3. The comparative analysis of the data obtained (Likhteshtein, 1976a, b, 1979, 1988; Likhtenshtein et al., 2000) revealed an apparent discrepancy between the physical labeling approach and certain other physical methods. Thus, the measurements of the temperature dependence of the heat capacity (c$_p$) of proteins, α-chymotrypsin, lysozyme, myoglobin, collagen, etc. at T 180-210 K at various degrees of hydration indicated only a monotonic increase of c$_p$ and did not detect pronounced phase transitions (Privalov aand Gill, 1998; 1982; Realdi and Battisel, 1993; Battisel et al., 2000). However, spin, fluorescence and Mössbauer labelling, H-D exchange, non-elastic neutron scattering and absorption spectra of heme in heme proteins detected sharp transitions within this temperature range. Parallel results were confirmed in experiments on the T-dependencies of such physical parameters of proteins as heat capacitiy and circular dichroism at the physiological temperature interval before thermal denaturation.

The above-mentioned discrepancy was easily confirmed by the following proposal (Likhtenshtein, 1976b). This type of nanosecond intermolecular mobility consists of movement of the relatively large and rigid parts of the protein macromolecules. Such hinge-like oscillation of the tightly packed polypeptide blocks does not give a measurable contribution to the overall heat capacity and the helicity degree of polypeptide chains, but it strongly affects the mobility of the Mössbauer labels firmly bound to the protein blocks, the mobility of spin and fluorescence labels and native chromophores located in cavities between the blocks, etc. At a later stage, the mechanism proposed was confirmed by independent experimental investigation and theoretical calculations. Similar concepts of hinge-bending or domain motion (Lumry and Gregory, 1986; Faber and Mathews, 1990; Zavodsky et al., 1995; Rojnuckarin, 1998; Gryk et al., 1998;; Lillimoen et al., 1998; Brown, 2001) and the knot-matrix principle of protein structure (Lumry and Gregory, 1986) were also introduced and confirmed in independent experiments and by molecular dynamics simulation (Karplus and McCammon, 1986; Karplus and Petsko, 1990; Zhou et al., 1998; Smith et al., 1989, 1998). Depending on protein specifics, the correlation time of domain motion can vary in temporal regions from milliseconds to nanoseconds.

As an example, we will consider the molecular dynamical behavior of egg white lysozyme. The temperature dependence of mobility of fluorescence, spin and Mössbauer labels attached to lysozyme was found to be similar to other investigated proteins: the monotonic increase typical for rigid polymers in dry states and in samples with water content (wt) was less than the critical value (wt_{cr}) and drastically burst when wt > wt_{cr} at T > 200 K took place (Frolov et al., 1978; Likhtenshtein, 1979). At similar conditions, experiments on the temperature dependence of heat capacity indicated only a monotonic steady increase for rigid organic material. Recently, in the fully dried lysozyme crystal, similar monotonic behavior of heat capacity was observed in temperatures between 8 and 30°C. At D_2O content more than 24 wt %, a slight deviation from the monotony was observed at temperatures above approximately 185 K, which most probably is due to the eutectic melting of $NaCl/2H_2O$ present in the samples to prevent water crystallization (Miyazaki et al., 2000).

Experimental results from studies of Arrhenius dependence of different characteristics of lysozyme are presented in Fig 4.1. (Alfimova and Likhtenshtein, 1979; Likhtenshtein, 1993; Likhtenshtein et al., 2000). The discontinuities on the curves indicate local conformational transitions and are apparently due to the appearance of a more open conformation of the protein. As can be seen from Fig. 4.1., these methods reveal conformational transitions at a temperature of about 30°C, whereas the temperature dependence of the partial heat capacity decreases monotonically in this temperature region. Recently, the presence of the conformational transition in lysozyme was confirmed independently. It was shown that the segmental motion of Trp 108 is hindered by the local cage structure at T < 30°C, although relieved from restricted motion by thermal agitation or by the formation of a ligand complex.

The internal motion of T4 lysozyme in the crystal was interpreted as an inter-domain motion corresponding to opening and closing of the active site cleft (Weaver et al., 1989). Hinge-bending and substrate-induced conformational transition in T4 lysozyme in solution were confirmed in a study by site-directed labelling (Mchaourban et al., 1997).

Both singles and pairs of nitroxide spin labels were introduced into different domains of the protein followed by monitoring distances between the labels by ESR technique. In the absence of a substrate, the results are consistent with a hinge-bending motion, which opens the active site cleft. When substrate binding takes place, the relative domain movement occurs. The concept of the hinge-bending motion of lysozyme domains was independently confirmed by an analysis of the extended molecular dynamics simulation of lysozyme in vacuum and aqueous solution. The analysis reveals so-called essential substrates containing only a few degrees of freedom from the non-harmonic opening and closing of the enzyme active site (Smith et al., 1989).

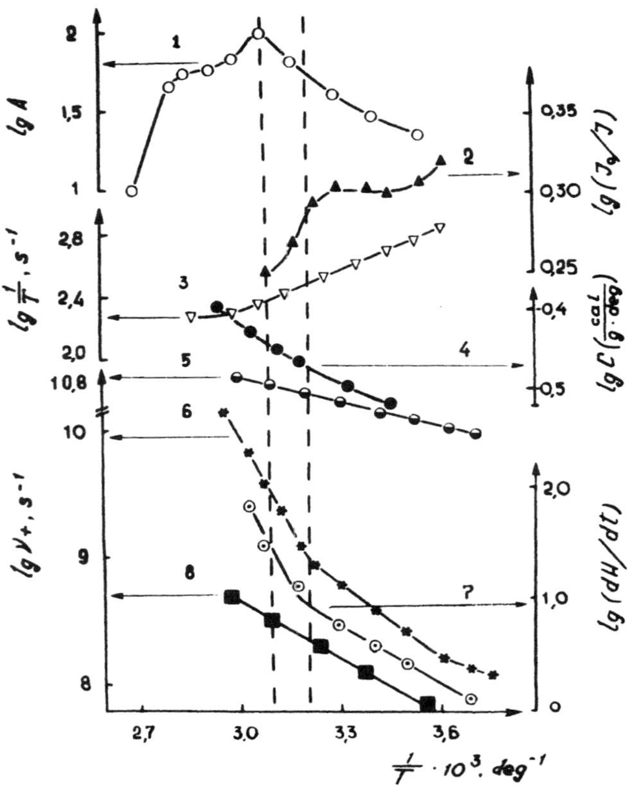

Figure 4.1. Arrhenius dependence of different characteristics of lysozyme: (1) enzyme activity; (2) relative fluorescence intensity; (3) water proton relaxation in the presence of the sample spin labelled by His-15; (4) partial spin capacity; (5) H-D exchange, (6,7) spin labels rotation and (8) the lysozyme globule rotation. Likhtenshtein et al., 2000. Reproduced with permission.

Long-range fluorescence energy transfer by the Förster mechanism is widely used for determination of intramolecular distances in macromolecules. The time dependence of the rate of energy transfer is a function of the donor/acceptor distance distribution and fluctuations between the various conformations, which may occur during the lifetime of the excited state. A method has been developed, based on global analysis of both donor and acceptor fluorescence decay curves, which allows determination of the parameters of the equilibrium distance distributions and intramolecular diffusion constants (Beechem and Haas, 1989). Simulation studies of typical intramolecular energy transfer experiments reveal that both static and dynamic conformational distribution information can thus be obtained at a single temperature and viscosity. This method was used for the investigation of the refolding transition of *Escherichia coli* adenylate kinase (AK) by monitoring the refolding kinetics of a selected 20 residue helical segment in the CORE domain of the protein (Ratner et al., 2002). Residues 169 and 188 were labeled by 1-acetamido-methyl-pyrene, and by bimane, resectively. The experiments combines double-jump stopped-flow fast mixing initiation of refolding and time-resolved Förster energy transfer spectroscopy for transformation of the fast-folding species formed in the first phase, to the slow-folding species. Refolding of the fast-folding species of the denatured state of AK was also a two-phase process.

During the first fast phase, within less than 5 ms, the fluorescence emission of both probes increased, but the distance distribution between the labeled sites was unchanged. Only during the second slow refolding step did the intramolecular distance distribution change from the characteristic of the denatured state to the narrow distribution of the native state.

The greater sensitivity of spin labels located near the boundary between the helical polypeptide chains of sperm-whale myoglobin to the pH change compared to that for spin labels located on the polypeptides was shown in detailed investigations (Atanasov et al., 1977). These provided direct evidence that the main mechanism of the conformational transition in the protein involves the relative displacement of fairly rigid spiral chains by restricted hinge-bending movements. The molecular dynamics simulation of myoglobin showed that at $T > 180$ K, the internal motion involves a combination of vibrations within substrates. A fast transition between them and α-helices are involved in the hinge-like motions for account of mobility of loops (Karplus and Petsko, 1990).

As shown in Section 4.1.2, investigation of the intramolecular mobility of proteins in the wide temperature range (40 - 350 K) and their correlation frequency ($\tau_C = 10^{-2} - 10^{10}$ s^{-1}) by physical labeling and complementary methods does not reveal sharp phase transitions, but rather a gradual softening of the protein globules. Thus, the dynamical behavior of serum albumins, for example, was found to be similar to that in amorphous systems. Protein crystals, on the other hand, expose X-ray structures with well-defined positions of atoms in polypeptide chains. The dynamic behavior of the protein molecules was described in terms of a "crystalline-amorphous" model (Likhtenshtein, 1986, 1988). According to the model, the protein globule is made up of rigid blocks (α-helical portions, β-structures, closely-packed side groups) and softer, amorphous regions (unordered, loose portions and water molecules). The blocks are bound by relatively flexible hinges and fairly weak interactions in the contacts between the blocks and the amorphous regions. Thus, the block system is embedded in a viscous amorphous medium. The globule is surrounded by a glycerol-like sheath composed of exposed surface groups and water molecules. The concept of proteins as systems possessing the properties of amorphous, glassy bodies was developed on the basis of data on the temperature dependency of the heat capacity in the region of helium temperature (Goldansky et al., 1983), as well as theoretical considerations (Shaitan et al., 2001; Vitkup et al., 2000). Analogous concepts were worked out for protein bodies, such as rubber-like systems (Lumry and Gregory, 1986).

4.1.7. PROTEINS DYNAMICS AND THEIR FUNCTIONAL ACTIVITY

Data on transglobular transitions at substrate-enzyme and substrate analogue-enzyme interactions and the considerable body of other evidence of such effects on other proteins indicate that the capacity of a protein globule to change conformation as a result of intramolecular dynamics is an inherent property of these macromolecules. It was suggested that the processes of complex formation between antigens and antibodies such as allosteric transitions, mechanical transformations, electron transfer, etc., only occurred because of the ability of protein globules to quickly and reversibly change their conformation (Lumry and Eyring, 1954; Lamry and Biltonen, 1969; Lumry and Rajender, 1970; Likhtenshtein, 1966, 1976a, b; Amadei et al., 1993; Faber and Mathews, 1990; Karplus and Petsko, 1990; Zhou et al., 1998; Schulten,, 2000). More detailed information on the role of protein dynamics was obtained from experiments in which the dependence of kinetic parameters of functional activity and the stability of proteins and enzymes were compared to the quantitative parameters of various dynamical modes.

In the search for such a correlation, α-chymotrypsin was modified by a spin label attached to the methionine-92 group in the region of the active site and by a Mössbauer label in the enzyme globule periphery (Likhtenshtein, 1976b, 1988; Frolov et al., 1978; Krinichny et al., 1987). The protein tryptophane group also served as an intrinsic fluorescence label. Agitation of the label mobility in the nanosecond region at relative humidity about $P_{rel} = 0.6$ correlates with a sharp increase in the hydrolysis degree of the cyanomoyl α-cymotrypsin covalent compound (Roslyakov and Churgin, 1972). This result highlighted the significance of nanosecond dynamics in the chemical step of the enzyme reaction.

Photosensitive systems are convenient objects for analysing a possible correlation between the dynamic and functional properties of proteins. After a short light pulse, it is possible to observe a chemical reaction and to trace the dynamical state of the matrix with the aid of internal and external physical labels.

The dynamic state of sperm-whale myoglobin monitored by spin, fluorescence, and Mössbauer labels (Likhtenshtein, 1988, 1993) as a function of temperature was compared with the results of kinetic studies on the photodissociation and reassociation of CO-deoxymyoglobin (Frauenfelder et al, 1991). The three independent labelling methods showed sharp increases in nanosecond mobility in the vicinity of the label in a temperature region of approximately 200-220 K. These temperatures were close to the temperatures of the dramatic increases in the relative quantum yield of the photodissociation, as well as to the fraction of non-dissociated molecules for 10^{-2} s following a short light flash. Fig. 4.2.a, b show that a dramatic increase in the rate of long distance electron transfer (LDET) between hemes of myoglobin donor-acceptor groups on the protein globule peripheral portions occurs within the same temperature interval as the animation of the nanosecond dynamics. A similar effect was observed for LDET between a heme group and an excited Zn-porphyrin of modified hemoglobin (Peterson-Kennedy, 1984).

A detailed investigation of the possible role of media (protein and membrane) dynamics in electron transfer was carried out on the reaction centre (RC) extracted from *Rhodopseudomonas spheroidas* in the isolated state and in the composition of the photosynthetic membrane (Berg et al., 1979a, b; Likhtenshtein, 1979a, b; Likhtenshtein et al., 1979; Kotelnikov et al., 1983; Kochetkov et al., 1984; Parak et al., 1983; Knox, 1989; Likhtenshtein, 1988(a, b), 1993, 1996; Likhtenshtein et al., 2000).

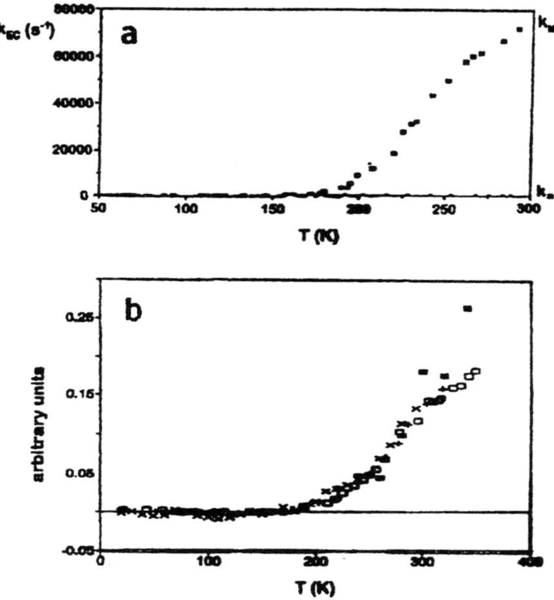

Figure 4.2. Temperature dependence of the rate constant of electron transfer (k_{ET}) in myoglobin modified covalently by donor-acceptor groups (a) and the deviation of various dynamic quantities from normal harmonic behaviour obtained by molecular dynamic simulation, inelastic neutron scattering, Mössbauer spectroscopy and spectral broadening analysis (b). (Likhtenshtein et al., 2000). Reproduced with permission.

Spin, Mössbauer, fluorescent and phosphorescent labels were introduced into the various portions of the system being studied. They were covalently bound to the RC surface groups, adsorbed by the hydrophobic segments of the protein and membrane, and ^{57}Fe atoms were incorporated by way of biosynthesis into iron-containing proteins. Then, in the same samples, the dependence on temperature, moisture content and viscosity was measured for the label mobility and the rate constant of electron transfer

(ET) between the components of the photosynthetic chain. The emergence of an electron from the primary photosynthetic cell, e.g. the transport from the reduced primary acceptor Q_{A-} to the secondary acceptor QB followed by the release of hydroquinone Q_BH_2 was shown to take place only under conditions in which the labels record the mobility of the protein moiety in the membrane with $\upsilon_c > 10^7$ s^{-1}. The rate of another important process, the recombination of the primary product of the charge separation, i.e. reduced primary acceptor (Q_A^-) and oxidized primary donor, bacteriochlorophyl dimere (P^+), falls from 10^2 to 10^3 s^{-1} when dynamic processes with $\upsilon_c = 10^3$ s^{-1} occur.

Very fast electron transfers from P^+ to bacteriochlorophyl (Bchl) and from (Bchl)- to QA do not depend on media dynamics and occur via conformationally non-equilibrium states (Fig.3.18). The dual fluorophore-nitroxide molecules (D-A) are also convenient objects for analysing the activity-dynamics relationship. The marked irreversible photoreduction of the nitroxide fragment of the dual probe incorporated into the binding site of HSA only took place when the nanosecond dynamical processes around the probe traced by ESR and fluorescence methods were detected (Rubtsova et al., 1993, Fogel et al., 1994; Likhtenshtein, 1986; Lozinsky et al., 2002). Similar results were reported for another model protein system, i.e. α-chymotrypsin with spin labeled methionin-92 groups (Belonogova et al., 1997). In the latter enzyme, the excited tryptophan group serves as an electron donor.

Thus the above-mentioned data clearly indicate that hinge-bending (blocks) nanosecond dynamics plays a key role in protein function and in enzyme catalysis in particular. However, a detailed discussion of the problem lies beyond the scope of the present chapter, which only intends to give a general appreciation of this role. Here we are limited to considering several typical examples.

Indirect evidence in favor of the role of enzyme dynamics in hydrogen tunneling in mesophilic and thermophilic alcohol dehydrogenase was obtained and confirmed theoretically (Antoniou and Schwartz, 2001). The authors suggested that hydrogen tunneling makes a significant contribution at temperatures above 25°C and 65°C for mesophilic and thermophylic enzymes respectively. At these conditions the enzymes undergo a transition to a less rigid structure and the reaction coordinate for the tunneling rate-determining step is coupled to dynamic modes of enzymatic environment.

The most specific feature of enzymes is their multi-centre nature. It is this feature, which is responsible for the main advantages of enzymes, such as the binding and orientation of substrates, synchronous elementary acts and the possibility that a multi-step process occurs with an optimal rate for each step. However, an analysis of concrete reactions shows that these advantages cannot occur in rigid structures. Chemical enzymatic processes are accompanied by multi-contact substrate-enzyme interactions and by significant changes in sizes of reaction complexs. Some bonds are broken, new ones are formed, and the covalent binding is changed to van der Waals contacts and vice versa. It is obvious that the structure of the protein matrix must fit the varying shapes of the reaction complexs in all their procedural steps. Even such a simple process as electron transfer must be completed with a structural reorganisation in which electronic-conformational interaction takes place. This general property of the protein may be defined as dynamic adaptability.

4.2. Electrostatic effects in proteins and enzymes

Electrostatic interactions play a key role in the structure and function of biological molecules. The association of proteins in solution and in membranes, protein-nucleic acids and nucleic acid - nucleic acid interactions, enzyme-substrate complexation, chemical reactions in enzyme active sites, charge-transfer, voltage gating of membrane channels, folding and unfolding processes of biopolymers, etc., are all drastically affected by the strength and distribution of the electrostatic field around various regions in biological molecules. At one time or another, much of the wide methodological and theoretical arsenal of chemical physics has been used to study electrostatic interactions in biological and chemical systems.

4.2.1. THEORETICAL CALCULATIONS

Significant progress has been achieved in the theoretical calculation of these interactions. The most advanced theoretical approach to the problem relies upon the use of the Poisson-Debye equation for polarizable solutes of known structure embedded in a dielectric medium (Klapper et al., 1986; Sharp and Honig, 1990; Bashford and Karplus, 1990; Bajorath et al., 1991, Aqvist et al., 1991; Tidor and Karplus, 1991; Sharp et al., 1992; Gilson, 1993; Loewenthal et al., 1993; Yang et al., 1993; Scott et al., 1994; Anni et al., 1994, Hecht et al., 1995; Honig and Nicholls, 1995;

For the classical treatment of electrostatic interaction in solution the Poison-Boltzman equation (PBS) is commonly used

$$\nabla\left[\varepsilon(\check{r})\nabla\phi(\check{r})\right] - \left[e(\check{r})\kappa(\check{r})2\sinh[\phi(\check{r})]\right] + 4\pi p(\check{r})/kT = 0 \qquad (4.1.)$$

where $\phi(\check{r})$ is the dimensionless electrostatic potential in units k_BT/q, q is the charge, $\varepsilon(\check{r})$ is the static dielectric constant, p is the fixed charge density, and $\kappa(\check{r}) = 8\pi q^2 I/\varepsilon k_BT$ (I is the ionic strength). $\check{r}$ denotes the position vector. In the accepted model, one supposes the existence of two dielectric continuums: one of low dielectric constant (ε_0^s) for solutes and one of high ($e_0^{aqu} = 80$) for the surrounding bulk aqueous phase. The main problem is the choice of the ε_0^s value for different portions of such a complex mosaic system as biopolymers.

To illustrate results of the theoretical calculation of electrostatic potential in proteins, we will consider some typical examples. A macroscopic electrostatic model is used to calculate the pKa values of the specific titratable groups in lysozyme (Bashford and Karplus, 1990). The model makes use of detailed structural information. The solvation self-energies and interactions between permanent partial charges and titratable charges are considered. According to (Bajorath et al., 1991) *Escherichia coli* dihydrofolate reductase (DHFR) carries a net charge of -10 electrons. Yet it binds ligands with net charges of -4 (NADPH) and -2 (folate or dihydrofolate). The results show that the enzyme is covered by an overall negative potential except for the ligand binding sites. These sites are located inside a cavity of positive potential that enables the enzyme to bind the negatively charged ligands. This property contributes significantly to electronic polarization of the ligand folate and, therefore, affects the catalytic process. The experimental data on site-specific titration curves for 12 histidine residues in carbon monoxy sperm whale myoglobin by the 2D double quantum NMR technique were found to agree with theoretical predictions obtained with using a numerical Poisson-Boltzmann model and a Monte Carlo treatment (Bashford et al., 1993).

That asymmetry in packing the peptide amide dipole results in larger positive than negative regions in proteins of all folding motifs was theoretically demonstrated (Gunner et al., 2000). The following conclusion have been made: 1) the average side chain potential in 305 proteins is 109 ± 30 mV; 2) the larger oxygen at the negative end and smaller proton at the positive end of the amide dipole yield positive potential potentials; 3) twice as many amides have their oxygens exposed than their amine protons; 4) 30% of the Asp, Glu, Lys, and Arg are buried, while 60% of buried residues are acids and only 40% bases; and 5) the positive backbone potential stabilizes ionization of 20% of the acids by >3 pH units (-4.1 kcal/mol).

It was shown that optimization of conformational relaxation, specific ion-binding, local hydrogen bonding networks, desolvatation and taking into consideration the flipping of side chains of asparagine, histidine and glutamine around their 2, 2 and 3 torsion angles can improve results of pK_a calculations. (Alexov and Gunner, 1997; Gunner and Alexev, 2000). These optimizations are applied to some well characterized proteins: BPTI, hen egg white lysozyme and superoxide dismutase. The significance of multi-conformational structure and hydroxyl group motion for the local dielectric constant and electrostatic potential was demonstrated as a result of calculating electrostatic, Lennard-Jones potentials, and torsion angle energies at each proton position of hen egg lysozyme (Alexov and Gunner, 1997). Detailed analysis of effects of functional group charges and dipoles and their distribution over protein globules on the electrostatic potential in proteins has revealed some general features of the systems under consideration.

4.2.2. EXPERIMENTAL APPROACHES

Methods of investigation of electrostatic potential around charged molecules
Two types of experimental methods for the investigation of local electrostatic fields in the vicinity of specific parts of biological molecules were proposed. The first group of methods is based upon electrostatic measurements utilizing static local parameters, such as the pK of a chosen protein or polypeptide functional group or the spectral characteristics of a chromophore attached to a biopolymer, *i.e.* the Stark effect (Lockhart and Kim, 1991, 1992; Sitkoff *et al.*, 1994 and references therein). For example, the electric field at the backbone amide groups and amino terminus of an alpha helix in water has been determined by measuring the Stark effect in the absorption band for a covalently attached, neutral probe molecule. It was shown that the field at the interface between the helix and the solvent is an order of magnitude stronger than expected from the dielectric properties of bulk water. The dielectric screening effects are an order of magnitude greater for the backbone-charge interactions than for the backbone-dipole interactions. The results obtained by these various methods agree with the theoretically predicted values in most cases. Nevertheless, it is necessary to bear in mind that

experimentally determined pK and Stark effect parameters may be effected by factors other than local electrostatic fields (such as local donor-acceptor interactions, local dielectric constants, steric accessibility to solvent, etc.).

A dielectric cavity model for a protein globule is used as a basis to consider the extended states which are mostly formed by the polarization field of the protein macromolecules (Balabaev et al., 1990),. In a protein solution the size of such a state can be compared with the size of the macromolecules. Typical values of the predicted electron energies of absorption bands and luminescence are found to be approximately 1000 nm for the ground state absorption band and approximately 2000 nm for the excited state. Covalently bound pyridoxal phosphate (PLP) has been shown to be a fluorescent probe, sensitive to the electrostatic field potential of the protein multipole. The non-covalent interactions, in which charge transfer and energy transfer occur between PLP-ALME and different electron-donor and electron-acceptor groups have been analyzed (Donchev et al., 1992). PLP has been used to for the experimental. determination. of local electrostatic potentials in singly substituted cytochromes c modified by pyridoxal phosphate at Lys 79 or at Lys 86 and for the calculation. the pKa values of all ionizable groups and the electrostatic potentials in the modified proteins (Miteva et al., 1997). The results obtained by afore mentioned various methods agree with the theoretically predicted values in most cases. Nevertheless, it is necessary to bear in mind that experimentally determined pK and Stark effect parameters may be effected by factors other than local electrostatic fields (such as local donor-acceptor interactions, local dielectric constants, steric accessibility to solvent, etc.).

The physical basis of the second type of approach rests upon the effect of the local electrostatic potential upon dynamic interactions at encounters with charged quenching molecules resulting in fluorescence (phosphorescence) (Vogel et al., 1986; Anni et al., 1994) or between a stable radical, *e.g.* nitroxide, and another charged paramagnetic species (Likhtenshtein et al., 1972; Likhtenshtein, 1976, 1988, 1993). In such cases, the relaxation parameters, *i.e.* the life-time of the fluorescence (phosphorescence) chromophore or spin-spin and spin-lattice relaxation rates of paramagnetic species are dependent upon the frequency of encounters, and, therefore, on local electrostatic fields

In particular, it was established (Likhtenshtein et al., 1972; Likhtenshtein, 1976, 1988, 1993) that the spin-exchange rate constants (k_{ex}) in solution between nitroxide radicals of different charges (I-III) and positive (diphenylchromium) or negative (ferricyanide) complexes are strongly dependent upon the following factors which are in approximate agreement with the Debye theory: (1) the product of the charges (Z_1Z_2), (2) the distance between the charges within the encounter complex, and (3) the ionic strength. It was also shown (Likhtenshtein et al., 1970, 1972; Likhtenshtein, 1976, 1988, 1993; Salikhov et al., 1971; Zamaraev et al., 1981) that k_{ex} values depend upon steric factors in the vicinity of encounter particles, as well as upon the electronic structure (spin, spin-relaxation parameters) of the paramagnetic complexes. A general limitation of the last two methods is that they are applicable only to systems with pronounced luminescent or paramagnetic properties (Tsui et al., 1990; Hecht et al., 1995).

Calculations of local charge Z_x in the vicinity of a paramagnetic particle (such as the active site of metalloprotein or a spin label) colliding with a nitroxide or metallocomplex with known charge Z_p can be carried out with the use of the Debye equation:

$$\frac{k^+}{k^0} = \frac{k^-}{k^0} = \frac{Z_p Z_x \alpha}{\exp(Z_p Z_x \alpha) - 1} \qquad\qquad (4.2.)$$

where k^+, k^- and k^0 are the rate constants of encounters for positively charged, negatively charged, and neutral uncharged particles, respectively; and $\alpha = e^2/k_B T \varepsilon_0 r$, where e is the charge of an electron; k_B is the Boltzmann constant; temperature T = 293 K, ε_0 is the dielectric constant of water, and r is the distance between the charges in the encounter complex (Debye, 1942). The values of (k^+/k^0) and (k^-/k^0) are determined by measuring the rate constants of spin exchange using equations 4.3 and 15 which describe the effect of paramagnetic species on spin phase and spin-lattice relaxation rate of the radical.

The equation 4.2 allows one to calculate the $Z_p Z_x$ product using the appropriate experimentally-measured log (k^+/k^0) or log (k^-/k^0) value and an r value estimated for the encounter complex. From the value of $Z_x Z_p$ one can ascertain the Z_x charge in the vicinity of the region of the paramagnetic complex encountered by the charged nitroxide spin-probe since the Z_p charge of the nitroxide spin-probe is known.

This approach can be applied to two types of problems. It can be used to investigate the electrostatic fields in the vicinity of a radical, say nitroxide spin label or spin probe using a second paramagnetic species with a different charge, ferricyanide anion or diphenylchromium cation, for example. (Likhtenshtein, 1976, 1993; Likhtenshtein et al., 1972). The second approach involves monitoring the effect of a paramagnetic species, such as a complex of paramagnetic ions with a protein or the active site of a metalloenzyme, on the spin relaxation parameters of nitroxide spin probes of different charges freely diffusing in solution. It can be illustrated by the study of interaction between ferricyanide anion and nitroxides of different charges:

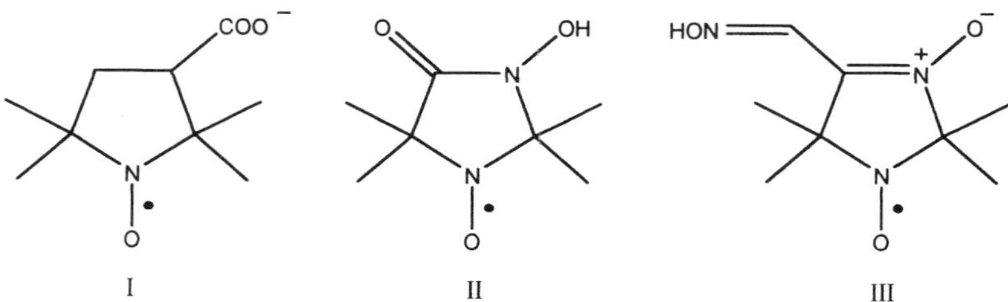

I   II   III

The measurements have been performed in aqueous solutions. The experimental values of k^+, k^-, and k^0, were found to be 38×10^8, 2×10^8 and 6×10^8 $M^{-1}s^{-1}$, respectively. From the experimental value of log k^+/k^- = 16 the distance between the NO fragment and the ferricyanide ion (r = 6 Å), one can find a product of charges of radicals ($Z_N = +1$) and ferricyanide anion (Z_{FC}) $Z_N Z_{FC}$ = -2.9±0.1 and therefore Z_{FC} = -2.9±0.1.

A new experimental approach has been developed to study the distribution of local electrostatic potential around specific protons in biologically important molecules. The approach is the development of a method denoted as "spin label/spin-probe" proposed in the early 1970's (Likhtenshtein et al., 1972). The effectiveness of nitroxides and paramagnetic metal complexes as relaxation reagents for protons has been widely demonstrated for both static and dynamic systems (Wien et al., 1972; Syrtsova et al., 1972, 1974; Lezina et al., 1976; Krugh, 1971; Likhtenshtein, 1976, 1993; Sletten et al., 1983; Niccolai et al., 1984). In contrast to nitroxides, metal complexes and luminescence chromophores show a certain preferred affinity towards some functional groups and therefore their use is limited.

The proposed method is based upon the quantitative measurement of the contribution of differently charged nitroxide probes to the spin-lattice relaxation rate $(1/T_1)$ of protons in a particular molecule, followed by the calculation of local electrostatic potential using the classical Debye equation (Likhtenshtein et al., 1999; Glaser et al., 2000). In parallel, the theoretical calculation of potential distribution with the use of the *MacSpartan Plus 1.0* program has been performed.

Apparent local electrostatic potential $U(R_0)$ can be determined from the experimental dependence of the proton spin-lattice relaxation rate on the concentration of the nitroxide probes [R•]

$$k^i = \frac{d\left[\dfrac{1}{T_1 dC}\right]}{[R\bullet]} \tag{4.3.}$$

The ratio of experimental apparent rate constants k_+/k_0 or k_-/k_0 (Hwang *et al.*, 1975; Hwang and Freed, 1975) can be given as:

$$\frac{k_{+-}}{k_0} = \beta_{el}\beta_I \tag{4.4.}$$

where in ambient temperature

$$\beta_{el} = \frac{\dfrac{U(R_0)}{0.6}e^{\frac{U(R_0)}{0.6}}}{1 - e^{\dfrac{U(R_0)}{0.6}}} \tag{4.5}$$

and

$$\beta_I = 10^{\frac{\sqrt{I}}{1+\sqrt{I}}} \tag{4.6.}$$

where I is the ionic strength. Estimating I and using β_{el}, $U(R_0)_{exptl}$ can now be calculated from equation 4.6. Nitroxide radicals IV-VI of different charges

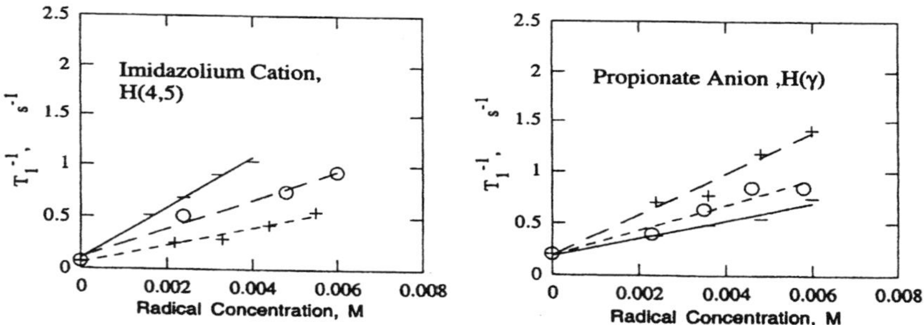

have been used for studying electrostatic effects in the vicinity of definite protons in specific molecules (Likhtenshtein et al., 1999).

As these radicals have similar chemical structures, they differ in the presence or absence of a small-sized functional group in a ring position remote from the paramagnetic nitroxide group. Therefore, it is obvious that they have very similar paramagnetic parameters, affected by the spin-lattice relaxation, i.e. magnetic moment, distance between radical and proton R'$_0$, and the diffusion coefficients of the radicals (Hwang and Freed, 1975; Alexandrov, 1975; Berdnikov et al., 1980). On the basis of the analysis of molecular models for these radicals, we can suggest that they are comparable for all radicals used in this study. The only marked difference expected for the radicals is the value and sign of their electrostatic charge [0, −1 and +1] for the corresponding radicals IV-VI. Accordingly, marked differences in the experimental data of k_i and $U(R_0)$ were obtained (Fig. 4.3.).

Figure 4.3. Spin relaxation rate of charged molecules as a function of nitroxide spin probe concentration. Neutral, negative, and positive charged probes denoted are respectively denoted as 0 , -, and + (Likhtenshtein et al., 1999). Reproduced with permission.

Experimental data

The general conclusions from the referred study are as follows:

1. Proton nuclei located at different positions within the small molecules and amino acids that were investigated exhibit similar degrees of spin-probe accessibility as shown by the similar values of slope $d(1/T_1)/dC$ for these protons in the presence of the neutral spin-probe IV. This experimental observation is consistent with the theoretical estimation of spin-probe accessibility as studied by computer-assisted molecular modeling of the various amino acid/spin-probe encounter complexes in our study.

2. In small charged molecules and in charged amino acids, the charge of functional groups and their charge-type clearly results in local electrostatic potentials experienced by neighboring nuclei, and is amenable to solution-state investigation by charged nitroxide spin-probes. These local electrostatic potentials appear to be concentrated around the ionized functional group in aspartic acid, while the results for more conformationally heterogeneous histidine and lysine show noticeable local electrostatic charged fields around proton nuclei located some distance away from the functional groups.

The method used in this investigation did not reveal a local electrostatic potential for the glycine α-H nuclei located close to the zwitterionic environment.

The above mentioned results illustrate the reliability of the new technique that was utilized in these investigations and show that it has the potential to develop into a method for the quantitative study of local charge distribution in polypeptides and proteins. Deviation from standard molecular values of $U(R_0)_{exp}$ and Z_{app} for a proton in such molecules can indicate the sign and magnitude of electrostatic effects in various regions of the specific molecule. While the differently charged spin-probes have only been used so far on a rather limited number of examples reported herein, the results show that this new methodology holds great promise for the investigation of local electrostatic fields in a wide range of biologically important molecules.

Electron-carrier horse heat cytochrome c and dioxygen-carrier sperm-whale myoglobin served as models for determining local electrostatic charges in the vicinity of paramagnetic active sites of metalloenzymes and metalloproteins (Likhtenshtein, 2000). Calculations of local charge Z_X in the vicinity of a paramagnetic particle can be performed using 4.2 for encounters between two charged particles in solution. Neutral TEMPOL, positively-charged nitroxide VI or negatively-charged nitroxide V were used to probe the local charge in the proteins' paramagnetic heme region. The experimental dependence of peak line-broadening, $\Delta\Delta H_{pp} = (\Delta H_{pp})_X - (\Delta H_{pp})_0$, for spin-probes with different charges (IV-VI) on the concentration of $Fe(CN)_6^{3-}$ or heme protein (Fe^{3+}cyt c or Fe^{3+}Mb) has been measured (Likhtenshtein et al., 2000). The values of k^i and the resulting charges Z_H calculated with Eq. 4.2. are presented in Table 4.2.. It was shown that cytochrome c causes a larger peak line-broadening ($\Delta\Delta H_{pp}$) for the negatively-charged nitroxide spin-probe (V) compared to that observed for neutral X. Myoglobin results in a larger line-broadening for the neutral nitroxide spin-probe (IV) than for the negatively charged species (V). The spin-exchange rate constants in Table 4.2. show that the effect of the heme proteins on k^i is considerably weaker than that exerted by free hemin or by ferricyanide in solution.

According to the experimental data on rate constants of spin exchange at encounters between heme groups and nitroxides presented in Table 4.2., the accessibility of the heme group of cytochrome c to the encounters with neutral spin-probes IV is ~31-33 times lower than that observed for free hemin. At present, it is difficult to separate the effect of heme group immersion into the protein globular structure from that of association in the relatively concentrated solutions (2-10mM) utilized in these studies.

TABLE 4.2. Apparent spin-exchange rate-constants (k^+, k^-, and k^0) of the positively charged (**VI**), negatively charged (**V**) and neutral (**IV**) nitroxide spin-probes with hemin, ferricyanide anion, and heme proteins in aqueous solutions and apparent local charges (Z_H) in the vicinity of the heme groups[a] (Likhtenshtein, 2000). Reproduced with permission.

Paramagnetic species	pH	$k^+ \times 10^{-8}$ $(M^{-1}s^{-1})$	$k^- \times 10^{-8}$ $(M^{-1}s^{-1})$	$K^0 \times 10^{-8}$ $(M^{-1}s^{-1})$	Z_H (± 0.1)
Hemin[b]		c	c	24^d	
$K_3Fe(CN)_6$[e]	6.9	38		6^f	c
Cytochrome c (Fe^{3+})[g]	10.7	c	0.97 ± 0.04	0.72 ± 0.07^f	+0.5
Cytochrome c (Fe^{3+})[e]	6.9	c	0.84 ± 0.11	0.71 ± 0.12^f	+0.3
Cytochrome c (Fe^{2+})[e]	6.9			~0	
Myoglobin[g]	7.0	c	0.56 ± 0.07	0.77 ± 0.14^h	-0.5

[a] 20 °C. [b] Pyridine solvent (Grebenshchikov *et al.*, 1972). [c] Not determined. [d] 4-hydroxy-2,2,6,6-tetramethyl-1-piperidinyloxy spin-probe used, data taken from (Likhtenshtein, 1976). [e] Phosphate buffer, ionic strength 0.09 M. [f] neutral probe **IV** used. [g] Distilled water. [h] Neutral probe **IV** used.

The region of the cytochrome c active center is surrounded by a cluster of positively charged lysine residues. The existence of such a structural moiety is the basis for the specific affinity of this electron carrier to cytochrome c oxidase. However, in spite of this, our experiment did not locate significant local electrostatic charges on the protein interface in the vicinity of the heme group at pH 10.7 (isoelectric point) or pH 7 with an ionic strength of 0.09 M (Table 4.2.). Therefore, while the charged lysine ε-amino groups of cytochrome c contribute significantly to the direct electrostatic interaction with the surface of cytochrome c oxidase, they apparently do not induce a markedly positive charge on the hemin. The existence of a large positive charge in this region could prevent electron transfer from Fe^{2+} cyt c.

While the differently charged spin-probes have only been used so far on a rather limited number of examples reported herein, the results show that these new methodologies hold great promise for the investigation of local electrostatic fields in a wide range of biologically significant molecules.

A similar approach was employed in Hecht et al. (1995) for determining the electrostatic potential near the surface of calf thymus DNA. Spin-spin interaction between an ^{14}N-nitroxide derivative of 9-aminoacridine attached to DNA and free ^{15}N-labeled nitroxides of different charges was monitored by electron-electron double resonance (ELDOR). The electrostatic potential near the surface of DNA was calculated using a nonlinear Poisson-Boltzman equation. The calculated results agreed with the experimental potentials.

The effect of dipole-dipole interaction between the Fe^{3+} heme group of myoglobin and water protons was used to study heme hydration and displacement in the pre-denaturational conformational transition of the molecule (Derzhansci et al. 1970).

The role of electrostatic interactions and particularly salt bridges in the stabilization of protein and its interactions with other molecules is widely investigated (Sheinerman and Honig, 1999; Sindler et al., 1998; Xiao and Honig, 1999; Nohaile et al., 2001). As an illustration, it was shown that a barnase and its intracellular inhibitor barstar association rate constant of 10^5 M^{-1} s^{-1} is increased to over 5 x 10^9 $M^{-1}s^{-1}$ by electrostatic forces (Schreiber and Fersht, 1994). The importance of buried salt bridges in the stability of protein was demonstrated by the example of the unfolding of barnase (Tissit et al., 1996). Replacing the Asp residues in the bridges Arg-69-Asp-93 and Arg-83-Asp-75 led to lowering the enzyme stability by up to 5.4 kcal/mol. Nevertheless theoretical calculations and experiments indicate that hydrophobic interactions are more stabilizing than salt bridges in protein folding (Sindler et al., 1998). The loss of stability is related to a substantial reduction in the degeneracy of the lowest-energy state.

Other factors also affect protein stability and hyperstability (Vetriani et al, 1998; Jaenicke, 1996, 1998, 2000; Daniel and Danson, 2001). These include the formation of a network of surface ionic pairs, hydrogen bonding, local interactions, the stabilization of polypeptides helices (the packing and docking of domains, association of subunits, conjugation with prosthetic groups and carbohydrate moieties, etc).

4.3. Enzymes from extreme thermophilic bacteria.

4.3.1. OVERVIEW

In recent years, increasing attention has been focused on proteins derived from extreme thermophylic bacteria (Daniel and Cowan, 2000; Vetriani et al., 1998; Jaenicke, 1996; 1998, 2000; Adams and Kelly, 2001; and references therein). The increasing use of these proteins in biotechnology has given new impetus to studies focused on their structure and stability. At the same time, thermostable proteins prove challenging as the ideal candidates for investigating the relationships between the structure and intramolecular dynamics of the enzyme on the one hand, and their function and stability on the other.

Proteins isolated from thermophylic and especially from hyperthermophylic micro-organisms are unusually stable with respect to high temperatures, organic solvents and detergents (Nucci et al. 1993; Britton et al., 1999; Daniel and Cowan, 2000; Jaenicke, 1998, 2000; D'Auria et al., 1999). A series of homologous proteins and enzymes with widely different stabilities was shown to be similar in sequence, subunit composition, and enzymatic activity, e.g. the nature of the catalytic group of the active site, the chemical mechanism of the reaction and specificity. Other than exhibiting high stability, these enzymes also exhibit very poor catalytic behavior at ambient temperature, although they are dramatically activated at high temperatures above 50°C and can reach maximum activity at 80-90 °C and even 115-120 °C under effect of pressure (200- 500 atm) (D'Auria 1999; Sun and Clark, 2001).

A number of challenging problems regarding the physico-chemical molecular level are posed to biochemists and biophysicists, i.e. (1) the specificity of the protein intramolecular structure giving such high thermostability and resistance to outer effectors; (2) the physical reasons for such poor catalytic activity at ambient temperature, and (3) the peculiarity of the intramolecular dynamics of the protein globule and particularly the active site.

Investigation of thermostable protein dynamics by indirect methods such as the kinetics of proteolysis and H-D exchange as well as buried chromophore fluorescence quenching, has led to the conclusion that at ambient temperature their globules are essentially less flexible than for non-thermostable proteins (Vetriani *et al.*, 1998; and references therein).

An approach to the hyperthermostability problem is based on an analysis of the structural models from hyperthermophylic and mesophylic micro-organisms. On reviewing the relevant literature, it can be stated that multiple factors affect protein hyperstability Vetriani et al., 1998; Jaenicke, 1998, 2000). These include the formation of a network of surface ionic pairs, hydrogen bonding, hydrophobic interactions, local interactions, the stabilisation of polypeptides helices (the packing and docking of domains, association of subunits, conjugation with prosthetic groups and carbohydrate moieties, etc.). A cumulative effect appears to be the result of a simple estimation indicating that for an increase in the equilibrium constant of a protein denaturation at 80 °C by 3 orders of magnitude, a shift in the free energy of bonding of about 5 kcal/mole is sufficient to make it difficult to isolate the most essential interactions from dozens of others. According to Jaenicke (2000) global comparisons of the amino acid compounds and sequences of proteins from mesophiles and extremophiles have not resulted in general rules of protein stabilization. Each protein optimizes internal packing and external solvent interactions by very different mechanisms.

Nevertheless, many authors have stressed a marked contribution of salt bridges in the protein stability of some enzymes (Vetriani et al., 1988; Aguilar et al., 1997; Jaenicke, 1998; Britton, 1999; Likhtenshtein et al., 2000). Theoretical calculation of the electrostatic contributions to the folding free energy of several hyperthermophilic proteins and their mesophilic homologs indicated that these interactions are more favorable in the hyperthermophilic proteins (Xiao nd Honig, 1999). Although due to the large free energy for burying charged groups, buried ion pairs are found to be destabilizing, ion pairs located on the protein surface provide stabilizing interactions. The electrostatic free energy strongly depends on the location of these groups within the protein structure, on favorable interactions with additional polar groups and the formation of stabilizing ion pair networks.

Biochemical and biophysical aspects of hyperthermophilic enzymes are as wide-ranging as all correspondent aspects of mesophilic enzymes but also include specific peculiarities. In this section some specific features of one of the typical hyperthermophylic enzymes, β-glycosidase *Sulfolobus solfataricus,* will be considered.

4.3.2. β-GLYCOSIDASE *SULFOLOBUS SOLFATARICUS*

β-glycosidase from the hyperthermophylic archaeon *Sulfolobus solfataricus* and its recombinants appear to be convenient objects for studying the relationship between intramolecular dynamics and enzyme activity (Nucci et al., 1993; Moracci et al., 1996; D'Auria et al., 1998, 1999; Bismuto et al., 1999). The enzyme is barely active up to

30°C, showing its maximal activity above 95°C and thermostability with a $t_{1/2}$ of 85 h at 75 °C. Using a special stainless steel optical pressure cell, enzyme assays and fluorescence measurements up to pressure of 160 atmosphere boiling the sample have been performed (D'Auria et al., 1999). The enzyme showed maximal activity at 125 °C.

Sulfolobus solfataricus, a hyperthermophilic archaeon first isolated from hot mud pools in the Solfatara crater north of Naples, grows optimally at 87°C (De Rosa et al., 1975). The recombinant enzymes were purified to homogeneity and characterised, showing structural and functional features similar to the native one β-glucosidase from *Sulfolobus solfataricus* MT4 expresses a glycohydrolase activity. Subsequent enzymatic analysis has revealed a much more general exo-β-glycosidase substrate specificity with galactose, glucose, fucose or xylose accepted at the non-reducing end of the substrate, and groups ranging from mono, di and trisaccharides to aromatic and long aliphatic hydrocarbon chains, acceptable as the β-1,4 linked substitute. The thermostable enzyme, as well as other glucosidases, operates by means of a two-step reaction involving a glucosyl-enzyme intermediate, supported by two carboxylic residues. Replacement of one of them, Glu387 for Gln, resulted in a complete destruction of enzyme activity, while the changing of Glu206 for Gln led to a 60-fold reduction of the enzyme reaction's maximum velocity (Moracci et al., 1996). It was suggested that the former group acts as general acid/base catalyst and the latter as a nucleophile.

The β-glycosidase structure was determined with the resolution of 2.4 Å (Aguilar *et al.*, 1997) and its structural, intramolecular, dynamical and functional properties in a wide temperature range and in the presence of chemical perturbants were investigated by means of a broad arsenal of physico-chemical methods. According to the chrystallographic model, the enzyme active site located in the radial channel contains a high concentration of residues, which are highly conserved in all family-1 glycohydrolases. One of these, Glu387, has been implicated in catalysis directly by its formation of a covalent bond with a substrate. The position of Glu387 in the overall fold is very similar to the position at which sites are generally found in other classes of enzymes. The interface between the non-crystallographically related monomers in the biologically active tetramer converts the radial channel to a tunnel running to the surface of the tetrameric enzyme. The full length of this tunnel is approximately 30 Å, suggesting that it could accommodate up to five β-1,4 linked sugar units.

The structural model of the protein (Aguilar et al., 1997) showed two features which differ significantly from the relevant homologous enzymes: a) an unusually large proportion of surface ion-pairs involved in networks which cross-link sequentially separated structures on the protein surface and b) an unusually large number of water molecules buried in hydrophobic cavities in the protein core. The cyanogenic β-glycosidase from clover, a mesophilic enzyme, has around 41% of its charged residues involved in ion-pairs, over 65% of which are isolated pairs. In contrast, in the Ssβ-Gly tetramer, a significantly higher proportion (~58%) of the charged groups are involved in ion-pair interactions in general, and nearly 60% of these ion-pairs occur as part of multiple ion-pair networks involving three or more charge centers.

An additional insight into the contribution of various interactions for protein stability and rigidity may be gained by a comparative data analysis of the differential scanning calorimetry (DSC) of the hyperthermostable and mesophilic enzymes. Accordingly, the polar and non polar interactions and vibrations in a relatively low molecular weight, M_r, (up to 25 kDa) contribute differently to the experimental heat capacity, ΔCp, and its temperature derivative: $\alpha = d(\Delta Cp)/dT$ (Khechinashvili et al., 1995). In this case, the non-polar interactions contribute essentially more than polar interactions and vibrations. The dependencies of ΔC_p^{NP} (in kJ mol^{-1} K^{-1}) on M_r were described by the equation:

$$\Delta C_p^{NP} = 1 + 2.1 \times 10^{-4} M^r + 1.9 \times 10^{-8} M_r^2 \qquad (4.7.)$$

and that for α (our estimation) by:

$$-\alpha = 1 + 1.6 \times 10^{-4} M^r + 3.5 \times 10^{-8} M_r^2 \qquad (4.8.)$$

Taking into account the β-glycosidase molecular weight of $M_r = 240$ kDa and suggesting the same tendency for non-polar contributions as for low molecular proteins, the following values were obtained for the hyperthermophylic enzyme: $\Delta C_P = 1100$ kJ mol^{-1} K^{-1} and $-\alpha = 1100$ kJ mol^{-1} K^{-2} (Likhtenshtein et al., 2000). At the same time, the experimental values are found to be $\Delta C_p =$ about 200 kJ mol^{-1} K^{-1} and $-\alpha < 10$ kJ mol^{-1} K^{-2} [115], which is markedly lower than the expected ones if only non-polar interactions had contributed. This estimation demonstrates the decisive role played by polar interactions in enzyme stability. The lower values of ΔC_p^{NP} and α also indicate a lower value of the protein globule energy fluctuation parameter $\sigma^2{}_{Ev}(T)$, i.e. it highlights globule rigidity.

Physical labeling studies on hyperthermostable β-glycosidase shed additional light on the issue of protein rigidity and intramolecular dynamics. In order to evaluate the conformational flexibility of the enzyme and the mechanisms behind thermal and chemical perturbant activation, the protein was modified by spin and fluorescent labels before its label mobility was monitored by ESR and fluorescence spectroscopies (Shames *et al.*, 2000; Likhtenshtein et al., 2000). The peripheral terminal NH_2 groups located away from the active site for 27 Å were labelled by thiocyanide derivatives of fluorescein and stilbene (FITS and SITS correspondingly). Furthermore, the SH moiety which lay at a distance of 19 Å from the active site, close to the entrance of the active site tunnel, was modified covalently by the nitroxide spin labels with maleimido (MAR·) and iodoacetamido (IAR·) chemically active groups and non-covalently by the hybrid dansyl -nitroxide probe (DR·).

The following peculiarities of the hyperthermostable β-glycosidase, which are different from that for proteins from mesophylic micro-organisms, were revealed in the results of the spin labelling experiments.

(1) The modification of NH_2 and SH groups occurred at a rate that is essentially lower than that typical for mesophylic proteins. This agrees with the enzyme structural model showing a solvent exposure of about 1% and 38% for SH and NH_2 groups, respectively.

(1) The modification of NH_2 and SH groups occurred at a rate that is essentially lower than that typical for mesophylic proteins. This agrees with the enzyme structural model showing a solvent exposure of about 1% and 38% for SH and NH_2 groups, respectively.

(2) Arrhenius plots of the spin labels rotation frequency and polarisation of the fluorescent labels, which are attached to the SH and NH_2 groups correspondingly, exhibit an inflection at T_{in} of about 314 K (Fig. 4.4).

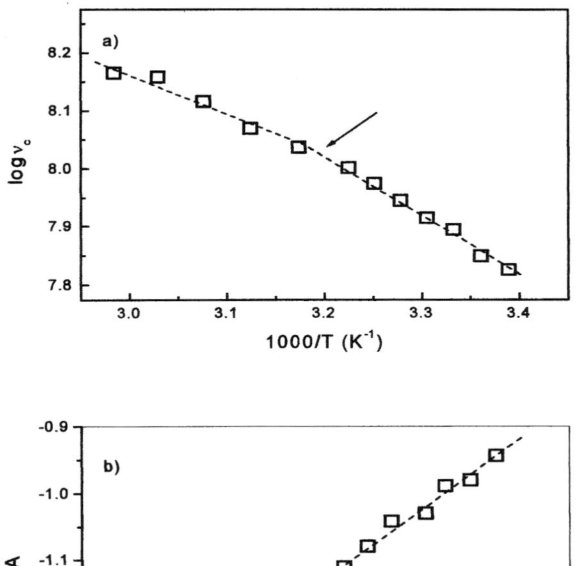

Figure 4.4. Arrhenius plots for (a) the temperature dependence of the rotation frequency nc of MAR labeled b-glycosidase and (b) the temperature dependence of the polarization of FMA labeled b-glycosidase. The arrows indicate the inflection points (Likhtenshtein et al., 2000). Reproduced with permission.

The latter point to a conformational transition of the protein at T_{in}. The time-resolved fluorescence studies indicated that the intrinsic Trp fluorescence emission of the protein was represented by a bimodal distribution with Lorential shape and was strongly affected by the protein conformational dynamics (Bismuto et al., 1999; D'Auria et al.,1999). Parameters of the temperature dependence of the bimodal lifetime distribution, such as fraction relative intensity, the position of centres, and the distribution line widths,

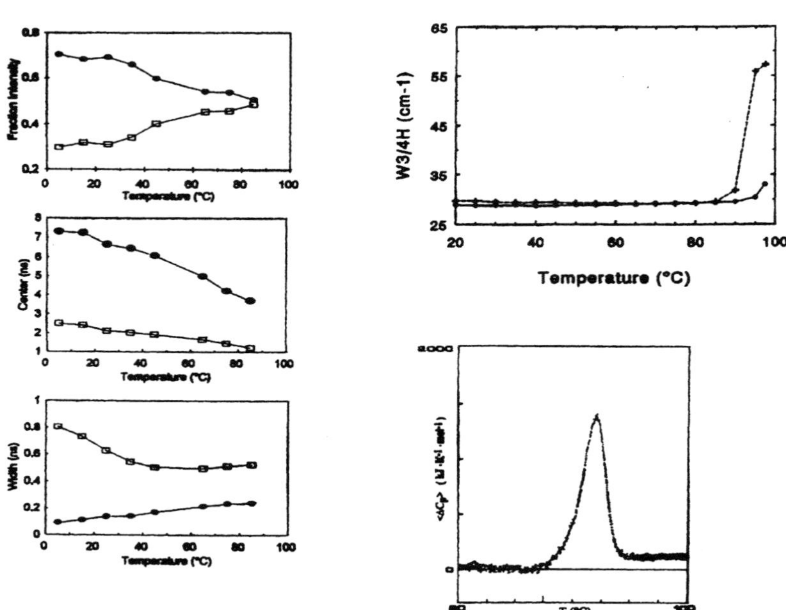

Figure 4.5. Left side. Temperature dependence of the bimodal lifetime distribution parameters of Sulfolobus solfataricus β-glycosidase. Long-lifetime component (squares); short lifetime component (circles). Right upper side W3/4H dependence on temperature: thermal denaturation of Sulfolobus solfataricus β-glycosidase at pD 7.4 (continuous line) and pD 10.0 (dashed line). The lines were obtained by monitoring the amide I width calculated at ¾ of the amide height (W3/4H) as a function of the temperature. Right bottom side <Cp> dependence on temperature for Sulfolobus solfataricus β-glycosidase. (Likhtenshtein et al., 2000). Reproduced with permission.

(3) The experimental values of the activation parameters for the label nitroxide rotation, E_{app} and $\Delta S^{\#}_{app}$, for different spin labels, exhibit linear dependence. Such a compensation dependence is typical for activation parameters of the rotational diffusion of nitroxide spin labels attached to proteins, as well as for enzymatic processes (Likhtenshtein, 1966, 1979; 1976a, b; Lumry and Rajender, 1970; Lumry and Gregory, 1986). The theory behind this phenomenon is based on a model which suggests that rotation of the nitroxide fragment can occur only after the rate limiting step for the rearrangement of the surrounding portion of the protein matrix has provided free volume for the label.

It is necessary to stress that the values of energy activation of the spin label rotation (E_{app}) range from 1,5 to 5.0 kcal/mole and from -1 to -16 e.u. for entropy activation. Such a set of activation parameters is typical for relatively rigid structures such as cross-linked polymers. This behaviour is contrary to the dependencies inherent in "regular" proteins (Likhtenshtein, 1976a). The aforementioned data indicate the essential rigidity of the hyperthermostable protein globule.

(4) Intensification of protein dynamics and conformational transition due to the effect of temperature increase and perturbants monitored by physical labeling and time-

resolved fluorescence techniques led to a more flexible enzyme structure, which is probably responsible for enhanced enzymic activity (Nucci et al., 1993; D'Auria et al., 1999; Shames et al., 2000; Likhtenshtein et al., 2000). Nevertheless, these effects are not accompanied by a marked change in integral protein properties such as heat capacity, degree of helicity and number and properties of intramolecular hydrogen bonds. Such an apparent discrepancy between the integral and local properties was found to be a general feature of "regular" proteins and enzymes, and appears to be a consequence of the hinge-like mechanism of protein dynamics. The fast reversible motion of relatively rigid blocks (polypeptide chains, hydrophobic and polar clusters and domains) can contribute significantly to mobility as well as to some local properties of biophysical labels, although they don't markedly affect the above-mentioned integral physical properties of proteins.

Two mechanisms of the effect of conformational flexibility on β-glycosidase activation caused by a temperature increase and the addition of activators can be inferred. The first mechanism is related to the steric hindrances to the substrate approach to the tunnel of the active site. Flexibility can make it easier for the substrate to access the catalytic group of the active site. The second mechanism concerns the chemical activity of the E387 group. According to the X-ray structural model (Aguilar *et al.*, 1997), this group in the enzyme resting state is connected by a hydrogen bond to histidine R79. Such a connection can dampen the nucleophylic activity of the E387 group. The conformational transition can break the hydrogen bond and therefore activate the carboxyl nucleophile. The fact is that the Michaelis-Menten constant K_M for substrate hydrolysis shows only a slight, if any, dependence on temperature (Nucci etal. 1993) evidences in favour of the latter mechanism.

We may also speculate concerning a reason for the increase in the protein rigidity and correspondent decrease in sensitivity of the spin labels' rotational diffusion to temperature increase above $T_{in} = 312$ K. Efficiency of the chemical processes requires optimum flexibility of the enzyme active site. If the low-temperature tendency toward an increase in the enzyme conformational flexibility in the active area would continue at high temperatures, such an optimization would be destroyed. Thus, the conformational transition may be necessary for maintaining a balance between activity and stability of the enzyme at high temperatures.

CHAPTER 5

AREAS RELATED TO ENZYME CATALYSIS

5.1. Antibody catalysis

Recent developments of catalysis by antibodies are based on two fundamental ideas advanced many years ago. Pauling (1946) proposed that the lowering of the activation energy in enzyme catalysis results from the enzymes affinity for the transition state exceeding its affinity for the substrate. Developing this idea, Jencks (1969, 1981) suggested that stable molecules, analogs of the transition state of a reaction could be used as haptens for the production of antibodies, which catalyze these reactions. These ideas were first realized in the 1980s by groups of Lerner and Schultz (Tramontano et. al., 1986; Pollack et al. 1989; Schultz, 1989; Lerner et al. 1991). Mechanistic and structural studies of antibodies provide insights into the molecular mechanism of enzymatic catalysis and the evolution of catalytic function. The ability to organize the immune response to generate selective catalysts for natural enzymatic reactions and for newly invented chemical processes underscores the chemical potential of large combinatorial libraries (Schultz and Lerner, 1995).

At present more than 100 reactions have been successfully performed with the use of catalytic antibodies (Schultz and Lerner, 1995; Hilvert, 2000; Rader and List, 2000; Blackburn and Garcon, 2000; DeSilva et al., 2000; Kurihara et al. 2000; Vayron et al., 2000; and references therein). Among them are reactions such as sigmatropic rearrangements, triterpen synthesis, hydrolysis, deprotonation, complexation of bivalent metals by protoporphyrin IX, acyl transfer and retroaldol reactions, the regio- and stereochemical of reactions, cleavage of acetals and glycosides, phosphate ester cleavage, amides and organophosphorus compounds hydrolysis, removal of the p-nitrobenzyl ester protecting group, the derivatization of primary amines with naphthalene-2,3-dicarboxaldehyde, etc.

Success in the synthesis of new catalytic antibodies (CAs) depends on the efficiency of each of the following steps: 1) hapten design, 2) immunogen synthesis, 3) preparation of the enzymatic tracer; 4) generation and purification of antibodies; and 5) kinetic assays.

At the most important step of designing a hapten, an analog of potential transition state, attention is focused on suggested distinctions between ground and transition states. These distinctions might be differences in conformation of substrates, changes in hybridization or in distribution of charges, dipoles and nucleophilic and electrophilic groups. For reactions involving several substrates, multisubstrate analogues can be used. Crystallographic and NMR (nuclear Overhauser effects) data on hapten-antibody complexes can confirm the complementarity of designed haptens and induced binding pockets.

Though the values of the Michaels complex ($K_m \approx 10^{-4}$ - 10^{-5} M) for reactions catalyzed by natural enzymes and catalytic antibodies were found to be of the same order of magnitude, the catalytic constants (k_{cat}) for CAs commonly 10^4 fold lower than that for correspondent enzymes. Experimental ratio values (k_{cat}/k_{uncat}) for CAs ranges within 10^2-10^6, while these values for similar enzymatic reactions can reach 10^{17}.

Examples of reactions catalyzed by catalytic antibodies, structures of corresponding transition states and haptens are presented in Figs. 5.1 and 5.2.

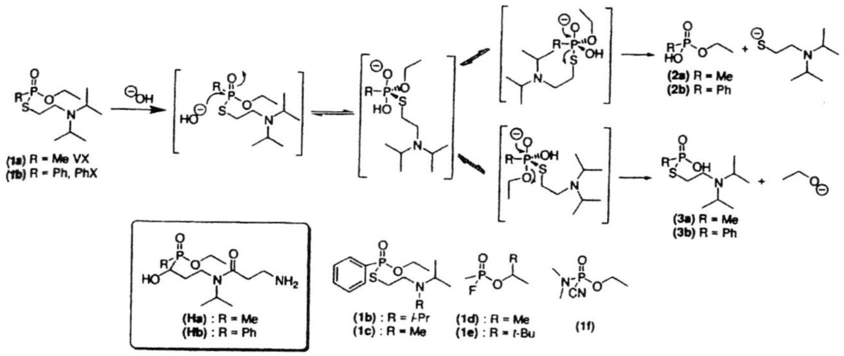

Figure 5.1. The oxy-Cope rearrangement catalyzed by antibody AZ-28, suggested transition state, and hapten (Hilvert 2000). Reproduced with permission.

In the case of the oxy-Cope rearrangement, NOE and X-ray structural analysis indicated preorganization of the normally extended hexadien substrate into cyclic conformation, ligand recognition is mediated by van der Waals contacts, π-stacking with aromatic rings and hydrogen bonding. The necessity of protoporphyrin IX distortion in the binding site of an antibody catalyzed in complexation with Fe^{2+} was proved by the X-ray structural analysis. The non-planar N-methylated porphyrins, which are inhibitors of ferrochelatase, makes extensive contacts with binding sites of the correspondent antibody.

The use of hydroxylated hapten mimicking the transition state in hydrolysis of the organophosphorus poisoning compound produces an antibody capable of hydrolyzing warfare nerve agents such as Sarin and Soman in *vivo* (Vayron, 2000a,b). Another recent example of antibody catalysis is the formation of steroid ring A of the lanosterol nucleus (Hasserodt et al., 2000). Antibodies generated by immunization with an 4-aza-steroid aminoxide hapten initiated the cationic cyclization of an oxidosqualene derivative.

Current and potential applications of catalytic antibodies in reactive immunization, therapy, biochemical analysis and biotechnology have been discussed (Schultz and Lerner, 1995; Rader and List, 2000; Blackburn and Garcon, 2000; Hilvert, 2000; Rader and List, 2000; Blackburn and Garcon, 2000; Vayron , 2000a,b).

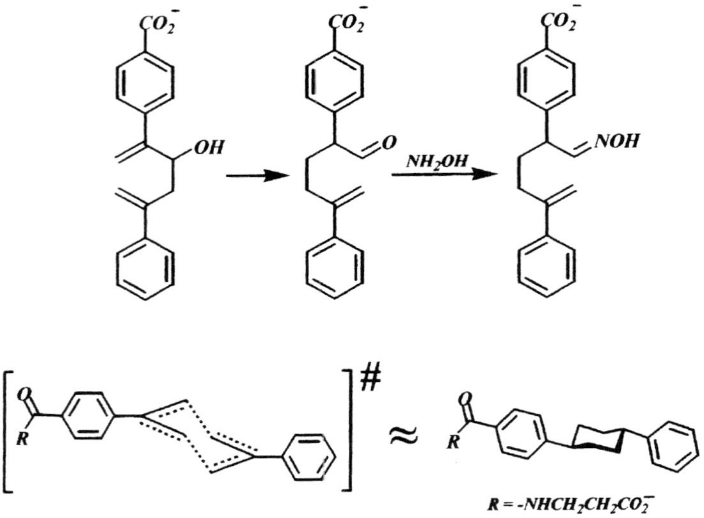

Figure 5.2. Hydrolysis reactions, hapten, and organophosphorus poisoning compound structures (Vayron et al., 2000). Reproduced with permission

5.2. Enzymes in organic solvents

In spite of a long-time paradigm that enzymes can be active only in their natural aqueous media and other solvents cause deactivation and denaturation of proteins, at present a growing number of investigations are devoted to enzymatic reactions in organic solvents (Klibanov, 2001; Ke et al., 1996; Koskinen and Klibanov, 1996; and references therein). Such enzymes as α-chymotrypsin, subtilisin ribonuclease, pancreatuc lipase, and horse radish peroxidase have been found to be markedly active in organic solvents (alcohols, amines, tiols,anhydrous alkanes, acetonitril, dichloromethane, methyl acetate, etc.).

While enzymes, as a rule, essentially lose their normal activity and specificity, they possess new useful features: 1) utilization of substrates non-soluble in water; 2) their ability to change substrate and inhibitor selectivity and specificity; 3) they alternate of reactions thermodynamics and kinetics reactions so that desirable products are favoured; 4) improvements of enzyme stability; and 5) the possibility to fix enzymes and reaction intermediates at states of certain pH and ionic strength in both solution and crystal form ('molecular memory effects').

The transfer of enzymes from water to organic solvents is accompanied by a decrease in their conformational flexibility, desolvation of substrate and catalytic groups, distortion of active centers, change in acidity and basicity, nuleophilicity and electrophilicity of functional groups, drastic change in distribution of electrostatic potential over protein globules including the area of enzyme active sites. For example, hydrolytic enzymes can utilize such 'unusual' substrates as alcohols, amines and tiols with the formation of corresponding products. In such conditions syntheses of esters from acids and alcohols becomes thermodynamically allowed. Drastic changes have also been observed in enantiomeric, prochiral, regio- and chemoselectivities.

Here we confine ourselves to a few typical examples of enzymatic systems in organic solvents (Klibanov, 2001; and references therein). α-chymotripsin is stable in unhydrous conditions for several hours at 100 °C. The α-chymotrypsin hydrophilic peptide substrate is transformed in organic solvent three times faster than hydrophobic substrate, while the latter in water is found to be non-reactive In water solution the dominant product of the conversion of prochyral 2-(3,5-dimetoxybenzyl)1,3-propandiol by this enzyme is the S-monoester, whereas in acetonitril R-enantiomer is formed.

The activity of enzymes in organic solvents is often dramatically low compared to that in water. This limitation can be largely overcome by crown ether treatment of enzymes. The marked activation (from 333 to 2480-fold) of subtilisin Carsberg in ethanol and acetone in the presence of salts (sodium iodide and sodium acetate) has been observed (Ru et al., 2000). Combination of co-immobilization of penicillin G acylase with polyethyleneimine and its chemical modification by polyaldehyde dextran allowed to increase of the enzyme activity in organic solvents (Fernandez-Lafuente et al., 1998). It was shown that activity of enzymes in organic solvents is greatly increased by crown ether treatment of enzymes. The complexation of 18-crown-6 with lysine ammonium groups of enzymes leads to violation of inter- and intra molecular salt bridges and, consequently, to improving thermodynamical and catalytical properties of the enzymes in new conditions (Van Unen et al., 2002).

5.3. Enzymes in synthetic chemistry

Isolation and investigation of over 3000 enzymes have established a powerful basis for synthesizing of myriad chemical compounds. The number of catalytic chemical processes can be infinitely expanded by the use genetic engineering, chemical modification, and a variety of media. A large body of publications exists on this subject (see for example Silversman, 2000; Dordick, 1991); Fersht, 1999; Jones, 1989; Drauz and Waldmann, 1995; Tramper,. (1996); Faber, 1997; Roberts, 1999; Adam et al., 1999; Klibanov, 2001; Koeller and Wong, 2001; Walsh, 2001; Arnold, 2001; and references therein). Recently it was shown that RNA and DNA possess catalytic activity as well (Narlikar and Hershlag, 1997; Sheppard et al., 2000). This Section is restricted with a brief over review on the use enzymes in synthetic chemistry and considering of several specific examples.

Among enzymes commonly used in organic synthesis in research laboratories, and pharmaceutical and biothechnological industry are the following: esterases (including lipases), amidases, proteases and acylases, dehydrogenases, mono-and dioxidases, peroxidases, kinases, aldolases, glycosidases, phosphorylases, phosphotases, transaminases, hydrolases, and isomerases, lyases, hydrases and sulphotransferases. Enzymes are also effective tools for protecting amino, tiol, carboxyl, and hydroxyl groups (Kadereit and Waldmann 2001). The growing application of biocatalysis takes place in industrial synthetic chemistry. For instance, optically active α-oxifunctional carboxylic acids, aldehydes, ketons, diols, halo, amino derivatives, epoxides and other compounds are important in in the production of grugs, pesticides, fungicides, herbicides, flavors, etc. Fig. 5.3 illustrates the advantages of biocatalitic synthesis of α-oxyfunctionalized carbonyl compounds.

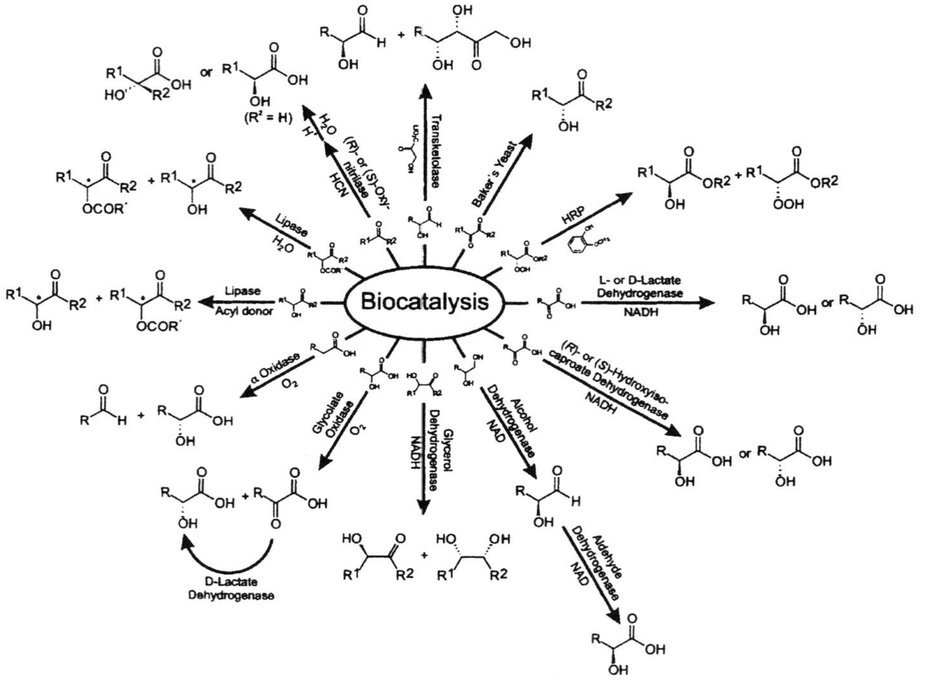

Figure 5..3. Biocatalytic synthesis of α-oxyfunctionalized carbonyl compounds (Adam et al., 1999) Reproduced with permission.

Recently a number of enzymatic systems have been developed at several chemical companies including lipases (synthesis of enantiotrope alcohols, R-amid, S-amin), nitrilases (R-mandelic acid), amidases (non-proteinogenic L-amino acids), aspartic acid ammonia lyase (L-aspartic acid), penicilin acylase (6-Aminopenicilanic acid), acylases (semisynthetic penicillins), etc.(Koeller and Wong, 2001; and references therin).

The following new trends in enzymatic synthesis can be delineated: the development of new enzymatic reactions; enzyme immobilization and stabilization; the use of organic solvents and two phase systems; site-directed mutagenesis; chemical modification of enzymes; antibody catalysis; catalysis by RNA and DNA; *de novo* design of biocatalists; employment of recombinant DNA for production of enzymes; and use computational and combinatorial methods

5.4. Enzymes design and redesign

Recent advantages in enzyme catalysis, protein chemistry and sequences, and the determination of three-dimensional structures and genetic engineering have laid a basis for the development of methods for enzyme design and redesign (Ferst, 1999; Clelend and Craik, 1996; Altamarino et al., 2000; Benson et al., 2000; Babitt, 2000; Ness et al., 2000; Ostermeier aand Bencovic, 2000; Fersht and Alamarino, 2001; DeGrado, 2001; Penning and Jetz, 2001; Lu et al., 2001; Oi et al., 2001; Tann and Oi, 2001; Tann et al., 2001; Saven, 2001; Arnold, 2000, 2001; Arnold and Volkov, 1999). The following directions in this area have sparked interest: 1) introducing novel functionality in native enzymes and protein by modifying their sequence and chemical composition; 2) directed evolution (mimicking the evolution of analogs *in vitro*); 3) producing semisynthetic enzymes by attaching new functionality; and 4) the design of protein sequences *de novo*.

A generation of new enzymes via covalent modification of existing proteins can be produced using several methods (Oi et al., 2001; an references therein). Chemical approaches for converting catalytic groups of enzymes have been described . For instance, the active site serine hydroxyl group of subtilisin was replaced by a thiol and the active site thiol was changed for a hydroxyl. An alternative approach involves the replacement of large portions of a protein via proteolysis or chemical cleavage. Ribonuclease A was cleaved by subtilisin into two fragments, S-peptide and S-protein, followed by the introduction of a pyridoxal cofactor to S-protein . The modified protein catalyzes convertion L-alanine to pyruvate. Flavin analogues were incorporated into the active site groove of papain that was used as the protein scaffold. These new semisynthetic enzymes catalyze the oxidation of dihydronicotinamides with activity of about 10% relative activity of the native NADH-specific FMN reductase.

Another protein and enzyme design process bases on the introduction of metal-binding sites into protein scaffolds (Lu et al., 2001). This approach includes two steps: 1) the choice of scaffolds such as *de novo* designed α-helical structures; and 2) the design and engineering of metal-containing active sites. This approach involves the redesign of existing metal-binding sites to new sites with different functions and the design and engineering of new metal-binding sites. In the frame of the first direction, experiments on the variation of proxymal and distal ligands and types of cofactors of heme proteins were performed. The most interesting results of these experiments were the successful transformation of heme-histidine proteins to heme-cysteine enzymes analogues, such as cytochrome P450 and chloroperoxidase. The human myoglobin with the proximal cysteine ligand exposes spectral properties typical for active sites of above mentioned enzymes. In the result of the modification, a 5-fold increase of in P450-like monooxydegenase activity was observed. Redesign of copper, non-heme iron and other metal-containing proteins have been also performed (Lu et al., 2001 and references therein). Design and engineering of new metal-binding sites involves rational design using the automated computer search algorithm and other empirical and semiempirical approaches, as well as design by combinatorial /evolution methods (selection of metalloproteins through phage display, search for metalloantibodies, and directed evolution of heme enzymes). For instance, the peroxidase activity of horse heart myoglobin was 25-fold improved using the random mutagenesis technique.

Biological redesign uses recent achievements in the recombinant DNA method, site-directed mutageneses, and growth of the databases of protein structures and sequences (Arnold, 2001). The main problem with this approach is the requirement of a detailed understanding of the structure and mechanisms of potential enzyme and its connection with the protein sequence. An example of such an approach came from work on dehalogenase (Kiang at al., 1999). The enzyme active site consists of a portion that provide 2-enoyl-coenzyme A (CoA) binding, an oxyanion pocket, and stations at which the enzyme binding and functional groups are in a position suitable for the catalylitic process. The site-directed diversification of eight amino-acid groups in 4-chlorobenzoyl-CoA-dehalogenase has led to the new ability to catalyze the hydration of crotonyl-CoA. Another approach to breeding new catalysts is the use random, mutagenesis, gene, recombinaton and screening *in vitro* conditions (Arnold, 2000, Ness et al., 2000). By such a method an enzyme desaturase, which normally introduces double bonds into phytoene was converted to a biocatalyst with the ability to produce other carotenoids containing double bonds at various positions. Nonheme chemistry was used as an exemplar for the emergence of superoxide dismutase, Fenton-like and dioxygen reductin functions in *Escherichia coli* thioredoxin lacking iron and oxygen binding sites (Benson et al., 2000).

Two approaches have been suggested for an alteration of large segments of protein sequence (domain swapping) (Penning and Jetz, 2000 and references therein). One of them can be used when two enzymes share common restricted sites in their DNAs. In thr second method, a target protein is composed from a series of synthetic or biosynthetic fragments.

Site directed mutagenesis, based on knowledge of three-dimensional structures and amino-acid sequences, has been successful in redesigning the substrate specificity of many enzymes including dehydrogenases, acetylholinesterase, proteases, aminotransferases, restriction enzymes, etc. (Fersht, 1992 and references therein) Malate dehydrogenase, which catalyzes lactate to pyruvate, was converted into malate dehydrogenase, which converts malate to oxaloacetate . Mutation of three residues in the area of the enzyme substrate pocket resulted in a 107-fold increase for the malate dehydrogenase reaction. Tripple mutation of a pyridoxal phosphate dependent enzyme, L-aspartate amino aminotransferase drastically altered the partitioning of the covalent intermediate aldimine: the ratio of b-decarboxylase activity to transaminase activity increased 25 million-fold .

It was experimentally shown that the indol-3-glycerol-phosphate synthase (IGPS) could switch its activity to that of phosphoribosylanthranilate isomerase (PRAI) (Altamarino et al., 2000: Fersht and Altamarino, 2001). Both classes of enzymes share similar α/β-barrels. Asn α/β-barrel protein served as an scaffold for introducing a new function. The PRAI function was evolved using the combined approach of rational design, *in vivo* mutation, recombination and in *vivo* selection. The new enzymes exhibit catalytic activity ($k_{cat}/K_m = 10^7$ $M^{-1}s^{-1}$) which is similar to the activity of native enzymes. The authors suggested the strategy of enzymes loop replacing may be of wider application.

The current status of the problem of *de novo* design of proteins and prospects in the area including energy landscape theory of protein folding, atomistic and minimal models, elements of protein design, and statistical approaches have been discussed in arecent review by Saven (2001).

CHAPTER 6

CHEMICAL MODELS OF ENZYMES

6.1. General principles

Outstanding catalytic and regulator properties of enzymes, which catalyze various chemical reactions with high rates, specificity and selectivity in mild conditions (ambient temperature, normal pressure, neutral aqua media) have long been of interest to chemists. A greater knowledge of the principles of the structure and mechanism of enzymes and the realization of these principles in chemistry would signify a new decisive step in the development of the theory of kinetics and catalysis and its application in industry (Shilov, 1997; Fersht, 1999, Groves, 1985, 2000; Silverman, 2000; Diekmann et.al., 2002)

The terms "mimicking enzymatic processes" or "chemical models of enzymes" have no monosemantic and exact definitions. In some cases mimicking involves preceding a specific fast chemical reaction catalyzed by an enzyme in mild conditions. In other cases, attempts to construct chemical structures similar to an enzyme active site and to imitate different steps of an enzymatic process are made. Depending on the knowledge of the detailed structure and action mechanism of a target enzyme, starting positions of chemist are also diverse.

At present, the following general steps of mimicking enzymatic processes may be formulated.

1. Previous detailed analysis of existing data on the structure and action mechanism of an enzyme, together with the experience and chemical intuition of the investigator, allow the composition a realistic working program which could provide optimal conditions for each stage of the enzymatic processes.

2. One must choose of basic (primary) catalytic groups directly involved in the catalytic process. These groups may be nucleophilic and electrophilic reagents, general acids and bases, complexes of transition metals of a given valence, etc. It is necessary to emphasize that the chemical reactivity of these reagents, as well as the activity of correspondent catalytical groups in the active sites of enzymes, have to be optimal to provide smooth thermodynamic relief in all steps of the process.

3. Selection of secondary groups, which can regulate the reactivity of the attacking groups. For instance, adjacent basic imidazol or carboxylate can strengthen nucleophilic properties of a hydroxyl or acid groups can assist in the reactions of electroplic reagants. For helping along redox processes with participation of transition metals, adjacent acid and basic charged groups can be useful. At multi-electron processes, the presence of transition metal clusters in the vicinity of primary metal atoms plays a key role.

4. Optimal disposition of primary and secondary catalytic groups within a single super molecule or on a polymer or membrane template according to its sterical adjusting for attacking substrates.

5. Including in the catalytic system are additional residues, which can form portions capable of bounding and precisely orienting the substrate molecule.

6. A matrix, carrying the model catalysis active site, should provide unimpeded entrance to reagents and exit to products, and free room for conversion of each intermediate (the dynamic adaptation). In other words, the matrix should exhibit optimum molecular dynamics similar to intramolecular dynamics of proteins.

7. Each stage of the catalytic process should obey the "principle of optimum motion" (Sections 2. and 2.9). Eventually, constrained pretransition-state complex that activates cleavage or formation of chemical bonds, have to be formed. The realization of this last requirement is the most challenging and difficult problem of the mimicking enzymes processes.

In the mimicking of an enzymatic process there is no need to copy the structure of protein and coenzyme groups and all stages of this process. In the course of evolution, Nature created enzymes in specific conditions in certain media and utilized certain "building materials". Besides chemical functions, enzymes bear many other obligations, serving as units of complicated enzymatic and membrane ensembles. These conditions have not always been the most favorable for catalytic properties and the stability of enzymes.

6.2. Reduction of dinitrogen

The process of assimilation of atmospheric nitrogen by microorganisms was known since 1838. Involvement of these molecules in a chemical reaction under mild conditions seemed to desagree with theoretical considerations and experimental evidence of the extraordinary chemical inertness of dinitrogen. The first break through in this problem was made in the pioneering work of Volpin and Shur (1964). These authors demonstrated the first reactions of dinitrogen reduction by such reducing agents as Al-AlBr$_3$, LiAlH$_4$-AlBr$_3$ in aprotic media in the presence of transition metals (FeCl$_3$, MoCl$_5$, CrCl$_3$).

In the 1970's, on the basis of the concept of the multi-electron mechanism of dinitrogen reduction in polynuclear transition metal complexes (Likhtenshtein and Shilov, 1970), dinirogen reduction of hydrazine and ammonia in protic media (methanol, water) involving relative weak reducing agents was discovered (Denisov et al., 1970; Shilov, 1984; Shilov and Likhtenshtein, 1971). The first systems discovered were heterogeneous and included metal hydroxides Mo(OH)$_3$-Ti(OH)$_3$ or V(OH)$_2$-Mg(OH)$_2$, which can be considered as giant clusters of transition metals. As a model of biological dinitrogen fixation, N$_2$ was reduced by Ti^{3+}, Cr^{2+}, or V^{2+} in the presence of Mo compounds in aqua and alcohol solutions, while CO strongly inhibited redaction. The principal product was hydrazine, although N$_2$ was reduced to NH$_3$ at higher temperatures. One of this system, complexes of V(II) and catechol in the protic media, including water, turned out to be homogeneous (Nikonova and Shilov., 1977; Shilov, 1997). In the presence of this complex the following reactions take place:

$$V^{(II)}_4 + N_2 = V^{(II)}_4 N_2$$

$$V^{(II)}_4 N_2 + V^{(II)}_4 + 8H^+ \rightarrow 8V(^{III}) + 2NH_3 + H_2O$$

Recently, a detailed analysis was performed of the EPR spectra of the V(II)-pyrocatechol complex active in the reduction of dinitrogen in solution. (Shestakov and Shilov, 2001). The hyperfine structure of the EPR spectrum of the test complex was explained as a consequence of strong exchange interactions. Conclusions were reached on the tetranuclear character of the active complex of the centrosymmetric structure with the romboid disposition of the vanadium atoms. These authors suggested that the vanadium four-nuclear complex reduces dinotrogen by thr four-electron mechanism. A hydrazine derivative and hydrogen are shown to be formed in the coordination sphere of tetramers, while ammonia is formed in the coordination sphere of an octamer (Dzabiev et al., 1999). Redaction of nitrogen to ammonia is accompanied by the evolution of diydrogen.

The systems involving Nb(III), Ta(III), Ti(II) and Cr(II) also reduced N_2 in protic media. Mo(III) complexes catalyzed reduction of N_2 by $Ti(OH)_3$ and sodium amalgam (Volpin and Shilov,1995).

Successful attempts have been made to model different steps of the nitrogenase reactions (Henderson and Leigh 1999; Sellmann, 1995; Sellmann et al., 1999; Leigh, 1995; 1998; Lee, 2002; Helleren et al., 1999, 2000; Hauser et al., 2002). Dinitrogen can displace a variety of ligands in metal complexes, including ammonia, water, chloride and dihydrogen (Leigh, 1995; Helleren et al., 1999). The substitution of dihydrogen in complexes $[FeH(H_2)(phosphine)_x]$ + [phosphine = $R_2PCH_2CH_2PR_2$ (R = Et or Me) or $P(CH_2CH_2PR'_2)3$ (R' = Me or Ph)] for ligands L (MeCN, PhCN, or Cl$^-$) has been shown in both acetone and THF. The stepwise protonation of dinirogen bond to molybdenum (0) has been established (Henderson et al., 1983). The $[(L) MoFe_3Cl_3(CH_3CN)]^{n-}$ cuban clusters have been found effective in the catalytic reduction of hydrazine to ammonia in the presence of cobaltocene as a source of electrons and lutidine hydrocloride as a source of protons (Coucouvanis , 2000;Coucouvanis et al., 1995).

A large new series of mono- and double cubane-type $[MoFe^3(S,Se)_n]$ and $[VFe_3S_4]^z$ clusters (z = 1+, 2+, 3+) with ligands $(Cl^-)_3$, $P(Et)_3$, $(HBpz)_3$ and other ligands has been prepared as a possible precursor species for clusters related to those present in vanadium-containing nitrogenase. Structure and redox conversions of the molybdenum-iron sulfide-bridged double cubanes have been characterized by X-ray crystallographic analysis, magnetic measurements, Mössbauer and ESR spectroscopies (Hauser et al., 2002 and references therin).

A study was conducted to elucidate the mechanism of FeMo-cofactor catalytic activity in non-enzymic conditions and to compare its catalytic behavior with that of the nitrogenase (Bazhenova et al., 2000). The kinetics were investigated of C_2H_2 redaction by multielectron donors, Zn and Eu amalgams, catalyzed by isolated FeMo-cofactor and inhibition of this process by CO. Results indicated that the FeMo-cofactor has a high level of self-sufficiency and can realize of some of its functions without the protein.

Thus, a number of systems of the catalytic and noncatalytic reduction of dinitrogen to hydrazin and ammonia and the successful synthesis of model iron- and iron-molibdenum (vanadium) clusters have been reported. These investigations have formed a basis for subsequent progress in mimicking the nitrogenase reaction.

6.3. Hydroxylation of organic compounds

Oxidation of organic compounds with dioxygen, for examples the conversion of alkanes to alcohols, is highly exothermic. Nevertheless, dioxygen is a weak one-electron oxidant (E_0 = -0,3 eV) and the thermodynamic barrier of the first stage of the reaction with the formation of superoxide O_2^- or HO_2^- is high. Involving dioxygen in a chemical reaction requires its conversion in radical or radicaloid forms, in which they act as strong one-electron oxidants, or into a form capable of performing two-electron oxidative processes (hydrogen peroxide, for instance). The most traditional way for oxygen activation is its previous reduction by a reducing agent, which is accompanied by protonation (Fig. 6.1).

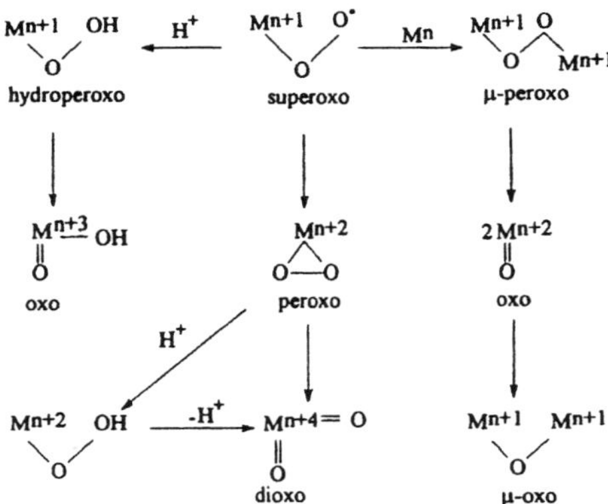

Figure 6.1. Various forms of "activated" oxygen and its complexes with metal. (Shilov, 1997) Reproduced with permission.

The most challenging problem for chemists was mimicking the biological hydroxylation of alkanes catalyzed by cytochrome P-450 and especially the conversion of methane to methanol. The first principle breakthrough in this direction was the pioneering work of Groves and his colleagues (Groves,1997, 2000; Groves and McGlusky, 1976; Groves Subramanian, 1984; Groves et al., 1994). The first synthetic analog which closely mimicked the chemistry of cytochrome P450 was chloro-α,β,γ,δ-tetraphenylporphinatoiron (III) [Fe(III)TPP(Cl)] with iodozylbenzene as the oxidant to effect the stereospecific epoxidation of olefins and hydroxylation of cyclohexane. This compound may be considered as an analog of oxoiron (IV) cation radical of protoporphyrin IX.

Numerous results of the use of iron-porphyrin complexes and strong oxidants $KHSO_4$, $NaOCl$, $ROOH$, ozone, etc; as model systems, have been reviewed (Gross and Simkhovich, 1998; Harris et al., 1998; Hegg et al., 1999; Nam et al., 1999; McLain et al., 2000; Groves and McGlusky, 1976; Groves, and Subramanian, 1984; Groves, 2000; De Visser et al., 2001; Ueno, 2001; Ogliaro et al., 2001; Diekmann et al., 2002). Several examples illustrate recent advantages in this area. A cytochrome P 450 model heme, which consists of an iron(III) meso-tetraphenylporphyrin with four chiral hydroxybinaphthyl moieties, was designed and prepared (Matsu-Ura et al., 2000). One of the hydroxyl groups was converted to a thioglycolate group, which provides the thiolate for binding with iron in one axial position. The other axial site is vacant, thus allowing for the formation of the adduct with dioxygen. Reaction with KO_2 under oxygen takes place. The bound dioxygen is stabilized by hydrogen bonding with the inner hydroxyl groups on the binaphthyl moiety.

The synthesis of a stable FeIII-porphyrin complex-alcenethiolate complex, in which the sulphur atom is sterically protected from reactive molecules such as O_2 and NO by bulky groups, has been reported (Suzuki et al., 2000). The electronic absorption and infrared spectra indicate that NO coordinates reversibly to the FeIII atom of the complex.

Direct hydroxylation of cyclohexane, alkyl cyclohexanes and cyclooctane by high-valent oxoporphyrin cation radical with strong electron-acceptor substituent $[Fe(TF_4TMAR)^{5+}]$ (I) (T4TMAR = meso-tetrakis(2,3, 5,6-tetrafluoro-4-N,N,N-trimethylaniniumyl)porphrinato] in the presence of H_2O_2 have been reported (Nam et al., 1999). In CH_3CN the hydroxylation in this system was found to be highly stereospecific, and the kinetic isotope effect was determined as 3.7. In the presence of $H_2^{18}O$, 40% of cycloxexanol-^{18}O was originated from $H_2^{18}O$. The high valent iron oxo porphyrin complex $[Fe(TF_4TMAR)\cdot^+Fe^{IV}=O]^{5+}$ is able to hydroxylate alkanes even at $-40\ ^{\circ}C$.

Complete selectivity of the single turnover hydroxylation of cholesterol at carbon 25 was induced by a membrane-bound manganese porphyrin (Groves, 1997). Ruthenium porphyrins catalyzed hydrocarbon hydroxylation with the high reactivity and turnover number of about 1000 per minute. In model system developed by Breslow and his coworkers (Breslow, 1986; Breslow et al., 1997), four cyclodextrin groups were attached to a synthetic manganese porphyrin (Fig. 6.2). A substrate steroid was captured by hydrophobic central cavities of the doughnut-shaped heptamylose sugars and the five-turnover hydroxylation occurred only at carbon 6 of the substrate.

Model diiron complexes mimicking active centers of enzymes (MMO, hemerythrin, ribonucleotide reductase, acyl-acyl carrier protein desaturase, toluene, monooxygenase, ω-alcane hydroxylase) have been synthesized (Wallar and Lipscomb, 1996; Hu and Gorun, 2000; Shilov, 1997; Du Bois J. et al., 2000; Khenkin, Shteinman,1995; Shteinman, 2001;and references therein). Several ligands for formation of chelate diiron complexes have been proposed including tris(pyrazol) borate, (polypyridyl)- with a single bridging phenoxyl, the dicarboxylate ligand m-xylenediamine bis(Kemp's triacid)imide, and 2.6-diarylbenzoic acid, dibenzofuran 4-6-diacetic acid, etc.

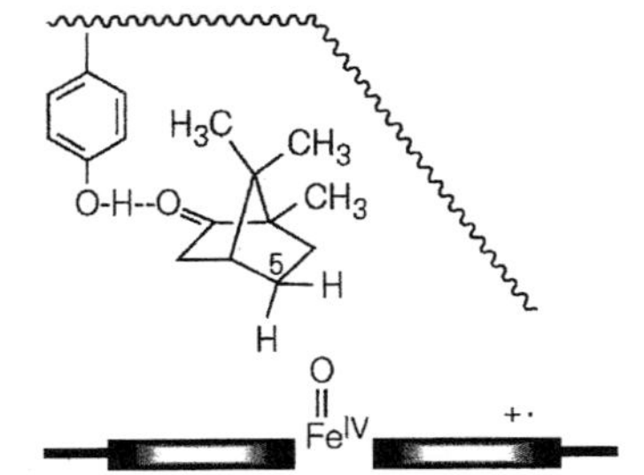

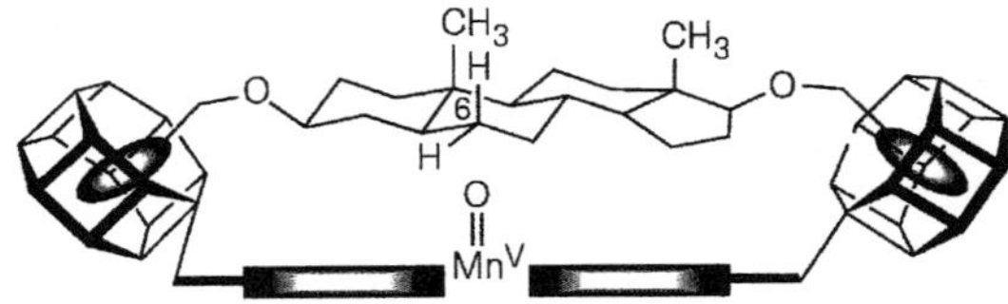

Figure 6.2. Scematic presentation of the Cytochrome P-450cam active site (a) and the Breslow model of steroid hydroxylase (Groves, 1997). Reproduced with permission.

First two complexes with a (μ-oxo)(μ-hydroxo)diiron (III) core $[Fe_2(O)(OH)(6TLA)_2(ClO_4)_3]$ (I) and $[Fe_2(O)_2(6TLA)_2(ClO_4)_2]$ (II), were isolated and characterized (Zang et al., 1995). Structure of a (-1,2-peroxo)bis(-carboxylato)diiron(III)model for the peroxo intermediate in the methane monooxygenase hydroxylase reaction cycle is presented in Fig, 6.3.

The Mössbauer spectrum and magnetic susceptibility proved diiron structure of the complex and found it to be similar to that in methane monooxygenase and relative enzymes. The crystal structures of synthetic diiron complexes of modeling compounds P and Q in the active site of MMO have been reported. Kim and Lippard (1996) have synthesized and structurally characterized a model for the peroxo intermediate in the methane monooxygenase hydroxylase reaction cycle, the complex [Fe2(μ-1,2-O2)μ-O2CCH2Ph)2-{HB(pz')3}2 where pz' = 3.5-bis(isopropyl)-pyrazol. In the complex, the two iron atoms are linked by two bridging phenyl acetate ligands and a peroxoligand is coordinated in a *cis*-μ-η1:η1 fashion. The transient complex [Fe2(O)2(5-MeTPA)2] (ClO4)3, TPA = tris2-(pyridylmethyl)amin, has been detected in reaction of H2O2 with a (μ-oxo)diiron (III)TPA complex in CH_3CN at –40 ˚C (Dong et al., 1995). The structure of the complex has been determined with the use of a set of physical methods including ESR, magnetization, EXAFS, X-absorption, Mössbauer and Raman spectroscopy. These properties consisted of a valence-delocalized low-spin (S = ½) Fe^{III} - low-spin (S = 1)Fe^{IV} pair coupled by both Heisenberg and double exchanges.

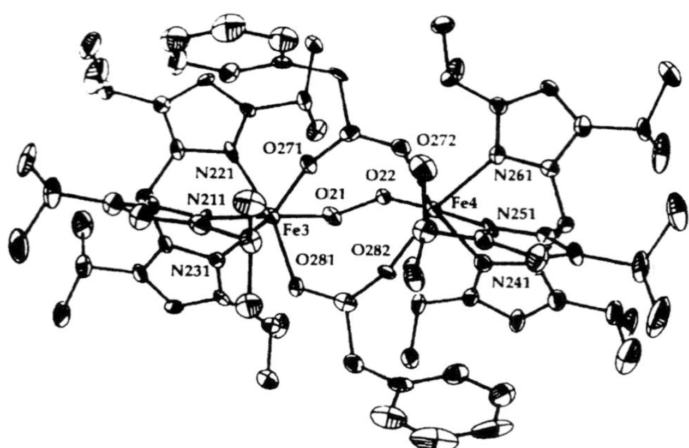

Figure 6..3. . Structure of a (-1,2-peroxo)bis(-carboxylato)diiron(III)model for the peroxo intermediate in the methane monooxygenase hydroxylase (Zang et al., 1995) Reproduced with permission.

The model $[Fe_2OL(OBz)](ClO_4)_2$ complex was prepared with the interaction of a polydentate ligand 2,6-bis[3-[N,N-di(2-pyridylmethyl)amino]propoxy]benzoic acid (LH) with $Fe(ClO_4)_3$ in the presence of NaOBz. (Trukhan et al., 1998). In this structure, one bridging carboxylate (in L) is fixed, and the other (in OBz) remains mobile, retaining the capability for substitution reactions and occupying two labile coordination sites. The complex catalyzes selective oxidation of methane to MeOH by H_2O_2. Oxidation of methane, ethane, hexane, and cyclohexane by hydrogen peroxide and tert-Bu hydroperoxide in acetonitrile catalyzed by binuclear μ-oxo-bridged iron complexes $[Fe_2OL_4(H_2O)_2](ClO_4)_4$ and $[Fe_2OL_2(PhCOO)_2(H_2O)_2](ClO_4)_2$, where L = bpy, 4,4'-$Me_2$bpy, 4,4'-$(ClCH_2)_2$bpy, phen, and 5-$NO_2$phen, was demonstrated (Gritsenko et al., 1995)

To mimic dinuclear active sites of some nonheme diiron proteins, ten new polydentate and potentially dinucleating ligands containing a carboxylate moiety designed to bridge two metal atoms, were synthesized (Trukhan et al., 2000). The reaction of these ligands with $Fe(ClO_4)_3 \cdot 9H2O$ leads to ferric μ-oxo-μ-carboxylato iron complexes [Fe2O(L)2 (H2O2)2](ClO4)2 and [Fe2O(L)(BzO)](ClO4)2 (L = ligand), containing one or two immobilized bridging carboxylates, respectively. X-ray analysis showed that some of these complexes are dimers or network polymers in the solid state.

It was shown (Ovanesyan et al., 2000) that iron complexes formed during the thermal treatment of FeZSM-5 zeolite perform single-turnover cycles of methane oxidation to methanol at ambient conditions when nitrous oxide is used as a source of oxygen. The long-living active intermediate is capable of transferring an accepted O atom into a C-H bond of methane to produce methanol at 100% selectivity. On the basis of joint Mossbauer and catalytic data, the structure and composition of iron active centers are suggested.

Commonly accepted mechanisms of the MMO reactions are based on the concept of the activation of dioxygen or the use of "shunts" such as H_2O_2. Nevertheless, the new mechanism of methane oxidation via an intermediate complex containing pentacoordinated carbon has been forwarded (Shilov, 1997, Karasevich et al., 1998, 1999). This suggestion is based on experiments on the multiple H-D exchange and methane oxidation catalyzed by platinum (II) complexes, ([H_2PtCl_6], for instance). Formation of methyl platinum (IV) chloride complex in methane oxidation was confirmed by its NMR spectrum.

6.4. Light energy conversion

There are two main objections to the mimicking of the photosynthetic process of light energy conversion in reaction centers via the mechanism of charge photoseparation on cation and anion radicals: 1) establishing factors affecting fast stages of primary electron transfer in donor-acceptor pairs using femto-, pico-, and nanosecond time domain techniques and 2) building donor-acceptor structures capable of retaining the photoseparated structures long enough for secondary chemical reactions of the charges to occur. Artificial reaction centers can also form the basis for optoelectronic devices. They may be incorporated into the lipid bilayer membranes of artificial vesicles, where they function as components of light-driven proton pumps that generate *trans*-membrane proton motive force for synthesis of ATP via an ATP synthase enzyme.

For this purpose a congruent and systematic set of well-designed models has been synthesized and the photochemical and photophysical propeties of these models were characterized (Sessler, 1992; McLendon and Hake1992; Gust et al., 1999, 2001; Miller et al., 2000; Wasielewski, 1992; 2002; Wasielewski et al., 1998, 2000; HammerstrÖm et al., 2001; Heinen et al., 2002; and references therein). The effect of the chemical structure of donor and acceptor centers, the energy of the donor center in its excited state, the distance between the centers and their mutual orientation, the nature and length of the spacer tethered donor and acceptor and solvent and temperature were investigated.

A series of Zn porphyrin-quinone dyads and two porphyrins-quinone tryads have been synthesized (Sessler, 1992; and references therein). In the first group of complexes the photoinduced charge separation (PCS) occurred on a time scale of < 1 ps, while in the triad the excitation formed a transition species for about 60 ps. In these systems the thermal recombination was found to be very fast. The distance dependence of PCS through norbornyl bridges of varying length has been examined (Verhoeven, 1999). The values of the decay factor β were determed as $1.0 - 1.25$ Å^{-1} for PCS and $0.8 - 1.0$ Å^{-1} for the thermal recombination. Similar multicomponent systems have been synthesized and investigated by elaborated time-resolved transient absorption and ESR techniques in 1990's (Wasielewski et al., 1998; Gust et al., 1999; and references therein)

Recently, new insight into detailed mechanisms of photochemical processes in donor-acceptor pairs (DA) has emerged. To study the role of bridge energy levels on electron transfer rates, a series of rod-like donor-bridge-acceptor (D-B-A) molecules in which a 4-aminonaphthalene-1,8-imide (ANI) electron donor is linked to a 1,8:4,5-naphthalenediimide acceptor (NI) via the 1,4 positions on a phenyl bridge was synthesized (Miller et al., 2000). In these compounds, the phenyl bridge was substituted at the 2 and 5 positions for small Me or methoxy groups to yield ANI-diMe-NI and ANI-diMeO-NI and these molecules differ only in the energy levels of the bridge molecular orbitals. The rate constants for charge separation and charge recombination within ANI-diMeO-NI in toluene were 32 and 1400 times larger, respectively, than the corresponding rate constants for ANI-diMe-NI. Solvents of higher polarity diminish these differences in rate constants. The authors suggested that the reaction 1*D-B-A → D-B+-A- occurs via a double electron-transfer process (Fig. 6.4).

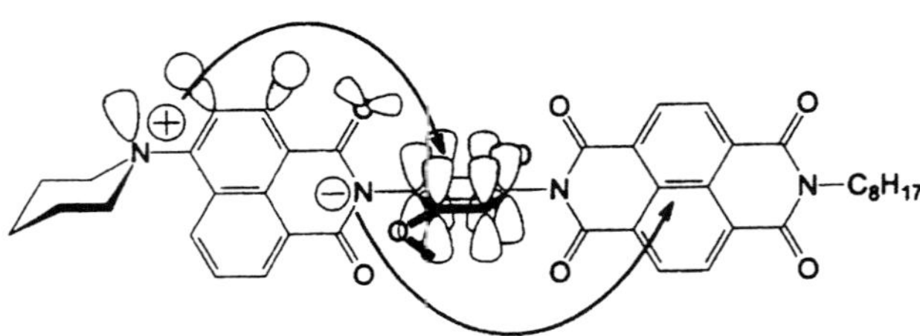

Figure 6.4. Proposed orbital interactions for the double electron transfer mechanism (Miller et al., 2000). Reproduced with permission.

There are investigation of charge separated process in a donor-acceptor pair, based on a tetracene donor linked to a pyromellitimide acceptor via a PPV oligomeric bridge of variable length and on zinc porphyrins linked to a perylene-3,4:9,10-diimide acceptor (PDI) via a series of Ph bridges, that progressively restrict rotational motion of the porphyrin relative to that of PDI (Wasielewski et al., 2000). The temperature dependence of the rates of electron transfer in these molecules did not obey the predictions of ET theories based upon the Condon approximation. These results revealed the importance of bridge dynamics in electron transfer in donor-bridge-acceptor molecules. A series of derivatives of green chromophore, 1,7-bis(pyrrolidin-1-yl)-3,4:9,10-perylene-bis(dicarboximide) (5PDI), that exhibits photophysical and redox properties similar to those of chlorophyll a (Chl a) has been synthesized (Lukas et al., 2002a.b). It was shown that 5PDI is both oxidized and reduced in CH_2Cl_2 at 0.57 V and -0.76 V vs SCE, respectively, making it a facile electron donor or acceptor. Rod-like covalent electron donor-acceptor pairs were prepared by linking the imide group of the 5PDI donor to pyromellitimide (PI), 1,8:4,5-naphthalenebis (dicarboximide) (NI), and 1,7-bis(3,5-di-tert-butylphenoxy)-3,4:9,10-perylene-bis(dicarboximide) (PDI) acceptors via an N-N bond. Measuring the formation and decay of their excited and radical ion pair states monitored by the femtosecond transient absorption spectroscopy, indicated high yield of photoseparated charges only in 5PDI-NI and 5PDI-PDI pairs but not in 5PDI-PI. This difference was explained by estimation of the ionic radii of the photogenerated ions, which for perylene chromophores 5PDI and PDI (strong electron acceptor) are 7.6 ± 0.5 Å, whereas those of the PI and NI (weak electron acceptors) are 5.6 ± 0.5 Å.

Rigid intramololecular donor (D)-acceptor (A1)-acceptor(A2)-X trichromophoric cascade 4,5-diaminoxanthene bridge B were prepared. D, is 4-(N-piperidinyl) naphthalene-1,8-dicarboximide (ANI), and the acceptors A1 and A2 are pyromellitimide (PI) and naphthalene-1,8:4,5-bis(dicarboximide) (NI), respectively (Lukas et al., 2002a.b). The femtosecond transient absorption experiments showed that electron transfer from 1*ANI to NI occurs by nonbonded superexchange interactions between 1*D and A2 that include contributions from both substituents on the NI acceptor and nearby solvent molecules. For charge separation, the estimated value for the decay factor $\beta = 1.1$-1.3 Å-1, gives evidence that solvents contribute to superexchange in BzCN. The distance dependent on the charge recombination rates with $\beta = 0.3$ Å^{-1}, indicates that solvent molecules mediate this process via a hole-transfer mechanism in toluene. The authors have concluded that mediation of electron transfer by nonbonded interactions can compete effectively with electron transfer via bonded pathways.

Intramolecular electron-transfer between donors ($[(bpy)_2 Ru^{III}]$, $[(NH_3)^5 Os^{II}]$) and acceptors ($[Ru^{III}(NH_3)_5]^{4+,}$ $[CoIII(NH_3)_5]^{4+}$) mediated by synthetic proline peptides of different length have been intensively investigated (Isied et al., 1992; and references therein). The following structure-function relationships in these systems can be noted: 1) for relatively short spacers, the number of the proline groups n < 5, the addition of each proline group dampened the rate constant of ET (k_{ET}) for about two order of magnitude. The subsequent addition of the proline groups contributed less and less to the damping. This effect can be explained suggesting flexibility of the long spacer bridges, which allows the electron transfer to occur in the shortest way.

The transient Q-band EPR experiments provide direct evidence for sequential electron transfer from the primary to the secondary radical pair of the triplet channel in a triad consisting of a zinc-9-desoxo-meso-methylpyrochlorophyllide donor (ZC), a pyromellitimide primary acceptor (PI), and a naphthalene-1,8:4,5-diimide secondary acceptor oriented in a liquid crystal (Heinen et al., 2002). At room temperature this process occurs with an exponential time constant of $\tau T = 50 \pm 1$ ns. In the singlet-initiated channel, the intramolecular electron-transfer rates are too fast for direct EPR detection. The species decay with a time constant of $\tau S = 36 \pm 1$ ns by charge recombination to the singlet ground state.

For the problem of utilization of light energy, donor-acceptor structures are capable to retain the photoseparated state long enough for the occurrence of secondary chemical reactions of those charges of special interest. The triads, tetrads and pentads are structures contain several quinones and/or porphyrin components through which a charge-separated state was stabilized for temporal ranges of micro- and submilliseconds (Gust et al., 1993, 1999; Wasielewski 1992; 2002; Wasielewski et al., 1998, 2000; and references therein).

Dual fluorophore-nitroxide molecules (FN) appear to be a convenient model for establishing factors affecting the intramolecular fluorescence quenching, electron transfer, and conversion of light energy to chemical (Bystrayk et al., 1986; li et al., 1999; Rubtsova et al., 1993, Fogel et al., 1994; Likhtenshtein, 1993, 1995; Lozinsky et al., 2001, 2002). A series of dual molecules of various structures of a fluorophore, nitroxide and a spacer were synthesized and rate constants of excited singlet state quenching (k_f) have been measured by the steady-state and time-resolved pico-second fluorescence techniques in solutions of different polarities. In parallel, the rate constant of photoreduction of nitroxide hydroxylamine under excitation of the donor fluorescence fragment (k_{pr}) has been measured by the steady state ESR and fluorescence methods. The photoreduction occurs without a violation of the fluorophore structure. This process is, in fact, the photoinduced electron transfer from solvent molecules, which are very weak reducing agents, to nitroxide with the formation of a hydroxyl derivatives (FNH) with moderate reducing power (Fig. 6.5). Therefore, photochemical reactions in dual molecules may be considered as processes mimicking light energy conversions in photosynthetic reaction centers.

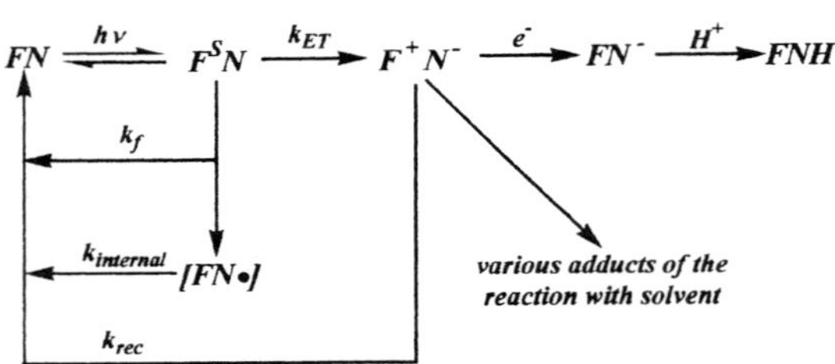

Figure 6..5. Photochemical and photophysical processes in a dual fluorophore-nitroxide molecule. (Lozinsky et al. 2001). Reproduced with permission.

Effects of factors affected by the rate of the aforementioned processes, namely, superexchange along a spacer covalent chain, redox potential of nitroxide moiety, flexibility of spacer groups and flourophore structure and solvent nature and temperature, have been quantitatively investigated. Experiments on the temperature dependence of k_{pr} for a dual molecule in media containing 75% glycerol, 20% water, and 5% ethanol indicated that this value can be experimentally determined only under conditions in which molecular dynamics of a solvent in the vicinity of the electron donor (fluorophore in the excited singlet state) and of the electron acceptor (nitroxide), monitored by fluorescence and the ESR technique respectively, occurs on a nanosecond temporal scale (Bystryak et al., 1986). Other necessary conditions for effective light energy conversion were found to have a relatively high dielectric constant of solvents ($\varepsilon_0 > 4$) and their aprotic nature. It was shown that in the series of dansyl derivatives of the dual molecules with a fixed distance between a chromophore and nitroxide groups, the experimental quenching constant k_f does not depend on a parameter with the relative oxidizing ability of nitroxide and solvent polarity, whereas a clear linear Marcus correlation observed (Lozinsky et al., 2001, 2002;).

To investigate the effect of a protein on electron transfer and the energy conversion, the dual probes (R_1) were incorporated to the hydrophobic pocket obovin serum albumin (Rubtsova et al., 1993; Vogel et al., 1994; Likhtenshtein, 1996; Lozinsky et al., 2001). Experimental temperature dependence on the rate constant of photoreduction k_{pr} was found to be similar to that in the above-mentioned solvent. Values estimated from experiments of parameters of local molecular dynamics with the correlation frequency at

20 °C (vc≈1 ns), the apparent dielectric constant in the vicinity of the donor ($\varepsilon_0 = 11$) and acceptor ($\varepsilon_0 = 65$) sites of the probe, and the calculated resonance integral, $V = 1.5$ 10^{-3} eV, allowed the constraction of an energetic diagram of photoreduction (Fig. 6.6).

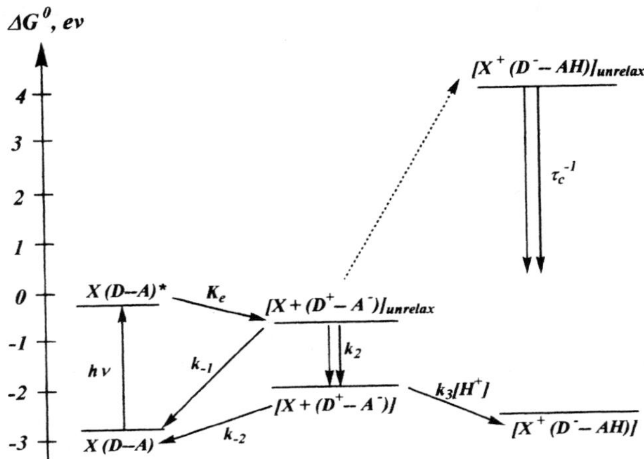

Figure 6.6. Energy diagram of photochemical and processes in a dual fluorophore-nitroxide molecule incorporated in bovin serum albumin (Likhtenshtein, 1996). Reproduced with permission.

Charge photoseparation can be performed with the use of artificial lipid membranes known as vesicles (Shilov, 1997; and references therein). This approach can be illustrated by a system in which the irreversible electron donor (D, EDTA) and photosensitizer (S, Ru(bpy)$_3^{2+}$) were incorporated into the inner water pool of lipid vesicles. The first acceptor (A$_1$,octadecyl viologen) was placed in the vesicular wall, while the second electron acceptor (A$_2$) was placed in the bulk solution. The quantum yield of the electron transfer from D to A$_2$ via the excited S* and A$_1$ was found to be 0.1 – 0.3 under conditions of steady state photolysis. Processes of conversion of exitation energy to electrochemical potential energy in the form of transmembrane charge separation, the utilization of this energy for proton transfer across the membrane and the synthis of ATP have been chemically mimicked in artificial membranes (Gust et al., 1999). Artificial systems of supermolecules, prepared from porphyrins and other chromophores, electron donors and acceptors, were vectorially inserted into the lipid bilayers of liposomes, where they function as constituents of transmembrane light-driven proton pumps. The proton motive force thus produced can be used to synthesize ATP via catalysis by F$_0$F$_1$-ATP synthase isolated from chloroplasts.

6.5. Water oxidation

The life giving process of water decomposition in containing manganese photosynthetic systems still remains one of the most challenging problems to biochemists and chemists. The evolution dioxygen from water in a cluster of transition metals in the biological systems at the absorption of light quanta of low energy can occurs by a sequence of elementary steps: four one-electron steps of oxidation of the manganese complex and, most probably and by one four-electron step of O_2 evolution (Section 3.5.2). In approaching this problem, a number of artificial manganese clusters and other transition metal clusters were synthesized and investigated (Shafirovich, 1995; Britt, 1996; Shilov, 1997; Rüttinger and Dismukes, 1997; Rüttinger et al., 2000; Wikaira and Gorun 1999;).

The crystallographic structures of the $[Mn_2(2OHsalpn)_2]^{2-}$ complex of different oxidative states (-,0,+) have been determined (Gelasko et al., 1997). These molecules form dimers with both of the ligands spanning both Mn ions with the alkoxide on the backbone of the ligand bridging the metals. The following metal-metal distances were obtained: Mn(II)-Mn(II) = 3.33 Å], Mn(II)-Mn(III) = 3.25 Å, Mn(III)-Mn(III) = 3.36 Å, Mn(III)-Mn(IV) = 3.25 Å. Significant structural changes in the polyhedra of X-ray structures of a series of dimanganese complexes and terpyridine dimanganese oxo complexes across the range of metal oxidation states, have been observed. The authors suggested that these changes are reminiscent of the carboxylate shift in metal carboxylate in the natural complex. It also illustrates how alkoxide ligands can participate in an analogous alkoxide shift to generate a binding site for an incoming ligand, such as MeOH, or a substrate, such as H2O2.

A series of dimanganese complexes, [Mn2III,IV(μ-O)2(terpy)2(H2O)2]3+(1), $[Mn_2III,IV(μ-O)_2(terpy)_2(CF_3CO_2)_2]^+$, (2), and $[Mn_2III,III(μ-O)(terpy)_2(CF_3CO_2)_4]$ (terpy = 2,2':6,2"-terpyridine) have been crystallographically characterized (Baffert et al., 2002). The electrochemical behavior of complex (2) in CH_3CN shows that while this complex could be oxidized into its stable manganese(IV,IV) species its reduced form manganese(III,III) is very unstable.

A model water oxidation complex $[H_2O(terpy)Mn(O)_2Mn(terpy)OH_2](NO_3)_3$ (terpy is 2,2':6',2"-terpyridine), containing a di-μ-oxo manganese dimer, was synthesized and structurally characterized (Limburg et al., 1999). This complex catalyzes the dioxygen evolution. Oxygen-18 isotope labeling showed that water is the source of the oxygen atoms in the evolved dioxygen. Another functional model for photosynthetic water oxidation, the complex, $[(terpy)(H_2O)MnIII(O)_2MnIV(OH_2)(terpy)](NO_3)^3$ (terpy = 2,2':6,2"-Terpyridine,) has been synthesized and characterized (Limburg et al., 2000, 2001). This complex catalyzes O_2 evolution from either KHSO5 (potassium oxone) or NaOCl via an intermediate complex $[(terpy)(SO_4)MnIV(O)_2MnIV(SO_4)(terpy)]$. The efficiency of the catalyst was relatively low: Vmax = 2420 mol O2 (mol 1)-1 hr-1 and K_M = 53 mM for oxone (7.5 µM), and V_{max} = 6.5 mol O2 (mol 1)-1 hr-1 and K_M = 39 mM for hypochlorite (70 µM), with first-order kinetics observed for both oxidants. Isotope-labeling studies using $H_2^{18}O$ and $KHS^{16}O_5$ show that O_2 evolution proceeds via an intermediate that can exchange with water. The rate-limiting step of O_2 evolution is proposed to be the formation of a formally MnV:O moiety which could then competitively react with either oxone or water/hydroxide to produce O_2. Dioxygen evolution in systems containing cubane-type tetramers, $[Ru_4(CO)_{12}(\mu3\text{-Se})_4]$ and $[(dpp)_6Mn_4O_4]$ (dpp- =diphenyl phosphinate anion) , have been indicated (Rüttinger et al., 2000). The former system released O_2 under UV-light absorption in the gas phase. The structure of oxocubane core $Mn_4O_4^{6+}$ complex which mimics of the photosynthetic water oxidation system is presented in Fig. 6.7

Mn(IV) bound to lipid vesicles is an active catalyst for O_2 evolution in the presence of one-electron oxidants, such as $[Ru(bpy)_3]^{3+}$ and $[Fe(bpy)_3]^{3+}$ where bpy is 2,2'-bipyridyl (Luneva et al., 1987; Shilov, 1997). The evaluation of the O_2 forming center is discussed. It is speculated that if a lipid membrane is formed in the presence of Mn^{2+}, the Mn^{2+} may be incorporated into the membrane forming the catalyst for O_2 evolution from H_2O.

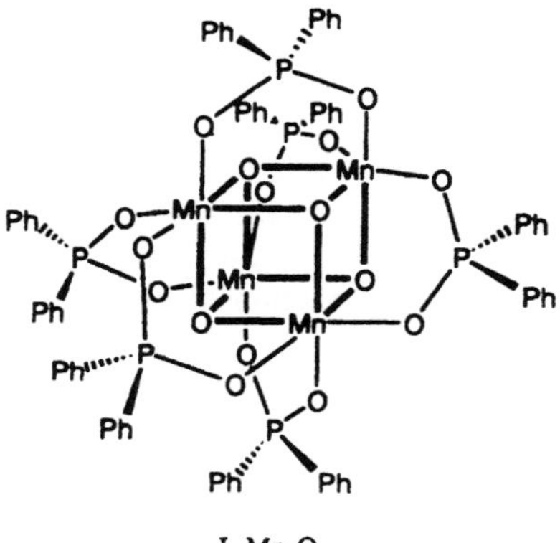

$$L_6Mn_4O_4$$

Figure .6.7. The structure of oxocubane core $Mn_4O_4^{6+}$ complex (Rüttinger et al., 2000). Reproduced with permission)

6.6. Organic reactions

Works on mimicking the organic enzyme catalyzing reactions can be conditionally subdivided into two groups. The first group of studies is related to some general features of enzyme catalysis such as proximity, orbital steering and strain effects, pretransition states, molecular recognition, etc. The second group of investigations deals with the functional modeling of specific enzymatic reactions or their separate stages.

In 1970's it was suggested and demonstrated on simple chemical models that the preorientation of the catalytic group of an enzyme and of reactive groups of the substrate is responsible, at least partially, for an increase in the enzyme reaction velocity as compared with a random arrangement (Storm and Koshland, 1970; Staninets and Shilov, 1971; Page and Jenckes, 1971). There is a significant acceleration of intramolecular reactions, which cause anhydride formation (up to 4×10^4 fold) as a result of the precise preorientation of carboxylate moieties in cyclohexanes of different flexibility of the ring (Staninets and Shilov, 1971). Similar results were obtained by Storm and Koshland

(1970). A comparison of the experimental data on the reactivity of a number of compounds with theoretical values calculated accounting for the entropy factor, has led to the following conclusions (Likhtenshtein, 1977c): (1) the amount by which the reaction rate is speeded up either approaches the maximum possible entropy factor or exceeds it by one to eight orders of magnitude; (2) the greatest effect of experimental values over theoretical values is observed for cases in which the structure of the cyclic complex has the least mobility; and (3) the experimental values of the acceleration effect depends on the catalyst used and, hence, on the reaction mechanism. The aforementioned analysis clearly demonstrates the significant contribution of the mechanical strain in the pretransition ground states in the reaction enthalpy and its relation to "rock" or "nutcracker" mechanism postulated by (Lumry and Eyring, 1954)

The importance of pretransition states in enzymatic and intramolecular reactions, when the initial ground state conformations are "activated", has been proved in subsequent investigations (Menger, 1985; Houk et al., 1990; Bruice and Lightstone, 1999; and references therein). According to (Bruice and Lightstone, 1999; Bruic and Benkovic 2000), the formation of the near attack conformation (NAS), which is defined as a conformation required for juxtaposed reactants to enter the transition state, is a key stage of model and enzymatic reactions. In the frame of this concept, the rate constant for bond making and breaking in these reactions depends to a great extent on the fraction of the enzyme-substrate complex present as NACs. A few typical examples of NACs have been described. Values of the rate constants for the intramolecule anhydride formation from mono-p-bromphenyl esters (k_{an}) varies of about eight order of magnitude depending on the position of the reactive groups in the molecule (Fig. 6.8). It was found that log k_{an} = 7.48 + log P, where P is the theoretically calculated. The computational observation of NASs formation has been done also for enzymatic reactions: the S_N2 replaces of Cl from 1,2 dichloroethane by Asp 124-CO_2 at the active site of haloalcane dehalogenase and for the anisotropic motion of enzyme bound NAD(P)H in lactate, malate and alcohol dehydrogenase, which is brought about by bulky substituents.

The most promising direction for enzyme modeling is to synthetically mimick the nature of the binding site and the active site in terms of the close similarity of catalytic groups, stereochemistry, interatomic distances and the mechanism of the action of the enzyme. Mimicking of the "proton-transfer relay' proposed for the mechanism of the action of chymotrypsin is a brilliant example of such work (D'Souza and Bender, 1987 and references therein). The miniature organic model of chymotrypsin built on the basis of cyclodextrin and the mechanism of hydrolysis m-tert-butylphenyl acetate is presented in Fig. 6.9.

The catalytic activity of "artificial chymotrypsin" in the hydrolysis of m-tert-butylphenyl acetate (k_{cat} = 2.8x10^2 s^{-1}, K_M = 13x10^5M) was found to be close to the activity of chymotrypsin in the hydrolysis of p-nitrophenyl acetate (k_{cat} = 1.1x10^2 s^{-1}, K_M = 4x10^5M). Another example of mimicking enzyme catalysis by β-cyclodextrin is general acid-base-catalyzed hydrolysis and nitrosation of amines by alkyl nitrites (Iglesias, 1998).

Detailed information about mimicking various enzymatic organic reactions is presented in a recent comprehensive book of Silverman (2000). Here we confine ourselves to two illustrative examples.

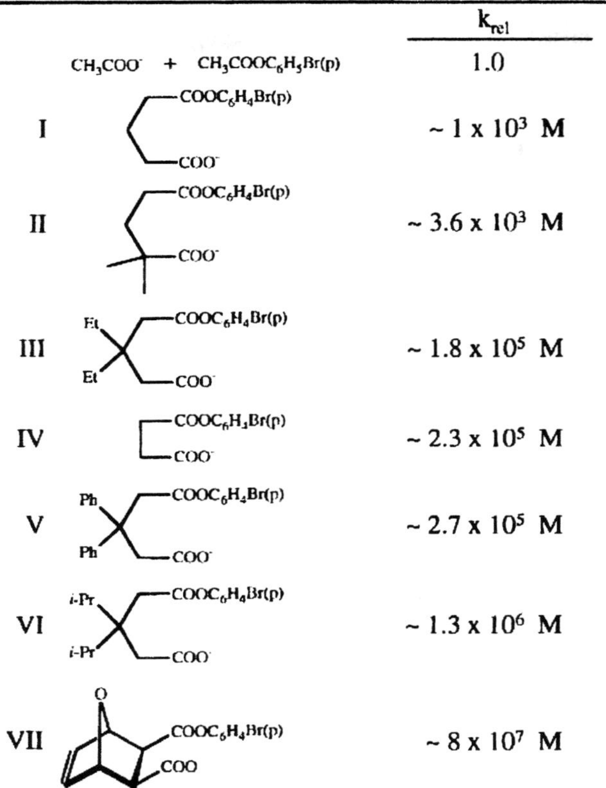

Figure 6.8. Chemical formulas of monophenyl esters and relative rate constants for correspondent anhydrid formation (Bruice and Lightstone, 1999). Reproduced with permission.

A model for redox and molecular recognition of flavin was proposed (Niemz and Rotello, 1999). The redox behavior of flavin and its interaction with receptors, a series of acylated diaminopyridines, in $CDCl_3$, have been investigated using a combination of cyclic voltampery, NMR, simultaneous electrochemistry and ESR, and UV/vis electrochemistry. Variation of the acyl substituents enabled control of the host-flavin recognition by modulation of both hydrogen bonding via change of acidity and electrostatic through-space effects.

Below references are given which can provide a key to the relevant literature concerning the mimicking of various reactions catalyzed by enzymes: (Shilov, 1997; Iglesias1998; Gust et al., 1999; Hegg et al., 1999; Wikaira et al., 1999; Silverman, 2000; Kopf and Karlin, 2000; Hu et al., 2000; Ju et al., 2000; Naruta et al., 2001; Hammarstrom et al., 2001; Ogliaro et al., 2001; Diekmann et al., 2002; and references therein.).

In spite of marked benefits discovered in the field of modeling structure and action mechanism of enzymes, more sophisticated models are needed to reach efficiency in the biological process. Further studies on modeling of the structure and action mechanism of nitrogenase promise deeper insights into the enzyme mechanism and promote the creation of new catalysts for the large number of enzyme reactions.

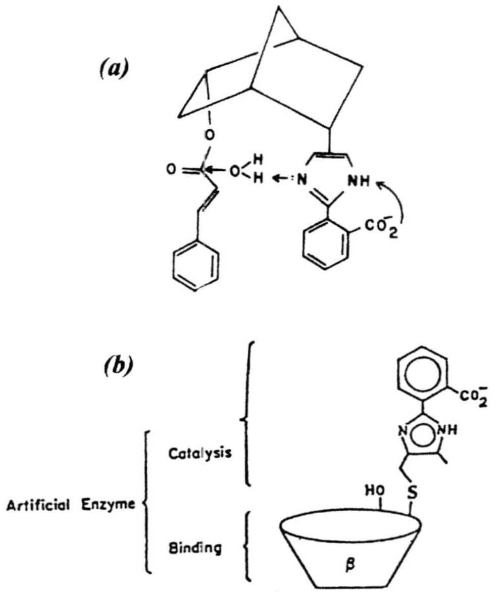

Figure 6..9. The mechanism of action of "artificial chymotrypsin" (a); Complete model of acylchymotripsin (a) and miniature organic model of chymotrypsin (b) (D'Souza and Bender, 1987). Reproduced with permission.

REFERENCES

Abrahams, J.P., Leslie, A. G., Lutter, R., and Walker J E. (1994) Structure at 2. 8 Å of F1-ATPase from bovine heart mitochondria, *Nature* **370**, 621-628.

Abu-Saud, H.M., Ichimori, K., Presta, A., and Stuehr, D.J. (2000) Electron transfer, oxygen binding, and nitric oxide feedback inhibition in endothelial nitric oxide synthase, *J. Biol. Chem.* **275**, 17349-17357.

Adak, S., Santolini, J., Tikunova, S., Wang, Q., Johnson, J.D., and Stuehr, D.J (2001a) Neuronial nitric-oxide synthase mutant (Ser-1412 → Asp) demonstrates surprising connections between heme regulation, NO complex formation and catalysis, *J. Biol. Chem.* **276** 1244-1252.

Adak, S., Wang, Q., and Stuehr, D. J (2001b) Molecular basis for hyperactivity in tryptophane 409 mutant of neural NO synthase, *J. Biol. Chem.* **275** 17434-17439.

Adam, W., Lazaris, M., Chantu Saha-Moeler, C. R., and Schreier, P. (1999) Biocatalytic synthesis of optically active α-oxyfunctionalized carbonyl compounds, *Acc. Chem. Res.* **32**, 837-845.

Adams R. D., (1998) Catalysis by di-and polynuclear metal cluster complexing (eds.), *Chemistry of Metal Clusters*, F. Allert Cotton.

Adams, M. W. W. and Kelly, R. M.(eds.) (2001) *Methods in Enzymology* (eds.), Hyperthermophylic Enzymes **330** (Part A), **331** (Part B) and **334** (PartC), Academic Press, San Diego.

Ädelroth, P., Paddock, M. L., Tehrani, A., Beatty, J. T., Feher, G., and Okamura, M. Y. (2001) Identification of the proton pathway in bacterial reaction centers: decrease of proton transfer rate by mutation of surface histidines at H126 and H128 and chemical rescue by imidazole identifies the initial proton donors, *Biochemistry* **40** 14538 -14546.

Aguilar, C.F., Sanderson, I., Moracci, M., Ciaramella, M., Nucci, R., Rossi, M., and Pearl, L.H. (1997) Crystal structure of the β-glycosidase from the hyperthermophilic archeon *Sulfolobus solfataricus*: resilience as a key factor in thermostability, *J. Mol. Biol.* **271**, 789-802.

Ahluwalia, A., Papper, V., Chen, O., Likhtenshtein, G.I. and De Rossi, D.A. (2002) Fluorescence method for characterization of order and orientation of antibodies immobilized on a silica plate, *Anal. Biochem.* **305**, 121-134.

Alakhverdiev, C.I., Kulikov, A.V., Klimov, V.V., Bogatyrenko, V.R., and Likhtenstein G.I. (1989) Determination of the depth of immersion of P680, pheophitin and secondary donor in photosystem 2 in pea subchloroplasts. *Biofizika,* **34**, 434-439.

Alexandrov, I. V. (1975) *Theory of Magnetic Relaxation.* Nauka. Moscow.

Alexandrov, I. V. (1976) Dependence of the rate of the concerted chemical reactions on the number of degree of freedom involved in the transition, *Teor. Exper. Khim. (Theor. Experim. Chem.* **12**, 299-306.

Alexov, E.G. and Gunner, M.R. (1997) Incorporating protein conformational flexibility into the calculation of pH-dependent protein properties, *Biophys. J.* **72**, 2075-2093.

Alderton, W.K., Cooper, C. E., and Knowles, R.G. (2001) Nitric oxide synthases: structure, function and inhibition, *Biochemical J.* **357**, 593-615

Alfimova, E.Ya., and Likhtenshtein, G.I. (1979) Investigation of structure and conformational change of proteins by the inductive resonance energy transfer, *Advans. Mol. Relax. Interact. Proc.* **14**, 47-89.

Alhambra, C., Corchado, J. C., Sanchez, M. L., Gao, J., and Truhlar, D.G. (2000) Quantum dynamics of hydrid transfer in enzyme catalysis, *J. Am. Chem. Soc.* **122**, 8197-8203.

Allen, A. D., Bottomley, F., Harris, R. O., Reinsalu, V. P. and Senoff, C.V. (1967). Ruthenium complexes containing molecular nitrogen. *J. Am. Chem. Soc.* **89**, 5595-5599.

Allison, W. S. (1998) A molecular motor that hydrolyzes ATP with sequential opening and closing of catalytic sites coupling rotation of its g subunit, *Acc. Chem. Res.* **31**, 819-826.

Altamirano, M.M., Blackburn, J. M., Aguayo, C., and Fersht, A.R. (2000) Directed evolution of new catalytic activity using the α/β-barrel scaffold, *Nature* **403**, 617-622.

Amadei, A., Linssen, B. M., and Berendsen, H. J. C. (1993) Essential dynamics of proteins, *Proteins: Structure, function and Genetics* **17**, 412-425.

Ananyev, G.M., Sakiyan, I., Diner, B.A., and Dismukes, G.C. (2002) A functional role for tyrosine-D in assembly of the inorganic core of the water oxidase complex of photosystem II and the kinetics of water oxidation, *Biochemistry* **41**, 974-980.

Anderson, J.M. (2001) Does functional photosystem II complex have an oxygen channel, *FBBS Lett.* **488**, 1-4.

Anderson, K.S. (1999) Fundamental mechanisms of substrate channeling, in Schramm, V. L. and Purich, D. L. (eds.), *Methods in Enzymology* **308**, Enzyme kinetics and Mechanism, Part E, Academic Press, San Diego, pp. 111-145.

Ando, K. and Hynes, J. (1999) Acid-base proton transfer and ion pair formation in solution, in Prigogine, I. and Rice, S.A. (eds), *Adv. Chem. Phys.* **110**, John Wiley & Sons, Inc. 381-430.

Angerhofer, A., Wasielewski, M.R., Gaines, G. L., III, O'Neil, M. P., Svec, W. A., and Niemczyk, M. P. (1991) Fourier-transform EPR on model systems of the primary charge separation in photosynthesis, *Z. Phys. Chem.* **172**, 17-30.

Angove, H.C., Bursey, E., and Burgess, B.K. (1998) *A. vinelandii* Fe protein: MgATP induced conformational change and reduction to an all ferrous state, *Curr. Plant Sci. Biotechnol. Agric.* **31** (Biological Nitrogen Fixation for the 21st Century), 47-48.

Angove, H.C., Bursey, E., and Burgess, B. K. (1998) *A. vinelandii* Fe protein: MgATP induced conformational change and reduction to an all ferrous state, *Curr. Plant Sci. Biotechnol. Agric.* **31** (Biological Nitrogen Fixation for the 21st Century), 47-48.

Anni, H., Vanderkooi, J.M., Sharp, K. A., Yonetani, T., Hopkins, S C., Herenyi, L. and Fidy, J. (1994). Electric field and conformational effects of cytochrome c and solvent on cytochrome c peroxidase studied by high resolution fluorescence spectroscopy, *Biochemistry* **33**, 3475-3486.

Antoniou, D. and Schwartz, S.D. (2001) Internal enzyme motions as a source of catalytic activity: rate-promoting vibrations and hydrogen tunneling, *J. Chem. Phys. B* **105**, 5553-5558.

Aquist, J., Luecke, H., Quiocho, F. A. and Warshel, A. (1991). Dipoles localized at helix termini of proteins stabilize charges, *Proc. Natl. Acad. Sci. USA* **88**, 2026-2030.

Aramini, J. M. and Vogel, H.J. (1998) Quadrupolar metal ion NMR studies of metalloproteins, *Biochemistry and Cell Biology* **76**, 210-222.

Arechada, I., and Jones, P. C. (2001) The rotor in the memrane of the ATP synthase and relatives, *FEBS Lett* **494**, 1-5.

Ariens, E.J. (1989) OSAR: Quantitative Structure-Activity Relationssships in Drag Design, p. 3. A. R. Liss

Armstrong, R.N. (2000) Mechanistic diversity in a metalloenzyme superfamily, *Biochemistry* **39**, 13625-13632.

Arnold, F.H. (2001) Combinatorial and computational challenges for biocatalyst design, *Nature* **409**, 253-257.

Arnold, F.H. (2000) Evolutionary Protein Design (eds.), *Adv. Protein. Chem.* **55**

Arnold, F. H. and Volkov, A. A. (1999) Directed evolution of biocatalysts, *Curr. Opin. Chem. Biol.* **3**, 54-59.

Asplund, M.C., Zanni, M.T., and Hochstrasser, R. M. (2000) Two demansional infrared spectroscopy of peptides by phase-controlled femtosecond vibrational photon echoes, *Proc. Natl. Acad. Sci. USA* **97**, 8219-8224.

Astashkin, A.V., Hara, H., and Kawamori, A. (1998) The pulsed electron-electron double resonance and "2 = 1 " electron spin echo study of the oriented oxygen-evolving and Mn-depleted preparation of photoystem II, *J. Chem. Phys.* **108**, 3805-3812.

Atanasov, B. P. Postnikova, G.B., Sadykov, Y. C., and Volkenstein, M.V. (1977) *Mol. Biol.* **11**, 537 (in Russian).

Atilgam, A.R., Durell, S.R., Jernigan, R.L., Demirel, M.C., Keskin, O., and Bahar, I. (2001) Anisotropy of fluctuation dynamics of proteins with an elastic network model, *Biophys. J.* **80**, 505-515.

Auria, S. D., Moracci, M., Febbraio, F., Tanfani, F., Nucci, R., and R., M. (1998) Structure-function studies on β-glycosidase from Sulfolobus solfataricus molecular bases of thermostability, *Biochimie* **80**, 949-957.

Austin, R.N., Chang, H.–K., Zylstra, G.J., and Groves, J.T. (2000) The non-heme diiron alkane monooxygenase of *Pseudomonas oleovorans* (AlkB) hydroxylates via a substrate radical intermediate, *J. Am. Chem. Soc.* **122**, 11747-11748.

Averbach, A.Z., Pekel, N.D., Seredenko V. I., Kulikov, A.V. and Gvozdev, R.I., (1995) Flavin-dependent alcohol oxidase from the yeast, *Pichiapinus. Biochem. J.* **310**, 601-604.

Babbit, P. (2000) New functions from old scaffolds: how nature re-engineers enzymes for new functions, *Adv. Protein Chem.* **55**, 1-28.

Babbitt, P.C. and Gerlt, J. A. (2001) New functions from old scaffolds: how nature reengineers enzymes for new functions *Advanced in Protein Chemistry* **55** (Evolutionary Protein Design), 1-28.

Babcock, G.T. and Wikstroem, M (1992) Oxidation activation and conservation energy in cell respiration, *Nature* **356**, 301-309.

Bach, RD., Mintcheva, I., Esteve, and Schlegel, H.B. (1995) Theoretical model for and alternative mechanism the cytochrome P450 hydroxylation of quadricyclane, *J. Am. Chem. Soc.* **117**, 10121-10122.

Bach, R.D., Mintcheva, I., Esteve, and Schlegel, H.B. (1995) Theoretical model for and alternative mechanism the cytochrome P450 hydroxylation of quadricyclane, *J. Am. Chem. Soc.* **117**, 10121-10122.

Backgren, C., Hummer, G., Wiksstroem, M., and Puustinen, A. (2000) Proton translocation by cytochrome c oxidase can take place without conserved glutamic acid in subunit I., *Biochemistry,* **39**, 7863-7867.

Baffert, C., Collomb, M.-N., Deronzier, Alain, Pecaut, J., Limburg, J., Crabtree, R. H., Brudvig, and Gary W. (2002) Two new terpyridine dimanganese complexes: a manganese(III, III) complex with a single unsupported oxo bridge and a manganese(III, IV) complex with a dioxo bridge. Synthesis, structure, and redox properties, *Inorg. Chem.* **41**, 1404-1411.

Bagryansky, V. A., Borovkov, V. I., Molin, Yu. N. (2002) Singlet-triplet oscillations of spin-correlated radical pairs caused by the Larmor precession in weak magnetic fields, *Doklady Physical Chemistry* **382**, 62-65.

Bahnson, B.J. and Kleinman, J.P. (1995) Hydrogen tunneling in enzyme catalysis, in Purich, D. L. (eds.), *Methods in Enzymology,* **249**, Enzyme Kinetics and Mechanisms, Part D, Acad. Press, San-Diego, 393-396.

Bahnson, B.J., Park, D-H., Kim, K., Plapp, B.V., and Klinman, J. (1993) Unmasking of hydrogen tunneling in the horse liver alcochol dehydrogenase reaction by site directed mutagenesis, *Biochemistry* **32**, 5503-5507.

Bajorath, J., Kitson, J., D.H., Kraut, J., and Hagler, A.T. (1991) The electrostatic potential of escherichia coli dihydrofolate reductase, *Proteins* **11**, 1-12.

Bakhshhiev, N.A. (1989) *Solvatochromism, Problems and Methods* (eds.), Leningrad University Press, Leningrad.

Balabaev, N.K., Lakhno, V. D., Molchanov, A. M., and Atanasov, B. P. (1990), Extended electron states in proteins, *J. Mol. Electron.* **6**, 155-166.

Balabin, I.A. and Onuchic, J.N. (2000) Dynamically controlled protein tunneling pathes in photosynthetic reaction centers, *Science* **290**, 114- 117.

Bamwenda, G.R., Uesigi, T., Abe, Y., Sayama, K., Arakawa, H. The photocatalytic oxidation of water to O_2 over pure CeO_2, WO_3, and TiO2 using Fe^{3+} and Ce^{4+} as electron acceptors, *Appl. Catal., A* (2001), 205(1, 2), 117-128.

Basch, H., Musaev, D.G., Mogi, K. and Morokuma, K. (2001a) Theoretical studies on the mechanism of the methane $\rightarrow$ methanol conversion reaction catalyzed by methane monooxygenase: O-side vs N-side mechanisms, *J. Phys. Chem. A* **105**, 3615-3622.

Basch, H., Musaev, D.G., Mogi, K. and Morokuma, K. (2001b) A density functunal study of the completion of the methane monooxygenase catalytic cycle. Methanol complex to MMOH resing state, *J. Phys. Chem. B* **105**, 8452-8460.

Bashford, D., and Karplus, M. (1990) pK_as of ionizable groups in proteins: atomic detail from a continuum electrostatic model, *Biochemistry* **29**, 10219-10225.

Battistel, E., Attanasio, F., Rialdi, G. (2000) Thermal stability of immobilized α-chymotrypsinogen, *Journal of Thermal Analysis and Calorimetry* 61(2), 513-525.

Bazhenova, T.A., Bazhenova, M.A., Petrova, G.N., and Shilov, A.E. (2000) Catalytic behavior of isolated FeMo-cofactor of nitrogenase in non-protein surroundings, *Current Plant Science and Biotechnology in Agriculture* **38** (Nitrogen Fixation: From Molecules to Crop Productivity), 49-50.

Bec, N., Gorren, A.C.F., Voelker, C., Mayer, B., and Lange, R. (1998) Reaction of neutral nitric-oxide synthase with oxygen at low temperature, *J. Biol. Chem.* **273**, 13502-13508.

Becker, O. M., Levy, Y., and Ravitz, O. (2000) Flexibility, conformation space, and bioactivity, *J. Phys. Chem. B* **104**, 2123-2135.

Beechem J.M. and Haas, E. (1989) Simultaneous determination of intramolecular distance distributions and conformational dynamics by global analysis of energy transfer measurements, *Biophys. J.* **55**, 1225-1236.

Belonogova, O. V., Likhtenshtein, G. I. and Krinichnyi, V I. (1997) Electron transfer in donor-acceptor pairs in modified α-chymotrypsin. Effect of microviscosity, macroviscosity and local polarity, *Photochem. Photobiol. A: Chem.* **107**, 35-42.

Belonogova, O.V., Likhtenshtein, G. I., Levashov, A.V., Khmelnitskij, Yu. L., Klyachko, N. L., and Martinek, K. (1983) A spin-lavel study of the state of the active center microenvironment of a-chymotrypsin solubilized in octan , using the surfactant aerosol OT, *Biokhimia* **48**, 379-

Belova, V.S., Gvozdev, R.I., Malashenko, Yu. R., Sadkov, A.P., and Yurchenko, V.V. (1976) The isotope effect in the enzymatic oxidation of methane, *Biochemistry* (Moscow) **41**, 1903-1904.

Benson, D.E., Wisz, M.S., and Hellinga, H.W. (2000) Rational design of nascent metalloenzymes, *Proc. Natl. Acad. Sci. USA* **97**, 6292-6297.

Beratan, D.N. and Onuchic, J.N. (1987) Electron tunneling through covalent and non-covalent pathways in proteins, *J. Chem. Phys.* **86**, 4489-4498.

Beratan, D.N., Onuchic, J.N., Betts, J. N., Bowler, B. E., and Gray, G.H. (1990) Electron- tunneling pathway in ruthenated proteins, *J. Am. Chem. Soc.* **112**, 7915-7921.

Berdnikov, B. M., Doctorov, A.B., and Makarshin, L.L. (1980) Dipole-dipole broadening of free radicals ESR spectra in the presence of paramagnetic ions, *Theoretical and Experimental Chemistry* (Kiev) **16**, 765-771.

Berg, A. I., Kononenko, A.F., Noks, P. P., Khrymova, I. N., Frolov, E. N., Rubin, Likhtenshtein, G. I., Uspenskaya, N., and Khideg, K., (1979a) *Molekulyarnaya Biologiya* **13**, 469-477.

Berg, A.I., Kononenko, A.F., Noks, P.P., Khymova, I.N., Frolov, E.N., Rubin, A.B., Likhtenshtein, G.I., Goldansky, V.I., Parak, F., Bukl M., and Mossbauer, R.L. (1979b) *Molekulyarnaya Biologiya* **13**, 81-89.

Berliner, L. (1976) *Spin Labeling. Theory and Applications* (eds.), Academic Press, New York, **1.**

Berliner, L. (1979) *Spin Labeling. Theory and Applications* (eds.), Academic Press, New York, **2.**

Berliner, L. (1998) *Spin Labeling. The Next Millennium* (eds.), Academic Press, New York, **14.**

Berliner, L. J., Eaton, S. S., and Eaton, G. R. (eds.), (2000) *Biological Magnetic Resonance* **19**, Distance Measurements in biological Systems by EPR, Kluwer Academic/Plenum Publisher, N. Y.,

Bernasconi, C.F. (1992) The principle of nonperfect synchronization: more then qualitative concept, *Acc. Chem. Res.* **25**, 9-16.

Berry, S.M., Gieselman, M.D., Nilges, M. J., van der Donk, W.A, and Lu, Y. (????) An Engineered Azurin Variant Containing a Selenocysteine Copper Ligand, ????

Berti, P. J. (1999) Determining transition states from kinetics isotope effects, , in Schramm, V. L. and Purich, D. L. (eds.), *Methods in Enzymology* **308**, Enzyme Kinetics and Mechanism, Academic Press, San Diego, pp. 355-397.

Bertini, I., Luchinat, C., and Parigi, G. (2002) Solution NMR of Paramagnetic Molecules. Application to metallobiomolecules and models (eds.), Elsevier Science, Amsterdam.

Beth, J.N., Beratan, J.N., and Onuchic, J.N. (1992) Mapping electron tunneling pathways: an algorithm that finds the "minimum length"/maximum coupling pathway between electron donors and acceptors in proteins, *J. Am. Chem. Soc.* **114**, 4043-4046.

Bishop, P.E., Jarlenski, D.M.L., and Heatherington, D.R. (1980) Evidence for an alternative nitrogen fixation system in Azotobacter Vinilandi, *Proc. Natl. Acad. Sci. USA* **77**, 7342-7346.

Bismuto, E., Nucci, R., Rossi, M., and Irace, G. (1999) Structural and dynamic aspects of β- glycosidase from mesophilic and thermophilic bacteria by multitryptophanyl emission decay studies, *Proteins: Struct., Funct., Genet.* **35**, 163-172.

Bixon, M. (1992) Electron transfer: theory, *Israel J. Chem.* **32**, 422-425.

Bixon, M. and Jortner, J. (1999) Electron transfer - from isolated molecules to biomolecules, in Jortner, J. and Bixon. (eds.), *Advances in Chemical Physics* **107**, Part 1, John Wiley & Sons. NY, 35-202.

Blackburn, G.M. and Garcon, A. (2000) Catalytic antibodies, in Kelly, D. R. (eds.), *Biotechnology* (2nd Edition) 8b 403-490. Publisher: Wiley-VCH Verlag GmbH, Weinheim,

Blake, R.C. and Coon M.J (1980) On the mechanism of action of cytochrome P450, spectral intermediates in the reaction of P450 LM2 with peroxy compounds, *J. Biol. Chem.* **255**, 4100-4111.

Blankenship, R.E. (2001) Molecular evidence for the evolution of photosynthesis, *Trends in Plant Science* **6**, 4-6.

Blough, N., and Simpson, D.J. (1988) *J. Am. Chem. Soc.* **110**, 1915-1917.

Blomberg, M.R., Siegbahn, P.E. M., Babcock, G. T., and Wikstrom, M. (2000) Modeling cytochrome oxidase: a quantum cchemical study of the O-O bond cleavage mechanism, *J. Am. Chem. Soc.,* 12848-12858.

Blow, D. M., Fersht, A. R., and Winter, G. (1987) (eds.), Cambridge Univ. Press, Cambridge, UK,

Blum, D. J., Ko, Y. H., Hong, S., Rini, D., Pedersen, P. L. (2001) ATP synthase motorcomponenets:proposal and animation of two dynamic models for stator function, *Biochem. Biophys. Res. Comm.* **287**, 801-807.

Blum, H., Leigh, J.S., Salerno, J.C. and Ohnishi, T (1978). The orientation of bovin adrenal cortex cytochrome P-450 in submitichondrial particle multilayers, *Arch. Biochem. Biophys,* **187**, 153-157.

Bogatyrenko, V.R., Sabo, Ya., Chamorovskii, S.K., Zakharova, N.I., Kononenko, A.A. and Kulikov A.V. (1991) Study of localization of bacteriochlorophyl dimer and cytochrome c in reaction centers from *Chromatium minutissium* by ESR, *Biofizika* **36**, 289-290.

Boichenko, V.A., Hou, J-M., and Mauzerall, D. (2001) Thermodynamics of electron transfer in oxigen photosynthetic reaction centers: volume change, enthalpy and entropy of electron-transfer reactions in intact cells of the cyanobacterium Synechocystis PCC 6803, *Biochemistry* **40**, 7126-7132.

Bolduc, J.M., Dyer, D.H., Scott, W.G., Singer, RM., Sweet, R. M., Koshland, D. E., and Stoddard, B.L. (1995) Mutagenesis and Laue structures of enzyme intermediate isocitrate dehydrogenase, *Science* **268**, 1312-1318.

Bolen, J.T., Cambasso, N., Muchmore, S.W., Morgan, T.V., and Mortenson, L. E. (1993) Structure and Environment of metal clusters of the nitrogenase molybdenum iron protein from *Clostridium pasterianum*, in Stiefel, E.I., Coucouvanis, D., and ewton, W.E. (eds.), *Molibdenum Enzymes, Cofactors, and Model Systems*, Am. Chem. Soc., Wahington, DC.

Book, L.D., Ostafin, A.E., Ponomarenko, N., Norris,. J.R., and Scherer, N. F. (2000) Exciton Delocalization and Initial Dephasing Dynamics of Purple Bacterial LH2, *J. Phys. Chem. B* **104**, 8295-8307.

Vogel, P. D.. (2000) Insights into ATP synthase structure and function using affinity and site-specific spin labeling, Journal of Bioenergetics and Biomembranes 32, 413-421.

Borbat, P.P. and Freed, J.H. (2000) Double-quantum ESR and distance measurements, in in Berliner, L, Eaton, S., and Eaton, G. (eds.), *Magnetic Resonance in Biology* **18**, Kluwer Academic Publishers. Dordrecht, pp. 383-460.

Bordwell, F.G. (1970) Are nucleophylic bimolecular concerted reactions involving four or more bonds a myth? *Accounts Chem. Res.* **3**, 281-290.

Boussac, A., and Rutherford, A.W. (2000) Comparative study of the g = 4 EPR signals in the S2 state of photosystem II, *Biochim. Biophys. Acta* **1457**, 145-156.

Bowman, M.K. and Norris, J.R. (1982) Cross relaxation of free radicals in partially ordered solids. *J. Phys. Chem.* **86**, 3385-3390.

Boyer, P. D. (2001) Toward an adequate scheme for the ATP synthase catalysis, *Biochemistry* (Moscow) **66**, 1058-1066.

Braunheim, B. B. and Schwartz, S. D. (1999) Computational methods for transition state and inhibitor recognition, in Schramm, V. L. and Purich, D. L. (eds.), *Methods in Enzymology* **308**, Enzyme kinetics and Mechanism, Part E, Academic Press, San Diego pp. 398-426.

Breslow, R. (2001) ***Biomimetic selectivity***, Chem Rec 1, 3-11.

Breslow, R.. (1996) **Biomimetic chemistry.** Bifunctional binding and catalysis, NATO ASI Series, Series E: Applied Sciences **320** (Chemical Synthesis), 113-135.

Britt, R.D. (1996) Oxygen evolution, *Adv. Photosynth.* **4** (Oxygenic Photosynthesis: The Light Reactions), 137-164.

Britton, K.L., Yip, K.S.P., Sedelnikova, S.E., Stillman, T. J., Adams, M. W.W., Ma, K., Maeder, D. L., Robb, F.T., Tolliday, N., Vetriani, C., Rice, D.W., and Baker, P.J. (1999), Structure determination of the glutamate dehydrognase from the hyperthermophile *Thermococcus litoralis* and its comparison with that from *Pyrococcus furiosus*, *J. Mol. Biol.* **293**, 1121-1132.

Brooks, C.L. III, Karplus M. and Pettitt, B. M. (1988) Proteins: A Theoretical Perspective of Dynamics, Structure and Thermodynamics, Wiley, N. Y.

Brown, L.J., Klonis, N., Sawyer, W. H., Fajer. P.G.; and Hambly, B.D (2001) Independent movement of the regulatory and catalytic domains of myosin heads revealed by phosphorescence anisotropy, *Biochemistry* **40**, 8283-8291.

Bruice, T.C. and Benkovic, S.J. (2000) Chemical basis for enzyme catalysis, *Biochemistry* **39**, 6267-6274.

Bruice, T.C. and Lightstone, F.C. (1998) Ground state and transition state contributions to the rates of intramolecular and enzymatic reactions, *Acc. Chem. Rec.* **32**, 127-136.

Bruno, W.J. and Bialek, W. (1992) Vibrational enhanced tunneling as a mechanism for enzymatic hydrogen transfer, *Biophys. J.* **63**, 6890-699.

Buchingam, A.D. (ed.)(1992) Structure and Activity of Enzymes (1992) *Faradya Discuss.* **93** (special issue).

Buck, M., Boyd, J., Redfield, C., MacKenzie, D.A., Jeenes, D.J., Archer, D.B., and Dobson, C. M. (1995) Structural determination of protein dynamics: analysis of 15N NMR relaxation measurements for main-chain and side-chain nuclei of hen egg white lysozyme, *Biochemistry* 34, 4041-4055.

Budil, D.E., Earle, K.A., Lynch, W.B., and Freed, J.H. (1989) Electron paramagnetic resonance at 1 millimeter wavelengths. In Hoff, A. J. (eds.), *Advanced ESR: Application in Biology and Biochemistry*, Elsevier, Amsterdam.

Bugg, T. (1997) *An Introduction of Enzyme and Coenzyme Chemistry*, Blackwell Science, Cambridge, MA.

Bulen, W.A. and LeComt, J.R. (1966) The nitrogenase system from Azotobacter: two-enzyme requirement for N2 reduction, ATP-dependent H2 evolution and ATP hydrolysis, *Proc. Natl. Acad. Sci.* **56**, 979-986.

Burgess, B.K. and Lowe, D.J. (1966) Mechanism of molybdenum nitrogenase, *Chem. Rev.* **96**, 2983-3011.

Burka, L.T., Guengerich, F.P., Willard, R.J., and Macdonald, T.L. (1985) Mechanism of cytochrome P450 catalysis. Mechanism of N-demethlylation and amine oxide deoxygenation, *J. Am. Chem. Soc.* **107**, 2549-2551.

Burlingame, A. L. and Carr, S. A. (eds.), (1999) *Mass Spectrometry in the Biological Science*, Totowa, New York, Humana.

Burshtein, A.I. (2000) United theory of photochemical charge separation. In Prigogine, I. and Rice, A. (eds.), *Advances in Chemical Physics* **114**, John Wiley and Son, inc. 419-587.

Bystryak, I.M., Likhtenshtein, G.I., Kotel'nikov, A I., Hankovsky, O., and Hideg, K. (1986) The influence of the molecular dynamics of the solvent on the photoreduction of nitroxyl radicals, *Russian J. Phys. Chem.* **60**, 1679-1683.

Calvo, R., Abresch, E.C., Bittl, R., Feher, G., Hofbauer, W., Isaacson, R. A., Lubitz, W., Okamura, M.Y., Paddock, M.L. (2000) EPR study of the molecular and electronic structure of the semiquinone biradical $Q_A^-.Q_B^-$. in Photosynthetic Reaction Centers from Rhodobacter sphaeroides. *J. Am. Chem. Soc.* **122** (30).

Cannon, W.R., Singleton, S.F., and Benkovic, S.J (1996) *Nature Struct. Biol.*, **3**, 821-

Carrel, T.G., Tyryshkin, A.M., and Dismukes, G.C. (2002) An evaluation of structural models for the photosynthetic water-oxidizing complex derived from spectroscopic and X-ray diffraction signatures, J. *Biol. Inorg. Chem.*, **7**, 2-22.

Carrea, G. and Riva, S. (2000) Properties and synthetic application of enzymes in organic solvents, *Angew. Chem.* **33**, 2226-2254.

Case, G.D., and Leigh, J.S. Jr. (1976) Intramitochondrial position of cytochrome haem groups determined by dipolar interaction with paramagnetic cations. *Biochem. J.* **160**, 769-783,

Cassidy, C.S., Lim, J., and Frey, P.A. (1997) A new concept for the mechanism of action in chymotrypsin: the role of the low barrier hydrogen bond, *Biochemistry* **36**, 4576- 4584.

Cavanagh, J., Venters, R.A. (2001) A structural double-mutant cycle: estimating the strength of a buried salt bridge in barnase. Protein dynamic studies move to a new time slot, *Nat. Struct. Biol.* **8** (11), 912-914.

Cha, Y., Murray, C. J., and Klinman, J. P. (1989) Hydrogen tunneling in enzyme reactions, *Science (Wash. DC)* **243**, 1325-1330.

Champion, P.M., Stallard, B.R., Wagner, G.G., and Gunsalus, I.C. (1982) Resonance Raman detection of a Fe-S bond, *in Cytochrome P-450: Structure and Function, National Symposium*, Minsk, p. 7.

Chan, J.M., Wu, W., Dean, D.R., and Seefeldt, L.C. (2000) Construction and Characterization of a heterodimeric iron protein: defining rolee for adenosin triphosphate in nitrogenase catalysis, *Biochemistry* **39**, 7221-7228.

Chance, B.C. (1949) The properties of the enzyme-substrate compounds of horse-radish and lacto – peroxidases, *Science* **109**, 204-208.

Chance, B. Devault, D. (1964) Kinetics and quantum efficiency of the chlorophyll-cytochrome reaction, *Ber. Bunsenges. Physik. Chem.* **68**, 722-726.

Chang, S-L., Wallar, B.J., Lipscomb, J.D., and Mayo, K.H. (2001) Residues in *Methylosinus trichosporium* OB3b methane monooxygenase component B involved in molecular interactions with reduced- and oxidized-hydroxylase component: A role for the N-terminus, *Biochemistry* **40**, 9539-9551.

Changenet, P., Choma, C.T., Gooding, E.F., DeGrado, E.F., DeGrado, W.F., and Hochstrasser, R.M. (2000) Ultrafast dielectric response of proteins from dynamics Stokes shifting of coumarin in caldmodulin, *J. Phys. Chem.* **B 104**, 9322-9329.

Chen, J., Wu, Wei, Dean, D.R, and Seefeldt, L.C. (2000) Construction and characterization of a heterodimeric iron protein: defining roles for adenosine triphosphate in nitrogenase catalysis, *Biochemistry* **39**, 7221-7228.

Cheng, X. (1995) Structure and function of DNA methyltransferase, *Annu. Rev. Biophys. Biomol. Struct.* **24**, 293-318.

Cherepanova, E. S., Kulikov, A.V. and Likhtenstein, G.I. (1990) Localization of paramagnetic centers relative to aqueous and lipid phases by ESR, *Biol. Membr.* (Moscow) **77**, 51-56.

Chiu, H-J, Peters, J. W., Lanzillota, W N., Ryle, M. J., Seefeldt, L. C., Howard, J.B., and Rees, D. C. (2001) MgATP-bound and nucleotide-free structure of a nitrogenase protein complex between the 127 D-Fe-protein and the MoFe-protein, *Biochemistry* **40**, 641-650.

Christiansen, J., Cash, V. L., Seefeldt, L.C., and Dean, D. R. (2000) Isolation and characterization of an acetylene resistance nitrogenase, *J. Biol. Chem.* **275**, 11459-11464.

Christie, P. D., Lee, H. -I., Cameron, L. M., Hales, B. J., Orme-Johnson, W. H., and Hoffman, B. M. (1996) Identification of the CO-Binding cluster in nitrogenase MoFe protein by ENDOR of 57Fe isotopomers, *J. Am. Chem. Soc.* **118**, 8707-8709.

Chu, H.A., Sackett, H., and Babcock, G.T. (2000) Identification of a Mn-O-Mn cluster vibrational mode of the oxygen-evolving complex in photosystem II by low-frequency FTIR spectroscopy, *Biochemistry* **39**, 14371-14376.

Clela, J.W. and Craik, C S. (1996) *Protein Engineering: Principles and Practice* (eds.), Wiley-Liss, N. Y.

Cleland, W. W. and Northrop, D. B. (1999) Energetics of substrate binding, catalysis, and product release, in Schramm, V. L. and Purich, D. L. (eds.), *Methods in Enzymology* **308**, Enzyme Kinetics and Mechanism, Part E, Academic Press, San Diego, pp. 3-27.

Cole, R. B. (1997) Electrospray Ionization Mass Spectrometry: Fundamentals, Instumentation and Practice, Wiley, New York.

Coon, M.J., White, R.E., and Blake, R.C. (1981) Oxygen activation by cytochrome P450, in King, T.E. (ed.) *Oxidases and related systems,* **1**, University Park Press, Baltimore, pp. 93-118.

Cordier, F. M., Caffrey, B. B., Cusanovich, M.A., Marion D., and Blackledge M. (1998) *J. Mol. Biol.* **281**, 341.

Cornish-Bowden, A. (2001) *Fundamentals of Enzyme Kinetics*, Portland Press, London.

Cornish-Bowden, A. (1995) *Analysis of Enzyme Kinetic Data,* Oxford University Press, Oxford.

Coucouvanis, D., Han, J., and Moon, N. (2002) Synthesis and characterization of sulfur-voided cubanes. Structural analogues for the MoFe3S3 subunit in the nitrogenase cofactor, *J. Am. Chem. Soc.* **124**, 216-224.

Coucouvanis, D., Mosier, P.E.; Malinak, S.; Laughlin, L.; Demadis, K.D. (1995) Catalytic reduction of hydrazine and acetylene to ammonia and ethylene and stoichiometric reduction of CN⁻ to ammonia and methane by Fe/M/S clusters (M =Mo, V) with structural features similar to those of the Fe/Mo/S site in nitrogenase, *Plant Sci. Biotechnol. Agric.* (Nitrogen Fixation: Fundamentals and Applications) **27**, 137-42.

Couture, M., Adak, S., Stuehr, D.J., Rousseau, D. L. (2001) Regulation of the properties of the heme-NO complexes in nitric-oxide synthase by hydrogen bonding to the proximal cysteine, *J. Biol. Chem.* **276**, 38280-38288.

Craig, D.B., Arriaga, E. A., Wong, J.C. X., Lu, H., and Dovichi N. I. (1996) Studies on single alkaline phosphatase molecule: reaction rate and activation energy of a reaction catalyzed by a single molecule and the effect of the thermal denaturation – the death of enzyme, *J. Am. Chem. Soc.* **118**, 5245-5253.

Crane, B.R, Arvai, A.S., Ghosh, D.K., Wu, C., Getzoff, E.D., Stuehr, D.J., and Tainer, J.A. (1998) Structure of nitric oxide synthase oxygenase dimer with pterin and substrate, *Science* **279**, 2121-2126.

D'Auria, S., Nucci, R., Rossi, M., Gryczynski, I., Gryczynski, Z., and Lakowicz, J. R. (1999) The β-glycosidase from the hyperthermophilic archaeon *Sulfolobus solfataricus*: enzyme activity and conformational dynamics at temperatures above 100°C, *Biophys. Chem.* **81**, 23-31.

D'Souza, V. T. and Bender, M. L. (1987) Miniature organic models of enzymes, *Acc. Chem. Res.* **20**, 146-152.

Daggett, V. D., Kollman, P. A. and Kuntz, I. D. (1989) Free energy perturbation calculations of charge interactions with the helix dipole, *Chemica Scripta.* **29A**, 205-215.

Dance, I. (1998) Understanding structure and reactivity of new fundamental inorganic molecules: metal sulfides, metallcarbohedranes, and nitrogenase, *Chem. Commun.* 523-530.

Daniel, R. M. and Cowan, D. A. (2000) Biomolecular stability and life at high temperatures, *Cell. Mol. Life Sci.* **57**, 250-264.

Dauber-Osguthorpe, P., and Osguthorpe, D. J. (1990) Analysis of intramolcular motions by filtering molecular dynamics trajectories, *J. Am. Chem. Soc.* **112**, 7921-7935.

Davis, W. B. Ratner M.A., and Wasielevski, M.R. (2001) Conformational gating of long distance electron transfer through wire-like bridges in donor-bridge-acceptor molecules, *J. Am. Chem. Soc.* **123**, 7877-

Davydov, R., Makris, T.M., Kofman, V., Werst, D.E., Sligar, S.G., and Hoffman, B.I. (2001) Hydroxylation of camphor by reducing oxi-cytochrome P450cam: Mechanistic implication of ESR and ENDOR studies of catalytic intermediate in native and mutant enzymes, *J. Am. Chem. Soc.* **123**, 1403-1415.

de Visser, S. P., Ogliaro, F. Harris, N., and Shaik, S. (2001), Multi-State Epoxidation of Ethene by Cytochrome P450: A Quantum Chemical Study, *J. Am. Chem. Soc.* **123**, 3037-3047.

de Visser, S., Ogliaro, F. and Shaik, S. (2001b) How does ethene inactivate cytochrome P450 en route to its epoxidation? A density functional study, *Angewandte Chemie, International Edition* **40**, 2871-2874.

de Visser, S., Ogliaro, F., Shaik, S. (2000a). Stereospecific oxidation by Compound I of Cytochrome P450 does not proceed in a concerted synchronous manner, *Chem. Commun.* (Cambridge, U. K.) 2322-2323.

Dean, D.R., Setterquist, R.A., Brigle, K.E., Scott, D.J., Laird, N. F., Newton, W.E., (1990) Evidence that conserved residues Cys-62 and Cys-154 within the *Azotobacter vinelandii* nitrogenase iron-molybdenum protein α-subunit are essential for nitrogenase activity but conserved residues His-83 and Cys-88 are not. *Mol. Microbiol.* 4(9),

Debye, P., (1942) Reaction rates in ionic solutions, *Trans. Electrochem. Soc.* **82**, 265-272.

DeGrado, W.F. (2001) Protein design (eds.), *Chem. Rev.* **101** (10), Special Issue.

Deng, H. and Callender, R. (1999) Raman spectroscopic studies of the structure, energies, and bond distortions of substrates bound to enzymes, in Schramm, V. L. and Purich, D. L. (eds.), *Methods in Enzymology* **308**, Enzyme kinetics and Mechanism, Part E, Academic Press, San Diego, pp. 176-215.

Denisov, E. T., Sarkisov, O. M, and Likhtenshtein G. I. (2000) *Chemical Kinetics* (In Russian), Khymia, Moscow.

Denisov, N. T., Shuvalov, V.F., Shuvalova, N. I., Shilova, A. K. and Shilov, A.E. (1970) Catalytic reduction of molecular nitrogen in proton media, *Kinet. Katal.* **11**, 813-14.

Denk, W., Strickler, J.H., and Webb, W.W. (1900) Two photon laser scanning fluorescene microscopy, *Science* **248**, 73-76.

De Rosa, M, Nicolaus, A., Gambacorta, B., Buonocore, V., and Poerio, E. (1980) Immobilized bacterial cells containing a thermostable β-galactosidase, *Biotechnol. Letters* **2**, 29 -34

DeRose, V.J. C.-H., Kim, W.E., Newton, D. R.D., and Hoffman B. M. (1995) Electron Spin Echo Modulation Spectroscopic Analysis of Altered Nitrogenase MoFe Proteins of *Azotobacter vinelandii*, *Biochemistry* 34, 2809-2814

DeRose, V.J., Liu, K.E., Lippard, S., and Hoffman, B.M. (1996) Investigation of the dinuclear Fe center of methane monooxygenase by advanced paramagnetic resonance techniques, on the geometry of DMSO binding, *J. Am. Chem. Soc.* **118**, 121-134.

DeSilva, B. S., Orosz, G., Egodage, K. L., Carlson, R. G., Schowen, R. L., Wilson, G. S. (2000) Catalytic antibodies for complex reactions: hapten design and the importance of screening for catalysis in the generation of catalytic antibodies for the NDA/CN reaction, *Appl. Biochem. and Biotechn.* **83**, 195-208.

Di Donato, M., Borrelli, R., Capobianco, A., Monaco, G., Improta, R., Brahimi, M., and Peluso, A. (1999), Proton assisted electron transfer *Adv. Quantum Chem.* **36**, 301-322.

Di Pace, A., Cupane, A., Leone, M., and Vitrano, E. and Di Pace A; Cupane A; Leone M; Vitrano E; Cordone, L. (1992) Protein dynamics. Vibrational coupling, spectral broadening mechanisms, and anharmonicity effects in carbonmonoxy heme proteins studied by the temperature dependence of the Soret band lineshape *Biophys. J.* **63**, 475-484.

Diaz, N., Suarez, D., and Merz, K.M., Jr. (2001) Molecular dynamics simulation of the mononuclear zinc-β-lactomase from *Bacciluscereus* complexed with benzylpenicillin and quantum chemical study of the reaction mechanism, *J. Am. Chem. Soc.* **123**, 9867-9879.

Diekmann, S., Weston, J., Anders, E., Boland, W., Schonecker, B., Hettmann, T, Von Langen, J., Erhard, S., Mauksch, M, Brauer, M, Beckmann, C., Rost, M, Sperling, P., and Heinz, E. (2002) Metal-mediated reactions modeled after nature, *Reviews in Molecular Biotechnology* **90**, 73-94.

Dismukes, G. C. (2001) Splitting water, *Science* **292**, 447-448.

Donchev, A.A., Kossekova, G.P., and Atanasov, B.P. (1992), Effect of some charged and neutral quenchers and heme-containing proteins on the fluorescence of pyridoxal phosphate-N-acetyl-lysyl-methyl ester, *Dokl. Bulg. Akad. Nauk.* **45**, 71-74.

Dong, J., Fujii, H., Hendrich, M.P., Leising, R.A., Pan, G., Randall, C.R., Wilkinsom, E.C, Zang, Y., Que, L. Jr., Fox, B. G., Kaufmann, K., and Munck, E. (1995) A high valent nonheme intermediate. Structure and properties of [Fe$_2$(O)$_2$(5-MeTPA)$_2$] (ClO$_4$)$_3$, *J. Am. Chem. Soc.* **117**, 2778-2792.

Dordik, J.S. (1991) *Biocatalysis for Industry*, Plenum Press, New York.

Drauz, K. and Waldman, H. (1995) *Enzyme Catalysis in Organic Synthesis*, Wiley, Weinheim

Druzhinin, S.Yu., Fogel, V.R., Syrtsova, L.A., Likhtenstein, G.I. and Kotelnikov, A I. (1986) Study on the cofactor center localization in nitrogenase by triplet labeling method, *Biofizika.* **31**, 16-21.

Druzhinin, S.Yu., Syrtsova, L.A., Denisov, N.N., Shkondina, N.I., and Gak, V.Yu. (1998) Xanthene dyes as photochemical donors for the nitrogenase reaction, *Biochemistry* (Moscow) **63**, 996-1006.

Druzhinin, S.Yu., Syrtsova, L.A., Nadtochenko, V.A., and Likhtenshtein, G.I. (1989) *Biochemistry* (Moscow) **54**, 1638-1645.

Druzhinin, S.Yu., Syrtsova, L.A., Rubtsova, E.T., and Shkondina, N.I. (1996) Photostimulation of intermolecular transfer of electrons in nitrogenase, *Biokhimiya* (Moscow) **61**, 2165-2172

Druzhinin, S.Yu., Syrtsova, L. A., Uzenskaja, A.M., Likhtenstein, G. I. (1993) *Biochem. J.* **290**, 627-631.

Druzhinin, S.Yu., Syrtsova, L.A., Uzenskaya, A M., Likhtenshtein, G. I. (1991) *Biokhimiya* (Moscow) **56**, 1036-1041.

Duncan, T.M., Bulygin, V.V., Zohu, Y., Hutcheon, M.L., and Cross, R.L. (1995) Rotation of of subunits during catalysis by Escherichia coli F1-ATPase, *Proc. Natl. Acad. Sci. USA* **92**, 10964-10968.

Dunford, H.B. and Stillman, J.S. (1976) On the function mechanism of action of peroxidases, *Coord. Chem. Rev.* **19**, 187-251.

Dunietz, B.D., Beachy, M.D., Cao, Y., Whittington, D. A., Lippard, S.J., and Friesner, R.A. (2000) Large scale *s* quantum chemical calculation of the intermediates in the soluble methane monooxygenase catalytic cycle, *J. Am. Chem. Soc.* **122**, 2828-2839.

Durrant, M.C. (2001) Controlled protonation of iron-molybdenum cofactor by nitrogenase: a structural and theoretical analysis, *Biochem. J.* **355**, 871-891.

Duyvis, M. G., Wassink, H., and Haaker, H. (1998) Nitrogenase of *Azotobacter vinelandii*: kinetic analysis of the Fe protein cycle, *Biochemistry* **37**, 17345-17354.

Dvorsky, R., Sevcik, J., Caves, L. S. D., Hubbard, R.E., and Verma, C. S. (2000) Temperature effect on protein motion: a molecular dynamics study of RNAase-*Sa J. Phys. Chem. B* **104**, 10387-10397.

Dzhabiev, T.S., Mironova, S.A., and Shilov, A.E. (1999) Kinetic evidence of nitrogen reduction in the coordination sphere of a polynuclear complex, *Kinetics and Catalysis* (Translation of Kinetika i Kataliz) **40**, 764-768.

Dzuba, S.A. and Hoff, A.J. (2000) Photo-induced radical pairs investigated usin-out of phase electron-spin echo, In Berliner, L. J., Eaton, S. S., and Eaton, G. R. (eds.), (2000) *Biological Magnetic Resonance*, **19**, Distance Measurements in biological Systems by EPR, Kluwer Academic/Plenum Publisher, N. Y., pp. 469-596.

Dzuba, S.A. and Kawamori, A. (1996) Selective hole burning EPR: spectral diffusion and dipole broadening, *Concepts in Magnetic Resonance* **8**, 49-61.

Eady, R. R. (1996) Structure-function relationships of alternative nitrogenases, *Chem. Rev.* **96**, 3013-3030.

Eastman, M.P., Bruno, G.V. and Freed, J. H. (1970) Studies of Heisenberg spin exchange. II Effect of radical charge and size, *J. Chem. Phys.* **52**, 2511-2522.

Eaton, G.R and Eaton, S.S. (1989) Resolved electron-electron spin-spin splittings in ESR spectra. *Biol. Magn. Reson.* **8**, 339-397.

Eaton, S.S. and Eaton, G.R. (2000) Distance measurement by CW and pulsed ESR, in Berliner, L, Eaton, S., and Eaton, G. (eds.), *Magnetic Resonance in Biology*, **V. 18**, Kluwer Academic Publishers. Dordrecht, pp. 2-28.

Edman, L., Mets, U., and Rigler, R. (1996) Conformational transition monitored for single molecules in solution, *Proc. Natl. Acad. Sci. USA* **93**, 6710-6715.

Efrima, S. and Bixon, M. (1974) On the role of vibrational relaxation in the electron transfer reactions with large negative free energy, *Chem. Phys. Lett.* **25**, 34-37.

Egava, T., Shimada, H., and Ishimura, Y. (1994) Evidence for compound I formation in the reaction of cytochrome P450cam with m-chloroperbenzoic acid, *Biochem. Biophys. Res. Commun.* **201**, 1464-1469.

Ekiel, I., Banville D., Shen, S.H., and Gehring, K. (1998) Effect of peptide binding on amide proton exchange rates in the PDZ2 domain from human phosphatase hPTP1E, *Biochemistry and Cell Biology* **76**, 334-340.

Elmerich, C. (2001) Nitrogenase: biochemical, molecular and genetic aspects, *Nitrogen Assimilation by Plants* 149-167.

Elson, E.L. and Rigler, R. (2000) *Fluorescence correlation spectroscopy. Theory and applications.* (eds.), Springer, Heidelberg.

Endeward, B., Plato, M., Will, S., Vogel, E., Szyczewski, A.;,Moebius, K.. (1998) Liquid-phase EPR, ENDOR, and TRIPLE resonance studies on corrole and isocorrole cation radicals, *Applied Magnetic Resonance* **14**, 69-80.

Englander, S. Hydrogen exchange. Walter, Krishna, Mallela M. G. (2001) *Nat. Struct. Biol.* **8**(9), 741-742.

Ermolaev, V. L., Bodunov, E. N., Sveshnikova, E. B., and Shakhverdov, T. A. (1977) *Radiationless Transfer of Electronic Excitation Energy*, Nauka. Leningrad.

Evans, D.J., Henderson, R.A. and Smith, B.E. (1999) Catalysis by nitrogenases and synthetic analogs. *Bioinorg. Catal.* (2nd Ed., Revis. Expanded) 153-207.

Evance, M.C.W., Rich, A.M., and Nugent, J.H.A. (2000) Evidence for the presence of a component of the Mn complex of the Photosystem II reaction center which is exposed to water in the S2 state of the water oxidation complex, *FEBS Letters*, **477**, 113-117.

Ewert, U., Crepeau, R.H., Dunnmam, Curt.R., Xu,D., Lee, S.and Freed, J.H. (1991) Fourier transform electron spin resonance imaging, *Chem. Phys. Letters* **184**, 25-33.

Eyles, S.J., Speir, J. P., Kruppa, G.H., Gierasch, L. M., and Kaltashov, I.A. (2000) Protein conformational stability probed by Fourier transform ion cyclotron resonance mass spectrometry, *J. Am. Chem. Soc.* **122**, 495-500.

Faber, H.R. and Mathews, B.W. (1990) A mutant T4 lyzozyme displays five different crystal conformations of 'hinge-like" motion *Nature* **348**, 263-.

Fainberg, B. D. and Huppert, D. (1999) Theoretical and experimental study of ultrafast solvation dynamics by transient four-phonon spectroscopy, in Jortner, J. and Bixon. (eds.), *Advances in Chemical Physics* **107**, Part 1, John Wiley & Sons. NY., pp 191-262.

Farber, G.K. (1999) Crystallographic analysis of solvent-trapped intermediates of chymotrypsin, in Schramm, V. L. and Purich, D. L. (eds.), *Methods in Enzymology* **308**, Enzyme kinetics and Mechanism, Part E, Academic Press, San Diego, pp. 201- 218.

Farver, O. and Pecht, I. (1999) Copper protein as model system for investigating intramolecular electron transfer processes, in Jortner, J. and Bixon. (eds.),, *Advances in Chemical Physics* **107**, Part 1, John Wiley & Sons. NY., pp. 555-590.

Feher, G. (1992) Three-dimensional structure of the reaction center by X-diffraction from single crystals, *Is. J. Chem.* **32**, 375-378.

Feix, J.B. and Klug, C.S. (1998) Site-directed spin labeling of membrane proteins and peptide-membrane interaction, in Berliner, L. (eds.) *Biological Magnetic Resonance* **14**, Spin Labeling: the Next Millennium, Plenum Press, N.Y., pp. 250-315.

Fernandez-Lafuente, R., Rosell, C. M., Caanan-Haden, L., Rodes, L., Guisan, J.M. (1998) Stabilization of immobilized enzymes against organic solvents: complete hydrophilization of enzymes environments by solid-phase chemistry with poly-functional macromolecules, *Prog. Biotechnol.* **15** (Stability and Stabilization of Biocatalysis), 405-410.

Fersht A. (1999) Structure and Mechanism of Protein Science : A Guide to Enzyme Catalysis and Protein Folding. W.H. Freeman and Co. UK.

Fersht, A. and Altamirano, M. (2001) Design of novel enzymes by mutagenesis of α/β-barrel proteins. *PCT Int. Appl.* **83**, pp.

Fersht, A. and Winter, G. (1992) Protein engineering, *Trends Biochem. Sci.* **17**, 292-294.

Fierke, C.A. and Hammes, G.G. (1955) Transient kinetic approaches to enzyme mechanism, in Purich, D. L. (eds.), *Methods in Enzymology* **249**, Enzyme Kinetics and Mechanism, Part D, Academic Press, San Diego, pp. 37-6.

Filatov, M., Harris, N., and Shaik, S. (1999) On the "rebound" mechanism of alkane hydroxylation by cytochrome P450: electronic structure of the intermediate and the electron transfer character in the rebound step. *Angew. Chem., Int. Ed.* **38**, 3510-3512.

Filizola, M. and Loew, G.H. (2000) Role of protein environment in horseradish peroxidase compound I formation: molecular dynamic stimulation of horseradish peroxidase-HOOH complex, *J. Am. Chem. Soc.* **122**, 18-25.

Filizola, M. and Loew, G.H. (2000) Role of protein environment in horseradish peroxidase compound I formation: molecular dynamic stimulation of horseradish peroxidase-HOOH complex, *J. Am. Chem. Soc.* **122**, 18-25..

Fiorini, M., McKendry, R., Cooper, M. A., Rayment, T., and Abell, C. (2001) Chemical Force Microscopy with active enzymes, *Biophys. J.*, **80**, 2471-2476.

Fischmann, T. O., Hruza, A., Niu, X. D., Fossetta, J. D. Lunn, C. A., Dolphin, E., Prongay, A. J., Reichert, P., Lundell, D. J., Narula, S. K. and Weber, P. C. (1999) Structural characterization of nitric oxide synthase isoforms reveals striking active-site conservation, *Nature Struct. Biol.* **6**, 233-242.

Fisher, K., Hare, N. D., and Newton W. E. (1998), Mapping the catalytic surface of *A. vinelandii* MoFe protein by site specific mutagenesis, *Curr. Plant Sci. Biotechnol. Agric.* **31** (Biological Nitrogen Fixation for the 21st Century), 23-26.

Fisher, M.W.F., Zengand, L.M., Zuiderweg, E.R.P. (1998) *Proc. Natl. Acad. Sci.*, **95**, 8016.

Flatmark, T., Stokka, A. J., and Berge, S. V. (2001) Use of Surface Plasmon Resonance for real time measurements of the global conformational transition in human phenylalanine hydroxylase in response to substrate binding and catalytic activation, *Anal. Biochem.* **294**, 95-101.

Fogel, V. R., Rubtsova, E. T., Likhtenshtein, G. I., and Hideg, K. (1994) Factors affecting photoinduced electron transfer in a donor-acceptor pair (D-A) incorporated into bovin serum albumin, *J. Photochem. Phot Photobiol. A: Chem.* **83**, 229-236.

Förster, T.H. (1948) Zwishenmoleculare Energiewanderung and Fluoreszent, *Annalen der Physik*, **2**, 55-75.

Fourkas, J. T. (2001) Multidimentional Raman spectroscopy, in Prigogine, I. and Rice, S. A. (eds.) *Adv. Chem. Phys.*, **117**, John Wiley & Sons, Inc. 235-274.

Frank, P., Angove, H. C., Burgess, B. K., and Hodgson, K. O. (2001) Determination of ligand binding constants for the iron-molybdenum cofactor of nitrogenase: monomers, multimers, and cooperative behavior, *J. Biol. Inorg. Chem.* **6**, 683-697.

Frauenfelder, H. and McMahon, B. H. (2001) The energy landscape, *Springer Series in Chemical Physics* **67** (Single Molecule Spectroscopy), 257-276.

Frauenfelder, H., McMahon, B. H., Austin, R. H., Chu, K., Groves, J. T. (2001) The role of structure, energy landscape, dynamics, and allostery in the enzymatic function of myoglobin McMahon, B. H., Austin, R. H., Chu, K., and Groves, J. T., *Proceedings of the national academy of sciences of the united states of America* **98**, 2370-2374.

Frauenfelder, H., Sligar, S.G., and Wolynes, P.G. (1991) The energy landscapes and motions of proteins. *Science* **254**, 1598-1610.

Fray, P. A. (2001) Radical mechanism of enzymatic catalysis, *Annu. Rev. Biochem.* **70**, 121-148.

Freed, J. H. (2000) New technologies in electron spin resonance. In *Ann. Rev. Phys. Chem.* **51**, 655-689.

Freed, J. H. and Möbeus, K. (1992) Magnetic resonance. High-field EPR-ENDOR. *Israel J. Chem.* **32**, 475-481.

Frey, P., Whitt, S., and Tobin, J. (1994) A low barrier hydrogen bond in the catalytic triad of serin protease, *Science* **264**, 1927-1930.

Frolov, E. N., Belongova, O. V., and Likhtenshtein, G. I. (1977) Investigation of the mobility of spin and Mössbauer labels bound to macromolecules, in E. A. Burshtein (eds.), *Equilibrium Dynamics of the Native Structure of Protein*, Izdatelstvo Akademii Nauk SSSR, Pushchino, pp. 99-142.

Frolov, E.N., Mokrushin, A. N., Likhtenshtein, G. I., Trukhtanov, V. A., and Goldansky V.I. (1973) Investigation of dynamic structure of proteins using gamma-resonance labels, *Dokl. Akad. Nauk SSSR* **212**, 165-168.

Fyfe, P.K.; Jones, M.R. Re-emerging structures: continuing crystallography of the bacterial reaction center. Biochim. Biophys. Acta (2000), 1459(2-3), 413-421.

Gamov, C.A. (1926) Zur Quanum theorie des Atoms, *Z. Phys.* **51**, 204-212.

Garbutt, J. R., Goward, G.R., Kirby, C.W., and Power, W.P. (1998) Solid-state ^{2}H NMR study of methyl-d3-cobalamin, *Biochemistry and Cell Biology* **76**, 423-428.

Gassner, G.T., Lippard, S.J. (1999) Component interactions in the soluble methane monooxygenase system from *Methylococcus capsulatus* (Bath). *Biochemistry* **38**, 12768-12785.

Gates, B C. (1991) *Catalytic Chemistry*, John Wiley and Sons, New-York.

Gehlen, J.N., Daizadeh I., Stuchebrukov, A. A., and Marcus, R. A. (1996) Tunneling matrix element in Ru-modified blue copper proteins: pruning the protein in search of electron pathway, *Inorg. Chim. Acta* **243**, 271-282.

Gentile, L.N., and McIntosh, L. P. (1998) Assigning the NMR spectra of aromatic amino acids in proteins: analysis of two Ets pointed domains, *Biochemistry and Cell Biology* **76**, 379-390

Gerber, S.A., Scott, C. R., Turecek, F., and Gelb, M. H. (1999) Analysis rates of multiple enzymes in cell lysates by electrospray ionization mass spectrometry, *J. Am. Chem. Soc.* **121**, 1102-1103.

Gerken, S., Brettel, K., and Witt, H.T. (1988) Optical characterization of the immediate electron donor to chlorophyll a_{II}^+ in O_2-evolution photosystem II complex. Tyrosine as possible electron carrier between chlorophyll aII and the water-oxidizing manganase complex, *FEBS Letters* **237**, 69-79.

Gerlt, J. A. (1999) Stabilization of reactive intermediates and transition states in enzyme active sites by hydrogen bonding, *Comprehensive Natural Products Chemistry* **5**, 5-29.

Gerlt, J. and A. Gassman, P.G. (1992) Understanding enzyme-catalyzed proton abstraction from carbon acids: details of stepwise mechanisms for β-elimination reactions, *J. Am. Chem. Soc.* **114**, 5928-5934.

Gherman, B.F., Dunietz, B.D., Whittington, D.L., Lippard, S.J., and Friesner, R.A. (2001) Activation of the C-H bond of methane by intermediate Q of methane monooxigenase: a theoretical study, *J. Am. Chem. Soc.* **123**, 3836-3837s.

Gibasiewicz, K., Dobek, A., Breton, J., and Leibl, W. (2001) Modulation of primary radical pair kinetics and engergetics in Photosystem II by redox state of the quinone electron acceptor Q_A, *Biophys. J.* **80**, 1617-1630.

Gibbson, C. Montgomery, M. G., Leslie, A. G. W., and Walker, J. E. (2000) The structure of the central stalk in bovin F1-ATPase at 2. 4A resolution, *Nature Struct. Biol.* **7**, 1055-1061.

Gilson, M. K. (1993) Multiple-site titration and molecular modeling: two rapid methods for computing energies and forces for ionizable groups in proteins, *Proteins* **15**, 266-282.

Glaser, R., Novoselsky A., Shames A., and Likhtenshtein G.I. (2000) NMR Studies of Electrostatic Fields Around Charged Monosaccharides and Related Molecules, *Isr. J. Chem.* special Lemieux Wolf Prize Laureate issue **40**, 263-269.

Goldansky, V. .I., Krupyansky Yu. F., and Flerov B. N., (1983) *Doklady Akademy Nauk SSSR*, **272** 978 (in Russian).

Goller, A. H., Clark, T. (2001) SAM1 semiempirical calculations on the mechanism of cytochrome P450 metabolism, *THEOCHEM* **541**, 263-281.

Goodman, J.L., Pagal, M.D., and Stone, M.J. (2000) Relationship between protein structure and dynamics from a database of NMR-derived backbone order parameters, *J. Mol. Biol.* **295**, 963-978.

Gorcester, J., Millhauser, G.L., and Freed, J.H. (1990) Two-dimensional electron spin resonance, in Kevan, L. and Bowman, M. (eds.), *Modern Pulsed and Coninuous-wave Electron Spin Resonace*, N. Y. Wiley, 119-194.

Govindjee (2000) Milestones in photosynthesis research, *Probing Photosynthesis,* 9-39.

Gray, G.H. and Winkler, J.R. (1996) Electron transfer in proteins. *Annu. Rev. Biochem.* **65**, 537-561.

Gray, H. B., Ellis, W. R. (1994) Electron transfer, in Bertini, I., Gray, H. B., Lippard, S. J., and Valentine, J. S., *Bioorganic Chemistry,* University Science Books. Mill Valey. pp. 316-362.

Grigorov, L.N. and Chernavsky, D. S. (1972) Quantum-mechanical model of electron transfer from cytochrome to chlorophyll in photosynthesis, *Biofizika,* **17**, 195-102.

Griller, D. and Ingold, K.U. (1980) Free-radical clocks, *Acc. Chem. Res.,* **13**, 317-323.

Grinberg, O.Ya., Dadali, A.A., Dubinski, A.A., Wasserman, A. M., Buchachenko, A. L., and Lebedev, Ya.S. (1979) Determination of components of g- and A-tensors and rotational mobility of nitroxide radicals using 2-mm EPR spectroscopy, *Teor. Exp. Chem.* **15**, 583-589.

Gritsenko, O.N., Nesterenko, G. N., and Shteinman, A.A. (1995) Effect of substituents in the ligand on oxidation of alkanes by binuclear oxo-bridged iron complexes, *Izv. Akad. Nauk, Ser. Khim.* **12**, 2518-2520.

Gross, Z. and Simkhovich, L. (1998) Hydroxylation of simple alkanes by iodosylbenzene is catalyzed more efficiently by second than by third generation iron(III) porphyrins, *Tetrahedron Letters* **39**, 8171-8174.

Groves, J. T. (2000) Reactivity and mechanisms of metalloporphyrin-catalyzed oxidations, *Journal of Porphyrins and Phthalocyanines* **4**, 350-352.

Groves, J. T. (1997) The importance of being selective, *Nature* **389**, 329-330.

Groves, J.T. (1985) Key elements of the chemistry of cytochrome P450, *J. Chem. Education* **62**, 928-931.

Groves, J.T. and McGlusky, G.A. (1976) Aliphatic hydroxylation via oxygen rebound. Oxygen transfer by iron, *J. Am. Chem. Soc.* **98**, 859-861.

Groves, J.T., Gross, Z., and Stern, M.K. (1994) Preparation and reactivity of oxiirin (IV) porphyrins, *Inorg. Chem.* **33**, 5065-5072.

Groves, J.T. and Subramanian, D.V. (1984) Hydroxylation by cytochrome P450 and metaloporphyrin models. Evidence for allylic reaction, *J. Am. Chem. Soc.* **106**, 2177-2181.

Groves, J. T.; and Wang, C. C-Y. (2000) Nitric oxide synthase: models and mechanisms, *Current Opinion in Chemical Biology* **4**, 687-695.

Grubmeyer, C.T., Gross, J.W., and Rajavel, M. (1999) Energy coupling through molecular determination, in Schramm, V. L. and Purich, D. L., *Methods in Enzymology* **308**, Enzyme kinetics and Mechanism, Part E, Academic Press, San Diego, pp. 28-47.

Gryk, M.R., Abseher, R., Simon, B., Nilges, M., and Oshkinat, H. (1998) Heteronuclear relaxation study of the pH domain of b-spectrin: restriction of loop motion upon binding inisitol triphosphate, *J. Mol. Biol.* **280**, 879-986.

Guallar, V., Gherman, B. F., Lippard, S.J. and Friesner, R. A. (2002) Quantum chemical studies of methane monooxygenase: comparison with P450, *Current Opinion in Chemical Biology* **6**, 236-242.

Guengerich, P.P. and Macdonald, T.L. (1984) Chemical mechanism of catalysis by cytochrome P450: a unify view, *Acc. Chem. Res.* **17**, 9-16.

Guergova-Kuras, M., Boudreaux, B., Joliot, A., Joliot, P., and Redding, K. (2001) Evidence for two active branches for electron transfer in photosystem I, *Proc.. Natl. Acad. Sci. U. S.A.***98**, 4437-4442.

Gunner, M.R.and Alexov, E. (2000) A pragmatic approach to structure based calculation of coupled proton and electron transfer in proteins, *Biochim. et Biophys. Acta* **1458**, 63-87.

Gunner, M.R., Saleh, M. A., Cross, E., Ud-Doula, A., and Wise, M. (2000) Backbone dipoles generate positive potentials in all proteins: origins and implications of the effect, *Biophys. J.* **78**, 1126-1144.

Gust, D. and Moor, T.A. (eds) (1989) Covalently linked donor-acceptor photosynthetic model systems. *Tetraedron* **45** (special issue)

Gust, D., Moore, T.A., and Moore, A.L. (1993) Molecular mimicry of photosynthetic energy and electron transfer, *Acc. Chem. Res.* **26**, 198-205.

Gust, D., Moore, T. A., and Moore, A. L. (1999) An artificial photosynthetic membrane, *Zeitschrift fuer Physikalische Chemie* **213**, 149-155.

Gust, D., Moore, T.A., and Moore, A.L. (2001) Mimicking Photosynthetic Solar Energy Transduction, *Acc. of Chem. Res.* **34**, 40-48.

Gutfreund, H. (ed.) (1995) Kinetics for the Life Sciences: *Receptors, Transmitters and Catalysis,* Cambridge University Press, Cambridge, UK

Gvozdev, R.I., Nikonova, E.L., Pilyashenko-Novokhatny, A.I., Shushenacheva, E.V., Grigoryan, A.N., Belova, V.S., and Shirokova, L.A. (1982) The role of CO-binding in enzymatic oxidation of methane by the bacterium, *Methylococcus capsulatus, Biochemistry* **47**, 1118- 1124.

Ha, N-C., Kim, M-S., Lee, W., Choi, K.Y., and Oh, B-H. (2000) Detection of large pK_a perturbation of an inhibitor and catalytic group at an enzyme active site, a mechanistic basis for catalytic power of many enzymes, *J. Biol. Chem.* **275**, 41100-41106.

Haas, E.M., Wilked, E., Katchalski-Kazir A.and Steinberg I.Z. (1974) *Proc. Natl. Acad. Sci.* **72**, 1807.

Hahn, J.E., Hodgson, K.O., Andersson, L.A., and Dawson, J.H. (1982) Endogenous cystein ligation in ferric and ferrous cytochrome P-450. Direct evidence from X-ray absorption spectroscopy, *J. Biol. Chem.* **257**, 10934-10941.

Hakansson, K., Emmett, M.R., Hendrickson, C.L. and Marshall, A.G. (2001) High-sensitivity electron capture dissociation tandem FTICR mass spectrometry of microelectrosprayed peptides, *Analytical Chemistry* **73**, 3605-3610.

Hamaguchi, H. and Gustafson, T.L. (1994) Ultrafast time-resolved spontaneous and coherent Raman spectroscopy: the structure and dynamics of photogenerated transient species, *Ann. Rev. Phys. Chem.* **45**, 593-662.

Hamilton, G.A., Giacin, J.R., Hellman, Th.T., Snook, M.E., and Weller, J.W. (1973) Oxenoid model for enzymatic hydroxylation, *Ann. Acad. Sci. New York* **212**, 4-32.

Hammarstrom, L., Sun, L., Akermark, B., and Styring, S. (2001) A biomimetic approach to artificial photosynthesis: Ru(II)-polypyridine photo-sensitizers linked to tyrosine and manganese 8. electron donors, *Spectrochimica Acta, Part A*: Molecular and Biomolecular Spectroscopy 57A, 2145-2160.

Hammarström, P., Owenius, R., Martenson, L-G., Carlsson, U., and Lindgren, M. (2001) High resolution probing of local conformational change in proteins by the use of multiple labeling:unfolding and self – assembly of human carbonic anhydrase II monitored by spin, fluorescent, and chemical reactivity probs, *Biophys. J.* **80**, 2867-2885.

Hammes, G.sG. (2000) Thermodynamics and Kinetics for the Biological Sciences, John Wiley and Sons, New-York.

Hammond, G.S. and Saltiel, J. (1962) Photosensitized cis-trans isomerization of the stilbens, *J. Am. Chem. Soc.* **84**, 4983-4984.

Hammond, M.S., Houliston, R.S., and Meiering, E.M. (1998) Two-dimensional ^1H and ^{15}N NMR titration studies of hisactophilin, *Biochemistry and Cell Biology* **76**, 294-301.

Hanley, J., Sarrou, J., and Petrouleas, V. (2000) Orientation of the Mn(II)-Mn(II) dimere wwhich result from the reduction of the oxygen-evolving complex of Photosysem II by NO: an electron paramagnetic resonance study, *Biochemistry* **39**, 15441-15445.

Harris, D., Loew, G.H., and Waskell, L. (1998) Structure and spectra of ferrous dioxygen and reduced ferrous dioxygen model cytochrome P450, *J. Am. Chem. Soc.* **120**, 4308-4318.

Harris, N., Cohen, S., Filatov, M., Ogliaro, F., and Shaik, S. (2000) Two-state reactivity in the rebound step of alkane hydroxylation by cytochrome P-450: origins of free radicals with finite lifetimes. *Angew. Chem., Int. Ed.* **39**, 2003-2007.

Harvey, I., Arber, J.M., Eady, R R., Smith, B. E., Garner, C. D., and Hasnain, S. S. (1990) Iron k-edge x-ray-absorbtion spectroscopy of the iron-vanadium cofactor of the vanadium nitrogenase, *Biochem. J.* **266**, 929-931.

Hasserodt, J., Janda, K.D., and Lerner, R.A. (2000) Anibodies mimic natural oxidosqualene-cyclase action in steroid ring A formation, *J. Am. Chem. Soc.* **122**, 40-45.

Hata, M., Hirano, Y., Hoshino, T., and Tsuda (2001) Monooxidation mechanism by cytochrome P-450, *J. Am. Chem. Soc.* **123**, 6410-6416.

Hauser, C., Bill, E., and Holm, R. H. (2002) Single- and double-cubane clusters in the multiple oxidation states [VFe$_3$S$_4$]$^{3+, 2+, 1+}$], *Inorganic Chemistry* **41**, 1615-1624

Hayashi, Y. and Yamazaki, I. (1979) The oxidation-reduction potentials of Compound I/Compound II and Compound II/ferric couples of Horseradish peroxidases A2 and C*, *J. Biol. Chem.* **254**, 9101-9106.

Hecht, J. L., Honig, B., Shin, Y. and Hubbell, W. L. (1995) Electrostatic potential near the surface of DNA: comparing theory and experiment, *J. Phys. Chem*, **99**, 7782-7786.

Hegg, E.L., Ho, R.YN., and Que, L. Jr. (1999) Oxygen activation and arene hydroxylation by functional mimics of α-keto acid-dependent iron(II) dioxygenases, *J. Am. Chem. Soc.* **121**, 1972-1973

Heinen, U., Berthold, T., Kothe, G., Stavitski, E., Galili, T., Levanon, H., Wiederrecht, G., and Wasielewski, M.R. (2002) High time resolution Q-band EPR study of sequential electron transfer in a triad oriented in a liquid crystal, *J. Phys. Chem. A* **106**, 1933-1937

Heinze, M.G., Kolterman, A., and Schille, P. (2000) Simultaneous two-photon exitation of distinct labels for dual-color fluorescence crosscorrelation analysis, *Proc. Natl. Acad. Sci. USA* **97**, 10377-110382.

Helleren, C.A., Henderson, R. A., and Leigh, G.J. (1999) The mechanism of displacement of dihydrogen and dinitrogen from iron, ruthenium and osmium hydrides and implications for models of nitrogenase action, (1999) *Journal of the Chemical Society, Dalton Transactions: Inorganic Chemistry* **8**, 1213-1220.

Helleren, C.A., McMahon, C.N., and Leigh, G.J. (2000) The use of chemical models to probe the mechanisms of substrate reduction reactions of nitrogenases *Current Plant Science and Biotechnology in Agriculture* **38** (Nitrogen Fixation: From Molecules to Crop Productivity), 55-56.

Henderson, R.A. (1995) Mechanistic studies on iron-sulfor-based clusters, in Tichonovich, I. A., Provorov, N. A., Romanov, V. I., and Newton, W. E. (eds.), Nitrogen Fixation: Fundamentals and Applications, Kluwer Academic Publishers, Dodrecht, pp. 117-122.

Henderson, R.A., Leigh, G.J. (1999) The mechanism of displacement of dihydrogen and dinitrogen from iron, ruthenium and osmium

Hendrickson, C L. and Emmet, M. R. (1999) Electrospray ionization Fourier Transform ion cyclotron resonance mass spectrometry, in Strauss, H. L., Babcock, G. T., and Leone, S. R. *Annu. Rev. Phys. Chem.* **50**, 517-536.

Hill, C.L. (1989) *Activation and Functionalyzation of Alkanes.* John Wiley and Sons, New-York.

Hill, R.B., Bracken, C., DeGrado, W. F., and Palmer, A. G. III (2000) Molecular motion and protein folding: characterization of the backbone dynamics and folding equilibrium of α^{2}D using ^{13}C NMR spin relaxation, *J. Am. Chem. Soc.* **122**, 11611-11619.

Hiller, W., Messinger, J., and Wydrzynski, T. (1988) Kinetic determination of the fast exchanging substrate water molecule in the S$_3$ state of Photosystem II, *Biochemistry* **37**, 16908-16914.

Hiller, R., Zhou, Z.H, Adams, M.W.W., and Enlander, S.W. (1997) Stability and dynamics in a hyperthermophilic protein with melting temperature close to 200°C, *Proc. Natl. Acad, Sci. USA* **94**, 11329-11332.

Hilvert, D. (2000) Critical analysis of antibody catalysis, *Ann. Rev. Biochem.* **69**, 751-793.

Hofbauer, W., Zouni, A., Bittl, R., Kern, J.;,Orth, P., Lendzian, F., Fromme, P., Witt, H.T. and Lubitz, W. (2001) Photosystem II single crystals studied by EPR spectroscopy at 94 GHz: the tyrosine radical YD, *Proc. Natl. Acad.Sci. USA* **98**, 6623-6628.

Hoff, A.J. (1992) Time-resolved resonance Raman spectroscopy, *Israel J. Chem.* **32**, 483-484.

Hoff, A.J. and Deisenhofer, J. (1997) Photophysics of photosynthesis. Structure and spectroscopy of reaction centers of purple bacteria, *Physics Reports* 287, 1-247.

Hoff, A.J. and Scherz, A. (1992) Structure of the antenna complex and energy transfer, *Jsrael Chem. J.* **32**, 373-375.

Holm, R.H., Kennepohl, P. and Solomon, E.I. (1996) Structural and functional aspects of metal sites in biology, *Chem. Rev* **96**, 2239-2314.

Honig, B. and Nicholls, A. (1995). Classical electrostatics in biology and chemistry, *Science* **268**, 1144-1149.

Hopfield, J. J. (1974) Electron transfer between biological molecules by thermally activated tunneling, *Proc. Natl. Acad. Sci. USA* **71**, 3640-3644.

Hou, J.-M., Boichenko, V.A., Diner, B.A., Mauzerall, D. (2001) Thermodynamics of electron transfer in oxygenic photosynthetic reaction centers: Volume change, enthalpy, and entropy of electron transfer reactions in manganese-depleted photosystem II core complexes, *Biochemistry* **40**(24), 7117-7125.

Houk, K. M., Tucker, J. A., and Dorigo, A. E. (1990) Quantitative modeling of proxymity effect on organic reactivity, *Acc. Chem. Res.* **23**, 107-113.

Howard J. B. and Rees D. C. (1996) Structural bases of biological nitrogen fixation, *Chem. Rev.* **96**, 2965-2982.

Hu, Z. and Gorun, S.M. (2000) Methane monooxygenase models, in Meunier, B. (eds.), *Biomimetic Oxidations Catalyzed by Transition Metal Complexes*, Imperial College Press, London, pp. 269-307

Hustedt, E.J. and Beth, A.H. (Structural information from CW-Esr spectra of dipolar coupled nitroxide spin labels, in Berliner, L, Eaton, S., and Eaton, G. (eds.), , *Magnetic Resonance in Biology*, **V. 18**, Kluwer Academic Publishers. Dordrecht, pp. 155-184

Hwang, J-K, and Warshel, A. (1996) How important are quantum mechanical nuclear motion in enzyme catalysis? *J. Am. Chem. Soc.* **118**, 11745-11751.

Hwang, L.P. and Freed J H. (1975) Dynamics effect of pair correlation function on spin-relaxation by translational diffusion in liquids, *J. Chem. Phys.* **63**, 4017- 4025.

Hyde, J.S., Swartz, H. M. and Antholine, W. E. (1976) The spin probe-spin label methods. In: *Spin Labeling. Theory and Application*. **2**. (Berliner L. eds.) Academic Press, New York, pp. 72-113.

Hyde, J.S., Subczynski, W.K., Froncisz, W., and Lai, C.S. (1983) Spin label oximetry: measurement of oxygen concentration in biological samples, *Bull. Magn. Reson.* **5**, 180-182.

Iglesias, E. (1998) Cyclodextrins as enzyme models in nitrosation and in acid-base-catalyzed reactions of alkyl nitrites, *J. Am. Chem. Soc.* **120**, 13057-13069.

Imahori, H., Guldi, D. M., Tamaki, K., Yoshida, Yutaka, L., Chuping, S., Yoshiteru, F., and Shunichi (2001) Charge Separation in a Novel Artificial Photosynthetic Reaction Center Lives 380 ms, *J. Amer. Chem. Soc.* **123**, 6617-6628.

Ioaninnidis, N. and Petrouleas, V. (2000) Electron paramagnetic resonance signals from S_3 state of the oxygen0evolving complex. A broading radical signal induced by low temperature near-infrared light illumination, *Biochemistry* **39**, 5246-5254.

Itoh, S., Iwaki, M., and Ikegami, I. (2000) Modification of photosystem I reaction center by the extraction and exchange of chlorophylls and quinines, *Biochim. Biophys. Acta* **1507**, 115-138.

Isaev, A. and Scheiner, S. (2001) Proton conduction by a chain of water molecules in carbonic anhydrase, *J. Chem. Phys. B*, **105**, 6420-6426.

Isied, S. S. (1997) Long-range intramolecular electron transfer reactions across simple organic bridges, peptides, and proteins, *Advances in Chemistry Series* **253** (Electron Transfer Reactions), pp. 331-347.

Iverson, G., Kharakats, Y. I., Kuznetsov, A.M. and Ulstrup, J., (1999) Fluctuation and coherence in long-range and multicenter electron transfer, in Jortner, J. and Bixon M. (eds.) *Advances in Chemical Physics*. Part 1, John Wiley & Sons. NY., pp. 453-514.

Jaenicke, R.J. (2000) Stability and stabilization of globular proteins in solution, *Biotechnol.* 79, 193-203.

Jaenicke, R, (1998), What ultrastable globular proteins teach us about protein stabilization, *Biochemistry* (Moscow) **63**, 312-321.

Jaenicke, R, (1996) Stability and folding of ultrastable proteins: eye lens crystallins and enzymes from thermophiles, *FASEB J.* **10**, 84-92.

Jencks, W P. (1981) On the attribution and additivity of binding energy, *Proc. Natl. Acad. Sci. USA* **78** (40), 4046-4050.

Jenks, W.P. (1969) *Catalysis in Chemistry and Enzymology*, McGraw-Hill, New York.

Jeshke, G., Pannier, M., and Spiess, H. W. (2000) Double electron-electron resonance, in Berliner, L, Eaton, S., and Eaton, G. (eds.), , *Magnetic Resonance in Biology*, **V. 18**, Kluwer Academic Publishers. Dordrecht, pp. 493-512.

Jiang, F., Tsai, S-W., Chen, S., and Makinen, M.W. (1998) ENDOR determined structure of a complex of α-chymotrypsin with a spin-labeled transition-state inhibitor analogue, *J. Phys. Chem. B*, **102**, 4619-4627.

Jin, Y. and Lipscomb, J.D. (2000) Mechanistic insights C-H activation from radical clock chemistry: oxidation of substituted methylcyclopropanes catalyzed by soluble methane monooxygenase from *Methylosynus trichosporium* OB3b, *Biochim. Biophys. Acta* **1543**, 47-59.

Jockel, P., Schmid, M., Choinowski, T., and Dimroth, P. (2000) Essential role of tyrosine 229 of the oxaloacetate decorboxylase β-subunitin the energy coupling mechanism of the Na^+ pump, *Biochemistry*, **39**, 4320-4326.

Johnson, K.A. (1995) Rapid quenching kinetics analysis in polymerases, adenosin tri phosphotase, and enzyme intermediates, in Purich, D. L. (eds.), *Methods in Enzymology* **249**, Enzyme Kinetics and Mechanism, Part D, Academic Press, San Diego, pp. 3-37.

Johnson, J.L., Nyborg, A.C., Wilson, P.E., Tolley, A.M., Nordmayer, F.R., and Watt, G.D. (2000) Mechanistic interpretation of the dilution effect for Azotobacter vinilandii and Clostridium pasterianum nitrogenase catalysis, *Biochim. Biophys. Acta* **1543**, 36-46.

Jones, J. B. (1989) Enzymes in organic synthesis, *Tetraedron* **42**, 3351-3403.

Jordan, P., Fromme, P., Witt, H.T., Klukas, O., Saenger, W., and Krau, N. (2001) Three-dimentional structure of cyanobacterial photosystem I at 2.5 Å resolution, *Nature* **411**, 909-917.

Jortner, J., Bixson, M. (eds.), (1999) Electron transfer- from isolated molecules to biomolecules, *Advances in Chemical Physics*, Parts 1 and 2. John Wiley & Sons. NY.

Joshi, YD., Sidhu, G., Pot, I., Brayer, G. D., Withers, S. G. and McIntosh, L. P. (2000) Hydrogen bonding and catalysis: A novel explanation for how a single amino acid substitution can change the pH optimum of a glycosidase, *J. Mol. Biol.* **299**, 255-279.

Juffer, A.H. (1998) Theoretical calculations of acid-dissociation constants of proteins , *Bchemistry and Cell Biology* **76**, 198-209.

Kadereit, D. and Waldmann, H. (2001) Enzymatic protecting group techniquee, *Chem. Rev.*, **101**, 3367-3396.

Kalko, S.G., Gelpi, J.L., Fita, I., and Orozco, M. (2001) Kalko, S.G., Gelpi, J.L., Fita, I., Orozco, M., *J. Am. Chem. Soc.* **122**, 9665-9672.

Kanelis, V., Farrow, N.A., Kay, L. E., Rotin, D., and. Forman-Kay, J.D. (1998) NMR studies of tandem WW domains of Nedd4 in complex with a PY motif-containing region of the epithelial sodium channel, *Biochemistry and Cell Biology* **76**, 341-350.

Kangas, E. and Tidor, B. (2001) Electrostatic complementarity at ligand binding site: application to chorismate mutase, *J. Phys. Chem.* **105**, 880-888.

Karapetyan, N.V., Holzwarth, A.R., and Rogner, M. (1999) The photosystem I trimer of cyanobacteria: molecular organization, excitation dynamics and physiological significance, *FEBS Letters* **460**, 395-400.

Karasevich, E.I.,Kulikova, V.S., Shilov, A.E., and Shteinman, A.A. (1998) Biomimetic alkane oxidation based on metal complexes, *Usp. Khim.* **67**, 376-390.

Karasevich, E.I., Shestakov, A.F., and Shilov, A.E. (1999) Novel mechanism of aliphatic hydroxylation in enzymic and biomimetic systems. Problems of the reaction dynamics. Problems of the reaction dynamics, *Experimental and Toxicologic Pathology* **51**, 335-341.

Karplus, M. and Cammon M. (1986) Dynamics of protein structure, *Sci. Am.* **251**, 4-12.

Karplus, M. and Petsko, G.A. (1990) Molecular dynamics simulations in biology, *Nature* **347**, 631-639.

Karush, J. (1950) Heterogeneity of the binding site of bovin serum albumin, *J. Am. Chem. Soc.* **72**, 2705-2713.

Käss, H., Fromme, P. Witt, H.T. and Lubitz, W. (Orientation and electronic structure of the primary donor radical cation in Photosystem I: a single crystal EPR and ENDOR study, *J. Phys. Chem. B* **105**, 1225-1239.

Kauffmann, K.E., and Munck, E. (1998) Combining Mossbauer spectroscopy and magnetometry. ACS Symp. Ser. 692 (Spectroscopic Methods in Bioinorganic Chemistry), 16-29.

Kay, E., (1998) Protein dynamics from NMR, *Biochemistry and Cell Biology* **76**, 145-152.

Kay, L.E., Torchia, D. A., and Bax, A. (1989) Backbone dynamics of proteins as studied by ^{15}N inverse detected heteronuclear NMR spectroscopy: application to Staphylococcal nuclease, *Biochemistry* **28**, 8972-8979.

Ke, T., Wescott, C.R., and Klibanov, A. M. (1996) Prediction of the solvent dependence of enzymic prochiral selectivity by means of structure-based thermodynamic calculations, *J. Am. Chem. Soc.* **118**, 3366-74

Kettling, U., Koltermann, A., Schwille, P., and Eigen, M. (1998) Real time enzyme kinetics monitored by dual-color fluorescence cros-correlation spectroscopy, *Proc. Natl. Acad. Sci.* **95**, 1416-1420.

Kharkatz, Yu., I. (1976) Calculation of the solvent reorganization energy in reactions accompanied by inner-sphere charge transfer, *Electrokhimia*, **12**, 592-595.

Khechinashvili, N.N., Janin,J., and Rodier, F. (1995) Thermodynamics of the temperature induced unfolding of global proteins, Prot. Sci. 4, 1315-1324.

Khenkin, A.M. and Shteinman, AA. (1995) Chemical models of nonheme iron hydroxylases, *Ross. Khim. Zh.* 39, 41-49

Kiang, H., Luo, L., Taylor, K. L., and Dunaway-Maariano, D. (2000) Interexchange of catalytic activity within the 2-enoyl-coenzyme A hydratase/isomerase super family based on a common active site template, *Biochemistry* **38**, 7638-7652.

Kim, J. and Rees, D.C. (1992) Crystollographic structure and functional implication of the nitrogenase molybdenum-iron protein from *Azotobacter vinelandii, Nature* **360**, 556-560.

Kim, K. and Lippard, S.J. (1996) Structure and Mössbauer spectrum of a (μ–carboxylato)diiron(III) model for the peroxointermediate in the methan monooxygenase hydroxylase reacton circle, *J. Am. Che. Soc.* **118**, 4914-4915.

Kim, S., Sacksteder, C.A., Bixby, K. A., Barry, B.A. (2001) A Reaction-Induced FT-IR Study of Cyanobacterial Photosystem I, *Biochemistry* **40**, 15384-15395.

King, B. A. (2001) Ultrafast dynamics in the photosynthetic reaction center and green fluorescent proteins. 172 pp. AN 2001:914004

Kirmaier, C., Cua, A. He, C. Holten, D. Bocian, David F. (2002) Probing M-branch electron transfer and cofactor environment in the bacterial photosynthetic reaction center by addition of a hydrogen bond to the M-side bacteriopheophytin, *Journal of Physical Chemistry* **B 106**, 495-503.

Klapper, I.K., Hagstrom, R., Fine, R., Sharp, K., and Honig, (1986) Focusing of electric fields in the active site of Cu-Zn superoxide dismutase: effects of ionic strength and amino acid modification, *Proteins,* **1**, 47-59.

Klibanov, A.M. (2001) Improving enzymes by using them in organic solvent, *Nature* **409**, 241-246.

Kobayashi, K., Iwamoto, T., and Honda, K. (1994) Spectral intermediate in the reaction of ferrous cytochrome $P450_{cam}$ with superoxide anion, *Biochem. Biophys. Res. Commun.* **201**, 1348-1355.

Kobayashi, K., Iwamoto, T., and Honda, K. (1994) Spectral intermediate in the reaction of ferrous cytochrome $P450_{cam}$ with superoxide anion, *Biochem. Biophys. Res. Commun.* **201**, 1348-1355.

Kochetkov, B.B., Likhtenshtein, G.I. Koltover, V.K., Knox, P.P., Kononenko, A.A., Grishanova, P.G., and Rubin, A.B. (1984) *Izvestiya Akademii Nauk SSSR (Seria Biologicheskaya),* (4) 572-579.

Koeller, K.M. and Wong, C-H. (2001) Enzymes for chemical syntheses, *Nature* **409**, 232-239.

Kokorin, A.I., Zamaraev, K.I., Grigoryan, G.L., Ivanov, V. P., and Rozantsev, E.G. (1972) Distance estimation between nitroxyl radicals. *Biofizika* **17**, 34-41.

Kolbasov,d. and Scherz, A. (2000) Asymetric electron transfer in reaction centers of purple bacteria strongly depends on different electron matrix elements in the active and inactive brunches, *J. Phys. Chem. B* **104**, 1802-1809.

Kopp, D.A., Gassner, George T., Blazyk, J.L., and Lippard, S.J. (2001) Electron-transfer reactions of the reductase component of soluble methane monooxygenase from *Methylococcus capsulatus* (Bath). *Biochemistry* **40**, 14932-14941

Koshland, D.J. (1959) Mechanism of tranfer of enzymes, in Boyer, P. D., Lardy, M., and Myrback (eds.), *The Enzyme* V. 1, Academic Press, N. Y., pp. 305-346.

Koskinen, A. M. and P., Klibanov, A. M., (Eds.) (1996) *Enzymic Reactions in Organic Media*, Pergamon, London

Kotel'nikov, A.I., Likhtenshtein, G.I. and Gvozdev, R.I. (1975) The use of phenomenon of saturation of the ESR signals for study of relief of a macromolecule in the vicinity of paramagnetic center. *Studia Biophysica,* **49**, 215-221.

Kotelnikov, A.I., Likhtenshtein, G.I., Fogel, V.R., Kochetkov, V.V., Noks, P.P., Kononenko, A.A., Grishanova, N.P., and Rubin, A.B. (1983) *Zhurnal prikladnoi Spectroskopii* **17** 846 (in Russian).

Kotovych, G., Cann, J. R, . Stewart, J. M., and Yamamoto, H. (1998) NMR and CD conformational studies of bradykinin and its agonists and antagonists: application to receptor binding, *Biochemistry and Cell Biology* **76**, 257-266.

Kramer, H.A. (1940) Brownian motion in a field of force and the diffusion model of chemical reactions, *Physica* **7**, 284-304.

Kresge, A.J. and Silverman, D.N. (1999) Application of Marcus rate theory to proton transfer in enzymy atalyzed reactions, in Schramm, V. L. and Purich, D. L. (eds.), *Methods in Enzymology* **308**, Enzyme kinetics and Mechanism, Part E, Academic Press, San Diego, pp. 276- 297.

Krinichnyi, V.I. (1991) Investigation of biological systems by high resolution 2-mm wave band ESR, *J. Biochem. Biophys. Metods* **23**, 1-30.

Krinichnyi, V.I. (1994) 2-mm wave band ESR spectroscopy of condensed systems, Boca Raton, CRC Press.

Krinichnyi, V.I., Grinberg, O.Ya., Bogatirenko, V.R., Likhtenshtein, G.I., and Lebedev, Ya.S. (1985) Study of microenvironment effect on magnetic resonance parameters of spin-labeled human serum albumin in 2-mm range, *Biofizika,* **30**, 216-203.

Krinichnyi, V.I., Grinberg, O.Ya., Judanova, E.I., Borin, M. L., Lebedev, Ya. S., and Likhtenshtein, G. I. (1987) Study of molecular mobility of biological membranes by 2-mm band EPR spectroscopy, *Biofizika* **32**, 59-65.

Krupyanskii, Y.E., Parak, F., Gaubman, E. E., Wagner, F M., Goldanskii, V.I., Mossbauer, R., Suzdalev, I., and Vogel, H. (1980) Investigation of the dynamics of metmyoglobinby Rayleigh scattering of Mossbauer spectroscopy, *J. Phys.* **41**, 489-490.

Kulikov, A.V. (1976) Determination of distance between the nitroxide label and paramagnetic center in spin-labeled proteins from the parameters of the saturation curve of the ESR spectrum of the label at 77K. *Molecul. Biol.* (Moscow) **10**, 109-116.

Kulikov A.V., Bogatyrenko V. R., Likhtenstein G. I., Allakhverdiev S. I., Klimov V. V., Shuvalov V. A., Krasnovskii A. A., (1983) Magnetic interaction of Mn with anion radical of pheophytin and cation radical of chlorophyll in reaction centers of photosystem 2, *Biofisika,* **28**, 357-363.

Kulikov A.V., Bogatyrenko, V R., Melnikov, A.V., Syrtzova, L.A. and Likhtenshtein, G.I. (1979) Determination of distance between cation radical of bacteriochlorophyl dimer and anion of quinone in photosynthetic reaction center from *R. rubrum. Biofisika* **24**, 178-185.

Kulikov, A.V., Cherepanova, E.S, and Bogatyrenko V. R. (1981) Determination of the closest distance between a radical and a paramagnetic ion. *Theoretical and Experimental Chemistry,* **17**, 618-627

Kulikov, A.V., Cherepanova, E.S., Likhtenshtein, G. I., Uvarov, V.Yu. and Archakov A. I. (1989) ESR Study of localization of cytochrome P450 in microsomes relative to aqueous and lipid phases, *Biologich. Membrany* **6**, 1085-1094.

Kulikov, A.V., Cherepanova, E. S., Bogatyrenko. V. R., Nasonova, T. A, . Fisher, V. R. and Yakubov, H. M. (1987). Determination of the depth of immersion of radicals into biological matrices by ESR. *Bull. Acad. Sci. USSR, Division of Biol. Sci.* N 5, 7762-769.

Kulikov, A.I. and Likhtenshtein, G. I. (1977) The use of spin-relaxation phenomena in the investigation of the structure of model and biological systems by method of spin labels. *Adv. Molecul. Relax. Proc.* **10**, 47-78.

Kulikov, A. V. and Likhtenstein, G. I. (1974) Application of saturation curves for evaluating distances in biological objects by the method of double spin-labels. *Biofizika.* **19**, 420-424.

Kulikov, A.I., Likhtenshtein, G. I., Rozantzev, E. G., Suskina, and Shapiro, A. V. (1972) Nitroxide bi- and polyradicals as standard models for distance estimation between the nitroxide moities. *Biofisika,* **17**, 42-49. (In Russian).

Kulikov, A. I., Yudanova, E. I. and Likhtenshtein, G. I. (1983). Investigation of the spin-exchange of nitroxide radicals using the continuous ESR spectrum saturation technique. *J. Phys. Chem.* (Moscow) **56**, 2982-2987. (In Russian).

Kurihara, S., Tsumuraya, T., Suzuki, K., Kuroda, M., Liu, L., Takaoka, Y. and Fujii, I. (2000) Antibody-catalyzed removal of the p-nitrobenzyl ester protecting group: the molecular basis of broad substrate specificity (2000) Chemistry--A European Journal , **6**, 1656-1662.

Kurreck, H, Elger, G., Von Gersdorff, J., Wiehe, A., and Moebius, K. (1998) EPR studies on photoinduced electron transfer in triad model compounds of photosynthesis *Applied Magnetic Resonance* *14, 203-215.*

Lacshmi, K.V. and Brudvig, G.W. (2000) Electron paramagnetic resonance distance measurement in photosynthetic reaction centers, in Berliner, L, Eaton, S., and Eaton, G. (eds.), , *Magnetic Resonance in Biology,* **V. 18**, Kluwer Academic Publishers. Dordrecht, pp. 513-568.

Lacowicz, J. (eds.), (1997) *Topics in fluorescence spectroscopy.* Plenum Press, NewYork.

Lakowicz, J. (1983) *Principles of Fluorescence Spectroscopy,* Plenum Press, New York,.

Lakowicz, J. and Weber, G. (1973) Quenching of protein fluorescence by oxygen. Detection of structural fluctuations in proteins on the nanosecond time scale, *Biochemistry* **12**, 4171-4179.

Landau, L. (1932) Zur Theorie der Energie Uebertragung, *Phyz. Zur.*, Sovietunion **2**, 46-51.

Lange, R., Bec, N., Anzenbacher, P., Munro, A. W., Gorren, Antonius CF., and Mayer, B. (2001) Use of high pressure to study elementary steps in P450 and nitric oxide synthase, *J. Inorg. Biochem.* **87**, 191-195.

Lanzilotta, W.N and Seefeldt, L.C. (1997) Changes in the midpoint potential of the nitrogenase metal centers as a result of iron protein-molybdenum-iron protein complex formation, *Biochemistry* **36**, 12976-12983.

Lanzilotta, W.N., Christiansen, J., Dean, D.R., and Seefeldt, L.C. (1998) Evidence for coupled electron and proton transfer in the [8S⋅7S] cluster of nirogenase, *Biochemistry,* **37**, 11376-11384.

Larson, T.M., Wedekind, J.E., Rayment, I., and Reed, G.H. (1996) A carboxylate of the substrate bridges the magnesium ions at the active site of enolase: structure of the yeast enzyme complex with the equilibrium mixture of 2-phosphoglycerate and phosphoenol piruvate at 1. 8 A resolution, *Biochemistry* **35**, 4349-4358.

Lau, E. and Bruice, T.E. (1998) Active site dynamics at the Hhal methyl transferase: inside from computor simulation, *J. Mol. Biol.* **293**, 9-18.

Lau, E.Y. and Bruice, T C. (2000) The active site dynamics of 4-chlorobenzoyl-CoA dehalogenase, *Proc. Natl. Acad. Sci. (USA)* **98**, 9527-9532

Lazaridis, T., Lee, I., and Karplus, J.A. (1997) Dynamics and unfolding pathways of a hypertermophilic and mesophilic rubredoxin, *Prot. Sci.* **6**, 2589-2605.

Loveless, T.M., Saah J.R. and Bishop PE (1999) Isolation of nitrogen-fixing bacteria containing molybdenum-independent nitrogenases from natural environments, *Applied and environmental microbiology*, **65**, 4223-4226.

Lear, J.D., Gratkowski, H., DeGrado, W.F. (2001), De novo design, synthesis and characterization of membrane-active peptides, *Biochem. Soc. Transact.* **29**, 559-564.

Lee, S.C. (2002) Iron-imide clusters and nitrogenase: Abiological chemistry of biological relevance? In Leigh, G. J. and Winterton, N. (eds) Modern Coordination Chemistry Royal Society of Chemistry, Cambridge, pp. 278-287.

Lee, S-K., Fox, B.G., Froland, W.A., Lipscomb, J.D., and Münck, E. (1993) A transient intermediate of the methane monooxigenase catalytic cycle containing an Fe(IV)Fe(IV) cluster, *J. Am. Chem. Soc.* **115**, 6450-6451.

Lee, D., Hung, P.-L., Spingler, B., and Lippard, S. J. (2002), Sterically hindered carboxylate ligands support water-bridged dimetallic centers that model features of metallohydrolase active sites, *Inorganic Chemistry* **41**(3), 521-531.

Leigh, G.J. (1998) Fixing nitrogen any which way, *Science* **279**, 506-507.

Leigh, G.J. (1995) The chemical mechanism of biological nitrogen fixation and the chemistry model systems, in Tichonovich, I. A., Provorov, N. A., Romanov, V. I., and Newton, W. E. (eds.), *Nitrogen Fixation: Fundamentals and Applications*, Kluwer Academic Publishers, Dodrecht, 129-136.

Leninger, A.L., Nelson,D.L.,Cox, M.M. (1993) *Principles if Biochemistry*, Worth Publishers.N.Y.

Lerner, R.A., Benkovic, S.J. & Schultz, P.G. (1991) At the crossroads of chemistry and immunology: catalytic antibodies. *Science* **252**, 659–667.

Levanon, H. and Stehlik, D. (1992) Time-resolved continuous wave-vs. Fourier transform-ESR, *Israel J. Chem, 32*, 474-476.

Levich, V.G. and Dogonadze, R. (1959) Quantum mechanical theory of electron transfer in polar media. *Dokl. Acad. Nauk.* **78**, 2148-21

Levich, V.G., Dogonadze, R., German, E., Kuznetsov, A.M., and Kharkats, Yu. I. (1970) Theory of homogeneous reactions involving proton transfer, *Electrochem. Acta* **15**, 353-368.

Leyh, T.S. (1999) On advantages of imperfect linkage, in Schramm, V. L. and Purich, D. L. (eds.), *Methods in Enzymology*, **308**, Enzyme Kinetics and Mechanism, Part E, Academic Press, San Diego, pp. 219-245.

Lezina, V.P., Stepanyants, A. U., and Likhtenshtein, G I. (1976) Study on the interaction of steroids with serum albumin by the NMR spin-echo technique. *Mol. Biol.* (Moscow) **10**, 1166-1175.

Li, B., Gutierrez, P. L., and Blough, N. V.. (1999) Trace determination of hydroxyl radical using fluorescence detection, *Methods in Enzymology* **300** (Oxidants and Antioxidants, Part B), 202-216.

Lie, S., Pulakat, L., and Gavini, N. (2000) Activation of vanadium nitrogenase expression in DJ54 revertant in the presence of molybdenum, *FEBS Lett* **482**, 149-153.

Likhtenshtein, G. I. (2000) Depth of immersion of paramagnatic centers, in Berliner, L, Eaton, S., and Eaton, G. (eds.), *Magnetic Resonance in Biology*, **V. 18**, Kluwer Academic Publishers. Dordrecht, pp. 309-347.

Likhtenshtein, G.I. (1996a) Role of orbital and dynamic factors in electron transfer in reaction centers of photosynthetic systems. *J. Phochem. Photobiol. A: Chem.* **96**, 79-92.

Likhtenshtein, G.I. (1996b) Spin and fluorescence immunoassay in solution, in Levkovits and Nezlin, R. (eds.), *Immunology Methods Manual*, Pergamon Press, London 540-550.

Likhtenshtein G. I. (1995) Biophysical labeling method in molecular biology, in Meyers R. A. (ed.), , *Encyclopedia of Molecular Biology.* Vol. 3, Chernow Editorial Series, New York, pp. 385-390.

Likhtenshtein, G. I. (1993) *Biophysical Labeling Methods in Molecular Biology.* Cambridge N. Y., Cambridge University Press.

Likhtenshtein G.I. (1990) The use of nitroxides in the solution of some problems of chemical biophysics, *Pure Appl. Chem.* **62**, 281-288.

Likhtenshtein G.I. (1988a) *Chemical Physics of Redox Metalloenzyme Catalysis*, Springer-Verlag, Berlin.

Likhtenshtein G.I. (1988b) Structure and Molecular Dynamics of Metalloenzymes studied by physical labels methods, *J. Molec. Catal.*, **48**, 129-138.

Likhtenshtein G.I. (1986) Water and dynamics of proteins and membranes, *Studia Biophysica*, **111**, 89-100.

Likhtenshtein G.I. (1986) On mechanisms of redox reactions with participation of metalloenzymes and their models, in Shilov, A. E. (eds.), *Fundamental research in homogeneous catalysis,* Gordon and Breach, New York, pp 325-334.

Likhtenshtein G. I. (1985a) Amorphous-crystaline model of intermolecular dynamics in global proteins, *Biofizika*, **30**, 37-30.

Likhtenshtein, G. I. (1985b) The role of multielectron and synchronous processes in enzyme catalysis. *Proc. 16th FEBS Cong.* Part A, VNU Science Press, pp 9-15.

Likhtenshtein, G. I. (1980) Structure and mechanism of action of nitrogenase active center, in Newton, W. E. and Orme-Johnson, W. H. (eds.), Nitrogen Fixation, **V 1**, Free-living Systems and Chemical Models, University Park Press, Baltimore, pp. 195-210.

Likhtenshtein G.I, (1979a) *Multinuclear Redox Metalloenzymes*, Moscow, Nauka.

Likhtenshtein G.I. (1979b) Study of protein dynamics by spin-labeling, Mösbauer spectroscopy, and NMR, in Losche, A. (eds.), *Special Collogue Amper on Dynamic Processes in Molecular Systems*, Leipzig, Karl-Marx University, pp 100-107.

Likhtenshtein, G.I. (1977a) On the principle of "optimum motion' in elementary acts of chemical and biological processes, I. Estimation of the synchronization factor for model processes. *Kinetika I Kataliz (Kinetics and Catalysis)*, **28**: 878-882.

Likhtenshtein, G.I. (1977b) On the principle of "optimum motion' in elementary acts of chemical and biological processes. III. Analysis of probabilistic mechanisms of some chemical and boichemical processes, *Kinetika I Kataliz (Kinetics and Catalysis)*, **28**: 1255-1260.

Likhtenshtein, G.I. (1977c) Kinetic analysis of the orientation effects in model chemical systems, *Russian J. Phys. Chem.* **41**, 842-846.

Likhtenshtein, G. I. (1976a) *Spin Labeling Method in Molecular Biology.* N. Y., Wiley Interscience.

Likhtenshtein G. I. (1976b) Water and protein dynamics, in Alfsen, A. and Bertran, A. J. *L'eau et les Systemes Biologoque*, CNR, Paris, pp. 45-43.

Likhtenshtein, G.I. (1974) *Spin Labeling Method in Molecular Biology.* Nauka. Moscow.

Likhtenshtein, G.I. (1970a) Study on the proteins microstructure by method of spin- label paramagnetic probe, *Mol. Biol.* (Moscow) **4**, 782-789.

Likhtenshtein, G.I. (1970b) On the nature of compensation phenomena in liquid phase reactions, Russian *J. Phys. Chem.* **44**, 1980-1990.

Likhtenshtein, G.I. (1968) Determination of the topography of proteins group using specific paramagnetic labels. *Molec. Biol.* (Moscow) **2**, 234-240.

Likhtenshtein, G.I. (1966) Regularities in the energy and entropy properties of enzymatic processes, *Biofizika* **11**, 24-32.

Likhtenshtein, G.I., Adin, I., Krasnoselsky, A., Vaisbuch, I., Shames, A., and Glaser, R. (1999) NMR studies of electric field distribution around biologically important molecules, *Biophysical J.* **77**, 443-453.

Likhtenshtein, G.I., Akhmedov, YuD. Ivanov, L.V., Krinitskaya, L.A. and Kokhanov, Yu.V. (1974) Investigation of the lysozyme macromolecule by a spin-labeling method. *Mol. Biol.* (Moscow) **8**, 40-48.

Likhtenshtein, G.I., Bishara R., Papper, V., Uzan, B., Fishov. I., Gill, D. and Parola A. H. (1996) Novel fluorescence-photochrome labeling method in the study of biomembrane dynamics, *J. Biochem. Biophys. Methods* **33**, 117-133.

Likhtenshtein, G.I., and Bobodzhanov, P. Kh. (1968) Investigation of the structure and local conformational changes of proteins and enzymes using double paramagnetic labels. *Biofizika* , **13**, 757-764.

Likhtenshtein, G.I., Bogatyrenko, V.R., and Kulikov, A.V. (1993) Low temperature protein dynamics studied by spin-labeling methods, *Appl. Magn. Reson.* **4**, 513-521.

Likhtenshtein, G.I., Febbrario, F., and Nucci R. (2000) Intramolecular dynamics and conformational transitions in proteins studed by biophysical labeling methods. Common and specific features of proteins from thermophylic microorganisms. *Spectrochemica Acta Part A. Biomolecular Spectroscopy* **56**, 2011-2031.

Likhtenstein, G.I., Grebentchikov, Yu.B., Rosantev, E.G. and Ivanov, V. P. (1972) Study on the electrostatic charges in proteins by method of paramagnetic probes. *Mol. Biol.* (Moscow), **6**, 498-507.

Likhtenshtein, G.I., Kulikov, A.V., and Kotelnikov, A.V. (1993) Relaxation process involving nitroxyl radiacal in molecular biology, in Zhdanov, R.I. (eds.), *Bioactive Spin Labels*, Springer-Verlag, Heidelberg, 125-151.

Likhtenshtein, G.I., Kulikov, A.V., Kotelnikov, A.I. and Bogatyrenko V.R. (1982) Structure and action mechanism of reaction centers of photosynthetic bacteria. *Photobiochem. Photobiol.* 3, 178-182.

Likhtenshtein, G.I., Kulikov, A. V., Kotelnikov, A.I., and Levchenko, L.A. (1986) Methods of physical labels - a combined approach to the study of microstructure and dynamics of biological systems. *J. Biochem. Biophys. Meth.* **12**, 1-28.

Likhtenshtein, G.I. Khudjakov, D.V., and Fogel, V.R. (1992) Photochrome-labeling methods in study of dynamics of biological systems, *J. Biochim. Biophys Methods, 25, 219-229.*

Likhtenshtein, G.I. and Shilov, A.E. (1976) On the chemical mechanism of coupling of ATP hydrolysis reactions, *Dokl. Acad. Nauk. SSSR* **229**, 1127-1130.

Likhtenshtein, G.I. and Mullokandov E.A. (1977) On the principle of "optimum motion' in elementary acts of chemical and biological processes, II. Mechanisms of the reduction of molecular nitrogen and liberation of molecular oxygen from water, *Kinetika I Kataliz (Kinetics and Catalysis)*, **28**: 883-888.

Likhtenshtein, G. I. and Shilov, A.E. (1970) On the thermodynamics of fixation of molecular nitrogen, *Zhurnal Fiz. Khem. (Russian J. Phys. Chem.)* **44**, 849-856.

Likhtenshtein G.I. and Therneley, R.N.F. (1995) Nitrogenase catalysis, in Tikhanovitch, I. A., Provorov, N. A., Romanov, V. I., and Newton, W. E. (eds.), *Nitrogen Fixation: Fundamentals and Applications*, Kluwer Academic Publishers, Dodrecht.

Likhtenshtein, G.I. and Troshkina T.V. (1968) On the kinetics of the cooperative processes in proteins, Molecul. Biol. (Moscow) 2, 654-663.

Lillemoen, J. and Hoffman, D.W. (1998) An investigation of the dynamics of ribosomal protein L9 using heteronuclear NMR relaxation measurements, *J. Mol. Biol.*, **281**, 539-551.

Limburg, J. Vrettos, J.S., Liable-Sands, L.M., Rheingold, A.L., Crabtree, and R.H., Brudvig, G.W. (1999) A functional model for O-O bond formation by the O_2-evolving complex in photosystem II, *Science* **283**, 1524-1527.

Limburg, J., Brudvig, G.W., and Crabtree, R H. (2000) Modeling in oxygen-evolving complex in Photosystem II,in Meunier, B. (eds.), *Biomimetic Oxidations Catalyzed by Transition Metal Complexes*, Imperial College Press, London, 509-541

Limburg, J., Vrettos, J. S., Chen, H., de Paula, J. C., Crabtree, R.H., Brudvig, G.W. (2001) Characterization of the O_2-Evolving Reaction Catalyzed by $[(terpy)(H_2O)MnIII(O)_2MnIV(OH_2)(terpy)](NO_3)^3$ (terpy = 2, 2':6, 2"-Terpyridine), *J. Am. Chem. Soc.* **123**, 423-443

Linderstrom-Lang, K. H. and Schellmann, . (1959) Protein structure and enzyme activity, in Boyer, P. D., Lardy, M., and Myrback (eds.), *The Enzyme* **V. 1**, Academic Press, N. Y., pp. 443-510.

Lipardi, G. and Szabo, A. (1982) Model-free approach to the inter[retation of nuclear magnetic resonance relaxation in macromolecules. 1. Theory and range of validity, *J. Am. Chem. Soc.* **104**, 4546-4569.

Liu, K.E., Valentine, A.M., Wang, D., Huynh, B.H. Edmondson, D.E.; Salifoglou, A. Lippard, S.J. (1995) Kinetic and spectroscopic characterization of intermediates and component interactions in reactions of methane monooxygenase from Methylococcus capsulatus (Bath), *J. Am. Chem. Soc.* **117**, 10174-10185.

Lippard, S.J. and Berg, J.M. (1994) *Principles of Bioorganic Chemistry*, University Science Books, Mill Valey, CA.

Loach, P.A. (1980) Bacterial reaction center (RC) and photoacceptor complex preparations, in San-Pietro, A. (ed) *Methods in Enzymology*, Vol. **69**, Photosynthesis and Nitrogen Fixation, part C, Academic Press, N.Y. pp. 155-172.

Lockhart, D.J., and Kim, P. S. (1992) Internal Stark effect measurement of the electric field at the amino terminus of an α-helix, *Science* **257**, 947-951.

Loew, G. H. and Harris, D. L. (2000) Role of the heme active site and protein environment in structure, spectra, and function of the cytochrome P450, *Chem. Rev.* **100**, 407-419.

Loewenthal, R., Sancho, J., Reinikainen, T. and Fersht, A R. (1993) Long-range surface charge-charge interactions in proteins: comparison of experimental results with calculations from a theoretical method. *J. Mol. Biol.*, **232**, 574-583.

Lovell, T. Li, J., Liu, T, Case, D.A., and Noodleman, L. (2001) FeMo cofactor of nitrogenase: a density functional study of states MN, MOX, MR, and MI, *J. Am. Chem. Soc.* **123**, 12392-12410.

Lowe, D.J., Fisher, K., and Thorneley, R.N.F. (1993) Pre-steady-state absorbance changes show that redox changes occur in the *Klebsiella pneumonia* MoFe-protein that depend on substrate and components ratio: a role for P-centers in reducing dinitrogen, *Biochem. J.* 292, 93-.

Lozinsky, E., Martin, V.V., Berezina, T.A., Shames, A., Weis, A.L., and Likhtenshtein, G. I. (1999) Dual fluorophore-nitroxide probes for analysis of vitamin C in biological liquids, *J. Biochem. Biophys. Meth.* **38**, 29-42.

Lozinsky, E., Novoselsky, A., Shames, A.I., Saphier O., Likhtenshtein G. ., and Meyrstein, D. (2001) Effect of albumin on the kinetic of ascorbate oxidation. *Biochim. Biophys. Acta* **1526**, 53-60.

Lozinsky E., Shames A., and Likhtenshtein G.I. (2001) Dual fluorophore-nitroxide molecules: Models for study of intramolecular fluorescence quenching and novel redox probes. *In: Recent Research Development in Photochemistry and Photobiology.*, V. 2, Transworld Research Network. Trivandrum. pp. 41-55.

Lozinsky, E., Shames, A.I., Martin, V.V., Weis, A., and Likhtenshtein G.I. (2002) *Phys. Chem. Chem. Phys.* (submittied)

Lu, Y., Berry, S. M., and Pfister, T. D. (2001) Engineering novel metalloproteins: Design of metal-binding sites into native protein scaffolds, *Chem. Rev. 101*, 3047-3080.

Lubitz, W., Lendzian, F., Plato, M., Scheer, H., and Moebius, K. (1997) The bacteriochlorophyll a cation radical revisited. An ENDOR and triple resonance study, *Applied Magnetic Resonance* 13, 531-551.

Lüdemann, S. K., Lounnas, V., and Wade, R. (2000) How do substrates enter and products exit the buried active site of cytochrome P450cam. 1. Random expulsion molecular dynamics investigation of ligand access channels and mechanisms, *J. Mol. Biol.* **303**, 797-811.

Lukas, A. S., Bushard, P. J., and Wasielewski, M.R. (2002a) Electron transfer involving nonbonded superexchange interactions in rigid donor-acceptor arrays, *J. Phys. Chem. A* **106**, 2074-208.

Lukas, A S., Zhao, Y., Miller, S E., and Wasielewski, M.R. (2002b) Biomimetic electron transfer using low energy excited states: A green perylene-based analogue of chlorophyll a, *J. Phys. Chem. B* **106**, 1299-1306.

Lumry, R. (1979) Dynamical aspect of a small molecule protein interaction, in Briabanti, A, (eds.) Bioenergetics and thermodynamics, NATO Advanced Study, Parma, Italy, pp. 435-454.

Lumry, R. (1995) On the interpretation of data from isothermal processes, in Johnson, M. and Ackers (eds.), *Methods in Enzymology* **259**, Energetics of Biological Macromolecules, Acad. Press, San-Diego, pp.

Lumry, R. (1995) The new paradigm for protein research, in Gregory, R. B. (eds.), *Protein-solvent interactions*, Marcel Dekker, Inc. New York, pp.

Lumry, R. (2002) *Biochem. Biophys. Acta* (in press)

Lumry, R. and Biltonen, R. (1969) Thermochemical and kinetical aspects of protein conformation, in Timashev, S. N. and Fasman, C. D. (eds) *Structure and stability of biological molecules,* **V. 2**, Biological macromolecules series, Dekker, New York, pp 146-306.

Lumry, R. and Eyring, H. (1954) Conformational changes in proteins, *J. Phys. Chem.* **58**, 110-120.

Lumry, R. and Gregory, R.B. (1986) Free energy management in protein reactions: concepts, complications, and compensation, in Welch, G. R. (eds.) *The fluctuating enzymes.* Wiley, New York, pp 3-185.

Lumry, R. and Rajender, S. (1970) Enthalpy-entropy compensation phenomenon in water solutions of proteins and small molecules: ubiquitous property of water, *Biopolymers* **9**, 1125-1227.

Luneva, N.P., Knerel'man, E. I., Shafirovich, V.Ya., and Shilov, A.E. (1987) A manganese cluster bound to a bilayer membrane: a chemical model for the oxygen-forming center of photosynthesis, *J. Chem. Soc., Chem. Commun.* (19) 1504-1505.

Macedo-Ribeiro, S., Martins, B. M., Pereira, P J. B., Buse, G., Huber, R., and Soulimane, T. (2001) New insights into the thermostability of bacterial ferredoxins: high-resolution crystal structure of the seven-iron ferredoxin from *Thermus thermophilus, J. Biol. Inorg. Chem.* 6, 663-674.

Machonkin, T. E. and Solomon, E. T. (2000) The thermodynamics, kinetics, end molecular mechanism of intramolecular electron transfer in human ceruloplasmin, *J. Am. Chem. Soc.* **122**, 12547- 12560.

Makinen, M.W. (1998) Electron nuclear double resonace determined structure of enzyme reaction intermediates: structural evidence for substrate destabilization, *Spectrochimica Acta Part A:* **54**, 2269-2281.

Makinen, M. W., Mustafi, D., and Kasa, S. (1998) ENDOR of spin labels for structure determination: from small molecules to enzyme reaction intermediate, in Berliner, L. (eds.), *Biological Magnetic Resonance* **14**, Spin Labeling: Next Millennium, Plenum Press, N. Y. pp181-249.

Malandrinos G., Louloudi, M., Deligiannakis, Y., and Hadjiliadis, N. (2001) Two-dimential hyperfine sublevel correlation spectroscopy applied in the study of a Cu+2-[pentapeptide]hydroxyethyl) thiamin pyrophosphate]-pentapeptide] system as a model of thiamin-dependent enzymes, *J. Phys. Chem. B,* **105**, 7223-7233.

Malmström, B.G., Andreason, L.E., and Reinhammer, B. (1975)Copper-containing oxidases and superoxide dismutases, in Boyer P. D. (eds.), *The Enzymes,* 3rd edn. **12**, Acad. Press, New York, pp 507-579.

Marbrouk, P.A. (1995) The use of nonaqueous media to prove biochemically significant enzyme intermediates: the generation and stabilization of horse redish compound III in neat benzene solution at room temperature, *J. Chem. Am. Soc.* **117**, 2141-2146.

Marcus, R.A. (1956) On the theory of oxidation-reduction reactions involving electron transfer, *J. Chem. Phys.* **24**, 966-978.

Marcus, R.A. (1968) Theoretical relations among rate constants, barriers, and Bronsted slopes of chemical reactions, *J. Phys. Chem.* **72**, 891-899.

Marcus, R.A. (1999) Electron transfer past and future, in Jortner, J., Bixon, M. (eds.), *Advances in Chemical Physics* **107**, Part 1, John Wiley & Sons. NY., pp. 1-6.

Marcus, R.A. (1956) On the theory of oxidation-reduction reactions involving electron transfer, *J. Chem. Phys.* **24**, 966-978.

Marcus, R. A. and Sutin, N. (1985) Electron transfer in chemistry and biology, *Biochim. Biophys. Acta* **811**, 265-322.

Mariani, P., Carsughi, F., Spinozzi, F., Romanzetti, S., Meier, G., Casadio, R. and Bergamini, C. M. (2000) Ligand-induced conformational changes in tissue transglutaminase: Monte Carlo analysis of small-angle scattering data, *Biophys. J.* **78**, 3240-3251.

Maritano, S., Fairhurst, S.A., and Eady, R.R. (2001) Novel EPR signals associated with FeMoco centres of MoFe protein in MgADP-inhibited turnover of nitrogenase, *FEBS Lett.* **505**, 125-128.

Martin, L. L., West, L. C., and Wu, B. (2001) An extrusion strategy for the FeMo cofactor from nitrogenase: towards synthetic iron-sulfur proteins, *Eur. J. Biochem.* **268**, 5676-5686.

Martin, Y, Kim K., and Lin, T.C. (1996) *Advances in Quantitative Structure-Properties Relationship*, p. 3. JAI Press, Greenwich, CT.

Masel, R.I. (2001) *Chemical Kinetics and Catalysis*. Wiley-Interscience. New-York.

Matsu-Ura, M., Tani, F., Nakayama, S., Nakamura, N., and Naruta, Y. (2000) Hydrogen-bonded dioxygen adduct of an iron porphyrin with an alkanethiolate ligand: an elaborate model of cytochrome P450, *Angewan. Chem., Internat.* Ed. **39**, 1989-1991.

Maturano, M. D., Bongibault, V., Klaebe, A., and Fournier, D. (1997) A chemical model for the enzymic monodealkylation of (methyl and ethyl) parathion by glutathione-S-transferase, *Tetrahedron* 53, 17241-17246

Maturano, M. D., Bongibault, V., Klaebe, A., and Fournier, D. (1997) A chemical model for the enzymic monodealkylation of (methyl and ethyl) parathion by glutathione-S-transferase, *Tetrahedron* 53, 17241-17246

Mayer, S. M., Lawson, D. M., Gormal, C A., Roe, S., and Smith, B.E. (1999) New insights into structure-function relationships in nitrogenase: A 1. 6 A resolution X-ray crystallographic study of Klebsiella pneumoniae MoFe-protein. *J. Mol. Biol.* **292**, 871-891.

McAuley, K.E., Fyfe, P.K., Cogdell, R.J., Isaacs, N.W., and Jones, M.R. (2000) X-ray crystal structure of the YM210W mutant reaction center from *Rhodobacter spheroiddes*, *FEBS Letters* **467**, 285-290.

McCammon, J.A., and Gilson, M.K. (1994) Prediction of pH-dependent properties of proteins, *J. Mol. Biol.* **238**, 415-436.

McCommon, J.A. and Harvey, S. (1987) *Dynamics of Proteins and Nucleic Acids.* Cambridge University Press, Cambridge.

McCommon, J. A., Gelin, B. R., and Karplus, M. (1977) *Nature* **267**, 565-590.

McConnell, H.M. and McFarland, (1970) Physics and chemistry of spin labels, *Quarterly Review of Biophysics* 3, 91-136.

McDonald, T. L., Gutheim, W. G., Martin, R. B., and Guengerich, F. P. (1989) Oxidation of substituted *N, N*-dimetylanylines by cytochrome P-450: estimation of the effective oxidation-reduction potential of cytochrome P-450, *Biochemistry* **28**, 2071-2077.

McDonald, T.L., Gutheim, W.G., Martin, R.B., and Guengerich, F.P. (1989) Oxidation of substituted *N,N*-dimetylanylines by cytochrome P-450: estimation of the effective oxidation-reduction potential of cytochrome P-450, *Biochemistry* **28**, 2071-2077.

Mchaourab, H.S., Fang, C.J, and Hubbel, W. L. (1997) Conformation of T4 lysozame in solution. Hinge bending motion and substratereduced conformational transition studied by site-directed spin labeling, *Biochemistry* **36**, 307-316.

Mchaourab, H.S. and Perozo, E. (2000) Determination of proteins folds and conformational dynamics using spin-labeling ESR spectroscopy, in Berliner, L, Eaton, S., and Eaton, G. (eds.), , *Magnetic Resonance in Biology*, **V. 18**, Kluwer Academic Publishers. Dordrecht, pp. 185-248.

McLain, Jennifer L., Lee, Jinbo, Groves, John T. (2000), Biomimetic oxygenations related to cytochrome P450: metal-oxo and metal-peroxo intermediates, in Meunier, B. (eds.), *Biomimetic Oxidations Catalyzed by Transition Metal Complexes*, Imperial College Press, London, 91-170.

McLendon, G. and Hake, R. (1992) Interprotein electron transfer, *Chem. Rev.* **92**, 481-490.

McNulty, J.C. and Millhauser, G.L. (2000) TOAC: the ridid nitroxide side chain, in Berliner, L, Eaton, S., and Eaton, G. (eds.), , *Magnetic Resonance in Biology*, **V. 18**, Kluwer Academic Publishers. Dordrecht, pp. 277-308.

Medzhidov, A.A., Likhtenshtein, G I. and Kirichenko, L.A. (1969) Metallocomplexes with the paramagnetic ligands. *Bulletin of the Academy of Science of USSR (Chemistry)* N 3, 698-902.

Meinike, C., Sole, A., Pospisil, P., Dau, H. (2000) does the structure of the water-oxidizing Photosystem II-Manganese complex at room temperature differ from its low-temperature structure? A comparative X-ray absorption study, Biochemistry 39, (24)

Mekler, V., and Likhtenshtein, G., I. (1986) Study of dynamic contacts of macromolecules according to kinetics of photoisomrization of fluorescent label sensitized by the dye in a triplet state, *Biofizika* **31**, 571-586.

Mekler, V.M. and Umarova, F.T. (1988) The use of triplet-sensitized photochromism phenomenon for the study of dynamic interaction of membrane proteins, *Biofizika* 33, 720-722.

Melkozernov, A.N., Lin, S., Blankenship, R.E., and Valkunas, L. (2001) Spectral inhomogenity of Photosystem II and its influence on excitation equilibrium and trapping in the cyanobacterium Synechcysts sp. PCC6803 at 77 K, *Biophys.J.* **81**, 1144-1154.

Menger, F.M. (1985) On the source of intramolecular and enzymatic reactivity, *Acc. Chem. Res.* **18**, 128-134.

Merkx, M., Kopp, D. A., Sazinsky, M. H., Blazyk, J. L., Muller, J., and Lippard, S.J. (2001) Dioxygen activation and methane hydroxylation by soluble methane monooxygenase: a tale of two irons and three proteins. *Angew. Chem., Int. Ed.* **40**, 2782-2807.

Meunier, B. (ed.), Biomimetic Oxidations Catalyzed by Transition Metal Complexes, Imperial College Press, London.

Michel, H. and Deisenhofer J. (1986) X-ray diffraction studies on a crystalline bacterial photosynthetic center. A progress report and conclusions on the structure of the photosystem II reaction center. *In Encyclopedia of Plant Physiology, New Series*, v. 19, (Stachelin, L. A. and Arntzen, C. J (eds) pp. 371-381. Berlin, Springer-Verlag.

Michel, H. and Deisenhofer J. (1988) Relevance of the photosynthetic reaction center from purple bacteria to the structure of photosystem II, *Biochemistry* **27**, (1)

Mildvan, A.S., Harris, T.K., and Abeygunawardana C. (1999) Nuclear magnetic resonance methods for the detection and study of low-barrier hydrogen bonds on enzymes, in Schramm, V. L. and Purich, D. L. (eds.), *Methods in Enzymology*, **308**, Enzyme Kinetics and Mechanism, Part E, Academic Press, San Diego, pp. 219-247.

Miller, S. E., Lukas, A. S., Marsh, E., Bushard, P., and Wasielewski, M.R. (2000) Photoinduced charge separation involving an unusual double electron transfer mechanism in a donor-bridge-acceptor molecule, *J. Am. Chem. Soc.* **122**, 7802-7810.

Milov, A.D., Maryasov, A.G., and Tsvetkov, Y. D. (1998) Pulsed electron double resonance (PELDOR) and its applications in free radical research, *Appl. Magn. Reson.*, **15**, 107-143.

Mino, H., Kawamori, A., and Ono, T-A. (2000) Pulsed ESR studies of doublet signal and singlet-like signal in oriented Ca^{2+}-depleted PS II membranes: location of the doublet signal center in PS II, *Biochemistry* **39**, 11034-11040.

Mitchell, P. (1976) Possible molecular mechanism of the proton-motive function of cytochrome systems, *J. Theor. Biol.* **62**, 327-367.

Miteva, M.A., Kossekova, G. P., Villoutreix, B O., and Atanasov, B.P. (1997), Local electrostatic potentials in pyridoxal phosphate labeled horse heart cytochrome c, *J. Photochem. and Photobiol., B: Biology* **37**, 74-83.

Mith, B.E., Durrant, M. C., Fairhurst, S A., Gormal, C.A., Gronberg, K.L.C., Henderson, R. A., Ibrahim, S.K., Le Gall, T., and Pickett, C. J. (1999) Exploring the reactivity of the isolated iron-molybdenum cofactor of nitrogenase. *Coord. Chem. Rev.* **185-186**, 669-687.

Miyashita, O. and Go, N. (2000) Reorganization energy of protein electron transfer reaction: study with structural and frequency signature, *J. Phys. Chem.* **104**, 7516-7521.

Miyzaki, Y., Matsua, T., and Suga, H. (2000) Low-temperature heat capacity and glassy behavior of lysozyme crystal *J. Phys. Chem. B* **104**, 8044-8052.

Moebius, K.; (Ed.). (2001) High-Field and High-Frequency Electron Paramagnetic Resonance. [In: *Appl. Magn. Reson.*, 2001; 21(3-4)].

Mortenson, L.E., Morris, J.A., and Jeng, D.Y (1967) Purification, metal composition, and properties of mollibdoferredoxin and azoferredoxin, two components of thenitrogen-fixing system of *Clostridium pasterianum* , *Biochim. Biophys. Acta* **141**, 516-538.

Moracci, M., Cabaldo, L., Ciaramella, M., and Rossi, M. (1996) Identification of two glutamic acid residues essential for catalysis in the β-glycosidase from the thermoacidophilic archaeon *Sulfolobus solfataricus Protein Eng.* **9** 1191 -1195

Moser, C. C. and Dutton, P. L. (1992) Engineering protein structure for electron transfer function in photosynthetic reaction centers. *Biochim. Biophys. Acta,* **1101**, 171-176.

Muh, F., Bibikova, M., Schlodder, E., Oesterhelt, D., and Lubitz, W. (2000) Conformational relaxation following reduction of the photoactive bacteriopheophytin in reaction centers from *Blastochloris viridis,* Influence of mutations at position M208, *Biochim. Biophys. Acta* 1459, 191-201

Müller, J., Lugovskoy, A. A., Wagner, G., and Lippard, S.J. (2002) NMR structure of the [2Fe-2S] ferredoxin domain from soluble methane monooxygenase reductase and interaction with its hydroxylase. *Biochemistry* **41**, 42-51.

Mukamel, S. (2000) Multidimentional femtosecond correlation spectroscopies of electronic and vibrational exitations, *Annu. Rev. Phys. Chem.* **51**, 691-729.

Mukamel, S., Pirytinski, and Chrnyak, V. (1999) Two-dimentional Raman echoes: femtosecond view of molecular structure and vibrational coherence, *Acc. Chem. Res.* **32**, 145-154.

Mullins, L.S. and Raushel, F. M. (1995) Isotope exchange as a probe of enzyme action, in Purich, D. L. (eds.), *Methods in Enzymology,* **249**, Enzyme Kinetics and Mechanisms, Part D, Acad. Press, San-Diego, 398-425.

Münck, E., Rhodes, H., Orme-Johnson, W.H., Davis, L.C., Brill, W. J., and Shah, V.K. (1975) Nitrogenase, VIII. Mossbauer and ESR spectroscopy, *Biochim. Biophys. Acta,* **400**, 32-53.

Munro, Andrew W., Noble, Michael A., Robledo, Laura, Daff, Simon N., Chapman, Stephen K. Determination of the Redox Properties of Human NADPH-Cytochrome P450 Reductase. Biochemistry (2001), 40(7), 1956-1963.

Munro, I., Pecht, I., and I. Stryer, I. (1979) Proc. Natl. Acad. Sci. USA **76**, 55-.

Murahashi S.I. (1999) *Transition Metal Catalyzed Reactions* (Chemistry for the 21st Century) YUPAC, pp 512

Musser, S.M. and Theg, S.M. (2000) Proton transfer limits protein translocation rate by the thylakoid DpH/Tat machinery, *Biochemistry,* **39**, 8228-8233.

Nabedryk, E., Breton, J., Okamura, M.Y., and Paddock, M. L. (2001) Simultaneous replacement of Asp-L210 and Asp-M17 with Asn increases proton uptake by Glu-L212 upon first electron transfer to Q_B in reaction centers from *Rhodobacter sphaeroides,* Biochemistry **40**, 13826-13832.

Nagano, T. (2000) First synthetic NO-heme-thiolate complex relevant to nitric oxide ynthase and cytochrome P450nor, *J. Am. Chem. Soc.* **122**, 12059-12060.

Nakabayashi, T., Okamoto H., and Tasumi, M. (1997) Probe-wavelength dependence of picosecond time resolved anti-Stokes Raman spectra of cantaxantin: determination of energy states of vibrationally excited molecules generated via internal conversion from the lowest exited single state, *J. Phys. Chem. A* **101**, 3494-3500.

Nam, W., Goh, Y. M., Lee, Yoon J., Lim, M. H., and Kim, . (1999) Biomimetic alkane hydroxylations by an iron(III) porphyrin complex with H_2O_2 and by a high-valent iron(IV) oxo porphyrin cation radical complex, *Inorg. Chem.* **38**, 3238-3240.

Narasimhulu, S., and Willcox, J. K. (2001) Temperature-jump relaxation kinetics of substrate-induced spin-state transition in cytochrome P450 (Comparison of the wild-type and C334A mutant P450CAM and P4502B4), Arch. Bioch. and Bioph. **388**, 198-206.

Narlikar, G. J. and Hershlag, D. (1997) Mechanistic aspect of enzymatic catalysis: lessons from comparison of RNA and protein enzymes, *Ann. Rev. Biochem.* **66**, 19-59.

Naruta, Y., Sasaki, T, Tani, F, Tachi, Y., Kawato, N., and Nakamura N (2001) Heme-Cu complexes as oxygen-activating functional models for the active site of cytochrome c oxidase, *J. Inorg. Biochem.* **83**, 239-46.

Neet, K. E. (1995) Cooperativity of enzyme function: equilibrium and kinetic aspects, in Purich, D. L. (eds.), *Methods in Enzymology,* **249**, Enzyme Kinetics and Mechanisms, Part D, Acad. Press, San-Diego, 519-567.

Neil, R., Kestner, N. R., Logan, J., and Jortner, J. (1974) Thermal electron transfer reactions in polar solvents, *J. Phys. Chem.* **78**, 2148-2166.

Ness, J.E., del Cardayre, S.B., Minshull, J., Stemmer, W.P. (2000) Molecular breeding – the natural approach to enzyme design, *Adv. Protein Chem.* **55**, 261-292.

Newcomb, M., Shen, R., Choi, S.-Y., Toy, P. H., Hollenberg, P.F., Vaz, A. D.N., and Coon, M.J. (2000) Cytochrome P450-Catalyzed Hydroxylation of Mechanistic Probes that Distinguish between Radicals and Cations. Evidence for Cationic but Not for Radical Intermediates. *J. Am. Chem. Soc.* **122**, 2677-2686.

Newton, W.E. "Nitrogen Fixation in Perspective", in *Nitrogen Fixation: From Molecules to Crop Productivity* (F. O. Pedrosa, M. Hungria, M. G. Yates and W. E. Newton, Eds.) Kluwer Academic Press, Dordrecht, The Netherlands, 2000, pp. 1-8.

REFERENCES

Newton, M.D. (1999) Control of electron transfer kinetics: models for medium reorganization and donor-acceptor coupling, in Jortner, J., Bixon, M. (eds.), *Advances in Chemical Physics* **107**, Part 1 John Wiley & Sons. NY., pp. 303- 376.

Newton, W.E. (1996) "Nitrogen Fixation", in *Kirk-Othmer Encyclopedia of Chemical Technology*, 4th Edition, Vol. **17**, John Wiley & Sons, NY, pp. 172-204.

Newton, W.E. (1997) "Molybdenum-Nitrogenase: Structure and Function", in Legocki, A., Bothe, H., and A. Puhler, (eds.), *Biological Fixation of Nitrogen for Ecology and Sustainable Agriculture*, Springer-Verlag, Heidelberg, pp. 9-12.

Newton, W.E., Fisher, K., Kim, C.-H., Shen, J., Cantwell, J.S., Thrasher, K S., and Dean, D.R. (1995) Probing catalytic function through amino-acid substitutions in *Azotobacter vinelandii* molybdenum-dependent nitrogenase. *Curr. Plant Sci. Biotechnol. Agric.* **27** (Nitrogen Fixation: Fundamentals and Applications), 91-96.

Newton, W. E., Schultz, F. A., Gheller, S. F., Lough, S., McDonald, J. W., Conradson, S. D., Hedman, B., Hodgson, K. O. (1986), Iron-molybdenum cofactor of Azotobacter vinelandii nitrogenase: oxidation-reduction properties and structural insights. *Polyhedron* **5**, 567-72.

Nicholson, H., Anderson, D.E., Dao-Pin, S., and Matthews, B.W. (1991) Analysis of the interaction between charged side chains and the a-helix dipole using designed thermostable mutants of phage T4 lysozyme, *Biochemistry* **30**, 9816-9828.

Nicollai, N., Rossi, C., Valensin, G., Mascagni, P., and Gibbons, W. A. (1984) An investigation of the mechanisms of nitroxide-induced proton relaxation enhancements in biopolymers. *J. Phys. Chem.* **88**, 5689-5692.

Niemz, A. and Rotello, V.M. (1999) From enzyme to molecular device. Exploring the interdependence of redox and molecular recognition, *Acc. Chem. Res.* **32**, 44-52.

Nikonova, L.A. and Shilov, A.E. (1977) Dinitrogen fixation in homogeneous protic media, in Newton, W., Posgate, J. R., and Rodrogues-Barrueco, G. (eds.), *Recent developmentsin nitrogen fixation*, Academic Press, N. Y., pp. 41-52.

Nishimoto, E., Yamashita, S., Szabo, A. G., and Imoto, T. (1998) Internal motion of lyzozyme studied by time-resolved fluorescence depolarization of tryptophan residues, *Biochemistry* **37**, 5599-5607.

Nitzan, A. Jortner, J., and Rentzepis, P.M. (1972) Intermediate level structure in highly excited states of large molecules, *Proc. Royal Soc. London* **A327**, 367-391.

Nogi, T., Miki, K. (2001) Structural basis of bacterial photosynthetic reaction centers. Journal of Biochemistry (Tokyo, Japan) **130**, 319-329.

Noguchi, T., Inoue, Y., and Tang, X-S. (1999) Hydrogen bonding interaction between primary quinone acceptor Q_A and a histidine side chain in Photosystem II as revealed by Fourier transform infrared spectroscopy, *Biochemistry* **38**, 399-403.

Noguchi, T. and Sugiura, M. (2000) Structure of an Active Water Molecule in the Water-Oxidizing Complex of Photosystem II As Studied by FTIR Spectroscopy, *Biochemistry* **39**, 10943-10949.

Nohaile, M. J., Hendsch, Z. S., Tidor, B., and Sauer, R.T. (2001) Altering dimerization specificity by changes in surface electrostatics., *Proc. Natl. Acad. USA* **98**, 3109-3114

Noji, H. and Yoshida, M. (2001) The rotary machine in the cell, ATP synthase, *J. Biol. Chem.* **276**, 1665-1668.

Norel, R., Sheinerman, F., Petrey, D. and Honig, B. (2001) Electrostatic contributions to protein-protein interactions: fast energetic filters for docking and their physical basis, *Protein Science* **10**, 2147-2161.

Northrop, D.B. and Cho, Y-K. (2000) Effect of high pressure on solvent isotope effects of yeast alcohol dehydrogenase, *Biophys. Journ.* **79**, 1621-1628.

Nucci, R., Moracci. M., Vaccaro, C., Vespa, N., and Rossi M (1993) Exo-glucosidase activity and substrate specificity of the beta-glycosidase isolated from the extreme thermophile Sulfolobus solfataricus, *Biotechnology and Applied Biochemistry* **17**, 239-50.

Nyborg, A.C., Johnson, J.L., Gunn, A., and Watt, G.D. (2000) Evidence for a two-electron transfer using the all-ferrous protein during nitrogenase catalysis, *J. Biol. Chem.* **274**, 39307-39312.

Ogilvie, I., Aggeler, R., and Capaldi, R. (1997) Cross-linking of the d subunit to one of the three subunits has no effect on functioning, as expected if d is a part of the stator that links the F1 and Foparts of the Escherichia coli ATP synthetase, *J. Biol. Chem.* **272**, 1662-16656.

Ogliaro, F., Cohen, S., de Visser, S. P., Shaik, S. (2000) Medium polarization and hydrogen bonding effects on compound I of cytochrome P450: what kind of a radical is it really? *J. Am. Chem. Soc.* **122**, 12892-12893.

Ogliaro, Francois,

Ogliaro, F., De Visser, S.P., Groves, J.T., and Shaik, S. (2001) Chameleon states. High-valent metal-oxo species of cytochrome P450 and its ruthenium analogue, Angew. *Chem., Intern. Ed.* **40**, 2874-2878.

Ohrme-Johnson, W.H. (1992) Nitrogenase structure: where to now? *Science* **257**, 1639-1640.

Ohrme-Jhonson, W.H., Hamilton, W.H., Jones, T L., Tso, M. -Y. W., Burris, R.H., and Shah, V.K., and Brill, W.J. (1972) Electron paramagnetic resonance of nitrogenase 3145 and nitrogenase components from *Clostridium pasterianum* W5 and *Azotobacter vinelandii* OP, *Proc. Natl. Acad. Sci. USA* **69**, 3142-3145.

Ohrme-Jhonson, W.H., Munck, E., Zimmerman, R., Brill, W. J., Shah, V K., Rawling, J., Henzel, M.T., Averill, B.A. and Ohrme-Jhonson, N.R. (1978) On the metal centers in nitrogenase, in Singer, T. P., Ondarza, R.N. (eds.), *Mechanism of Oxidizing Enzymes*, Elsevier, N. Y. pp. 85-107.

Qi, D, Tann, C-M., and Distefano, M.D. (2001) Generation of new enzymes via covalent modification of existing proteins, *Chem. Rev*, **101**, 3081-3112.

Rabenstein, B., Ullmann, G. M., Knapp, E.-W. (2000) Electron transfer between the quinones in the photosynthetic reaction center and its coupling to conformational changes, *Biochemistry* **39**, 10487-10496.

Okamura, M.Y., Paddock, M.L., Graige, M.S., and Feher, G.. (2000) Proton and electron transfer in bacterial reaction centers, *Biochim. Biophys. Acta* **1458**, 148-163.

Önfelt, B., Lincoln, P., Norden, B., Baskin, J. S., and Zewail, H. (2000) Femtosecond linear dichroism of DNA-interacting chromophores: solvation and charge separation dynamics of [Ru(phen)2dppz]+2 systems, *Proc. Natl. Acad. Sci. USA* **97**, 5708-5713.

Oriz de Montellano, P.R. (eds.) (1995) *Cytochrome P450: Structure, Mechanism and Biochemitry*, 2nd ed., Plenum Press: N. Y.

Oriz de Montellano, P.R. and Stearns, R.A. (1987) Timing of the radical recombination step in cytochrome P-450 catalysis with ring-strained probs, *J. Am. Chem. Soc.* **109**, 3415-3440.

Ostermeier, M. and Bencovic, S.J. (2000) Evolution of protein function by domain swapping, *Adv.* Protein. Chem. 55, 29-78.

Ovadi, J. (1991) Physiological significance of metabolic channeling, *J. Theor. Biol.* **152**, 1-22.

Ovanesyan, N S., Dubkov, K. A., Pyalling, A.A., and Shteinman, A.A. (2000) The Fe active sites in FeZSM-5 catalyst for selective oxidation of CH_4 to CH_3OH at room temperature, *Journal of Radioanalytical and Nuclear Chemistry* **246**, 149-152.

Page, M. T. and Jencks, W. P. (1971) Entropic contribution to rate acceleration in enzymatic and intramolecular reactions and the chelate effect, *Proc. Natl. Acad. Sci. USA* , 1678-1683.

Palm, T., Coan, C., and Trommer, W.E. (2001). Nucleotide-binding sites in the functional unit of sarcoplasmic reticulum Ca^{2+}-ATPase as studied by photoaffinity spin-labeled 2-N3-SL-ATP, *Biol. Chem.* **382**, 417-423

Palmer, A.G. III (2001) NMR probes of molecular dynamics: overview and comparison with other techniques *Ann. Rev. Biophys. Biomolec. Struct.* **30**, 129-155.

Palmer, J.G., Doemeny, P. A., and Schrauzer, G. N. (2001), The chemical evolution of a nitrogenase model, XXIII. The nature of the active site and the role of homocitric acid in MoFe-nitrogenase. *Z. Naturforsch., B: Chem. Sci.* **56**, 386-393.

Palmer, A.G., Williams, J., and McDermott, A. (1996) Nuclear magnetic resonance studies of biopolymer dynamics, *J. Phys. Chem.* **100**, 13293-13310.

Papper, V. and Likhtenshtein, G.I. (2001) Substituted stilbenes: A new view on well-known systems. New applications in chemistry and biophysics, *J. Phochem. Photobiol.* A: **140**, 39-52.

Papper, V., Likhtenshtein G.I., Pines D. and Pines E. (1998) *Trans-4-4'*disabstituted stilbenes: Linear free-energy relationship in photochemistry and photophysics. *In: Recent Research Development in Photochemistry and Photobiology*. V. 1 Transwold Research Network. Trivandrum. pp. 205-250.

Papper, V., Likhtenshtein, G.I., Medvedeva N., and Khoudyakov, D.V. (1999) Quenching of cascade reaction between triplet and photochrome probes with nitroxide radicals, *Photochem. Photobiol. A: Chem.* **122**, 79-85.

Papper, V., Medvedeva, N., Fishov, I., and Likhtenshtein, G.I. (2000) Quenching of cascade reaction between triplet and photochrome probes with nitroxide radicals: novel labeling method in study of membranes and surface system, *J. Appl. Biotech. Biophys.* **88**, 1-17.

Parak, F., Knapp, E.W., and Kucheida, D. (1982) Protein dynamics. Mössbauer spectroscopy on deoxymyoglobin crystal, *J. Mol. Biol.*, **161** 177-194. paramagnetic center in spin-labeled proteins from the parameters of the saturation curve of the ESR spectrum of the label at 77K. *Molecul. Biol.* (Moscow) **10**, 109-116.

Park, J.H. and Trommer , W.E. (1989)Advantages of ^{15}N and deuterium spin probes for biomedical electron spin probes investigation, *Biological Magnetic Resonance* **8**, 547-595.

Parkhomyuk-Ben Arye, P., Strashnikova, N. V., Likhtenshtein G. I. (2001) Stilbene photochrome-fluorescence-spin molecules: covalent immobilization on silica plate and applications as redox and viscosity probes, *J. Biochem. Biophys. Methods* (in press)

Pauling, L. (1963) *Die Natur der chemishe Bindung.* Verlag Chemie, Weinheim.

Pauling, L. (1948) Chemical achievement and hope for the future. *Am. Sci.* **36**, 51–58.

Peisach, J.. (1995) ESEEM spectroscopy - probing active site structures of metalloproteins,   *Bioradicals Detected by ESR Spectroscopy* 203-215.

Peisach, J., Appleby, C.A., and Blumberg, W.E. (1972) Electron paramagnetic resonance and temperature dependent spin state studies of ferric cytochrome P-450 from Rhizobium japonicum, *Arch. Biochem. Biophys.* **150**, 725-732.

Peluso, A., Di Donato, M., and Saracino, G.A.A.. (2000) An alternative way of thinking about electron transfer in proteins: Proton assisted electron transfer between the primary and the secondary quinones in photosynthetic reaction centers, *J. Chem. Phys.* **113**, 3212-3218.

Penning, T.M., and Jez, J.M (2001) Enzyme redesign, *Chem. Rev.* **101**, 3027-3046.

Persson, M., Harbridge, J. R., Hammerström, P., Mitri, R., Ma?rtenson, L-G., Carlson, U., Eaton, G., and Eaton, S. (2001) Comparison of electron paramagnetic resonance methods to determine distances between spin labels on human carbonic anhydrase II, *Biophys. J.* **80**, 2886-2897.

Perutz, M F. (1992) What are enzyme structure telling us? *Faraday Discuss.* **93**, 1-11.

Perutz, M.F., (1989) Mechanisms of cooperativity and allosteric regulation in proteins. *Quart. Rev. Biophys.* 22, 139- 236.

Peters, J. W.K. Fisher, W.E. Newton, and D.R.Dean, "Involvement of the P Cluster in Intramolecular Electron Transfer within the Nitrogenase MoFe Protein", *J. Biol. Chem.* **270**, 27007-27013 (1995).

Peters, J.W., Stowell, M.H. B, Soltis, S. M., Finnegan, M. G., Johnson, M. K. and. Rees, C.D. (1997) Redox-dependent structure change in the nitrogenase P-cluster, *Biochemistry*, **36**, 1181-1187.

Peterson-Kennedy, S.E., J.L. Mc Courty and B.M. Hoffman, *J. Amer. Chem. Soc.,* **106** (1984) 5010.

photolysis and X-ray crystallography study, *Biochemistry*, **39**, 10967-10974.

Pierick, J., Wassink, H., Haaker, H., and Hagen, W. R. (1993) Redox properties and ESR spectroscopy.of the P-clusters of MoFe-protein, Eur. J. Biochem. 212, 51-61.

Podust, Larissa M., Poulos, Thomas L., Waterman, Michael R. Crystal structure of cytochrome P450 14α-sterol demethylase (CYP51) from *Mycobacterium tuberculosis* in complex with azole inhibitors. Proceedings of the National Academy of Sciences of the United States of America (2001), 98(6), 3068-3073.

Pollack, S.J., Hsiun, P. & Schultz, P.G. (1989) Stereospecific hydrolysis of alkyl esters by antibodies. *J. Am. Chem. Soc.* **111**, 5961–5962.

Ponce, A., Gray, H.B., and Winkler, J. R. (2000) Electron tunneling through water: oxidative quenching of electronically exited Ru(try)$_2^{2+}$ (try=2, 2':6, 2''-terpyridine) by ferric ions in aqueous glasses at 77 K. *J. Am. Chem. Soc.* **122**, 8187-8191.

Pople, J.A. and Curtiss, L.A. (1991) The energy of N_2H_2 and related compounds, *J. Chem. Phys.* **95**, 4385-4388.

Postgate, J. (2002) Biological nitrogen fixation, in Leigh, G. J. and Winterton, N. (eds) Modern Coordination Chemistry Royal Society of Chemistry, Cambridge, pp. 233-251.

Poulos, T.L., Finzel, B. C., Gunzalus, I. C., Wagner, G. C., and Kraut, J. (1985) The 2. 6 Å crystal structure of Pseudomonas putida cytochrome P-450. *J. Biol. Chem.* **200**, 16122-16130.

Priestly, N.D., Floss, H. G., Froland, W.A., Lipscomb, J.D., Williams, P. G., and Morimoto, H. (1992) Cryptic stereoscopy of methane monooxygenase, *J. Am. Chem. Soc.* **114**, 7561-7562.

Privalov, P.L. and Gill, J.G. (1998) Stability of protein structure and hydrophobic interaction, *Adv. Prot. Chem.,* **39**, 191-234.

Proserpio, D.M., Rappe, A. K., and Gorun, S.M. (1993) Theoretical modeling of the mechanism of dioxygen activation and evolution by tetranuclear manganese complexes, *Inorg. Chim. Acta* 213, 319-24.

Prosser, R.S., Volkov, V.B., and Shiyanovskaya, I.V. (1998) Solid-state NMR studies of magnetically aligned phospholipid membranes: taming lanthanides for membrane protein studies, *Biochemistry and Cell Biology* 76, 443-454.

Pudlak, M. and Pincak, R. (2001) The role of accessory bacteriochlorophylls in the primary charge transfer in the photosynthetic reaction centers. *Chem. Phys. Lett.* **342**, 587-592.

Rader, C. and List, B. (2000), Catalytic antibodies as magic bullets, *Chemistry--A European Journal* 6, 2091-2095.

Radziska, A. and Wolfenden, R. (1995b) A proficient enzymes, *Science* **267**, 90-93.

Raitsimring, A. (2000) "2+" pulse sequence as applied for distance and spatial distribution mearsurements of paramagnetic centers, In Berliner, L. J., Eaton, S. S., and Eaton, G. R. (eds.), (2000) *Biological Magnetic Resonance*, **19**, Distance Measurements in biological Systems by EPR, Kluwer Academic/Plenum Publisher, N. Y., pp. 461-492.

Raman, C.S., Li, H., Martasek, P., Southan, G., Masters, B. S. S., Poulos, and Thomas, L. (2001), Crystal Structure of Nitric Oxide Synthase Bound to Nitro Indazole Reveals a Novel Inactivation Mechanism, Biochemistry **40** 13448-13455.

Ratner, V., Kahana, E., and Haas, E.. (2002), The natively helical chain segment 169-188 of *Escherichia coli* adenylate kinase is formed in the latest phase of the refolding transition, *J. Mol.. Biol.* **320**, 1135-1145.

Reat, V., Dunn, R., Ferrand, M., Finney, J.L., Daniel, R.M., and Smith, J.C. (2000) Solvent dependene of dynamic transition in protein solution, *Proc. Natl. Acad. Sci. USA* **97**, 9961-9966.

Rector, K.D., Jiang, J., Berg, M.A., and Fayer, M.D. (2001) Effect of solvent viscosity on protein dynamics: infrared vibrational echo experiment and theory, *J. Phys. Chem.* **105**, 1081-1082.

Rees, D.C. and Howard, J.B. (2000) Nitrogenase: standing at crossroads, *Curr. Opin. Chem. Biol.* **4**, 559-566.

Rees, D.C., Komia, H., Yeates, TO., Allen, J. P., and Feher, G. (1989) The bacterial photosynthetic reation center as a model of membrane proteins, *Annu. Rev. Biochem.* **38**, 607-633.

Rees, D.C. and Howard, J.B. (2000) Nitrogenase: standing at crossroads, *Curr. Opin. Chem. Biol.* **4**, 559-566.

Rhee, K-H. (2001) Photosystem II: the solid structure era, *Biophys. Biomolec. Structure* **30**, 307-328.

Rialdi, G. and Battistel, E. (1993) Thermodynamic properties of immobilized enzymes, *Calorim. Anal. Therm.* **24**, 401-404.

Rich, P., Tiede, D. M, Bonner, W. D, (Jr). (1979) Studies on the molecular organization of cytochromes P-450 and b$_5$ in the microsomal membrane. *Biochim. Biophys. Acta* **546**, 307-315.

Richardson, WH., Peng, C., Bashford, D., Noodleman, L., Case, D. A. (1997) Incorporating solvation effects into density functional theory: calculation of absolute acidities, *Int. J. Quantum Chem.* **61**, 207-217

Rigby, S.E.J., Evans, M.C.W., and Heathcote, P. (2000) Electron nuclear double resonance (ENDOR) spectroscopy of radicals in photosystem I and related type 1 photosynthetic reaction centers, *Biochim. Biophys. Acta* **1507** 247-259.

Robert, A. and Meunier, B. (2000) Asymmetric biomimetic oxidations, in Meunier, B. (eds.), *Biomimetic Oxidations Catalyzed by Transition Metal Complexes,* Imperial College Press, London, pp. 543-562.

Roberts, S.M. (1999) Biocatalysis for Fine Chemical Synthesis, Wiley, Weinheim.

Rocchia, W., Alexov, E., and Honig, B. (2001) Extending the Applicability of the nonlinear Poisson-Boltzmann equation: multiple dielectric constants and multivalent ions, *J. Phys. Chem. B* **105**, 6507-6514.

Rod, T. H. and Norskov, J. K. (2000) Modeling the nitrogenase cofactor, *J. Am. Chem. Soc.* **122**, 12751-12763.

Rod, T.H., Hammer, B., and Norskov, J. R. (1999) Nitrogen adsorption and hydrogenation on a MoFe$_8$S$_9$ complex, *Phys. Rev. Letters* **82**, 4054-4057.

Rogniaux, H., Sanglier, S., Strupat, K., Azza, S., Roitel, O., Ball, V., Tritsch, D., Branlant, G., and Van Dorsswlaer, A. (2001) Mass spectrometry as a novel approach to probe cooperativity in multimeric enzymatic systems, *Anal. Biochem.* **291**, 48-61.

Rojnuckarin, A., Kim, S. and Subramanian, S. (1998) *Proc. Natl. Acad. Sci. USA* **95**, 7406-7410.

Rose, I.R. (1995) Partition analysi: detection enzyme reactions cycle intermediates, in Purich, D. L. (eds.), *Methods in Enzymology*, **249**, Enzyme Kinetics and Mechanisms, Part D, Acad. Press, San-Diego, 315-340.

Rosenzweig, A.C., Frederic, C.A., Lippard, S. J., and Nordlund, P. (1993) Crystal structure of a bacterial non-heam iron hydroxylase that catalyses the biological oxidation of methane, *Nature* **366**, 537-543.

Roslyakov, B. Ya. and Khurgin, Y. I. (1972) Study of cyanamoyl-a chymotrypsin hydrolysis in the solid state, *Biokhimiya*, **37**, 493-447.

Rozek, A., Sparrow, J.T., Weisgraber, K.H., and. Cushley, R. J. (1998) Sequence-specific ^{1}H NMR resonance assignments and secondary structure of human apolipoprotein C-I in the presence of sodium dodecyl sulfate, *Biochemistry and Cell Biology* **76**, 267-275.

Rozovscy, S. and McDermott, A. E. (2001) The times scale of the catalytic loop motion in triosephosphate isomeraze *J. Mol. Biol.* **310**, 259-270.

Ru, M.T., Hirokane, S.Y., Lo, A. S., Dordick, J. S., Reimer, J. A., and Clark, D.S. (2000) On the salt activation of lyophilized enzymes in organic solvent, effect of salt kosmotropocity on enzyme activity, *J. Am. Chem. Soc.* **122**, 1565-1571.

Rubtsova, E.T., Fogel V.R., Khudyakov, D V., Kotel'nikov, A.I., and Likhtenshtein, G.I. (1993) Influence of the molecular dynamics of a protein medium on kinetics of intramolecular electron phototransfer, *Biophysics* **38**, 211-216.

Rupp, E., Nowak, F., Fiechter, S., Reck, G., Eyert, V., Alonso-Vante, N., and Tributsch, H. (2001) A new cubane-type $Ru_4(CO)_{12}(\mu3-Se)_4$ tetramer tailored for water photooxidation catalysis. Europ. J. Inorg. Chem. (10), 2489-2495.

Rutherford, A.W. and Faller, P. (2001) The heart of photosynthesis in glorious 3D, *Trends in Biochemical Sciences* **26**, 341-344.

Rüttinger, W. and Dismukes, G.C. (1997) Synthetic water-oxidation catalysts for artificial photosynthetic water oxidation, *Chem. Rev.* **97**, 1-24.

Rüttinger, W., Yagi, M., Wolf, K., Bernasek, S. and Dismukes, G.C. (2000) O_2 Evolution from the Manganese-Oxo Cubane Core $Mn_4O_4^{6+}$ A Molecular Mimic of the Photosynthetic Water Oxidation Enzyme? *J. Am. Chem. Soc.* **122**, 10353-10357.

Ruzicka, F., Huang, D-S., Donnelly, M I., and Frey P.A. (1990) Methane monooxygenase catalyzed oxygenation of of 1, 1-dimethylcyclopropane. Evidence for radical and carbocationic intermediates, *Biochemistry* **29**, 1696-1700. s

Sabbert, D., Engelbrecht, S., and Junge, W. (1996) Intersubunit rotation in active F-ATPase, *Nature,* **381**, 623-626.

Saito, H. and Ando, I.C. (1989) High resolution solid-state NMR studies of synthetic and biological molecules, in Webb, G. A. (eds.), *Annual Report on NMR Spectroscopy* **21**, Academic Press, London, 210-290.

Salikhov, K. M., Doctorov, A. B., Molin, Yu. N., and Zamaraev, K. I. (1971) Spin relaxation of radicals and complexes upon encounters in solution *J. Magnet. Reson.* 5, 189- 196.

Salikhov, K.M., Semenov, A.G., and Tsvetkov, Yu.D., *Electron Spin Echo and Its Application.* Nauka, Novosibirsk (1976) p. 342

Salikhov, K.M., Kandrashkin, Yu.E., and Salikhov, A.K. (1992) Peculiarities of free induction and primary spin echo signals for spin-correlated radical pairs, *Appl. Magnet. Reson.* **3**, 199-217.

Saltiel, J. and D'Agostino, J. (1972) Separation of viscosity aand temperature effects on the singlet pathway to stilbene isomerization, *J. Am. Chem. Soc.* **94** 6445-6456.

Saltiel, J., Waller, A.S., and Sears, D. F., Jr. (1992) Dynamics of cis-stilbene photoisomerization: the adiabatic pathway to excited trans-stilbene, *J. Photochem. Photobiol., A* **65**, 29-40.

Sakata, Y. and Fukuzumi, S. (2001) Charge Separation in a Novel Artificial Photosynthetic Reaction Center Lives 380 ms, J. the Am. Chem. Soc. **123**, 6617-6628.

Santolini, J., Adak, S., Curran, C.M.L. and Stuehr, D.J. (2001) A kinetic simulation model that describes catalysis regulation in nitric-oxide synthase, *J. Biol. Chem.* **276** 1233-1243.

Saven, Jeffery G. (2001), Designing protein energy landscapes, *Chem. Rev.* **101**, 3113-3130.

Scalf, M., Westphall, M.S., Krause, Z., Kaufman, S.L., and Smith, L.M. (1999) Controlling charge states of large ions, *Science* **283**, 194-197.

Schaefer, J., and Stejkal, E.D. (1976) Carbon-13 nuclear magnetic resonance of polymers spinning of the magic angle, *J. Am. Chem. Soc.* **98**, 1031-1032.

Schindelin, H., Kisker, C. and Rees, D.C. (1997) The molybdenum cofactor: a crystallographic perspective, *J. Biol. Inorg. Chem.* **2**, 773-781.

Schlichter, J., Friedrich, J., Parbel, M., and Scheer. H. (2001) Influence of isotopic substitutin on the conformational dynamics of frozen proteins, *J. Chem. Phys.* **114**, 9638-9644.

Schlichting, I, Berendzen., J., Chu, K., Stock, A.M., Maves, S., Benson, D., Sweet, R.M., Ringe, D., Petsko, G., and Sligar,S.G. (2000) The catalytic pathway of cytochrome P450 at atomoc resolution, Science 287, 1615-1622.

Schlichtich, I. and Goody, R.D. (1997) Triggering methods in crystallographic enzyme kinetics, in Carter, C. V and Sweet R. M. (eds.), *Methods in Enzymology*, Macromolecular Crysallography, Part B, 277, 467-.

Schmidt, A., Dordick, J.S., Hauer, B., Kiener, A., Wubbolts, M., and Witholt, B. (2001) Industrial biocatalysis today and tomorrow, *Nature* **409**, 258-267.

Schramm, V.L. (1999) Enzymatic transition state analysis and transition-state analogs, in Schramm, V. L. and Purich, D. L. (eds.), *Methods in Enzymology* **308**, Enzyme kinetics and Mechanism, Part E, Academic Press, San Diego , pp. 301-354.

Schramm, V. L. (2001) Atomic motion in enzymatic reaction coordinates. Shi, Wuxian. *Current Opinion in Structural Biology* **11**, 657-665.

Schreiber, G. and Fersht, A.R. (1994) Rapid, electrostatically assisted association of proteins, *J. Mol. Biol.* **238**, 415-436.

Schulten, K, (2000) Perspectives: electron transfer: exploiting thermal motion. *Science* (Washington, D. C.) **290**, 61-62.

Schmidt, K.A., Neerken, S., Permentier, H.P., Hager-Braun, C., and Amesz, J. (2000) Electron transfer in reaction center core complex from green sulfur bacteria *Prosthecochloris aestuarii* and *Chlorobium tepidum, Biochemistry* **39**, 7212-7220.

Schultz, P.G. & Lerner, R.A. (1995) From molecular diversity to catalysis: lessons from the immune system. *Science* **269**, 1835–1842.

Schultz, P.G. (1989) Catalytic antibody, *Acc. Chem. Res.* 22, 287-294.

Schünemann, V., Jung, C., Trautwein, A. X., Mandon, D., and Weiss, R. (2000) Intermediates in the reaction of sudstrate-free cytochrome P450cam with peroxy acid, *FEBS Lett.* **179**, 149-154.

Schwille, P., Kummer, S., Heikal, A. A., Moerner, W.E. and Webb, W.W. (2000) *Proc. Natl. Acad. Sci. USA* **97**, 151-156.

Scott, D.L., Mandel, A.M., Sigler, P.B., and Honig, B. (1994) The electrostatic basis for the interfacial binding of secretory phospholipases A2, *Biophys. J.* **67**, 493-504.

Scourotis, S.S. and Beratan, D.N. (1999) Theories of structure-function relationships for bridge-mediated electron transfer reaction, in Jortner, J., Bixon, M. (eds.), in *Advances in Chemical Physics* **107**, Part 1, John Wiley & Sons. NY., 377- 452.

Seefeldt, L.C. and Dean, D.R. (1997) Role nucleotide in nitrogenase catalysis, *Acc. Chem. Res.* **30**, 260-266.

Seiter, M.S., Bauer, M. P., Vogel, P.D. and Trommer, W.E. (1996) Synthesis of novel spin-labeled photoaffinity derivatives of NAD+ and ATP and their characterization as coenzymes and substrates of several enzymes, *Synthesis* (2) 269-273.

Sellmann, D. (1995) Chemistry of N_2H_2 and other nitrogen hybrids related to N_2 fixation in the coordination sphere complexes, in Tichonovich, I. A., Provorov, N. A., Romanov, V. I., and Newton, W. E. (eds.), Nitrogen Fixation: Fundamentals and Applications, Kluwer Academic Publishers, Dodrecht, pp. 123-128.

Sellmann, D., Utz, J., Blum, N., and Heinemann, F. W. (1999) On the function of nitrogenase FeMo cofactors and competitive catalysts: chemical principles, structural blue-prints, and the relevance of iron sulfur complexes for N_2 fixation, *Coord. Chem. Rev.* **190-192,** 607-627.

Sergeev, P.V., Magai, I.V., Lexina, V.P., Stepanyants, A. U., and Likhtenshtein, G.I. (1976) Investigation of the interaction of steroids with human serum albumin by the spin-echo-paramagnetic probe technique, *Mol. Biol.* (Moscow), **10**, 1166-1174.

Sessler, J.L (1992) Photosynthetic model systems, Israel J. Chem 32. 449-468.

Setif, P., Seo, D., and Sakurai, H. (2001) Photoreduction and reoxidation of the three iron-sulfur clusters of reaction centers of green sulfur bacteria. *Biophys. J.* **81**, 1208-1219.

Shafirovich, V.Ya. (1995) Chemical models of reaction centers for photoinduced charge separation and photosynthetic enzyme systems, *Ross. Khim. Zh.* **39**, 80-88.

Shaitan, K.V., Mikhailyuk, M.G., Leont'ev, K M.,Saraikin, S.S., and Belyakov, A.A. (2002) Molecular dynamics of bending fluctuations of the elements of protein secondary structure, *Biofizika* **47**, 411-419.

Shames, A., Nucci, R., D'Auria, S., Febbrario, F., Vaccaro. C., Lozinsky, E., Rossi, M., and Likhtenshtein, G.I. (2000) Study of conformational transitions in β-glucosidasefrom thermophylic *Sulfolobus solfiaricus* by methods of spin labels, *J. Appl. Magn. Res.* **18**, 515-526

Shan, S. and Hershlag, D. (1999) Hydrogen bonding in enzymatic catalysis: analysis of energetic contributions, in Schramm, V. L. and Purich, D. L. (eds.), *Methods in Enzymology*, **308**, Enzyme kinetics and Mechanism, Part E, Academic Press, San Diego, pp. 246-275.

Sharp, K., and Honig, B. (1990) Electrostatic interactions in macromolecules: theory and applications, *Ann. Rev. Biophys. Chem.* **19**, 301-332.

Sharp, K., Jean-Charles, J., and Honig, B. (1992) A local dielectric constant model for solvation free energies which accounts for solute polarizability, *J. Phys. Chem.* **96**, 3822-3828.

Sharrok, M., Debrunner, P. G., Schultz, C., Lipscomb, J. D., Marshall, Y., Gunsalus, I. C. (1976) Cytochrome P-450 and its complexes. Mössbauer parameters of the heme iron, *Biochim. Biophys. Acta* **420**, 8-26.

Shaw, G.L, Davis, B., Keeler, J., Fersht, A. (1995) Backbone dynamics of chymotrypsin inhibitor 2: effect of breaking the active site bond and its implications for the mechanism of inhibition of serin proteases, *Biochemistry* **34**, 2225-2233.

Shestakov, A.F. and Shilov, A.E. (2001) On the nuclearity of the vanadium(II)-pyrocatechol complex active in the reaction of molecular nitrogen reduction, *Kinetics and Catalysis* (Translation of Kinetika i Kataliz) **42**, 653-656.

Shevion, M., Peisach, J., and Blumbrg, W E. (1977) Imidazol, the ligand trances to mercarcaptide in ferric cytochrome P-450. An ESR study of proteins and model compounds, *J. Biol. Chem.* **252**, 3637-3645.

Shilov A.E. (1997) Metal Complexes in Biomimetical Reactions. N_2 Fixation, Activation and Oxidation of Alkanes, Chemical Models of Photosyntheses, CRC Press, Boca Raton, New-York, , pp. 302

Shilov, A.E.(1984) Dinitrogen fixation in model systems, in *Mechanisms of Catalysis.* Part II, Nauka, Novosibirsk, pp. 135-155.

Shilov, A.E. (1983) Activation of saturated hydrocarbons by transition metal complexes, Reidel, Dordrecht.

Shilov, A.E., Denisov, N. T., Efimov, N. O., Shuvalov, N., Shuvalova, N.I., and Shilova, A.K. (1971) New nitrogenase model for reduction of molecular nitrogen in protonic media, *Nature* **231**, 460-461.

Shilov, A.E., Likhtenshtein, G.I. (1971) Biological fixation of molecular nitrogen and its chemical modelling, *Russian Biological Bulliten* (4) 518-537.

Shinkarev, V.P., Crofts, A.R., and Wraight, C.A. (2001) The electric field generated by photosynthetic reaction center induced rapid reversed electron transfer in the bc1 complex, *Biochemistry* **40**, 12584-12590.

Shoemaker, K.R., Kim, P.S., York, E.J., Stewart, J.M., and Baldwin, R.L. (1987) Texts of the helix dipole model for stabilization of a-helices, *Nature* **326**, 563-567.

Shteinman, A.A. (2001) The role of metal-oxygen intermediates in biological and chemical monooxygenation of alkanes, *Russian Chemical Bulletin* **50**, 1795-1810.

Shutilova, N. I. (2000),   Mechanism of photosynthetic oxidation of water in a dimeric oxygen-evolving complex of photosystem II of chloroplasts,   *Biofizika* **45**, 51-57.

Shuvalov, V.A. and Krasnovsky, A.A. (1981) Photochemical electron transfer in the reaction centers of photosynthesis, *Biofizika* **26**, 544-556.

Siddarth, P. and Marcus, R.A. (1993a) Electron-transfer reactions in proteins: an artificial intelligence approach to electron coupling, *J. Phys. Chem.* **97**, 2400- 2405.

Siddarth, P. and Marcus, R. A. (1993b) Electron-transfer reaction in protein: electronic coupling in mioglobin, *J. Phys. Chem.* **97**, 6111-6114.

Siddarth, P. and Marcus, R.A. (1993c) Correlation between theory and experiment in electron-transfer reaction in protein: electronic couplings in modified cytochrome c and myoglobin derivatives. *J. Phys. Chem.* **97**, 13078-13082.

Siegbahn, E.M. and Crabree, R.H. (1997) Mechanism of C-H activation by diiron methane monooxigenases: quantum chemical studies, *J. Am. Chem. Soc.* **119**, 3103-3113.

Siegbahn, P.E.M., Westerberg J., Svensson, M., Crabtree, R.H. (1998) Nitrogen fixation by nitrogenases: a quantum chemistry study, *J. Phys. Chem. B*, **102**, 1615-1623.

Siemann, S.,   Schneider, K.,   Drottboom, M., and Muller, A. (2002) The Fe-only nitrogenase and the Mo nitrogenase from Rhodobacter capsulatus. A comparative study on the redox properties of the metal clusters present in the dinitrogenase components, *European Journal of Biochemistry* **269**, 1650-1661.

Silverman, R. B. (2000) The Organic Chemistry of Enzyme-catalyzed Reactions. Academic Press, San Diego.

Siminovitch, D.J. (1998) Solid-state NMR studies of proteins: the view from static ^2H NMR experiments, *Biochemistry and Cell Biology* 76, 411-422.

Sindelar, C.V., Hendsch, Z.S., and Tidor B. (1998) Effects of salt bridges on protein structure and design, *Protein Science* 7, 1898-1914.

Sitkoff, D., Lockhart, D. J., Sharp, K. A., and Honig, B. (1994) Calculation of electrostatic effects at the amino terminus of an α-helix, *Biophys. J.* **67**, 2251-2260.

Sjoergen, T., Svenson-Ek, M., Hajdu, J., and Brzezinski, P. (2000) Proton-coupling structural change upon binding of carbon monoxide to cytochrome cd_1: a combine flash

Sletten, E., Jackson, J.I., Burns, P D. and La Mar, G.N. (1983) Effects of cross relaxation on the analysis of T_1 data in paramagnetic proteins. *J. Magn. Reson.* **52**, 492-496.

Sloan, D.L., and Mildvan, A.S. (1974) Magnetic resonance studies of the geometry of bound nicotinamide adenine dinucleotide and isobutyramide on spin labeled alcohol dehydrogenase, *Biochemistry* **13**, 1711-1718.

Slupsky, C.M., Gentile, L.N., and McIntosh, L.P. (1998) Assigning the NMR spectra of aromatic amino acids in proteins: analysis of two Ets pointed domains, Biochemistry and Cell Biology **76**, 379-390

Smith, B.E. (1999) Structure, function and biosynthesis of the metallosulfur clusters in nitrogenases, *Adv. Inorg. Chem.* **47**, 159-218.

Smith, B.E. (2000) Chemistry and biochemistry of nitrogenase, *Curr. Plant Sci. Biotechnol. Agric.* **38** (Nitrogen Fixation: From Molecules to Crop Productivity), 11-12.

Smith,B.E., Durrant, M.C., Fairhurst, S.A., Gormal, C.A., Gronberg, K.L. C., Henderson, R. A., Ibrahim, S.K., Le Gall, T., and Pickett, C.J. (1999) Exploring the reactivity of the isolated iron-molybdenum cofactor of nitrogenase. *Coord. Chem. Rev.* **185-186**, 669-687.

Smith, L.J., Mark, A. E., Dobson, C.M. and Gursten, W. F. (1998) Molecular dynamic simulation of peptide fragments from hen lysozyme: insight into non-native protein conformation, *J. Mol. Biol.* **280**, 703-719.

Smith, B. E., Roe, S. M., and Yousafzai, F K. (1995) The structures of the nitrogenase proteins-an overview, in Tikhanovitch, I. A., Provorov, N. A., Romanov, V. I., and Newton, W. E. (eds.), *Nitrogen Fixation: Fundamentals and Applications*, Kluwer Academic Publishers, Dodrecht.

Solomon, E.I., Sundaram, U.M., Machonkin, T. E. (1996) Multicopper oxidases and oxygenases, *Chem. Rev.* **96**, 2563-2605.

Song, J. and Ni, F. (1998) NMR for the design of functional mimetics of protein-protein interactions: one key is in the building of bridges, *Biochemistry and Cell Biology* **76**, *177-18*.

Sono, M., Roach, M.P., Coulter, E.D., and Dawson, J.H. (1996) Heme-containing oxygenases, *Chem. Rev.* **96**, 2841-2887.

Spiro, T.G. (eds.) (1988) Biological Application of Raman Spectroscopy, Wiley, New York.

Sporlein, S., Zinth, W., Meyer, M., Scheer, H., and Wachtveitl, J. (2000) Primary electron transfer in modified bacterial reaction centers: optimization of the first events in photosynthesis, Chem. Phys. Lett. 322(6), 454-464.

Srere, P.A. (1987) Complex of sequential metobolic enzymes, *Annu. Rev. Biochem.* **56**, 89-124.

Stahl, S.S., Fransicsco, W. A., Merkx, M., Klinman, J.P., and Lippard, S.J. (2001) Oxygen kinetic isotope effects in soluble methane monooxygenase, *J. Biol. Chem.* **276**, 4549-4553.

Stahl, S.S., Fransicsco, W.A., Merkx, M., Klinman, J.P., and Lippard, S.J. (2001) Oxygen kinetic isotope effects in soluble methane monooxygenase, *J. Biol. Chem.* **276**, 4549-4553.

Stainhoff, H.-J., Radzwill, N., Thevis, W., Lenz, V., Brandenburg, D., Antson, A., Dodson, G., and Wollmer, A. (1997) Determination of interspin distances between spin labels attached to insulin: comparison of electron paramagnetic resonance data with the X-ray structure , *Biophys. J.* **73**, 3287-3298.

Staninets, V. I. and Shilov, E.A. (1971) Addition reactions involving the intramolecular formation of the ring, *Usp. Khim.* **40**, 491-512.

Stavrev, K.K., Urahata, S., Herz, T., Han, J., and Coucouvanis, D. (2001) Theoretical study on the electronic structure and properties of synthetic MoFe3S3 compounds. *Int. J. Quant. Chem.* **85**, 469-474.

Sterpone, F., Ceccarelli, M. (2001) Dynamics of hydration in hen egg white lysozyme, *J. Molec. Biol.* **311**, 409-419.

Stoddard, B.L. (1999) Visualization enzyme intermediates using fast diffraction and reaction trapping methods isocitrate dehydrogenase, *Biochemical Society Transactions* **27**, 42-48.

Storm, D.R. and Koshland, D. E. (1970) A source for the special catalytic power of enzymes: orbital steering, *Proc. Natl. Acad. Sci. USA* **66**, 445-452.

Stowell, M.H.B., McPhillips, T.M., Rees, D.C., Solitis, S.M., Abresch, E. and Feher, G. (1997) Light-induced structural changes in photosynthetic reaction center: implications for mechanism of electron-proton transfer, *Science* (Washington, D. C.) **276**, 812-816.

Strashnikova, N.V., Medvedeva, N., and Likhtenshtein, G.I. (2001) Depth of immersio of fluorescence chromophore in biomembranes studied by quenching with nitrioxideradicals, *J. Biochem. Biophys. Meth.* **48**, 43-60.

Strop, P., Takahara, P. M., H-J Chiu, Angove, H. C., Burgess, B.K., and Rees, D. C. (2001) Crystal structure of the all ferrous [4Fe-4S] form of the nitrogenase iron protein from *Azotobacter vinelandii Biochemistry* **40**, 651-656.

Stuchebrukov, A. A. and Marcus, R.A. (1995) Theoretical study of electron transfer in ferricytochromes, *J. Phys. Chem.* **99**, 7581-7590.

Stuehr, D. J. (1999) Mammalian nitric oxide synthase, *Biochem. Biophys. Acta* **1411**, 217-230.

Stuehr, D. J., Adak, S., Santolini, J., Wei, C.-C., and Wang, Z. (2001) Mechanism of oxygen activation in the NO synthases, and a kinetic model for catalysis. *NATO Sci. Ser., Ser. A* **317**(Nitric Oxide), 23-26.

Stuehr, D.J. and Ghosh, S. (2000) Enzymology of nitric oxide synthases. *Handbook of Experimental Pharmacology* **143** (Nitric Oxide), 33-70.

Sumi, H., (1999) Solvent fluctuation control of solution reactions and its manifistation in protein functions, in Jortner, J., Bixon, M. (eds.), *Advances in Chemical Physics.* **107**, Part 2 , John Wiley & Sons. NY., pp. 611- 646.

Sumi,H. and Ulstrup, J. (1989) Dynamics of protein conformation transition in enzyme catalysis with special attention to proton transfers in serine proteinase, *Biochem. Biophys. Acta* **955**, 26-42.

Sun, M.M.C. and Clark, D.S (2001) Pressure effect on activity and stability of hyperthermophilicenzymes, *Methods in Enzymology* **334**, 316- 326.

Sundin, A. 1991. *MacMimic version 2. 1*. InStar Software, Lund, Sweden.

Sutin, N. (1999) Electron transfer reaction in solution: a historical perspective, in Jortner, J., Bixon. M. (eds.), *Advances in Chemical Physics*. **107**, Part 1, John Wiley & Sons. NY. Pp. 7-33.

Suzuki, N., Higuchi, T., Urano, Y., Kikuchi, K., Uchida, T., Mukai, M., Kitagawa, T., and Nagano, T. (2000) First synthetic NO-heme-thiolate complex relevant to nitric oxide ynthase and cytochrome P450nor, *J. Am. Chem. Soc.* **122**, 12059-12060.

Swain, C.G., Stiver, E. C., Reuwer, J. F., and Schaad, L. J. (1958) Use of hydrogen effects to identify attacking nucleophile in enolization of ketons, *J. Am. Chem. Soc.* **80**, 5885-5893.

Syrtsova L.A., Likhtenstein, G. I., Pisarkaya, T. N., Berdinskii, V.L., Lezina, V.P. and Stepanyants A. U. (1974) Estimation of the distance between the ATPase and substrate-binding sites in nitrogenase by the NMR-^{1}H method. *Mol. Biol.* (Moscow) **8**, 656-662.

Syrtsova, L. A. and Timofeeva, E. A. (2001) Electron transfer coupled with ATP hydrolysis in nitrogenase, *Russian Chemical Bulleten*, **50** 1789-1794.

Syrtsova, L. A., Druzhinin, S.Y., Rubtsova, E.T., Shkondina, N.I. (1998), New possibilities for studying mechanism of nitrogenase reaction with photodonors of electron, *Curr. Plant Sci. Biotechnol. Agric.* **31** (Biological Nitrogen Fixation for the 21st Century), 49-50.

Syrtsova, L.A., Druzhinin, S. Yu., Khramov, A. V., and Moravsky, A.P. (1995) Photostimulation of nitrogenase reaction in vitro for investigation of nitrogenase mechanism action *Curr. Plant Sci. Biotechnol. Agric.* **27** (Nitrogen Fixation: Fundamentals and Applicaaaation.

Syrtsova, L.A., Druzhinin, S.Yu., Uzenskaya, A.M., Khramov, A. V., Moravskii, A. P., and Likhtenshtein, G I. (1988), Kinetics of proton release in the process of nitrogenase electron transfer coupled with ATP hydrolysis, *Biofizika* **33**, 31-5.

Syrtsova, L.A., Levchenko, L.A., Frolov, E. N., Likhtenshtein, G. I., Pisarscaya, T. N., Vorob'ev, L. V., and Gromoglasova, V.A. (1971) Structure and function of thenitrogenase components from *Azotobacter vinelandii*, *Mol. Biol.* (Moscow) **5**, 726-734.

Syrtsova, L. A., Nadtochenko, V. A., and Timofeeva, E.A. (1998) Kinetics of all stages of electron transfer in nitrogenase in the presence of a photodonor. Biochemistry (Moscow) 63(8), 1007-1013.

Syrtsova, L.A., Nadtochenko, V.A., Denisov, N.N., Timofeeva, E. A. Shkondina, N. I., and Gak, V.Yu. (2000) Kinetics of elementary steps of electron transfer in nitrogenase in the presence of a photodonor. Biochemistry (Moscow) **65**, 1145-1152.

Syrtzova, L. A., Likhtenshtein, G.I., Nazarova, I.I., Pisarkaya, T.N., and Nazarov V.V. (1972) Study on the ATP-ase active center of nitrogenase by NMR method *Doklad. Akad. Nauk USSR* **206**, 367-370.

Szilagyi, R. K., Musaev, D. G., Morokuma, K. (2001) Theoretical studies of biological nitrogen fixation. I. density functional modeling of the Mo-Site of the FeMo-cofactor, *Inorg. Chem.* **40**, 766-775.

Tanaka, S. and Marcus, R.A. (1997) Electron transfer model for electric field effect on quantum yield of charge separation in bacterial photosynthetisc reaction centers, *J. Phys. Chem.* **101**, 5031-5045.

Tang, J., Thurnauer, M.C., and Norris, J.R. (1994) Electron spin echo envelope modulation due to exchange and dipolar interactions in a spin correlated radical pair, *Chem. Phys. Lett.*, **219**, 283-290.

Tang, X.-S., Randall, D.W. Force, D.A., Diner, B.A., and Britt, R.D. (1996) Manganese-tyrosine tnteraction in the Photosystem II oxygen-evolving complex, *J. Am. Chem. Soc.* **118**, 7638-7639.

Tann, C. -M, Qi, D., and Distefano, M. D. (2001), Enzyme design by chemical modification of protein scaffolds, *Curr. Opin. Chem. Biol.* **5**, 696-704.

Tarek, M., Martina, G.J. and Tobias, D. (2000) Amplitude and frequency of protein dynamics: analysis of discrepancies between neutron scattering and molecular dynamics simulations, *J. Am. Chem. Soc.* **122**, 10459-10451.

Taylor, J.C., Leigh, J.S. and Cohn, M. (1969) The effect of dipole-dipole interaction between nitroxide radical and a paramagnetic ion on the line shape of the ESR spectra of radical. *Proc. Natl. Acad. Sci. USA* **64**, 219-206.

Teutloff, C., Hofbauer, W., Zech, S. G., Stein, M., Bittl, R., and Lubitz, W. (2001), High-frequency EPR studies on cofactor radicals in photosystem I, *Applied Magnetic Resonance* **21**, 363-379.

Tezcan, F.A., Crane, B.R., Winkler, J. R., and Gray, H.B. (2001) Electron tunneling in protein crystals. *Proc. Natl. Acad. Sci. USA* **98**, 5002-5006.

Thoden, J.B., Huang, X, Rausel, F. M., and Holden, H. M. (1999) The small subunit of Carbomoyl Phosphate Synthetase: snapshots along the reaction pathway, *Biochemistry* **38**, 16158-16166.

Thoden, J.B., Holden, H.M., Wesenberg, G., Raushel, F. M., and Rayment, I. (1997) Structure of carbamoyl synthase: a jorney of 96 A from substrate to product, *Biochemistry* **36**, 6305-6316.

Thorneley, R.N.F., Asby, G., Howarth, J.V., Millar, N.C., and Gutfreund, H. (1989) A transient kinetic study of the nitrogenase of Klebsiella pneumonia by stopped-flow calorimetry. Comparison with the myosin ATPase, *Biochem. J.* **264**, 657-661.

Thorneley, R.N.F.and Dean, D.R. (2000), Chemistry and biochemistry of nitrogenase (part 1). *Curr. Plant Sci. Biotechnol. Agric.* **38** (Nitrogen Fixation: From Molecules to Crop Productivity), pp. 31-32.

Thorneley, R.N.F. and Lowe, D.J. (1985) Kinetics and Mechanism of the nitrogenase systems, in Spiro,T.G. (ed.) Molybdenum Enzymes, John Wiley and Sons Inc., N.Y. pp. 2211-284.

Thornley, R.N.F. and Lowe, D.J. (1984) The mechanism of *Klebsiella pneumonia* nitrogenase action. Determination of rate constants required for the simulation of the kinetic of N_2 reduction and H_2 evolution, *Biochem. J.* **224**, 895-901.

Tidor, B., and Karplus, M. (1991) Simulation analysis of the stability mutant R96H of T4 lysozyme, *Biochemistry* **30**, 3217-3228.

Tikhanovitch, I.A., Provorov, N A., Romanov,V.I., and Newton, W.E. (eds.), (1995) *Nitrogen Fixation: Fundamentals and Applications*, Kluwer Academic Publishers, Dodrecht.

Tissot, A. C., Vuilleumier, S., and Fersht, A. R. (1996) Importance of two buried salt bridges in the stability and folding pathway of barnase, *Biochemistry* **35**, 6786-6794.

Torrent, M., Musaev, D. G., Basch, H. and Morokuma, K. (2002) Computational studies of reaction mechanisms of methane monooxygenase and ribonucleotide reductase, *J. Comput. Chem.* **23**, 59-76.

Torrent, T., Musaev, D., aand Morokuma, K. (2001) The flexibility of carboxylate ligands in methane monooxyganase and ribonucleotide reductase: a density functional study, *J. Phys. Chem,* **105**, 322-327.

Tramontano, A., Janda, K.D. & Lerner, R.A. (1986) Catalytic antibodies. *Science.* **234**, 1566–1570.

Tramper, J. (1996) Chemical versus biochemical conversion: when and how to use biocatalysis, *Biothechnol. Bioeng.* **52**, 290-295.

Tripp, B.C. and Ferry, J.G. (2000) A structure-function study of a proton transport pathway in the γ–class carbonic anhydrase from *Methanosarcina thermophila, Biochemistry,* **39**, 9232-9240.

Trommer, W.E. and Vogel, P.D.. (1992) Photoaffinity spin labeling, in Zhdanov, R.I. (eds.), *Bioactive Spin Labels,* Springer-Verlag, Heidelberg, pp. 405-427.

Trukhan, V.M., Gritsenko, O.N., Nordlander, E., and Shteinman, A.A. (2000) Design and synthesis of new models for diiron biosites, *J. Inorg. Biochem.* **79**, 41-46.

Trukhan, V.M., Polukhov, V. V., Sulimenkov, I. V., Ovanesyan, N.S., Koval'chuk, N. A., Dodonov, A.F., and Shteinman, A.A. (1998) First structural-functional model of methane monooxygenase, *Kinet. Catal.* **39**, 788-791.

Tsai, A.M., Neumann, D.A., and Bell, L.N. (2000) Molecular dynamics of solid-state lysozyme as affected by glycerol and water: a neutron scattering study, *Biophys. J.* **79**, 2728-2732.

Turner, D. L. (1989) Recent development of multple pulse NMR, in Webb, G. A. (eds.), *Annual Report on NMR Spectroscopy* **21**, Academic Press, London, pp. 162-209.

Turzo, K., Laczko, G., Filus, Z., and Maroti, P. (2000) Quinone-dependent delayed fluorescence from the reaction center of photosynthetic bacteria, *Biophys. J.* **79**, 14-25.

Uchida, T., Ishikawa, H., Ishimori, K., Morishima, I., Nakajima, H., Aono, S., Mizutani, Y., and Kitagawa, T. (2000) Idification of histidine 77 as the axial heme ligand of carbonmonooxy CooA by picisecond time-resolved resonance raman spectroscopy, Biochemistry 39, 12747-12752.

Ueno, T., Kousumi, Y., Yoshizawa-Kumagaye, K., Nakajima, K., Ueyama, N., Okamura, T., and Nakamura, N. (2001) Role of α-Helix Conformation Cooperating with NH···S Hydrogen Bond in the Active Site of Cytochrome P-450 and Chloroperoxidase: Synthesis and Properties of [MIII(OEP)(Cys-Helical Peptide)] (M = Fe and Ga), *J. Am. Chem. Soc.* **120**, 12264-12273.

Van Gastel, M., Boulanger, G.W., Canter, G.W., Huber, M., Murphy, M.E.P.,

Van R., Bart J., Crielaard, W., van Stokkum, I. H. M., Hellingwerf, K. J., and Westerhoff, H. V. (2002) Simplicity in complexity: the photosynthetic reaction center performs as a simple 0.2 V battery, *FEBS Letters* **510**, 105-107.

Van Unen, D.-J., Engbersen, J. F. J., and Reinhoudt, D.N. (2002) Why do crown ethers activate enzymes in organic solvents? *Biotechn. and Bioeng.* **77**, 248-255.

Varfolomeev, S.D. and Gurevich, K.G. (1999) *Bikinetika. A Practical Course.* Grand. Moscow, 1999.

Vaughan, Cara K., Harryson, Pia, Buckle, Ashley M., Fersht, Alan R. (2002), *Acta Crystallographica*, Section D: Biological Crystallography **D58**, 591-600

Vayron, P., Renard, P.-Y., Taran, F., Creminon, C., Frobert, Y.,G.,J., and Mioskowski, C. (2000a), Toward antibody-catalyzed hydrolysis of organophosphorus poisons, Proc. Natl. Acad. Sci. USA **97**, 7058-7063.

Vayron, P., Renard, P.-Y., Valleix, A.,and Mioskowski, C. (2000b), Design and synthesis of an α,α-difluorophosphinate hapten for antibody-catalyzed hydrolysis of organophosphorus nerve agents *Chemistry--A European Journal* **6**, 1050-1063.

Vaz, A., McGinnity, D.F., and Coon, M.J. (1998) Epoxidation of olephins by cytochrome P450: evidence from site-specific mutagenesis for hydroperoxo-iron as an electrophyloc oxidant, *Proc. Natl. Acad. Sci., USA* 95-355-3560.

Vaz, A.D.N., McGinnity, D.F., and Coon, M.J. (1998) Epoxidation of olephins by cytochrome P450: evidence from site-specific mutagenesis for hydroperoxo-iron as an electrophyloc oxidant, *Proc. Natl. Acad. Sci., USA* 95-355-3560.

Verbeet, M.Ph., and Groenen, E.J.J. (2001) A single-crystal electron paramagnetic resonance study at 95 GHz of the type 1 cooper site of the green nitrate reductase of *Alcaligenes feacali, s J. Phys. Chem.* **B 105**, 2236-2243.

Verhoeven, J. W. (1990) From close contact to long-range electron transfer, Jortner, J., Bixon. M. (eds.), *Advances in Chemical Physics,* **107**, Part 1, John Wiley & Sons. NY. pp. 603- 645.

Vetriani, C., Maeder, D.L., Tolliday, N., Yip, K. S., Stillman, T. J., Britton, K. L., Rice. D. W., Klump, H. H., and Robb, F. T. (1998) Protein thermostability above 100 degrees C: a key role for ionic interactions, *Proc. Natl. Acad. Sci. USA* **95**, 12300-12305.

Vincent, M., Gilles, A-M, Li de la Sierra, I., Briozzo, P., Barzu, O., and Gallay, J. (2000) Nanosecond fluorescence dynamics Stockes shift of tryptophan in a protein matrix, *J. Phys. Chem.* B **104**, 11286-11295.

Vitkup, D., Ringe, D., Petsko, G.A. and Karplus, M. (2000) Solvent mobility and the protein 'glass' transition, *Nature Struct. Biol.* **7**, 34-35.

Vocadlo, D. J., Davies, G. J., Laine, R. and Withers, S. G (2001) Catalysis by hen egg-white lysozyme proceeds via a covalent intermediate, *Nature* **412**, 855-838.

Vogel, P.D.. (2000) Insights into ATP synthase structure and function using affinity and site-specific spin labeling, *Journal of Bioenergetics and Biomembranes* 32, 413-421.

Vogel, V.R.; Rubtsova, E. T.; Kotel'nikov, A. I.; Likhtenshtein, G. I. (1986) Study of protein collisions in solutions by triplet labels, *Biofizika* **31**, 152-154.

Vogel, V.R., Rubtsova, E. T., Likhtenshtein, G. I., and Hideg K. (1994) Factors affecting photoinduced electron transfer in a donor-acceptor pair (D-A) incorporated into bovine serum albumin, *J. Photochem. Photobiol. A: Chem.* **83**, 229-236.

Volpin, M.E. and Shur, V.B. (1970) Nitrogen fixation by transition –metal complexes in aprotic media, *Organomet. React.* **1**, 50-78.

Vos, M. H., Borisov, V. B., Liebl, U., Martin, J-L., Konstantinov, A. (2000) Femtosecond resolution of ligand-heme interaction in the high-affinity quinol oxidase bd: a di-heme active site? *Proc. Natl. Acad. Sci. USA* **97**, 1554-1559.

Vos, M.H., Rappaport, F., Lambry, J.-Ch., Breton, J., and Martin, J.-L. (1994) Probing low-frequency vibrational motion in bacterial reaction by femtosecond,absorption spectroscopy, *Springer Proc. Phys.* 74 (Time-Resolved Vibrational Spectroscopy VI), 219-22.

Wachtveitl, J., Huber, H., Feick, R., Rautter, J., Muh, F., and Lubitz, W. (1998) Electron transfer in bacterial reaction centers with an energetically raised primary acceptor: ultrafast spectroscopy and endor/triple studies, *Spectrochim. Acta, Part A* **54A**, 1231-1245.

Waggoner, A. S. (1986) Fluorescent probe for analysis of cell structure, function, and health by flow imaging cytometry. Application of Fluorescence in Biomedical Science, Alan Liss, New York.

Waldeck, D.H. (1996) Photoisomerization dynamics of stilbenes, *Chem. Rev.* **91**, 415-436.

Wales, M E, Wild J R (1991) Analysis of structure-function relationships by formation of chimeric enzymes produced by gene fusion, *Methods in Enzymology,* **202** 687-706.

Wallar, BJ., and Lipscomb, J.D. Dioxygen activation by enzymes containing binuclear non-heme iron clusters, (1996) *Chem. Rev.* **96**, 2625-2657.

Walsh, C. (2001) Enabling the chemistry of life, *Nature* **409**, 226-231.

Wand, A. (2001) Dynamic activation of protein function: a view emerging from NMR spectroscopy. . *Nature Structural Biology* **8**, 926-931

Warshel, A., Hwang, J-K and Aqvist (1992) Computer simulations of enzymatic reactions: examination of linear free-energy relation ship and quantum-mechanical corrections in the initial proton-transfer step of carbonic anhydryse, *Farad. Dissc.* **93**, 225-238.

Wasielewski, M.R. (2002) High time resolution Q-band EPR study of sequential electron transfer in a triad oriented in a liquid crystal, *J. Phys. Chem. A* **106**, 1933-1937

Wasielewski, M.R. (1992) Photoinduced electron transfer in supramolecular systems of artificial photosynthesis, *Chem. Rev.* **92**, 435-461.

Wasielewski, M.R., Davis, W. B., Miller, S. E., and Ratner, M. A. (2000) Effects of bridge dynamics on electron transfer in donor-bridge-acceptor molecules: From photosynthesis to molecular wires, *Abstr. Pap. - Am. Chem. Soc.* 220th INOR-289.

Waterman, M.R. and Mason, H.S. (1970) The redox potential of liver cytochrome p-450, *Biochem. Biophys. Res. Commun.* **39**, 450-454.

Watt, G.D. and Reddy, K.R.N. (1994) Formation of an all ferrous Fe4S4 cluster in the iron protein-component of *Azotobacter vinelandii* nitrogenase, *J. Inorg. Biochem.* **53**, 281-294.

Wasielewski, M.R. (2002) High time resolution Q-band EPR study of sequential electron transfer in a triad oriented in a liquid crystal, *J. Phys. Chem. A* **106**, 1933-1937.

Wasielewski, M.R. (1992) Photoinduced electron transfer in supramolecular systems of artificial photosynthesis, *Chem. Rev.* **92**, 435-461. Wasielewski, M. R. (1992) Photoinduced electron transfer in supramolecular systems of artificial photosynthesis, *Chem. Rev.* **92**, 435-461.

Wasielewski, M. R., Davis, W.B., Miller, S.E., and Ratner, M A. (2000) Effects of bridge dynamics on electron transfer in donor-bridge-acceptor molecules: From photosynthesis to molecular wires, *Abstr. Pap. - Am. Chem. Soc.* 220th INOR-289.

Wasielewski, M.R., Wiederrecht, G.P., Svec, W A., Niemczyk, M.P., Hasharoni, K., Galili, T., Regev, A., and Levanon, H.. (1998), Using synthetic model systems to understand charge separation and spin dynamics in photosynthetic reaction centers, in   Editor(s): Garab, G. (ed.) *Photosynthesis: Mechanisms and Effects*, Proceedings of the International Congress on Photosynthesis, 11th, Budapest, Aug. 17-22, 54193-4200. Kluwer Academic Publishers, Dordrecht, Neth A

Weaver, L.H. T.M. Gray, M.G. Gruetter, D.E. Anderson, J.A. Wozniak, F.W. Dahlquist, B.W. Matthews, (1989) High-resolution structure of the temperature-sensitive mutant of phage lysozyme, Arg 96 → His. *Biochemistry*, **28**, 3793-3797.

Weber, G (1989) Perrin revised: parametric theory of the motional depolarization of fluorescence, J. Phys. Chem., **93**, 6069-6073.

Weber, J. and Senior, A. E. (1997) Catalytic mechanism of F1-ATPase, *Biochim. Biophys. Acta* **1319**, 19-58.

Wei, C-C., Wang, Z-Q., Wang., Q., Meade, A. L., Hemann, C., Hille, R., and Stuehr, D.J. (2001) Rapid kinetic stadies link tetrahydrobiopterin radical formation to heme-dioxy redyction and arginine hydroxylation in inducible nitric-oxide synthase, *J. Biol. Chem.* **276**, 315-319.

Weiner, L.M. (1986) Magnetic resonance study of the structure and function of cytochromeP-450, *Crit. Rev. Biochem.* **20**, 139-200.

Whittington, D.A., Sazinsky, M.H., and Lippard, S J. (2001) X-ray Crystal Structure of Alcohol Products Bound at the Active Site of Soluble Methane Monooxygenase Hydroxylase. *J. Am. Chem. Soc.* **123**, 1794-1795

Wien, R.W., Morriset, J.D. and McConnell, H.M. (1972) Spin-label induced nuclear relaxation. Distances between bound saccharides, histidine-15, and tryptophan-123 on lysozyme in solution *Biochemistry* **11**, 3707-3716.

Wikaira, J., Gorun, S M. (1999) Biological and biomimetic catalysis of manganese redox enzymes and their inorganic models, in Reedijk, J. and Bouwman, E. (eds) *Bioinorganic Catalysis* (2nd Edition, Revised and Expanded) Marcel Dekker, Inc., New York, N. Y., pp. 355-422.

Wilks, H.M., Hart K.W., Feeney R, Dunn C R, Muirhead H, Chia, W.N., Barstow, D.A., Atkinson T., Clarke A.R., and Holbrook J.J. (1988 A specific, highly active malate dehydrogenase by redesign of a lactate dehydrogenase framework. Science **242** , 1541-1544.

Willems, J-P., Valentine, A.M., Gurbiel, R., Lippard, S.J., and Hoffman, B.M. (1998) Small molecule binding to the mixed-valent diiron center of methane monooxygenase hydroxylase from *Methylococcus capsulatus* (Bath) as revealed by ENDOR spectroscopy. *J. Am. Chem. Soc.* **120**, 9410-9416.

Williams, R.J.P. (1982) The nature of local chemical potential, *FEBS lett.* **150**, 1-3.

Winkler, T., Kettling, U., Koltermann, A., and Eigen, M. (1999b) Confocal fluorescence coincident analysis: an approach to ultra high-throughput screening, *Proc. Natl. Acad. Sci. USA* **96**, 1375-1378.

Winlker, J. J., Dmochowski, I. J., Dawson, J. H., Winkler J. R., and Gray, H. B. (1999a) Substrates for rapid delivery of electrons and holes to buried active sites in proteins, *Angew. Chem. Int. Ed.* **38**, 90-92.

Wishart, D. S and Nip, A. M. *(1998) Protein chemical shift analysis: a practical guide*, Biochemistry and Cell Biology 76, 153-163.

Witt, H.T. (1996) Primary reactions of oxygen photosynthesis, Ber. Bunsensges. Phys. Chem. **100**, 1923-1942.

Witt, H., Schlodder, E., Teutloff, C., Niklas, J. Bordignon, E., Carbonera, D., Kohler, S., Labahn, A., and Lubitz, W. (2002) Hydrogen bonding to P700: site-directed mutagenesis of threonine A739 of Photosystem I in *Chlamydomonas reinhardtii, Biochemistry* **41**, 8557-8569

Wolfenden, R. and Snider, M. (2001) The depth of chemical time and power of enzymes as catalysts, *Acc. Chem. Res,* **34**, 938-945.

Wolthers, Kirsten R., Schimerlik, Michael I. (2002) Neuronal nitric oxide synthase: substrate and solvent kinetic isotope effects on the steady-state kinetic parameters for the reduction of 2, 6-dichloroindophenol and cytochrome C^{3+}, *Biochemistry* **41**, 196-204.

Wong, C.H., Whitesides, G.M. (1994) Enzymes in Synthetic Organic Chemistry, Pergamon, Oxford

Wu, G. (1998) Recent developments in solid-state nuclear magnetic resonance of quadrupolar nuclei and applications to biological systems, *Biochemistry and Cell Biology,* 76, 429-442.

Wütrich, K. (1986) *NMR of Proteins and Nucleic Acids.* A Wiley-Interscience Publication, N. Y.

Xiao, L. and Honig, B. (1999) Electrostatic Contributions to the Stability of Hyperthermophilic Proteins, *J. Mol. Biol.* **289**, 1435-1444.

Xiao, W. and Shin, Y-K (2000) ESR spectroscopy ruler: the deconvolution methods and its applications, in Berliner, L, Eaton, S., and Eaton, G. (eds.), , *Magnetic Resonance in Biology,* **V. 18**, Kluwer Academic Publishers. Dordrecht, pp. 249-276.

Xie, X.S. and Trautman, J.K. (1998) Optical studies of single molecules at room temperature, *Annu. Rev. Phys. Chem.* **49**, 441-480.

Xie, Yuchun, Das, Prasanta Kumar, Klibanov, Alexander M. (2001) Excipients activate peroxidases in specific but not in non-specific reactions in organic solvents, *Biotechnology Letters* **23**, 1451-1454.

Xu, Q., Baciou, L., Sebban, P., and Gunner, M.R.. (2002) Exploring the Energy Landscape for QA- to QB Electron transfer in Bacterial photosynthetic reaction centers: effect of substrate position and tail length on the conformational gating step, *Biochemistry* **41**, 10021-10025.

Xue, Q.F. and Yeung, E.S. (1995) Difference in the chemical reactivity of individual molecules of an enzyme, *Nature* **373**, 681-683.

Yachandra, V.K., DeRose, V., Latimer, M.J., Mukerji,I., Sauer, K., and Klein, M. (1993) Where plants make oxygen: a structural model for the photosynthetic oxygen-evolving manganse cluster, Science 260, 675- .

Yagi, M, and Kaneko, M.. (2001) Molecular catalysts for water oxidation. *Chem. Rev.* (Washington, D. C.) **101**, 21-35.

Yakovlev, A.G., Shkuropatov, A.Y. and Shuvalov, VA. (2000) Nuclear wavepacket motion producing a reversible charge separation in bacterial reaction centers, *FEBS Letters* **466**, 209-212.

Yakovlev, A.G. and Shuvalov, V.A. (2001) Charge separation in photosynthetic reaction centers under femtosecond excitation, *Biochemistry* (Moscow) **66**, 211-220.

Yamamoto, K., Mizutani, Y., and Kitagawa, T. (2000) Nanosecond temperature jump and time-resolved Raman study of thermal unfolding of ribonuclease A, *Biophys. J.* **79**, 485-495.

Yennawar, H. P., Yennawar, N. H., Farber, G. K. (1994) *X-ray structure of γ-chymotrypsin in hexane, Biochemistry,* **33**, 7326-7336.

Yoshida. S., Sakak. S., and Koboyashi. H. (1994) *Electronic Processes in Catalysis: A quantum Chemical Approach in Catalysis.* John Wiley and Sons, New-York, .

Yoshizawa, K.. (2002) Theoretical study on kinetic isotope effects in the C-H bond activation of alkanes by iron-oxo complexes, *Coordination Chemistry Reviews* **226**, 251-259.

Yoshizawa, K. (2000) Two-step concerted mechanism for methane hydroxylation on the diiron active site of soluble methane monooxygenase, *J. Inorg. Biochem.* **78**, 23-34.

Yoshizawa, K., Kamachi, T., and Shiota, Y. (2001) A theoretical study of the dynamic behavior of alkane hydroxylation by a Compound I model of cytochrome P450, *J. Am. Chem. Soc.* **123**, 9806-9816.

Zamaraev, K. I., Molin, Yu. N., and Salikhov, K. M. (1981) *Spin Exchange. Theory and Physicochemical application.,* Springer-Verlag. Heidelberg.

Zanes, ?T. L., Doetsch, V., and Schmitz, U. (eds.), (2001) *Methods in Enzymology.* Nuclear Magnetic Resonance of Biological Molecules. **338** (Part A), **339** (Part B)

Zang, Y., Dong, Y., Que, L. Jr., Kauffmann, K., and Münck E. (1995) The first Bis(m-oxo)diirin complex. Structure and magnetic properties of [Fe$_2$(μ-O)$_2$(TLA)$_2$(ClO$_4$)$_2$, *J. Am. Chem. Soc.* **117**, 1169-1170.

Zavodsky, S., Kardos, J., Svingor, A., and Petsko, G. A. (1995) *Proc. Natl. Acad. Sci. USA*, **95**, 7406-.

Zech, S.G., Hofbauer, W., Kamlowski, A., Fromme, P., Stehlik,D., Lubitz, W., and Bittl, R. (2000) A structural model for the charge separated state P700$^+$A$_1^-$ in Photosystem I from the orientation of the magnetic interaction tensors, J. *Phys. Chem. B* **104**, 9728-9739.

Zener, C. (1933) Dissociation of excited molecules by external perturbation, *Proc. Royal. Soc.* **A140**, 660- 668.

Zhong, D., Douhal, A., and Zewail, A.H. (2000) Femtosecond studies of protein-ligand hydrophobic binding and dynamics: human serum albumin *Proc. Natl. Acad. Sci.* **97**, 14056-14061.

Zhou, H.X., Wlodek, S. T., McCommon, J. A. (1998) Conformational gating as a mechanism for enzyme specificity, *Proc. Natl. Acad. Sci. USA* **95**, 9280-9283.

Zouni,A., Witt, H.T., Kern, J., Fromme,P., Krauß, N., Seanger, W., and Orth, P. (2001) Crystal structure of Photosystem II from *Synechoccus elongates* at 3.8 Å resolution, *Nature* **409**, 739-743.

Zundel, G. (2000) Hydrogen bonds with large proton polarizability and proton transfer processes in electrochemistry and biology, in Prigogine, I. and Rice, S. A. (eds) *Adv. Chem. Phys.* **111**, John Wiley & Sons, Inc. 1-218.

Index